VERDI

HIS MUSIC, LIFE AND TIMES

Books by George Martin

The Opera Companion:
A Guide for the Casual Operagoer

Verdi: His Music, Life and Times

The Opera Companion
to Twentieth-Century Opera

The Damrosch Dynasty:
America's First Family of Music

The Battle of the Frogs and the Mice:
An Homeric Fable

The Red Shirt and the Cross of Savoy:
The Story of Italy's Risorgimento, 1748–1871

Causes and Conflicts: The Centennial History
of the Association of the Bar of the City of New York,
1870–1970

Madam Secretary: Frances Perkins

VERDI

HIS MUSIC, LIFE AND TIMES

BY GEORGE MARTIN

*Illustrated with drawings by
Everett Raymond Kinstler,
photographs, maps, and
Delfico cartoons*

DODD, MEAD & COMPANY   NEW YORK

First published as a Dodd, Mead Quality Paperback in 1983
Copyright © 1963 by George Martin
All rights reserved
No part of this book may be reproduced in any form
without permission in writing from the publisher
Published by Dodd, Mead & Company, Inc.
79 Madison Avenue, New York, N.Y. 10016
Distributed in Canada by
McClelland and Stewart Limited, Toronto
Manufactured in the United States of America

Library of Congress Cataloging in Publication Data

Martin, George Whitney.
  Verdi, his music, life, and times.

  Bibliography
  Includes index.
    1. Verdi, Giuseppe, 1813-1901. 2. Composers—Italy—
Biography. I. Title.
ML410.V4M266   1983   782.1'092'4 [B]   83-14239
ISBN 0-396-08196-7 (pbk.)

Musical examples from *Aida, Don Carlo, I Masnadieri, Macbeth, Rigoletto, La Traviata* and the *Requiem* are reproduced by courtesy of G. Ricordi & C., Milan. Quotations from *Giuseppe Verdi: His Life and Works* by Francis Toye, copyright 1946, are reproduced by permission of the publishers Alfred A. Knopf, Inc.

To the memory of

GIUSEPPE VERDI

man and musician

1813—1901

CONTENTS

PART III

The political atmosphere in Italy and Paris. Orsini attempts to assassinate Napoleon. The censors reject the libretto. The law suit, and the production cancelled. The opera in Rome and the political excitement. Discussion of *Un Ballo in Maschera*.

PART IV

41. THE LAST YEARS: THE *PEZZI SACRI* AND HIS DEATH
    (1897–1901; age, 84–87)   560

The Casa di Riposo. Boito arranges the première of the *Pezzi Sacri*. Discussion of the *Te Deum*. La Scala reorganized. Toscanini. Queen Margherita's prayer. His death in Milan and the two funerals.

APPENDICES

ILLUSTRATIONS

VERDI LETTERS

MAPS

PHOTOGRAPHS
following page 234

following page 498

CARTOONS BY MELCHIORRE DELFICO
following page 362

Verdi, Strepponi and Loulou arrive in Naples.
Neapolitans hoping to get into a rehearsal
Stratagems of friends to get into a rehearsal
Rehearsals
Verdi meets a friend, Il Barone Genovesi.
Verdi and Genovesi cook rice and macaroni.
Sight-seeing trip with friends to the Blue Grotto on Capri
Verdi sick in bed
Mercadante presents Verdi to the pupils of the Conservatory.
De Sanctis shows Verdi a spot for his honeymoon.
Verdi and Delfico admire the Bay of Naples.
Delfico pays homage to Strepponi.
Verdi and Loulou

PREFACE

I HAVE tried in this biography to present Verdi as a man and a musician set firmly in the history of his times. If the first duty of a biographer is to imprint on the reader's mind the personality and character of the man presented, surely the second is to recreate the atmosphere in which the man existed. For great men are *of* their age, responding with insight and spiritual energy to its peculiar strains and challenges. Verdi's "times," for example, offer important clues to the emotional basis of his patriotism, his anti-clericalism, his sense of purpose and even his popularity.

I have written for the general reader and omitted footnotes and citations. But no student should have difficulty locating the source of a statement or quotation if he studies the bibliography for a moment and then uses the indexes in the works listed. Still, to be exact: I have used or quoted in the book three of Verdi's letters previously unpublished, and these will not appear in the indexes elsewhere. Two, one in Italian and the other in French, I have used as illustrations of Verdi's handwriting. The third, a description of Verdi's trip from St. Petersburg to Berlin, I have quoted at length. The most interesting of a number of other unpublished letters I have read are scheduled to appear soon as the basis of an article in "Verdi," the bulletin of the Istituto di Studi Verdiani. These letters are a series to Enrico Tamberlic about the composition and production of *La Forza del Destino* in St. Petersburg. The originals of all of these unpublished letters are, at present, in my possession.

Besides reading unpublished letters I have been to Italy and done original research. Bits and pieces of it are scattered throughout the book. As Catherine Drinker Bowen once observed, persons attending a lecture on arctic exploration have a right to ask if the speaker has himself been to the Pole and back.

In writing I have tried to avoid drifting into fiction when the facts are thin, and there are some important episodes in Verdi's life about which remarkably little is known. I have not put words into Verdi's mouth or thoughts into his head that he did not utter or write. Where I have speculated on what he may have said or thought, I have indicated that I am doing so. In the same way I have deliberately avoided closing "open" questions. It is not clear, for example, why Verdi delayed marrying his mistress or whether he had affairs with various ladies. In such cases I have tried to present what evidence exists rather than merely stating my conclusions drawn from it.

The translations of all letters and texts are my own as are also the analyses of Verdi's music and the opinions expressed about it. In making the translations I have not used the usual dots . . . to show that words in the quoted passage have been omitted. My reason is that Verdi used dots regularly in his letters, and I wanted to preserve their flavor and appearance as closely as possible. Where I have omitted words in a quotation, I have indicated the fact in this fashion: (etc.). I have also used this (etc.) to indicate that the letter continues beyond the part I have quoted.

In studying Verdi's music I have started, whenever possible, with actual performances of it. Beyond that I worked generally from the Ricordi vocal scores; the Ricordi and International Music Company orchestral scores; and recordings, either on discs or tapes, of all the operas except *Il Corsaro* and *Alzira* and of most of the shorter works except for the earlier songs. The musical quotations are all taken from the Ricordi vocal scores, and I am grateful for permission to use them.

In my research many persons have helped me both in the United States and Italy, and I am delighted here to express my thanks to them publicly. I also, at this point, would like to acknowledge my use of the scholarly research done by Frank Walker and published in articles in various musical magazines from 1950 on. These taken with his recent book on Verdi constitute the most important body of research done on Verdi in recent years. More specifically I wish to thank the following without whose help the book would be very different from what it is: Signorina Gabriella Carrara Verdi for her kindness to me in the Villa Verdi at Sant' Agata where she answered all the questions I could think of then and many more by mail that I have thought of since; Edith S. Lynch of New York who studied several of Verdi's earliest songs and sang them to me; Giovanni Secchi of Busseto who helped me with the maps of that town and the countryside around it; Mario Peracchi of Busseto and the Monte di Pietà (now the Monte di Credito su Pegno) who spent many days helping me to decipher illegible scripts; Signora Eva Prina of Genoa and New York against whose patience and specialized knowledge I endlessly tested my view of nineteenth century Italy and the customs of its people; Luigi Filiberti of Parma and New York who helped me with the problems of translation; Elliott B. Nixon of New York who has read the proofs, correcting substance as well as type; Delight Ansley of New York who by her skill and enthusiasm created a useful index; and finally my editor, Allen T. Klots, Jr., who patiently read drafts of many of the chapters and invariably made wise suggestions for revising them.

GEORGE MARTIN

New York, 1963

Part I

ITALY IN 1813

Jagged borders show extent of the French Empire under Napoleon who was also King of Italy. Murat was one of his Marshals. Napoleon's sister, Elisa Baciocchi, ruled Lucca.

CHAPTER 1

LE RONCOLE

1813–1823; AGE, 0–10

VERDI was born on 10 October 1813 in Le Roncole, a tiny village in the Duchy of Parma. It was a Sunday, and the following Tuesday Verdi's father, Carlo Giuseppe Verdi, trudged the three miles to Busseto to register his first-born. The clerk wrote in French, and the baby was recorded as Joseph Fortunin François; for Parma was then incorporated into France as part of Napoleon's Empire. So it happened that for the civil and temporal world Verdi was born a Frenchman; for that of the spirit he had been enrolled the previous day in the Roman Catholic Church and in Latin as Joseph Fortuninus Franciscus. But he always referred to himself merely as Giuseppe Verdi: he was clearly Italian and not a man for fancy middle names. His family, after he was grown, his friends, and even his wife, in a farewell note to him over the signature to her will, addressed him simply as "Verdi."

Le Roncole in 1813 was a village of peasants, perhaps a hundred of them, clustered in fifteen or twenty small houses around a church dedicated to St. Michael the Archangel. The village lay beside the main road from Busseto, the nearest market town, to Parma, the capital of the Duchy. The peasants worked the land which they owned, the last vestiges of feudal rights and duties having been swept away in the Napoleonic upheaval at the turn of the century. It was good land made fertile by the ancient floodings of the river Po, but in 1813 life on it was simple and hard. War and conscription for the Napoleonic armies had upset the village's economy. It offered little else except, as part-time work, the necessary hand crafts, such as carpentry or cobbling. Verdi's father ran the one shop which also served as an inn and tavern. To survive he peddled salt, wine and groceries to the outlying farms and worked his own garden. His wife, Luigia, tended the store and did spinning. Over all in the summer blew the hot dust off the flat fields, and in the winter down the valley of the Po came a cold fog from the Alps. Le Roncole was one of those villages which in later generations thousands of despairing Italians would abandon for the hope of the New World.

The Verdi house, serving as tavern, shop and home, was one of the larger and better ones in the village. It is preserved today by the Italian Government as a national monument. As Verdi knew it, the ground floor had the kitchen and shop to one side with the tavern and sitting room to the other; a hallway running the length of the building divided them. All four rooms were small. A cramped stair led to two attic rooms, one for the parents, the other for Verdi although he may have shared it for some years with his younger sister, Giuseppa, who was born on 20 March 1816. The first years for the family, in spite of the poverty and politics which saw war again in the valley and inflation in the money, must have been happy. With the fall of Napoleon, the Congress of Vienna in 1815 gave the Duchy of Parma to his estranged wife, the ex-Empress Marie Louise, and backed by Austrian guns, she brought peace to Parma, the first real peace in almost twenty years. Verdi's parents were still young and in good health; his father was twenty-eight and his mother twenty-six when he was born. With settled times they must have reasoned that business would improve and the family prosper. And it did, but still first the parents, then the brother, had to admit that Giuseppa was mentally retarded. Verdi was a sensitive boy; he must have wondered early about the ways of the Deity in the world.

His parents, like most of the peasants, were illiterate, or very nearly so, and could teach him little except the lore of the peasantry and how to use his hands around a store and in the garden. To learn, they sent him when he was seven to the priest, the most educated man in the village. The schooling was of the simplest sort—reading, writing and arithmetic—all skills helpful to his father in the store. But the schooling was irregular, being constantly interrupted by the demands of village life on both Verdi and the priest. Verdi accompanied his father on buying trips to Busseto, helped with the store and garden, and served as an acolyte in the church; the priest said Mass, heard confession, tended the sick, blessed the dying and took part in all the

ITALY IN 1815

After the Congress of Vienna. The Emperor of Austria was also King of Lombardy-Venetia, and his close relatives ruled Parma, Modena, Tuscany, and the Two Sicilies. Lucca became part of Tuscany in 1847.

village festivals. For both the school was secondary to the business of life.

Sometime before his eighth year, perhaps for one of his birthdays, Verdi's father bought and gave him a spinet, an upright harpsichord with strings plucked by little points of leather at the end of hammers. The spinet was popular during the eighteenth century and then was supplanted by the piano, which had one great advantage: it could play soft and loud. The origin of its full name, "pianoforte," is simply a running together of the Italian words for soft and loud, "piano . . . forte." By 1820, the time of the gift, the piano had displaced the spinet in all the musical capitals of Europe and even provincial Busseto was shifting to it—which may explain how Carlo Verdi was able to buy a spinet at all, even though this one was old, battered, without pedals and with broken hammers. It was an extraordinary gift for a peasant; a secondhand trumpet would probably have been a great deal cheaper, and the trumpet at the time was a popular instrument.

But the gift was made, and Verdi kept the spinet all his life. It is now in the La Scala Museum in Milan, very small and battered. The fact of the gift is the first real evidence of Verdi's musical ability. At the same age, Mozart had given concerts to a critical and discerning public, and he had written minuets for the piano which are still published and played. There is no such record for Verdi, only the fact of the spinet and a note, discovered years later, tacked inside it and which reads:

By me, Stefano Cavaletti, these key-hammers were renewed and lined with leather, and I fitted pedals, which I gave as a present; as I also repaired gratuitously the said key-hammers, seeing the excellent disposition the young Giuseppe Verdi shows to learn how to play this instrument—which suffices to give me complete satisfaction.   —Anno domini 1821.

A generous action, and evidence that others in the village besides his parents were fond of the boy and impressed by his musical ability. But how he demonstrated it is uncertain. The only other keyboard instrument in the village was the organ in the church, and again the fact of the spinet, a keyboard instrument, suggests that Verdi as a tiny boy must have made impressive and successful efforts to play the organ. But legend and fact are inextricably mixed in an oral tradition in which chance remarks assume a significance after the event—although the stories are all possible, and those involving Verdi are in keeping with his reported character: self-contained, shy and, when crossed, fierce.

The stories begin even before his birth. It is said that a wandering musician appeared at the tavern one night and prophesied to the expectant mother that she would have a son. He promised that he and his friends would return to serenade her on the night of the birth. The serenade is supposed to have taken place; it probably did. Nothing would be more natural than for two or three itinerant musicians brooding over their wine in a tavern to strike up a tune on the safe delivery of their host's first son in a room overhead. The prophecy is natural, too: everyone in rural Italy or any agricultural community hopes for and predicts the first-born to be a son.

Then there is the story of the bell tower when Verdi was still a babe in arms. It was 1814, and the Cossacks, who were reported to eat babies alive, pursued the retreating French through Le Roncole. The women of the village hid in the church, and Verdi's mother in a frenzy of love and caution climbed with him at her breast to the top of the tower. It is awful to contemplate what might have happened to his eardrums if anyone, at that time of confusion and alarm, had rung the bell. But perhaps his mother had thought of everything and pulled the rope up after her. At any rate the story is commemorated by a plaque on the tower which was placed there in 1914, or sixty-three years after the chief actor, his mother, had died. Verdi himself had been dead then for thirteen years; during his life he never mentioned the story.

The most familiar of the wandering musicians in Le Roncole was Bagasset, who played a fiddle for weddings, festivals or just the joy of it. Verdi, as a child, is supposed to have followed Bagasset everywhere, sitting quietly beside the fiddler as he played. It is also said that as late as the 1850s Bagasset could be found on occasion at Verdi's farm at Sant' Agata. All of which is highly probable; Verdi had a long memory for old friends.

And there is the story which everyone tells a little differently. Verdi, supposedly about seven, was serving as an acolyte at Mass. On this particular Sunday he became so absorbed in listening to the organ that he did not hear the priest whispering for the water and wine. Three times the priest is supposed to have hissed at the daydreamer while the congregation watched with amusement. Finally the priest either kicked, shoved, or nudged the boy who, according to one version, fell in a faint, or to another, picked himself up and, shouting, "God damn you," ran out of the church. There probably is some truth in the story, for it was current in Verdi's lifetime, and at least once in his old age he repeated it in the rougher version to a friend. But old men tend to dramatize their youth, and Verdi's memory was on occasion demonstrably faulty.

Lastly, there is the more musical story of Verdi attacking the spinet with a hammer because he could not find again the chord of C major. But this story is told in one form or another of almost every composer,

and the same action in amateurs who have even more difficulty in relocating chords is taken merely as a sign of bad temper.

One reason it is impossible to state almost anything for certain about Verdi's earliest years in Le Roncole is that he was surrounded and nurtured by men and women, most of whom could not write or did so only with great difficulty. There are no family letters or accounts, children's diaries or schoolbooks, and even when, years later, he had become famous, those of his earliest friends and parents who had survived still could not record their memories and impressions. Verdi himself had no interest in doing so. In all his life, and then only at persistent request, he only once committed his memories to paper, and those were of his first years in Milan. About Le Roncole he would say no more than he did once to a friend: "My youth was hard."

Verdi's father, after he gave his son the spinet, also arranged for him to play the organ with Pietro Baistrocchi, the village organist at Le Roncole. The position of organist was well recognized in even the smallest villages of Italy. It carried a salary, generally not enough to live on, and was frequently combined with other duties in the church or village. In Baistrocchi's case he also claimed to be a schoolteacher. As an organist he cannot have been very good. He is supposed to have

CARLO VERDI'S FARM

been unable to read music which would preclude his being able to teach any but the simplest harmony or theory, so that probably he did no more than show Verdi how an organ worked and give him some suggestions for practicing and phrasing music. Happily Baistrocchi was old and did not mind that his pupil in a year or two obviously played better than his teacher, and he allowed Verdi to substitute for him at several church services. When the old man retired, Verdi, although only ten, succeeded him as village organist.

The position was to be important to Verdi, and he held it until he went to Milan in 1832, nine years later. He probably augmented the salary by playing at weddings and festivals, and in most villages the organist was allowed once a year at the harvest festival to take a collection for himself. He must have been an appealing boy, for the villagers were proud of him. When there was talk of another organist being sent in by the bishop to succeed Baistrocchi, they protested loudly and successfully on behalf of their "maestrino."

At this point Verdi's career might have remained had his father not once again taken the initiative and arranged to have him go to school in Busseto. Probably Verdi nagged his parents about it day and night; perhaps they thought it better for the son and the retarded daughter to grow up apart; perhaps the death of the priest in Le Roncole was decisive, but whatever the reason, his father was sympathetic. He apparently recognized that if Verdi was to hold his job as organist and perhaps add to it that of schoolmaster or priest while at the same time fending off protégés of the bishop, he would have to be better educated, better than he could be if he stayed in Le Roncole. So, just as he had done to get the spinet, Carlo Verdi walked again to Busseto to talk to friends and see what could be arranged.

CHAPTER 2

BUSSETO, I

1823–1829; AGE, 10–16

THE man Carlo Verdi consulted first was Antonio Barezzi, the grocer and wine merchant from whom he bought most of the supplies which he in turn peddled in the village of Le Roncole. Barezzi ran a sort of department store in which he made a specialty of wine which he pressed himself. Business had been good—there is demand for food and drink even in troubled times—and Barezzi was rich, a representative of the new middle class that was rising to prominence in northern Italy.

In 1823 Barezzi was only thirty-six, two years younger than Carlo Verdi, but he was already a man of importance in Busseto for he was the president of the Philharmonic Society and many of its performances and rehearsals were held in a large room in his house. The Society's orchestra was both less and more than the typical symphony orchestra of today. It performed, or at least part of it performed, as a sort of Municipal Band on all public occasions, and in return the town paid its musical director a salary. The Society also provided the orchestra for any visiting opera troupes that might perform in the piazza or any of the larger halls in the town; it provided musicians for the churches when needed, and it gave concerts both outdoors and in, often in Barezzi's hall. The men with a few exceptions such as the director were all amateurs, and they played, perhaps not very smoothly or subtly, for the joy of it; many played several instruments, the choice depending on whether the Society was providing a brass band or a string orchestra. Almost every family in Busseto had a son, a brother or a cousin in the Philharmonic Society, and its orchestra was the talk and pride of the town—particularly when, as not infrequently happened, the orchestra was invited to the neighboring towns. Of all this excitement Barezzi was a recognized leader and patron.

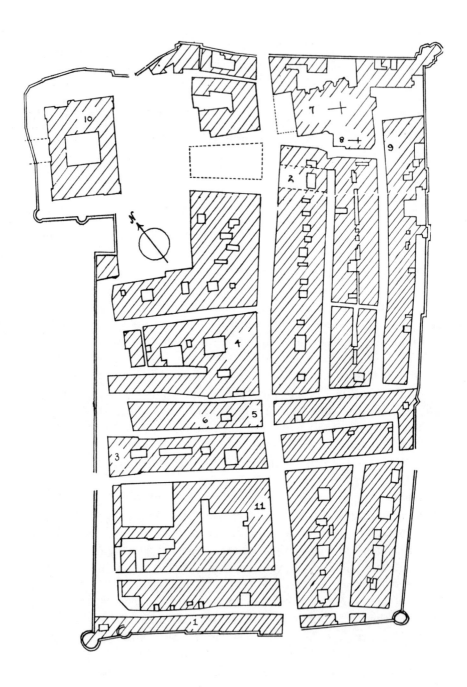

The plan shows the town as it was throughout Verdi's life. It is just the same today except that outside the walls in every direction, streets with houses have developed, particularly to the south. In Verdi's time there were almost no houses outside the walls except that about two hundred yards directly out the north gate was a small church surrounded by three or four buildings. To the south about a quarter of a mile in an open field was a large church attached to a Franciscan monastery, and and next to it in a small park stood the summer villa and stables of the Marquis of Pallavicino. The town gates at the north and south ends of the main street were torn down about 1853 in spite of many outraged protests. Later the walls were pierced on the east and west.

1. By local tradition Pugnatta, the cobbler with whom Verdi lived from 1823 to 1831, had a basement shop and apartment somewhere on the south side of this street.
2. Palazzo Barezzi.
3. Palazzo Tedaldi, where Verdi and Margherita Barezzi lived immediately after their marriage.
4. Palazzo Ex-Cavalli or Orlando, where Verdi lived for several years while the Villa Verdi at Sant' Agata was being built and where he composed Rigoletto.
5. Monte di Pietà, built in 1679.
6. The town library, part of the Monte di Pietà and based on a collection seized by the town from the Jesuits when that Order was banned in 1767.
7. The Chiesa Colleggiata di San Bartolomeo, the town's largest church, built in 1339 and known locally in Verdi's time as the "Cathedral." Here Don Ballarini was the Provost.
8. The Cappella Santa Trinità, a tiny chapel technically separate from the "Cathedral" beside it. It was the parish church for the Barezzi family and here Verdi and Margherita were married. Built in 1110, it is the town's first and oldest church.
9. By local tradition the Jewish community was here so that the unfortunate Sig. Levi could have been murdered directly behind the Palazzo Barezzi. In 1961 reportedly only one Jewish family lived in Busseto.
10. The Teatro Verdi built in 1868, over his objection, and opened with Rigoletto. It is a tiny theatre; the orchestra seats about 150.
11. The Church of the Jesuits, banned in 1767. The church was later desanctified and is now used by the town for exhibitions. It is by far the most beautiful of the churches in Busseto, airy, light and rococo, whereas the others are Lombard.

It is likely that Carlo Verdi several years earlier had consulted Barezzi about the spinet; he probably, on one of his buying trips into town, asked Barezzi to listen to his son play. There is no direct evidence on the conversations between the two men at any point during these years, but their actions seem to indicate clearly that Carlo Verdi recognized and was disturbed by his son's unusual abilities and that Barezzi from the very first took a kindly interest in the boy. Certainly Barezzi never exclaimed to anyone that on such and such a day, like a revelation, he discovered a great talent. On the contrary, he seems almost to have expected Carlo Verdi's visit and without hesitation urged the father to send his son into Busseto to school. He approved of the arrangements to board the boy with a cobbler and, further, agreed to keep a close eye on him. He must have recognized that Verdi, being so interested in music, would inevitably hang around his house and that in the eyes of the town he, Barezzi, would be *in loco parentis*. But he seems never to have worried about the responsibility or been nervous about the difficulties of sponsoring a child of obvious talent but whose temperament was still unknown. It was enough that both he and the peasant boy cared passionately about music; he would do what he could. So that autumn of 1823, in time to begin the school in November, Verdi and his spinet came in a cart to Busseto.

For the next seven and a half years Verdi lived with a cobbler, Pugnatta. The agreement was that Verdi could have board and lodging for thirty centesimi a day. His father paid about half of this, and to the balance Verdi contributed all his earnings as organist at Le Roncole. The seemingly trivial job, which he held for nine years, was paradoxically one of the most important of his entire career, for without it he never would have come to Busseto. Every Sunday and every feast day Verdi walked the three miles to and from Le Roncole—supposedly always barefoot in order to preserve his shoes. One time in winter when he was only ten or eleven he is supposed to have missed his footing and slipped into the deep ditch that lined many of the roads in Parma. These were designed partly for drainage and partly to keep animals and creeping vegetation off the road. This particular time the ditch was filled with water, the bank was steep and slippery, and Verdi, unable to get himself out, was about to become a typical farm accident when a peasant woman passing heard his cries and helped him.

Pugnatta, the cobbler, is a shadowy figure, almost totally unknown except that he is supposed to have been very poor and almost illiterate.

Although he shared house and table with Verdi for many years, he never established any relationship with the boy and thereby missed his chance for at least one sort of immortality. What did he think of all the music? Did he, like Hans Sachs, cobble in time to mark Verdi's mistakes on the spinet, or did he night after night stagger to the tavern to complain to his friends: "Gran dio, all day and night . . . that spinet!" The only story, repeated by old inhabitants of Busseto, is that the stews from Pugnatta's kitchen pot were thin and to eke them out Verdi persuaded a neighbor who sold roasted chestnuts to let him roast strips of cereal mash on the grill.

Verdi's relationship, or lack of it, with Pugnatta suggests the intensity of the concentration Verdi lavished on his music and schoolwork. It is also a little saddening. For Verdi, Pugnatta simply did not exist in anger or in laughter, meanness or kindness. Verdi might be so poor that he had to walk barefoot to Le Roncole, but culturally and intellectually even at ten he had already left forever his family's type and class of man. He would remain always, even in trying circumstances, a loving and dutiful son to his parents, but he would grow in the next ten years as the son of another man. He never again would make a friend among the peasants and the cobblers, and the friendships with them that he had would quickly fade as his life changed and theirs remained the same.

When Verdi came to Busseto, it was a town of some two thousand persons and the political and commercial capital of its area. It had several churches, one of which the inhabitants called a cathedral, by which they meant only that it was the church where the bishop said Mass when he came. The cathedral had an organ, larger than the one at Le Roncole, four singers, a choir and a string quartet. There was the school, known as the Gymnasium, also a music school, and even a Jewish community with its own school. Also, and most important for Verdi, there was a public library. Outside the town the local aristocrat, the Marquis of Pallavicino, had a summer villa set in a tiny park and surrounded by a moat. In town the buildings rose sometimes as high as three or four stories and were generally built around an interior courtyard. Barezzi's house was one of these. On the ground floor was the store set back behind an arcade. Immediately above was the large room where the Philharmonic rehearsals and concerts were held, and then above and behind that were the family's quarters. It was all on a scale vastly larger than anything in Le Roncole and offered in what it represented a life of far greater possibilities, so much greater in fact that the difference was one of kind rather than degree. The move to Busseto into Barezzi's patronage, even more than the later move to Milan, was the most decisive act in Verdi's life.

From his trips into the town with his father Verdi must already have been familiar with its streets and buildings. Certainly he knew Barezzi's store; so that his new surroundings cannot have been strange. In any event he had his spinet to play, and at least once a week, he knew, he would see his family in Le Roncole. Still ten is young to be partially self-supporting and away from home. Did he cry? Was he homesick? He never said, and no one knows. But almost certainly not; he was eager and from the first did well at the school where his teacher was Don Pietro Seletti, a priest and a canon at the cathedral. Verdi started in the lower grammar school with the basic subjects of reading and writing. Later he took up Latin and Italian literature and history. He did well enough in these for the priest to want the boy to go into the Church, a career at the time easily and traditionally joined with music.

When he was not in school Verdi seems to have been either practicing on his spinet, reading in the public library or just hanging around places where music was being made, the cathedral, Barezzi's house, or the music school. He probably behaved just as he had in Le Roncole with the fiddler Bagasset, sitting quietly and watching and, when called upon, eagerly doing whatever was asked of him, beginning with arranging chairs and music stands. A town of two thousand is, after all, a very small town, and there can hardly have been more than a hundred musicians actively making music in public places. These must very soon have come to know Verdi and granted him a niche in their lives and doings.

The best musician and the most important to Verdi was Ferdinando Provesi, who was at this time fifty-three and the music director of the Philharmonic Society, head of the music school and organist at the cathedral. The town had appointed Provesi to his posts in 1813, and since then with the backing of Barezzi he had reorganized the choir, the Philharmonic Society and music school to everyone's greater enjoyment. More than any other man he was responsible for the variety and unusually high standard of music in Busseto. Barezzi must have very early introduced Verdi to Provesi, for Provesi, at first from a distance with suggestions and then personally, directed Verdi's musical education. At his suggestion Barezzi taught Verdi how to play the flute,

PROVESI

the clarinet, the horn and an old-fashioned sort of bass clarinet known as a "serpent." Provesi himself worked with Verdi on harmony and counterpoint and the piano which the boy had started by himself from a book of instructions. He practiced on the piano in Barezzi's house. As he got more and more proficient on the instruments he began filling in for players absent at the Philharmonic rehearsals and copying out the parts. He also fell behind in his work at the grammar school.

This caused trouble, and his teacher Seletti, the priest, complained to Verdi, the school officials, and apparently to anyone else who would listen, that the boy was spending too much time on music. Word of it got, as Seletti intended, to Provesi, who replied in kind, which meant that cutting epigrams and satiric poems were discreetly circulated by

SELETTI

the two men among mutual friends and enemies. The row was partly political: Provesi was a republican and radical, imbued with the ideas of the French Revolution, and Seletti was a reactionary favoring Austrian intervention to support the Pope's Temporal Power in Italy. In the middle and the immediate bone of the growling was Verdi, still only twelve or thirteen years old. He attempted to please both by skimping his work first for this one, then that, but of course this merely and inevitably drew the thunder and lightning onto his own head. Nothing is more agitating, even physically painful, to a teacher than to realize that, somehow, he is failing to hold the full attention of his best and favorite student. It is like a personal repudiation.

One day in anger and disappointment Provesi is supposed to have complained to Verdi that the work assigned was not being done. The reply was a confession by way of extenuation: there was not enough time in the day to go to the grammar school, the music school, support one's self by playing the organ in Le Roncole and do the tens of other little musical jobs that by then Verdi had accreted to himself. Even worse, there was talk at the grammar school of expelling him if he did not work harder at Latin and less at music, in fact give up the music school. After thinking, Provesi replied: "Listen, my son, if you continue to work as you have in the past you will become a first-rate maestro. I could not predict as much for you in the field of scholarship, not because you lack ability, but because of your inordinate love of music." He added, however, that a musician must know many things, and he urged Verdi to continue with his academic studies, offering to teach them himself if the grammar school expelled him.

Still, while Provesi's remarks may have helped Verdi to see more clearly that he was inevitably to be a musician and not a priest, they had not reached the ears of the grammar school faculty and probably would not have penetrated those of Seletti in any event. What was needed was an incident, a fact, and preferably one that did not stem from Provesi or Barezzi. Happily this came along at a special church celebration. The organist hired for the occasion, a man named Soncini, failed to appear, and Seletti suggested that Verdi take his place. Perhaps Seletti was joking, but Verdi's performance, improvised and without music, was so good that the priest conceded and urged the boy to put music first. Thereafter there were no more complaints from the grammar school, and in due time Verdi graduated. He and Seletti remained friends, for the priest was a reasonable man and reputed to be a good violinist. And when Verdi first arrived in Milan, an unknown young man from a little provincial town, he stayed with Seletti's nephew.

As the years passed Verdi became Provesi's assistant in name as well as fact. He gave lessons when Provesi was ill; he assisted at the organ, at the Philharmonic Society, taught Barezzi's children, and continued to be organist at Le Roncole, every Sunday and feast day, out and back. By the time he was fifteen he was an accomplished even if inexperienced maestro. Provesi acknowledged him to be the better pianist.

When he was about fifteen Verdi began to compose, probably at first piano pieces, songs and airs for solo instruments. One of the first full orchestral works seems to have been a new overture for Rossini's *Il Barbiere di Siviglia*. A visiting troupe was to present the opera and the Philharmonic Society, as usual, was to provide the orchestra. Verdi by this time had conducted many rehearsals and knew all the members of the Philharmonic Society; they, more than the boys in school or the peasants in Le Roncole, were his friends. So he wrote an overture which they rehearsed and played at the performance. It was a great success.

To substitute an overture to an opera in 1828 was not the presumptuous thing it would be today. Then there was hardly a concept of a standard repertory with masterworks that could not be tampered with. Most music was new music, and the older operas were constantly rearranged to suit the talents of a particular troupe or the needs of a public occasion. Rossini himself had used his own overture to *Il Barbiere di Siviglia* for two previous operas, both of which had failed. So Verdi's action was neither flamboyant nor presumptuous; it was offered and received in the spirit of what might be expected of any practicing musician; the only extraordinary thing was that he was fifteen.

That same year he composed a cantata called *I deliri di Saul*. Barezzi has left an enthusiastic note describing it as "for full orchestra and solo baritone voice, the first work of some account, composed at the youthful age of fifteen, in which he shows a vivid imagination, a philosophical outlook and sound judgment in the arrangement of the instrumental parts." This was played and sung throughout the villages and towns surrounding Busseto and added considerably to Verdi's local fame. The music was never published as Verdi always forbade the publication of his early works: the past, he considered, was his private affair.

By now Verdi had learned almost everything Busseto had to teach him. He was sixteen; he was not yet fully self-supporting. He felt that

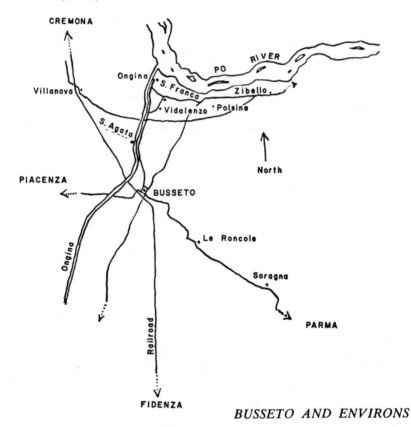

BUSSETO AND ENVIRONS

a great deal had been done for him by others and he should, if possible, free them of the burden. When the organist at a nearby village, Soragna, announced his retirement, Verdi asked to be considered for the job. The salary combined with that at Le Roncole would have provided a modest living. His petition to the vestry of the church is preserved:

Roncole, 24 October 1829

Most Illustrious Gentlemen:

It having come to the knowledge of Giuseppe Verdi, a resident of the commune of Roncole, that the position of organist at the Parish Church at Soragna, by reason of the voluntary resignation of Signor Frondoni, will soon be vacant, he offers himself as a replacement for the present incumbent, subject of course to the necessary investigation, either private or public, of the applicant's ability to discharge the holy duties.

He asks, therefore, that the said most Illustrious Gentlemen will admit him among the competitors for the above-mentioned position of organist, assuring them of the most attentive and conscientious service and every effort possible to deserve the general approval in the event that he is selected for the post.

With confidence and expression of his deepest respect he declares himself, Gentlemen, your most obedient and devoted servant,

GIUSEPPE VERDI

Verdi, however, in spite of the support of his friends and testimonials by Provesi, was not hired—which probably in the long run was best for him. Le Roncole and Soragna between them offered less stimulation than Busseto. Probably, although no one recognized it yet, he was ready to move on to Milan or Parma, both centers of music. Just as Carlo Verdi had thought in terms of his son becoming the organist and perhaps schoolteacher or priest at Le Roncole, so now Barezzi and Provesi seem to have thought in terms of Verdi succeeding Provesi in the various musical posts in Busseto. The boy, after all, was already Provesi's assistant, and the older man was increasingly ill and wanted to retire. What Verdi wanted for himself is not known, but it would be strange if he did not dream of writing the great Italian opera. Opera at that time was the dominant form of musical expression in Italy, and any artist, particularly a young one, dreams of a magnum opus that will stir his fellows and bring him fame and fortune. But a practical plan to realize his ambition was something else again. Verdi, who was having trouble making ends meet in Busseto, probably never considered Milan at all and saw life in terms of a day-to-day job in Busseto: schoolwork, a rehearsal, a new composition, a new paying pupil for the piano. After he failed to win the post at Soragna, life in Busseto went on as before.

CHAPTER 3

BUSSETO, II

1829–1832; AGE, 16–18

SOMETIME when he was sixteen Verdi read Manzoni's novel *I Promessi Sposi*. The book made a profound impression on him, and when he was fifty-three he wrote a friend about it and Manzoni with all the enthusiasm of youth: "You know well what and how much has been my veneration for that Man who, according to me, has written not only the greatest book of our time but one of the greatest books that ever came out of a human brain; and it is not only a book, but a consolation to humanity. I was sixteen years old when I read it for the first time. Since then I have read many another which (even when by the greatest authors) on rereading at an older age have seemed less good than I remembered it. But for that book my enthusiasm endures, ever the same; or even, on knowing men well, has grown greater. It's that this is a *true* book; as true as the *truth.*" Several years later, in 1874, Verdi translated his veneration into music when he composed his *Requiem* to commemorate the first anniversary of Manzoni's death.

I Promessi Sposi is the great Italian novel; it has been described as representing for Italians all of Scott, Dickens and Thackeray rolled into one and infused with the spirit of Tolstoy. Because of the times and conditions in Italy in 1827, when it was first published, it had then and increasingly each year thereafter an extraordinary extra-literary effect. This was partly because of its language.

In 1827 there was no *national* Italian language; the basis of what ultimately became it was still only a dialect, the Tuscan, spoken in and around Florence. Elsewhere different areas and even towns each had their own dialects, and it was perfectly possible for a Neapolitan to be unable to understand a Venetian unless they had in common some other language or dialect, usually Tuscan which was descended from the language of Dante. The court and official languages of the various Italian states at the time were French in Piedmont and Naples, Latin in the Papal States, and German in the Austrian dependencies of Lombardy-Venetia, Parma, Tuscany and Modena. And what was spoken at court often had no relation to what was used at home. In Milan, for example, Manzoni and his family always spoke to each other in French or the Milanese dialect; at Nice, Garibaldi and his family used French or a Ligurian dialect; and at Busseto, Verdi and the Barezzis all spoke a Parmigiano dialect. For almost all Italians in the nineteenth century Italian, as it exists today, was a second or sometimes even third language. Simple folk like Verdi's parents spoke only their local dialect.

The dialects tended to keep Italy divided and the people of different areas suspicious of each other. During the nineteenth century, as Italians began to feel themselves a nation and struggled to achieve unity and independence, a movement loosely called the Risorgimento, the development of a common language out of the Tuscan dialect had a strong cohesive effect. To it Manzoni's novel contributed greatly by bringing the language and grammar up to date.

When Manzoni, along with most educated Italians, had decided that of all the dialects the Tuscan was the richest and the most beautiful, he had only just begun on the problem of writing a popular novel in it. There was, for example, no authoritative dictionary. Probably the best was the *Vocabulario della Crusca* which had been compiled by the academy of that name. The dictionary consisted almost entirely of words culled from the works of Tuscan writers of the fourteenth to sixteenth century. It was, therefore, dated and had almost no words for any concrete object or thought that had come within the province of literature since the sixteenth century. However excellent a dictionary it might be for poets writing epics of chivalry and courtly love, for novelists writing in the nineteenth century it was hopelessly inadequate.

To this was added the additional problem of flowery construction. Throughout the eighteenth century academies had flourished in Italy —Busseto had had two—which had attempted to foster the arts and graces of life and also to preserve and purify the language. But the result had been to create yet another dialect, literary talk. It perhaps was pure, capable of subtleties, power and refinement; it certainly was involved, and no one, not even writers and educated aristocrats, consistently talked it. The great bulk of Italians, the peasants and middle class, did not talk it at all. Writers of all sorts, literary and political, despaired over this; language was a barrier, not a bridge to communication.

Manzoni's book was the first to break down the barrier. It succeeded, in its early editions, by using a happy mixture of literary talk for the descriptive passages with Milanese dialect for the dialogue. The vocabulary was a mixture of Lombard, Tuscan, French and Latin with made-up words he derived from one or the other by analogy or extension. The style was simple and straightforward. The story is of war, famine and plague and is subtitled "A Tale of XVII Century Milan." Manzoni wove into his tale, which was based in part on contemporary documents, many strands, at least one of which was sure to appeal to every Italian: there was the irresponsibility of the governing classes, the simple honesty of the peasants who were its heroes, the beginnings of the Milanese silk industry, the adaptability of human nature to disaster, and finally, throughout, a devastating indictment of evil. For the first time in many years on the Italian peninsula everyone who could read, even boys like Verdi in provincial towns, read the same book.

It sped through edition after edition (to date there have been some 520) until the definitive one Manzoni issued in 1840 after revising much of the language. He had visited Florence in 1827 and become convinced that Tuscan Italian was the best language for all of Italy. Thereafter in each edition he substituted more and more Tuscanisms, which gave rise to the quip that he had "washed his linen in the Arno." This referred to Emilia Luti, a Florentine governess, who besides teaching his children and doing a little family laundry became the oracle for testing words and phrases. But beside words Manzoni fixed whole ways of constructing sentences in the popular mind. The book became almost a primer and dictionary of the emerging Italian language, and from the first schools used it as such. Childish, piping voices recited the famous passages, as in other lands their counterparts do Homer, Racine or Shakespeare. Today children in the Italian government schools begin studying it at nine. In the 1830s when they first began to do so the fact had tremendous political significance. Without it or something like it the ultimate unification of Italy might not have been possible.

Verdi's response to *I Promessi Sposi* was not primarily political. Yet he, like many Italians, was probably moved by it to ally himself emotionally with the liberal, patriotic party. The novel tells its tale

MANZONI

without propaganda, but when the hero leaves the ill-governed Duchy of Milan for the better governed Republic of Venice, it suggests that man should try to improve his lot in this world and that forms of government are important. And in Manzoni's other works which Verdi also read, Manzoni is more explicit. These were two verse tragedies on patriotic, noble themes and an Ode, *Il Cinque Maggio,* on Napoleon's death (5 May 1821).

The Ode took Italy and Europe by storm, outdoing in popularity other odes on Napoleon by Lamartine, Béranger, Wordsworth and Byron. Goethe translated it into German, Gladstone into English and the Emperor of Brazil, Don Pedro II, into Portuguese. As Manzoni wrote to a friend, "The news shook me as if something essential was now lacking from the world. I was seized with an urge to write about him and had to throw off that Ode." He seems to have had an almost direct inspiration, for he wrote the Ode in three days; only "almost," however, because he kept his wife at the piano in the next room continually playing military marches.

Verdi probably discovered the Ode and the tragedies when he read

I Promessi Sposi or perhaps, under Provesi's guidance, even earlier. Certainly they too made a deep impression on him, for at some time, perhaps about 1840, he set the Ode and some of the choruses of the tragedies to music. He never allowed them to be published, but on the other hand, one time when he was destroying much of his early music, he saved them because of what they had meant to him.

Throughout Verdi's early life Napoleon's name was the most hated, discussed and beloved in Italy; his picture often hung over the fireplace or door, and thousands of baby boys were named after him. For many parents it was enough merely that the man who was the greatest explosion of human energy in modern times was an Italian by heritage, for Corsica had not become French—and then most unwillingly—until March 1769, five months before Napoleon was born. For others his meteoric career embodied the democratic doctrine that talent, not wealth or birth, should determine a man's position in society and that no phase of art, government or law was necessarily a perquisite of pedigree or privilege. More practically, he drove the Austrians out of Northern Italy and set up the Cisalpine Republic out of the former duchies of Milan, Parma and Modena, the legations of Bologna and Ferrara, the Romagna, and some scraps of Venice and Switzerland. Far more important than the actual boundaries was that the area included Milan, Parma and Bologna and contained the most energetic and progressive populations in Italy. They never forgot their brief experience of freedom and self-government, and some of them never ceased to work to have it again.

Those who hated Napoleon found it easy to find reasons. His soldiers frequently forgot they were bringing liberty and freedom and behaved like the oppressors they replaced. Napoleon in 1805 cancelled the Republic's constitution and had himself solemnly crowned in the Cathedral of Milan as King of Italy. He conscripted Italians into his armies by what amounted to slave raids, and only a third of his army he took into Russia was French. Those with money or pull—Rossini was one—could buy their way out of service, but the peasants could not, and they hated Napoleon. All groups suffered, but again particularly the peasants, from the inflationary effect on money of his commissary purchases and confiscations. The Church and the devout hated him as an atheist who declared boldly that the purpose of religion was to attach "to heaven an idea of equality which prevents the rich man from being massacred by the poor." And anyone proud of

Italian art, but particularly the titled possessors of it, hated him for his organized and educated looting. By deliberate policy Napoleon ordered all that was best and movable to be sent to the new Rome, Paris. Off from Venice, for example, in 1797 went the four bronze horses, the lion of St. Mark's, a bust, a bas-relief, an exceptionally precious cameo, sixteen pictures, 230 incunabula and 253 manuscripts. Every city, including the Vatican, was forced to surrender its best art works. Understandably the owners were unhappy and nurtured their grudges. To all Italians it was humiliating.

In time much came back. On 23 and 24 October 1815 forty-one carts with more than 200 draft horses left Paris for Italy. The four bronze horses bound for St. Mark's in Venice traveled over the Alps in four specially constructed wagons, each pulled by six horses, and were unveiled in place just eighteen years to the day after they had been removed. But much also remained in Paris, and as recently as 1926 the Musée du Louvre in its catalogue was still insisting that soldiers were, after all, soldiers, and if they carried off pictures, well: "Leur avidité était singulièrement idéaliste." But as always with Napoleon, there was good mixed with the bad. The Louvre put the works on public display, and for the first time artists from all of Europe, tourists and the general public could see masterpieces of art heretofore locked in private collections. Napoleon's raids into Italy greatly accelerated the democratization of art so typical of the present century.

Although Napoleon's defeat restored some of its art to Italy, the country had no more freedom than before. The Congress of Vienna gave Austria the two provinces of Milan and Venice which were organized into a dependent Kingdom of Italy. Parma was given to Marie Louise, and the tiny Duchy of Lucca to the unimportant Spanish-Bourbon line which before Napoleon had ruled in Parma. Other Austrian dependents were restored to the thrones of Modena and Tuscany. Only in the Kingdoms of Naples and Piedmont-Sardinia did the restored monarchs have any real independence.

Beneath the surface of this imposed order ideas that Napoleon had first introduced to Italy, such as nationalism and constitutional government, continued to fester. And his defeat and subsequent death did not ease the antagonism between Italians over these ideas. On the one hand favoring them were the liberal aristocrats, artists of all kinds and some of the middle class; opposing them were the Church, the aristocrats who had a direct interest in maintaining the petty principalities and much of the peasantry which was apt to adopt the opinions of its parish priests. But there were all shades of opinions. Perhaps the largest group was of republicans who admired the early Napoleon of liberal laws and constitutions; others favored the political theory of Napoleon as Emperor, a despot based on popular consent; still others wanted a constitutional monarchy. Busseto as a small town in the Duchy of Parma, the quietest of the small states, was outside the main political stream of the times. But Verdi cannot have been unaware of the issues; his reading shows he was not, and his two teachers, Provesi and Seletti, held differing opinions. Inevitably Verdi must have absorbed more than music from Provesi, and although he always said he knew nothing about politics and in his youth refrained from political acts and conspiracies, he was a republican in sympathy, anti-Austrian and anti-clerical.

Conspiracies were constantly going on, and revolutions were attempted periodically. Usually only a few men were involved and casualties were very small. One of the first and most important provided the movement with a martyr, Conte Federico Confalonieri. He was famous in northern Italy for introducing the spinning jenny which started the area's cotton industry, and he had also built the first steamboat to navigate the Po. He was a republican, and the attempted revolution took place in Milan in April 1821.

The plan was to drive the Austrians out of Milan by concerted action with a party of constitutionalists in the Kingdom of Piedmont. The timing was bad to begin with, but in addition everything conceivable went wrong, including an inexplicable hesitation and betrayal by the liberal Prince of Piedmont, Carlo Alberto. His aide-de-camp, the Marchese di Collegno, was so horrified at the turnabout that he slapped the prince's face, then broke his sword at his feet and went into exile.

Meanwhile consternation and suspense reigned in Milan. Confalonieri was seized and convicted of treason, for which the penalty was death. His wife, the Contessa Teresa, hoping to intercede for him, bounced and jigged across the Alps as fast as horse could pull carriage in order to plead with the Austrian Emperor, Francis I. The trip generally took five or six days. Metternich, the Emperor's Chancellor, was opposed to having the Emperor see her, but after several days her friends succeeded in arranging an interview. To the Contessa's pleas the Emperor replied: "Madam, as a special mark of my good will toward yourself, I inform you that a courier has already been dispatched with a sentence of death for your husband. If you wish to see your husband alive, I advise you to quit Vienna immediately." The poor woman then re-entered her carriage and attempted to overtake the courier in a race over the Alps back to Milan.

Happily the courier's carriage broke down, and the Contessa passed him. Then a second courier arrived in Milan before the first with orders to the commission countermanding the death sentence but without advising what punishment should be imposed. So the Contessa's brother hastened to Vienna with a petition from many of the leading citizens in Milan. In the end Confalonieri was sentenced to life imprisonment in Spielberg, the Austrian political prison in Bohemia. When he returned to Milan in 1840 on parole to see his dying father, his prison experience and reconversion to Catholicism had made him an ardent supporter of the status quo and peace-at-any-price. Some argued that he had achieved wisdom, others that prison had broken him.

Verdi was only eight years old and still in Le Roncole when Confalonieri was sentenced, and it is doubtful whether the peasants around him knew, cared about or discussed what was happening in Milan which was, after all, in a foreign state for which a passport was needed. But in larger Busseto he heard the issues discussed and argued, endlessly, for Confalonieri was only one of several martyrs, and the next attempted revolution affected Verdi's own state, the Duchy of Parma.

It began on 3 February 1831 in the Duchy of Modena, immediately to the south and west of Parma. Verdi was then seventeen. The revolutionaries this time issued a manifesto proclaiming as king of Italy Napoleon's only legitimate son, the Duke of Reichstadt, who was just short of twenty years old and kept prisoner, although with golden chains, by Metternich in Vienna. The manifesto called for a king "sprung from the blood of the immortal Napoleon." The Duke's mother, the ex-Empress Marie Louise, was the Duchess of Parma. The revolution, seeking to replace the mother with the son, reached Parma in a week and after Bologna, Ferrara, Ravenna and Forli had all announced for Napoleon II, as the young Duke was called in Italy. In Parma Marie Louise, who had refused to accompany Napoleon to Elba and seldom went to Vienna to see her son, was restricted by the revolutionaries to her palace. After four days she escaped—no one wished her harm—and fled to Piacenza where the Austrians were in control. At Busseto, which was on one of the main roads between Parma and Piacenza, everyone saw couriers and cavalry gallop by, watched coaches stop to change horses, and had his heart rise or sink with each rumor, depending on his political bias.

In Vienna Marie Louise's internment in Parma was described as a magnificent act of resistance and her escape to Piacenza as an epic adventure. The revolutionaries formed a provisional government, but within a month they had gone underground or into exile as the Austrian troops restored order in the two Duchies. Happily they did not know that in Vienna their candidate for king of Italy had talked wildly of leading a regiment to his mother's assistance. But he was never to see Italy, not even to visit his mother in Parma. She did not want it, and Metternich never would allow it. The name and heritage were too incendiary. Eighteen months later when Marie Louise was safely back on her throne, her son died in Vienna of tuberculosis, a pawn in Austrian politics and a prisoner in his own family.

When Marie Louise herself died in 1847 she was still, in spite of the revolutions, Duchess of Parma and had been so for as long as Verdi could remember. By Italian standards of the time her reign was long and mild. Its length perhaps was caused by Austrian second thoughts about her son. Under the original terms of the Congress of Vienna he had been in line to succeed his mother. But then his father, the first Napoleon, had escaped from Elba and had his Hundred Days to Waterloo. After his defeat there he abdicated and declared his son Emperor of France, Napoleon II. But the little boy, the Prince of Parma, was then in Vienna with his mother who preferred to go on to the backwater of Parma rather than to return to the maelstrom of Paris. The lesson of the Hundred Days, however, was not lost on Metternich and the other statesmen. Marie Louise was forced to renounce her son's right to succeed her in Parma, and the succession was given to the Spanish-Bourbon line which was languishing in Lucca. This act undoubtedly contributed to her longevity, for no one in Parma wanted to restore the Bourbons who had a reputation for cruelty.

The mildness of her reign was an expression of character, and the people of Parma were envied by others who groaned under the Bourbons in Naples, the Pope in Rome and the Duke in Modena. Her court was dominated by Austrians and her policy run by Metternich in Vienna. But she herself was neither viciously cruel nor personally vindictive. She had a trick of turning her ear inside out, and in a mild way she even patronized the arts. She built the Teatro Regio, which is still the opera house in Parma, and she herself often attended the per-

MARIE LOUISE

formances in it. Sometimes the circumstances were awkward. She re-fused to allow news of Napoleon's death at St. Helena, for example, to deter her from hearing a performance of Rossini's *Il Barbiere di Siviglia*. But by then she had no feeling left for the distant Emperor and gave his death mask, which had been brought to her by his doctor, to her steward's children to pull around the floor on a piece of string. What she really liked was men. Her first lover was an Austrian, Count Neip-perg, who seemed to be able to keep her contented or at least pregnant. By him she had a flock of illegitimate children, called Montenuovo, and within a month of Napoleon's death she married him. It is a com-mentary on the difficulty of communication in those days that she was able to keep the marriage and children a secret from her father, the Austrian Emperor, for a number of years. But Neipperg died in 1829, leaving Marie Louise disconsolate. Her desires continued as ardent as before, but no longer, it seemed, could any one man satisfy them. To control the traffic at her bedroom door and steer the less desirables down the hall one of her ministers posted a sentry. But then one morn-ing he, too, was discovered in her bed. The guard was doubled, but gossip had it the two men were fully occupied ministering to their sovereign's wants. She became a middle-aged frump, followed around by an old-fashioned court. To everyone, including the Parmigiani, she seemed utterly devoid of political importance or personal standing. What mattered were the Austrian bayonets supporting her.

The year of the revolution in Parma, 1831, was also the year Barezzi decided definitely that by hook or crook Verdi must go to Milan to study. After Verdi failed to win the post of organist at Soragna, he continued his studies and work in Busseto with Provesi. He was already famous locally; persons came from other towns to hear his works, and he often led the Philharmonic Society out on tours through the villages around Busseto. But he clearly was at a point where he either had to continue his studies, which meant leaving Busseto and was expensive, or had to establish himself in some combination of jobs that would make him financially independent. His father, Carlo Verdi, favored this last course: it was time now for the son to come home and help support the family. At least he would not have to peddle salt and till the ground as had his father.

Barezzi, however, did not agree. By now he was convinced that there was no limit to Verdi's talent and that he should have the best training available. This meant not Parma, which had a good music school and small court theatre, but Milan, which had the best Conservatory in Italy and La Scala, the greatest theatre. What Verdi felt is unknown except that obviously he did not go to Milan against his will. But he has left no clue how he resolved in his own mind his proposed departure and his duty to his family toward whom he was always extremely loyal. Did he remember Provesi's suggestion that anyone so inordinately fond of music as he courted disappointment and bitterness if his commitment to it was anything short of complete? Once again there is no record, but his life, letters in later years and even his opera librettos suggest that he was aware of this sort of conflict and could not take it lightly.

Barezzi's plan was to make use of one of the scholarships offered by the Monte di Pietà e d' Abbondanza. This was an institution in Busseto, founded in the seventeenth century after an epidemic of cholera. Many of the inhabitants gave property in memory of the children lost to found the institution whose purpose was to relieve poverty in general and to provide annual grants to poor children for their education. Urged on by Barezzi, Carlo Verdi swallowed his objections and on 14 May 1831 filed an application requesting the "Illustrious President and Administrative Councilors of the Sacred Monte di Pietà of Busseto" to grant his son a scholarship "whereby he may perfect himself in the art of music, in which he has given evidence of extraordinary ability both as to execution and composition." He protested that his humble circumstances and financial straits did not permit him to aid his son in his career and he placed the "liveliest hope" in "that monthly subsidy by means of which other poor young men are enabled to pursue their studies either in the fine arts or in the sciences." He further requested for the moment "a small subsidy" while awaiting "the fortunate moment for one of the fixed scholarships." Then, of course, for many months, while the institution made its investigation, nothing happened.

The same day that Carlo Verdi filed the application Barezzi invited Verdi to live at his house. For a number of years Verdi had become increasingly a member of Barezzi's family: he ate most of his meals with them; he helped Barezzi with the accounts in the store; he gave the children piano lessons. The move, however, was Signora Barezzi's idea. Two nights earlier a neighbor, Isaac Levi, had been murdered. Burglars, after the proceeds of a sale of a farm and aided by his servant, had woken him, gagged and carried him to his attic, and slit his throat. They were still at large, and Signora Barezzi, a sort of auricular witness to the crime, was terrified that her house would be visited next. She knew Verdi stayed up to all hours reading and composing and saw in the seventeen-year-old boy the perfect watchman. To Barezzi she argued that Verdi was in the house all day long; why not the night, too? Barezzi was delighted with the idea and immediately persuaded Verdi to move.

Barezzi's family then consisted of his wife, Maria, three daughters followed by a son, Giovanni, and a baby, Demetrio. The eldest daughter, Margherita, was only five months younger than Verdi; she was gentle, pretty and fond of music. In the months that they lived together in the same house, laughing and playing duets, he came to love her as she did him. He called her "Ghita." There are no first love letters or notes between them for they were never separated.

In time their attraction was noticed, but just how is not known. Did the Signora come on them one day holding hands at the piano? Did a younger brother see a kiss and tattle? Or was it just the added consideration he accorded her? The last is the most likely. By the customs of the time a kiss would have been a scandal and almost certainly have ended Barezzi's relations, at least the personal ones, with Verdi. Love in those days and in a family such as Barezzi's blossomed in the midst of family life, and however old the daughter might be a chaperon accompanied her to the theatre, the market or even into the street. Frequently the chaperon was a sister or brother, but still there were always two, and even today among simple families, particularly in southern Italy, the girl's first kiss is often at the altar after the priest has married her. But howsoever it was first discovered, Barezzi was delighted. The Signora undoubtedly laid down a few precepts for behavior, and the affair was officially if not formally recognized. Verdi, meanwhile, continued to live with the family, the fact being good evidence of the confidence the parents had in him. Margherita was, after all, the eldest daughter of one of the town's leading and most prosperous citizens. She was approaching marriageable age, and many parents would have feared that Verdi's continued presence might, in the eyes of the town, compromise their daughter. Certainly most small-town, prosperous grocers would have considered a penniless peasant who wanted to write music a most unsuitable match.

Barezzi, however, was an unusual man. It says much for his tact and the fullness of his love that his own children never resented Verdi's presence in their midst and even more perhaps that Verdi was never embarrassed by his position. The children and Verdi saw and liked each other even when grown. Barezzi's goodness to Verdi at times seems almost to obscure his character and manifest merely a rather fat, jovial simpleton who drifted through life without much purpose or character of his own. It is well to remember that he was an exceedingly success-ful businessman and one of the recognized leaders of his town, that he had the energy and interest to discover and foster a genius who was not a child prodigy, and that when Verdi was the most successful com-poser in Italy Barezzi asked for nothing from his protégé except news of how life was going. The key to his goodness to Verdi is twofold: his love of music and, developing out of these years in Busseto, his love for Verdi. The two in time combined in a faith which, while perhaps simple, was absolutely constant: Verdi would be a great composer.

The application to the Monte di Pietà had been submitted in May 1831, and by December still nothing had been heard. Barezzi and Provesi consulted, and Carlo Verdi petitioned again on behalf of his son. This time, however, he appealed directly to his sovereign, Marie Louise, setting forth the history and purpose of his previous applica-tion. The Duchess as sovereign had an interest in the administration of charities within her state and through her Minister of Interior looked into the matter and replied promptly: all four scholarships were presently held, and none would become available until October 1833. This was eighteen months off, and in January 1832 the Mayor of Busseto informed Barezzi and Carlo Verdi that the Monte di Pietà had awarded Verdi a scholarship beginning November 1833. The foundation did, however, in view of the expense of living and studying in Milan, agree to pay the full stipend in two years instead of the usual four. The only requirement of the scholarship was that Verdi must present each year "a certificate from the most prominent professors attesting to his ability, mastery, unusual talent and such progress as to leave no doubt that young Verdi showed extraordinary promise in music far above the

MONTE DI PIETÀ

average; moreover that he was a young man of good conduct and an assiduous worker."

Barezzi promptly offered to advance the equivalent of a year's stipend so that Verdi could begin at the Conservatory in November 1832 or a year before the scholarship from the Monte di Pietà became available. The school year at the Conservatory ran from November through June. Barezzi also financed, because there was no one else to do so, Verdi's trip to Milan in June to take the Conservatory examinations. To go to Milan, which was in a foreign state, Verdi needed a passport, and the Minister of the Interior of Parma issued him one at the end of May. Probably sometime that month Verdi walked for the last time to Le Roncole to play the organ; after nine years he resigned the post.

Early in June he set out with his father and Provesi. He had never been in a big city before; indeed he had never been beyond the area immediately around Busseto. His passport described him: Age: eighteen. Height: tall. Color of hair: chestnut-brown. Color of eyes: gray. Forehead: high. Eyebrows: black. Nose: aquiline. Mouth: small. Beard: dark. Chin: oval. Face: thin. Complexion: pale. Special peculiarities: pock-marked.

CHAPTER 4

MILAN

1832–1833; AGE, 19

MILAN, when Verdi first came to it in 1832, was the most prosperous and important city in northern Italy. It was the capital of the Kingdom of Lombardy-Venetia, and the king was the Austrian Emperor, Francis I. He ruled through an Imperial Governor who kept his seat in Milan and thereby assured the political dominance of that city over the tiny Duchy of Lucca, the neighboring Duchies of Parma and Modena and even to some extent over Tuscany. It was also the source of bayonets for the Pope when he needed, as in the revolution of 1831, to reconquer his subjects. Only Turin, capital of Piedmont-Sardinia and seat of the House of Savoy, did not look on Milan as the true political pole of northern Italy.

Milan also dominated its neighbors artistically. In literature it had Manzoni, although it could not claim the great poet, Giacomo Leopardi, who preferred Florence and Naples. But in music it was acknowledged throughout all of Italy to be supreme; from about 1820 on all that was best in music gravitated toward Milan, particularly to its principal theatre, the Teatro alla Scala, which is popularly shortened to La Scala and stands in the center of the city. Its name derives from its site where once stood the church of Santa Maria alla Scala, built in 1381 by Regina della Scala, the wife of one of the ruling family of Visconti; whatever may be the origin of the Visconti name, the theatre's name has no direct connection with stairs or steps.

The Austrians subsidized La Scala heavily in order, Italian patriots insisted, to keep the Milanese from thinking of their political grievances. But if this was so, the policy did not succeed, although the performances were the best in Europe. An entry in the records of the theatre, for example, reads: "20 January 1824. Scarcely a soul in the theatre; all boxes shut or deserted. Universal mourning for the tragic

PO VALLEY

With principal cities; national boundaries as of 1962. (One inch = 63 statute miles)

catastrophe of the sentences to be imposed tomorrow on various members of the principal families of Milan for implication in political affairs." And then two days later: "A great silence and terrible sorrow in the theatre and outside."

But La Scala was not the only theatre in Milan. At the time, partly because of the multiplicity of dialects, music more than literature was the common language of entertainment, and this meant theatres for opera. The Teatro della Canobbiana produced operas and ballets continuously for almost a hundred years, from 1779 until the late 1860s. Donizetti's still popular *L'Elisir d'Amore* had its première there in May 1832, only a month before Verdi arrived in Milan. A theatre more famous still was the Teatro Carcano, built in 1803. Donizetti's *Anna Bolena* had its première there in 1830 and Bellini's *La Sonnam-*

bula in 1831. Its acoustics at the time were considered perfect for music. The same architect had also built the Teatro Re in 1796, but its acoustics were mysteriously poor. Verdi's opera *I Due Foscari* was produced there in 1846, and that same year three other of his operas were produced at the Carcano. And there were still other theatres with more specialized functions such as the Conservatorio, connected with the Conservatory, and the Teatro dei Filodrammatici.

The Conservatory itself had been founded in 1807 by decree of Napoleon, and like most in Italy at the time it was essentially a charitable institution. Most of the students were there on scholarships and lived in a dormitory. They were young—acceptance was limited, except in rare circumstances, to students under fourteen—and talented; together with a good faculty the students had made it the best conservatory in Italy.

But in spite of its importance and exceptional activity Milan was still, by European standards, a remarkably small and backward city. In 1832 its population was well under 150,000; it had no industry, no railroad connections, and such trade as it did have was harassed by the multiple borders and tariff regulations of the tiny surrounding states. To visitors from England, France and the United States, where the governments were based on infinitely larger land areas unified by a common tongue, the Italian political conditions seemed out-of-date and permanently unstable. But to keep Italy on this backward condition and to prevent its unification was the purpose of the policy of the Austrian, Bourbon and Vatican governments throughout the peninsula. Even eighteen years later, in 1850, Milan had no important railroad connections, whereas in Britain there was an east coast-west coast loop from London to Glasgow, complete with cross connections and spur lines. Britain, with roughly the same population as Italy, 25,000,-000, had almost five times as much overseas trade. And in all of Italy in 1850 only one city, Naples, famous for the multiplicity of its beggars, had a population of more than 200,000. Small wonder that Paris, with a population in the millions, was the capital of the musical world and lured Rossini, Donizetti and Bellini out of Italy. When Verdi came to Milan it was still, as late as 1832, a charming, bustling, but essentially eighteenth-century city with narrow streets, walls and gates.

Provesi had accompanied Carlo Verdi and his son to Milan in order to introduce Verdi to Alessandro Rolla, a professor at the Conservatory and one of Italy's most distinguished elder musicians. Rolla was born in Pavia in 1757, but his early life was associated with Parma, where he had led the orchestra for twenty years, 1782–1802, and where he had known Provesi. Thereafter he had gone to Milan where, beginning in 1802, he made a great reputation as a conductor of opera at La Scala. He also composed ballets, songs, and all sorts of works for strings, including concertos for the violin and viola. These last two were his particular instruments, and even Paganini had studied with him. In 1808 Rolla had been appointed professor of violin and viola at the newly opened Conservatory, where he also served on its board of examiners. Provesi could not furnish Verdi a better sponsor provided he could persuade Rolla to take an interest in the boy.

While Provesi renewed his acquaintance with Rolla, Verdi and his father examined the city, the cathedral, the theatres, the outside of the Conservatory, the squares and streets; it was the first time either had seen a city. Barezzi had arranged for Verdi to board and lodge with Giuseppe Seletti, the nephew of Verdi's grammar teacher, Don Pietro Seletti. The younger Seletti, like his uncle, was also a teacher and lived at 19 via Santa Marta (which in 1943 was almost completely destroyed by bombs). After a few days, leaving Verdi in care of Seletti and introduced to Rolla, Provesi and Carlo Verdi returned to Busseto.

Verdi's application to the Conservatory was complicated by his age. He was eighteen, four years over the usual limit, and to be admitted he had to demonstrate an exceptional talent. Article Ten of the Conservatory's By-Laws specifically allowed such exceptions. His application was in two parts, an audition and a formal petition. The audition, curiously, came first, and at it he played the piano, a "Capriccio" by Henri Herz, and either played or submitted some of his own compositions. Very soon thereafter he filed the petition, addressed to the Imperial Governor and dated 22 June 1832. In it he pointed out his age, the exemption allowed exceptional talent under the By-Laws, and expressed the hope that the audition had shown him qualified to be admitted to the Conservatory as a paying resident student, in order "to perfect himself in music." The application was refused without explanation, and Verdi was not admitted to the Conservatory.

The formal reply to the petition which Rolla forwarded to Provesi offered no explanation or comment, and it is doubtful that Rolla knew of any that he withheld. Verdi, all his life, considered he had been judged and found wanting: not of exceptional talent. A visitor in Verdi's home in later years reported seeing the application rolled up and on its outside in Verdi's handwriting: "fu respinta! . . ." (It was rejected).

The simple words seem to quiver with repressed emotion. What words did he choose to write to Barezzi or Margherita? What words in his mind did he hear being said in Busseto by friends and scoffers? And finally, being practical, what could he do now?

Rolla advised him to take private lessons and recommended two teachers, Lavigna or Negri. Undoubtedly Rolla was kind, but he was seventy-six, too old to stir himself to help a young and not very prepossessing protégé of a distant friend. Although on the board of examiners, for example, Rolla never seems to have taken the trouble to discover the basis of the rejection or in the succeeding years, although he lived in Milan until his death in 1841, to have seen anything of Verdi.

For almost a hundred years the rejection served as the classic example of the pedantic board snubbing the budding genius, and certainly Verdi thought of it that way. The same year that he was rejected he saw an exception made for a singer, a bass, only a year younger than he, on the ground that a bass voice could not develop by fourteen. But Carlo Gatti, in his biography of Verdi, published in 1931, offered evidence that this view was unfair. He ferreted out of the archives notes of the board among themselves and back and forth to the Imperial Governor. These reveal that the board thought Verdi was talented, perhaps even exceptionally talented, that he held his hands incorrectly at the piano and that he showed promise of being a good composer. The difficulties were that the Conservatory was already overcrowded, that Verdi, coming from Parma, was a foreigner and that he was also overage. For these reasons the board decided not to make an exception to its general rule. Unfortunately, the rejection itself did not state the reasons, nor did Rolla discover and report them to Provesi, Barezzi, or, most of all, Verdi. He might have saved much anguish and bitterness. Years later, when the Conservatory wanted to honor Verdi by renaming itself after him, he was widely quoted as saying: "They wouldn't have me young; they can't have me old."

Artists were no more sensitive then than now, but in the days before telephone and telegraph the duration of their sufferings may have been longer. The mail coach left Milan for Parma and Busseto only twice a week, and an exchange of letters took eight or ten days. During this time Seletti undoubtedly tried to encourage Verdi, but the most important voice, the voice that was needed and could help, was Barezzi's. The letter does not exist, but it is not hard to imagine it: Verdi was to stay in Milan; all the reasons for going there were just as valid now as before. He should study with one of the teachers Rolla recommended and board with Seletti. All of this would probably cost twice as much as had been anticipated, but Verdi was not to worry; he, Barezzi, would advance what was needed. Verdi could keep the cost down by working through what would have been the Conservatory vacations. The rejection was, of course, a terrible blow but not fatal; others had succeeded without the benefits of the Milan Conservatory, and Verdi could too. In Busseto—he hardly needed to be told—they all loved him, their hearts went out to him, and they thought of him all the time—especially Ghita.

So, soothed and supported by Barezzi, Verdi stayed on in Milan. He never forgot or underestimated the magnificence of Barezzi's decisive generosity.

Of the two teachers Rolla recommended Verdi chose Vincenzo Lavigna and began a period of work so intense it has around it a black air of desperation. Both Lavigna and Seletti sent reports on Verdi to Barezzi and the Monte di Pietà, stressing his extraordinary industry and good behavior. The latter was to reassure those nervous folk in Busseto that Verdi had not succumbed to the supposed sins of the big city. But no matter what his inclination, his good behavior was one inevitable result of his industry; he worked twelve to fourteen hours a day and had no time for sinning, which takes considerable time and attention. It also takes some money, and Verdi had none.

For eighteen months he seems to have done nothing but study and go to the opera house. Barezzi, on Lavigna's advice, bought Verdi a season ticket to La Scala, but Verdi also went regularly to the Teatro Carcano and the Canobbiana. He studied the operas before and after from scores he had rented and played them over on a piano which Barezzi gave him and which can be seen today at La Scala Museum. During all this time Verdi seems to have seen or spoken to almost no one beside Lavigna and Seletti. This isolation, far more than the actual instruction, was the real cost to Verdi of being rejected by the Conservatory. He developed musically alone; he had the self-discipline to do it. But companionship is a good thing; so is the constant stimulation and criticism of fellow students, and these Verdi missed.

In his teacher, Lavigna, Verdi was fortunate, for the man's good and bad points alike worked for his benefit. Lavigna, then in his sixty-seventh year, had studied at the Conservatorio della Pietà in Naples but made his career in Milan. Beginning in 1809, he was an accompanist and coach at La Scala, and in 1823 he was appointed to the faculty of the Conservatory. He was also a composer and wrote more than ten operas and two ballets. His first and most popular opera was *La Muta per Amore* which had its première at La Scala in 1803. As a practical man of the theatre he was well suited to instruct Verdi and presumably was able to get his pupil into many rehearsals and even performances. Happily he was also a completely educated and trained musician, and he started Verdi with Palestrina and endless exercises of voice part-writing, fugues and canons; no fancy projects, just exercise after exercise. This probably was what Verdi needed most after the freedom of Busseto where he composed at will and without much reflection or criticism by others. Lavigna, however, enjoyed criticism. His hobby was analyzing Mozart's *Don Giovanni*. Each day he greeted Verdi by suggesting they have "another look at the introduction and the grand finale." In later life Mozart was not one of Verdi's favorite composers.

Lavigna's only fault—and it may not have been one—was that his taste was behind the times. His favorite composer was Paisiello, who lived 1740–1816 and wrote all but one of his operas in the eighteenth century. His most famous opera, *Il Barbiere di Siviglia,* 1782, had preceded Rossini's on the same libretto by thirty-three years, and a good argument can be made that it was the first universally popular opera, succeeding in every country from Russia to Mexico. It and other of Paisiello's operas are still revived and generally with success. For Lavigna to have liked Paisiello was a sign of his good taste, but years later Verdi said of him: "I remember that he corrected in Paisiello's style the entire instrumentation of a symphony I had written. 'This is a nice fix,' I said to myself, and from that time I never showed him any original compositions; and in the three years I studied with him I did nothing but canons and fugues, fugues and canons of every sort. No one taught me instrumentation and how to handle dramatic compositions." But on counterpoint, the setting of one note against another and thereby interweaving strands of melody, Verdi declared that Lavigna "was very strong." Verdi's operas reflect this. They are, of course, not all equally inspired, but even in the duller sections of the poor ones the notes head somewhere and are added, one to the other, with purpose and craftsmanship.

But Verdi may not have been altogether unlucky in Lavigna's clear preference for the style of a previous generation. Almost nothing is more dangerous to a developing genius or can more quickly deflect and blunt the impact of his originality than the help and direction of some older man who understands, or thinks he does, the purpose and style of the generation following his own. This is one reason why always throughout history the best patrons, like Barezzi, have provided the money and then left the artist alone. At least on this point there was no confusion between Verdi and Lavigna, and always Verdi's music had a quality peculiarly his own.

For his instruction in music Lavigna was paid, but he did more. As the weeks passed, he evidently grew fond of Verdi and sensed his solitude. To lessen it, he invited Verdi frequently to his house in the evening, for meals and to meet his friends. Lavigna's social circle was not very exalted, but it included many of the leading musicians in Milan. The talk was literate and passionate, and out of it Verdi slowly developed some valuable acquaintances and the beginnings of some social graces which he needed badly. His clothes, about which he could do very little, were ill-fitting and perhaps unpressed, and his figure he himself described as scrawny; his manners were polite but, out of shyness, abrupt and often awkward, and he had no gift for the happy phrase. He tended, as he had always done, to sit quietly and listen, hanging on the edge of a conversation like some uncertain cloud at which the others throw occasional, uneasy glances. Those who dismissed him as of no importance were wrong, of course, but Lavigna at the time could only suspect it, and he must have gone to bed many a night shaking his head and despairing over the lump of a peasant from Busseto.

From some of his exercise sheets which Verdi kept, carefully rolled and arranged by composer, it is clear that he studied the sonatas and concertos of Corelli (1653–1713), quartets and symphonies of Haydn (1732–1809), works of all kinds of Mozart (1756–1791) and Beethoven (1770–1827), and even the early chamber works of Mendelssohn (1809–1847). He, of course, studied the vocal works of the great early Italians, Palestrina (1525–1594) and Marcello (1686–1739). At La Scala, beginning in the autumn of 1832 when he arrived in Milan, he undoubtedly saw the operas presented which were by Mercadante (1795–1870, and known as "the Italian Beethoven"), Donizetti (1797–1848), Coccia (1782–1873) and Luigi Ricci (1805–1859). The dates of these men indicate the modernity of the Italian opera repertory at the time. The concept, so typical of the twentieth century, of a "standard repertory" made up of the works of dead men simply did not exist; at La Scala Verdi saw almost entirely new works. This is a reason why at this time he saw no Rossini (1792–1868). *William Tell,* Rossini's most recent opera, was written in 1829, and it was produced in Lucca and Florence in 1831. The Austrians, however, because of its political connotations, banned it in Venice and Milan. Rather than revive an old Rossini opera, La Scala waited confidently for his next; it could not guess that *William Tell* would be his last.

In July 1833 Verdi heard from Busseto that Provesi had died. He had not seen his teacher for a year, and the last time was when Provesi, old and in pain, had accompanied him in a coach to Milan to introduce him to Rolla and try to make his way smooth. More than anyone except Barezzi, Provesi had challenged Verdi as a boy to do his best and then made it possible. Now he had died and too soon: before Verdi had an opera produced or even a song published, anything to show the faith was justified.

Verdi could not go to the funeral; not only was there not the time, there was not the money. So in letters he read of how Provesi's friends in Busseto raised money by subscription to give him a magnificent funeral. Verdi must have grieved that he, Provesi's best pupil and assistant, was not there to choose the music, rehearse the choir, to honor his friend and teacher. Death as a real, emotional shock often comes earlier to artists than to others, for their best friends are often their teachers and much, much older.

The following month, in August, Verdi learned that his sister, Giuseppa, had died in Le Roncole. He was now his parents' only child. Again he could not travel from Milan to be with them. He did the only thing he could, which was to work even harder than before.

CHAPTER 5

THE COMPETITION FOR THE POST OF *MAESTRO DI MUSICA* IN BUSSETO

1833–1836; AGE, 19–22

PROVESI'S death precipitated a storm in Busseto which, although it had been gathering for years, broke suddenly over the question of his successor. Possibly if Provesi had survived another two years until Verdi had returned from Milan clutching an impressive certificate of ability from Lavigna, the trouble would have blown over, and Provesi's combined jobs as organist, choirmaster, director of the Philharmonic and the music school would all have fallen to Verdi as his assistant, able, waiting and in town. But Verdi's absence and the necessity of his staying on in Milan yet another year gave his and Provesi's enemies their chance.

As soon as Provesi died, the Philharmonic Society agreed to hold open its position of conductor until Verdi completed his studies. More usual, perhaps, would have been to announce a date on which applicants could compete for the post, but the Philharmonic's move was not unnatural, considering Verdi's previous relations with it. The Philharmonic then further suggested to the Provost of the cathedral who controlled the jobs of organist and choirmaster that he appoint a pupil of Provesi as provisional organist until a permanent one could be selected. But the Provost, Don Gian Bernardo Ballarini, disliked Provesi, Verdi and the Philharmonic Society and refused to appoint one of Provesi's pupils. Instead he selected "a certain Sormani." As Busseto was sufficiently small so that all the good musicians were either Provesi's friends or pupils, the services under Sormani often broke down and, in the words of one of Verdi's supporters, the treasurer of the Monte di Pietà, "most of the time there was no choir music on

Sundays." It was the recognizable beginning of a scandal, and the town began to choose up sides.

Meanwhile other candidates for the combined position came forward, some by mail, others in person. Of the latter the most important was Giovanni Ferrari, a choirmaster, who came from Guastalla with recommendations from its vice-mayor, its police commissioner and, most impressive, its bishop. Don Ballarini, the Provost, promised Ferrari his support and, after explaining the situation, advised him to call on Barezzi. Ferrari was politely received and invited to the Philharmonic Society's concerts, but he did not pick up its backing.

Although not yet officially the organist and choirmaster of the cathedral, Ferrari in November 1833 attempted through the Monte di Pietà to strengthen his position as organist *de facto*. The Monte di Pietà paid the organist a small stipend in return for which he was expected to teach young students at the music school and conduct concerts in the square or wherever requested. Ferrari petitioned the directors of the Monte di Pietà to declare him eligible for the stipend. That same month Verdi, probably on Barezzi's advice, had prepared

THE "CATHEDRAL" IN BUSSETO

a petition for the directors requesting that he be considered a candidate for the stipend. He forwarded it to Barezzi to present for him. But Barezzi, on being informed that the post of organist would be awarded by competition, did not submit the petition which then seemed premature.

In December Verdi forwarded directly from Milan to the Monte di Pietà a certificate from Lavigna stating that he was working hard and well and in another year would be able to assume the duties of a "maestro compositore di musica." And then again in February 1834, undoubtedly on Verdi's request, for the terms of his scholarship required only one certificate a year, Lavigna made out another certificate which Verdi forwarded to the Monte di Pietà.

Lavigna probably would have made out as many certificates as Verdi requested for Verdi was doing increasingly well and beginning to attract attention. One night in April at Lavigna's suggestion he went to the Teatro dei Filodrammatici to hear a rehearsal of Haydn's oratorio, *The Creation*. The singers were an amateur group under the direction of Pietro Massini, whom Verdi had met at Lavigna's house. Verdi sat down in one of the rear rows and waited for the rehearsal to begin, but soon it became evident that there was some sort of mix-up as all three of the assistant conductors were late. Massini asked Verdi to fill in at the piano, adding that he need only play the bass accompaniment. But as the rehearsal continued and Verdi warmed to the music he began to conduct with his right hand while playing with his left. At the end he had a real success and all the more, as he later said, "because so unexpected." Massini then gave Verdi charge of the public performance which went so well that it was repeated in the Casino de' Nobili before the Austrian Viceroy, Archduke Rainer, and the nobility of Milan.

The program on its front announced the oratorio, gave appropriate credit to Haydn, Massini and the Deity who was pictured with a crown of shooting stars and flames. Inside it read:

Maestro al Cembale
Verdi Sig. Giuseppe
Primo Violino Direttore e Capo dell' Orchestra
Rachell Sig. Michele
L'Orchestra
è composta di Dilettanti
e Professori

This first public appearance in Milan undoubtedly pleased Lavigna more than Verdi who, with the impatience of youth, was probably disappointed that not more came of it than did. But there were some substantial if unspectacular results. It cemented Verdi's friendship with Massini who soon became one of his most enthusiastic supporters and asked him to conduct and prepare a performance by the amateurs of Rossini's opera, *La Cenerentola*. He also prepared Meyerbeer's *Robert-le-diable,* although the performance seems to have been canceled. But as a result Verdi had for the first time since he left Busseto a chance to work with an orchestra, always a problem for students. He also began to meet people outside of Lavigna's purely musical circle. Count Renato Borromeo, one of the amateurs, asked Verdi to write a cantata for his daughter's wedding which Verdi did. But the small jobs did not add up to any recognized position and, most galling, no one paid him for any of his work; his debt to Barezzi regularly kept increasing.

In June Barezzi called Verdi back to Busseto. Ferrari had the advantage of being constantly present and was gaining support; the Philharmonic Society needed to see and exhibit its candidate. So although he had not completed his studies and had no final certificate from Lavigna, Verdi came and arrived on 18 June. That very day the officers of the cathedral appointed Ferrari organist and choirmaster— without announcing or holding any competition for the post. The timing of the appointment infuriated the Philharmonic Society and supporters of Verdi and alienated many others who might otherwise have held aloof from the squabble. At the time and even now it inevitably raises suspicions about the board of vestry's motives. At best the board members merely wanted to please the Bishop of Guastalla and perhaps were tired of inaction; at worst they knew Verdi was about to arrive, knew he was the better maestro, and, perhaps swayed by Don Ballarini, hoped to preclude him by an official appointment however hasty or improper. The other applicants, everyone recognized by now, were effectively rejected: it was to be Verdi or Ferrari.

On 21 June the Church reported the appointment of Ferrari to the Monte di Pietà which four days later granted Ferrari the stipend for teaching the students and leading the Philharmonic Society orchestra. Verdi's petition for the stipend which Barezzi now tried to file was declared to be too late. Did the directors of the Monte di Pietà feel they had to accept the Church's appointment of its own organist and choir-

YOUNG MEN WITH AND WITHOUT QUEUES

BEETHOVEN   MANZONI

master, however peculiar the circumstances, and that to withhold the stipend would be an unprecedented discrimination? Whatever its reasoning, within four days both Verdi and the Philharmonic Society filed protests with the Ducal Governor in Busseto. And the Philharmonic prevented Ferrari from earning the stipend by refusing to play under him. It also invaded the cathedral and removed all its music.

The situation quickly slid from bad to worse. Everyone in the small town had a new opinion, fact or quotation to tell his neighbor, and anything short of complete and abject agreement on the part of any listener was a sign of prejudice and betrayal. The feud, as almost always in nineteenth-century Italy, at once took on political overtones: liberals vs. clerics, Verdians vs. Ferrarians. The parties adopted or were inflicted with symbols: white cockades, "coccardini," for the liberal descendants of the French Revolution, and pigtails, "codini," for the clerics and those who longed for eighteenth-century privilege. When the French Revolutionary armies had first burst into the Milanese provinces in 1796, all the schoolboys had cut off their pigtails to show their sympathy with the followers of Rousseau. Forty years later the same symbols reappeared, partly because Busseto was a provincial town, but also partly because the issues represented were not yet resolved in Italy still un-united and held apart by Papal and Austrian interests.

Ferrari at once took up his duties at the cathedral and also began instructing the music students. Verdi led the Philharmonic in concerts and its band in outdoor recitals. The Society put on a grand "soirée" in Barezzi's house at which Verdi appeared along with a soprano who held a scholarship from the Monte di Pietà to study in Parma. He also appeared at another soirée in nearby Villanova. Meanwhile the Philharmonic Society refused to play in the cathedral on St. Bartholomew's Day, and Don Ballarini had to hire "foreign" musicians. This infuriated everyone either on the ground of principle or expense, and the sarcasm and intrigue grew even more bitter. In November a certain Luigi Seletti (not Verdi's old schoolteacher) filed a complaint with the police that Signora Barezzi and one of her sons had insulted him. The Signora in defending Verdi had said: "You infamous old man—everyone knows you hate even your own children." The Chief of Police attempted to soothe the injured father with a diplomatic letter. But Seletti was not so easily satisfied. More letters were exchanged, all of which everyone knew about.

Happily in December the ducal Governor let it be known that he would use his influence to have the combined position awarded by competition. The plain fact was, as he observed in a note to the secretary of the Philharmonic Society in Parma, that if the Church did not agree to a competition then its organist would either starve or resign, for the combined salaries from the Church and the Monte di Pietà would not support Ferrari and his family. And if the town and the Philharmonic Society, while withholding their contributions to the total wage, insisted on a competition, then in the end the Church would have to agree to it. Therefore, argued the Ducal Governor, he would use his influence now to have a competition. As soon as this became generally known, Verdi returned to Milan. He had been away for almost six months.

Throughout the winter Verdi continued to study with Lavigna. At La Scala he saw Donizetti's new and successful opera, *Gemma di Vergy,* and a revival of *Norma* with Giuditta Pasta for whom Bellini wrote the opera. By 1835, when Verdi heard Pasta, her voice which was never perfect was noticeably tiring—she was even said to have sung an entire opera flat—but her acting and dramatic stress were perhaps even more perfect than ever. Her voice, around which argument always raged, was famous for its peculiar "suffocated" tone.

The winter in Milan for Verdi passed exactly as the preceding one but without the excitement of conducting public performances at the Teatro dei Filodrammatici or the Casino de' Nobili. He continued, however, to see a great deal of Massini who one day gave him a libretto to set to music. Equally if not more important, Massini promised to have the opera produced at the Filodrammatici where he had influence. The libretto was by a friend of both men, Antonio Piazza, a journalist. Four and one half years later the libretto and music, after many revisions, probably became Verdi's first opera, *Oberto, Conte di San Bonifacio.* (*See* Appendix A, p. 577.)

But the situation in Busseto effectively poisoned the winter. No letter came without reference to it: what Ferrari was doing, when the competition would be announced, or who had said what to whom. Lavigna who frequently examined candidates for musical positions in nearby towns discovered an opening as organist in Monza, and he advised Verdi to hold it as an alternative to Busseto. The cathedral in Monza had held an open competition, and as none of the candidates had been good enough, the position was still open. Its board of vestry would have welcomed any musician Lavigna recommended to them.

Meanwhile in Busseto the exchange of letters and memoranda between the Mayor, the Ducal Governor and all the other parties concerned continued apace. In the course of them the Provost, Don Ballarini, was advised by the Ducal Governor to pay more attention to religion and less to intrigue. But finally on 25 June in the name of "Her Majesty, Our August Sovereign" the Governor announced a competition for the post of Master of Music in Busseto. He did not announce a date and dismissed the complaints filed with him by Verdi and the Philharmonic, but both the Verdians and Ferrarians considered it a victory for the Philharmonic Society. Barezzi was jubilant.

The Chief of Police promptly wrote the Mayor a memorandum outlining his plans for handling the inevitable disturbances following the announcement of the winner. He labeled the parties "codini" and "coccardini," identified the chief troublemakers in each, and promised to keep an eye on a tavern run by a certain Fantoni where the street brawls were apt to start.

Barezzi promptly wrote Verdi that it was time now to come home, and, the studies completed, Lavigna gave Verdi a final certificate with which to face the world. It read:

I the undersigned state that il Signor Giuseppe Verdi of Busseto in the State of Parma has studied counterpoint under my direction and pursued his studies, in a praiseworthy fashion, of fugues with two, three and four voices; also of canons, doublevoiced, etc., believing him to be equal in ability to any accredited Maestro di Cappella. I further add that his conduct while with me has at all times been most quiet (dolcissima), respectful (rispettosa) and moderate (morigerata) in his dress. So much I state to be the pure truth.

Milan, 15 July 1835

Professore di musica: VINCENZO LAVIGNA

The concern with conduct shows Lavigna's eighteenth-century background which was typical of Italian musicians at the time: the good musician was a presentable person, with manners and a certain grace, capable of taking a recognized place in society. The contrary concept of the musician as a Bohemian with wild hair and dirty fingernails was only just developing in Paris, and Henri Murger's "Scènes de la Bohème," on which Puccini based his opera, did not begin to appear for another ten years. It never would have occurred to Verdi to starve in a garret, dodging the rent, while he wrote a masterpiece. He expected to do just as he saw others do: to have a musical job which supported him and his family and into which he poured his energies. If he was to be a Church organist, he would write Church music, just as when he was leading the Philharmonic Society's band he wrote marches for it. This was the first step and for most musicians it was the last. Perhaps Verdi already hoped someday to be a purely operatic composer like Bellini or Donizetti. But at the moment he contented himself with the first step: a job, so he could marry Margherita and start paying off his debt to Barezzi. He left Milan at the end of July.

Arriving in Busseto, Verdi found the squabble continuing. The Philharmonic Society was willing to await the competition quietly provided Ferrari would not make any claims to the title or actual jobs as organist, choirmaster, or teacher. But Ferrari, still backed by Provost Ballarini, refused to recognize that such was the effect of the Governor's decree. The wrangle continued until finally Her Majesty prohibited any music in all the churches of Busseto.

As the summer wore on and the Governor still had not announced the date for the competition, Barezzi grew disgusted. Privately he advised Verdi who was working on his opera to take the job at Monza. So Lavigna went to work, and so did Massini, and even Barezzi discovered a business acquaintance there. In October the authorities in Monza accepted Verdi subject to final arrangements about the salary which, as Lavigna informed Verdi, promised to be better than he could get in Busseto. But weeks went by and Verdi did not appear in Milan or Monza to close the contract. In December Lavigna wrote a hurried note to Verdi, inquiring what possibly could be keeping him.

Verdi began his reply with a line from Canto VI of Dante's *Inferno:* "Nuovi tormenti e nuovi tormentati"—new souls in torment and new kinds of pain. The letter's language is just a little stiff and archaic. Verdi's education came to him late and much of it was his own reading; he still lacks the ease with written words of a man born to them.

Nuovi tormenti e nuovi tormentati: Just when I thought I was on the point of getting rid of my troubles and procuring an honorable, and easy, living, I find myself once more plunged to the depths where I can see nothing but darkness. Last Saturday was the day I should have gone to Milan and to that end I had sent a special delivery the day before to Parma to obtain a passport. When news of my departure leaked out in Busseto it stirred up such a whispering campaign as you cannot imagine. The party hostile to the Philharmonic seized this opportunity to insult the Philharmonic group; the latter flew into a rage and hurled insults at me and at Signor Barezzi. The Philharmonic Society reminded me of the pledges made, the insults they had been subjected to, and the benefits I had received from the home town, and said they would voluntarily assume an obligation to pay me a thousand francs annually. Annoyed by my refusal, they tried to frighten me and even threatened to hold me in Busseto by force if I made any move to leave. But for the fact that the people here would turn against my benefactor Barezzi on my account, I would have left at once and neither their reproaches nor their threats could have held me. For even though I did receive a small pension for my maintenance in Milan from the Monte di Pietà, that benefit should not have been granted at the price of my humiliation and slavery and if such was the case I am forced to look upon that benefit no longer as a generous act, but as a contemptible one. That is the only reason why I have remained in Busseto and to my many sacrifices is now added a fresh sorrow, that of having involved you and of not being able to reciprocate your many kindnesses. This alone grieves me and if I might atone at whatever cost, I would do so with the greatest pleasure. Beyond this I can add nothing in my excuse. In the meantime be assured of my eternal gratitude and if you will deign to reply, I will be greatly honored to exchange letters with you from time to time. I may perhaps come to Milan during Carnival, and then we shall discuss this matter at length. If I may be of any service to you in any way and at any time, I shall always consider it a great privilege. My kindest regards to your family.

With assurances of my esteem and gratitude I remain

Your affectionate friend and servant,

GIUSEPPE VERDI

Barezzi likewise in a letter to Seletti in Milan reported angry words and threatened violence at the meeting with the Philharmonic Society. He added that, of course, the threats had not influenced either him or Verdi, yet in view of the demonstration they had both given ground. For the next few months at least the position at Monza seemed an impossibility.

But the situation in Busseto did not improve. The distant bureaucracy in Parma seemed either to have forgotten or shelved the competition it had itself announced, and tempers remained high as everyone continued to jockey for position and tried to exert pressure. The Provost, of course, forbade Verdi to play in his cathedral, but the Franciscan Friars outside the town were not under the Provost's jurisdiction and they invited Verdi to play for their services. The result was that the Franciscan Church was full and the cathedral nearly empty—which represented a considerable switch in financial support between the two churches with attendant smug clerical smirks and ill will. And at a Municipal Council meeting one night a riot nearly broke out as six members walked out and a passionate appeal was made to support the Philharmonic Society on the ground that it saved the youth of Busseto from the evils of drink. The whole silly business was eventually celebrated by a local poet in a poem of nine cantos entitled "Gli uccelli accademici," or "The Academic Birds." In it Marie Louise appeared as the royal eagle, Barezzi and Margherita as a pair of blackbirds, Verdi as a parrot and Ferrari as the cuckoo in the nest.

Finally on 23 January 1836 the Mayor, "on orders from high authorities," posted a notice that the competition would be held in Parma before Maestro Giuseppe Alinovi, the Court organist. It was left to the various candidates to get themselves to Parma and appear before Alinovi.

A month later on 27 February Verdi presented himself; Ferrari, by this time discouraged and somewhat discredited, did not, but in his place appeared a certain Rossi, also from Guastalla. Verdi stayed with the man who was perhaps Provesi's best friend, Lorenzo Molossi, who was not only secretary of the Parma Philharmonic Society but also had a post in the government. In spite of all the controversy Verdi appeared at the examination with talent, training and excellent references. Rossi quickly and agreeably confessed himself unlikely to win.

The examination was in two parts, the first day at the piano, and the second composing a fugue in four parts on a theme set by Alinovi. At the piano Verdi played some of his own works, improvised on de-

ALINOVI

mand, transposed directly from orchestral scores to the piano, played some of Alinovi's works on sight, and ended playing a sonata for four hands with Alinovi. The next day he received the subject for the fugue at eight in the morning and turned the completed score back shortly after six in the evening.

Molossi quickly wrote to a friend in Busseto:

As Verdi's modesty prevents him telling you how things stand, I will say that yesterday about six o'clock he finished his work, and Alinovi, after studying it carefully, leaped to his feet and said to Verdi: "Till this moment my duty has been to examine critically, now it is to express admiration. This fugue is worthy of the most experienced Maestro; it deserves to be published. You should be a Maestro in Paris or London, not Busseto. I confess it, I could not have done in an entire day what you have done in a few hours."

That night Molossi took Verdi to a *conversazione* at which everyone made a fuss over him, and he was asked to play the piano. He chose some variations of his own and scored a success. Rossi, who was present, was also asked to play but declined. His examination began the next morning.

A few days later Alinovi announced that Verdi had won the competition, and the Mayor of Busseto, who had journeyed to Parma for it, wrote Barezzi an ecstatic letter. And when Verdi arrived back in Busseto he was greeted like a hero, serenaded and garlanded with flowers. But even the official appointment by the Department of Interior on 5 March did not end the squabble. The *codini* complained that the competition had been held secretly, that the Mayor had not informed the proper officials so that the notice to candidates had gone out late and in some cases not been received in time, and that the competition was therefore illegal. Others said that twenty-two was too young: the boy ought to serve an apprenticeship first and gain experience.

Some of the objections were met by the passage of time. No one seriously proposed another competition, and Verdi was plainly qualified for the job. Yet the Provost remained obdurate and refused to appoint Verdi organist or let him play in the cathedral. Still the job was Verdi's; but it was less clear that he had any joy of it. Provesi had died in July 1833; Verdi's contract with the town of Busseto, setting forth his duties, was dated April 1836.

CHAPTER 6

MAESTRO DI MUSICA

1836–1838; AGE, 22–24

ONE joy, however, Verdi realized from his new position and at once: he married Margherita. On 16 April 1836 at the Mayor's office the couple declared their intent to marry in the presence of both her parents and Verdi's father. His mother, it was recorded, was ill and could not attend. Three weeks later, on 4 May, they were married; both were twenty-three years old. They had known each other for thirteen years and been openly in love for four. Barezzi and his wife were pleased; less surprising, perhaps, was the pleasure of the humble parents of the young man. After the wedding the couple took a short trip ending in Milan where Verdi introduced his wife to his friends, Lavigna, Massini and others. She and Seletti's wife were already close friends. Back in Busseto they settled, with Barezzi's help, in the Palazzo Tedaldi.

Like all brides, Margherita's friends reported her to be beautiful. Her hair, a golden blond, was especially lovely, and she wore it, according to the fashion of the time, in a bun or swirled on the sides and top. A portrait of her at this age shows her hair as dark, but a strand of it in the wedding ring she gave Verdi is blond. In the portrait she seems a rather serious girl with attractive features and a suggestion of quiet humor in the eyes and mouth. She evidently was a decisive person, for her friends took seriously what she said. The marriage was visibly happy. She took pride in Verdi's work and position and looked forward to the time when he would be a great composer in Milan. Their home, like Barezzi's not far away, became a center in the town for music lovers and music making.

As Provesi's successor as Director of Music in Busseto, Verdi, although he could not play the organ in the cathedral or direct the choir, was busy. He had his opera to work on; he was head of the Music School and taught its pupils; and he was the director of the Philharmonic Society, conducting most of its rehearsals and performances. In addition, he taught private pupils and composed a great deal of new music for special occasions. He saved none of it except his settings of Manzoni's ode on the death of Napoleon and some choruses from Manzoni's verse tragedies. In later years whenever he found an early work, he burned it, and there is no reason, from the very few works that have survived, to regret his judgment. It was a time of apprenticeship, an exercise in the craft of making music, turning out so many bars of it on demand without deepening or even engaging the composer's enthusiasm.

In September Margherita let it be known to her close relatives that she was pregnant. But the pleasure for Verdi was soon spoiled by news from Milan that Lavigna had died suddenly on 14 September. Early in the year Lavigna had retired from his position at La Scala and his increased leisure had agitated and exhausted rather than rested him. Worse still, during the summer months he had no classes at the Conservatory as an epidemic of cholera in Milan had closed it. A number of the professors fell ill, and some of the classrooms were turned into an infirmary. Lavigna apparently wilted under the inactivity. He was seventy when he died and left a widow and fourteen-year-old daughter. Although there was nothing he could do, Verdi worried about them and mourned his teacher, who was also a friend.

On a meanly practical level, Lavigna's death was a blow to Verdi's hopes for his opera, *Oberto*. Lavigna's approval and backing would have carried weight in the theatres in Milan, and the news from there was increasingly discouraging. In October Massini wrote that there was no chance of producing the opera at the Teatro dei Filodrammatici until sometime in 1837 at the earliest, which, allowing time for the usual delays, intrigues and rehearsals, meant late in that year. But the opera was completed, and time was slipping by. Verdi had left Milan in July 1835, and it was already getting on to 1837. Lavigna had died. His other friends would soon forget him or lose interest, and his opera would slowly be entombed in Busseto. He wrote Massini and asked him about the position in Monza. Had it yet been filled? He confessed he felt no particular leaning toward church music, but how could he stay in Busseto, a small country town without resources or hope for a professional musician? At least, he wrote, "I would be better off in Monza because it is bigger and nearer Milan."

But there were other drawbacks to Busseto besides its country air and size. The split in the town over Provesi's successor, embroiled as it had become with Church and politics, had lasted too long and been too bitter to heal altogether. No one challenged Verdi's right to the post, but he recognized that some of his supporters enthused more over the defeat of the clerical party than over their candidate's musical accomplishments. And on the other side was Don Ballarini who was backed by many who cared nothing about music and much about the affront to the Church.

More directly agitating was a confusion with the Monte di Pietà over payment of his scholarship. The directors had promised to pay Verdi the equivalent of a monthly stipend for four years. With that sum seemingly assured, Barezzi had advanced an amount which in the end was perhaps three times greater. But then the directors suspended the monthly payments after only twenty-six of the forty-eight months on the theory that by then, January 1836, Verdi had established himself in his goal as Director of Music of Busseto and needed no further grants to attain it. Verdi's father then petitioned the Monte di Pietà for the balance. Barezzi, in a long letter to the directors, pointed out that Verdi had worked through what would normally have been vacations and had financed himself on borrowed money, all of which had been lent on the understanding that the full stipend would be available to repay at least part of the debt. After an investigation the directors compromised and agreed to pay the balance but, claiming to be hard-pressed at the moment, only at the end of the year 1837. Everyone agreed to this, but it was still an unhappy event for Verdi, who felt that his affairs were once again becoming a topic of public discussion.

With the coming of spring Margherita gave birth on 26 March to a girl who was christened Virginia Maria Luigia. Her two middle names, as was the custom of the times, were those of her two grandmothers; her first name was Verdi's choice and reflected his reading in Roman history, where Virginia is a virtuous girl who prefers death at her father's hand to dishonor by a corrupt judge. The story is a favorite in literature and was copied from the Latin of Livy's *History of Rome* (Book 3, Chapters 44–58), into Italian by Petrarch, into French by Jean de Meung in the *Roman de la Rose,* and into English by Chaucer through the Physician in *The Canterbury Tales*. According to the author's purpose, the story can be told to demonstrate the corruptness of judges, barbarity of the father, or the nobility or foolishness of the girl. Verdi, with his interest in Manzoni and Italian history, undoubtedly thought of Virginia, as did Livy, as a prototype of Roman republican virtue. Sometimes, too, Verdi thought of his child as just a baby and sang songs to her.

So the summer passed with Verdi happy in his family but restless in his position. He had contacts in Parma, and he tried to interest the opera house there in producing *Oberto*. The government official who ran Marie Louise's Teatro Regio Ducale was sympathetic to the idea of a new opera by a local composer, but months passed and nothing happened. Then the government hired a new impresario to manage the theatre, and when the gentleman arrived from Lucca on 1 November 1837, Verdi was in Parma to greet him. But although Verdi had managed to win the support of the orchestra and even some support from the Theatre Commission itself, he could not get a commitment out of the man. Two days later, back in Busseto, Verdi wrote to Massini in Milan:

. . . I thought at first I might be able to talk him into it, or as the saying is, "butter him up"; but whatever I said he would not give me a contract and always gave the same answer. If I hadn't been the first to see him, I'd suspect that someone had prejudiced him against me, but that was not possible. I returned home furious, very discouraged and without hope. Why should young men work hard? No one ever pays them for it. Tell me: couldn't you speak to Merelli and find if we could do something with any of the theatres in Milan? Tell him first of all that I should like to submit the score to the judgment of competent maestros, and if the decision is unfavorable, I do not want the opera produced.

Merelli was the new impresario at La Scala where he had succeeded Duke Carlo Visconti di Modrone in 1836. Verdi, as his letter states, would have been happy with any theatre in Milan; what he wanted was Merelli's influence. But nothing came of it; and the year ended with the opera *Oberto* finished and no hope of its being produced. Meanwhile Virginia grew, and Margherita was pregnant again.

During this time, the autumn of 1837, or perhaps even earlier, Verdi wrote six songs for solo voice and piano accompaniment which became, in 1838, his first published works. He was still in Busseto and had sent them as a group to a publisher, Canti, in Milan. They caused no stir at the time and are exhumed today only occasionally by students. They are neither good nor bad but merely competent, typical of the style of the day. They are also typical and prophetic of Verdi. Four are to texts of Italian poets; the other two—and the most interesting—attempt to set, in an Italian translation, two of Marguerite's songs from Goethe's *Faust*.

In *Faust* each song is a scene in which Marguerite appears alone, first at her spinning wheel and then at a shrine, and taken together, the scenes are Goethe's most intense expression of Marguerite. At her spinning wheel Marguerite grieves that her peace of soul has gone; Faust has destroyed it, and she will never know it again. For her now there is only yearning and the hope of dying on his kiss. Gounod and his librettists when they came to do their *Faust* in 1859 fudged this song, perhaps honestly recognizing that Gounod could not compose music profound enough to convey the girl's sense of loss of peace of soul. Instead they wrote a spinning song with an interesting but distracting accompaniment. In it Marguerite regrets that Faust will never come back to her, a much simpler and less profound emotion.

In the second song Marguerite prays to the Madonna to ease her sense of sin, for only the Madonna can guess at the heartache and pain that is beyond expressing except in tears. Goethe presents merely the girl at the shrine and then the poetry. Again, Gounod and his librettists did not dare do anything so simple; whether because they correctly estimated the French opera public or their own limitations is immaterial. They moved the scene into a cathedral, introduced Mephistopheles to make spooky gestures with a cape, and off-stage had a glorious choir to imitate first demons calling Marguerite to hell and then priests (with boys' voices added for ethereality) requesting mercy of the Lord.

Verdi's songs are less successful than Gounod's, but what is interesting is what he attempted to do. He tried to convey Marguerite's deepest sense of loss and sin as directly as Goethe had done. He expected the singer to stand in front of the piano and realize for the audience two states of soul. Later, in his operas, when he was more skilled and perhaps more inspired, he succeeded in doing just that. His characters constantly stand alone on the stage and express their deepest feelings directly to the audience. And the impact on an audience of such direct emotion is tremendous. Critics talk of Verdi's sincerity, his integrity, his force; they mean he presents not a portrayal or a report of an emotion but the emotion itself, directly and without trappings, as though he had succeeded artistically in presenting the naked heart of a man.

The songs further are typical and prophetic of Verdi in that they rely almost entirely on the human voice to express the emotion; the piano accompaniment is of the very simplest. He does not even use it to set a mood; in each the voice begins almost at once. Later in his operas Verdi was to be accused of using the orchestra merely as a guitar accompaniment for the singers. But even in his old age, when he was a master of operatic orchestration, in *Otello* and *Falstaff,* he kept the orchestra absolutely subordinate to the voice, suggesting that for him it was a fundamental preference and not merely a reflection of the contemporary style.

Typical of Verdi also are the melodies, rhythms, use of vowels and kindness to the singer in setting up the phrases and spots to breathe. Notice in the first example, the opening section of Marguerite's first song ("I have lost my peace"), how all the long or held notes, or those on which something happens and, therefore, a climax, are sung to easy vowel sounds, like "ah," or "i" (eye): pAHce, gwEYEee, trovAHrla.

The phrases follow the meaning and punctuation, and the singer, if off to a bad start, can sneak a breath after "pace." Of course, it is true that the verses existed and Verdi merely set them to music. But he chose these verses, not some others, and it is just this sort of care for vowel sounds and phrasing that fills his letters to his librettists in later years. Only because of it can singers, even poor ones, make the song seem effortless. And because of the deliberate disregard of it, much modern music seems and is more difficult to sing.

The second example from the middle of Marguerite's prayer to the Madonna shows Verdi trying for one of his broad melodies. This one

Saint-Saëns' aria for Dalila

is irretrievably spoiled for modern ears by its close resemblance, only one note different, to the phrase Saint-Saëns created almost forty years later, for Dalila to seduce Samson. Again, notice how Verdi with two initial small notes allows the singer to throw his voice up to the long high note that starts the downward phrase. Singers like this. The start of any note, like taking off in an airplane, is a tricky moment. Better to start on a low note, get the air moving evenly and smoothly through the throat, and then move up to the higher one. Verdi generally "prepared" for the high or difficult notes.

Both examples show Verdi's typical dotted-note rhythm—"hiccup style," say those who dislike it. In the second example, "La mia lacrima scendea" has the typical Verdi setting. The daDAH effect gives a feeling of forward motion to the line, but sometimes when he repeats it several times, it does sound as though that day his coffee had set badly. But it is a musical fingerprint identifying Verdi and turns up constantly, like 6/8 rhythm in Brahms or a crescendo chorus in Rossini.

The songs are most interesting, however, not for anything intrinsic, but for what they reveal about Verdi's taste and personality. Any music master in a provincial Italian town might possibly have set Goethe's poetry to music, but it is more likely that he would not, that he would choose something more conventional, sadness at sunset, or a mother's grief at a child's death. Verdi, however, found his way to Goethe, in translation, and responded to it. Shakespeare, again in translation, he revered as a god. All his life Verdi read, not only Italian but world literature. His education was haphazard, and his mind may not have neatly ordered questions of style, taste, or construction in literature; but it did respond instinctively to the good rather than the bad, and it constantly reached out for more.

Verdi's mind and heart also responded to what was human and personal in Goethe's *Faust*. The tragedy contains everything from farce to philosophy, and another composer might have found his way to "The Song of the Flea" or "The Song of the Rat," or to any of the peasant choruses or even to Marguerite's first song, "The King of Thule." Instead, Verdi passed by even the two main characters, Faust and Mephistopheles, to reach something purely personal, the girl's suffering. What interested him was the human being, and all his operas are about individual humans and their problems. His characters may sometimes be poorly motivated or without substance, but they are never symbols or concepts, such as Mozart has in *The Magic Flute.* In this Verdi reflects the truth of the adage that the Latin temperament is unsympathetic to conceptions. It does not see evil as an amorphous first sin or an impersonal force with a capital "E." For most Latins and for Verdi evil is always a specific person in time and place who hurts others or who, by intent or foolishness, creates an evil situation. Thus, in his opera *Macbeth,* Verdi succeeds with Shakespeare's Lady Macbeth but only makes something ludicrous out of the witches.

A result of this view of evil is that, however multitudinous evil may be, it is always separable into this problem or that: the jealous brother, the war, or Iago in *Otello.* And, further and most important: if evil is separable, specific and human, it can be cured or removed. A premise under all of Verdi's operas is that if only the good people had learned the truth sooner or been able to take some particular action, then the disaster never would have happened. And if action could prevent the disaster, then action is worth taking. Mentally, by temperament, Verdi, a self-made man, was drawn to strong stories in which the characters struggle to change their fate.

But for Verdi the disaster always does happen. Even in *Simone Boccanegra,* in which for once the soprano is allowed to marry the man she loves, the bride comes from the altar to discover her father dying of poison, and the gay wedding music is never heard at all. Verdi might well agree with Sophocles in *Oedipus at Colonus:* "Not to be born is best. . . ." For Verdi life is a vale of tears; and he has Aida, as she is dying, sing it literally: "O terra addio, addio valle di pianti."

William James, in *The Varieties of Religious Experience,* aptly characterized two extreme and contrasting attitudes toward life: "There are men who seem to have started in life with a bottle or two of champagne inscribed to their credit; whilst others seem to have been born close to the pain-threshold, which the slightest irritants fatally send them over." Verdi was somewhere in the second group, and Marguerite's two songs suggest how close he lived to his threshold of pain. Even though Verdi was young, in good health, happily married with a growing family, and the first large steps from peasant to musician successfully taken, still in all of *Faust* what struck the sympathetic and creative chord in him was the girl's tragedy, her suffering and pain.

The songs were good for prestige, but they added nothing to Verdi's pocket. The opera, *Oberto,* was still his best hope for establishing a reputation and financial independence. An opera could pass from town to town, and even in those days of no copyright laws the composer, by overseeing each new production, could earn something out of the performance. With songs it was infinitely more difficult. Indeed, a song that was truly popular became impossible to police. Luigi Denza wrote "Funiculì Funiculà" in 1880 to commemorate the opening of the funicular railway to the top of Mt. Vesuvius, and six years later Richard Strauss, thinking it was an anonymous folk song, used it as a finale to his "Aus Italien" symphonic fantasy, where it became a sort of wild, Germanic "Ride of the Vesuvians." But even if six songs were not an opera, they were a published work, considered worthy by an independent critic, the publisher, who actually invested money in them. Nothing is more encouraging to an artist.

On 11 July 1838 Margherita's second child was born, a boy. They named him Icilio Romano Carlo Antonio; the last two names, again according to custom, were those of his grandfathers. The first name, Icilio, is not common in Italy, although well known. It is the clan name of an important Roman family of whom the earliest and most distinguished member was Lucius Icilius, who happened to be, Livy records, affianced to the unfortunate Virginia. After her death Icilius, with her father, organized the plebeians so that they successfully asserted demands for better justice and government against the patrician party, of which the corrupt judge was a member. It is always possible that Virginia, a name popular in Italy in the nineteenth century, and Icilio just happened to be Margherita's two favorite names and that Verdi had no part in choosing them. But it is most unlikely.

On 12 August, Virginia, who was only in her seventeenth month, suddenly died of some childhood disease, which is not known. The family was stunned. Busseto seemed a place of disaster, and Verdi was determined to get away. Some sort of a trip, even a short one, was necessary for Margherita, and in Milan just then there was the excitement and distraction of a coronation. But there was no money; his salary as Director of Music had not allowed him to save anything, so he applied to his father-in-law for a loan. He did it in the way of the anguished proud, by letter, although Barezzi lived close by. At least the two men need not be face to face at the first moment of application. Verdi wrote:

At home the day of
5 September 1838

My very dear father-in-law:

I have tried always, for as long as I have been in Busseto, to inconvenience you as little as possible, and I believe I have succeeded to some extent. This time, in spite of myself, I must bother you. You know that Ghitta [Verdi consistently misspelled this common nickname by inserting an extra "t"] and I are going to Milan, and not just for pleasure, but to look out for my interests as a musician. As I will have to stay there the entire time I am away, the money I have is not enough to maintain us, and I think I shall need an additional 120 or 130 francs. If you wish to advance me that amount, on my return I will have my monthly salary to draw against, and I can give you a draft for that amount, keeping the rest for myself. This will be a straight loan and short-term. If you think favorably of this, will you lend me the sum at the Milanese exchange rate, and then tear up this note, keeping the loan a secret between us two. Further, to keep it a better secret, could you forgo entering it in your book, because I am most eager to repay you quickly, as is likewise your daughter. I salute you from the heart.

Yr. most affec.
G. VERDI

Barezzi granted the loan. The book that Verdi worried about was Barezzi's account book. Like many men with a family business, Barezzi ran his family and business out of the same pocket, recording personal and business transactions in the same ledger. When he toted up accounts and struck balances, his children often helped him, and anyone might make an entry during the day if Barezzi were away from the store. Verdi had helped Barezzi with the accounts and knew that the book was completely public.

Barezzi's financing and system of accounting, so open and simple, has a certain nostalgic charm. There was no foolishness then about the Married Woman's Property Act, or trust funds for the children. It was simply all his. And no member of his family would have thought of questioning whether he was using it wisely. Nor would any tax collector insist that he segregate income or itemize expenses. If Barezzi wanted to operate as a sort of personal foundation, issuing grants to musicians and subsidizing a Philharmonic Society, he could do it all out of his grocery-store ledger. And perhaps just because it was so simply all his, he had no shame or secrecy about it and used his wife and children, even hired hands, to help him with it.

On 7 September, Verdi and Margherita left for Milan. They expected to be gone just a few weeks, and Icilio remained behind with a nurse. Verdi took with him the manuscript score of *Oberto* and all the parts for solo voices, separately copied. He could not, even if he had wished, lose interest in *Oberto*. The opera, unproduced, was a burr on his back driving him to the impresarios, the theatres, the big cities. His friends wished him luck with it; some came to see him off on the coach. He was, after all, still the Director of Music at Busseto.

CHAPTER 7

THE CORONATION IN MILAN AND *OBERTO* PRODUCED

1838–1839; AGE, 24–26

VERDI and Ghita arrived in Milan in the middle of coronation week. The Emperor of Austria, Ferdinand I, had come to have himself crowned King of Lombardy-Venetia in the cathedral, and the celebrations were immense. Verdi's first letter to Barezzi is a typical traveler's note, breathless with unrecounted excitement:

My very dear father-in-law:

We arrived safe in Milan the evening of the 8th. We could find rooms neither for ourselves nor the horse, but fortunately through the kindness of Prof. Seletti we have an apartment. I won't tell you about the military reviews with the Emperor on horseback or the parades or the court ball or the decorations at the Cathedral. You will read descriptions in the papers. Lines are forming outside of La Scala, and I must go. Soon I will write you a very long letter. Greetings to all our friends. Ghitta is well. A kiss from the heart.

Your most aff.

G. VERDI

The coronation was the first the city had seen since June 1805, when Napoleon in the same cathedral had crowned himself King of Italy. Reference to that act, however, while perhaps popular, was, during the present festivities, not polite, and the city as a whole and particularly the aristocracy and clerical elements celebrated and enjoyed themselves without raising or attempting to answer any of the more profound political issues of the day.

They existed, however, and the coronation itself was an effort to answer them by a piece of applied statecraft on the part of Metternich, the Austrian Chancellor. Once there had been a Holy Roman Empire. It had existed from 962 to 1806, when Francis II of Austria, the last Emperor, had renounced the then empty title. The Empire had never been the same thing in any two years, but always in theory it had been a commonwealth or federation of Europe with an Emperor elected by the member states. It stood for unity and order among Christian nations. It was supposed to be the temporal counterpart of a Universal Catholic Church. It existed in theory by the consent of the states and perhaps, though remotely, by the consent of the people. It had always had, as the obvious heir of the classical Roman Empire, an immense appeal for Italians even though no one but a Hapsburg had been elected Emperor since 1438, and even though the Reformation had made a mockery of the Universal Catholic Church. But even so, it was a politically potent idea, appealing equally to those who yearned for an order to society with a rational political structure and to those who enthused about the brotherhood of man regardless of race or language.

When, beginning in 1803, Napoleon swept into Germany, capturing Imperial cities, duchies, palatinates and the myriad other political divisions that made up the geographical country, he effectively abolished the Holy Roman Empire. In its place he substituted a Confederation of the Rhine, including Bavaria, made up of larger political units and all subservient to him. In answer to this threat Francis II, the last Holy Roman Emperor, had in 1804 declared the Austrian Empire which consisted of Austria, Hungary, Czechoslovakia and parts of Poland and the Ukraine. After Waterloo, and by the Congress of Vienna, he added or recaptured to it Lombardy-Venetia, part of Yugoslavia and part of Rumania. In addition, in Italy he had relatives on the thrones or married to the sovereigns of the Kingdom of the Two Sicilies, Parma, Modena, Piedmont and Tuscany. The coronation, Metternich hoped, would demonstrate to the Italians that the sprawling Austrian Empire, transcending barriers of race and language and with a system of incorporated and nominally independent kingdoms and duchies, was the successor of the old Holy Roman Empire and deserved allegiance.

To the coronation, as if to give their consent, dutifully came the minor monarchs or their representatives, and the Milanese lined the streets, gaping at the display and cheering the horses and coachmen. There was Verdi's sovereign, the Duchess Marie Louise of Parma. As

Napoleon's widow, no matter how ordinary, even frumpy, she looked now, she had a glamor even she could not destroy. She had married the great man; she had borne his only legitimate son. There was Duke Francesco IV of Modena, the most hated and cruel of all the monarchs; Grand Duke Leopoldo II of Tuscany, the most liberal and popular; and most important both for the future and the present was Carlo Alberto, King of Piedmont-Sardinia, whose cousin Marianna was the wife of the Austrian Emperor and newly crowned King of Lombardy-Venetia. From the Kingdom of the Two Sicilies Ferdinando II, whose grandmother and second wife were both Austrian Grand Duchesses, sent a representative; the Pope sent a nuncio; and many of the more distant powers, ambassadors and special delegations. In Milan that week no one who was anyone moved from palace to post without a train of carriages and a troop of cavalry.

The flaw in Metternich's scheme, of course, was that it ignored nationalism which, since the start of the century, had become an increasingly powerful force in European politics. Napoleon had fostered it in Italy with the Cisalpine Republic and then the Kingdom of Italy. Since then it had been nourished by patriots and martyrs like Count Confalonieri, who after eighteen years was still imprisoned in Spielberg, the Hapsburg fortress in Moravia. More important, because in the end he influenced the whole peninsula, was Mazzini, a young revolutionary from Genoa. But by 1838 Mazzini, after repeated failures to rouse the Italians as a nation, had gone into exile in London. There he stayed for eleven years until in 1848 he returned and became the following year the First Triumvir of the ill-fated Roman Republic.

But if Metternich, who by diplomatic pressure had successfully hounded Mazzini out of Piedmont, out of France, out of Switzerland, to faraway England, thought distance would lessen Mazzini's influence, he was mistaken. Distance probably increased it; for Mazzini on the scene in person in action was ludicrous. When he attempted in 1834 to organize some four hundred international revolutionaries in Switzerland for an invasion of Piedmont, half his army never got into action at all. The Swiss police in a rare naval action kept it sitting without overcoats in open boats on Lake Geneva until the January breezes had congealed its revolutionary blood. The other half did cross the border, read a proclamation unheralded by drum roll because there were no drumsticks, and planted a tree of liberty. This last gave rise to obvious jokes by the Swiss who had come to watch—it was a fine Sunday afternoon—that January was a poor season for transplanting. Faced with disaster, the expedition on its second day disbanded. The men disappeared into the scenery as tourists, and the leaders began to explain in letters and memoirs that it was all someone else's fault.

Such perhaps was Mazzini in action in Italy, but as a pamphleteer living in exile he wrote with the power and force of an Old Testament prophet. From 1831 to 1834 he had lived at Marseilles and organized a new revolutionary group, *La Giovine Italia,* Young Italy. There were lodges and chapters throughout the peninsula. By action they accomplished nothing permanent, but through them Mazzini started to educate almost an entire generation of young Neapolitans, Romans, Genoese, etc., to think of themselves as Italians, to think of the entire Peninsula as one political unit, with Rome as its capital and its government a republic. In a sense he provided the broad base to support the liberal aristocrats like Count Confalonieri. Verdi seems never to have joined a lodge; neither did Metternich, but both had heard and understood Mazzini's message. It was in the air of Italy and it hovered above the crowds at the coronation in Milan.

But the divisions and loyalties were not yet sharp. In Piedmont where French was the official language and in its province of Savoy the only language, there was little emotional pull in Mazzini's concept of a united Italy. Instead there was a countering pride in the cosmopolitanism of the kingdom, its acquaintance with French rationalism and Swiss Protestant thinking. In Milan, by reason of history and position, the influence was more Austrian. Many of the families had sent their sons to Vienna to be educated, and there was considerable intermarriage. There was also the tradition: Andrea Maffei, for example, a forty-year-old poet and one of the leaders of Milan society, was the son of a Cavaliere of the old Holy Roman Empire. He wrote a cantata and verses in honor of the coronation. Then, too, Metternich was aware of the bitterness of many families over the continued imprisonment of Italians in Spielberg, and Ferdinand arrived in Milan promising a general amnesty for political prisoners. This caused the young poet Temistocle Solera to burst into print with a hymn to Ferdinand entitled "The Amnesty." Solera's father had been sentenced to Spielberg when his son was still a boy. Metternich, at least for the moment, apparently had succeeded in confusing the real issues and muddling the loyalties so that the Milanese seemed to themselves and to the rest of the world to be persuaded that the Austrian Empire in Italy was a good thing.

For the time being, at any rate, the city determined to have fun. The people turned out in force to watch the parades. The poets celebrated the monarch, who occasionally suffered from bouts of insanity, as the best of all monarchs; painters idealized him in oil on huge canvases, and sculptors modeled allegorical figures. At La Scala, Merelli announced a gala season in honor of their Majesties and more than doubled the price of admission. The repertory consisted of four operas by Rossini, one by Pier Antonio Coppola and four ballets. The most successful of these last was *Nabucodonoser* (Nebuchadnezzar), with sumptuous scenery and choreography by Antonio Cortesi. It was given in all thirty-five times, generally, as the custom then was, after the first act of an opera which continued, thereafter, far into the night. Merelli opened the season with a special gala performance on 2 September. On the sixth, Ferdinand was crowned in the cathedral, the inside of which had been completely transformed by Sanquirico, the leading stage designer at La Scala. On the ninth, the city gave a grand ball, and after a week of intense excitement the Milanese watched Ferdinand, followed by endless chamberlains and heralds in a long line of carriages, start for Venice where a new round of festivities began. He never returned, and his coronation was the last in the cathedral.

When it was all over Verdi began a letter to Barezzi with what sounds suspiciously like a contemporary political jingle:

The Emperor has departed, and the brothel is finished (L'Imperatore è partito e il bordello è finito). Milan is always beautiful but at this time . . . Ah! . . . It is useless for me to describe the spectacle, etc. . . .

Verdi, of course, was not invited to the functions, and his mind was not filled with questions of dress, tickets and protocol. He wanted to talk about his opera, but most of the important people wanted to talk only of how the ball went last night or of the preparations for the one on the morrow. He conferred with his friend Massini who had unfortunately resigned from his position as director of the amateur group and whose influence at the Teatro dei Filodrammatici had therefore waned. But Massini recommended Verdi again to Count Borromeo, for whom Verdi in 1834 had composed a wedding cantata, and to an engineer, Francesco Pasetti. Both agreed to speak to Merelli. Another supporter and most important was Vincenzo Merighi, a professor at the Conservatory and first cellist at La Scala. Merelli was known to respect his opinion.

The hope was to persuade Merelli to produce *Oberto* at the close of the season just starting as a benefit production for the Pio Istituto Teatrale. This was an organization, "The Holy Theatrical Institute," founded by Duke Carlo Visconti di Modrone, Merelli's predecessor, to help singers and actors in distress. It was, for obvious reasons, a popular charity with the La Scala audience. The argument was that Merelli would be guaranteed a full house and a receptive audience. If the opera was a success he could continue it; if not, then he could drop it, having given the Pio Istituto a première for its benefit. The argument had some force until Merelli reported that with the coronation season doing so well he did not intend that fall to give any benefits.

Discouraged, having already stayed longer than he intended and with his money running short, although Barezzi had sent him more, Verdi made arrangements to return to Busseto. Then suddenly he changed his plans and stayed over. Merelli, persuaded apparently by Merighi, had studied the score and agreed, if some changes were made, to produce *Oberto* for a Pio Istituto benefit in the spring season of 1839.

With this news Verdi and Ghita returned quickly to Busseto where he conferred first with Barezzi and then submitted his resignation as the town's Director of Music. His letter to the Mayor in which he requested to be released was a model of leaving the unpleasant unsaid. Most of it was devoted to a precise exposition of his right under the contract of employment to resign upon six months' notice and the expression of his regret at leaving and affection for the town. Only in the first paragraph does he regret that unhappy circumstances prevented him from being as useful as he had hoped to be.

The Mayor and the directors of the Monte di Pietà, however, were under no illusions about the unhappy circumstances. The churches in Busseto were still without music, and every Sunday and feast day was a new cause for argument, a further example of the stupidity of someone's position. The directors accepted Verdi's resignation with regret but stated frankly that it seemed to be a universal desire to have music again in the churches, particularly with Christmas coming on. The Mayor, too, in his letter regretted the division in the town. Neither letter suggested that Verdi was in any way responsible for the trouble, but each exuded a sigh of relief at his going. In effect, he was allowed to resign at once and given six months' salary.

Verdi and Ghita celebrated Christmas in Busseto and then prepared to leave. Ghita packed while he worked on his opera. According to the division of duty and honor in marriage and housekeeping at the time, the house always and the children, at least until they were six or seven, were entirely the wife's affair. Even in the simplest peasant's home in Le Roncole no man ever washed a plate, made a bed, or changed a diaper. On the other hand, no guest ever entered a house without paying recognized homage to its lady. She might, by custom, retire immediately after dinner to the kitchen or her drawing room, but while on the scene she was queen. Yet if Verdi never washed a plate, neither, probably, did Margherita, at least in Busseto. Labor then was cheap, and there was an endless supply of peasant spinsters and widows who, lacking a husband or family, had no place in the agricultural villages and who drifted toward the towns and cities to become seamstresses, washerwomen, cooks and maids of all work. Margherita, as Barezzi's daughter, probably had some domestic help from the first.

Verdi's consuming interest in his score made his departure from Busseto inevitable. Barezzi not only understood this but rejoiced in it; Verdi's talent needed scope, as Provesi and Lavigna had agreed. La Signora Barezzi, however, probably had some regrets. It was all very well for the men who sometimes traveled and might see each other, but for her and Margherita it was a real separation. She would not see her grandchild grow, and at the next pregnancy she certainly would have to go to Milan to be with her daughter. Margherita herself alternated between excitement and regret. She, after all, would keep house in either place, and perhaps it was pleasanter in Busseto. But then if Verdi's work took them to Milan, they must go, and although it was in a foreign state with a different dialect, they had after all been there twice.

So on 6 February 1839, Verdi, with Margherita and Icilio Romano, left Busseto for Milan. He had completed the revisions on his opera and was eager to get back to the city. By the added pressure of his presence he hoped to keep Merelli to his promise to produce *Oberto* as the benefit for the Pio Istituto. Verdi feared the argument of "out of sight, out of mind," and even more he feared the argument of changed circumstances. Merelli's Carnival season had not gone well.

Of the six operas staged three had failed and two of these were new operas. There were rumors that Merelli would try to recoup with a spring season of proven successes.

For it Merelli announced a strong company. Among the men were Napoleone Moriani, the best tenor in Italy, and a baritone, Giorgio Ronconi, who was a specialist in Donizetti. The soprano, about whom there was the most excitement and who was making her Milan debut, was Giuseppina Strepponi. She had studied at the Milan Conservatory and made her debut in 1835 in Trieste. From there she had sung in the smaller Italian houses, particularly at Florence, Venice and Trieste, and also with great success in Vienna, so that she came to Milan as an exciting international star. Like Ronconi she, too, was a specialist in Donizetti, and his operas presumably would dominate the season. When Merelli finally announced the schedule it included by Donizetti *Lucia di Lammermoor, Pia de' Tolomei* and *L'Elisir d'Amore* and by Bellini, *I Puritani.* Strepponi was to sing in all four.

This made a brutal schedule for any singer, but it was typical of the times, particularly in Italy. A prima donna in the 1830s was seldom the proud, independent diva of the 1890s, associating with royalty and singing only when she wanted. Strepponi's career, for example, was run by a theatrical agent who rented her out, without her approval, to any impresario making up a company for a season. The impresario, of course, was interested only in his season and expected her to sing four or five times a week. As a result vocal careers were often glorious but short. Artists struggled against the system, but only the greatest were able to break free. Strepponi was bound to it, for her earnings supported her family, a widowed and illiterate mother, four younger brothers and sisters, and also her own illegitimate child about whom almost nothing is known.

Her letters reveal a sense of desperation about her career of which Verdi and the general public were almost certainly unaware. They saw on the stage merely a rather short woman with a reasonable figure who was in her middle twenties, had a clear, limpid voice, excellent technique, and was also a remarkable actress. In the La Scala season about to start Strepponi was to be equally successful in both the comic *L'Elisir d'Amore* and the tragic *Lucia di Lammermoor.* It is no wonder that Verdi was eager to have her sing in *Oberto.*

Meanwhile his friends, Massini and Merighi, continued to urge the opera on Merelli, who in turn showed it to his singers who reported

MERELLI

favorably on it. Merelli then announced *Oberto* as the opera for the Pio Istituto benefit and assigned to it his three leading singers and a popular bass, Ignazio Marini. Verdi was given a rehearsal schedule, and overnight, from being a thin fellow who was always hanging around, he became someone of importance. Eighteen months before he had been reduced to begging merely that competent maestri examine the score; now the public would judge it in as fine a production as La Scala could give. Then, the rehearsals barely under way, the tenor fell sick, and the production was canceled.

Verdi began to despair. He almost hated the opera for the emotions it had tortured in him. And there was no money. How could he stay in Milan without a job and how could he go back to Busseto without one? But plainly with Margherita and the child there was really no choice. They would all have to return to Busseto. It would be the second time he had left Milan with his opera and without a commitment for its production and this time with less hope than last.

Then, as often happens in the theatre, black in an instant turned to white, and Merelli offered Verdi a contract to do *Oberto* as part of the regular schedule in the coming autumn season. This would not be a benefit performance, late in the season, and with the composer expected to contribute his services to the charity in gratitude for having his work done at all, but the opera would be one of the announced repertory. With any luck at all there would be a dozen performances and a correspondingly greater chance that other impresarios would hear it or of it and produce it at their theatres. Needless to say, Verdi accepted and any thought of returning with his family to Busseto was canceled.

It seems that Merelli, in making up his schedule for the autumn season, was able to count on only two new operas, one by Ricci and another by Panizza who had succeeded Lavigna as *maestro al cembalo.* Merelli wanted a third, and he sent for Verdi. He told Verdi that one night during a performance as he was standing in the wings he overheard a conversation between his soprano and baritone. In the course of it the soprano, Strepponi, spoke enthusiastically of *Oberto,* and the baritone agreed. Thereafter Merelli himself had studied the score and libretto in detail and concluded that while the libretto was weak the score was not. Merelli had earlier in his life written a number of librettos, and his suggestions for improving it were good; Verdi agreed to them without argument.

At that time librettos were always written in verse, and Merelli suggested that Verdi use the young poet, Temistocle Solera, to rewrite the changes and introduce a quartet into the second act. As well as being a poet Solera was also a composer, and he could be expected to produce verses that would sing well. Thus with Merelli's blessing and through his influence Verdi started to work with a poet and librettist of considerably greater stature than Piazza, the journalist.

Throughout the summer Verdi worked on the opera and other shorter works. Three of these he sent to his publisher, Canti. They were a nocturne for three voices, flute and piano, and two songs. None has any great virtues, and the two songs are far less interesting than the best of his previous efforts. One, "The Exile," to verses by his new librettist, Solera, describes the exile at sunset on a foreign shore, longing to see home again and to kiss his parents' cheeks. Verdi tried to make of it something splendid. He lavished on the opening sunset a long, moody piano introduction; he introduced the voice on unaccompanied recitative and, thereafter by his usual standards, built up an extremely varied interplay between voice and piano. The year 1839 was a time when many Italians were in exile, and the subject had an immediate appeal. But neither the verses nor the music, for all of whatever artistic effort went into them, are anything more than exercises in the expected emotions.

The second song, "The Seduction," is almost ludicrously bad. It attempts in four short pages to recount how an innocent girl, sweet as any flower, was ruined and not a stone or tree marked her grave. On the central verse, "fu sedotta" (she was seduced), the voice first rises, then drops an octave in horror. The verses were by a schoolmate from Busseto, Dr. Luigi Balestra, and unquestionably the most real emotion in the joint endeavor was that of friendship between the two men; Verdi's feelings for the unfortunate lady sound quite artificial.

The two songs are typical of the bad art of the period and good examples of the sort of composition that Verdi slowly but steadily improved on. All over Italy in the 1830s men of sensibility sighed over urns and maidens, rediscovered the wild beauties of nature, were charmed by ruins and in general behaved as members of the Romantic Age of which they were a part. At its best it could produce a man like Garibaldi or a work of art like Verdi's *Otello;* at its worst it produced men and art that attempted to rape all the big emotions without actually touching or feeling them.

Verdi and Ghita were still living in rented rooms, which was more expensive than renting a small house, and in September, the season for house hunting in Milan, they hoped to find one. But Verdi lacked the money for the down payment. So he wrote Barezzi:

4 September 1839

My very dear father-in-law:

Encouraged by your kindness so often exerted on my behalf, I take heart again to tell you what I need.

You know that at the moment we are at Saint Michael's, and I have not yet found a house because the landlords want the rent in advance. I haven't got it, and I turn to you. While I am working on my opera I cannot raise the money by other jobs. About the opera I will tell you secretly when you come here. For now I will only say that the news is good, and better than I ever dared to hope. As for the money I need about 350 lire. I hate to bother you now when I know how much you do for others. If I were able to do with less I swear I would do so. You know where my thoughts and hopes turn. Certainly not towards accumulating money but towards being someone among men and not being merely a useless tool like so many others. If I cannot get help from you I will be like the swimmer who sees the safety of the shore and heads for it, but . . . his strength fails, and he dies. Relying on your goodness, I thank you in advance and hoping to embrace you soon I send you, meanwhile, my greetings,

Yours,

G. VERDI

Barezzi forwarded the money which was actually, although unknown to Verdi, furnished by a supporter in Busseto, the Baronessa Soldati. With it Verdi rented a small house at 3072 via San Simone (today via Cesare Correnti) near the Porta Ticinese, and the family moved in. The area around the Porta Ticinese was one of the rougher sections of the city, and even to be seen in fashionable clothes in the evening was to risk being stoned. There the family lived very quietly.

Toward the end of October, as Verdi was about to begin rehearsals of *Oberto*, Icilio Romano fell ill. Again there was a lack of money for the doctor and medicine, and this time Verdi signed a note to cover a small loan from Signora Barezzi. But it was all to no avail. On 22 October Icilio Romano died. As with Virginia, the cause is unknown; both died at about sixteen months and suddenly. The timing of the second death was cruel. For Verdi had, at least, the distractions of the rehearsals, but for Margherita there was simply the empty house and the feeling that his attention was elsewhere.

For the première of *Oberto* on 17 November 1839 Barezzi, with his eldest son Giovanni and a number of close friends, came to Milan prepared to applaud no matter how the performance went. Merelli had assembled a good cast, although not as exciting as the one for the canceled production. The bass, Marini, was the same and the others were adequate. One of the sopranos, Mary Shaw, was English, and she wrote enthusiastic letters home which are said to have been the first news of Verdi to reach England. As was the custom of the time Verdi, as the composer, sat in the orchestra pit between the first double bass and first cello, from where he could hear every handclap or titter.

At the final curtain it was plainly a success but not a great success. It ran in the autumn season, which Merelli extended, for a respectable fourteen performances. The critics approved of it while, of course, pointing out flaws and similarities of style to other composers. One, while comparing Verdi to Bellini, complained, "There is an abundant, perhaps too abundant, wealth of melody." The libretto, which by then had been worked on by Piazza, Merelli, Solera and Verdi, was universally criticized as weak. The opera tells a romantic story of aristocratic types loving, leaving and dueling around castles set in a countryside described in the score as "delicious." The final curtain falls as the soprano, after learning that her lover has killed her father, contemplates death in her despair while a chorus, on her behalf, begs comfort from heaven. The opera's chief interest today lies in being Verdi's first, and as such it is occasionally revived in anniversary years or for festival performances.

But for a first opera it was a good beginning. Merelli immediately contracted with Verdi for three more to be produced at La Scala and the Court Theatre in Vienna. He agreed to pay four thousand lire an opera and to share the profits evenly on the sale of the copyright. This was an excellent contract for a beginner, and nothing could more concretely demonstrate Merelli's confidence in Verdi. Other impresarios began to approach Verdi for productions of *Oberto*, and it was given almost immediately in the 1840 Carnival season at Turin and in 1841 at Genoa and Naples.

The opera did not end Verdi's financial problems and it could not restore his children, but by insuring him work and the work he wanted it restored hope and equilibrium to his family. He and Ghita could have more children; they were both young and in good health. Now they definitely would stay in Milan and make a life for themselves away from Busseto. Sometimes around the house she caught him humming his own music, the quartet from *Oberto*.

CHAPTER 8

MUSICAL STYLES OF THE TIME AND *UN GIORNO DI REGNO*

1839–1840; AGE, 26

FOR Verdi's first opera under their new contract Merelli wanted an *opera seria,* that is, a serious opera as opposed to a comic one, an *opera buffa.* The terms by 1840 were dated and described rather inaccurately the new kinds of opera that were emerging. For the political and social changes that had sometimes violently and sometimes slowly transformed Italy during the Napoleonic era and after had also transformed opera. The audience thereafter expected and the composers and librettists provided something different from their predessors. Italian comic opera, for example, had existed before Waterloo and been universally admired, but after Waterloo, with Rossini, it suddenly became a European mania. One explanation is Rossini's genius. Another is that the audience, exhausted and its sensitivity blunted by the Napoleonic wars, wanted to relax with slapstick, farce, peace and laughter.

When Merelli, in order to balance his schedule, asked Verdi in 1840 for an *opera seria,* he probably had in mind an opera such as Bellini's *Norma,* 1831, or Donizetti's *Lucia di Lammermoor,* 1835, which were already quite different from what the eighteenth century understood by the term. The differences which began merely as matters of emphasis slowly became an actual change in kind, although in *Aida* in 1871 Verdi would compose a triumphal scene that would have set all the eighteenth-century opera buffs nodding with approval.

In the eighteenth century the term *opera seria* described the sort of opera that flourished before an aristocratic audience gathered at some royal or ducal court or perhaps, at one remove, in a public theatre in some capital city. The operas almost always were based on some mythological or remote historical incident, had a happy ending if only because the audience was going on to dinner and dancing, and had at least one scene of pure spectacle. For an opera *Ezio* in 1755 there was a Roman triumph with a victorious army marching in review, hordes of shuffling captives, cheering crowds and over a hundred horses passing across the stage. However many generations may lie between, the line descends directly to the Egyptian triumph in *Aida*.

But even more than the spectacle the glory of the eighteenth-century *opera seria* was the aria and the singer. The librettos used the mythological or historical stories merely to string together a series of arias in which the singer, often making little effort to stay in character, displayed his gorgeous voice and marvelous technique. It was a type of opera in which the singer was supreme, and the libretto offered little or no drama in the sense of carefully paced action leading to a crucial scene. Instead each aria made its own impact on the audience, unaided or hindered by what had gone before or came after.

Obviously this sort of opera required great singers, especially in that the singer was expected to improvise at each performance a whole new set of embellishments on each aria. The embellishments consisted basically of scales or runs and trills, but in infinitely complicated combinations; so that it might take the singer a hundred notes and several minutes to pass from one word to the next. The audience took a great interest in this, found it expressive, and judged a singer in large part by his ability to improvise and create embellishments that fitted the mood and text of the aria. The orchestra was of no importance, and if the singer was doing well, it might even stop altogether to let him carol away alone.

The best singers in this style throughout the eighteenth century and lasting until about 1820 were the castrati. These were men who as boys had been castrated to prevent their voices from dropping, so that they were male sopranos and altos. They were undoubtedly, as far as technique was concerned, the greatest singers the world has ever heard, and until they disappeared they were the most feted, idolized and admired musicians of their time. When Napoleon occupied Vienna in 1805, he heard the castrato Girolamo Crescentini and was so impressed he made him a Knight of the Iron Cross of Lombardy. He also invited Crescentini to come to Paris, and from 1806 to 1812 the castrato was the leading performer before the Imperial Court at the Tuileries.

But as the nineteenth century began, the fashion in singing and opera changed, although so slowly that it is clear only to hindsight. As late as 1824 Meyerbeer composed a successful opera, *Il Crociato in Egitto,* with a part for a castrato, Velluti, who, as it turned out, was to be one of the last of the castrati to sing in opera. The reasons for the change in taste and style are various, and their relative importance depends greatly on the historian's point of view. Historically, about 1810, there was a sudden drop in the number of castrati singing in the theatres, and by 1820 there were almost none. It seems that Napoleon's Italian campaigns, beginning in 1796, so discomposed the musical conservatories up and down the peninsula that for a number of years they hardly graduated any students. The conservatories often depended in part at least on grants from sovereigns or rich aristocrats who fled before Napoleon's revolutionary armies or used their money elsewhere. Faculties were dispersed; students never entered or were conscripted out of school, and the future musical life of Italy became a casualty of political disorder. When times became settled again, after 1815, the contemporary critics voiced a universal lament over the decline in standards of musical performance and training. In the meantime the tradition and succession of the castrati had been broken, and it never was resumed.

Socially the Napoleonic upheavals changed or greatly speeded the change in the composition of the opera audience. By loosening the exclusive grip of the aristocrats on the political and cultural life and by increasing trade it strengthened the rising middle class. The audience lost its aristocratic, white complexion and developed a more ruddy, bourgeois hue; "positively freckled," growled the old guard. As its base broadened socially, it became geographically more widespread. The century of an opera house in every little Italian town is the nineteenth, not the eighteenth. Fifty years earlier Barezzi would probably have felt less personally involved in opera, and Merelli, as director of the Court Theatre in Vienna and La Scala, would certainly have been at least a count. His predecessor at La Scala, for example, was Duke Guido Visconti di Modrone.

With the change in the audience came a change in the style of librettos for *opera seria.* There was less of Ariadne, Theseus and Hercules and more of the simpler types such as Lucia di Lammermoor and

Norma. To enjoy stories based on classical mythology, to be able to recognize the allusions and to associate them to the present requires an education in the classics, and this the more bourgeois audiences were apt to lack. Verdi, for example, never used a mythological story for an opera, probably not because he had analyzed the level and type of education in an average audience, but because the stories and dramas of the Greeks meant little to him. Whereas stories of Italian history in which he had educated himself struck an immediate response. Inevitably it would do the same in his audience, most of whom were well enough aware that as a repressed people they were the stuff of which history is made.

One result of this move away from mythology to national history, real or fictionalized, was to cut down the number of roles available to castrati. Their voices, however beautiful and excellently trained, were suitable only for non-realistic drama, mythology or remote history in which the audience was not personally involved. But inevitably as soon as the drama became realistic, about *Les Huguenots,* the family in the castle on the hill, or even the man next door, the castrati were doomed. No one in the audience would recognize his neighbor's voice among those of the castrati.

Then too in the field of love, always a subject for a serious opera, the point of view changed as eighteenth-century Enlightenment turned to nineteenth-century Romanticism. In the eighteenth century love was an addition to life, diverting but not necessary. Anything could be arranged, even publicly, as long as certain rules of behavior were observed. Perhaps the most famous arrangement was Voltaire's, by which for sixteen years, 1733–49, he lived happily with the Marquise du Châtelet and her husband. Even when he surprised the lady with a substitute for himself, she was able to smooth everyone's ruffled ego, and when she died shortly after giving birth to the third man's child, Voltaire and the husband were desolate. In opera librettos this view of love can be seen in Mozart's *Le Nozze di Figaro,* 1786, where the Countess, although genuinely grieved by the Count's philanderings, does not go mad of her grief or contemplate suicide but sets out to get him back by cheating at love games in the garden.

But by 1840, with the Romantic Age at its height, love, at least in opera librettos, was no longer a diversion but a necessary paroxysm, a divine passion excluding all but the beloved. Arrangements were inconceivable. The vile husband had to be challenged in the very keep of his castle so that on the way to it all his servants could be assaulted. The lady's charms increased the closer she teetered toward permanent insanity, and in both sexes suicides for love became as common as the smallpox.

This change in the fashion of sensibility greatly increased the actual violence in librettos and the style in which composers presented it. Classical restraint gave way to romantic frenzy, and again the castrati and even those who sang like them were the losers. Greek mythological stories abound in violence, but perhaps because it is never indulged in for its own sake it seems presented at one remove, in the middle distance. A castrato's rather cool, controlled tone seemed appropriate for Orfeo lamenting the loss of his Euridice, and the myth's final scene in which irate, fanatical women literally tear him apart, limb by limb, was generally omitted. Gluck in his opera, *Orfeo ed Euridice,* 1762, substituted a typical *opera seria* ending in which the lovers live happily ever after. But by 1840 the composers and the audience were abandoning restraint for the direct assault on the emotions, and for this the skill of the voice at trills and scales mattered less than its emotional qualities. So when Edgardo commits suicide at the end of *Lucia di Lammermoor,* the aria is technically simple but deliberately designed to release the throb of a tenor voice which more than any other, and much more than a castrato's, has a sense of push and strain to it.

The famous mad scene of *Lucia di Lammermoor* exhibits the merging of the old and new sensibility. It is frankly a demonstration of singing in the castrati tradition; the soprano can extend it with any number of embellishments she cares to add, and the audience even today judges her ability by her skill at it. At the same time it presents insanity in the best romantic tradition with shredded hair, rolling eyeballs and a chorus clucking its sympathy. By comparison *Boris Godunov,* 1874, has a mad scene for the bass voice which has the rolling eyes but in its almost spoken style of singing is vocally outside the castrati tradition.

The last, and most important, and the most purely musical transformation of the old *opera seria* occurred when the techniques of comic opera began to infiltrate it.

Comic opera, *opera buffa,* began its life as a poor relation. It was allowed to divert the audience during intermissions of *opera seria.* Music was, after all, a grand ennobling art, and its proper sphere was the expression of noble sentiments. But even as its practitioners mused on their great calling, *opera buffa,* almost behind their back, established itself as an important form quite different from *opera seria.* The first to have a world-wide success, a success that continues today, was Pergolesi's *La Serva Padrona,* or roughly "How the Maid became the Madame." It first appeared in 1733 in two parts or "intermezzi" to be played between the acts of Pergolesi's *opera seria, Il Prigionier superbo. La Serva Padrona* has only two characters, the master and the maid, although technically a mute servant makes a third. Each half or "intermezzo" has four arias or duets and considerable witty dialogue in recitativo, that is, where the characters swiftly converse back and forth on a musical tone without dropping into a speaking voice. It is a technique that works well in Italian, which has many vowel sounds which can be merged and run on, but is almost hopeless in any other language. The tunes in the little opera are simple and swift, and the voices merge easily in and out of duets. At the end the maid, Serpina, has so muddled her master, poor simple Uberto, that he has agreed to marry her.

In miniature the opera exhibits the structure and emerging strength of the *opera buffa* tradition. It tells a story, simple and domestic, about the man next door. It achieves a fast pace by carefully constructed scenes leading up to the little finale. The very fact that pace was deliberately sought precluded from the very first in the *opera buffa* tradition any extended improvising such as the castrati did in *opera seria.* In sum *La Serva Padrona* and its successors were more theatrical and less like a concert or a spectacle than *opera seria. Opera buffa* achieved this without sacrificing any of its musical qualities; in fact it developed a new one, the ensemble, in which all the characters chatter away at each other at once. This is quite a different thing from a chorus in which all the characters join in expressing the same thought. *Opera seria* in the eighteenth century made use of the chorus and sometimes even a duet, but it never had four characters express four differing sentiments as Verdi does in the quartet from *Rigoletto,* or six as in Donizetti's sextet from *Lucia,* or seven as in Mozart's *Le Nozze di Figaro.* Yet just this sort of ensemble became one of the glories of nineteenth-century serious opera and remains for many persons today opera's unique attribute and its most satisfying.

Mozart in his *Le Nozze di Figaro,* 1786, and *Don Giovanni,* 1787, was one of the earliest, and still today one of the most successful, to merge the best of *opera seria* and *opera buffa* into something new, but

his example was not immediately followed elsewhere. In Italy he has never been popular, and although musicians such as Lavigna and Rossini admired and studied him, his operas were and are seldom produced. In Italy the musical revolutionary was Rossini, and if he seems an unlikely man for such a role, it is because posterity willfully insists on seeing only half the man. It is true that he was irrepressibly gay, loved the good life, good-looking women and, above all, *pâté de foie gras*. But he also loved his music and, like a true revolutionary, did battle for his ideas.

When Rossini began to compose operas in 1810, the forms of *opera seria* and *opera buffa* were still distinct and exclusive. He composed both forms. But when in an *opera seria* he thought a castrato, Velluti, was improvising excessively, he protested. Thereafter by pleading, tact and tantrum he began to force the singers to stay in character and keep to the written note. When he made an *opera seria* out of Shakespeare's *Othello*, he kept the unhappy ending although everyone insisted that no *opera seria* ever had an unhappy ending. There was so much objection he had to provide an alternative ending in which Desdemona convinces Othello of her innocence, and they end with a sentimental duet. Four years later in 1820 he tried another unhappy ending for *Maometto II*. This time only Venice required the alternative, happy ending. His opera *Mosè in Egitto* with the Red Sea had an ending happy and spectacular enough to please everyone, but he insisted on giving the title role to a bass which had never been done in *opera seria* and rattled the traditionalists terribly. He constantly demanded more and better playing by the orchestra, which, considering the incredibly low standards prevailing in the opera houses, was the merest beginning. Once in Rome, when he discovered that the barber who had just shaved him was also the first clarinetist in the orchestra, he ran home in despair and made the parts easier. It is probable that at the time no orchestra in Italy outside of Venice, Milan, Rome or Naples could have played through a Mozart opera without breaking down. And of course every time Rossini added another toot on a horn or a roll on the drums, the singers all shrieked that he had a German heart and was sacrificing them to the orchestra.

But Rossini's greatest innovation in *opera seria* and the thing for which in his own lifetime he was most admired was his use of ensemble singing. Four or five voices blending together is of course beautiful in itself; but it also has an immense effect on the kind of libretto a composer can set. Clearly a plot can proceed faster when all the characters can talk at once than when each must explain his position and feeling in a solo aria or even a few solo remarks. An extreme example of this is Mozart's *Le Nozze di Figaro*. As long as Mozart keeps the plot developing aria by aria, as he does largely throughout the first act and the beginning of the second, it proceeds at a speed anyone can follow. But when he begins his finale to the second act, the plot development accelerates to a speed where an audience unfamiliar with it is often left puzzling over just what has happened. The finale begins with a duet and builds up to a septet with an eighth character brought on in the middle and sent off. In all it runs about twenty-two minutes, and through most of it everyone talks at once.

The result of incorporating these *opera buffa* techniques into *opera seria* was to make the librettos tighter and the drama thereby more effective. Rossini's contemporaries, at least in the beginning, considered that he had revitalized the old *opera seria* form, but posterity can see that, taking all his reforms together, he actually transformed it into something new: Italian romantic opera. Because of this he is a true revolutionary like Wagner and has a side to him which Bellini or Donizetti lacks. They took a form presented to them and within its terms created masterworks.

Rossini's last opera, *William Tell*, first produced in 1829, shows all the seeds which he and others less famous had planted now visibly growing above ground. It tells a non-mythological story familiar to everyone; its famous overture emphasizes the importance of the orchestra, and Rossini's scoring for the various instruments gives it rich, varied sound; it is filled with romantic touches of local color and nature; and the love between the tenor, a Swiss patriot, and the soprano, the sister of the Austrian tyrant, is beset with the necessary difficulties. In its anti-Austrian bias it touches on a political overtone that would sound in almost all of Verdi's early operas. No example, however, is perfect: *William Tell* has a happy ending, is too long, and is cursed with a bathetic text. So it became a musician's opera, a well from which others drew their inspiration. It exists today almost entirely in excerpts—its overture, an aria or two for a concert, and its ballet music. It was, however, the grand prototype of the sort of opera Merelli wanted when he asked Verdi for an *opera seria*. The first opera, *Oberto,* had, after all, been no more than it should have been: short and successful in part because of its very lack of pretensions. Now it was time to try for more.

For a librettist Merelli recommended Gaetano Rossi, who had written the text for Rossini's *Semiramide* in 1823 and would do so for Donizetti's *Linda di Chamounix* in 1842. A recommendation from Merelli, who controlled theatres in Milan and Vienna, was a commission, and Rossi set at once to work. He soon had the libretto in outline and most of the text written. Verdi did not like it. It was called *Il Proscritto, The Outlaw,* but the situations did not appeal to Verdi and he dawdled on the music. Nervously he waited for Merelli to return from Vienna.

What might have been a ticklish situation for a young composer evaporated on Merelli's return. He called Verdi into his office and announced that instead of an *opera seria* for the autumn season he needed an *opera buffa.* The change was not as drastic as perhaps it sounds. The tradition in Italy has always been that composers can do both. Nineteenth-century examples are Rossini and Donizetti, and in the twentieth century even lachrymose Puccini produced a comic masterpiece in *Gianni Schicchi.* The audience for both forms was the same, and on *opera buffa* the rising middle class seemed merely to have a sentimentalizing influence which drew it in spirit closer to *opera seria* or romantic opera. Donizetti's *L'Elisir d'Amore,* for example, is considerably sweeter and more charming than any of Rossini's comedies which preceded it by ten or twenty years. It is also, as a symptom of the general decline in technique, considerably easier to sing. The very fact that Verdi, who was preparing to object to a libretto for an *opera seria,* did not object to the sudden change in form suggests that he expected to be able to compose in both forms like his predecessors. For a libretto Merelli offered Verdi several old works by Felice Romani, who had done the librettos for *La Sonnambula* and *L'Elisir d'Amore,* and suggested Verdi take his choice. The fact that it would not be an original story was of no importance; originality, or rather individuality, of music has always been the key to success in opera.

None of the secondhand librettos, however, pleased Verdi, and he again was in the awkward position of hanging back just when he wanted most to press forward. Finally in desperation he selected one called *Il Finto Stanislao,* or *The Fake King Stanislaus.* The story, set in France in 1733, is remotely connected with the historical King Stanislaus who left exile in France for Poland where he was elected King. Romani invented a story involving a courtier who stayed behind in France and who, in order to protect his sovereign on his journey to Warsaw, pretended to be the King. This caused complications with the lady he wished to marry who sees through the sham, and so on. In 1818 an Austrian composer named Adalbert Gyrowetz had set it for a première at La Scala where it had not been a great success.

Verdi and Merelli renamed the opera *Un Giorno di Regno,* or *King for a Day,* and Verdi began to work on it. Almost at once he fell ill with angina; Margherita put him in bed, and all work stopped for several weeks.

He soon recovered, and then toward the end of May it was Margherita's turn to fall ill and Verdi's to nurse. She had encephalitis, and instead of getting better it got worse. Verdi sent for Barezzi who arrived on 18 June just before she died. She was twenty-seven. The two men buried her in the cemetery of San Giovannino outside of Milan. Then Barezzi closed up the little house on the Via San Simone and took Verdi back to Busseto.

Merelli, not altogether unkindly, insisted on his contract. The autumn season began in the middle of August, and the opera was announced. Verdi begged to be released, but Merelli refused. So to make good on his bond Verdi went back to Milan alone, to reopen the house and to finish the opera.

Un Giorno di Regno was produced on 5 September 1840 and was a grand fiasco. The audience, when it did not remain in hostile, bored silence, hissed and booed. Verdi sat in the orchestra pit as custom required. After the curtain, as was expected of him, he stood backstage and received the congratulations and reassurances. Several of his Milanese friends were conspicuously absent. The next day the critics were unkind, the public circulated jokes about *King for a Day,* and the remaining performances of the opera were canceled.

Verdi retreated to his house and began publicly to behave with a rigid self-control that revealed his private, black despair. Even before the fiasco at La Scala his friends in Busseto had worried over him; one had described him after Margherita's death as reduced "almost to the point of mental aberration." Now he plainly passed over some indefinite line into a form of nervous breakdown in which he could do no work, music was no consolation to him, and he arranged his life in a way that, while perfectly controlled, made little sense.

First he undertook to break his contract with Merelli. Merelli argued that he still had confidence in Verdi, that he had revived *Oberto* to replace the canceled performances of *Un Giorno di Regno,* and that one fiasco meant nothing. But calmly and politely Verdi announced that he would not compose again and he wished to have the contract destroyed. In the end Merelli, perhaps recognizing that there was a time to stand firm and a time to give in, did as Verdi asked, although protesting that any time Verdi would compose an opera, he, Merelli, on two months' notice would produce it.

Then Verdi sent all the furniture which Margherita had collected to Barezzi in Busseto, closed the house and rented a furnished room on the Piazzetta San Romano (which does not exist today). There he stayed week after week. Occasionally he said something about taking students, but in fact he did nothing. He never called on anyone, and almost no one called on him. Lavigna would have, but he was dead. Seletti tried to keep an eye on him, but most of the time Verdi was alone. The truth was that he did not have many friends in Milan and in his present state was not good company. Most of the time he ate alone at a trattoria on the piazza or had a sea biscuit dipped in water in his room.

Today it is hard to see just why the audience turned so strongly against *Un Giorno di Regno.* Twenty years later Verdi wrote of it: "From that day I have never set my eyes on *Un Giorno di Regno;* it is certainly a bad opera, although many other operas no better have been tolerated." Subsequent performances, particularly in the last ten years, have demonstrated the fairness of this judgment. That night at La Scala perhaps was one of those evenings when the audience might just as well have withheld judgment or granted a tolerant and amused success to a beginner. Instead, unfortunately for Verdi, its emotions accelerated in the other direction, and it plainly and loudly indicated that it would have none of the opera.

The critics granted that the performance was poor, a thing about which the Italian audience with its tradition of hearing the best in singing is far less tolerant than those of other nations. Also the libretto was at fault. The opera was announced as an *opera buffa,* and yet there is almost nothing comic in it. In spirit it is far closer to a senti-mental romance, the sort of thing the Viennese adored in Strauss and Lehár: attractive aristocrats and *haute bourgeoisie* waltzing through the confusion of a mistaken identity out to a happy ending. The music suits this mood, the best aria being a bittersweet wonderment by a soprano about when the baritone will declare his love. The only truly comic scene is the farcical preliminaries to a duel between two pom-pous, middle-aged men. For this Verdi succeeded in making the music sparkle. But for an audience expecting an opera with the vivacity of Rossini or the melodic charm of Donizetti it was understandably a dis-appointment. It was plainly the sort of opera that should have had its première in the provinces or one of the smaller theatres in Milan, but not at La Scala. In this instance Verdi's luck in starting at the top was a misfortune.

CHAPTER 9

AUTOBIOGRAPHICAL SKETCH
AND *NABUCCO*

1840–1842; AGE, 26–28

ALL his life Verdi believed passionately in privacy for himself and others. When he was sixty-eight, he argued to a friend who had sent him a biographical article on Bellini: "Why should anyone drag out a musician's letters? They are always written in haste, without care, without his attaching any importance to them, because he knows that he has no reputation to sustain as a writer. Isn't it enough that he should be booed for his music? No, sir! The letters too! Oh, what a plague fame is! The poor little great celebrated men pay dearly for popularity. Never an hour of peace for them, either in life or in death."

And later to a German editor who inquired he wrote:

"Never, never shall I write my memoirs!"

"It is quite enough that the musical world has tolerated my music so long! Never shall I condemn it to read my prose."

But happily, as with most general rules, there was an exception: one day in 1879 Giulio Ricordi, a friend of forty years and his publisher, persuaded him to describe his early days in Milan. The description was to be used in a short biography that Ricordi planned to publish. Verdi talked, and it is not clear whether Ricordi wrote in his presence or immediately after. But in either event Ricordi, who was quite familiar with Verdi's turn of phrase, certainly reproduced the sketch almost verbatim.

The sketch is famous not only for the moving simplicity of its style but for its inaccuracies. Verdi, for example, in a slip certain to excite a psychoanalyst puts his son's death before his daughter's. He also telescopes the death of his wife and two children into a three-month period. Actually, of course, they died over a period of three years. His biographers have struggled with this. Several point out that although

Ricordi apparently sent Verdi the proofs and Verdi made corrections, there is no evidence that the corrections were made in the type. Another, Dyneley Hussey, exclaims: "It is extraordinary that these tragic events, which left an indelible mark upon Verdi's character, should not have impressed themselves accurately upon his memory. . . . It is, perhaps, of small importance whether these events occurred within a space of two months or three years, but it is at least puzzling that Verdi's recollection of them should have been at fault." But is it surprising that the memory of a sixty-seven-year-old man, startled one afternoon into recounting events forty years old, should rearrange them? Man, after all, lives chronologically only for tax purposes or in biographies. In his own life he lives emotionally; and this is particularly true of artists who must harvest their emotions into crops for the market, suffering through the dry seasons and harvesting double in the good ones. In retrospect the three years for Verdi, in spite of the success of *Oberto*, made a single emotional disaster, for what was the moderate success of one opera compared to the loss of his entire family? Certainly there is no question that he felt the cumulative loss profoundly and that his view of life was shaped by it.

What follows is roughly the last two thirds of the sketch, beginning with the composition of *Un Giorno di Regno* and with the inaccuracies left just as Verdi stated them:

At that time I was living in a small apartment near the Porta Ticinese, and with me was my family, my young wife Margherita Barrezi and our two small children. Just as I got down to work [on *Un Giorno di Regno*] I had a bad attack of angina that put me in bed for a long time. Hardly had I begun to get better, when I remembered the rent, fifty *scudi,* would be due in three days. At the time the sum was fairly large for me although I cannot call it serious. But my painful illness had prevented me from amassing it in advance and the fact that the mail went only twice a week to Busseto prevented me from writing to my excellent father-in-law in time for him to help me. I wanted to pay the rent, regardless of inconvenience, on the day due. So, much as I hated to go to a third person, I decided to ask the engineer Pasetti to approach Merelli for fifty *scudi,* either as an advance on my contract or as a loan for eight or ten days, but long enough to write to Busseto for the money.

There is no need here to go into just why Merelli, without fault on his part, could not advance me the fifty *scudi.* But I was terribly upset to miss, even by a few days, paying the rent on the day due. My wife, seeing my distress, took her few trinkets of gold, left the house, and, I don't know how, succeeded in raising the money which she brought to me. I was deeply moved by this proof of her love and swore to myself, that I would restore everything to her, which I was soon able to do, thanks to my contract.

But then my misfortunes began: my boy fell sick at the beginning of April. The doctors could not diagnose his trouble, and the poor little fellow slowly wasted away in the arms of his frenzied mother. But that was not enough. After a few days my little girl fell ill in her turn! . . . and the sickness ended in death! . . . . Still even that was not enough. In the first days of June my young wife was seized with acute encephalitis, and on 19 June 1840 a third coffin went out of my house! . . .

I was alone! . . . alone! . . . In the short space of two months three persons dear to me had gone, for ever: my family was destroyed! . . . In the midst of this terrible anguish, to keep my bond, I had to write and finish a comic opera!! . . .

Un Giorno di Regno did not please. Certainly some of the fault was the music; part, too, in its execution. With a mind tortured by my domestic disaster, embittered by the failure of my work, I persuaded myself that I had nothing more to find in music and I decided never to compose again! . . . I even wrote to the engineer Pasetti, who had shown no sign of life after the failure of *Un Giorno di Regno,* asking him to obtain from Merelli a release for me from my contract.

Merelli called me in and treated me like a capricious child! . . . He refused to believe that I could turn my back on music because of a single failure, and so on. But I held firm until finally he gave me the contract and said:

"Listen, Verdi, I cannot force you to compose. But my faith in you is no less than before. Who knows, some day you may decide to start again? Then give me two months warning before a season, and I promise your opera will be produced."

I thanked him; but even these words could not shake my decision, and I left.

I settled in Milan near the Corsia de' Servi. I was discouraged and gave no thought to music. Then one evening in the winter as I was leaving the Galleria De Cristoforis, I ran into Merelli who was on his way to the theatre. It was snowing with large flakes. Taking me by the arm, he asked me to accompany him to his office at La Scala. We chatted as we went, and he told me of his troubles with a new opera he had to produce. He had commissioned Nicolai to compose it, but Nicolai was unhappy over the libretto.

"Just imagine," cried Merelli, "a libretto by Solera, stupendous! . . . magnificent! . . . extraordinary! . . . grandiose, effective, dramatic situations; beautiful verses! . . . But that thick-headed maestro will have none of it and says the libretto is impossible! . . . I don't know where to look to find another quickly."

"I can help you there," I remarked. "You gave me the libretto for *Il Proscritto,* and I haven't composed a note: it's yours to make use of."

"Oh! bravo . . . what luck."

Talking this way, we had reached the theatre. Merelli called Bassi, who was poet, stage manager, callboy, librarian, etc., and asked him to look at once in the library files for a copy of *Il Proscritto,* and one was found. But while the search was on, Merelli took another manuscript which he showed me and said:

"Look, here is Solera's libretto! Such a good plot, and it is turned down! . . . Take it . . . read it."

"What should I do with it? . . . no, no, I don't want to read any librettos."

"Eh . . . it won't bite you! . . . read it and then give it back to me." And he put the manuscript in my hands. It was a thick bundle written in a large hand, as was the style then. I made it into a roll, took leave of Merelli and started for home.

On my way I felt a sort of vague uneasiness, a great sadness, an anguish that swelled up in my heart! . . . And at home I threw the manuscript with a violent gesture on the table and stood rigid before it. The libretto, falling on the table, opened itself and without my quite realizing it my eyes fixed on the page before me at one particular line:

"Va, pensiero, sull' ali dorate" (Go, thought, on golden wings). [These were the words which Verdi made into a great chorus and which the crowd lining the streets at his funeral sang fifty-eight years later.]

I glanced through the verses following and was deeply moved, particularly in that they almost paraphrased the Bible which I have always loved to read.

I read a bit, then another. Then firm in my resolution never to compose again, I forced myself to stop, closed the book, and went to bed. But oh! *Nabucco* kept running in my head, and sleep would not come. I got up, I read the libretto, not once but two, three times so that by morning, it's fair to say, I knew Solera's libretto by heart.

Even so, I determined to stick to my decision, and the next day I returned to the theatre and handed the manuscript to Merelli.

"Beautiful, eh?" he said.

"Very beautiful."

"Well then, put it to music!"

"No, never. I want no part of it."

"Put it to music, put it to music!"

Saying this he took the libretto, stuffed it into my overcoat pocket, seized me by the shoulders, and not only shoved me out of his office but closed the door and locked it in my face.

Now what?

I went home with *Nabucco* in my pocket. Today, a verse; tomorrow, another; one time a note, another a phrase . . . . little by little the opera was done.

We were in the autumn of 1841. I remembered Merelli's promise and, going to see him, announced that *Nabucco* was written; he could give it in the next season of Carnival-Lent.

Merelli declared himself ready to keep his promise, but at the same time he pointed out that he couldn't possibly give the opera in the coming season because he had already accepted three new operas by famous composers. To give a fourth new opera by a near beginner would be dangerous for all but especially for me. It made more sense, therefore, to wait until spring when he was not so tied up, and he promised to engage good artists for me. But I refused. Either in Carnival or never . . . and I had good reasons, for it would not be possible to find two singers better suited to my opera than Strepponi and Ronconi, both of whom I knew were under contract and on whom I set great hope.

Merelli, however much he wanted to oblige me, as an impresario was not altogether wrong: four new operas in a single season was a great risk! . . . But I, too, had good artistic reasons to oppose his. In short, what with "yes" and "no," objections, half promises, the program for the Scala season came out . . . but *Nabucco* was not announced.

I was young and my blood boiled! I wrote a bad letter to Merelli in which I let loose all my resentment—I confess as soon as I sent it I had an attack of remorse and feared I'd ruined everything.

Merelli sent for me. When he saw me he said gruffly: "Is this the way to write a friend? . . . But bah! You are right. We will give this *Nabucco*. But you must realize that I have already spent heavily for the other three operas, and I cannot afford new costumes or scenery for *Nabucco*. I will have to patch up as best I can with whatever is in the warehouse."

I agreed to everything, so eager was I for the opera to be given. A new announcement came out on which, finally, I read: NABUCCO.

I remember a comical scene that I had with Solera a little earlier. In the third act he had written a love duet for Fenena and Ismaele. I didn't like it because it cooled the action and seemed to me to detract a bit from the biblical grandeur that characterized the drama. One morning when Solera was with me, I told him so. But he didn't want to agree, not so much because he found the comment unjust as because it annoyed him to rework something already finished. We argued back and forth: I stood firm and so did he. He asked me what I wanted in place of the duet, and I suggested the prophecy of Zacharias. He didn't think that a bad idea and with "buts" and "ifs" he said he would think about it and then write it. That was not what I wanted, because I knew many, many days would pass before Solera sat down to write a verse. So I locked the door, put the key in my pocket and said half serious and half joking: "You can't leave here until you've written the prophecy. Here is the Bible, you have the words ready made."

Solera, who had a violent temper, didn't take kindly to my joke. An angry gleam came into his eye, and I passed a nervous moment for the poet was of size that could quickly set to right an obstinate maestro. But all of a sudden he sat at the table and in a quarter of an hour the prophecy was written.

Finally in the last days of February 1842 the rehearsals began, and twelve days after the first piano rehearsal the première took place, on 9 March. The singers were Strepponi, Bellinzaghi, Ronconi, Miraglia and Derivis.

With this opera it is fair to say my artistic career began. And if I had many difficulties to contend with, it is also certain that *Nabucco* was born under a lucky star. For even the things that might have defeated it turned out well. For example, I wrote a furious letter to Merelli who might well have sent the young maestro packing. But the opposite happened. The patched-up costumes were splendid! . . . The old scenery, touched up by the painter Perroni, made an extraordinary effect. The first scene in the temple, for example, made such an effect that the audience applauded for at least ten minutes. At the dress rehearsal nobody yet knew when or where the stage band was to come on. The conductor Tutsch was embarrassed. I pointed out a measure to him, and at the première the band entered on the crescendo with such precision that the audience burst into applause.

But it is not always good to trust in lucky stars! And experience taught me later how right is our proverb: "Fidarsi è bene, ma non fidarsi è meglio." (To have faith is good, but not to rely on it is better.)

The opera tells of Nebuchadnezzar, whose name for purposes of song is reduced to Nabucco. In the first act he defeats the Jews at Jerusalem, blasphemes in their temple, and carries them all off captive to Babylon. There, overcome by his success, he declares himself God and is knocked insane by a thunderbolt. In the ensuing scramble for power Nabucco's illegitimate daughter, Abigaille, easily pushes aside her legitimate half sister, Fenena, who has lost the support of the important priests of Bel by declaring the Jewish God, Jehovah, to be supreme. Just as Abigaille is about to kill Fenena and all the Jews, Nabucco recovers his mind, contracts with Jehovah to establish Judaism as the state religion and with divine aid rights all the wrongs.

STREPPONI

Solera's libretto may be naïve and bombastic, but it created excellent opportunities for music in the operatic style of the time: prayers by almost every character, a mad scene, warlike and lamenting choruses, and even a Dead March as the Jews are almost executed. Undoubtedly the familiarity of the opera's structure contributed to its immediate success with the public, and it may even have helped Verdi to have the opera produced by making an equally swift appeal to the singers.

After the season's schedule appeared without *Nabucco* on it and in response to Verdi's furious letter, Merelli had suggested that inasmuch as Verdi wanted Strepponi for the opera he should show it to her. If she approved of it, then Merelli would produce it. According to an account which Verdi later declared to be true, he at once made an appointment with the lady and with his friend Pasetti, who owned a carriage, went around one afternoon to her house. Verdi played the score through at the piano and Strepponi, over his shoulder, tried a phrase here and there. At the end she declared that she liked it and suggested they call on Ronconi, the baritone Verdi wanted for the title role. Verdi allowed as how a carriage was waiting at the door, and with a laugh Strepponi put on her coat and went with them that afternoon. At Ronconi's house Verdi again played the piano as Ronconi alternately listened and hummed while Strepponi and Pasetti occasionally interjected exclamations of approval or explanation. Ronconi, too, was excited by the music, and there in his room a conspiracy of three was joined to pressure Merelli into producing the opera in the Carnival season when the two singers would be in Milan.

Good operas at that time, and *Nabucco* was one, were all sooner or later produced, so that it is easy to overemphasize the value of the singers' support. Merelli, as Verdi admits, was both perceptive and decent in all his dealings about the opera, and Verdi himself showed wisdom in his willingness to compromise on secondhand scenery and costumes. As soon as he was great enough to have the power, he made fierce demands about the productions of his operas.

But the support of Strepponi and Ronconi did insure, at very least, that the opera was produced in the most important of La Scala's seasons and with a good cast. Inevitably this meant, if the opera was a success, that other houses and impresarios would at once begin to bid for it. There would be no slow climb to the top such as Mozart's operas, succeeding first in Prague, had to undergo in Vienna.

Merelli scheduled the première for 9 March 1842, but even before it word began to leak out of the theatre about the extraordinary new opera. Today only a historical ear can hear anything new-fashioned in *Nabucco,* but at the time the music was considered revolutionary. When the rehearsals moved out of practice rooms onto the stage, it became impossible backstage to get anything done. Painters, machinists, candlemen, ballet dancers and friends of friends who could wangle their way into the theatre stood around openmouthed, watching and listening. "Che fotta noeuva," they exclaimed in Milanese dialect. ("What new thing is this?") By opening night the opera was already a success. As Verdi slipped into the composer's traditional seat in the orchestra, between the first double bass and the first cellist, his friend Merighi, the cellist, said to him, "Maestro, I would give anything to be in your place this evening."

In fact the première was a regular *furore.* The audience at the end of Act I made so much noise that Verdi, remembering *Un Giorno di Regno,* for a moment doubted their intent. And in the third act, in spite of a specific police prohibition against repeats, the audience insisted that the chorus, "Va, Pensiero," be sung again. The police disliked repeats because they were apt to become demonstrations against the Austrian officials and gentry scattered throughout the boxes, and so there was a general prohibition against any. Of course if the audience were insistent enough, the conductor could always shrug his shoulders, repeat and later plead that it seemed more unwise to balk the audience than to satisfy it.

The police in this case, however, were right to worry although, as so often happens when a mass sentiment is stirred, they could do nothing to control it. In the opera the chorus is sung by the Hebrews, captive in Babylon, as they think of their native land. In one sense it is not a true chorus for, as Rossini observed, it really is an aria sung by massed voices; except for a few notes where they divide, all the voices sing the tune. But this only increased its popularity. The tune did not pass from voice to voice and get out of a man's range; any man could sing it all, and for the Hebrews held captive every Italian understood his own people. Solera's text was moving enough alone, but when sung it became for the time the perfect expression of a people's longing for freedom:

Va, pensiero, sull'ali dorate;
   Va, ti posa sui clivi, sui colli,
Ove olezzano tepide e molli
    L'aure dolci del suolo natal!

Go, thought, on golden wings;
   Go, rest yourself on the slopes
    and hills,
Where, soft and warm, murmur
    The sweet breezes of our native
     soil.

Del Giordano le rive saluta,
   Di Sïonne le torri atterrate . . .
Oh mia patria sì bella e perduta!
   O membranza sì cara e fatal!

Greet the banks of the Jordan,
   The fallen towers of Zion . . .
Oh my country so beautiful and lost!
   O memory so dear and fatal!

Arpa d'ôr dei fatidici vati,
   Perchè muta dal solice pendi?
Le memorie nel petto raccendi,
   Ci favella del tempo che fu!

Golden harp of the prophetic bards,
   Why do you hang mute on the
    willow?
Rekindle memories in our breast,
   Speak to us of the time that was!

O simile di Solima ai fati
   Traggi un suono di crudo lamento.
O t'ispiri il Signore un concento
   Che ne infonda al patire virtù!

O as with the fates of Solomon
   You make a sigh of cruel lament.
O may the Lord inspire you to a
    song
    That infuses suffering with
     strength!

The line "Oh mia patria sì bella e perduta!"—such very simple words —inevitably misted the eyes of the audience, just as Solera undoubtedly intended it to do. The success of *Nabucco* as an allegory for Italian patriots can hardly have surprised Solera or Verdi. Both knew that in an occupied country with strict censorship the ears of the oppressed become extraordinarily sensitive to allusion, the only form of public communication the police cannot control. When in 1833 the Grand Duke of Tuscany, Leopoldo II, at the request of Austrian Emperor Francis I, had suppressed the famous Florentine journal *Antologia*, he had silenced the last forum on the peninsula for liberal thought and independent criticism. Since then Italians had been forced to communicate with each other underground in secret societies or publicly by allusion.

But *Nabucco* did not succeed purely by a patriotic tug on the Italian heart; it had considerable musical virtue, particularly an urgency that was new. Rossini in his comedies had made music actually laugh and sparkle; Bellini had spun out long langorous melodies, and Donizetti had charmed the audience with his ease and grace. Verdi's music had a vitality to it that seemed unable to stop for beauty. Even the slow arias had the same emotional intensity so that from the first critics and the audience recognized that it was not just a question of speed but of a quality in the music itself. "Ruvidezza" was the word they used to describe it, "roughness" or "coarseness," and from the first it offended many men of taste who felt it was uncouth and unmusical.

The same feeling of rough urgency exists in *Oberto* and also in *Un Giorno di Regno*. *Nabucco* is a better opera than its predecessors and the feeling is stronger, but all three are plainly by the same man. *Nabucco* is better than *Oberto* partly because it is simply more inspired; the Biblical subject with its cry for freedom appealed to Verdi, and perhaps also the bludgeonings which his own emotions had undergone in the preceding year had left them better sensitized to re-create emotions in his characters. But beyond the general inspiration some specific good points can be isolated. In Abigaille and Nabucco he created two unusual but typically Verdian roles, and, whether intentionally or not, he focused attention on them when he forced Solera to delete the love duet for Ismaele and Fenena. Lovers are always something of a convention in opera, but a scheming princess like Abigaille is not. In the same way mad scenes for sopranos are a commonplace; those for a baritone like Nabucco are not. In both instances

SOLERA

the very lack of example before him may have helped Verdi to write music that would make the two characters come alive, although he succeeded equally well for a third character, the prophet Zacharias, for whom there was a very obvious example in Rossini's Moses. Both composers made their prophets basses; each gave his prophet a prayer which became famous. Probably Verdi had his music already in mind when he forced Solera to write the verses; he certainly knew that he was inviting comparison to Rossini, and he must have been confident that his music, while different, was not inferior. Three strong characters, to say nothing of the excellent choruses, are a good start for an opera, and they were more than *Oberto* had.

But over and above the individual parts *Nabucco* has a unity of style or atmosphere that Verdi had not had before and would not attain again for some time. Felice Romani, Verdi's former librettist now turned critic, wrote of it at the time in the Milanese *Figaro:* "Verdi has imbued his opera with an austere, grandiose atmosphere which is lost so seldom that he could easily make it absolutely perfect if he would only revise one or two places in a little calmer state of mind."

This is high praise from a critic and suggests why *Nabucco* has survived as an entity into the repertory today. It does hang together in spite of some bad moments, particularly in the last act where the plot is swept hastily under the carpet to get it out of the way of the falling curtain. But the opera itself makes an impact rather than merely one or two arias and ensembles for which the singers and audience obviously wait and then all go to sleep until the next big number. The feeling of unity is partly the result of the simplicity of the story. Zacharias and the Hebrew people are the constant against which the principals play out their more merely human story, and the fear, captivity and fate of the Hebrew nation act as a keel to the opera, keeping it upright and sailing. Everything that happens in the opera turns on or comes back to the fate of the Hebrews, and the main characters never get fogbound for long in their own personal relations. The opera has therefore, particularly for its time, a strong sense of direction.

Although *Nabucco* is not one of Verdi's greatest operas, it has survived continuously down to today and often been honored by special productions. In the 1930s it was revived in Germany; in 1933 the Florentines used it to open the first of their May Festivals; and in 1946 the Milanese, probably in part for its political connotations, chose it to reopen La Scala after the damage of World War II had been repaired. And it had its first performance at the Metropolitan in New York when it opened the 1960–61 season there. In the decade of its première it was performed around the world, including New York and Havana, and during the 1850s it reached the cities in South America.

When Merelli first presented it in the spring of 1842, it was the fourth and last première of his Carnival season and there was time for only eight performances before the season ended. As it turned out, however, the most skilled showman could not have scheduled the timing better. All the leaders of society and music in Milan managed to see at least one of the eight and then had the summer in which to discuss the opera excitedly in the presence of those less fortunate who had, perforce, to remain silent. The consequent build-up in interest and publicity was tremendous, and when Merelli scheduled it for his autumn season, he gave it a good cast and all the best dates.

In the autumn neither Strepponi nor Ronconi sang in it. The baritone perhaps was a loss; Strepponi was not. In the spring she had been in bad voice and apparently made little impression as Abigaille, which must have been a blow to Verdi who had specially requested her. But in the years since her previous Milan season Strepponi had used her voice hard, and her health was poor following the birth of a second illegitimate child. Probably the father of both was the tenor, Napoleone Moriani.

Yet even if Strepponi did not shine in the performances of *Nabucco,* Verdi evidently was grateful for her support, liked her as a person and considered her a friend. When, after the third performance of *Nabucco,* Merelli gave Verdi a contract for a new opera, it was all filled in and signed except for Verdi's commission, which was left blank. In answer to Verdi's startled inquiry Merelli replied in the best P. T. Barnum style that it was up to the composer to set his price. Verdi said nothing but pocketed the contract and went off to think. After a while he went to see Strepponi. He was, he realized, inexperienced in this sort of behavior; he was only three operas away from Busseto—all at La Scala and all with Merelli. Strepponi, on the other hand, had sung in twenty-seven opera houses, including most of the principal ones of Italy and Austria. He explained his problem, and she took it seriously. After a moment she advised that while, of course, he should take advantage of his good fortune, it would be wise not to overvalue himself. She suggested he ask for the same commission Bellini had received for *Norma* in 1831. This was a good fee in 1842 but not exorbitant, and Verdi took her suggestion.

When *Nabucco* reopened in the autumn at La Scala, it was, if possible, even more successful than in the spring. Between 13 August and 4 December it had fifty-seven performances, which at the time was a record for a single season, and it is said that the chorus, "Va, Pensiero," was encored at every one. Barezzi, who had seen the first performance in March, came back for the last in December.

The number of performances is particularly impressive in that Milan in 1842 was still a city of less than 150,000 inhabitants. La Scala has been renovated and the seating changed several times since then until today it seats about 2300, not including standing room; in 1842 with a top gallery since eliminated it may have held about 2600. So that possibly something like 20,000 more seats were sold to *Nabucco* in its first year than there were inhabitants in the town. Visitors undoubtedly came but probably not many. There were still no rail connections, and travel by coach was uncomfortable. Besides, the tradition of the time was that the opera rather than the audience traveled.

The success of *Nabucco* made a change in Verdi's life as swift and dramatic as any in an opera. Ties, hats and even sauces were named after him. More important, it guaranteed him, for the first time in his life, financial independence and security. The opera plainly would go on for many years; Merelli already planned a production for Vienna in 1843 and other houses clamored for it. There would be new commissions—there was already one—and at very least new productions of *Oberto* and *Nabucco* to oversee. He continued living in his rented room, and he began to pay off his debts. It was exciting after twenty-nine years: from the organ loft at Le Roncole to the orchestra pit at La Scala. For his mother and father it meant the end of worry and work; Carlo Verdi could hardly believe it; a miracle, he sometimes called it. For Barezzi, who remembered Provesi and Lavigna and who perhaps now knew Verdi better than his parents did, it was no miracle but the overdue reward for many years' work. For Verdi certain hard realities remained: the hooting at *Un Giorno di Regno* and the gravestones in the cemetery of San Giovannino. A new life might begin; he was eager for it. But he had learned from experience that the stars were seldom benevolent; they exact their pay in pain. "Fidarsi è bene, ma non fidarsi è meglio."

ST. MICHAEL'S CHURCH, LE RONCOLE

Part II

CHAPTER 10

NEW FRIENDS IN MILAN AND
I LOMBARDI

1842–1843; AGE, 28–29

THE success of *Nabucco* lifted Verdi into the literary and social life of Milan, first with the gentlemen and then, after he had won their approval, with their ladies. Solera, his librettist, Verdi had known for more than three years, since the production of *Oberto* in 1839, but Solera had not led him into the life of the city. Partly this was because of Verdi's temperament, alternately shy and fierce, and wholly incapable of the role of bright young man in coffee shops and living rooms, and partly it was because of Solera himself.

Although Solera was well-known in Milan, his poetry read and discussed, and his cantatas produced at La Scala, he was regarded by the men with amusement and by the ladies, who tended to keep their distance, as something of a wild man. He was enormous with flashing eye, booming voice and, in his youth, a great shock of hair; and he lusted for all the experiences of life. As a boy he had been educated in Vienna but had run away from school to join a circus. His father was imprisoned by the Austrians, and understandably Solera became an Italian patriot, republican and a loud and witty spokesman against the established order. He was a true bohemian, and part of his charm was that he remained so throughout his life whether rich or poor, successful or not. Always, no matter what his fortune, he wore a monocle. At one time, by his own report, he was a favorite of the Queen of Spain. But when he died, he was penniless, forgotten, and a few friends were trying to raise a subscription for him.

But after *Nabucco* Verdi began to meet other men outside the small, working world of the theatre, and being by nature rather silent, he was a good listener and therefore popular. The men of Milan used to meet in coffee shops or at the theatres where the intermissions were long and the performances as much of a social as a musical event. Obviously when a man went for the fourth or fifth time in a month to *Nabucco,* he did not feel pressed to break off a conversation in the foyer to be in his seat for the start of any act. The conversations ranged from art to penal reform, and although the groups sometimes had a specific bias to them, they just as often did not. The tradition was that all men of culture mixed together freely and deliberately in order to exchange, polish and enrich their ideas. There was none of the specialization of knowledge and association that separates artists of all kinds today.

For Verdi the most important of his new acquaintances was Andrea Maffei, a poet specializing in translations, particularly of English and German works, and also a gentleman of considerable social standing. His wife, Clara, ran the city's most important salon, and their circle of friends reflected his interest in literature and hers in politics. After Maffei had met Verdi a number of times and presumably had reported that the young man's manners were simple but good, Verdi was invited to attend one of the Contessa Maffei's evenings. These varied in formality; the Contessa might for a special occasion issue invitations, or, more generally, she would simply be "at home" in the evening. Dinner in Milan at the time was early, between four and five, and was eaten at home with the family. After it the parents and perhaps the eldest children would go for a drive in the carriage. The city was still very small and in fifteen minutes in any direction from the center of town there was open country. After the drive the children would be dismissed and the parents would dress for the evening, perhaps an opera beginning at nine, sometimes a ball, or, most often, calling on friends like the Maffeis who were apt to be "at home."

They were an oddly matched pair and unhappily married. In 1842, the year Verdi met them, Maffei was a man of forty-four with an aristocratic but somewhat debauched air, whereas the Contessa was only twenty-eight and without any of the beauty, distinction, or even arrogance generally associated with a great hostess. Her charm lay in her gentle manners and in her open and enthusiastic affection for people. Her friends used to joke that she had "an especial predilection for—all." But she was not merely gushy; she ordered her thoughts and talked extremely well, so that the men considered her an intellectual

ANDREA MAFFEI

equal. She did not, however, push her opinions herself but exerted her influence on the political life of the city through the men she entertained. She and Maffei married in 1834 and two years later, when she was twenty-two, she started her salon which ran continuously, except when the Austrians forced her from Milan, for fifty years. She made it so much a part of the city's life that today a marble plaque on her house commemorates it.

Neither she nor her husband were native Milanese. He came from Trent, where Italy and Austria began to meet and many of the inhabitants were bilingual, and he had been educated in Munich. She came from an old family in Bergamo, and the title, Contessa, was actually her father's but extended by courtesy to her. Nor was her husband, Andrea, technically a noble but merely a gentleman of leisure. His family, however, was well-known, his father being a Cavaliere of the old Holy Roman Empire and he himself being one of the Austrian Empire. Andrea's birthplace, education and service to the Austrian Empire made him unenthusiastic about Italian independence, and this was one of the difficulties between him and his wife. During the decade of the 1840s she became convinced that independence was a necessity and that it should be hurried into being; inevitably her salon reflected this view.

Their other difficulties were more personal. Maffei, who had been born in 1798, appears today like a man condemned by fate to live in the wrong century. Goldoni, the Venetian playwright, had described life in Milan in the eighteenth century as "La mattina una messetta, l'apodisnar una bassetta, la sera uña donnetta" (A little mass in the morning, a little cards in the afternoon, a little woman in the evening). In a society which accepted such a life and could, therefore, by its social pressures to some extent control it Maffei might have continued to be an acceptable husband. But in the nineteenth century, with a different relationship between husband and wife emerging, his gambling and women became impossibly difficult, and although he often protested he was about to reform, the moment always escaped him. The Contessa, on the other hand, had a liaison with Carlo Tenca, the editor of the literary periodical *Rivista Europea*, which she conducted with discretion, and which, perhaps in part because it was so clearly based on affection, was accepted by the Milanese. In 1846 the Maffeis agreed to separate, and it is evidence of the friendship Verdi had developed with both that he was asked to be a witness to their separation agreement. All his life he remained equally the friend of both.

The Maffeis gathered around them the intellectuals of Milan, and it speaks well for Verdi's self-education that he could hold the interest of such people. They would not have endured for long anyone who was a bore or opinionated or merely the composer of a popular opera. Verdi must have talked in turn and been interesting; his ideas perhaps were more original than polished but thereby more refreshing. Certainly he must have talked and argued endlessly with Maffei about his favorite poet, Shakespeare, and Maffei's favorites, Schiller and Milton. (*See* Appendix B, p. 578.)

It was the sort of combined stimulus and discipline that Verdi desperately needed. He was twenty-nine and he had never been out of the Po Valley except for a production of *Oberto* in Genoa. The largest city he had ever been in was Milan; he had never seen a statue by Michelangelo, sailed overnight on a boat, or traveled on a train. He was a provincial from Busseto who thought that behind everyone somewhere there was a farm, perhaps owned outright, perhaps enormously large, but still: land. At the Maffeis' and from others he began now to hear of other sources of wealth and power, of the Industrial Revolution, why it made England rich and Italy poor, and what could be done about it; of Paris, and why so many Italian exiles went there. It was not then the City of Light. Napoleon III had not yet rebuilt it, and it was an ugly, stinking, dark, horribly overcrowded medieval city in which movement was almost impossible: of the sixteen bridges across the Seine ten were privately owned and charged high tolls. But in Italy it was recognized as the city of potential power to be used against Austria, and the politics in Paris and changes of government there were followed as closely as any in Italy.

Then there were discussions of form: how a novel should be put together, a poem, a song, or even an opera. In defending his ideas against the questions of men whose taste he respected Verdi was forced again and again to re-examine his ideas, not only about what he wanted for Parma and Milan, but also about what he wanted to do in an opera. Was it to be a succession of beautiful arias like a concert? Or was it to be a drama in which melody and technique were subordinate to the play's development. And if a little of each, then how much of each?

Another salon where Verdi went frequently was that of Mme. Giuseppina Appiani. She was a widow of about forty-five with six children and about to be a grandmother. Several of her husband's family and one of her sons were artists, and her salon had an artistic rather than political or literary basis. As such it complemented rather than competed with the Contessa Maffei's. Ultimately it was far less important both to Verdi and to the life of the city, but for roughly twenty years, 1830–1850, it was a recognized artistic center in the city and in the field of music was one of the most important. This was because Mme. Appiani managed to charm in succession the city's three leading composers: Bellini, Donizetti and Verdi. Bellini, in fact, wrote his *La Sonnambula* while staying in her house, and in the year of *Nabucco* Donizetti, also her guest, composed *Linda di Chamounix*.

In the succession from Donizetti to Verdi a kind Fate helped Mme. Appiani by providing a nicely timed solution to what might have been a difficult social problem. Throughout the autumn of 1841 and winter of 1842 Donizetti was the chief ornament of her salon. Of an evening he would chat, gossip, play the piano and behave exactly as every hostess hopes a lion will behave. Then in March came *Nabucco,* and suddenly there was a new lion whose music had stirred everyone to talk. The situation required tact and action: salons survive only if the hostess provides the setting and assembles an up-to-date and fascinating cast of characters.

With Donizetti a good friend, Mme. Appiani's own sense of delicacy, to say nothing of society's, would have prevented her from capturing Verdi except that Donizetti, who stayed in Milan especially

DONIZETTI

to hear the première of *Nabucco*, left almost immediately after for Bologna. From there he went on to Vienna to become, like Mozart and Haydn before him, Imperial and Royal Composer of Chamber Music and Director of His Majesty's Private Concerts. The post carried a large salary and the appointment was possibly the greatest honor the government could offer a composer. No one could say that Mme. Appiani had deserted Donizetti in his hour of need or thrust him aside like an old shoe. Instead she was able quite naturally to start entertaining Verdi. Her salon, as well as offering juicy gossip by mail from the scene in Vienna, continued, as always, to present the newest and best in the musical life of Milan.

But life was not all play for Verdi. Throughout the autumn of 1842 he worked on his next opera which, by his contract with Merelli, was to be the *opera d'obbligo* of the Carnival season. It was the custom at the time for an impresario to contract with the directors of the opera house to provide each year one wholly new opera or, at very least, one that had never before been heard in the particular house, and Merelli had such an agreement with La Scala. Inevitably in an opera city like Milan attention focused on the *opera d'obbligo*, and a commission to compose it was a mark of esteem. It also, if possible after the success of *Nabucco*, added to the pressure under which Verdi worked. The Milanese had a possessive curiosity about their *opera d'obbligo*, and no one hesitated to ask him directly about it: Was it on the same theme? Would it be in the same style? Did he plan another comic opera?

There are no secrets in the theatre world, and almost as soon as Verdi and Solera everyone else knew that they had selected as their subject Tomasso Grossi's poem "I Lombardi alla Prima Crociata" (The Lombards on the First Crusade). Grossi was a Milanese, still alive, and his long poem, which had first appeared in 1826, had stirred up considerable discussion. It told of the Lombards going to free Jerusalem from the Saracens, falling out among themselves, and finally winning out. Those who liked it called it a modern epic; those who did not complained that the characters were too trivial for the theme, that the sweep of history was sacrificed to an overblown romance between a Christian Maid and a Saracen Warrior. All the old arguments took on new life as the première drew closer and reached a fury of discussion when it became known that the police, on orders of the Archbishop, had refused to license the production.

The difficulty arose over a scene showing the Saracen Warrior, converted by the Christian Maid, being baptized. Baptism was a sacrament, said the Archbishop, who was a Cardinal, and it was sacrilegious to portray it on the stage. As in Busseto, the people began to divide into camps and argue the point furiously. Probably most of the city was against its Archbishop, who otherwise was popular. The Chief of Police was caught between the Archbishop's displeasure and the certainty of riots at the theatre if the license was refused or the libretto cut too severely. He summoned Verdi, who refused to appear. Then he summoned Merelli and Solera, both of whom protested that they had no influence with the composer while pointing out that he was the most popular man in Milan. The Archbishop, meanwhile, threatened to appeal to the Emperor. Finally Torresani compromised. He is supposed to have said, "I will not be the one to clip the wings of such a promising genius." He proposed that the first line of the Maiden's Prayer be changed from "Ave Maria" to "Salve Maria," and Verdi, through Merelli, agreed. The Archbishop was told that, while in order to prevent riots the baptismal scene was allowed to remain, certain other important religious changes had been made.

The day of the première, 11 February 1843, crowds began gathering outside the theatre early in the afternoon. They brought sandwiches and wine, and by evening there were many more than could possibly be admitted. Verdi, never inclined to be optimistic, became increasingly nervous. The rehearsals had not gone well, and all sorts of extra-musical pressures were building up around the opera. He confessed his fears to his soprano, Erminia Frezzolini, who was not yet twenty-five and who calmly assured him: "If I must die on the stage, your opera will triumph."

It did. The police succeeded in preventing one encore and then gave up. The audience at once cast itself as the Lombards and the Austrians as the Saracens defiling the Holy Land; it understood that the Crusade was in the future and greeted with frenzy a chorus in the last act which calls the Lombard crusaders from despair to battle. Solera and Verdi had arranged for the tenor to bawl, "La Santa Terra oggi nostra sarà" (The Holy Land today will be ours), to which the chorus and the audience answered, "Sí! . . . Guerra! Guerra!" (Yes! . . . War! War!) The police shrugged in despair: and the Archbishop had worried about the baptismal scene! After *I Lombardi* Verdi was a marked man with the censors, and his librettos were cut, rewritten and in at least one opera, *Ballo in Maschera,* tragically mangled.

As a popular opera *I Lombardi* had as great a success as *Nabucco,* perhaps even greater. It was, for example, the first Verdi opera heard in such distant cities as New York and St. Petersburg; in a French version which Verdi made in 1847 and retitled *Jérusalem* it was the first of his operas to be produced at the Paris Opéra, probably the most important house at the time. There it began a second life, not only in such French-speaking cities as Brussels and New Orleans, but, after being translated back into Italian as *Gerusalemme,* it started another round in Italy with La Scala in 1850.

Musically *I Lombardi* was less successful than *Nabucco,* and the Milanese critics managed, above the excited, popular clamor, to say so. Fundamentally their complaint was that Verdi had sacrificed the drama to the theatrical effects. What Verdi and Solera had done was to write a nineteenth-century Hollywood extravaganza with a cast of thousands and lush Biblical scenery. Immediately after a scene in the Saracen harem comes one in the Valley of Jehoshaphat in which, the score insists, the Mount of Olives must be "prominent." In the infamous baptismal scene the water is too much for the Saracen Warrior, who promptly dies, only to reappear in a vision, complete with aria, to the distraught Christian Maid who converted him. In the final scene the side of the crusader's tent is raised so that the dying Hermit can see the banners of the Cross flying over the walls of Jerusalem in the first pink light of dawn.

This sort of slick, technicolor effect is the penalty which music, or any art, must pay when it begins to enjoy, for however long, popular support. In the 1840s there were no movies, no television and, for a number of reasons, including the problem of dialect, little that was truly popular in the theatre or literature. At least in Italy opera was the popular form, and the struggle of the good musicians such as Rossini and, in time, Verdi was to improve it or even perfect it musically—just as in painting Raphael had done with his Madonnas and in writing for the theatre Shakespeare with the history play.

When the music is bad in *I Lombardi* it is boring or ludicrous. There is a conspirators' chorus in the first act which Francis Toye has translated brilliantly, as he says, "doggerel for doggerel":

> With one blow we like to send our
> Fellows' souls in heaven to shine;
> Then with gore-encrusted daggers
> We sit calmly down to dine.

Verdi wrote tippy-toe conspirator music, alternating with loud crashes on the brass and drums, and it is all perilously close to Gilbert and Sullivan. Any modern audience, on being asked to take it seriously, would burst out laughing or yawn just as did the more sophisticated and musical parts of the audience even in 1843.

But beside the bad there is considerable good music in *I Lombardi,* the most famous being two choruses with long, broad phrasing like "Va, Pensiero," the Maiden's Prayer in Act I, and the prelude to the conversion scene in Act III which is a long violin solo, almost a violin concerto and unique in Verdi's operas. There is also a famous trio typical of Verdi in that as one lover dies, the other survives despairing, while a third person, generally a hermit or father figure of some sort, urges resignation under the blows of life. The scene reoccurs in various forms in many of Verdi's operas, *La Forza del Destino* and *La Traviata* being the most obvious. Generally the scene is musically one of the most successful and moving; clearly it struck some special response in Verdi. Nothing is more dangerous than amateur psychology, particularly when practiced on creative artists, but it is impossible to ignore the obvious comparison to Verdi's own experience of watching first his children, then Margherita die. Who then is the older man urging resignation: is it Barezzi or, as seems more likely, is it Verdi by some sort of self-projection desperately disciplining himself?

In Verdi's day the dedication to a patron with which a musical work was published was still a sign of the composer's position in the world, and Verdi, like any other artist of his time struggling for recognition, hoped to shine in some reflected glory by capturing an illustrious name for the title page of his operas. The vocal score of the first, *Oberto,* had been dedicated to his friend Pasetti who, although he owned a carriage, was hardly an impressive patron. The unfortunate *Un Giorno di Regno* had a history unlikely to interest anyone of note, but with *Nabucco* Verdi's position changed. His publisher, Ricordi, had nervously delayed publication until after its success was proven, and as a result the vocal score, when it appeared, announced that the opera had been: "Set into music and humbly dedicated to H.R.H. the Most Serene Archduchess Adelaide of Austria, 31 March 1842, by Giuseppe Verdi."

The spectacle of Italy's revolutionary composer who wrote what has been well described as "agitator's music" humbly dedicating an opera to a Serene Austrian Archduchess is somewhat startling except in context. Verdi was at the start of his career with his most revolutionary operas still to come; loyalties in Milan were still divided and confused, and in spite of the title Adelaide was very little Austrian. It is true that her first cousin, Ferdinand, was the Austrian Emperor and that her father, the Archduke Rainer, was at various times the Austrian Viceroy in Milan. But Rainer had lived almost his entire life in Milan, had married a princess of the Piedmontese House of Savoy, and was one of the few Austrian officials to enjoy any popularity. For his daughter, Adelaide, Milan was home and the Milanese her oldest friends. A month after the première of *Nabucco* and the publication of its score she married the Duke of Savoy, Vittorio Emanuele, who eighteen years later in 1860 became the first King of Italy. In time her son and then her grandson each became Verdi's sovereign, so that ultimately history made the curious dedication peculiarly appropriate.

For the score of *I Lombardi* Verdi could now do the obvious, and he addressed himself to his sovereign, Marie Louise of Parma. His first letter, to her Major-Domo Count di Bombelles, who was also her second morganatic husband, received no answer. His second, sent two days after the very successful première and calling her now his "Most" August Sovereign, succeeded, and the score appeared with the title page shown opposite. The printer's arrangement of her titles

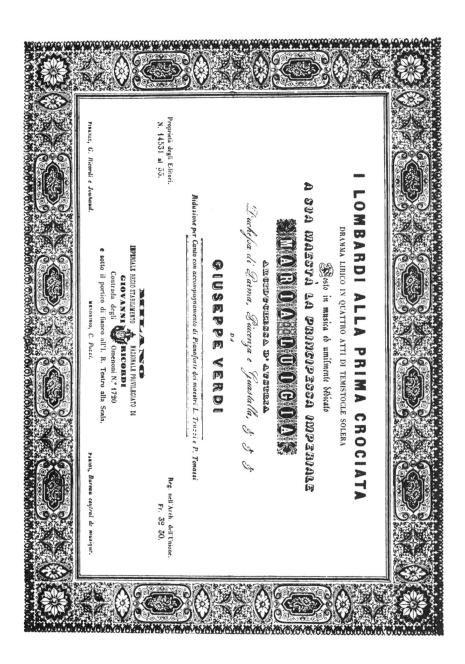

I LOMBARDI ALLA PRIMA CROCIATA

DRAMMA LIRICO IN QUATTRO ATTI DI TEMISTOCLE SOLERA

posto in **musica** ed umilmente dedicato

A SUA MAESTÀ LA PRINCIPESSA IMPERIALE

MARIA LUIGIA

ARCIDUCHESSA D'AUSTRIA

Duchessa di Parma, Piacenza e Guastalla, S. S. S.

DI

GIUSEPPE VERDI

Riduzione per Canto con accompagnamento di Pianoforte dei maestri L. Truzzi e P. Tonassi

Proprietà degli Editori.
N. 14531 al 55.

MILANO
IMPERIALE REGIO STABILIMENTO   NAZIONALE PRIVILEGIATO DI
GIOVANNI RICORDI
Contrada degli Omenoni N.° 1720
e sotto il portico di fianco all'I. R. Teatro alla Scala.

FIRENZE, *C. Ricordi e Jouhaud.*

MENDRISIO, *C. Pozzi.*

PARIGI, *Bureau central de musique.*

Reg. nell'Arch. dell'Unione.

Fr. 32 50.

reflected the true source of her power. The fact that she was the reigning Duchess of Parma, "etc.," was less important than her being an Austrian archduchess.

There was a certain justice in this dedication. Marie Louise through her government had assisted Verdi to study in Milan by investigating and backing his father's petition to the Monte di Pietà, and in Parma itself she had supported the Conservatory and the arts in general with her personal interest and funds. It was only fitting that her subject should acknowledge this and she, on her part, recognize the honor he had brought to Parma.

Sometimes in April, soon after the vocal score to *I Lombardi* had gone to the publisher, Verdi went to Parma to supervise a production of *Nabucco* at the Teatro Regio. It was a happy time for him. Marie Louise was gracious; the Parmigiani were immensely proud of their native son, and the opera played twenty-two times in six weeks. As in Milan, more seats were sold than there were inhabitants in the town.

Strepponi again sang Abigaille. It was the first time she had sung anywhere since the first performances of *Nabucco* in Milan. After them she had retired for a year in a desperate effort to recover her voice. She had put herself in the hands of a doctor living in Parma, and it is possible that Verdi, who had a high opinion of doctors there, recommended the man. Certainly he must have known of Strepponi's decision to cancel her spring season in Vienna, and quite likely he recommended her for the production at Parma. Probably at the same time he had been meeting Mme. Appiani and the Contessa Maffei he had continued to see something of Strepponi.

Her personal life at the time was in as bad repair as her voice. Without work, she had to spend her capital to support herself and her family, and her letters show that she could not marry the unidentified father of her two children as he was already married. (*See* Appendix C, page 580.) She twice contemplated marrying other men for security and twice rejected the idea. Her children presumably were living somewhere in the country with their grandmother, for Strepponi only once writes of them as being with her. She was in the unenviable position of being a prima donna with a failing voice, relatives and illegitimate children. There seemed little she could do except go back to singing.

At Parma, with her voice refreshed by a year's rest, she made a triumphant return, although a schedule of Abigaille every other night was bound soon to take a toll. But for the moment the public thought her wonderful. Marie Louise heard the opera twice and at the end of the season at a benefit night for Strepponi presented her with a gold bauble decorated with enamel and pearls. The public paid homage with enormous bouquets, honorary poems and endless applause. In gratitude she stayed beyond the season to sing without fee at a concert to aid a local orphanage.

The Parmigiani, who sincerely believe that anything of any importance happened first in Parma, date the beginning of love between Verdi and Strepponi from these six weeks when they were both in Parma. It seems unlikely. Verdi did constantly put off his return to Milan, but he had many friends in the city beside Strepponi, and when they worked together on his *Ernani* at Bergamo a year later he did not stay the season and made neither before nor after it any effort to be where she was or to have her in his productions. More likely he stayed in Parma simply because he was enjoying himself and to have an interview with Marie Louise on her return from a trip to Piacenza. At the interview she gave him a gold pin with his monogram set in diamonds, and he promised to send her a copy of the vocal score of *I Lombardi* just as soon as it was available. At the time Marie Louise was fifty-two and Verdi almost thirty; in age they were not so far apart, but in background and experience extremes met.

TEATRO REGIO

CHAPTER 11

VENICE AND *ERNANI*

1843–1844; AGE, 29–30

FOR his next opera after *I Lombardi* Verdi signed a contract with the Teatro La Fenice in Venice, then as now one of Italy's most important theatres. The board of managers there through its director, Conte Carlo Mocenigo, had offered to open its Carnival season in 1843–44 with *I Lombardi,* directed and conducted by Verdi, and then in the following month, as its *opera d'obbligo,* to produce his new one. It was an attractive offer and led to Verdi's first break with La Scala. He gave as his reason that he had now done an opera for Milan each year for four years and that it was time to give the Milanese a rest from Verdi. This may have been only a half-truth. Immediately after the première of *I Lombardi* in Milan Verdi had accompanied Merelli to Vienna for the première there of *Nabucco.* It had not been a great success. Apparently Merelli had presented a cast of undistinguished if not actually poor singers, for Donizetti had reported to Appiani and her salon that "the Italian troupe had been received almost with scorn." Verdi had left Vienna after the first performance on 4 April, disappointed and undoubtedly reflecting that one way to insure good productions by Merelli was to show that the composer was not to be taken for granted. By May Verdi and Conte Mocenigo were discussing the terms of their contract and about to come to an agreement.

Merelli more than anyone else in the theatre had supported Verdi's rather shaky beginning at La Scala, and he had done so with tact and financial generosity. With the years telescoped into successive pages of a book and taken out of the context of the times, Verdi's contract with Conte Mocenigo appears to be something of an ungrateful desertion. No one at the time thought of it as such. Between *Oberto* and

I Lombardi there were four years of association. In the same period of time at the beginning of his career twenty-five years earlier Rossini had worked with six theatres to produce twelve operas. The tradition of opera composition and production in Italy was slowly changing, but the initiative in 1843 still lay with the impresario. He hired a composer to write a specified opera which was to be produced in a particular theatre and season for a particular audience, using the impresario's company of singers. Composers were expected to travel from city to city writing operas, and only rarely did an established composer write an opera first and then try to place it.

A letter from Verdi to Conte Mocenigo about the contract shows how a production was planned. It is also typical of Verdi's constant effort, perhaps a result of his grocery-store training, to be extremely explicit in all his business dealings.

25 May 1843

Dear Conte:

I have received the contract. I think I see some points in it which might be objectionable, and since neither you nor I would like to get ourselves into litigation, I have made some modifications which of course you can accept or refuse.

I cannot bind myself to Article 2 of the contract, because the Director might refuse both the first and the second libretto and so we might never see the end of it. The Director may be quite sure that I shall endeavor to have a libretto written that I can feel, so as to compose it as well as possible. Hence, if the Director does not have confidence in me, let him have the libretto written himself and charge it to me, always provided that the cost is not more than I can pay.

I cannot bind myself to Article 3, because (as I wrote in my last letter from Udine), I always do the instrumentation during the piano rehearsals, and the score is never completely finished before the rehearsal preceding the dress rehearsal.

In Article 7, the phrase "after completion of the third performance" must be deleted, because the third performance might never be confirmed for many reasons and I ought not to be bound by it.

A tenth article must be added, as noted below.

2. The libretto in question will be published at the expense of the Maestro.

3. Maestro Verdi pledges himself to be ready to put on the new opera about a month after the production of *I Lombardi,* providing, however, that as many rehearsals as are necessary for a good production are held.

7. He is to be paid 12,000 (twelve thousand) Austrian lire, in three

equal installments, the first on arrival in the city, the second at the first orchestral rehearsal, the third after the dress rehearsal is held.

10. The artists who are to take part in the new opera of Maestro Verdi shall be chosen by the Maestro himself from the roster of the company.

I am not sending back the contract because it would be too voluminous. But I shall return it or destroy it, as you direct. If you reply to this letter by return mail, you may address your letter to Parma, otherwise to Milan.

With the highest esteem, I remain yours devotedly.

G. VERDI

The choice of the libretto, as always, caused difficulty. Throughout the summer Verdi and Conte Mocenigo considered and rejected many; first, something on Catherine Howard, but Verdi did not feel drawn to the English characters. He liked Cola di Rienzi as a subject but dismissed it out of fear that the Austrian-Venetian police would never permit an opera on the man who in 1347 established a republic at Rome and tried to unite Italy. Verdi did not know, nor would he have cared, that only the previous year Wagner had composed and produced his opera *Rienzi* at the Dresden Court Theatre. In England there was Bulwer Lytton's immensely popular historical novel and also a play, both on Rienzi. As a leader sprung from the people, Rienzi was at the time a favorite symbol and hero of liberals and republicans throughout Europe.

For lack of an outstanding bass or baritone in the company at the Teatro Fenice Verdi rejected subjects based on Charlemagne, King Lear, Byron's *The Corsair* and Victor Hugo's *Cromwell* which, he felt, had too many characters and scenes. But this last led him and Conte Mocenigo to Hugo's *Hernani,* on which they finally agreed. By then it was September, and Verdi had only three months to compose the opera. Quickly he sketched the outline and dramatic situations, leaving the actual verses to the Fenice's house poet, a Venetian named Francesco Maria Piave.

Hugo's play, first presented at the Comédie-Française in 1830, was famous throughout Europe as a battleground over which the young Romantics in Paris had routed the old guard defending the citadels of French classic drama. The old guard wanted drama to observe the unities of time, place and action and to present passion with restraint in the heightened but distant poetic language of Corneille and Racine. Of all this *Hernani* was the antithesis. It presented violent passion in strong, familiar vernacular and with a multitude of deaths, three sui-

HUGO

cides in thirty seconds, all gruesomely on-stage instead of off, whence a messenger might come in Greek style and report the catastrophe to the audience.

The skirmishings over the play, which all of literary Paris followed, began during the rehearsals in the sacred halls of the Comédie-Française. The actors, nervous and inept in the new style, tended to cling to tradition and be contemptuous of the play and its author until one day Hugo, exasperated beyond bearing, asked the leading actress, Mademoiselle Mars, to surrender her part. In a short speech, very French in its clarity and balance, he politely explained: "Madame, you are an extremely talented woman, but there is something you do not seem to realize, of which, therefore, I must inform you—I, too, am an extremely talented man. I should like that to be quite clearly understood. In future you will treat me as I deserve to be treated." The lady had only a second to guess at the future; she kept the part and Hugo had the victory.

But to insure it at the première and to prevent the actors, while performing before a hostile audience, from slipping back into their old style of declamation, Hugo and his friends organized platoons of art students and literary types to act as a claque. They were led by Théophile Gautier who wore a rose-pink doublet, trousers of very pale sea-green and a dress coat with facings of black velvet. As expected, the old guard in the expensive seats was shocked, commented unfavorably on the haircuts of the young men and, after the performance began, was unable to make its displeasure with the play heard above the organized roar of approval. After several nights of this, by the curious logic of the literary world the Romantic movement in French literature was considered to be established and observance of the traditional conventions in the novel, verse and drama no longer necessary.

The play tells of three men, all of whom love the same woman, Doña Sol. She is, of course, beautiful with black hair, flashing eyes, and imperious manner. Sarah Bernhardt, who made a specialty of "glances" and quick facial responses to such words as "honor," used to tour in the role. The men are the Duke of Silva, an extremely haughty Spanish grandee, who is also the uncle and guardian of Doña Sol. Everyone but himself considers him too old for the lady. There is the King of Spain, Don Carlos, who later is elected Holy Roman Emperor and is supposed to be the historical Emperor Charles Fifth, and lastly there is John of Aragon, son of the Duke of Segovia. Poor John, however, has been proscribed and lives in the hills as a bandit under the name of Hernani, but he alone of the three has the love of Doña Sol. (His assumed name is something of a puzzle. There is a Spanish town, where Hugo once had been, named "Ernani," and this is the spelling Verdi used in his opera. Just why Hugo felt impelled to start his character's name with an "H" is unknown; perhaps Hugo simply liked the initial.)

The play proceeds at a leisurely pace by a series of confrontation scenes which allow the men to berate each other in lengthy speeches while Doña Sol flutters between them. The speeches are longer than any modern man could bear not to interrupt, and so much talk of honor, pride and vengeance is fatiguing. Over the years the excesses of the Romantic writers have fitted best into poems and novels: in a poem the excess of feeling is an end in itself; and in a novel, where all need not be dialogue, far greater variety is possible. In a novel the reader can set his own pace, and length, as in Hugo's *Notre Dame de Paris, Les Miserables,* or any of Dumas' continued romances, becomes an asset: the characters are more alive simply because they live longer in the reader's mind. But the theatre requires a different discipline, and the plays of the Romantics tended to strike audiences almost at once as discursive, unmotivated and requiring a personality like Mlle. Mars or Sarah Bernhardt to make them come alive. In them there is always a good deal of standing around by some characters while another explains the condition of his soul; in fact they read and play like opera librettos, which is a reason why they attracted composers.

Even before the Comédie-Française performances Bellini began to compose an *Ernani,* but when the Austrian censor, on the basis of the libretto by Romani, refused to license a production of it—it contained a conspiracy scene—Bellini transferred what he could of his work into *La Sonnambula.* There had also been an unsuccessful version done in Paris in 1834 and still another, likewise ill-fated, was announced in Genoa for the same season that Verdi prepared his for Venice. But none of this mattered; musical originality was the important thing.

Verdi's libretto preserves most of the dramatic situations of the play but without the supporting detail that made the motivation of the characters comprehensible even if not plausible. When everyone knew the play well, this was not serious, but today the opera strikes an unprepared audience as an incredibly confused scramble of bombastic scenes in which the only certainty is that someone soon will throw off a disguise. Verdi did, however, change Doña Sol's name to "Elvira," which with its unequal syllables has more musical possibilities. The first act of the opera opens with the proscribed nobleman (tenor) hiding as "Ernani" in the hills. He appeals to his men to help him kidnap Elvira from Silva's castle, and the scene then changes to Elvira's bedroom. As she is yearning for Ernani, Don Carlo (baritone) enters in disguise, protests his love and is about to carry her off when Ernani enters. The men are exchanging threats, with Elvira glancing from one to the other, when Silva (bass) enters. He, as might be expected, complains of so many men in milady's chamber and prepares to kill them when Don Carlo throws off his disguise and reveals he is the King of Spain. This causes general stupefaction and provides a grand choral finale during which the principals mutter and plot their next move.

Bernard Shaw, who liked the opera, parodied this scene in the first act of his *Arms and the Man* in which he has a most unheroic Swiss soldier, who is running away from battle and prefers eating chocolates to dying, climb up a drainpipe into the heroine's bedroom. This in turn in 1908 was made by Oscar Straus into an operetta, *The Choco-*

ACT 1 SCENE 1
(in the hills; Silva's castle in the background)

chorus · drinking song

ERNANI

- recitative (short) · he appeals to his friends.
- aria (slow) * · his love for Elvira whom Silva will marry to-morrow.
- chorus (very short) · they will abduct her.
- aria (faster) * · two excited verses of his love for Elvira with chorus joining end of each in a tiny finale.

SCENE 2
(Elvira's bedroom in the castle)

ELVIRA

- recitative (short) · Silva is away; she awaits Ernani.
- aria (slow) * · her love for Ernani who will save her.
- chorus (very short) · her ladies-in-waiting congratulate her on her marriage.
- aria (faster) * · two excited verses of her love for Ernani with chorus joining end of each as all, including Elvira, go out.

DON CARLO

- recitative (short) · he loves Elvira.
- recitative (with Elvira) * (very melodic) · You here! He offers her love, but she inquires about honor and spurns him.
- aria (slow) · his love for Elvira.

which becomes a

A little finale

- duet (faster) * · his love for her; she refuses to be Queen or mistress.
- recitative · exclamations as Ernani enters.
- trio (still faster) * · the men berate each other with Elvira protesting between them.

SILVA

- recitative (short) · what do I see? (while the others stand around)
- aria (slow) * · he had loved and trusted Elvira.
- recitative (very short) · he threatens the men.
- aria (faster) · two excited verses of his challenge; in the end of each his retainers join.

Bigger Finale

- recitative (short) · Don Carlo reveals he is the King.
- everyone (slow) * · general surprise and sung without orchestra.
- everyone (faster) * · each, including chorus, comments on situation.

* The public considered these numbers to be particularly successful.

	recitative	Carlo makes up a reason for Silva why he is in disguise and asks to spend the night; he saves
GRAND FINALE		Ernani by pretending the bandit is a messenger.
	everyone (faster)	they all sing their secret thoughts to a march which grows louder and louder as drums roll
	everyone (fastest)	and trumpets toot.

late Soldier, in which the heroine sings the still popular "My Hero." This is a waltz just as Verdi's Elvira invokes her Ernani with a waltz, "Ernani, Involami." But the difference in style and difficulty is a good microcosm of musical history, showing how far more sophisticated was the musical taste of the popular audience in 1844 than 1908.

Verdi set his first act to music in the operatic style of the time. (It is demonstrated in the scheme on the opposite page.) It is a form of Italian opera which he, more than anyone else, developed into something different, so that his own later operas tended to put his earlier ones out of fashion. For many years the critics and public, although the latter perhaps more reluctantly, assumed that this change was a progression from bad to better. Today an articulate minority of critics and perhaps even a majority of the public challenges the assumption. Verdi in his old age, these argue, started Italian opera down a side street where it is still lost.

A person need never have set foot in an opera house to see some of the crudities of this construction. The singer-characters go on- and off-stage almost as if in a concert. Each arrives to a short recitative which sets the scene and then has two set arias, a slow one followed by a fast, which psychologically is a good order for exciting applause. The fast is called a "cabaletta," perhaps because it gallops along like a horse ("cavallo" in Italian and "caballo" in Spanish). Even Don Carlo, who is allowed only a single aria, is still a part of the same musical pattern which is also the form of the finales. In all the pattern is repeated six times to make up the act—which is theatre at its simplest, to say nothing of a finale that any vaudeville trouper would happily recognize as "a flag finish."

But a concert, however much music it may offer, has little drama, and the musical pattern Verdi employs, and which was typical of the day, almost precludes the introduction of any. In order to preserve the pattern the composer must restrict any real development in the drama to the end of the fast aria or, more usual, to the recitative, during which the characters hurriedly change positions on center stage for the next set number. This is a difficulty with the form; and no matter how skillfully the composer may vary the musical patterns he uses, the difficulty appears whenever he and his audience prefer the musical values of any sort of pattern over the requirements of the drama. Thus there is no perfect solution to the problem of the operatic form; there is only a better or worse balance, according to the fashion of the moment, between the musical and dramatic values.

Within this general problem of operatic form Verdi had some more personal difficulties, such as his inability to characterize his men and Elvira. Except for range and agility, the arias would almost be interchangeable between all four lovers. The melody Verdi has given to Silva is not more haughty or more suitable for an old man than the one he has given to Ernani; it is merely more suitable for bass voice. In the same way there is little relation between words and music: a fast aria could as well be used to pant words of love as to hurl a challenge. And lastly the orchestration is rough, almost brutal. Verdi was still hearing much of his music in the brass band sounds of a concert in the piazza at Busseto. It would be years before he could orchestrate with the sophistication Rossini had shown in *William Tell* or Donizetti only the previous year in *Don Pasquale*.

What the opera had, and in incredible abundance, was melody: great, glorious swinging tunes that a man could roar or sob at home or whistle in the street. In the scheme (p. 130) all those arias or concerted numbers marked with an asterisk were considered to be extremely successful, and the arias until about 1920, or for almost eighty years, turned up regularly on concert programs. Even today those of Elvira and Silva are staples in the soprano and bass repertory. And the third act, which together with the fourth was considered even more successful than the first, had two superb arias for the baritone, a grand choral finale hailing Don Carlo as Emperor Carlo Quinto and what may have become, at least in Italy, the best-known number in the opera: a chorus in unison of conspirators, "Si ridesti il Leon di Castiglia" (Let the lion awake in Castille). Throughout Italy followers of Mazzini and all shades of anti-Austrians substituted "Venezia" or "Italia" for Castille and identified Verdi and his music with their cause.

This was easy to do with *Ernani,* for in the preface to the play Hugo bluntly identified Romanticism as "liberalism in literature" and thereby gave the play a political purpose and connotation. There is no evidence that Verdi intended to do the same for his opera or saw in it anything more than a story he felt he could successfully set to music. In fact his version of it emphasizes the humanity of the four lovers at the expense of their possible political symbolism: the celebration of the bandit against the government; a demonstration, in the vengeance of Silva, of the sterility of feudal ideas; or Hugo's idea, in Don Carlo's soliloquy, of a liberal monarch. In *Nabucco* Verdi had dealt with a people and their longing for freedom, in *I Lombardi* with Italians in a period of glory. In his *Ernani* the political background was dominated by the human tragedy of four persons caught up in it. This was to be typical of Verdi, as in *Aida.* But he was, at this time, a republican, and he was drawn to this play and not some other. Once embarked on it, he made the most of such a theatrical opportunity as a meeting of conspirators beside the tomb of Charlemagne. Both he and Conte Mocenigo, after all, hoped to have a popular success, and the political symbolism Hugo put into the play, even though reduced, was bound to strike a sympathetic chord in Italian audiences or even German and French; for 1848, when there would be revolutions in almost every European country, was only four years off. The Austrian-Venetian censors to their sorrow, however, approved the libretto after demanding only a few lines be changed.

Other changes Verdi resisted. As a successful composer he was beginning to have some power in an opera house, and he began to exert it. There was trouble over a hunting horn. Silva, the haughty Duke, puts allegiance to the ancient laws of hospitality before that he owes the King by refusing to turn his guest, Ernani, over to Don Carlo. In

a fury Don Carlo carries off Elvira as a hostage. Silva then challenges Ernani to a duel, but, in return for time to pursue Don Carlo and revenge them both, Ernani promises to commit suicide whenever the old man blows the horn which Ernani then gives him. In the last act, during the festivities following the marriage of Ernani and Elvira, Silva appears (in disguise) and, as the lovers enthuse over their happiness, blasts on the horn. Obviously the horn is important, and Silva must appear on-stage with it. But for some reason Conte Mocenigo got entangled in the idea that it was beneath the dignity of the Fenice to have a hunting horn on-stage. Verdi insisted, pointing out that to have it behind the scenes, or in the pit, or substituting something else, would destroy the effect. And by absolutely refusing to compromise he won his point.

To the horn and what it represents in the play Verdi was able to add the purely musical value of a theme or motif to which Ernani sings his promise to die. It is a short theme, duly solemn, and Verdi uses it to bind the opera together. It begins the prelude to the opera on an ominous note, occurs again in Act II when Ernani makes the promise and twice in the last act when Silva insists that he die. It is one place where the opera has an advantage over the play.

Verdi's next artistic battle was considerably more serious, involving the local Mlle. Mars, a soprano named Sophia Loewe. Like most sopranos, she had a reputation for being difficult, and during the rehearsals for *I Lombardi* Verdi treated her politely but distantly. He wrote to a friend: (We have) "exchanged a few complimentary words and that was the end of it. I haven't been to pay her a single visit yet, nor do I intend to unless it should be necessary. In all, I can only speak well of her, for she does her duty very conscientiously, without the slightest shadow of caprice." But this happy if standoffish relationship soon came to an abrupt, noisy end.

Part of the trouble undoubtedly was that the production of *I Lombardi* was not a success, and La Loewe became nervous about *Ernani.* Just why *I Lombardi* failed in Venice is a mystery; perhaps it had been so praised in advance that the Venetians out of local pride turned against it. Verdi reported in a letter to Mme. Appiani only the following:

You are impatient for news of *I Lombardi,* so I am sending it promptly: it is hardly a quarter of an hour since the curtain fell. *I Lombardi* was a grand fiasco: one of the really classic fiascos. Everything displeased or was simply tolerated, except the cabaletta of the vision. That is the simple but true story; and I tell it without joy, but without sorrow either.

A fiasco in Italian glass-blowing terminology is a bottle in the blowing of which something has gone very wrong, so that the bottle cannot stand by itself but must be propped up in a straw basket. The secondary meaning of the word as used in opera houses is perfectly clear, and the effect of one is always to shorten tempers all around. After a "really classic fiasco" an explosion is inevitable.

It came between Verdi and Loewe over the last act of *Ernani*. Verdi had written a final trio which he felt was an improvement on Hugo's play because the situation was one in which the opera could move more swiftly than the play to the inevitable climax. Silva, Ernani and Elvira are face to face, Silva demanding Ernani's life, Elvira begging Silva to have pity on them, and Ernani protesting his fate to heaven. In the play Hugo must write the perfectly obvious speeches successively; in the opera Verdi could combine them into a single musical number. The operatic form in such a situation has an advantage over the requirements of the theatre.

Loewe, however, perhaps remembering her success with the cabaletta of the vision in *I Lombardi,* thought it might save *Ernani* if Verdi inserted a similar cabelleta for her after the final trio and before the last few measures in which Ernani kills himself. She told the librettist Piave to write the verses, and he, never having worked with Verdi before, had them all finished when he was told brusquely to throw them away. In the end Verdi won, but at a cost, for at the première he had a sullen soprano who had to some extent infected the rest of the cast. Again to Mme. Appiani he reported:

Ernani which was produced yesterday had quite a success. If I had singers who were, I don't say sublime, but at least able to sing in key, *Ernani* would have been just as successful as *Nabucco* and *I Lombardi* were in Milan . . .

Guasco [the tenor] had no voice at all and was so hoarse that it was frightening. It is impossible to flat worse than Loewe did last night. Every number, great and small was applauded, excepting Guasco's Cavatina [the slow aria]. But the ones that made the biggest effect were Loewe's Cabaletta, the Cabaletta of a duet that ends as a trio, the whole finale of the first act, all of the act of the conspiracy, and the trio in the third act.

There were three curtain calls after the first act, one after the second, three after the third, and three or four at the end of the opera. This is the true story.

Within a week I shall be in Milan.

The contemporary reports bear out Verdi's appraisal. The première was a success, but after two or three performances, when the singers got over their colds or had decided that perhaps their bread was buttered on the composer's side, *Ernani* became a great success. Two months after the season at the Fenice ended, another Venetian theatre, the Teatro San Benedetto put it on again with a different and better cast. The Venetians went again and again. What they liked was the melody. One critic, after discussing the individual numbers and especially congratulating the composer on saving his climax of interest and inspiration for the final trio, said: "The music made such a strong impression that, even on Sunday, people coming out of the theatre were already humming the tenor and baritone arias." And he added: "To impress itself on the mind at a first hearing and become popular is the privilege of good music." With *Ernani* Verdi had exactly hit the temper of the time, theatrically and musically.

VENICE

He did not wait to be feted and praised in Venice, but immediately after the first three performances at the Fenice, which tradition required the composer to conduct, he left for Milan. And instead of paying a farewell call on the leading soprano and exchanging a flurry of breathless compliments before witnesses, which was also a tradition, he took his leave of La Loewe by card, which was only just polite. The entire Fenice company, including the lady, realized that, unlike Mlle. Mars, La Loewe had made a mistake. But Verdi's quick departure was not caused by the agitation of his troubles in the opera house. Even before the première of *I Lombardi* when everything had been going well he wrote a friend: "Venice is beautiful, it is a poem, it is divine, but . . . I wouldn't stay here of my own accord."

The previous spring he had not stayed in Vienna after the first performance of *Nabucco,* and on his return to Milan he had left at once for Busseto and then on to Parma for the performances there of *Nabucco* with Strepponi. Then back to Busseto; on to Milan. Not all the quick departures were required by business, and his letters are those of a restless man, always examining timetables, making arrange-

ments in advance, leaving new addresses behind. The glories of Venice and Vienna seem to have made no impression on him, and even his anger at La Loewe was easily put aside when he worked with her some months later in another production of *Ernani*, this time at Bologna. Margherita and the children had been dead four years. The success of his last three operas had made him at thirty the most sought-after composer in Italy. But his actions and letters, although he never discusses his feelings, suggest a not very happy man.

CHAPTER 12

THE YEARS IN THE GALLEY, I

1844–1845; AGE, 30–31

BACK in Milan after the successful production of *Ernani* in Venice, Verdi began a life that in later years he described as "anni di galera" (years in the galley). Beginning with the production of *Oberto* in 1839, he had composed an opera each year; actually there were eighteen months between the ill-fated *Un Giorno di Regno* and the fresh start with *Nabucco*. There were five operas in all with the last three fantastically successful. Clearly he could repeat his success; equally clearly it hardly mattered whether he did or not, for the public would happily pay the cost of producing anything he might compose, good or bad. Impresarios, publishers and agents from cities as far away as London besieged him by letter and in person with proposals to produce the old operas or commissions to write new ones. To keep it all straight he started making copies of his letters so that he could refer accurately to this clause in that contract, to the other man's proposal and his refusal. He also made copies of some of the letters to his librettists and personal friends, and he continued to do so until his death in 1901. There are some gaps in the collection, one lasting nine years, and the important and irrelevant mix together. But the collection is an extraordinary record of an artist's life and the greatest single source of material on Verdi. He, of course, had no idea the collection would ever be published, but it was, twelve years after his death, and under the simple title *Copialettere,* or *Copybook.*

Besides the men of the theatre world, Milanese society now tried to take up Verdi. Wealthy ladies without a pretense of Mme. Appiani's interest in music sent around their footmen with invitations or offered their carriages for drives in the country. He almost invariably refused these invitations, but even to refuse took time. He had to walk to the door, listen to the coachman explain and think of a polite excuse; and for the men calling on business there were times when it would have been convenient to be "out." What Verdi needed, short of a wife, was a secretary, and even as Barezzi had once, perhaps inadvertently, provided the former, he now again provided the latter in the person of Emanuele Muzio, a young man from Busseto.

Muzio was the son of a poor cobbler in Zibello, a village near Busseto. Like Verdi, he too had worked with the Philharmonic Society, had been granted a scholarship by the Monte di Pietà and sent with help from Barezzi to Milan to attend the Conservatory. He arrived in April soon after Verdi returned from Venice, and then, as he wrote Barezzi:

Milan, 22 April 1844

To Antonio Barezzi:

Maestro Verdi has been giving me lessons in counterpoint for several days because no foreigner nor any one from the Milanese province can attend the Conservatory; and if eventually I am able to attend, it will be through a special favor which the Viceroy and the Governor of Milan grant to Signor Verdi. Furthermore, he will be so kind as to make out a recommendation for me, which I shall send you just as soon as I receive it. Many students would pay as much as two or three talers a lesson if Signor Verdi would give lessons, but he does not give any to any one, except a poor devil like me, whom he has already done a thousand favors, now in addition is giving him lessons, not once or twice a week but every morning. It amazes me. And very often when he asks me to do something for him, he even offers me lunch. My Maestro has such greatness of soul, generosity and wisdom and such a heart, that to find its match, I would have to place yours next to his, and then I could say: these are the two most generous hearts in all the world.

EMANUELE MUZIO

Muzio was only eight years younger than Verdi, but the difference in experience and sophistication, though real enough, was magnified to the young provincial's eye. Even though he had seen and met Verdi in Busseto in the days before *Nabucco,* had heard often from Barezzi the story of Verdi's early trials and failures, he never felt they shared a common background and history. For Muzio, Verdi's success, though it may have come late, was so great and brilliant that it proved a sort of divinity from birth; for Muzio, Verdi was simply not like other men.

After the première of *Ernani* in Vienna on 30 May most of Verdi's friends and admirers heard of its success by the same mail, and Muzio wrote to Barezzi:

You, sir, should have been in the house of Signor Verdi on the day when the news arrived of the most happy results, to see how for a whole hour, first one would come with a letter from Donizetti, then another who had received the news from some Count, I don't remember his name, and then another who had a letter from Merelli, and so many others that they never seemed to come to an end, and to hear the wonderful things they wrote about the Signor and his *Ernani* you would have surely wept, sir, because you are very sensitive, and then to see them all sitting there, now one reading his letter and then another reading his, and with their papers in their hands they were like so many boys in school reciting their lessons; and the Signor there in the middle of them at his table seemed a teacher, and I big-eyed in my corner seemed the dunce of the school. It was a thing which gave pleasure and delighted.

But the interruptions did not always give pleasure. When the Grand Duchess of Tuscany sent around a chamberlain to Verdi to express her admiration of him, Verdi hotly declared afterward to the dazzled Muzio that it was "a lot of nonsense." Another time Signora Lucca, the wife of a hopeful publisher and a lady with the reputation of being able to handle difficult temperaments, put on a rather lengthy scene in which she described her husband's hopes for a contract and misery at the prospect of not getting one. She even went so far as to insist that in bed he did nothing but sigh, and Verdi, by making the obvious commiserating remark, was able to get rid of her.

Among the men of business, in the end Ricordi got the Italian copyright to *Ernani,* Lucca had to content himself with continued negotiations, and the Teatro Argentina in Rome got the contract for the new opera. Verdi then suspended his negotiations with Naples, Milan and Venice, although indicating that he liked some of the suggested librettos and would bear them in mind.

The contract for Rome specified that Verdi's opera would be the *opera d'obbligo* to be put on in the autumn season and that he would stage it. The contract was signed in the spring, so that Verdi had the four summer months in which to prepare the opera. The first libretto he submitted, on Lorenzino de' Medici, was rejected by the papal censors; the second was accepted. It was based on Byron's play *The Two Foscari,* a historical melodrama of political intrigue in Venice during the fifteenth century. Verdi and Piave had outlined it the year before for Venice, but Conte Mocenigo had rejected it in favor, ultimately, of *Ernani*.

Verdi began work at once. He harried Piave to finish the libretto, suggested dialogue to start off an aria, and wanted the Doge's character to be made more forceful; Verdi always was requesting strong characters. He also wanted a gondolier's song to join with a general chorus to which he added a bid for popular appeal: "Couldn't it be arranged for all this to happen toward evening and thus have a sunset, too, which is always so beautiful?" He closed by answering one of Piave's questions. "Certainly, agree to write for Pacini. But try not to do the *Lorenzino,* because you and I want to do it together some other time. But if you can't get out of it, then do *Lorenzino* too. Do what is best for you."

Lorenzino was the libretto rejected by the censors, and Pacini, who was the court musician for Marie Louise, was one of the leading composers in the older generation. In a long life, 1796–1867, he wrote about seventy operas, often completing them in a few weeks. His contemporaries considered him a great melodist but very weak on orchestration and drama. His opera *Lorenzino de' Medici,* with libretto by Piave, was successfully produced at the Fenice in Venice in March 1845, and so Verdi lost a libretto.

But he liked the libretto for *I Due Foscari,* and the composition of it went well except that his health broke down—he had headaches and stomach pains—and he lost a number of days in bed. Muzio ran errands for him, fended off what visitors he could and kept Barezzi, that generous man, informed of everything, including his own needs:

Milan, 24 June 1844

To Antonio Barezzi:

He is pestered by everyone. He says he doesn't want to receive anyone, but he's so kind that he'll never stick to it.

A composer, whose name I don't remember, wrote Signor Verdi a letter in which he begged and even implored him not to put *I Due Foscari* to music, because he too had set it to music and feared that the same thing would happen to it as happened to Mazucato's *Ernani.* Signor Verdi answered that he had already proceeded too far with the work so that he couldn't grant him his ardent request. (etc.)

This morning I began the imitations. My teacher used the same studies which he used under Lavigna, but which he has improved upon. He guides me with his knowledge and clears the road along which I have started. The lesson lasts only a quarter of an hour; I'll leave it to you to guess what the reason may be. My funds are low; I added up my expenses and find I have money enough to live until the middle of July, but on the 15th of that month I must pay for the rent of my room and the piano, and that will take all my money. Please help me at your convenience. My teacher tells me that when I'm in need I must tell him freely; but I haven't the courage, because already he does too much by teaching me so well and so willingly. This morning he asked me, "How do you feel after studying with me?" I told him, "I'm a new-born person." I continue to live as economically as possible. I don't spend a cent uselessly, but the expense of paper, light, etc., is so great that it seems impossible. The Maestro says that if I don't write a great deal and well, I'll never learn. I must do all these things and study very hard.

EMANUELE MUZIO

Thinking the country air might do him good, Verdi went down to Busseto to stay with Barezzi. But in a few weeks he was writing to Mme. Appiani: "I shall soon be back in Milan. The moment my health is better I shall leave for the Lombard capital. The air of my home town is not good for me." In fact, that summer no air in either place seemed entirely satisfactory. Verdi's health taken over the years was good, and in his old age, when it was extraordinarily good, journalists periodically wrote articles speculating on the cause of it. But in these first years of success it sometimes failed, and the pattern of its failure is interesting. He suffered usually from headaches, stomach pains with nausea and severe sore throats which occurred, almost invariably, when he was trying to compose a new opera, and no medication or change of air ever seems to have alleviated them. The conclusion seems inescapable that the psychical agitation of creation had its physical counterpart, and Verdi, although he never ceased complaining of his troubles, came to realize that he must simply endure them.

The sore throat is interesting because the response to opera by any audience is made, fundamentally, in the throat; the ear serves largely as a conduit. Of course the ear distinguishes whether a high note is beautiful or ugly, but the excitement of the high, climactic note is generated by the muscular response in the listener's throat. From his own experience he knows that to reach the note or to hold it requires a tremendous physical tension, and his own muscles respond sympathetically. Verdi, at this time, composed his operas entirely vocally, that is, he created the melodic lines for the entire opera with only the barest piano accompaniment. Then during the rehearsals he filled in the orchestration. Toward the end of his life he began to do more of the orchestration as he went along—and his troubles with sore throats decreased. But at this time he still composed vocally; whether singing aloud, to himself, or merely hearing it in his head makes little difference—the strain on the muscles of his throat would be almost the same, and such concentrated singing over several months would irritate any throat.

This phenomenon of the sore throat is not restricted to composers or even singers who may be mentally reviewing a role. Veteran opera-goers such as Vincent Sheehan or Nietzsche, who have never sung a note during a performance, have reported the same symptom after a bout of operagoing. They have sat and listened with their ears, but they have "responded" with their throats. Probably most students of Verdi are content with this explanation of his sore throats. But the same argument can be pushed further to explain the stomach pains and nausea although, of course, being more of an extreme, it has fewer adherents. Verdi, after all, was pre-Freud and psychosomatic analysis.

The theory here is that the seat of all deeply felt emotions is the middle part of the body, the stomach, diaphragm, heart and lungs. Any adult unfortunate enough to have heard another break down under some sort of tension knows that the first sounds heard are not the con-ventional high-pitched screams, blasphemous words, or even tearful sniffles; they are stomach noises, heaves and curious, strangled gurgles that rise in the throat like escaping bubbles of agony. The more con-ventional noises may follow immediately after, but they are percep-tibly "after." Meanwhile anyone who has heard the unconventional sounds has had his own muscular response: his heart has "stopped," or his stomach "sunk," and he has put out a hand or crossed the room, all before his mind has consciously registered that his brother is in trouble.

Verdi attempted to put just these breakdowns and the very strongest sorts of emotions to music. To do it, when he had time, he learned the libretto by heart, repeating the verses over and over to himself. He literally dredged himself for an emotional response to the situation on the stage. Perhaps it is not surprising that his stomach sent up signals of distress in pain and nausea.

On the last day of September Verdi left Milan for Rome where he orchestrated *I Due Foscari,* staged it and, as always, conducted the first three performances. The reception on opening night was enthusiastic but somewhat testy. The impresario, with a new Verdi opera, had raised the price of admission, and the audience was irritated. On the second and third nights, at regular prices, the enthusiasm was immense. One critic counted thirty curtain calls. For many years the opera was as popular in Italy as *Ernani* or *Nabucco,* and like them, it, too, went around the world. Then, perhaps after twenty years, it began to fall behind, although it was frequently revived and still is on occasion.

As an opera *I Due Foscari* has considerable virtue as well as some interesting faults. The virtue, as in *Ernani,* lies in the melodies, particularly the finales to Acts II and III which Verdi succeeded in making into scenes rather than merely choral finishes. Throughout the opera Verdi clearly attempted to shift the balance between musical pattern and drama toward the drama. The pattern is still basically that of *Ernani,* a slow aria followed by a fast, but Verdi cut out the repeated verses and varied the pattern more by having trios, duets, or even another character sing the fast sequel. Thus the opera is more musically compact than *Ernani.*

To increase the drama in the music, Verdi gave themes to the characters, including even the Council of Ten, which assembles periodically throughout the opera. But this was only partly successful. Themes do best when they change and develop even as do the characters they represent; otherwise they are a trap, arresting the character with a particular face toward the audience and keeping him always turned that way. Thus Lucrezia, the heroine and wife of young Foscari who is condemned to exile, has a theme that rushes excitedly up the scale. It generally precedes her entrance, so that she always seems to arrive on-stage breathless, hair astray, and prepared to throw herself at someone's feet. The music inevitably inspires the would-be wits to chant: "Here comes Lucrezia"—which is bad for drama. Verdi in his later operas used themes—in *Aida* the priests have one, as does Aida herself—but he never again used them so rigidly or invented themes so little susceptible to variation.

In a sense *Ernani,* by trying for less than *I Due Foscari,* was more successful; but neither had the artistic unity of *Nabucco,* held together by its religious theme running through all the choruses and the plot. But each new opera proclaimed that *Nabucco* was a sport, scientifically speaking, in Verdi's development. Whether he was conscious of it or not, what interested him was individuals; opera for him meant individuals musically rounded and psychologically true. There was some of this in *Nabucco,* but there was also a good deal of oratorio, massed singing in which the characters are more leaders of the chorus than

LA SCALA

individuals. What *I Due Foscari* had was the beginning of real musical personality in the character of the Doge who must condemn his own son to exile. A contemporary Roman critic observed, "Each character speaks his own language; each expresses his own passions in a manner eminently dramatic." To an audience of today, trained by the later Verdi operas to expect this as a matter of course, the praise seems exaggerated. But to an audience used to the balance between musical pattern and drama tipped toward the musical pattern Verdi's opera seemed extremely dramatic.

Verdi returned to Milan toward the end of November and into a situation in which he again and again lost his temper and laid the basis for his nickname of "the Bear of Busseto." He had agreed with Merelli to write a new opera for the Carnival season, 1844–45, and also to produce a revival of *I Lombardi* to open the season on 26 December. His old friend Erminia Frezzolini, who had created the role of Giselda in *I Lombardi,* was to sing in both, together with her husband Poggi, a tenor. Solera was to write the libretto for the new opera based on Schiller's tragedy, *Die Jungfrau von Orleans,* i.e., Joan of Arc.

Verdi began composing in December but had hardly more than started when he had to stop to conduct the rehearsals of *I Lombardi.*

The trouble began in the opera house. Verdi complained about the orchestra which was too small and badly arranged in the pit; the singers took too many liberties with the music; the chorus was lazy; and scenery and costumes were dilapidated, clashing, or both. In short, La Scala showed all the symptoms of a traditional opera house resting on its laurels. At the rehearsals, Muzio reported to Barezzi, Verdi "shouted like a madman and stamped his feet so much he looked as though he were playing the organ; he sweated so profusely that the perspiration dripped down on the score." Frezzolini wept constantly because her voice was frayed; her husband nervously sang wrong notes, and a baritone whom Merelli had miscast in a part for a basso profondo could not make himself heard in the concerted numbers. Verdi, who was by then exhausted, refused to attend opening night. But the revival was a success, and it was repeated fifteen times.

Meanwhile everyone in the theatre had fought with at least one other person beside Verdi, who held the dubious distinction of having fought with them all. It is impossible to know exactly where the right lay. Certainly the standards at La Scala were slipping. In spite of the myth assiduously circulated by Milanese, La Scala has not always been the first opera house of the world or even in Italy; like all other theatres it has had its ups and downs, and some of the down periods have been very poor indeed. Hindsight now can see that the great theatre was starting a decline. Some of the fault was undoubtedly Merelli's, but he had several unusual problems about which Verdi was probably not very sympathetic. Solera's wife, for example, against Verdi's advice undertook to sing Donizetti's *Gemma di Vergy* and had such a fiasco that Merelli had to withdraw the production after two evenings and dismiss the lady—which can hardly have soothed anyone's temper. And besides losing a production, Merelli lost one of his leading sopranos when the lady simply tore up her contract and went off to sing in other theatres.

Added to these artistic difficulties may have been some emotional ones. Gossip at the time tattled that Verdi had an affair with almost every lady he knew. Most often mentioned were Mme. Appiani, the Contessa Maffei, and the sopranos Strepponi and Frezzolini. But little evidence survives of an affair at this period of Verdi's life. There are no love notes, no letters, no days or weeks in his life unaccounted for; there are not even any explicit remarks about such an affair in the letters of his friends. If in fact he was conducting one, he did it with incredible discretion, for the prying eyes of the theatre world never blink.

But the gossip has refused to die, and Italians who like to think of themselves as lovers treat the possibility of chastity on Verdi's part during this period as some sort of slur on the national honor. "Non fa senso," they protest. "It doesn't make sense." Verdi was single, healthy, reasonably attractive personally, and in his position and prestige very attractive. "All men . . ." the Italians start, and then conclude with a series of generalizations about the Italian character and customs of the time. It was assumed, for example, that all single and most unhappily married men found a release for their sexual energy in an affair. The lady would be the man's equal, generally, in social position and education. For a man continually to find his release in a bordello was not only bad taste but incomprehensible: there were so many suitable ladies available and willing in his own class. Almost invariably the lady was married, a widow or an actress; to have an affair with a young, unmarried girl society considered a seduction and unforgivable. The affair also had to be more than a one night's frolic, and there was a hard word for a lady who changed her men frequently. There was also a perceptible difference between a lady involved in an affair and a mistress. The former, theoretically, met her gentlemen on terms of complete equality; the mistress was to some extent "kept." But the line with widows and actresses was very blurred and generally drawn by society in favor of the widows and against the actresses.

For a man to marry his mistress was indelicate, creating an impossible situation when he tried to introduce her to his friends' wives. To marry the lady of an affair was sometimes possible although society was apt to exact some sort of penalty such as living elsewhere for several years, say in Paris. But then if there were children, particularly if they were charming, society declared it a love match and all was forgiven. But such marriages were rare; more often the affair disintegrated after several years. If it continued for longer it became a liaison, and society made certain adjustments in its favor such as including both parties in large dinners, always provided, of course, the lady's husband was not present. The generally less familiar Italian words for these relationships are: a mistress, "una mantenuta"; an affair, "un' avventura"; and a liaison, "una relazione."

For the Italian man involved in an affair there was no moral penalty of which his Church could not absolve him and very few if any social penalties. For the ladies it was more difficult, and they sometimes, particularly the widows and actresses, tended to get a little hard. Their friends tired of defending them while their enemies never tired of accusing and judging them. In the end they often lived alone, without friends, and miserably aware that no one, not even the men, cared for them. But still almost any affair could be arranged within society as long as it was done with discretion and observed certain rules. Among them was one that the lady never went to the man's apartment, unaccompanied, for any reason whatsoever. Usually, like Mme. Appiani, the lady had an establishment where she entertained her circle of friends and where the favored gentleman felt free to return after the others left; or the two might meet at some villa in the country. Certainly none of the four ladies with whom Verdi's name was mentioned ever visited him alone in his apartment in Milan. But the one rule for an affair that stood before all others was that of discretion. The famous affair, 1833–39, of Liszt and the Comtesse d'Agoult caused such a sensation because it was conducted like a blow in the face of society.

It is hard to see how Verdi could have had an affair on these terms without leaving some trace of it. Frezzolini, for example, had a husband who gossip said was jealous of Verdi. But if this was the cause of some of the scenes at the theatre that winter, it is extraordinary that no one, stagehand or singer, recorded a jealous explosion. Poggi, the husband, was, after all, a temperamental tenor. For a different reason an affair with the Contessa Maffei seems unlikely. The following year she separated from her husband in order to keep her property free of his gambling debts and herself free to conduct her affair with Carlo Tenca. This affair, which must have started some time before, was a true liaison and lasted until Tenca's death in 1883. Verdi knew and was friends with all the parties; there is no sexual role for him in the Maffei triangle.

An affair with Strepponi seems equally impossible, for the two were hardly ever in the same town. After the performances of *Nabucco* at Parma Strepponi attempted to keep her career going but at a slower pace. She restricted herself almost entirely to *Nabucco* except for a long and disastrous season at Palermo during the winter Verdi was losing his temper in Milan. Her voice had almost completely gone; the critics and public were unkind, and in her letters to friends she was discouraged, tired of life, and in one she wonders whether suicide or a complete withdrawal may not be the only solution to her problems.

There is no suggestion of the happiness that later begins to run through her letters. And if she and Verdi wrote any letters to each other, they are still undiscovered.

The most likely candidate in the past has always seemed Mme. Appiani, for here some suggestive notes and letters do exist. Her side of the correspondence is lost or perhaps was destroyed by Verdi so that most of the notes have no context. But at various times he wrote:

"Agreed. I shall go at three o'clock; but now I must know where I am to go. Meanwhile, a thousand thanks. Write."

And again: "I am furious, desolate, but you must give up playing Queen Bee (alla sultanità). I thank you notwithstanding and press your hands." (This is a usual closing and with "hands" in the plural because the Italians, on meeting and parting, frequently clasp both hands straight on rather than crossing with the right to the right.)

From London in 1847 he wrote in a letter: "I am still an example of fidelity . . . Don't laugh, by God, or I'll fly into a rage!"

Earlier from Busseto he had written in a letter: "Be patient for once and be assured that no person will rule my life nor will I make myself a slave to any thing."

And finally from Venice over Christmas 1845 he replied to Mme. Appiani who had sent him a pair of suspenders and addressed him as "carissimo": "I am not dearest, never, never: nor do I pretend to be. I pretend to be many things, but not to be amiable or good-looking, certainly not. I am neither more nor less than a fool though at heart I am not such a bad fellow, and I think often of you and your family, although you, without actually believing it, accuse me of the contrary." (etc.)

There are difficulties about these notes. In all that survive, although Verdi wrote often, he never wrote an endearment or any reference to her physical charms. He never addressed her in the intimate second person singular, and even when he brought himself to say that he missed her, he was apt to dilute the statement by including her family, Milan, or city life.

Further, there is a difficulty about the lady herself. In 1951 Frank Walker in an article in *Music and Letters* (*See* Bibliography) demonstrated that there were two ladies named Mme. Appiani. Both were widows with children, but one was considerably younger, prettier and with fewer children. Donizetti knew both, but Verdi knew only the elder. She was the one with the salon, and by 1845 she was a grandmother surging on fifty and apparently with an intimate non-musical friend who seems far more likely than either Verdi or Donizetti to have been her lover. Gatti and other biographers who have followed his lead have confused the two ladies, attaching the face, figure and fewer children of the younger to the middle-aged dowager running the salon. Walker, by unraveling the confusion, has made an affair between Verdi and the Mme. Appiani whom he knew seem less likely.

In fact Verdi's notes, when read with the elder lady in mind, seem less a display of love than an effort at gallantry. He sounds as if he were trying to reproduce the light, smooth tone of talk he undoubtedly heard in Mme. Appiani's house. But his rough, country tongue had not yet mastered it, and some of the remarks come out with a startling blunt quality that Mme. Appiani perhaps found charming.

With such meager evidence speculation begins early and runs long. And the danger to avoid for those who indulge in the sport is the weighing of evidence and likelihood in terms of their own experience rather than Verdi's, as manifested in his life. It may not "make sense" but probably Verdi, so typically Italian in his music, was not so in his relations with women. He did not seem to slip easily in and out of conditions of intimacy with them, perhaps because his simple, peasant background made him uncertain and cautious in the sophisticated society of Milan. Even among the men he made few friends and slowly, but most of these he kept throughout his life. And finally when he began to have an affair with Strepponi he conducted it in a way that was very typical of him and broke all the accepted rules. In the light of this it seems uncharacteristic and therefore hard to believe that sometime during the period of 1842–47 he conducted an affair with Mme. Appiani so expertly and discreetly that its very existence cannot be established beyond a reasonable doubt.

But even assuming some sort of intimacy with one of the ladies during that winter, Verdi cannot have paid her much attention, for his schedule at the theatre left no time for a dalliance. When the previous year he had gone to Venice to put on *I Lombardi* and *Ernani,* he had arrived with the new opera almost completed, and he had had from 26 December, the opening night of the season, to 9 March to prepare the *Ernani* production for its première. Now at La Scala he had only from 26 December to 15 February not only to prepare the production of *Giovanna d'Arco* but also to compose the greater part of it. The result was a conventional opera in which the best parts were all incidental rather than crucial. The overture, for example, which uses no music from the opera, is effective, and in one of its quieter sections Verdi wrote more skillfully for the wind instruments than he ever had before. But the character of Joan of Arc is nothing more than a routine soprano role with the required number of fast and slow arias, and the libretto throughout is a travesty on the historical story, which, considering much of Italy longed for a Joan to lead it against the Austrians, everyone knew well. In the opera she is wounded leading the French in battle and dies in a French castle, banner in hand, the stage picture being a sort of feminine version of the death of Wolfe at Quebec with a vision of the Virgin added.

The critics were not very enthusiastic about the opera and complained of all the singers except Frezzolini. The public, however, supported it, and for a while Merelli was able to produce it four times a week. There were plenty of banners on-stage and also some good tunes which were immediately taken up by the barrel organs and town bands. One of the most popular of these was the "Devil's Waltz," which is typical of what was bad in the opera. Joan hears heavenly and hellish voices, those from hell urging her to desert her mission for earthly love. The words Solera provided as a chorus to express this idea are:

Tu sei bella, tu sei bella!	You are pretty, you are pretty!
Pazzerella che fai tu?	Silly girl, what are you doing?

The Italian words make a sound exactly like some Neapolitan jingle, and that is just the sort of music Verdi provided for them. In the theatre everyone's foot starts tapping and he smiles at his neighbor as the demon chorus comes on to terrify Joan.

Immediately after the première Merelli tried to persuade Verdi to stage a production of *Ernani* which was to be presented toward the end of the season. But Verdi refused, stating publicly that he would have nothing more to do with La Scala. He was not the only composer to be angry with Merelli. In 1843 Merelli had announced Donizetti's *Fausta* in a new production revised by the composer. In fact, as Donizetti complained, he had not revised it. Merelli on his own had merely added a finale from another Donizetti opera and an aria by another composer. Now in the winter of 1845, aside from the troubles with Verdi over *I Lombardi* and *Giovanna d'Arco*, Merelli gave *I Due Foscari*, Verdi's most dramatic opera to date, with the third and last act preceding the second. Verdi did not forgive him. In his new contracts with Ricordi, his publisher, he began to insist on reserving the right to himself to decide in which theatres his operas should appear. Meanwhile he refused all of Merelli's offers for a new opera and prepared to write instead for Naples, Venice and Florence.

Verdi's bitterness with Merelli and La Scala was deep and, unfortunately for the theatre, lasted long. After the première of *Giovanna d'Arco* in that winter of 1845 Verdi refused to give another première to La Scala until that of his revised *La Forza del Destino* in 1869, almost a quarter of a century later. For many years after 1848 he refused even to drive through the city in order to avoid meeting the theatre's officials or a well-intentioned ambush by partisan Milanese who might question his actions and urge him to return. Meanwhile La Scala, the theatre in the popular mind most closely associated with Verdi, watched his most popular operas, *Rigoletto, Il Trovatore* and *La Traviata*, have their premières in Venice and Rome.

CHAPTER 13

THE YEARS IN THE GALLEY, II

1845–1846; AGE, 31–32

ONE reason Verdi refused to direct the La Scala production of *Ernani* in that ill-fated winter of 1845 was that he had contracted previously to compose and stage a new opera for the Teatro San Carlo in Naples, and the première was set down for June. Time was already short, and Verdi's health, bad all winter, now grew worse. His headaches and stomach troubles were so aggravated by nervous exhaustion that he finally had to ask the impresario at Naples, Vincenzo Flauto, for a postponement. With his letter he enclosed a doctor's certificate as evidence that he was not malingering. But Flauto replied evasively, suggesting that the Neapolitan sun and air would cure whatever might ail Verdi and urging him to come at once as per the contract. The tone of Flauto's letter irritated Verdi who complained to the librettist in Naples, Salvatore Cammarano: "It seems that an artist is not allowed to be sick." But in the end the postponement was granted, and Verdi left for Naples in June with the opera almost completed although, as always, without the orchestration. Largely because Cammarano had offered himself as a sort of lightning rod to draw off the temperamental sparks between the two men when Verdi arrived in Naples, his relations with Flauto and others in the theatre were perfectly cordial.

Cammarano, who was twelve years older than Verdi, was a well-known poet and very popular in Naples where he was held in the sort of general affection often reserved for eccentrics. He liked to compose on the porch of the Church of San Francesco di Paolo, and, tall, thin and with spectacles, he would lean thoughtfully against a pillar and occasionally scribble a verse. When he was tired, he would sit down and go to sleep, and no one would disturb him. In the theatre world he was famous as the librettist of Donizetti's *Lucia di Lammermoor,* which had had its première at the San Carlo in 1835, just ten years earlier. There is a tone of respect in Verdi's letters to Cammarano absent in those to Solera or Piave.

Cammarano and Flauto had settled on a libretto based on Voltaire's classical tragedy *Alzire ou les Américains,* a play in which the Spanish governor of Peru, after being excessively cruel to an Inca chief, suddenly on his death bed tries to make everything right by giving his widow, an Inca princess, to the chief she had always loved. The Inca chief is so impressed by this display of peace, pardon and virtue that he immediately is converted to Christianity. Voltaire has always been a popular source for opera librettos, a modern example perhaps being Leonard Bernstein's *Candide* in 1956, but *Alzire* was a curious and bad choice. One difficulty with it was that there has always been a strong suspicion that Voltaire intended the play to be taken not seriously but ironically: Listen to what these Christians preach and look at how they behave in Peru. In this view the conversion of the Inca chief at the end is the final hilarious improbability or possibly added merely to get the play by the censors. This, of course, would be very

characteristic of Voltaire, and no one has ever doubted that he intended to make fun of parts of the Old Testament in his mock tragedy *Saul*. The view of *Alzire* more generally held, however, is that Voltaire intended to show that true Christian forgiveness, as the essence of the religion, is a superior virtue to any of those embodied in the noble savage. But whichever view of the play may be correct, Cammarano and Verdi took it seriously and then excluded all the philosophical background, leaving on-stage a wildly improbable love story filled with exotic violence and in which the villain of the triangle, the Spaniard, suddenly as he is dying becomes the extreme of virtue. As a climax it is dramatically ludicrous. When in *Rigoletto* Verdi switches the audience's dislike of Rigoletto in Act I into sympathy at the end of Act IV, he does it slowly, scene by scene, each time adding a little more to Rigoletto's character and the audience's understanding of it. With the plot of *Alzira* this was impossible.

But even out of the difficult libretto Verdi might have been able to make a successful melodrama if he could have dredged up some sort of inspiration for the music. But he could not; it is conventional and, as it plods along, dull. Like *Giovanna d'Arco,* which by comparison is inspired, the best part of *Alzira* is the overture, an appendage having

NAPLES

nothing to do with the characters of the opera; they hardly exist except as counters to set up the successive scenes. For this failure of inspiration Verdi's poor health was probably in large part responsible, and it in turn was caused by the pace he had set for himself. He had contracted to produce an opera for the San Carlo's summer season, and he did it. But it was the third opera he had staged within a year while composing at least two and a half of them within the same period. The premières were: *I Due Foscari,* 3 November 1844; *Giovanna d'Arco,* 15 February 1845; and *Alzira,* 12 August 1845. The pace was more than three times as fast as he had composed his earlier and more successful operas, and at least for him it was plainly too fast. The difference between *Ernani* or *I Due Foscari* and *Alzira* is immense, and he himself recognized it. In later years he would say of *Alzira:* "Quella è proprio brutta," or, "That one is really ugly." And he never urged that it be revived, nor did he ever attempt to compose at such a pace again.

In a theoretical way it is doubtful whether even with musical inspiration Verdi could have done anything of interest with Voltaire's play. He certainly at this time was quite capable of writing a rousing series of repetitions and variations of "Onward, Christian Soldiers, Marching as to War," but that hymn, while perhaps perfectly expressing the Spanish attitude toward the Incas, hardly expresses anything about the essence of Christianity, forgiveness, which was, by its presence or perversion, the essence of Voltaire's play. Verdi was certainly quite incapable of taking the play ironically and writing sardonic music. He himself did not have that view of life, and neither he nor anyone else at the time thought music could be used for such a purpose. For the nineteenth century music was charming, exciting or ennobling; sometimes it was humorous, but it was never sarcastic. The librettists invariably went to Voltaire for his tragedies, among them *Sémiramis, Olimpie* and *Zaïre.* It was not till the twentieth century that a composer attempted *Candide.*

Verdi was probably equally incapable of doing justice to Voltaire's theme taken seriously. To do so would have required a man who felt the religious theme deeply and was able to translate it into music, and there is no evidence that at the time Verdi was such a man. While in Busseto he had composed conventional church music apparently only because his job had required it; as soon as he moved to Milan he stopped. And, after the death of his children and Margherita, he seems almost never to have gone into a church except to admire the art or to hear some music. He believed strongly in the Christian ethics, but as these were also, inevitably, the professed ethics of Italian secular life, his code and actions in terms of them seem not to have had any religious basis. His life and associations, the influence of Provesi, the fracas in Busseto over his appointment, and the political role at all levels of the Church, inclined him to be "out of sorts" with organized religion.

His wide reading was a symptom of his independent mind and perhaps had made him something of a free thinker. To the devout even to consider a libretto by Voltaire was not only shocking but sinful. When, for example, Manzoni re-entered the Catholic Church, following the conversion of his Calvinist wife, he finally, after repeated urgings, handed over his magnificently bound eighteenth-century edition of Voltaire's complete works to his family confessor. The priest then solemnly burned it in Manzoni's presence volume by volume. Manzoni is supposed to have withheld three of the volumes, but none were found in his library after his death. Manzoni had an equivocal character and could let his ideas out one door only to reintroduce them by another, and *I Promessi Sposi*, although at least in part censored by the confessor, often reflects Voltaire's rationalism and irony. But the confessor was in a position of tremendous power and could often influence Manzoni's behavior, if not his thoughts. In this same year, for example, the confessor reported to his superior about Manzoni: "He has returned to the confidence he first had in me, which had rather cooled, as I had declared myself too openly. He scarcely talks politics any more, or talks of them with moderation." It is impossible to think of Verdi moderating his talk, burning his books, or submitting to this sort of authority: "Understand that no person will rule my life nor will I make myself a slave to anything." In his personal as well as his musical life he was, to an extraordinary degree, self-taught and also self-disciplined. He did not confess to a priest, and he did not go to Mass.

Lacking any personal experience of the mystical side of the Church and being strongly antipathetic to its authoritarian side, Verdi probably could not have made anything but a melodrama out of *Alzire*, in which case he would have done better to stick to an Italian subject about which he knew more and which did not attempt to present such a complicated issue as the clash of civilizations or the role of the Church. Perhaps he subconsciously felt this, for with the unhappy exception of *Stiffelio*, in his next thirteen operas he avoided anything but the most conventional religious choruses, generally in the background where the Church with its costumes, processionals and prayers has always been a standard stage picture in Italian opera. When in 1862 he took a libretto, *La Forza del Destino,* in which the religious feelings of some monks and a harrassed woman are squarely in the forefront of the opera, he composed some of his most beautiful music for them; but there is nothing specifically Christian about it. The agonized Leonora could just as well be a pagan girl rushing into a group of Druid priests. On the other hand, in the same opera Verdi most successfully created a comic Chaucerian monk, fat, peevish, lazy, full of gossip and very human; Fra Melitone is conceivable only as a Christian friar. Clearly for Verdi, at least at this period, the reality of the Church was not in the vision in *I Lombardi,* the heavenly voices in *Giovanna d'Arco,* or even the theme of *Alzira;* these were the conventions of opera which, in spite of his best endeavor, remained for him always uninspired. The reality, as he saw it, was the monk cloaking his common humanity in the ill-fitting garb of a man of God.

The première of *Alzira* was not a fiasco. Verdi's operas were popular in Naples, particularly *Elvira d'Aragona* which, with changes to satisfy the censors, was *Ernani.* Naturally everyone went to see the new Verdi opera, and it had a respectable run with mixed notices. But when it opened in Rome in October, the audience sat through it almost in silence, and at Parma the following February it achieved only nine performances. After that, except for a very occasional revival, it dropped into a complete oblivion from which Verdi steadfastly refused to rescue it. After the Rome production he wrote a friend: "I am very thankful to you for your news about poor, unfortunate *Alzira,* and even more for the suggestions you are kind enough to make. In Naples, I too saw those weaknesses, before the opera was put on, and you can't imagine how long I thought them over! The ill is too deep-seated, and retouching would only make it worse."

One failure, however, did not affect Verdi's market value and, just as before, as soon as he returned to Milan, he was besieged by agents and publishers. One of the most important of these was Leon Escudier to whom Verdi, before leaving for Naples, had turned over the French rights to all his operas. Paris, with a population of more than a million, even excluding the surburbs, was the musical capital of the world, and a successful production at the Paris Opéra was the pole toward which all operatic composers finally turned. But a successful production was

not easy to achieve; there was intrigue on all levels, social, governmental and artistic, and a composer needed a good agent and often
a lawyer. Berlioz, the best French composer of the period, never did
achieve it, and Wagner, who had first presented *Tannhäuser* to Dresden
in 1845, succeeded in getting it to the Opéra only in 1861. Even then,
because Wagner refused to add a ballet in the second act, the production was the victim of organized demonstrations, and Wagner had to
withdraw the opera after the third performance. To the Opéra's shame
Tannhäuser did not reappear there until 1895.

Verdi succeeded where Wagner failed partly because Paris was always more ready to accept Italian music than German, partly because
of Escudier's industry and ability, and partly because, in spite of an
increasingly famous temperament, Verdi often demonstrated an ability
to compromise on smaller issues to gain the larger. With Merelli he
had insisted that *Nabucco* be presented in the Carnival season when the
singers Strepponi and Ronconi could appear in it, but then, having
won his point, he immediately agreed to secondhand scenery. Where
there was no larger issue as at Venice in the row over the horn and
the aria for the soprano, he could be the Bear from Busseto, obdurate,
rude and even ruthless. At the Opéra he recognized there was a tradition of ballet, and if asked he would write one to be inserted, even into
Otello; but the larger issue of a successful production was perfectly
clear.

There was also a tradition at the Opéra that all operas would be
presented in French, and with regard to this Verdi demonstrated an
admirable restraint. Escudier had started negotiations between the
Opéra and Verdi for a new opera, but these Verdi broke off, in spite
of the tremendous prestige involved, because he felt he could not compose to a French text. Later, after he had lived in Paris and become
more fluent in the language, he set two French librettos, but without
much success, so that his fears in 1845 were justified. Some of the
most successful lines in Verdi's operas occur where the music and text
fuse into a single sound so that, once heard, it becomes almost impossible to repeat the words without giving them Verdi's rhythm and
melody. He strove for just this sort of fusion by repeating the words
over and over to himself, and inevitably in a strange language the
subtleties of rhythm and sound would often be lost or jarring.

Meanwhile, beginning with *Nabucco* in October 1845, Escudier
arranged for productions in Paris, but in Italian, of *Nabucco, Ernani*

and *I Due Foscari*. As it turned out, this was the best way Verdi could have launched himself in the French capital: without pretension and with the fusion between text and music at its best for being untranslated. Also there was trouble over two of the operas. A French playwright succeeded in collecting a royalty on *Nabucco* by proving that Solera had stolen the subject from him, and, more important, the great Hugo refused to allow *Ernani* to play under that title so that it became *Il Proscritto*. Because the operas were presented at the small Théâtre Italien neither incident caused much excitement. But if either had occurred at the Opéra, particularly the one with Hugo in the opposition, the quelling of an Italian upstart might have become a *cause célèbre* in which all Paris would have reveled and which would have kept Verdi, like Wagner, out of Paris for many years. As it was, he succeeded easily to the position held there previously by Rossini, Bellini and Donizetti and was recognized as the leading Italian composer. This meant that his operas were performed regularly in Paris where impresarios from outside Italy saw them, and following these first productions in Paris, Verdi's more successful operas began to appear regularly in foreign cities. Thus, although Verdi and Wagner were born in the same year, 1813, Verdi's success came almost a generation ahead of Wagner's.

Besides Escudier from France there was also an English impresario, Benjamin Lumley, who had come to Milan to see Verdi. Lumley had staged a successful *Ernani* at His Majesty's Theatre in the spring of 1845 and now made arrangements to put on *Nabucco* and *I Lombardi*. The former had to be presented as *Nino* with the Biblical characters renamed, for London refused to have the Scriptures on the stage in an opera, although it was happy to have them on the stage in an oratorio. The public in London at this time was very knowledgeable about singing and cared nothing about the drama in opera. The performances were still lighted by gas, making it difficult to darken the auditorium, and there was a great deal of moving about and talking through all except the most popular arias. The result inevitably was to make an opera less of a drama and more of a concert in which the artists, in the tradition of the castrati, performed the individual arias, improvising cadenzas and adding special endings. This reached some sort of extreme when Lumley again presented *Ernani* in 1847 and cast Marietta Alboni, a contralto, in the baritone role of Don Carlo.

In Italy Verdi was as sought after as ever. Giovanni Ricordi had published most of the operas, but a competitor, Lucca, had published *Alzira*. Now in the autumn following the première of *Alzira* Verdi, who played one man against the other, agreed to do another opera for Lucca. Negotiations had started in March, and Verdi signed the contract in October. Meanwhile he had given Lucca six songs, three to poems by Maffei, all of which Lucca published in 1845 in an album ponderously dedicated to Don Giuseppe Salamanca, Gentleman of the Bedchamber of Her Majesty Donna Isabella II, Queen of Spain.

With one exception the songs are remarkably like the first six published in 1838; they are still sentimental, overdramatic and almost entirely vocal, although the last is not necessarily a fault. The exception is "Lo Spazzacamino," or "The Chimney Sweep," and it is a street cry set to music. The child stands in the street, calls up at the windows, shrugs and moves on. Unlike the other songs which usually are to be sung "melanconico" or "con espressione," this is to be "bright" and "joking," and for once Verdi uses the piano, with a waltz figure, to contrast with the voice rather than merely to accompany it. It is a slight song, but its charm endures; and it is interesting because in a vein unusual for Verdi and which he began to explore only in his later operas. Today it is the only one of all his songs to survive in an occasional performance.

One of its first exponents was Strepponi who sang it in Paris in two concerts she gave there in November 1846 and by which she introduced herself to the city's musical public. That autumn she had retired altogether from opera in Italy and gone alone to Paris to establish herself as a singing teacher for ladies wishing "to acquire a complete knowledge of the art." The concerts and the song must have gone well, for she succeeded in making a place for herself in the city and was able to send money to her family in Italy. There Lucca's wife, Giovannina, kept an eye on Strepponi's son, Camillino; the other child by now must have died, for Strepponi does not mention him in her letters.

Verdi's contract with Lucca required him to deliver the new opera to the publisher to be performed "in one of the leading theatres of Italy by a first-class company in Carnival of 1848 or within the year 1849 and in any case after *Attila* is produced." The contract was one of the first between a composer and a publisher rather than an impresario and reflects Verdi's position in Italy. Neither he nor Lucca anticipated any difficulty in placing a new Verdi opera in a "leading theatre."

Attila was the opera on which Verdi was working when he signed the contract with Lucca in October and which he expected to produce on New Year's Eve at the Fenice in Venice. He had refused all of Merelli's offers in favor of Conte Mocenigo and contracted, just as two years before, to stage a Verdi opera new to Venice on opening night of the Carnival season and then later to produce a Verdi world première. Before it had been *I Lombardi* and *Ernani;* now it was to be *Giovanna d'Arco* and *Attila.* The Fenice company was still largely the same with Sofia Loewe the reigning diva and Carlo Guasco the tenor. In addition Verdi was promised as a bass Ignazio Marini, who had sung at the première of *Oberto.*

The opera *Attila* was to be based on a play by a Zacharias Werner, and it promised to have all the virtues that *Alzira* lacked. The subject involved an invasion of Italy by the Huns, the founding of Venice as the citizens of Aquileia take refuge in the lagoons of the Adriatic, and finally the death of Attila as the Huns withdraw. For a stage picture there was the meeting between Attila and Pope Leo I in which the Pope persuades Attila not to invade Rome, a historic event of 452 A.D. As a libretto it had all the obvious appeal of *I Lombardi.*

Verdi had first considered *Attila* as a possible libretto immediately after *Ernani,* and he and Piave had begun to work on it once, Verdi urging Piave to read Mme. de Staël's *De l'Allemagne* for the background. But then it had been put aside while Verdi did other operas for Rome, Milan and Naples, and meanwhile he had taken the libretto away from Piave and given it to Solera whose ability to write a flaming, patriotic line, in Verdi's opinion, was considerably greater than that of the mild-mannered Piave. But Piave at least was reliable, whereas Solera soon proved he was not. He was supposed to have the libretto ready on Verdi's return from Naples, but he did not. Then the weeks in September and October went by with Muzio trotting from Verdi to Solera and generally returning empty-handed. Once Muzio reported with provincial indignation at the ways of Bohemia that Solera was still in bed at eleven o'clock in the morning.

Toward the end of October Solera finally produced the finished libretto, and soon after he left for Spain where he continued his flamboyant life, reports coming back to Milan that he had graced the bed of the Queen. Later, in Venice, Verdi had to ask Piave to make some small changes in the libretto and write a few additional verses. *Attila* was the last libretto Solera did for Verdi; in all, of Verdi's first nine operas he had done four, *Nabucco, I Lombardi, Giovanna d'Arco* and *Attila,* and some work on a fifth, *Oberto.* During this period he was famous as Verdi's librettist, and it is only as such that history takes note of him. His departure broke another of Verdi's ties to La Scala and Milan. He was one of the few men in Verdi's world of success and fame that stretched back past *Nabucco* to the early days of Margherita and the children. With him went some part of Verdi's youth. But the two men were never intimate, and they parted probably without regret, for Verdi was in a state of nervous irritation at the delay in receiving the libretto.

To make matters worse Verdi promptly fell ill again, this time with a severe attack of rheumatism. Muzio wrote to Busseto, recounting the symptoms and reporting that Verdi "was now a little better; we rub him continually." But after a year of ill health Verdi did not recover quickly, and when he arrived at Venice in December, he could neither rehearse *Giovanna d'Arco* nor even attend the Christmas Eve performance of it at which the Emperor of Russia was present. He did compose a new aria for Sofia Loewe to insert in the opera, and it was applauded. But as a whole the opera was not a success in Venice. As Verdi himself admitted: "É andata fredda fredda"; literally "it went cold cold." The best news for Verdi in Venice was that before he had arrived the Teatro di San Benedetto had successfully produced *Un Giorno di Regno.* Verdi was delighted.

But it was no consolation to Conte Mocenigo that a rival theatre had succeeded with a Verdi failure while with *Giovanna d'Arco* he seemed to be failing with what in Milan had been a success. The *Attila* première grew more important as each week it was postponed. Happily or unhappily Verdi was often so obviously ill that there seems to have been no hard feelings over the delay. He worked slowly at finishing the orchestration, rehearsing the singers, collecting notes on the scenery and costumes until finally on 17 March 1846, two and a half months late, the opera had its première. It was a success and, like *Ernani,* one that increased with each performance.

Solera's libretto is sloppy in detail; there is, for example, a "chorus of hermits," and some of the lines important for exposition are buried in passing phrases. A greater defect, for anyone not an Italian under

Austrian occupation, is that Attila is easily the most sympathetic character, and although the opera was performed outside Italy it did not rival the success of *Ernani*. Within Italy almost the entire opera became a battle cry. When the Venetian audience saw the Huns appear on the Adriatic shore, it burst into cries of "Italia! Italia!" Some of Solera's lines passed directly into the language, such as when the Roman says to Attila: "Avrai tu l'universo, resti l'Italia a me" (You take the universe, leave Italy to me). Verdi's music for the phrase was particularly happy, and the duet between Attila, bass, and the Roman, baritone, in which the words are a recurring phrase is vibrantly alive and with a masculine vigor that was peculiarly Verdi's. Invariably the audience shouted back at the stage: "A noi! l'Italia a noi!" (Italy for us!) It seems extraordinary that the censors allowed the line or any part of the libretto to pass.

At the time in Italy censorship varied from state to state and was, paradoxically, least serious in those two provinces which Austria actually occupied as its dependent Kingdom of Lombardy-Venetia. The presence there of the Austrian army gave its government confidence so that it was less easily alarmed than the smaller states, such as Modena or that of the Pope. These had to rely on "calling in" the Austrians, which took time and left a hazardous interim. But perhaps more important was that the censorship in Milan and Venice was intended to support a foreign administration; elsewhere, such as at Rome or Naples, it was intended to support a native administration. The difference strongly affected the loyalty and diligence of those Italians who worked in the various censors' offices. In Naples the censors recognized that a change in government would cost them their job, but in Milan and Venice they considered, perhaps incorrectly, that a change in government would simply cost the Austrians their jobs. It is not surprising then that the greatest trouble Verdi had with censors occurred in Naples.

What the censors objected to also varied with the states, so that as an opera traveled from city to city different changes would be made in it. *Ernani* appeared under at least three other titles as *Elvira d'Aragona*, *Il Corsaro di Venezia* and *Il Proscritto*. There was some pattern to it. The Papal States and its bishops elsewhere tended to object only to religious scenes, such as the baptism in *I Lombardi*. Austria cared little about these but much about scenes inciting patriotism and cries for a united Italy. Naples, where the Bourbon throne was insecure, censored anything that might undermine the principle of the Divine Right of Kings but sometimes considered that demonstrations of Italian patriotism could be turned to its own uses. Beyond this there was no pattern and often there seemed to be no purpose. Who in Naples was fooled or preserved from sin by changing *Giovanna d'Arco* in title and setting into *Orietta di Lesbo,* or in Palermo when *Attila* was retitled *Gli Unni ed i Romani?*

Verdi was pleased with *Attila* although all he would allow himself to write in a letter to the Contessa Maffei was: "It is not inferior to the others." He was accused by some critics, however, of writing a pot-boiler, and whether his accusers were hostile or friendly they at least assumed that he had more in him than merely to repeat *I Lombardi.* For many years, particularly in the first quarter of the present century, it was a cliché of Verdi criticism to say that after *Ernani* he entered a "bad period" when he turned out a series of operas that succeeded for political and not musical reasons. This allowed the critics to scold Verdi for not being a serious musician and to dismiss the operas as unworthy of attention. Today criticism tends to take a different view. It concedes that *Attila* succeeded in part for non-musical reasons, but it points out that the orchestration is much better than in *I Lombardi,* that while there is nothing perhaps as good as the trio in that opera the writing throughout *Attila* is far more uniformly good, and that for all of the Pope Leo scene the opera is less stagy and more of a human drama. Verdi, in fact, was attempting to use all he had learned and was continuing to move toward the sort of human opera at which he later excelled. If he moved slowly, it was partly because he had much to learn, not only about opera production, but about himself. Verdi at thirty-two probably had seen and partaken in only as many opera productions as either Mozart or Rossini by the time they were twenty-one.

CHAPTER 14

THE BUSINESS END OF ART
AND *MACBETH*

1846–1847; AGE, 32–33

MAFFEI, who had gone to Venice for the *Attila* première, accompanied Verdi back to Milan and left him in Muzio's care. To the anxious group in Busseto Muzio reported: "He has lost a good deal of weight, but his eyes are bright and his color fairly good; a rest will put him on his feet again."

Muzio's letters describe a pleasant convalescence, and a few weeks later he reported to Barezzi that Verdi "continues to keep well and to put on weight. He does nothing in the way of writing or study but amuses himself with walks or drives in one of the five or six carriages at his disposal. All the lords and ladies who pay court to him compete among themselves to amuse him. Sometimes around noon he goes out to the country either to Monza, Cassano or Traviaglio by boat, and returns home at five, then dines. In the evening he goes to bed early and sleeps well. If he continues to follow this routine he will soon be completely well again."

In fact Lucca, with whom Verdi had a contract to write an opera for the "Carnival of 1848 or within the year 1849," began to press and wanted to pay Verdi the first installment on the contract. Verdi refused; there was plenty of time, and as evidence that he was sick he sent Lucca a doctor's certificate which solemnly stated that Verdi in his present condition could not "write music, without grave risk to his health and perhaps even to his life." From Venice Verdi had sent a similar certificate to the English impresario Lumley. But neither Lumley nor Lucca was impressed.

From England Lumley sent letters describing his production of

I Lombardi, which the Court had attended and Queen Victoria applauded. Royal applause, Lumley assured Verdi, would cure any ill. Also London, in any season an exciting city, was at its best in summer. Verdi could come in short stages. To all of which Verdi replied: "My curiosity to see a city as extraordinary as London, my pride and interest were sufficient reasons why ordinarily I would not delay to fulfill my contract with Signor Lucca. But my illness holds me back and I need a complete rest." Still Lumley was eager and, undoubtedly supported by Lucca, remained unconvinced. In the end he sent his brother to Milan to talk to Verdi. But Verdi refused to discuss a trip to London or a new opera; there was plenty of time and his certificates, he insisted, were evidence of his good faith. Any new opera, at least for the moment, would simply have to be postponed. He resented the pressure, which he felt questioned his word, and he blamed Lucca, who was in Milan and to some extent acting as agent for the distant Lumley, who obviously had to rely on what others told him about Verdi's health and plans.

The certificates are not very convincing. Most persons tend to exaggerate their ills, Italians perhaps more than others. Only the past winter in Venice, Verdi, while finishing *Attila,* had described himself as "almost dying," and Garibaldi in his *Autobiography* describes how as a young man he was "mortally wounded." Lucca perhaps was justified in ignoring the certificates, but there were other signs of Verdi's ill health which Lucca might have noticed and considered. The *Attila* première, for example, had been in March, two and a half months late, and by July Verdi still had not signed a contact with anyone for a new opera. He was not discriminating against Lucca; he had, in fact, refused to write for the Paris Opéra although offered a new libretto, and he was replying vaguely to propositions from Naples. During all this time he was on a diet of "Gratz water," the recipe for which he noted in his *Copialettere:* "Water and milk, mixed; at first three and then four glasses a day. Exercise and perspiration essential."

In July Verdi, again accompanied by Maffei, went to Recoaro, a tiny watering place in the foothills of the Venetian Alps and famous for its iron baths. For both the trip was an act of frendship, Maffei to keep an eye on the ailing Verdi and Verdi to distract the agitated Maffei who the previous month had separated from his wife. The separation had surprised no one, not even Maffei, who knew his own faults well. But the finality of it had shaken him, and Verdi reported to the Contessa that her Andrea had passed some "very sad moments."

The sick man and the sad one were hardly a gay pair, and after several weeks of the mountain air, the walks and baths Verdi was bored. His sore throat still bothered him, and he complained of headaches from the sun. Journalists and gossips one minute had him dead, the next leaving for Paris, so that Muzio in Milan wrote Barezzi to tell Verdi's father that: "The Maestro left Milan in good health and if he had been ill he would not have undertaken that journey [to Recoaro], and he must not pay any attention to idle gossip." Poor Carlo Verdi may have been as much irritated by Muzio's big-city tone as consoled to learn the true state of his son's health.

Verdi returned from Recoaro to Milan at the end of July with three librettos in mind. One, for which Maffei had agreed to write the libretto, was to be based on Schiller's play *Die Räuber,* or *The Robbers.* This in time became the opera *I Masnadieri.* Another was to be based on Grillparzer's *Die Ahnfrau,* which Verdi called *Avola,* and although he did considerable work on the libretto he never composed for it. The third was to be an opera based on Shakespeare's *Macbeth.* As it turned out, this last was the first completed although Verdi first began composing for *I Masnadieri.* One of the three he planned to give Lucca and Lumley for a première in London and another to Alessandro Lanari, the impresario of the Teatro della Pergola at Florence.

Lanari had played the role of impresario with skill. In June at the Teatro della Pergola he had produced *Attila* with great success, and, whether it was originally his idea or not, when he arrived in Milan to see Verdi, the leading families of Florence had already subscribed to and presented Verdi with an album in which they expressed their "most respectful admiration and looked forward to the pleasure of knowing him." Inevitably Verdi felt a rush of sympathy for the Florentines, particularly as their city, the home of Dante and Michelangelo, had such a unique position in Italian history and culture.

But Lanari did more. He consulted with Verdi about the singers and conductors Verdi wanted to have in the Pergola company. There was, for example, a new conductor, Angelo Mariani, who was only twenty-five and had begun to make an international name for himself. By training he was a violinist but in 1844, in Messina, he began conducting and in 1846 in Milan he appeared, not at La Scala, but at the Teatro Re and then later at the Teatro Carcano. At both theatres he had conducted operas by Verdi, *I Due Foscari, I Lombardi, Giovanna*

MARIANI

d'Arco and *Nabucco*. In *I Lombardi* he had himself played the famous violin solo before the trio and made of it one of the most exciting events of the season. Verdi wanted Mariani, and Lanari tried to engage him. But Mariani's price was too high, and the following year instead of to Florence he went to Copenhagen where he conducted at the Court Theatre. Lanari, although his efforts had been unsuccessful, had created a sympathetic atmosphere which stimulated Verdi to work, and in the correspondence between the two men on the question of which libretto and which singers Verdi's increasing excitement is evident.

Lucca, on the other hand, seemed to have lost, at least temporarily, his touch in dealing with an artist. Not only did he try to hurry Verdi; he also argued with him about the subject. Verdi had first planned to do an opera, *Il Corsaro,* based on Byron's *The Corsair,* a romantic, swashbuckling poem about a Greek pirate fighting the Turks. The poem was very popular in Italy where its overtones of the fight for Greek independence vibrated strongly, and where Garibaldi with his amphibious expeditions in South America seemed to be the corsair in action. But Verdi had decided against it, preferring the dramatic situations in *I Masnadieri.* He considered that by his contract the choice of libretto was his alone, but even so he informed Lucca. To his surprise and indignation Lucca attempted to argue with him, but not for long, for Lucca was too experienced to think he could acquire a successful Verdi opera by arguing with the composer. But it was another irritation between the two men and another reason why Lanari rather than Lumley produced the next Verdi opera and Ricordi rather than Lucca published it.

The question was which opera would it be, *I Masnadieri* or *Macbeth?* Verdi was prepared to do either. By September he had started on the music for *I Masnadieri,* but he also had written the prose libretto for *Macbeth* and sent it to Piave to turn into verse. The decision depended on the singers Lanari could sign for the spring season. *I Masnadieri* needed a leading tenor, and *Macbeth* did not, for in his aural imagination Verdi heard Macbeth as a baritone.

The tenor Verdi wanted for *I Masnadieri* was Gaetano Fraschini, one of the great tenors of the time and who had sung in the première of *Alzira.* But he was under contract elsewhere. A second choice was Napoleone Moriani, but during the summer Verdi heard him sing at Bergamo and thought his voice had disintegrated. In the end Merelli signed the tenor with the poor voice for La Scala, and Lanari and Verdi, without regret, went ahead with *Macbeth.*

The decision once made, others fell more easily into place. Lumley came to Milan himself and had congenial talks with Verdi. They agreed that if Flauto in Naples would release Verdi from a promise to write for the Teatro San Carlo in the spring of 1847, then Verdi would go to London and produce *I Masnadieri* in late June or early July. This schedule allowed Verdi only three months after the première of *Macbeth* to compose and produce another opera, and inevitably some of the time would be taken up by the trip to England. But with the libretto in hand and the music started, Verdi was confident he could do it. He refused to consider doing *Il Corsaro* on the ground that the time was too short to start a new work. In the end Flauto stepped aside, probably wondering whether he had lost another *Alzira* or an *Ernani.*

The question of Verdi's contracts, promises and half promises to producers and publishers is very confused and reflects the eternal problem of the artist and businessman attempting together to produce a commercially successful venture. Impresarios must work by contract; it is the only way they can assemble a company. But the contracts in an important sense are meaningless. No impresario, even when backed by a court, can force a soprano to sing well or an orchestra not to play sloppily. Ultimately the artistic success of any venture depends on the atmosphere the impresario can create within his company and around the work. Good impresarios recognize this and tend to back away from ventures that start off antagonizing any important party, regardless of what the legal rights and duties of the parties may be. Probably Flauto recognized that at least for the spring of 1847 Verdi's mind and interests were elsewhere and no good would come of trying to force them down to Naples, regardless of what letters had been exchanged or promises made.

The composer at the time had a different problem. He might, like Verdi, have three or four librettos in mind, but which would actually work up into an opera he could not know until his inspiration made itself practical by a contract with an impresario. Opera composition was still thought of by everyone as being done essentially in the theatre rather than the study. Hindsight can see that this was already beginning to change, but Verdi and his colleagues simply thought of themselves as being merely better prepared to begin work when they arrived at the theatre, sketches in hand. But the orchestration and even the arias were often composed after rehearsals began. A result of this system was a constant correspondence between impresarios and composers about possible librettos and suitable singers. Out of these embryonic discussions arose many of the promises and half promises which either party broke or tried to enforce as it suited his interest.

Verdi did not take easily to this system. Under it flourished certain abilities, perhaps even virtues, that he lacked: glib talk, subtle harassment and frequently the substitution of something different for the thing promised, in short, an ability in a man to pledge his word and then be able to talk his way around it. Verdi, after the discussions had become specific, was always trying to reduce them to writing, so that both sides would know what their rights were. His efforts were a credit to his sense of honor: he wanted his word to be good. But it was often a style of business ill adapted to the problems of producing opera in the theatre and unnecessarily irritating in its legalistic tone. Verdi wrote to Lucca: "When you write be sure to remind Lumley of the stipulation I called to his attention in my letter of the 11th of November, namely that he give me the singers he promised in a confidential conversation. Mr. Lumley must now write me a letter specifically assuring me those singers and at the same time giving me the right to choose from his company." (etc.)

Confidential conversations are almost impossible to prove in court so that Verdi's tone is out of place. Probably Lumley merely sighed, noted for future reference that Verdi was strong on "his rights," and then went ahead promising to produce the two singers without any real certainty that he could. They were to be a soprano, Brambilla, and the tenor, Fraschini. When the opera was produced it was without either, and Verdi made no objection. Lumley, if he remembered the letter at all, probably smiled to think of the huffing and puffing that had blown itself out.

Verdi began composing *Macbeth* in October. At first it went slowly, but he kept at it steadily and his life developed a routine. He rose early and worked three or four hours in the morning either at the piano or a long table where Muzio also did his exercises or wrote letters for Verdi. Then he had lunch, always with Muzio, which was followed by an hour of billiards and then more work until the evening. Sometimes he went to the theatre, sometimes to visit Mme. Appiani or the Contessa Maffei, and even to these places he often took Muzio with him.

Muzio reveled in the life; and when Barezzi wrote him about a musical post near Busseto that was open and for which there would be the usual competition, Muzio would not consider it. He put his reasons in simple, human terms: Verdi had done everything for him and to leave his Maestro now would be ungrateful. He recognized that there were conflicting loyalties: "Some will say the needs of my family are great, I understand that myself. But they've been patient for two years now, and I hope that for another year at most they won't die of hardship. Please tell my mother about all these things, because I haven't the heart to write them to her." (etc.)

Barezzi did not urge Muzio to return. He understood the glamor of Verdi and music in Milan. Perhaps, too, he recognized that the standard of musical culture in country towns like Busseto was declining. There was less interest than in Provesi's day; fewer men played instruments and those who did often played them less well. Perhaps the political agitation of the period absorbed men's time and interest; perhaps the growth of the cities, a symptom of the Industrial Age, was already tending to pull the artists ever more tightly into fewer and bigger cities. Ten years earlier Busseto had not offered enough to hold Verdi; now there was even less to hold Muzio. But it must have been hard to explain to Muzio's mother.

So Muzio stayed on in Milan. In December he wrote Barezzi: "*Macbeth* is going better and better. What sublime music! I can tell you that there are things in it that thrill you. It costs him a great deal of hard work to compose music like that, but he succeeds very, very well."

Part of the cost for Verdi was that as soon as he got into the composition of the opera his sore throat returned. But now, having learned from *Alzira* and *Attila* what havoc ill health could cause, he paced himself more slowly. He made some small changes in *I Due Foscari* for the Paris production and in *Attila* for the production at La Scala, but until *Macbeth* was finished he refused to take on any new work. One such refusal he particularly regretted. It was an invitation to compose a cantata for performance in Rome to celebrate the election in June of the new Pope, Pius IX or, as he has been universally known, Pio Nono.

The old Pope, Gregory XVI, had died in June 1846, eighty-one years old and almost a recluse. He had been elected in 1831, the same year in which revolutionaries had driven Marie Louise from Parma to Piacenza, and in the first three weeks of Gregory's reign the same men had unseated his government in all his principal cities except Rome, Rieti and Orvieto. Gregory, who was a saintly Camaldolese monk with a reputation for learning, appealed to Metternich for Austrian troops and quelled the revolt by force. Thereafter he governed his rebellious cities also by force, using his priests and police as informers, organizing bully squads out of those who enjoyed violence, and making hundreds of secret arrests. Many of his citizens, including the future Pio Nono, protested. But Gregory made no effort to resolve the discontent of his subjects except by putting them in dungeons or driving them into exile. When he died, the Papal States were becoming a European problem, and many more than just Italians hoped for a more liberal successor.

The new Pope, Pio Nono, was young, only fifty-four; but in the first weeks of his reign that was almost all that was known about him. But from Imola, a small city near Bologna and of which Pio Nono had been the bishop, began to come reports that he was a good administrator, merciful and, above all, liberal. Then a month and a day after his election, on 17 July 1846, he astonished Rome and, as the news spread, Metternich and the whole of Europe by granting an amnesty to more than a thousand of the proscribed who had lead the revolution of 1831–32.

The political effect of this act was enormous, far greater undoubtedly than Pio Nono had expected. He probably viewed his amnesty as an

PIO NONO

act of local mercy affecting only the less culpable of the revolutionaries who were, after all, citizens of his state. But as news of it spread
he became, whether he liked it or not, the political symbol and leader
of reform for almost all groups of the disgruntled. Everywhere in Italy
his name was stitched into banners and scratched on walls. At Florence, as if to suggest a cantata by Verdi on the subject, the audience
at performances of *Ernani* changed the words of the finale to Act III
from "A Carlo Quinto sia gloria ed onor" to "A Pio Nono" (be glory
and honor). At Rome huge crowds gathered night after night before
the Quirinal Palace to receive his blessing. He was the most popular
Pope in memory, and through the summer everything he did or proposed increased his popularity. He talked of lighting the streets of Rome
with gas, of building railways and improving agriculture. Everywhere
liberals of all shades hailed him as a progressive Pope who would finally
lead the Papacy out of the Middle Ages.

For a number of reasons the political position of the Pope at the
time was peculiarly powerful. He was, of course, the political head
of a large state straddling the center of the peninsula. But more than
that, a priest named Gioberti had recently proposed in a book, *Il
Primato,* that the various states of Italy, in order to achieve independence from foreign interference, federate in a union under the Pope as
president.

The possibility of such a federation created tremendous excitement.
The idea seemed to offer something to all classes, priest, peasant and

political liberals in the towns. Everyone could unite behind a liberal Pope, making it easier to expel Austria and start a bloodless economic revolution. In the first years of his reign every action of the new Pope was awaited, watched and discussed by everyone. No historical event of the decade was as widely known in Italy and as generally acclaimed as his election. On the first anniversary of it beacons burned up and down the peninsula, and the *Te Deum* was sung in churches.

To all this excitement Verdi was asked to contribute a cantata, perhaps twenty minutes of "gloria ed onor a Pio Nono." It would have required only two or three good tunes with choral background, a potboiler in fact. The prestige would have been enormous, and the circumstances strongly appealed to his patriotism and sense of Italian history. But he refused; he was beginning to learn how to pace himself. He was nervous about his health, and also he was fully engrossed in *Macbeth*.

Verdi also refused, and under circumstances that do him little credit, either to conduct or direct the rehearsals of Merelli's production of *Attila* at La Scala. Merelli, gossip reported, was facing financial ruin. His last seasons in Milan and Vienna had not been successful, and he was even supposed to have mortgaged or sold his house in Milan to finance the Carnival season at La Scala. Against this background Verdi and Lucca, who controlled the Italian rights of *Attila,* tried to charge Merelli such an exorbitant fee that the Chief of Police stepped into the negotiations on Merelli's behalf and reduced it.

From any point of view Verdi's part in this seems mean. His later actions show that he was not interested in the money; he wanted to penalize Merelli, to kick the man who gave him his start when that man was down. Verdi's life contains few such vindictive acts, and the best explanation of this one seems to be artistic: Verdi felt Merelli was deliberately and unnecessarily putting on sloppy productions of opera. The productions at the Teatro Re and Carcano with the conductor Mariani had demonstrated what could be done even with smaller means. Why wasn't Mariani conducting at La Scala? Why for his leading tenor did Merelli continue to hire Moriani, whose voice was failing, instead of Fraschini, whose voice was fresh.

When Verdi saw Merelli's production of *Attila,* he admitted that the cast, including the unfortunate tenor, was good. But the production infuriated him. In the scene where dawn was supposed to break gradually over the Venetian lagoons, the sun was up before the music;

the sea remained calm when the music was rough; throughout the storm, the sun shone like a spring day; the hermits had no huts, the priests no altars, and Attila had to eat through his banquet without a torch or oak log burning. In short, a rotten production.

In negotiating his contract with Ricordi for publishing *Macbeth*, Verdi, after referring to the production of *Attila,* insisted: "I repeat, therefore, that I cannot and must not allow a performance of *Macbeth* at La Scala, at least not until there has been a change for the better. I felt obliged to let you know for your own guidance, that this stipulation which I now make for *Macbeth* goes for all my operas from now on." In fact Verdi's connection with La Scala had ended, not to be resumed until 1869. The theatre continued under various managements to produce his operas, but it had no premières or productions directed and conducted by Verdi, which even the tiny theatre in Rimini achieved.

As if determined to show Merelli what a good production might be, Verdi worked over every aspect of *Macbeth*. He wrote to London to find out how Banquo's ghost was usually brought on-stage. He studied costumes of the period, built models, drew diagrams of the staging and instructed the designer, who had started wrong, on Scottish history: "Macbeth's period is much later than Ossian and the Roman Empire." Then as a piece of show-off, for he must have known it would mean nothing to the designer, he added a list of contemporaneous English kings: "In England in 1039 the king was Harold, called 'King of the Hares' and a Dane; he was succeeded in the same year by Hardicanute, uterine brother of 'Odoardo il confessore' ecc." Actually Harold was known as "Harefoot," and Verdi by his unfortunate mis-translation had libelled an entire nation. But no doubt the designer was too stunned by the scholarship to question it.

As always there was trouble with the singers. This time it involved the bass hired to sing Banquo. The man saw no reason why *he* should reappear for a few minutes, and mute, as Banquo's ghost. It was an unimportant role; let someone unimportant do it. He was soon convinced otherwise. A disappointment for Verdi was that Sofia Loewe could not sing Lady Macbeth. Her voice had suddenly gone and the next year she retired from the theatre and married a Prince Liechtenstein. The substitute for Loewe was a Marianna Barbieri-Nini. Macbeth was to be sung by Felice Varesi, a baritone lucky in his three Verdi premières, for he was also the first Rigoletto and the first

Giorgio Germont in *La Traviata*.

By January Verdi had the opera completely sketched and had begun on the orchestration, which he usually did not start until he arrived at the theatre. He also on this opera began to change his method of composition, leaving until the last the final form of many of the arias. The usual method of composition at the time was to compose the arias first and then later connect them. Now Verdi began to reverse the order. Probably he had in mind exactly what the aria would be like, but by composing the introduction and closing bars first he tended to de-emphasize the aria and make the scene more of a unified piece, tipping the balance further toward drama and away from musical pattern.

Verdi arrived in Florence just a month before the première and began the rehearsals at once. He took Muzio with him to play the piano accompaniments. The soprano, Mme. Barbieri-Nini, years later wrote a description of that month of rehearsals. She stated that Verdi rehearsed the duet in the first act between herself and Varesi, the baritone:

More than one hundred and fifty times so that it might be, as Verdi used to say, more *spoken than sung*. And, imagine this. The evening of the final rehearsal, with a theatre full of guests, Verdi made the artists put on their costumes, and when he insisted on something, woe to anyone contradicting him. When we were dressed and ready, the orchestra in the pit, the chorus on stage, Verdi signalled to me and Varesi to follow him into the wings. There he explained that he wanted us to accompany him to the foyer for another piano rehearsal of that accursed duet.

"Maestro," I protested. "We are already in these Scottish costumes; how can we?"

"Put a cloak over them."

And Varesi, annoyed at the strange request, dared to raise his voice: "But we've already rehearsed it a hundred and fifty times, for God's sake!"

"I wouldn't say that again for within half an hour it will be a hundred and fifty-one!"

He was a tyrant who had to be obeyed. I can still remember the black look Varesi shot at Verdi as he followed the Maestro into the foyer. With his hand clutching the pommel of his sword he seemed about to murder Verdi even as later he would murder King Duncan.

But even Varesi gave in, and the hundred-and-fifty-first rehearsal took place, while the impatient audience made an uproar in the theatre. But anyone who merely said that the duet was enthusiastically received would be saying nothing at all; for it was something incredible, new, unimagined. (etc.)

The lady's count of rehearsals surely inflated with the years, but the picture of Verdi as a theatrical tyrant is accurate. He was constitutionally unable to keep from poking his finger in every pie, and his concept of an opera composer included far more than merely providing the music. Like Wagner in later years in Germany, Verdi now in Italy began a revolution in operatic staging. Even a dress rehearsal was a thing "unimagined." But Verdi, with the power of his popularity, was in a position to force old and reluctant performers to learn new tricks. And during the period of the *Macbeth* rehearsals he was only thirty-three.

The première on 14 March was a success. Barezzi, whom Verdi had urged to come, counted thirty-eight times that Verdi was called on stage. Barbieri-Nini has described how, after the sleep-walking scene, Verdi looked in on her on his way back to the pit:

The storm of applause had not yet died down, and I was standing in my dressing room, trembling and exhausted, when the door flew open—I was already half undressed—and Verdi stood before me. He gesticulated and his lips moved as if he wished to make a speech, but not a word came out. I was laughing, crying and could not say anything either. But I saw that his eyes, too, were red. He squeezed my hand hard, hard, and rushed out. That moment of real emotion paid me back many times over for the months of hard work and continuous agitation.

Ten days later Verdi wrote Barezzi who had returned to Busseto:

Florence, 25 March 1847

Dear Father-in-law,

For a long time I have wished to dedicate an opera to you who have been for me a father, benefactor and friend. It is a duty I should have done sooner, and I would have if circumstances had not prevented me. Now, here is this *Macbeth* which I love more than all my other operas and which I think the most worthy to present to you. It comes from my heart: let yours receive it, and let it be always a witness of the gratitude and affection borne for you by

Your most affectionate

G. VERDI

With the première behind him Verdi had a chance to enjoy the city, and the Florentines, true to their invitation, were eager to know and entertain him. The Grand Duke invited him to a reception at the Palazzo Pitti, and the intellectuals, sculptors, historians and poets took turns giving him tours of the city and its galleries. What impressed him most of all were the works of Michelangelo; his friends were impressed with his interest and knowledge of painting and sculpture.

At each performance the opera was cheered and in the summer it began the round of the Italian theatres. But it soon became clear that it was not to be one of his most popular. At Parma, for example, it had fewer performances than *Ernani, Nabucco, I Lombardi* or *I Due Foscari*. It was far from unsuccessful; like the others, it played all over the world. But neither London nor Paris produced it, and it became a specialty rather than a staple of the repertory. Over the years this grieved Verdi, and almost twenty years later, in 1865, he revised it for its first Paris production. But again it was not a great success. In this revised version it hung on the edge of the general repertory in Italy but nowhere else. Then in Germany in the 1930s it suddenly reappeared as part of a general Verdi revival and since then has been presented, often for the first time, in most of the important theatres. Verdi would be pleased; it has outlasted by many years *I Lombardi* or *I Due Foscari*.

The revision, at least for modern ears, was an improvement and it is now the familiar version of the opera. But the changes did not affect the first act, which contains the much-rehearsed duet, or the sleep-walking scene, the two which Verdi felt were the heart of the opera. So by examining these it is possible to see what Verdi was trying to do in 1847 and speculate on why the opera was a success and yet not popular.

A comparison of the first act in *Macbeth* (p. 182) and *Ernani* (p. 130) will show the transformation Verdi was working in the form of opera. In the first scene the pattern of slow to fast is the same, but in *Macbeth* Verdi introduces two characters at the same time who will have different reactions to the prophecies. The scene is inherently far more dramatic. Lady Macbeth is introduced in the same style as Elvira, but Lady Macbeth's cabaletta is triggered by the announcement of Duncan's arrival that night and reflects her decision to murder him. Elvira has no such dramatic reason for her fast aria. Verdi here is essentially only making better use of an old form. But with Macbeth's arrival he begins to use a new form of melodic recitative. Others, including himself, had used it briefly, but it was unusual to

ACT I SCENE 1
(a wood near a battlefield)

THE WITCHES	chorus (slow)	they gather to await Macbeth; as he approaches, they swirl in a dance.
MACBETH and BANQUO	recitative (long and varied)	the witches give their prophecies to the two men who exclaim at them; messengers arrive, hailing Macbeth as Thane of Cawdor.
	duet with (slow) chorus	Macbeth thinks of being King as Banquo watches him carefully. The messengers wonder that Macbeth is not more pleased at being Cawdor.
THE WITCHES	chorus (fast)	Macbeth will return to see them again.

SCENE 2
(a hall in Macbeth's castle)

LADY MACBETH	recitative (short)	she reads Macbeth's letter describing the prophecy and wonders if he has the will to realize his ambition.
	aria (slow)	she wishes he'd come quickly to draw strength from her.
	messenger	he announces that Duncan, the King, is coming with Macbeth to spend the night in the castle.
	aria (fast)	she calls on the spirits of evil to "unsex me here"; Duncan must die that night. (This has a typical cabaletta ending with a rush of sound up the scale to a high note held long and at full volume.)
SPECTACLE of DUNCAN'S ARRIVAL	recitative (short)	arriving a moment before the King, Macbeth agrees, in a quick aside with Lady Macbeth, to murder him.
	March	Duncan arrives, and all go to their rooms.
MACBETH	recitative (long, varied and melodic)	he sees a dagger before him. He follows it into Duncan's room where he murders the King.
MACBETH and LADY MACBETH	recitative (short)	she fears he won't do it.
	duet (slow)	he is shaken by the deed; she encourages him.
	recitative (short and melodic)	she takes the dagger from him to leave it beside Duncan.
	duet (fast)	she urges him to come away as he mutters about the deed. (Although the cabaletta, this ends not on a high, loud note but a low, soft whisper.)

put such an important sequence as Macbeth's seeing the dagger before him in anything but an aria. And in the duet which follows, the voices respond to each other conversationally more often than they join. This demanded closer attention from the audience than it was accustomed to pay, for it still expected, in an only half-darkened auditorium, to chatter to its neighbor through all but the favorite arias. The audience also found the cabaletta confusing in that instead of ending with a rush of noise and excitement it ended in whispers, after which applause seemed incongruous. This made it hard for the singers who were used and trained to flamboyant closings calculated to excite the audience to applause. Undoubtedly Verdi rehearsed his singers so hard because, instead of going off shaken by the deed with subdued voice and gesture, they tended, even subconsciously, to exult in the murder by coming down to the footlights with head back and broad gesture. It was, after all, the close of the cabaletta.

In musical terms the sort of transformation Verdi was attempting can be seen in the closing bars of Lady Macbeth's arias. In the first act Verdi presents her in the *Ernani* style of two arias, slow and fast. The slow one ends:

gnar.   Che tar - di? Ac-cetta il do - no, a-scen - di - vi a re -

gnar. Che tar - di? Che tar - di?   Ah!

a - scen-di - vi a re - gnar.

And the cabaletta, going at high speed and full voice, ends:

gnal,   il   pu - gnal,*   no,   no,   non

veg - ga   il   pu - gnal, ————

pu - gnal.

* The dagger.

Both of these are in the old-fashioned, diluted castrati tradition of great singing. Persons who dislike this style of opera are always quick to point out that Lady Macbeth hardly would go about her castle at full voice detailing her plans to murder the King. Those who like it reply that the musical form is satisfying and, in this case, correctly reflects the lady's increased excitement.

Verdi ends the sleepwalking scene in a way that shows traces of the old style of brilliant ending but is fundamentally different:

Audiences at the time found this sort of ending and dramatic approach to the scene confusing. Only twelve years earlier Donizetti had done a mad scene for *Lucia di Lammermoor* which was exactly in current style: after trills, runs and general singing exhibition, the lady sang a high E flat as long and loud as she possibly could and then fell in a faint. Verdi's sleepwalking scene, which is in the direct tradition of presenting the soprano romantically distraught, has hardly a loud note in it, no trills and no runs except the last shown above, which must be sung slowly in a sleepily worried fashion.

There was of course much in the opera that was exactly as expected. There was a conspirators' chorus, this time of assassins gathering to kill Banquo; a patriotic chorus of Scottish exiles which, as always, aroused great enthusiasm; and some jiggy witches' music, not much better than that for the Heavenly Voices in *Giovanna d'Arco*. To modern ears these parts of the opera sound dated and incongruous beside the more dramatic writing. And if this mixture of styles kept *Macbeth* from being as great as *Rigoletto* or *La Traviata,* both of which came after it and were more of a piece, it probably also made it possible for the opera, as a very early venture into dramatic writing, to survive at all.

Why Verdi was introducing so much more drama into opera is a mystery. It is possible by careful selection of operas stretching back to Rossini's *William Tell* to demonstrate triumphantly that a trend toward drama existed. But it is not very illuminating because Verdi, the largest figure in Italian opera, is the predetermined end. Others, like Bellini, went to Shakespeare and found *Romeo and Juliet;* only Verdi composed to *Macbeth,* a story without any love interest of any sort, even in the secondary characters. And he did it at the height of the Romantic Age, when the tragic view of life expressed in blood and thunder revolved, at least on the stage, almost entirely around thwarted love. Yet Verdi took as his hero a middle-aged man, happily married.

Another mystery is why Verdi imagined Macbeth, and so many other of his leading men, as baritones. Here there is no question of a trend. Verdi is unique in the roles he gave to baritones, and in a sense he created the voice. Before Verdi many roles could be sung by both bass and baritone; Don Giovanni and Figaro in Mozart's operas are examples and even today are sung by both types of voice. This is not possible in Verdi's operas; he wrote the general level of the baritone voice considerably up and the bass voice slightly down. At the time critics and singers, or at least many of them, shrieked that he was ruining the collective baritone voice. But it seems he did not; today baritones suitable for Verdi are easier to find than tenors of any sort. The convention in opera was to give the leading male role to the tenor voice, and there were many great tenors at the time, perhaps more than at any time since. Why then in his operas did Verdi hear so many of the crucial roles as baritones? Just among the title roles there are Nabucco, Macbeth, Rigoletto, Boccanegra and Falstaff, stretching steadily from his first great success to his last.

As there are no sure answers to these questions, it is permissible to speculate. Verdi's background is unique among musicians in that he was essentially a farmer's son, and he remained in the market town of an agricultural community until he was eighteen. Most composers are children of the urban middle class and often of musicians. Verdi, a country child, grew up isolated from the excesses of city life where the folk change the cut of their clothes every few years. In theatrical terms this meant that Verdi did not share in the excesses of the Romantic Age in the theatre. He did not have his view of reality shaped by what he saw in the theatre because there was no regular theatre in Busseto, only an occasional passing troupe. For Verdi the theatre world could never become almost or even more real than the actual life around him as it sometimes does for the city child caught up in it. Verdi might read the literature in his room in Busseto, but as a reflection of what human behavior truly was like there was always the agricultural community, living, working and dying around him. He could respond to these things with a tragic view of life so that he was a Romantic but his point of view by the time of *Oberto* was too individual and well set for him to become part of a movement. His view of reality included something more than just what was currently fashionable. His eye could be right in style in seeing an opera in *Hernani,* but it could also in Shakespeare see more than just *Romeo and Juliet.*

In the same way, perhaps, the agricultural community influenced Verdi's ear so that he imagined so many of his characters as baritones. The tenor voice is to some extent an artificial creation of the theatre; it exists rarely and almost never without training. Yet composers write for it as if it were one of the common male voices, and a city child who has gone frequently to opera will think of it as such. Verdi in his work with the Philharmonic Society and the churches of Busseto probably seldom had a real tenor to work with, only high baritones. And all around him, on the street and in Barezzi's store, he would have heard the lower tone to an extent impossible for a city child whose father goes away to work and who spends almost the entire day among the piping voices of other children or women.

No other composer has such a masculine tone to his operas as Verdi. But then, perhaps, no other composer grew up in an agricultural community like Busseto where the men so completely dominated the life of the town, in church, school, field and store. Even today market day in Busseto, Tuesday, is an extraordinary demonstration of the position of the grown men in the community. The farmers begin gathering shortly after ten, many of them wearing the same black peasant's hat that Verdi wore all his life. By eleven the town's main street is packed with men, more than a thousand of them, buying articles, making deals, visiting. No women pass among them; all children are kept indoors; no traffic goes through the street. It is an extraordinary sight and it gives off an even more extraordinary sound. A low hum, unbroken by a single high voice, begins to shake the fronts of the buildings until the whole town seems to reverberate. After twelve the men begin to go home. In the afternoon, after the siesta, the women reappear to sweep the street and the children to ride their bicycles up and down it.

No social anthropologist could devise a more stunning object lesson for children on the position of the grown man in the community. The demonstration takes place once a week, not off in some distant business district where the children never go, but right on the main street where everyone can see it. Verdi saw and heard it; from it, perhaps, he learned that there was more to life than just young love with a tenor bawling. When he needed a sound for a character like Macbeth, he may have subconsciously heard it in the range of the farmers confidently talking in the main street of Busseto.

CHAPTER 15

PARIS, LONDON AND
I MASNADIERI

1847; AGE, 33

THE production of *I Masnadieri* in London was to be Verdi's first première outside of Italy and as such had a particular excitement for him. The prospect of it was also exciting London which had never before had a première by an important Italian composer, not by Rossini, Bellini, or Donizetti. London loved and honored great singing, and its impresarios regularly imported the best. But with a large proportion of their funds invested in the singers the impresarios not unnaturally preferred to present them in tried and true operas that would last the season. Lumley, by commissioning an opera from Verdi and persuading him to appear in person to stage and conduct it, showed great enterprise, and the city rewarded him with intense excitement.

In Milan Verdi finished the opera comfortably in time, but leaving as always the orchestration and details until he arrived at the theatre. He paid Maffei for the libretto and also gave him a gold watch and chain for some patchwork verses Maffei had done for *Macbeth*. Actually, in the end, Maffei, whose name never appeared on the libretto, had done more than just patchwork, for he had completely rewritten the sleepwalking scene. Verdi's gift and payment, which were both generous and more than what had been agreed upon, embarrassed Maffei. In a letter to Verdi he wondered if he could return the gift without offense but decided he lacked the courage. Then he added: "But if I must keep it, at least do not deny me the pleasure of accepting, also from you, two small memories that you know well. I mean your kindness which lifted a weight from my spirit, and your affection for me which I hope has not diminished. I am only a little happy, dear

Verdi; the loneliness in which I find myself would be sweet to an egoist, but I need friendship and yours in particular; you could not take it from me without breaking my heart. Do not speak of sacrifice when you want something from me. My pen and poor talent are for all time your servants. Addio."

Macbeth, in its first year, seemed to be having a success. Impresarios from most of the Italian houses, except La Scala, were negotiating for it, and from London Lumley was offering five times what his rival at Covent Garden would pay if he could have exclusive English rights to it. But Ricordi, who controlled the rights, had a contract with Covent Garden which could not be broken. With *I Masnadieri* Verdi hoped to give Lumley a counterattraction.

He left Milan in the last week of May with Muzio. For both it was their first trip to Paris and London and, except on Verdi's part for a quick trip to Vienna for Merelli's production of *Nabucco,* the first time out of Italy. Verdi's French was usable if not yet fluent, but he knew almost no English or German. Muzio was no better off for languages, and his French was even less good.

They had expected at Strasbourg to take a coach for Paris, but they missed the connection, and, according to Muzio, Verdi "got the whim" to go down the Rhine to Brussels. In a letter to Barezzi, written the very day they arrived in Paris, Muzio describes the trip, identifying each monument they saw and carefully informing Barezzi that the Rhine was "one of the largest rivers of Europe, in the plains of which Napoleon had an army of three hundred thousand men—that being considered the key to France." With Marie Louise, Napoleon's widow, for their sovereign and the Duchy of Parma a political re-creation of the Congress of Vienna, Napoleon was still very real to the people of Busseto, even thirty years after Waterloo. In London the Duke of Wellington was still alive and known, on occasion, to attend the opera. In him Verdi and Muzio hoped to see one of the great monuments of the Napoleonic times in the flesh.

For both men the trip, by comparison, was a sad commentary on the political conditions in Italy. Muzio wrote: "We passed through all these provinces and kingdoms without being asked for our passports, which we still have in our portfolios. Moreover, our trunks were examined only once in Belgium. What a difference from traveling in Italy, where it is so inconvenient that you have to be showing your passport every minute, and always have your trunks open to show what's inside." It was also an experience in the wonders of the modern age. There was the first ride on a large steamboat, the first long ride in a train. "I forgot to tell you," Muzio added, "that from Cologne to Brussels, inasmuch as it's all mountainous country, we passed through twenty-four tunnels. In the cars the lights were always on because these tunnels are very long, some five miles, others three." And he ended with a list of the hours spent in the various types of travel:

From Milan to Fiora by coach		30	hours
"	Fluelen to Lucerne by steamboat on the Lake	2	"
"	Lucerne to Basel by coach	11	"
"	Basel to Strasbourg by rail	5	"
"	Strasbourg to Kehl by coach	¾	"
"	Kehl to Karlsruhe by rail	2	"
"	Karlsruhe to Mannheim by rail	3	"
"	Mannheim to Mainz by steamboat on the Rhine	4	"
"	Mainz to Coblenz, Bonn, Cologne on the Rhine	9	"
"	Cologne to Brussels by rail	11	"
"	Brussels to Paris by rail	13	"
		$91\frac{3}{4}$ hours	

The expense was quadrupled because, though the trip from Strasbourg to Paris cost 60 francs, we spent more than four times that going by way of the Rhine.

EMANUELE MUZIO

P.S. I was forgetting to tell you that we passed the field of Waterloo, where Napoleon fell, and we saw with great displeasure the monument they have erected to the English (on French soil!) in memory of that victory.

Verdi lingered in Paris for two days while sending Muzio ahead to see Lumley. There were rumors that Jenny Lind, whom Lumley had promised, had refused to sing in a new opera. By refusing to appear until the matter was settled Verdi, perhaps, hoped to put pressure on Lumley.

The tone of Verdi's letters during the months preceding the production of *I Masnadieri* is unusually snappish. In April he had written Lucca: "I am not disposed to tolerate the slightest slip-up. I have been pretty poorly treated in this whole business; and if the opera is not performed at the proper time and in the proper way, I tell you quite plainly that I shall not have it given." Later, a day or two after he arrived in London, he wrote to the Contessa Maffei: "It's true I arrived late and the impresario could complain, but if he says a single word that doesn't suit me, I shall give him back ten for an answer and leave immediately for Paris, whatever happens."

Verdi was always ready to sacrifice money for artistic integrity and, in this case, just plain temperament. He had not been "poorly treated"; Lumley had assembled an extraordinary cast for him with Jenny Lind; the great bass, Lablache; and a very popular tenor, Gardoni. If anyone was at fault, as Verdi confessed, it was himself. One reason for his quick temper undoubtedly was that he disliked Lucca with whom he constantly had to deal. Always, as soon as he talked directly to Lumley, whether in Milan or London, the problems disappeared. Another reason, and more pervasive, was that he was nervous. He was nervous about the opera; he had asked Maffei earlier to redo the second act which he felt was "absolutely cold for the stage." He was nervous about the première outside of Italy in a land whose language he could not speak. How could he talk to the orchestra, to the stagehands, to make his wishes understood? And the trip did nothing to calm him. With each new invention, longer tunnel, larger city, greater nation, Parma seemed smaller, he and Muzio more innocent and provincial.

In the two days he spent in Paris Verdi refused to allow his agent, Escudier, to introduce him to anyone. He went to the Opéra and reported a week later to the Contessa Maffei in a letter from London that he had "never heard worse singers or a more mediocre chorus. The orchestra itself (if our 'lions' will permit me) is hardly more than mediocre." This undoubtedly encouraged him; if the problems at the Opéra were the same as in Milan, or Florence, or Venice, then he could handle London.

He also, it seems likely, called on his oldest and best friend in the theatre, Giuseppina Strepponi. There is no direct evidence for this visit, but the circumstantial evidence is strong. Such a visit might explain in part why Verdi sent Muzio on ahead, why he refused Escudier's invitations, why in his first letters from London to all and sundry he talked of returning promptly to Paris, and lastly why after only two days in Paris he could write the Contessa Maffei in the same letter as above: "What I saw of Paris I rather liked, and I like particularly the free life one can lead in that country. I can say nothing about London, for yesterday was Sunday and I haven't seen a soul."

He actually, at the time he wrote the letter, had spent as many days in London as in Paris, had reportedly not seen a soul in either city, and yet was an authority on the kind of life it was possible to live in Paris but not on the kind of life it was possible to live in London. The day of the week, Sunday, can hardly have made such a difference. Plainly he must have talked with someone who did know about life in Paris. Outside of Escudier, some musicians and political exiles, Verdi knew no one in Paris except Strepponi. And if he talked with either the musicians or the exiles he certainly would have reported on their health to their friends in Milan.

Strepponi, on the other hand, was in a peculiarly good position to tell him about the "free life" possible in Paris. She had been living there now for more than a year, giving lessons twice a week, on Tuesdays and Fridays, and taking only the pupils she wanted. As a former diva she was welcome in all the literary and social salons, although as an "actress" the old-fashioned aristocratic society would have nothing to do with her. But in Paris it did not matter; the most interesting people were in the intellectual and artistic circles, not the Faubourg Saint-Germain. In fact there were two worlds, and they did not meet.

Verdi, of course, had known for as long as Strepponi had been there that she was in Paris. But he seems to have been in no particular hurry to see her. His original plans did not call for a stopover there, and his decision at Strasbourg to go down the Rhine delayed his arrival. But having reached Paris and knowing she was there, it seems likely that he then decided to call on her.

No one knows where love comes from, but it is generally accepted among intelligent women that men need it, especially when hard pressed, and will often then turn to a woman to find it. If, as seems likely, Verdi turned up at very short notice at her door, agitated over the possibility of losing Jenny Lind, over his opera and over the difficulties of dealing with the English, she may have sensed an opportunity for love and taken a decisive step toward it by suggesting the two of them stay quietly at home.

Opinions differ over just when Verdi and Strepponi became lovers in both the merely physical and the deepest spiritual sense. Italian biographers have generally argued that an affair between them began as early as 1842, continued in or about Milan until 1845 when Strepponi began to retire from the theatre, and survived the break when she went to Paris. Vincent Sheehan, following the Italians, even argues that she deliberately left Milan for Paris because "her woman's wisdom told her this was the one place where she would most certainly attract him and regain him." But Walker's careful reconstruction of her career, showing that she and Verdi were seldom in the same city during these years, has made an affair, even a casual one, less likely. Verdi knew she had gone to Paris, for he gave her a letter of introduction to his agent, Escudier. But Strepponi, even after being there several months, apparently had not heard from him, for in a letter to her friend, Giovannina Lucca, she asked: "Is Verdi at Milan? Tell me if his health has been good this year, and if he is in a good humor, for good humor, in him, is a sign of health." There is no reason to suppose she was trying to mislead her friend about her relations with Verdi.

The theory of this book is that no affair existed before June 1847; that Strepponi went to Paris not on some fanciful scheme to regain Verdi but simply because it was the musical capital of Europe and she could earn a living there; that Paris was also a place where she could live with dignity, away from her embarrassing relatives and an illegitimate child; that to kindle a desultory friendship into a roaring blaze of love requires some sort of special circumstance; and lastly that this special circumstance seems more likely on Verdi's way to London when he was nervous, agitated and given to "whims" rather than after London when his opera had had a successful première, Lumley was pursuing him with extravagant offers, and he was being received everywhere in Paris as the most important composer.

In the end the uncertain, private beginning of the affair is far less important than the established, public fact of it which caused no concern in the big city of Paris but in time became the principal subject of conversation in Busseto. But the curious will always wonder about love. How does it come, at what moment, why?

Assured of Jenny Lind for his opera, Verdi left at once for London. Muzio had reserved a tiny apartment. Aghast at the cost of three rooms and a maid, he had insisted on taking two rooms with a cot for himself in one. But Verdi overruled the attempted economy. Both men found London dazzling. Muzio wrote Barezzi: "Steam by land and by sea. The steam engine flew over the earth, and the steamboat flew over the sea. What chaos in London! What confusion! Paris is nothing in comparison. People shouting, the poor weeping, steam engines, steamboats flying along, men on horseback, in carriages, on foot, and everybody howling like the damned. My dear Signor Antonio, you can't imagine!"

Verdi was less wide-eyed but just as impressed. He wrote a friend about his stay: "Although the London climate was horrible, I took an

extraordinary liking to the city. It isn't a city, it is a world. Its size, the richness and beauty of the streets, the cleanliness of the houses, all this is incomparable; you stand amazed and feeling very small, when in the midst of all this spendor, you look over the Bank of England and the docks. Who can resist this people? The surroundings and the countryside about London are marvelous. I do not like many of the English customs, or rather, they do not suit us Italians. How ridiculous it looks when people imitate the English in Italy!"

With his opera to finish and his work in the theatre Verdi, as always before a première, refused most invitations. He went once to dinner at Lumley's where he met Prince Louis Bonaparte, then in exile from France but soon to become Napoleon III. Prince Louis was one of the few men who had any personal knowledge of Pio Nono, for he had been one of the leaders of the revolt around Bologna in 1831–32 against Gregory XVI and Pio Nono, then Bishop of Imola, had helped him to escape. Verdi also, like every Italian who came to London, met Mazzini and talked about conditions in Italy.

The première was a success. The newspapers had fanned the general excitement until a mob, far larger than the theatre could hold, gathered outside. At about quarter past four the people rushed the doors and broke into the theatre. Later the celebrities arrived, Victoria and Albert, the Duke of Wellington, Prince Louis Bonaparte and many of the Members of Parliament. Verdi conducted and was called to the stage many times. As the reviews appeared the next morning and during the week the critics generally approved. But some did not. *Punch* quipped that the opera was so noisy that each act was "a Riot Act, for it disperses every one till the ballet." And a very good critic, Henry E. Chorley in the *Atheneum,* made one of those mistakes that the public enjoys too much to forget: "We take this to be the worst opera which has been given in our time at Her Majesty's Theatre. Verdi is finally rejected. The field is left open for an Italian composer."

But Chorley was not altogether wrong; *I Masnadieri* is not one of Verdi's better operas. It is dramatically far less interesting than *Macbeth* and melodically less distinguished than *Ernani.* Maffei, who was a translator rather than a librettist, constructed a libretto that resembled the repertory of operas he had recently been seeing in Milan. The result was an average, conventional libretto in which the characters are brought on one at a time, as in *Ernani,* and given a slow and a fast aria to sing. Verdi in *I Due Foscari, Attila* and particularly *Macbeth* had begun to create a different style, and some of his music for *I Masnadieri* sounds as though he found it hard to go back. A little of the breath of life has gone out of it, and it sounds a bit like an exercise, skillful and brilliant, but still an exercise. Somehow Maffei's characters did not plumb Verdi's deepest emotions. The feeling of an exercise is increased by the special coloratura writing he put in for Jenny Lind, "the Swedish Nightingale." Muzio described her voice to Barezzi as "a touch harsh in the high notes, weak on the low ones; but by studying she has succeeded in making it flexible in the high tones and can handle any difficulties. Her trill is unapproachable; she has an agility without equal and, generally, to show off her skill she sings in excessive ornamentation, shakes and trills; a style pleasing the last century, but not in 1847." (etc.) Verdi, composing specially for this voice, created a soprano part dated in style even when written and which needed a Jenny Lind to make it effective. Paradoxically Verdi's own particular talent was restricted by Maffei's conventional libretto and Jenny Lind's unconventional voice.

But as in most of Verdi's less successful operas, there is much beautiful and effective music. It begins with a prelude consisting almost entirely of a cello solo, lovely in itself and which sets an appropriate melancholy tone to the beginning. It was greatly admired at the time.

Some of the arias are good, particularly a cabaletta for the soprano in which she rejoices that her lover lives and a duet in the last scene for the tenor and bass. This last is extremely melodic and the voices marvelously contrasted. As so often in Verdi, it is a duet between father and son, and it leads directly into the chief glory of the opera, the final trio, in which the soprano joins them and the chorus of robbers occasionally exclaims in the background. It is vintage Verdi of the period, the voices arching over and entwining with each other while the whole has a feeling of inexorable forward movement. Winding up like a barrel organ, say those who do not like it; thrilling, say those who do. But whatever the point of view, it is worth examining the trio briefly to see what made up the musical style that was peculiarly Verdi's.

The details of the stage situation are not important to the musical style; it is sufficient that the tenor is in despair, the soprano desperately trying to persuade him that all will come right in the end, and the bass, the tenor's father, fearing the worst. The chorus interjects from time to time to remind the tenor of his oath to be their leader, the oath representing honor and the soprano, love.

Verdi begins the trio with the tenor sobbing in broken phrases built around a single held note:

CARLO

Largo ♩ = 66
con dolore

Ca-duto è il re - ... pro-bol l'ha côlto Id-
(Fallen is the rep - ... robate! God has cut

stentate

di - o. So - gni di gau - dio, per sem-pre ad-
him down. Dreams of joy for-ever fare-

di - ol I ceppi, il car - ce - re, la scure, il
well! Chains, pri - son, the axe, the

ro - go, son questi i pro - nu-bi del nostro a - men of our love.)
st - ake, these are the brides - men of our love.)

The style closely resembles that of Verdi's first Goethe songs: the accompaniment kept to the very simplest and the voice in short phrases ending, generally, on turns. The turns now are simpler and easier to project, and the long held note adds an inherent contrast, but the basic idea is the same.

The tenor is followed by the soprano desperately pleading with

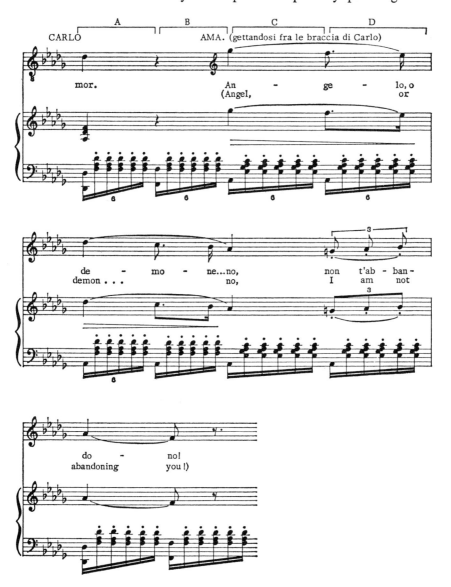

him. She has a long, broad melody like the second Goethe song. The swiftly falling line is inherently dramatic, if only because the audience waits to hear it turn up before it hits some sort of aural bottom.

Neither melody is particularly beautiful in itself, but each has a seed of drama in it. Taken together and put on the stage, they make a scene.

All three voices then join with the band of robbers, and a trio with chorus becomes a finale. It is blessed with that sense of pace that is a musical fingerprint of Verdi. The secret of it seems to be twofold. The basic count is a march, four-four time, but this is less important than the triple time Verdi imposes on each of the four beats. This is less complicated than it sounds. Triple time is nothing but the ONE-two-three that everyone dances in a waltz.

In the example of the soprano above, the four basic beats of the march are indicated by A, B, C, D. The triple time has been imposed by Verdi in the indication "6" which means it is to be played or counted as A-two-three-FOUR-five-six, B-two-three-FOUR-five-six. This is a variation of the imposed triple time and gives a feeling of sustained glide to the melodic line which the Goethe song, probably quite deliberately, lacks.

A simpler form of imposed triple time which Verdi uses as the trio begins is this:

This would be counted A-two-three, B-two-three, etc.

The fact that the triple time is imposed on a march is of far less importance than the fact that it is triple time: ONE-two-three. Now, why should this rhythm give such a feeling of forward movement? Most persons believe, because they are told, that the march, ONE-two-three-four, is the natural rhythm of forward movement. A march is a march is a march. Soldiers, and all.

In fact, children in school and soldiers in the army are taught to walk to a march probably only because they cannot handle a rhythm in which the beat falls first on one foot and then on the other. In a march, if a man starts with his left foot, the beat then always falls on the left foot. Always. In triple time the beat changes, always, from foot to foot. Altogether too much for the Enlisted Man. Suppose he came to a corner on the wrong foot?

But it was not too much for the Greeks. Indeed, they even managed to do it and do it backward. In their classical tragedies the chorus generally entered and went out to "marching anapaests," a metrical rhythm of two shorts followed by a long or three-two-ONE.

Some lines of English verse written in an approximation of anapaestic rhythm are W. S. Gilbert's from *Iolanthe:*

> When you're lying awake with a dismal headache, and
>   repose is taboo'd by anxiety
> I conceive you may use any language you choose to
>   indulge in, without impropriety;

But the question still remains why this ONE-two-three rhythm gives such a sense of movement, "pace" being only movement made regular by recurring beats. The Greeks did not say, and Verdi was an instinctive artist, but the answer may lie in the physical experience of the body. If a man stands in place and lifts his feet in march time, emphasizing the first beat, he will shift his weight very little as the beat will always fall on the left foot. If he does the same thing to triple time, he will shift his weight more. And if he actually marches to the two beats, the difference will become even more apparent. Indeed, to triple time he will assume almost a seaman's roll. This shift of weight his muscles remember, and his mind subconsciously associates it and the ONE-two-three count with a sense of movement. This physical memory and mental association Verdi arouses in the listener by starting a strong ONE-two-three beat in the orchestra. The response is in the listener, not in the orchestra; there is no more actual movement in a violin playing ONE-two-three than ONE-two-three-four.

Why Verdi particularly liked this rhythm is a mystery. Why does one man prefer red and another blue? But he plainly did, and in this period of his operas, roughly from 1844 to 1850, he turned to it again and again for his finales.

To it he added a musical figure, a sort of screw-turn, that became almost a mannerism of his style. He gave it generally to a low voice, bass or baritone, or sometimes the chorus, and he placed it where the other voices, soprano and tenor, are coming to the end of a phrase. The end of a phrase is a dangerous spot for a composer trying to give the music a feeling of inexorable sweep; the phrase ends because the singer must stop to take a breath. The danger is that the phrases may become separate units, set off by tiny gaps of silence, rather than merely parts of a continuous line which itself generates excitement in the listener partly by merely seeming to be longer than the longest possible breath could possibly sustain.

Into these inevitable gaps of silence at the end of phrases Verdi put his screw-turn, like the example from *I Masnadieri* below:

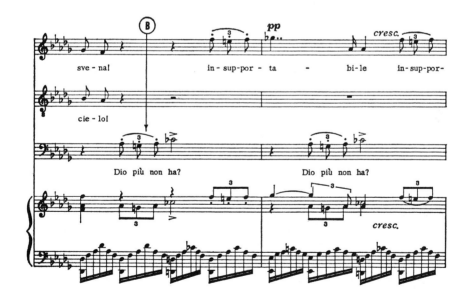

ta - bi-le vi-ta mi re - sta _____

dal mio pre - ci - pi -

tre-muoti e tur - bi - ni, no, Di - o

dam - mi ___ que - st'ul - ti-mo pe-gno d'a-

to so - gna - to ciell so-gna-to cie -

piu non ha, non ha? non

The screw-turn appears at "B" in its simplest form. Notice that the count for it is ONE-two-three-ONE, as though there were a little extra twist on the final note. In fact, Verdi indicates this with an accent mark. The screw-turn in a variation appears at "A" as the soprano and tenor in their falling line stop for breath. Its effect in both places is to keep the musical line going, as though winding it up before it can stop, or organ-grinding.

Taken together and combined with good melodies, the basic rhythm and recurring figure served Verdi well. (See Appendix D, p. 582.) Both effects were simple and easy to project in a theatre; they also tended to reinforce each other. Further, being based on a simple rhythm to which everyone from the musical aristocrat to the simplest peasant had the same muscular response, it tended to be a great leveler, binding all the audience into a single unit that appreciated, rocked and hummed together. This was one reason why musical aesthetes of the time found Verdi's music vulgar; there seemed so little room in it for subtle musical effect and appreciation. But for the great mass of people, particularly the Italians, it made going to the opera even more of a communal experience, which partly explains why Verdi's choruses became such popular battle songs in the Italian struggle for unity and independence.

CHAPTER 16

PARIS AND MILAN, 1848

1847–1848; AGE, 33–34

AFTER two performances of *I Masnadieri* Verdi left London for Paris with an offer from Lumley to become the musical director of Her Majesty's Theatre. The salary suggested, by Italian standards, was enormous, 60,000 lire per year; and in addition Lumley was to provide an apartment and a carriage. In return Verdi was to direct all the productions, conducting most of them himself, and to compose one new opera a year. At that time the season at Her Majesty's Theatre lasted from February until August, so that, excluding January for rehearsals, Verdi might have had four full months to himself; although presumably in those months, as well as composing the one opera, he would travel to and from Italy to sign up new singers and composers. Lumley wanted the contract to run for ten years.

The prosperity of England, the hustle and bustle of London and the opportunity there for personal wealth dazzled Verdi as it did all Italians who came to London. By contrast the Italian cities with their far more rigid societies, older methods of agriculture and business and myriad distinctions of tongue seemed small, petty and hopelessly provincial. Verdi did not like the climate in London; he missed the Italian sun and complained that the constant smell of coal made the city seem like one large steamboat. He was also not sure that he wanted to restrict himself to one opera a year. But he negotiated, even eagerly. He must be allowed to remake the orchestra, have new scenery for some of the productions; and the contract must run for only three years. Verdi suggested 1849, 1850 and 1851.

In the end nothing came of it. To do it Verdi needed to be released by Lucca from the duty to provide the publisher with an opera, and he offered Lucca 10,000 lire to cancel the contract. Lucca refused.

About the same time Lumley wrote Verdi that he would postpone any definite settlement until his next trip to Italy when they could discuss it more leisurely. It is just possible that Lucca influenced Lumley to hold off. More probable is that when Lumley saw his competition at Covent Garden having a particularly bad season, he decided that he, at Her Majesty's Theatre, could economize. But Verdi, whether he suspected Lucca of influencing Lumley or not, was furious at the publisher for insisting on his rights under the contract. With supreme inconsistency Verdi characterized Lucca as "avaricious" whereas, of course, it was Verdi's love of money that initiated the request to cancel the contract. Possibly Lucca could not cancel the contract because he in turn had contracted with various Italian theatres for the production of the opera. If so, he did not make it clear to Verdi who, by the end of the summer, was thoroughly disgusted and resolved never to do business with him again.

But even though the negotiations came to nothing, they indicate that Verdi's ability as a conductor and director were highly prized. And his hesitation at the prospect of composing only one opera a year, for during the season his other duties would have taken all his time, is most revealing. Always he thought of himself primarily as a composer, happy to use his other talents when he found himself in the opera house, but they were to be subordinate to the composing. Later in his life he would be offered all sorts of administrative posts which he refused easily; the only offer that ever seriously interested him was this one of Lumley's which never did come to the point of decision. If it had, Verdi might well have refused at the last minute to sign or insisted on impossible conditions regarding the orchestra, scenery, or his own duties. Lucca, in fact, may well have saved Verdi the embarrassment of backing out of a protracted negotiation. Verdi, however, at the time did not think so.

That summer in Paris Verdi enjoyed himself. He sent Muzio back to Milan to arrange for the publication of I Masnadieri while he himself lingered without any immediate plans other than doing an opera to satisfy Lucca and another for Naples, both due in the coming year. As always after an opera his throat was sore, and he nursed his health. In June he had explained in a letter to Mme. Appiani: "My health is really not bad in London, but I am always afraid that some misfortune may descend upon me." The memory of that bad winter in Venice when he had completed *Attila* two and a half months late did not leave him.

Except for the climate he preferred London to Paris, for he did not like the boulevard life. Of the two cities Paris has traditionally appealed more to women and London to men. Verdi, with a background of Busseto where no such thing as a Paris salon existed, may have found the feminine domination of Paris life confusing and distasteful. But he liked the anonymity of a big city where, as he wrote a friend, no one pointed at him on the streets and where he entertained no one and no one entertained him.

But this was only a half-truth. He must have gone out to dinners and salons occasionally, perhaps pushed by Strepponi, because he became a recognized member of the Italian colony in the city and the subject of magazine and newspaper articles. And like most men enjoying public success, he tended to favor himself as a subject of conversation and wrote Mme. Appiani: "Apropos of *Entre-Acte* [a magazine], there was a very funny article in it about me. I think Emanuele Muzio has taken it to Milan. Have him give it to you." Then he went on to describe the symptoms of Donizetti's insanity which the doctors considered, correctly as it turned out, to be incurable. He promised to write again if there was any change and reported that he would return to Milan at the end of November. He did not say, because it was not yet definite, that the Opéra had approached him for an opera in the autumn season.

The administration at the Opéra had changed, and the new directors were anxious in their first year to do something spectacular. Undoubtedly urged on by Escudier, Verdi's agent, they reasoned that present in Paris was the leading Italian composer whose operas were continually and very successfully produced in Italian at the Théâtre Italien but who had not yet had an opera in French at the Opéra. The result, after negotiations in which Verdi objected that time was too short to do a new work, was an agreement to refashion *I Lombardi,* which had not been done in Paris. For this patchwork job Verdi composed a lengthy ballet and several new arias set to a new French text in which the Lombards became Frenchmen and Milan, Toulouse. The new version was called *Jérusalem* and presented as something done "for the Opéra" so that no French feathers would ruffle at the prospect of the great national house being fobbed off with a dated, provincial piece.

The première was on 26 November, and as Verdi himself admitted, the production, the scenery and costumes were "absolutely magnificent, for here they spare no expense." About the music he said almost nothing; perhaps he realized, as most critics have since agreed, that the opera in its first somewhat gauche but honestly Italian version had more punch. The Parisian audience was cool toward it, perhaps because a series of political crises were distracting the city's attention. In the less politically minded French provinces the opera did well, and in the French version it penetrated some foreign cities that *I Lombardi* might not have. In the United States, for example, *I Lombardi* in the spring and summer of 1847 was the first Verdi opera produced in New York and Philadelphia, but *Jérusalem* in January 1850 was the first in the former French colony of New Orleans.

Verdi sold the publishing rights to Ricordi who arranged for an Italian translation of the French version. The vocal score appeared with a dedication, which must have been first approved by Verdi, to "the distinguished singer, Signora Giuseppina Strepponi."

Verdi's relations with Strepponi were gradually deepening. They still lived apart, each conducting an independent life: Strepponi busying herself with her pupils and Verdi with the rehearsals for *Jérusalem* and after that the composition of *Il Corsaro* for Lucca. But they saw each other regularly. Verdi had urged Barezzi to come for a visit to Paris, and the old man went for several weeks and had a wonderful time. In a letter to Verdi on his return to Busseto Barezzi talks constantly of Strepponi by name and only vaguely of Verdi's "other friends." Even Demaldè, the treasurer of the Monte di Pietà, who had not been to Paris but had met Strepponi many years before, wrote to Verdi specifically inquiring about her and commenting on her "fine mind and virtues." Plainly in Paris Verdi and Strepponi were often together, and in Busseto the fact was recognized, at least for the moment, with pleasure.

After Barezzi left Paris in January 1848, Verdi stayed on to finish *Il Corsaro*. Meanwhile the political situation in the city occupied more and more of everyone's attention, Italians as well as French, for any change of government there was sure to affect the balance of power in Europe and the future of the small Italian states. Verdi felt he was at the center of political events in Europe and wrote constantly to his friends, particularly the Contessa Maffei, of what was happening in Paris.

France in 1847 was a constitutional monarchy under Louis Philippe, the "citizen king," who had come to power after the revolution of 1830 which had deposed Charles X. Charles, for whom Rossini in 1824 had composed a coronation opera, was the brother of the beheaded Louis XVI and represented the senior Bourbon line in France; he also represented reaction and a return, wherever possible, by law and custom to the *ancien régime,* pre-Revolutionary France. Throughout the nineteenth century Frenchmen supporting Charles, his descendants and the program they represented were known as "legitimists."

The revolution of 1830 in Paris had been the work of the growing middle class which with the Industrial Age was rising to power and also of the workers whose conditions in the crowded city grew continually worse. The workers wanted a republic with universal franchise and a socialistic program. The bourgeois, however, succeeded in "stealing" the revolution with the election of Louis Philippe, a member of the junior line of the Bourbons descending from a Duke of Orleans, and Frenchmen who supported Louis Philippe, his descendants and philosophy were known as "Orleanists."

At first Louis Philippe had seemed a genuine compromise between the desires of the bourgeois and the workers, but as the years passed it became plain he favored big business and so did his legislation. When the workers and intellectuals like Hugo complained that only the rich could qualify to vote, Louis Philippe, through his minister Guizot, replied: "If you want a vote, get rich!" By which Guizot only meant that industry and thrift were the basis of the individual's and the country's prosperity. But to those who worked hard and somehow did not get rich and could not vote, it smacked of "Let 'em eat cake."

Opposition to Louis Philippe mounted imperceptibly, aggravated in 1846–47 by a business recession, poor crops and flamboyant oratory, the latter generally delivered at banquets and often warmer than the cold veal and salad. One such banquet in Paris had been scheduled by the opposition for 22 February 1848 and the government first forbade it, then authorized it, and then forbade it again, although weakly suggesting that perhaps the courts should decide. As 1847 ended, Paris, discussing in its salons and on its boulevards the rights and wrongs of the ridiculous incident, focused its attention on the government which began to quaver under the scrutiny. Political savants predicted a change in 1848.

Even before the new year one change of government affected Verdi as a citizen of Parma. Marie Louise, only fifty-six years old, died on 17 December. Although she had ruled Parma since 1815, living by far the greater part of her life there, to the end she remained an Austrian archduchess, and her body was buried in Vienna. That act demonstrated what everyone knew to be true: that the government of Parma was imposed on it by the Austrians; even after thirty-two years as its Duchess, which was more than half her life, Marie Louise was still a foreigner in Parma.

In Paris, even though she was an ex-Empress of France, her death and burial in Vienna passed almost unnoticed except for cynical observations. She was buried next to her son by Napoleon, the Duke of Reichstadt, who for a few days in 1815 had been Napoleon II. But as the wits pointed out, this mother had repudiated her son's inheritance, abandoned his father and even abandoned the son himself to a palace-prison in Vienna, while she went off to Italy with her lover. The glamor had gone out of Bonapartism even before Marie Louise's death; as a movement in France it seemed finished as everyone now struggled, not for "la gloire," but merely to "get rich." The Bonaparte pretender in England, Prince Louis Napoleon, the great man's nephew, was forbidden to return to France, and without any party to keep his name before the public he was almost forgotten. The republicans of France, led by Lamartine and Hugo, two of the country's great Romantic poets, posed as the true heirs of the Revolution and all that was best in Napoleon's social program. They seemed to Italians like Verdi, Mazzini and the Contessa Maffei to be the natural allies of the republicans in Italy.

At Parma the succession on Marie Louise's death reverted to the minor Bourbon line which had been swept away by Napoleon and given Lucca by the Congress of Vienna. Now from Lucca came Carlo Ludovico, who became Parma's Duke Carlo II. He was a middle-aged playboy whose only desire was to live the life of a "dandy." The English word had become Italian slang at the time, and the phrase "la vita di dandy" was understood by everyone to mean a good income, good clothes, if possible a title, and a life filled with making arrangements to go from one watering place to the next.

He was regarded at first with suspicion and then outrage when the terms of a secret treaty became known. In 1844, even before Marie Louise's death, Carlo had contracted to cede Guastalla, to the west of Busseto, with eight surrounding towns and an additional two in the mountains to the south, to Francesco IV of Modena, the most hated ruler on the peninsula. In return he was to be paid an annuity of 700,000 francs. His old Duchy of Lucca went to Grand Duke Leopold of Tuscany. The ceded towns with their citizens priced and sold protested and demonstrated against the transfer as much as they dared, but Carlo promptly signed new treaties with Austria which increased the Austrian garrison at Parma. For his Chief Minister he appointed an English jockey, Thomas Ward. Unable to protest effectively, the people grumbled, and the grumbling all over Italy constantly grew louder.

From Milan Verdi's friends with mixed glee and sorrow wrote him of a Tobacco Party organized by the liberals and modeled on the Boston Tea Party. Tobacco in Milan was an Austrian monopoly and a rich source of income. On New Year's Day the liberals with posters urged all Milanese not to smoke and pointed out that an old ordinance, never repealed, forbade anyone to smoke in the streets. The protest was generally taken up and the few, mostly Austrians, who continued to smoke in public were hissed. In reply the Austrian Viceroy issued cigars to the soldiers with orders to smoke ostentatiously. The people then attempted to snatch the cigars out of the soldiers' mouths and finally the inevitable happened: the soldiers fired on the people, killed five and wounded fifty-nine. The Mayor, trying to prevent the disaster, was struck in the face and arrested.

The Austrians at first tried to handle the situation by dividing the Milanese. The poor were told that the rich would always desert them; the middle class, that disorder would disrupt trade; and every effort was made with dinners, honors and private talks to persuade the leaders and aristocracy that their interests lay with those of Austria. From Vienna Metternich wrote to his minister in Milan: "We have bored them. A people which wants *panem et circenses* does not want to be bored. It wants to be governed with a strong hand—and amused." But the formula, if it had ever succeeded, no longer seemed apt. The Milanese of all classes struck together. Busts of Pio Nono, the liberal Pope, were carried through the streets in pious but political processions, and every feast and saint's day was celebrated. There were nights when, mysteriously, no one went to the theatre, others when at La Scala all the ladies wore the colors of Savoy, white and blue. One night all the men had white cravats and yellow gloves, the colors of the Pope. Finally on 22 February the Austrians put the city under martial law.

It became treason to wear certain colors or badges, to sing certain songs, to applaud or hiss certain passages at the theatres.

Communications in the year 1848 were still very slow, and although the telegraph had been invented, it was not yet in general use. News traveled generally by diplomatic courier and a few days slower by private letter. The railway from Milan to Venice was only just begun, and no line yet crossed a mountain range, either in Italy or connecting it to the outside. A letter from Milan to Paris took at least five days and from Venice to London, eleven or twelve. First reports, of course, were seldom accurate, and Verdi in Paris was probably as much as three weeks behind on what was happening in Italy.

He must have known that there had been a revolution in Sicily and that at Naples King Ferdinando had promised a constitution, and perhaps he knew that constitutions had been promised in Tuscany and Piedmont. But he seems to have known nothing in detail, and in a letter, early in March, to Mme. Appiani he complains that many letters between them have evidently been lost. So he proceeded to tell her all about the revolution which was going on before him in Paris and which, as he could see it with his own eyes, seemed to him the most important.

The isolation in which one revolution after another occurred in 1848 in places as far apart as Paris, Palermo and Warsaw is scarcely believable today. One effect of it was tragic: there was almost no co-operation between cities, even neighboring cities, and much that was gained was held for only a few weeks or months while the old order righted itself and returned with arms. On the other hand, the very spontaneousness of the various revolutions was a striking demonstration of the people's frustration; 1848 has with reason been called "the mad and holy year." Suddenly, everywhere the pot boiled over; and the slow communications of the time made it inconceivable that any central committee was directing the general upheaval. But this only added to the terror of the old order, for the enemy was now not one man like Mazzini, but the people.

Verdi's revolution in Paris, by comparison to most, was very mild. There was an incident: soldiers fired on the crowd. The city grew restive; citizens threw up barricades, and Louis Philippe went out to review his guard. But instead of shouting, "Long live the king!" the troops cried, "Hurrah for Reform!" And the king decided in the interest of peace in the country to retire to England. Probably he saved

France from a civil war, but the moderates, republicans and radicals who had been pressing for reforms could not have been more surprised and were not ready. In the confusion during the last week of February the Second Republic was declared. Lamartine, Hugo and the republicans everywhere were jubilant. In France, according to the oratory, the fountain of liberty had begun to flow again.

About the same time Verdi finished *Il Corsaro* and sent it off to Lucca. He refused to stage or conduct it himself: Lucca could do what he wished with it. Verdi, however, recommended Muzio as a good conductor and director. *Il Corsaro* is one of the rare Verdi operas on which he himself did not work at the première and, as might be expected from his lack of attention, it is also one of the worst of his operas. Everything had been against it, a poor libretto, bad relations with his publisher and the double distraction of love and politics in Paris.

The politics in particular now took almost all his attention. He wrote to Mme. Appiani about the Paris revolution:

I can't conceal from you that I am having a wonderful time and that nothing has disturbed my sleep so far. I do nothing, go walking, listen to the most ridiculous nonsense, buy nearly twenty papers a day (without reading them, of course) to avoid the persecutions of the vendors, for when they see me coming with a whole bundle of papers in my hand they don't offer me any. And I laugh, and laugh, and laugh. If nothing more important calls me to Italy, I shall stay here for the rest of April to see the National Assembly. So far I have seen everything that has happened, serious and comical (please believe me that "seen" means *with my own eyes*), and I don't want to miss the twentieth of April (etc.).

This last was the date set for the national elections, the first chance France as a whole would have to vote on the Second Republic and the revolution which Paris, unasked, had made for the country. The letter, dated 9 March, indicates that Verdi had not the faintest conception of affairs in Milan.

After the proclamation of martial law there the situation grew steadily worse. The Austrians offered some small concessions, but these had no effect on the Milanese who now had solidified into a stance of sullen obedience. When they could safely protest, they did. At La Scala the two greatest ballerinas of the century, Marie Taglioni and

Fanny Elssler, were alternating. On the night of 17 March when Elssler, who was a Viennese, was dancing, the chorus all wore medallions of Pio Nono. When Elssler saw the chorus, tight-faced and sullen, lined up against her, she fainted.

The next day a large crowd, vaguely demanding reform, but without any particular purpose, demonstrated in front of the Governor's palace. News had just arrived that a revolution had taken place in Vienna. No one had any certain knowledge of what had happened, and the rumors may have unsettled the soldiers who, as always, stood the gaff for a while and then fired on the crowd. The "Cinque Giornate," "The Five Days" so glorious in Milan's history, had begun.

Any revolution in Milan was certain to be bloody. The city had a population of 160,000, and the Austrian garrison had been steadily increased during the winter until it numbered 15,000. Many of these were illiterate Croats and Hungarians who could not speak the Milanese dialect and cared nothing for any one or thing in Italy. They knew quite well that they were in a hostile city and were prepared to fight their way out of Milan and out of Italy if necessary. There was no possibility, as in Paris, of the army joining the rebellion. Nor was Radetzky, the marshal in command, a Louis Philippe, to retire to avoid bloodshed. His motto, often quoted, was said to be: "Three days of bloodshed secure thirty years of peace."

The crowd before the Governor's palace on 18 March, after being fired on, dispersed; but the incident somehow determined the city's collective will to fight. The people built barricades in the streets, and when the soldiers came to destroy them, the people threw down on the soldiers tiles from the roofs, boiling water and furniture. The soldiers neither dared to stay in the streets nor dared to enter the houses to escape from them. Seventeen hundred barricades went up, isolating pockets of troops and making communication between them impossible. The city then had fewer open areas than today. The piazzas in front of both the Duomo and La Scala were partially filled with houses; there was no gallery or street running directly from the Duomo to La Scala and no street like today's Via Dante running from the Castello to the center of the town. Many streets, like the Via Morone on which Manzoni lived, were only six or eight feet wide with tall buildings on either side. Soldiers trapped in such canyons with barricades before and behind had almost no chance to escape.

In old towns with narrow streets it was always easy to start a revolution with barricades. The crisis generally came in the third or fourth day when, with the city's life totally disrupted, the inhabitants began to pull in different directions. The glory of the Milanese in their "Cinque Giornate" was that they continued united in their determination to drive the Austrians out. From his windows on the Via Morone Manzoni watched the young men going to the barricades; some were still in evening clothes and dancing pumps. One night two or three hundred demonstrators stopped under his windows. "Viva l'Italia! Viva Manzoni!" they cried. The great man had a well-known fear of crowds and he seldom went out in public. His friends had a hard time persuading him even to appear on a balcony with lanterns held behind him. He mumbled a few words and then withdrew. It was an agitating time for him. Not only were all his emotions for the city

DUOMO AT MILAN

and Italy stirred, but his sons were fighting in the streets and one, Pietro, was captured by the Austrians at the fighting near the Town Hall and held as a hostage.

Gradually the Milanese captured and improvised enough arms to attack the Austrians in their strongholds. One particularly difficult

assault was on the roof of the Duomo where a troop of Alpine sharp-shooters had barricaded itself. Others and most important were on the city gates. Finally the Milanese succeeded in capturing several, allowing food and volunteers to enter. By the third day the Austrians were penned into the Town Hall, Governor's Palace, various barracks and the Castello. "The nature of these people," Radetzky wrote, "has been transformed; fanaticism has invaded all ages, all classes and both sexes." At the Engineers' Barracks, the Milanese planned to burn the soldiers out, and they succeeded in laying some kindling and straw against the wooden door. Then an old man, a cripple, carrying a torch of burning straw, skipped and hopped his way across the open street to fling it against the door. How had the Austrians, the people of Mozart and Schubert, allowed themselves to get into a position where they inspired so much hate?

Radetzky wanted to bombard the city, but the foreign consuls pro-tested. He offered a truce, but the city's Council of War rejected it. On the fifth day, 22 March, Radetzky began to withdraw, and the next day the city was free of Austrian troops for the first time since 1815.

As soon as Verdi heard of the "Cinque Giornate," he raced to Milan and arrived in early April. One of his first letters, to "Citizen" Piave in Venice, reverberates like a manifesto. Verdi had just seen the "stupendous barricades" in the streets of Milan, and he wrote:

Honor to these brave men! Honor to all Italy, which at this moment is truly great!

Be assured, her hour of liberation has struck. It is the people that will it, and when the people will there is no absolute power that can resist.

They can do what they like, they can intrigue how they like, those that strive to impose themselves by brute force, but they will not succeed in defrauding the people of their rights. Yes, yes, a few more years, perhaps only a few more months, and Italy will be free, united and a republic. What else should she be?

In the same letter, after congratulating Piave on being a simple soldier, Verdi regrets that he can only be a "tribune, and a miserable tribune at that, because I am only spasmodically eloquent."

His meaning is not clear, but it sounds as though he expected to have some sort of political post if and when the republicans established a government in the city. This is quite probable. He knew personally, after all, not only Mazzini, who had arrived from London, but also the Contessa Maffei and her friends, most of whom were republicans.

It was a time of intense excitement in the city. Exiles by the hundreds returned, and even more young men departed to join volunteer regiments or the Piedmontese army in order to fight the Austrians. Verdi was no more inebriated than anyone else when he wrote Piave: "I am drunk with joy. Just think: there are no more Germans here!!"

CHAPTER 17

THE PATRIOTS IN MILAN
SOW THEIR DEFEAT

1848; AGE, 34

THE political maneuvering in Milan when Verdi arrived in April 1848 was intense and important. During the "Cinque Giornate" the leading Milanese, among them Manzoni, had signed an appeal to Carlo Alberto, King of Piedmont, to come to their aid. This was practical common sense: driving Radetzky and his army out of Milan did not drive it out of existence, and the only army in northern Italy to oppose it was that of Piedmont. On 23 March with great misgivings Carlo Alberto declared war on Austria, and his troops began to cross the Ticino River into Lombardy. The next day the Venetians succeeded in expelling the Austrians, and the ancient city of Doges promptly redeclared itself a republic with Daniele Manin as President. Carlo Alberto began to hesitate. Why should he fight to preserve Venice as an independent republic? Was Milan, and with it Lombardy, about to declare itself a republic?

The Milanese could not decide. To the fury of the Piedmontese, who were in a war largely at Milan's request, the city through its leaders, with Manzoni again among them, refused to declare itself annexed to Piedmont. Equally to the fury of republicans like Verdi and Mazzini, it refused to proclaim itself a republic. But the choice was not just between Mazzini, the republican, and Carlo Alberto, a monarch who had just granted his people a constitution. That spring Gioberti began a tour of the most important northern cities, expounding his idea of a federation of Italian states under the presidency of the Pope. He drew enormous crowds, far greater than Mazzini, and many

Milanese felt that Lombardy should continue to wait until Gioberti .had seen the Pope.

But Carlo Alberto was in a war and had to press on or sue for peace. The news from Vienna seemed to indicate that now, if ever, was the moment to drive the Austrians out of northern Italy. It was clear that the revolution in Vienna, started by university students, had forced Metternich from power and, as he had fled to England, probably for good. There were also rumors that the epileptic Emperor Ferdinand, after granting a constitution in April, had been forced to flee Vienna in May, and there were uprisings in Hungary. So Carlo Alberto and his generals continued forward with skirmishes and small battles and forced Radetzky into an area north of the Po known as the Quadrilateral. At its corners were the four heavily fortified towns of Peschiera, Verona, Mantua and Legnago, and behind their guns Radetzky hoped to regroup his army. The political situation was still unresolved, but the war at the end of April looked hopeful for the Italians.

Early in May Verdi went to Busseto to see his parents and Barezzi. Parma, too, had had a revolution but a mild one. After the "Cinque Giornate" in Milan Duke Carlo had issued a manifesto promising a constitution, aid to Lombardy, and offering to submit the political differences of his duchy to arbitration by Pio Nono, Carlo Alberto and the Grand Duke of Tuscany. But meanwhile the Austrian army had pulled back to Mantua, and the Parmigiani simply ignored him. In April he fled, after one of his chief cities, Piacenza, had already voted to join Piedmont. Part of the confusion of the times was that no one, including the ministers of Piedmont, had any idea of the legal or political effect of such a vote by an individual, un-independent city. The question cleared slightly when the rest of Parma, by a plebiscite in May, voted to join Piedmont.

Meanwhile in the small country towns of Parma like Busseto life continued almost as if the entire north side of the Po Valley from Milan to Venice was not in a state of siege. As the war developed Parma happily was out of it, being to the south and west and not across any important thoroughfare. At Busseto Verdi bought a farm. Four years earlier he had bought a small one at Le Roncole on which he had put his parents as caretakers, but he himself had almost never visited it and had taken no interest in the running of it. Now he contracted to exchange that as part of the purchase price of the new one. It too was near Busseto but to the opposite side, on the northwest, in the tiny village of Sant' Ágata. The land was good, and between it and the road ran a small creek called the "Ongina."

Just why Verdi should have chosen the spring of 1848 when the Po Valley was torn by war to enlarge his real estate holding is something of a puzzle. Perhaps the war had depressed the price of farms; perhaps the agitation of the times increased his desire to have something substantial to hold on to, to belong to. Verdi now was thirty-four; he had been in London, Paris and most of the more important Italian cities. The feeling of an Italian peasant for his "paese," his particular locality, is notoriously strong, and certainly Verdi was no exception to it. All his life he loved the land in that corner of Parma in which he was born. Whatever the reason for the purchase of the farm, it was not a whim. The purchase contract was complicated; it involved not only an exchange of properties but also required Verdi to guarantee certain mortgages covering other lots in which he was not interested. But from the first he took a greater interest in the new property than he had in the old. The existing buildings on the new farm were in poor repair, and Verdi ordered them to be put in shape with some alterations and then hurried back to Milan.

This property at Sant' Agata with a new building ultimately became his home and is still in his family. Of all the cities and theatres in Italy with which Verdi is associated, none has the sense of his presence that still hangs about his house and the garden which he planted around it.

In Milan the political maneuvering among patriots of various political persuasions grew more complicated and bitter even as the war seemed to go better. Facing Radetzky in the Quadrilateral were several Italian armies, the most important from Piedmont being on the west. But the Venetians also harassed him from the east, and on the south were two small armies from the Papal States. One was the Pope's regular army and the other, a band of several thousand volunteers. All of northern Italy south of the Po was now cleared of Austrian troops, and if Radetzky's army could be isolated from Austria, the area north of the Po might soon be likewise, either by a victory at arms or by concessions forced from Vienna.

But in the Quadrilateral Radetzky was safe. The distance between the four towns was such that he could mass his troops at any one by a day's march. From Peschiera to Verona is about twelve miles; from Verona to Legnago, twenty-five; Legnago to Mantua, twenty; and Mantua to Peschiera, twenty. Between Peschiera and Verona the valley of the Adige River enters the plain of the Po. As long as Radetzky controlled the valley of the Adige leading up to the Brenner Pass, which at 4490 feet was the lowest across the Alps, he could maintain his army forever in the heart of the Po Valley.

There was no secret about the strategic problem posed to the Italian armies: the Brenner Pass and Adige Valley was a traditional route for German invaders entering Italy. In May, with volunteers from other cities arriving daily in Milan, Carlo Alberto's army attacking the fringes of the Quadrilateral, and rumors of new uprisings in Vienna, many Italians thought, not unreasonably, that by summer the Austrian supply line would be cut and Radetzky forced to terms. Elsewhere others thought so too. From England in May came an offer of mediation on a basis of the Duchies of Modena and Parma to become part of Piedmont and Milan and Venice to remain part of Austria but with constitutional reforms and guarantees. Not surprisingly the Italian leaders rejected the offer; they were convinced they could do better.

But for those with a clear eye and good ear, like Mazzini and the Contessa Maffei in Milan, the political situation was alarming. Above the noise of the military bands and cheering crowds there was only the sound of argument, bitter and destructive, among the leaders of the various parties, states and towns. Verdi had written Piave in Venice: "Banish every petty municipal idea! We must all extend a fraternal hand, and Italy will yet become the first nation of the world." But it was just what the leaders could not do. They were unable to come to any agreement on the aims of the war beyond the simplest one of driving the Austrians out. But even to achieve this first step, to be taken against a superior Austrian Army, some sort of unity of purpose was clearly necessary to encourage the fainthearted, bind the weak together and take advantage of the heroism of the brave. Even in May it was possible to see that Carlo Alberto's army was moving too slowly and that what was holding it back, even more than poor leadership, was the unresolved political situation.

This appeared everywhere in a different guise yet was always the same fundamental question: what sort of political community would emerge in northern Italy after the Austrians were driven out. On the battlefield the Piedmont troops cried, as they had for hundreds of years, "Sempre avanti Savoja" (Always forward Savoy). The cry did not reassure those others about to die that their sacrifice was, after all, for a united Italy, not merely an expanding Savoy. In Milan the citizens, although unable to decide on the terms of union with Piedmont, were noisily certain that Milan must be the capital of any new northern Italian state, which did not reassure the people and royal family of Piedmont. Everywhere Gioberti continued to draw large crowds as he spoke in favor of a federation of states with the Pope as president. And everywhere republicans, Verdi among them, insisted that ultimately any new state in northern Italy must be a republic.

At the time the republicans were aided in their argument by the results of the April election in Paris. There Lamartine and the liberal republicans had won 500 of the 900 seats in the Chamber of Deputies, and Italian republicans insisted that France would support a sister republic in Italy against the Hapsburg monarchy. Another of their arguments, however, failed them: that their program was the only one that gave the people dignity and that the people would rise to support it. To some extent this was true of the towns, but by May it was clear that once again the country folk had adopted a wait-and-see attitude. They not only did not volunteer; they often kept their money in their pockets and even sometimes actively helped the Austrians. Their attitude of indifference was partly the result of the peasant's inveterate provincialism; to his ear the dialect of Piedmont was just as strange as the German of Austria. But it was also partly the failure of the towns to develop any policy other than that of merely getting the Austrians "out." Too often "out" meant merely outside the city walls, dumped in the country where a farmer, living in a small community or completely isolated, was the victim of any troop of Austrian cavalry that happened to clatter by. A barricade, so romantic and effective in a narrow city street, was a joke in an open field.

So it became increasingly clear that if the war was to be won at all it must be won quickly, before the Austrians could reinforce themselves, defeat the inexperienced army of Piedmont and the untrained volunteers, and then, controlling the country with cavalry, pick off the isolated towns one by one. But speed required unity of purpose, and there was none. The possibility of achieving it greatly lessened in May after Pio Nono, the liberal Pope, dramatically parted company with the liberal movement.

He did so in an Allocution published in Rome on 29 April and which in the following weeks was read, analyzed and discussed all over Europe. It was divided into three parts. In the first the Pope traced the history of the reform movement in general and referred to his own reforms in the Papal States. Significantly he said nothing about the constitution he had granted in March 1848; the implication was clear that he did not consider it a proper reform. The second part dealt with the war. He pointed out that he could not prevent his citizens from volunteering to fight with others against the Austrians. Then he continued: "Although some persons now desire that we, together with the other peoples and princes of Italy, make war against the Austrians, we deem it proper to disclose clearly in this solemn meeting of ours, that it is wholly foreign to our intentions, since we, however unworthy, exercise on earth the functions of Him who is the author of peace and lover of charity, and according to the office of our supreme Apostolate we follow and embrace all races, peoples, and nations with equal zeal of paternal love." Then finally he denied any part in a proposal to make Italy a united republic under his presidency, and he urged all Italians to reject such ideas and to continue loyal to their princes.

The Allocution was a public statement directed to northern Italians fighting what they considered to be a war for independence, and each man of them, depending on his political and religious convictions, was saddened, infuriated, embarrassed, or, like Verdi, simply strengthened in his republican prejudice that there was no hope for Italy in the Papacy. The Austrians, naturally, were jubilant. In Rome, overnight, popular demonstrations for the Pope ceased.

At the same time, but privately, Pio Nono appealed to Emperor Ferdinand to make peace on a basis of Italy and Austria each observing their "natural boundaries." The appeal provoked laughter in Vienna. Ferdinand remarked: "Austria possesses her Italian provinces by virtue of the same treaties which have reconstituted the Temporal Power of the Pope."

The remark, however cynical, cut through the fuzzy good intentions of the Pope and showed that Ferdinand, like Metternich, had thought harder about the problem of Italy than had Pio Nono. Short of something as wide as the English Channel, there are no natural boundaries, only boundaries which are observed or violated as the neighbors consider in their interest. Both the Papacy and the Hapsburg Empire were based on ideas supposedly transcending differences of language, culture, or climate. Neither could allow their north Italian subjects to form an independent kingdom on a national basis with "natural"

ROME

boundaries without by implication conceding the same right to all their other restive subjects and so preparing to pass out of existence.

For the Austrians there was not only the principle of the old Holy Roman Empire binding diverse nations together, there was also the very practical problem that the Austrian provinces, the Kingdom of Lombardy-Venetia, while containing only one-sixth of the population of the Austrian Empire, provided one-third of its wealth. This Aus-

tria was not prepared to give up. In the same way by far the richest part of the Papal States, the area from Pesaro to Bologna, was north of the Apennines, a "natural" boundary and in the Po Valley. The loss of it would mean not only a severe blow to the Papal finances but, inevitably, increased dependence on some outside power for whatever remained of the Papal States.

This was what Metternich had meant when he said that a liberal Pope was not a possibility. Liberalism in Italy, whether championed by a constitutional monarchist or a republican, inevitably meant, at very least in northern Italy, some form of Italian unity, whether by conquest or merger. A Pope could be liberal only if he was prepared to have his Temporal Power greatly reduced, if not actually extinguished. No Pope had yet been prepared to go that far, and Pio Nono by his Allocution declared to the world that he was not.

The theory of the Temporal Power was both practical and mystical with the two inextricably intertwined. In the Middle Ages in order for the Pope to be able to exercise his spiritual power (the appointment of cardinals, excommunication, etc.) with any degree of independence he had needed a fortified city, Rome, an army and also some land in which to maneuver the army, the Papal States. These last also provided the necessary agricultural area to support the city. But only with the walled city, the army and the surrounding countryside could the Pope prevent the emperors of the world from kidnapping his person and dictating his decisions. The danger was not theoretical; the event had happened twice within the memory of many, including Pio Nono. In 1798 and then in 1809 Napoleon had overrun the Papal States and taken first Pius VI and then Pius VII as prisoners to France. The first had died there; the second had been able to return to Rome only in 1814.

There is no doubt that Pius VII and his successors, including Pio Nono, all believed that the Papal States were literally a gift of God to his Church, the Patrimony of St. Peter. To them as seeming evidence of it was the fact that the Papal States were the most ancient sovereignty in Europe. It was therefore the duty of any Pope to defend every inch of his Patrimony; how could a Pope alienate a gift from God? A liberal Pope might introduce court reform, better housing, or start a program of public works, but he could not allow his subjects to vote directly or by representative to merge the Papal States in some larger secular community. Yet after he granted a constitution in March 1848, for the first time admitting laymen into his government, the vision of just such a sacrilege began to haunt Pio Nono and, unable to see any solution except in reaction, he issued his Allocution.

If the Papacy had been a purely local church like the Church of England, it might have, given time, been able to work out some sort of imaginative adjustment to an emerging national state in Italy. But its success as a world church in the minds of men over the centuries hindered any such adjustment. The Pope, as Pio Nono stated, was the father of all Christians and all his children were citizens of the Holy City. There all had a right to come, all were equally loved and made welcome, and all could share equally in the spiritual refreshments of their eternal home on earth. In a divided, harassed world it was a powerful idea. Catholics from all over the world were quite ready to come to Rome in order to fight the Italians to preserve it. Romans were not considered Italians, and Rome, in the opinion of most Catholics in 1848, was not an Italian city.

Many Romans, however, did not see why they should not be allowed to choose for themselves between Catholic and Italian citizenship and, whenever given a chance, stated their preference for the latter. By 1870 a majority of Catholics around the world were prepared to have Rome become an Italian city. In 1848 they were not, and even if Pio Nono himself had wished to make such an adjustment, probably his cardinals and the Catholic faithful would have prevented it.

On a military level Pio Nono's Allocution made little difference to the patriots. The army of volunteers from the Papal States continued to be just that, and the Pope's regular army began taking its orders from Carlo Alberto. But politically it compounded the confusion which threatened to dissipate all the military gains. The problem of the Papacy's Temporal Power which had already plagued Italy for a thousand years was to continue to do so and with a new virulence because of Pio Nono's seeming betrayal of the patriotic cause.

In the last days of May, while Milan still had not officially declared its political intent, Verdi decided to return to Paris. The republicans were daily losing ground in Milan, and their cause was plainly lost. The city, led by the constitutional monarchists, would soon annex itself and Lombardy on some sort of terms to Piedmont. There was nothing to keep him, and at Paris he had left all his business affairs up in the air, some of which urgently needed to be settled. He had come with high hopes and left with disappointment. From Paris Strepponi, almost certainly reflecting his views, wrote bitterly to a friend in Florence: "They forget how much it costs to overturn a throne, and they raise another, as if man cannot live without a king!"

As he crossed the border into Switzerland, Verdi wrote to Cammarano in Naples, urging him to work up an idea for an opera which Cammarano had suggested. It was to be a propaganda piece extolling a united Italy defeating a German invader. If he could not work for a united Italy in Milan as a republican politician, he would do so from Paris as a musician.

CHAPTER 18

VERDI AT ROME AND
LA BATTAGLIA DI LEGNANO

1848–1849; AGE, 34–35

BACK in Paris Verdi for the first time, as far as can be determined, lived openly with Strepponi. Together in the summer they rented a house with a garden in Passy, then still a small village outside of Paris. In a letter Strepponi wrote in 1867 to the Contessa Maffei she stated that the idea of a country house was hers: she liked to garden and perhaps she thought rest and quiet would benefit Verdi while he worked on his opera.

Cammarano's idea was to build an opera around the defeat of Frederick Barbarossa, Holy Roman Emperor and German King, by the cities of the Lombard League. The battle took place in 1176 at Legnano, which in time had become Legnago and one of the four cities of the Quadrilateral. The hopeful parallel for the events of 1848 was obvious, and throughout the summer Verdi and Cammarano corresponded about the libretto.

It was the only opera at the moment Verdi had under way although he had been under contract to compose and produce an opera at the Teatro San Carlo in October. But the management there, undoubtedly because of the political troubles in Naples, had failed to furnish the libretto in the time specified, and Verdi had canceled the contract. Perhaps it would have been more generous on his part to consider the political troubles an act of God which throughout their duration suspended the running of the contract; certainly Flauto at the San Carlo thought so, and he threatened litigation. It was an error of judgment. Verdi was not to be threatened. He was capable of generous acts but on his own motion, or, more rarely, by an appeal to his heart, never by a suggestion that he had a duty to perform. As usual, in Verdi's relations with the San Carlo poor Cammarano was caught in the middle.

Possibly a reason Verdi, given the chance, was so quick to cancel the contract was that he liked Cammarano's idea for a patriotic opera and feared that its production would be forbidden at Naples. And considering the temper of the times, King Ferdinando would never have permitted it.

Meanwhile in Paris Verdi saw a revolt put down with savage brutality. What had happened was that once again, as in 1830, the workers of Paris saw, or thought they saw, the fruits of their revolution being plucked, this time by the liberal republicans, for the benefit of the middle class. The workers were interested in socialistic programs such as guaranteeing a worker a right to a job, and although the constitution of the Second Republic promised these aims, they did not seem about to be realized. So the workers began to riot, first in March, then in April, and finally in June they took to the barricades. It was bloody. The Archbishop of Paris was killed trying to utter a message of peace. The government, with a controlling majority of republicans, voted dictatorial powers to a general of the Algerian campaign, Godefroy Cavaignac, a fellow republican but of the old Roman type, high-minded and austere. Within three days he had quelled the revolt. In the ensuing months thousands of the workers were deported without trial. Cavaignac was called ever after "the Butcher of June." The episode was not one on which republicans anywhere liked to dwell; the lesson seemed to be that, given the chance, republicans could not govern except by the sword. The unrest in Paris may have been a reason Strepponi and Verdi rented the house in Passy.

In Italy during June and July events hurried to disaster. Early in June Lombardy had finally voted 561,002 to 681 for immediate fusion with Piedmont. But the vote had little meaning as all the difficult questions were left for a Constituent Assembly to be called after the war was won. At the end of June Piedmont voted to accept the fusion, but likewise postponing the important decisions. And finally in July Venice, too, voted to fuse with Piedmont. Carlo Alberto proclaimed a Kingdom of Upper Italy which included also Parma and Modena. It existed about two weeks or until the battle of Custozza, a series of engagements lasting from 23 to 27 July and in which Radetzky outmaneuvered and defeated the Piedmont generals. The Austrian army,

ANTONIO BAREZZI
(*from an oil painting*)

VERDI IN 1842
(*from a drawing*)

MARGHERITA BAREZZI
(*from an oil painting*)

THE CONTESSA
CLARA MAFFEI

STREPPONI IN 1845
(*from an oil painting*)

VERDI IN 1853

STREPPONI

VERDI IN 1859

VERDI IN 1867

TERESA STOLZ IN 1870

VERDI IN 1876

STREPPONI IN 1878

regrouped and reinforced, numbered 140,000, the Italians about 65,000.

The defeat, although not severe, was decisive, and the Piedmont armies everywhere retreated. In Paris Verdi, as one of the most distinguished Italians present, signed an appeal to General Cavaignac to intervene with troops. But the French government busied itself with its own affairs. In Italy Carlo Alberto agreed to an armistice, the terms of which required him to pull his army back to Piedmont, leaving all of the Po Valley to the Austrians. Those cities which for some reason were peculiarly defensible, like Venice, might conceivably hold out on their own. But the great majority of them, like Milan and Parma, would be immediately reoccupied by Radetzky. As the Piedmont troops retreated through Milan, the crowds there, who had stayed snugly at home during the battles, shrieked that they were betrayed. They called the soldiers cowards, Carlo Alberto a Judas, and surrounding the King's headquarters, they tried to hold him prisoner. He refused to let his troops fire on the crowd and escaped in a private carriage. If the "Cinque Giornate" in March was Milan's glory, that first week of August was its disgrace. Politically it greatly increased the bitterness and suspicion between the Piedmontese and the Lombards.

At once the leaders, soldiers or anyone who might be subject to reprisal by the Austrians began to leave Milan. Manzoni went to his wife's country villa on the Piedmont side of Lago Maggiore. Muzio and the Contessa Maffei both went to Switzerland. To Muzio, whose resources were small, Verdi was able to forward some money by making a joke of it. To the Contessa he wrote:

Paris, 24 August 1848

Cara Clarina:

Your letter gave me the greatest pleasure, for I didn't know what to think about you. Now that I know you are saved and safe, I am happy.

You want to know the French opinion on events in Italy? Dear God, what can I find to say!! Those who are not opposed to us are indifferent: And I must add that the idea of a United Italy frightens the petty nonentities who are in power. France will certainly not intervene with arms, if it is not swept along against its will by some unforeseen event. Anglo-French diplomatic intervention can be only unjust, shameful for France, and ruinous for us. . . . Indeed, such intervention would tend to make Austria abandon Lombardy and content itself with Venetia. Supposing that Austria could be induced to give up Lombardy (at present she looks as if she might, but perhaps she would sack and burn down everything before leaving), that would be one more dishonor for us; the devastation of Lombardy, and still another prince in Italy. No, no, no! I have no hopes of France, nor of England. If I have hopes of anybody, it is—what do you think?—of Austria. Something serious must be happening there, and if we use the opportunity and wage the war that should be waged, the war of insurrection, then Italy may yet be freed. But God forbid that we should rely on our kings or on foreign peoples!

Italian diplomats are arriving here from every direction, yesterday Tommaseo, today Picciotti. They will have no success; it seems impossible that they should still have hope in France. There you have my opinion. Please don't attach any importance to it, for you know I don't understand politics.

For the rest, France herself stands before a catastrophe, and I don't know how she will surmount it. The investigation of the events of May and June is the most despicable, repulsive thing in the world. What a pitiful, puny age. Nothing great happens—not even great crimes. I believe that a new revolution is coming, you can smell the *odor* of it everywhere. And the next revolution will overthrow this poor republic completely. Let us hope it will not happen, but there is reason enough to fear it will. (etc.)

In Italy the effect of the armistice was to infuriate the republicans in the towns who felt that Piedmont and those supporting its policy had betrayed a national movement. Venice, Brescia and some others held out. In the Papal States Bologna, operating for the moment independently of Rome, also repulsed the Austrians. But at Parma the Austrians re-entered the city in the name of Duke Carlo. Radetzky, however, was not able to press his advantage after Custozza to a great extent for there was still trouble in Vienna where a second time Emperor Ferdinand had to flee. He went to Innsbruck in the Tyrol, always a stronghold of the Hapsburgs. About the same time on 25 October *Il Corsaro* had its première at Trieste, a city so firmly held by the Austrians that Lucca was able to interest the local impresario in a new Verdi opera. In spite of a good cast it was not a success. A duet and chorus were admired, but the only "performer" the audience chose to honor with a curtain call was the scene painter.

In Paris Verdi was entirely caught up in his new opera and events in Italy. He sent Mazzini, who had fled from Milan to Switzerland, music for a patriotic poem, "Suona la Tromba" ("Sound the Trum-

MAZZINI

pet"), by a young Genovese, Goffredo Mameli. "I am sending you the hymn," he wrote, "and though it is a little late I hope it will arrive in time. I have tried to be more popular and easy than may have been possible for me. Do with it what you wish. Burn it, if it doesn't seem good enough." (etc.) Then he closed, "May this hymn soon be sung among the music of the cannon on the Lombardy plains," and added, "Accept the most heartfelt greetings of a man who holds you in great honor!" Mazzini published the hymn, but it never became popular. The music is not particularly successful and, coming after the armistice, the fighting was over. Also, another man, Michele Novaro, had set Mameli's poem "Fratelli d'Italia," "Brothers of Italy," earlier and with greater success. This became one of the great songs thoughout the Risorgimento and ultimately, in 1946 when Italy became a republic, the country's national anthem.

To Cammarano in Naples Verdi wrote a steady stream of letters about the new opera which was to be called *La Battaglia di Legnano,* or *The Battle of Legnano.* He had suggestions and requests for almost every scene. Some were vague: "After a beautiful recitative, have the husband arrive and do a moving little duet. Have the father bless his son, or something of the sort." But in others he requested specific lines, advising whether he wanted to repeat words or not, or requested another solo voice in an ensemble, or a new scene to give the soprano greater importance. Generally his remarks are aimed at keeping the story short, swiftly paced and full of passion. At least for this opera, in which he was striving for broad effects, "la patria," he deliberately emphasized dramatic scenes rather than dramatic characters.

But in the same letter to Cammarano he could not resist giving all sorts of advice, which he hoped would reach Flauto, the impresario, for the first production in Naples of *Macbeth*. He had specific suggestions for the staging in the apparition scene—"the *kings* must not be dolls"—and "the place they pass over must be like a mound, and you must be able clearly to see them ascend and descend." He had seen a production of the play in London, and he prided himself on understanding Shakespeare. But beyond these technical points the greater part of his suggestions are aimed at developing character, particularly that of Lady Macbeth. "Tell them," he wrote Cammarano, "that the most important numbers of the opera are the duet between Lady Macbeth and her husband and the sleepwalking scene. If these two numbers are lost, then the opera falls flat. And these two numbers absolutely must not be sung:

> They must be acted and declaimed
> With very hollow voice,
> Veiled: otherwise it will
> make no effect.
> The orchestra with mutes."

The style of routine performances at the time required the orchestra and singers to go all out on the big duet and soprano number, and Verdi could not quite bring himself to leave the opera to its fate. To Flauto he wrote hopefully: "You should be at the rehearsals yourself and don't grudge an extra one. This opera is a little more difficult than my others, and its mise-en-scène is important. I confess, I care more for it than the others and I should be sorry to see it fall on its face."

Ricordi, who was to publish the new opera, had arranged for its première at the Teatro Argentina at Rome in January 1849. Rome with the Pope and a seemingly popular liberal government had probably impressed Ricordi as the most stable of the major operatic cities outside the area of Austrian censorship or guns and the most likely to give the new opera a good start. But even at Rome the political

situation had deteriorated to the point where, by the end of
the Pope had fled.

After his Allocution Pio Nono's position had gradually become
intolerable. In the early months of the summer the most important
layman in the Pope's new liberal ministry, Terenzo Mamiani, had
tried to create a new form of Papal government by separating the spiritual and temporal power. But it had not been a success. The government offices, courts and police were almost entirely staffed by
priests, and any division between spiritual and temporal duties and
offices meant depriving the priests of their jobs and power. Naturally
these men interpreted the Allocution as an indirect order to drag their
feet and hinder reform. On the other hand, reformists of all shades
felt that in the Allocution Pio Nono had betrayed them, and this feeling increased when, after three audiences with the Pope, Gioberti
was unable to announce any support for his plan of federation. Caught
between those Romans out of power pushing forward and those in
power pushing back, Mamiani could do nothing but resign. Pio Nono
replaced him with Count Pellegrino Rossi, an arrogant, strong man,
but also a brilliant administrator. Rossi's policy was not to divide the
spiritual and temporal power but to reform the traditional Papal government, men and offices, to make it more efficient and honest. While
doing it he intended to quell the crowds in the street with the police.
This was becoming more difficult, for after the armistice in the north
the volunteers, furious at the Pope and now with arms, began to pour
back into the city. Like Mamiani, Rossi soon found himself without
friends. By sheer force of character he sustained himself until 15
November when, like Caesar in March, he ignored warnings, started
for the Council Chamber and was stabbed as he started up the first
steps.

The murder was the work of the extreme republicans, many of
whom came from the poorest section of the city, the Trastevere. For
months they had been organized in clubs and sought through their
leaders to put pressure on the Pope to join Piedmont against Austria.
What they held most against Rossi was that he opposed any sort of
united Italy in the north and would send no help to Piedmont, Venice,
or any of the other towns still holding out. With Rossi dead the extreme
republicans began to rule Rome through their control over the crowds
in the street, which now were joined by the soldiers and carabinieri.
For the next two days the Pope was besieged in the Quirinal Palace

by an armed crowd numbering at times as much as six thousand. Bullets spattered through the windows; a bishop was shot dead. What was left of the government, now thoroughly cowed, agreed to disband the Pope's Swiss Guard and replace it with a Civic Guard. Thereafter Pio Nono was a prisoner.

His escape was well arranged. He was still allowed to see the foreign ambassadors, and those from the great Catholic countries called often. On 24 November the French Ambassador had a private audience with the Pope. Through the door the Civic Guard could hear the Frenchman's voice droning on and on. Meanwhile the Pope, dressed as a simple priest, followed his valet through a secret passage, down to a courtyard where a carriage was waiting. He left Rome by the Lateran Gate, accompanied by the Bavarian Ambassador. They were challenged, passed and continued on to Gaeta, a seaport town across the border of the Kingdom of the Two Sicilies. There others joined them. King Ferdinando of Naples was delighted to pose as the protector of the Pope, put a palace at his disposal and urged him to remain as long as he wanted. Pio Nono at once made it plain that he had no intention of returning to Rome on any conditions except his own and prepared to spend the winter. The Gaetans, who saw in him a source of income, were delighted.

The Romans were not. The simplest people, at least, were disturbed. Although most of them could not read the bulletins that the Pope's adherents posted, their leaders could not conceal from them that the Pope had fled voluntarily. The people were quite prepared to bully him and even perhaps to be bullied in return. But after fourteen centuries of the Papacy in their way they loved Pio Nono, and his voluntary departure left a void which all the republican oratory could not fill. For the moderates the Pope's departure was a disaster. No day-to-day co-operation was possible with a government miles away at Gaeta, and that part of the clerical government that remained in Rome was likewise immobilized. The extreme republicans controlled the government and announced a Constituent Assembly with representatives elected by direct and universal suffrage; it was to meet on 5 February 1849 to decide on a new form of government for the Papal States. The Pope condemned the election and forbade Catholics to vote. As a result the republicans won almost all the seats, and it was certain that the Assembly, when it met in February, would declare the Papal States to be a republic. From all over Italy republicans began to pour into Rome. Among them were Mazzini and Garibaldi. Verdi arrived early in January to direct the rehearsals of his opera.

On 27 January 1849 he conducted the première of *La Battaglia di Legnano*. The occasion was a "furore." Probably under the circumstances any opera would have succeeded that waved a flag and allowed the chorus to sing of "la patria." But *La Battaglia di Legnano* did more. In the finale of its third act the hero, locked in a tower room, hears the sound of trumpets as his friends march off to fight Barbarossa. To join them and save his honor he leaps from the window into the moat. The music is stiring: the man's agitation is contrasted with the sounds of the distant march. At one of the early performances a soldier in the gallery was so carried away by it all that, tearing off his coat, he, too, leaped from the gallery and landed sprawling in the orchestra. No one seems to have been injured.

The impresario repeated the opera as often as the singers' voices would allow, and generally at each performance the entire fourth act was repeated. The excitement in the audience continued to be extraordinary. Cockades were worn, streamers flown, and almost every chorus interrupted with cheering. For the first few performances while Verdi remained in Rome he was called endlessly onto the stage; in the cheering "Viva Verdi" alternated with "Viva Italia," and he became the personal symbol of the patriotic movement. He did not enjoy it and left Rome for Paris as quickly as he could.

The extraordinary thing about *La Battaglia di Legnano* is not its success in 1849 but its quality as an opera. As a propaganda piece it set an extremely high standard, far higher than anything similar that Broadway or Hollywood produced in either World War. For intensity of feeling perhaps Noel Coward's "Cavalcade" equaled it.

What Verdi and Cammarano did, and it is the usual method of a propaganda piece, was to combine two stories: one, historical, and the other, a private romance. But they were unusually successful in intertwining the two so that a single scene or line is often able to carry a double meaning. The tenor is locked in the tower room, for example, by the baritone who believes the tenor has seduced his wife. When the tenor leaps to join his troop, because not to do so would be to break his vow to fight for Italy, the private story and the public lesson are well merged. In the last act the finale is built about the line: "Chi muore per la patria alma sì rea non ha," or, "He who dies for his country does not have a guilty soul." It, too, does double duty, allowing the baritone to believe the tenor's dying protestation that the wife is pure while at the same time presenting the propaganda. The result is an extremely swift story of action in which the four acts, taking only just two hours, still build considerable intensity.

The propaganda is ubiquitous. Every character at some point sings about "la patria," and the scene Verdi requested, in which the father was to bless his son "or something of the sort," became a farewell from the baritone to his wife, whom he still believes to be faithful. The father holds his infant son in his arms and sings: "Tell him that he has Italian blood" and that "after God he must honor the country." It has always been easier to sing mawkish sentiments than to say them, perhaps because the forward motion of music prevents the sentiment from coagulating into indigestible blobs. Verdi's melodies were vigorous and the arias kept short, so that the effect was generally more of excitement than sentiment.

Some of the worst excrescences of modern propaganda films and musical comedies Verdi, by his very nature, avoided. Barbarossa, the enemy, appears in the second act as a dignified, noble man, which historically he was, and not as a brutish caricature. The villains of the piece are the town fathers of Como who refuse to join the Lombard League. They are presented in council and, like Barbarossa, as honest men, though wrong headed. There are no bugle jokes about getting up in the morning or snickers about latrine duty. Verdi felt strongly about "la patria." It aroused the noblest emotions in him, and he could see that it did in others. Young men from the towns were going out to die in what seemed like a hopeless cause. Verdi could not have conceived of any reason why he should cheapen their sacrifice by making the enemy unworthy or by suggesting with little jokes that it was fun after all. Nor would he evade the central issue by suggesting it did not end in death. Because he himself believed simply and without embarrassment in such concepts as honor and "la patria," he could deal directly in them and persuade others that to die fighting for Italy was a joy greater than life itself. In the same way he could not have understood the argument put forward by some artists during World War II that their first duty was to preserve their artistic talent pure and not prostitute it for purposes of political propaganda. Verdi was quite prepared to parade his deepest feelings before the public for the cause of Italy. For him the conflict of artistic integrity versus public purpose did not arise because he so firmly believed in the nobility of the cause.

The chief lesson Verdi preached was that of a united Italy. He was a republican but not a doctrinaire, and the historical setting allowed him to avoid the political question which at the moment Italians could not decide. His heroes in the opera were men of medieval towns and historically they undoubtedly cried: "Verona" or "Milano." In Verdi they cry "Italia." This lesson, seemingly so simple, most Italians would grasp only in the future as they reviewed the disasters of 1848 and 1849. Verdi grasped it earlier, probably through some mixture of his reading in Mazzini, of his own political speculation, and by the chance of being born in the countryside and free from the town-bred Italian's inordinate municipal pride. But his understanding of it and his power to communicate it made him a leader of the Risorgimento, and because he was a musician and dealt so directly with the emotions, he was particularly dear to the people.

Musically *La Battaglia di Legnano* is in the old tried-and-true form of introductory chorus, recitative and arias slow and fast. Verdi, after all, consciously strove for a sure success. But it was his thirteenth opera, not including the revision of *I Lombardi,* and he had by then honed the form to a sharp perfection without any redundant notes. The last act, which runs only fifteen minutes, manages to include a prayer for the soprano, choruses of hope for priests and people, announcement of victory, a victory chorus, arrival and death of the hero and final chorus. All are characterized separately in the music without the scene seeming confused or hurried. Verdi could do it now where he could not before because his melodic lines were fusing ever more closely with the words, so that whereas before a stanza might be needed, now sometimes a single phrase would carry his idea. The melodies just as melodies were not as exciting as those in *Ernani,* but the orchestration of them was subtler. Compared to Verdi's earliest operas and considering its purpose, *La Battaglia di Legnano* is remarkably free of clashing cymbals and blaring trombones. Even its overture, built around a march representing the Lombards and a contrasting soft theme, is held down to a reasonable level of brass noise.

His audience, of course, did not worry about the artistic questions; they found it a glorious night at the theatre and were pleased. One performer particularly so was the tenor, Gaetano Fraschini. *La Battaglia di Legnano* was the third Verdi première in which he had sung; the other two had been *Alzira* and *Il Corsaro.*

CHAPTER 19

THE DISASTER AT ROME
ENDS AN ERA

1849; AGE, 35

AS expected, the Constituent Assembly at Rome on 9 February 1849 proclaimed that the new form of government for the Papal States would be that of a republic, based on a constitution and with the capital at Rome. By so doing the Assembly cut through the complicated question of the Temporal Power of the Pope simply by voting it out of existence. In the future, priests, cardinals and the Pope himself, if he chose to return to Rome, would be citizens like all other men, each with one vote. News of the Assembly's action was not the sort to which men remained indifferent. Republicans, naturally, exulted. From Paris Verdi wrote Piave that he regretted leaving Rome so soon after the première of *La Battaglia di Legnano;* he had missed the historic occasion. Others felt the occasion was infamous. From Gaeta Pio Nono issued a formal appeal to the great Catholic countries, France, Spain, Austria and Naples, to intervene with arms and restore him to power.

Throughout February little happened. The sympathies of governments in Europe were entirely with the Pope, but the great powers moved slowly. Both Spain and Naples were too weak to restore the Pope alone, and France and Austria were suspicious of each other. The republicans hoped that France, as a sister republic, would recognize the new state and by diplomacy prevent Austria from intervening. It seemed not impossible. In the Po Valley Radetzky still had not retaken Brescia, Bologna, or Venice, and in his rear, in Vienna, the Emperor Ferdinand had been forced, in December, to abdicate in favor of his nephew, Franz Josef, who was only nineteen. With troubles at home and a new and inexperienced Emperor, Austria seemed unlikely to start on a foreign crusade.

In Paris, too, in December there had been a change of government but by an election under the Second Republic. There, to everyone's astonishment, Prince Louis Napoleon had become president, defeating the nearest candidate, General Cavaignac, almost five to one. The General, an earnest man, had refused to shake hands with the winner. No one quite knew what to make of the election. Louis Napoleon was not well known in France, and it is possible that he won because of it. The other candidates were all stamped with notorious failures: Lamartine had just shown that the republicans could not govern without calling in the dictator, General Cavaignac; the people were tired of the middle-of-the-road Orleanists under Louis Philippe and disgusted with the reactionary legitimists. There was left only Louis Napoleon and some candidates from the socialist and radical parties. The election is important in French history because, by giving Louis Napoleon the presidency, it gave him the position from which he could, and in four years did, make himself by a coup d'état Emperor of the French. But in 1849 he was still an ambiguous figure, styling himself Prince-President and wearing the uniform of a general in the National Guard. What the Italian republicans liked to recall about him was his fighting for their cause at Bologna in the uprising of 1831–32. They were less happy to remember that he had escaped the Austrians only by the help of that Bishop of Imola who was now Pio Nono. It seemed not impossible that he would use his influence as Prince-President to support the republicans in Rome. Verdi, however, who had met the man and was in Paris, thought differently. He wrote to Piave that there was no hope in France, now less than ever.

Verdi's letters throughout this period, as might be expected, are almost feverish with excitement over events in Italy, and every other sentence is sprinkled with dots and exclamation points. He rejoiced in every heroic deed as a credit to Italy and kept insisting that as soon as he had wound up his affairs in Paris, he would "fly" to Italy. In fact he never did, and even when as at Rome he might have stayed, he chose to hurry away. Yet no one thought him any less of a patriot because he had never actually fired a shot. His reasons, which of course he never listed neatly on paper, seem to have been both public and personal. His feeling for Strepponi continued to deepen, and she remained steadily in Paris. In January while in Rome he had written to the directors of the Opéra in Paris about a void contract he had with them and asked them to return their signed copy of it to the Signora Strepponi at 13 bis rue de la Victoire. She in turn was to give to the directors his signed copy. The rather legalistic letter is also curiously romantic, for it is the first recorded time Verdi publicly gave Strepponi's address as his own. And the fact that he was prepared to use her as his agent, although he had a recognized agent in Escudier, is further evidence of his increasing reliance on her. Undoubtedly a private reason for Verdi's absence from Italy was Strepponi's presence in Paris.

More public was the situation in the Po Valley. There the Austrians had re-occupied most of the cities, and the leading revolutionaries had fled. The hotels just across the Swiss border were crowded with Italians waiting to see whether the Austrians would proscribe them, confiscate their property, or merely impose fines. Even Muzio, hardly a revolutionary leader, found he was penalized indirectly. When he had first come to Milan in 1847, leaving Verdi with Strepponi in Paris, he had started conducting operas, particularly Verdi's, in the smaller cities like Mantua. But with the war his opportunities ceased, and his mother again put pressure on him to compete for the post of music master of Busseto. Reluctantly he agreed. He undoubtedly would have been the most able candidate, but his friend the Mayor advised him not to bother to come to Busseto. The post was controlled by Austrian sympathizers, and Muzio would not be seriously considered. With the Austrian army back in Parma the animosity or at least official nervousness over a man of Verdi's stature would have been even greater. It was not the time for him to return to Parma except as an obscure, private citizen.

Meanwhile he planned to do another opera with Cammarano and for the Teatro San Carlo at Naples. This was an act of friendship on Verdi's part. He would have preferred to do an opera with a theatre in Venice, Florence, or even Rome, in any of which he found it easier to work than Naples. But Cammarano had been late in delivering a libretto to the San Carlo management, and it was disciplining him with threats of law suits, prison and, worst of all, future unemployment. A strong man or even a free one might have ignored the threats, but Cammarano had six children and, as a poor poet, limited resources. His greatest asset was his working relation with Verdi, and to Verdi he appealed. Fortunately for Cammarano, Verdi could put himself in a position to help. He could cancel the contract with the Paris Opéra, and he could write Piave that there was no time at the moment for an opera on Rienzi and the medieval Roman Republic. Fortunately for Verdi, as he recognized, Cammarano was the best of his librettists. He constructed the dramas more carefully than either Solera or Piave, and although he never achieved the occasional brilliant line that Solera managed, his verses as a whole were smoother and clearer.

The subject the two men had agreed upon was a historical novel by a Florentine, Francesco Domenico Guerrazzi, called *The Siege of Florence*. The opera, like *La Battaglia di Legnano,* would be a banner for freedom and Italy, particularly as Guerrazzi had taken a leading part in proclaiming a Tuscan Republic only ten days after that of Rome. Through the winter Verdi and Cammarano corresponded about the libretto until in April it was presented in a summary to the Neapolitan censors. It was rejected on the ground that the general political situation in Italy and particularly that of Florence made the subject "inopportune."

The men can hardly have been surprised. Ferdinando of Naples, who was sheltering a fugitive Pope at Gaeta and threatening the Roman Republic with his troops, was hardly going to permit a republican propaganda piece to open the opera season. The opera house, after all, was not only royal but actually attached to the palace. And even if Florence had been on another continent, the situation in the rest of Italy in the spring of 1849 was enough to make a government hold its breath.

In Piedmont Gioberti had become for a while Prime Minister. Everyone knew that he and Pio Nono were having diplomatic conversations, and many hoped that some sort of federation of Italian states would emerge, guaranteeing the Pope his spiritual independence while allowing his former subjects to continue with their constitution. Verdi saw no hope in the negotiations. He seems to have distrusted Gioberti and felt that the Papacy was incapable of any self-reform.

In the end the negotiations came to nothing, and Gioberti was forced to resign. With his retirement the scheme for some sort of federation with the Pope as president ceased to exist as a practical possibility. In the future moderates would have to choose between extremes, the Papacy maintaining its Temporal Power across the center of the peninsula or some sort of united Italy in which all of the Papal States, except perhaps Rome itself, had been seized by force of arms. Barring some imaginative new proposal or a change in position on the part of either extreme, a peaceful solution to the problem of the Papal States had become impossible.

With the fall of Gioberti's administration at Turin the pressure in Piedmont to renew the war with Austria increased. The country was filled with Lombard exiles; its King, Carlo Alberto, had a mystical belief that he was born to liberate Italy, and the army as well as many of the people felt the national honor had been smudged in the campaign of 1848. On 14 March 1849 Carlo Alberto denounced the armistice and prepared to go to war.

Immediately, south of the Po, the Austrian army again began to retract north into the Quadrilateral. In Parma Duke Carlo II, the dandy, seeing the Austrians pull out a second time, admitted that he was not born to rule and abdicated. There was talk in the various Republics of Rome, Tuscany and Venice of sending aid to Piedmont, but none had any troops to spare, and before any could have arrived in the north Radetzky had crossed the Ticino River into Piedmont and on 23 March at Novara crushed the Piedmontese army. Carlo Alberto vainly sought death in the battle. To obtain better terms for his country he abdicated in favor of his eldest son Vittorio Emanuele. Then he rode away alone, passed through the Austrian lines in disguise, and retired to a Portuguese monastery at Oporto. There before the summer was over he died.

The two campaigns, ending first in Custozza and then Novara, had been a disaster for the small Kingdom of Piedmont, demoralizing its citizens, depleting its treasury and thrusting a new king to the fore under the most difficult circumstances. He saved Piedmont from conquest by Austria, which would have been delighted to add it to its Italian provinces, partly by inspiring France with the danger to it of such an extension of Austrian power and partly by agreeing to abandon the patriots elsewhere to whatever fate they could fashion for themselves against the Austrian army. At Venice, for example, the withdrawal of his fleet from the Adriatic meant inevitable defeat. Irate republicans tried to say that he had betrayed the patriotic cause, but most north Italians saw that he could do nothing else. One thing Vittorio Emanuele refused to do, although Radetzky pressed it, and that was to modify or abrogate the constitution his father had granted only a year before. This stand, which he made a point of honor, endeared him to the liberal Piedmontese and was of incalculable importance in the coming decade. Because of it there existed in Italy where all Italians could see it a constitutional monarchy which functioned well and dignified its citizens by allowing them a voice in their affairs.

After Novara, with no possibility of interference from Piedmont, Radetzky began to mop up the spots of resistance. At Parma there was no fight. The army re-entered as before, only this time in the name of Duke Carlo III. But at Brescia the resistance was fierce, and the Austrian brutalities under General Haynau became a European scandal. At Venice in April a siege began which lasted, while the city slowly and gallantly starved, until August. And in May the Austrians took Bologna which opened to them the entire Adriatic coast and backside of the Roman Republic. But by then Rome itself was in a state of siege. The time was not "inopportune" for Verdi and Cammarano to write another opera like *La Battaglia di Legnano;* it was simply too late. By common consent they put it aside and never went back to it.

Meanwhile in the siege at Rome an important issue was in the balance, whether the city should be Catholic or Italian. France, although itself a republic, had answered Pio Nono's call for help and sent an army to retake his city for him. The Romans put a band on the city walls to play *La Marseillaise,* but the French guns were not turned to cabbages by the irony of it. The siege, after several weeks of skirmishing outside the walls, lasted a month, and then on 3 July 1849 the French entered the city. Yet the ultimate victory belonged to Mazzini and Garibaldi, the men who had inspired and defended the Republic, and not to Pio Nono who had defeated it.

Mazzini, with his sad, long face and dressed always in somber black, was a figure every bit as arresting as Pio Nono, personally a genial man and generally clothed in white and gold. Of the two, which was the saint? Undoubtedly Mazzini was the more eloquent, and his words and writings stirred the imagination of Italy. He talked of a "Third Rome," not the old Rome of classical times, or Papal Rome with its churches and basilicas, but a new Rome of modern Italians. The simplicity of Mazzini's life, the purity of his ideals and the years he had suffered for them held the country's attention; even more, he inspired men to die for his vision of Rome, and thereby the city acquired a new glory. In the future when Lombards, Tuscans, Piedmontese, or Venetians talked of a united Italy, they talked increasingly of its capital, of necessity, being Rome. Such was the victory Mazzini fashioned out of the defeat of the Roman Republic. Like himself, it was mystical and prophetic.

Around the black and white figures of Mazzini and Pio Nono rode a third: Garibaldi, in his red shirt. He, too, was a spellbinder with a unique quality, particularly in his eyes and voice. His eyes were a light, clear blue, but when he was moved they became darker like the sea and with excitement they were said to turn black. His voice was calm and deliberate; its tone, low, veiled and often tremulous with inner emotion. The shape and structure of his face was like that of a lion, yet, for many, it was curiously Christlike. Men of all kind instinctively responded to him, put down what they were doing and followed him. He, too, from the defeat at Rome fashioned a victory, the Retreat from Rome, and it was like himself, a brilliant improvisation.

Although it was plain that the Roman Republic was finished, Garibaldi could not bring himself to capitulate to foreigners on Italian soil. Instead he retreated into the mountains with a small army to continue the fight. His plan was unfeasible; with 4,000 men he could not oppose some 70,000 French, Neapolitan, Spanish and Austrian troops. Much of his army deserted, and what did not he finally had to abandon in the sanctuary of the tiny Republic of San Marino. He himself tried to push on to Venice with a few companions. Finally, alone, he was passed through the republican underground back across the peninsula and escaped in a boat. Eventually he landed in New York. He did not see Italy again for another ten years.

As a military action Garibaldi's Retreat from Rome was an ill-conceived, pointless failure. As propaganda for a free, united and republican Italy, it was a superb success. The hearts of all but the most prejudiced Italians went out to the man being hunted by foreign troops across the center of Italy. Thousands of simple peasants saw him stop by a village well, talked with him by a roadside, and realized that he was not the "roaring beast" Pio Nono and their village priests had described. And in the next ten years his lieutenants wrote accounts of the siege at Rome and retreat from it which were read not only in northern and central Italy but all over Europe. Public opinion which had supported Pio Nono in 1849 began slowly to turn against him.

But that was still in the future. For the present 1849 seemed to patriotic Italians to be a year of disaster. In March Austria had defeated Piedmont; in July Rome fell, and in August Venice would finally capitulate. Verdi in July wrote to his friend, Vincenzo Luccardi, who was in Rome:

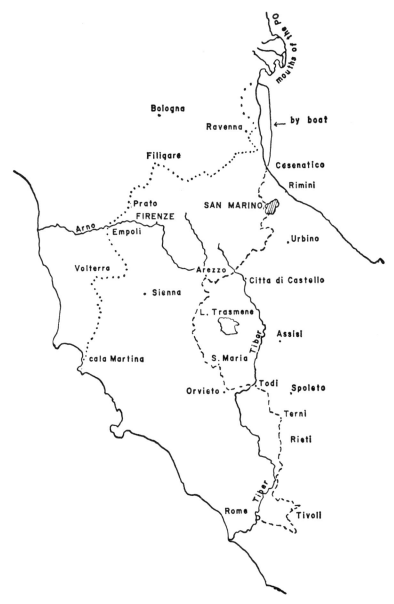

GARIBALDI'S RETREAT FROM ROME

*3 July to 3 August and escape from the Austrians 3 August to
2 September 1849*

For three days I've been impatiently awaiting your letters. You can well imagine how the catastrophe at Rome has sunk me in despair, and you were wrong not to write me at once. Let us not talk of Rome!! What would be the use!! Force still rules the world! And Justice? What good is it against bayonets!! We can only weep over our misfortunes and curse the authors of so much disaster!

So tell me about yourself! Give me news of your doings. What are you working on now? Tell me everything that our new masters will let you say. And tell me about my friends! Write to me at once, immediately. Don't delay an instant for I have an inferno within me.

When Venice fell, he wrote a similar letter to Piave. Everywhere Italians tried to pick up their lives again, but after the eighteen months from the Cinque Giornate to the fall of Venice the lives were nowhere the same. The period had been one of those in which gradual changes accelerate until they seem to make a visible line of demarcation after which everything is different: domestic habits, civic life, custom and thought. It was to be true for Italians generally and also for Verdi. After 1848–49 both his personal life and operas were to be different from what they had been before.

Part III

CHAPTER 20

LUISA MILLER AND STIFFELIO

1849–1850; AGE, 35–37

AFTER the Neapolitan censors rejected the outline for an opera based on Guerrazzi's *The Siege of Florence,* Cammarano suggested to Verdi that they use Schiller's play *Kabale und Liebe,* or *Intrigue and Love.* As Verdi sometime before had mentioned it as a possibility, they quickly agreed, and Cammarano was able in May, even before Rome fell, to send the first act of the proposed libretto to Verdi in Paris. The production at the Teatro San Carlo in Naples was planned for the end of October.

Schiller's play has some political and social overtones, and these Cammarano eliminated, so that the opera presents simply a story of human emotions, a tragedy of thwarted love in a "pleasant village" in the Tyrol. A father in the minor nobility refuses to allow his son to marry an untitled girl and, by his intrigue to separate the lovers, drives them both to suicide. No censors, political or religious, could find anything objectionable in the libretto, and the opera, entitled after its heroine *Luisa Miller,* played everywhere in Italy without cuts or changes, one of the very few of Verdi's earlier operas to do so.

He composed much of the music in Paris, where he stayed until the middle of August and then left for Busseto. By then the Austrians had regained control of all the cities in the Po Valley and Tuscany, and everywhere the revolutionary leaders were in hiding or flight. Sometimes, as in Parma, Modena and Tuscany, the Austrians hid their rule behind a puppet, but in Lombardy and Venetia there was direct military rule by Marshal Radetzky. His personal attitude he expressed in a letter to his daughter in November 1849: "These Italians have never loved nor will they love the Germans; but, persuaded that they cannot liberate themselves by force, they have surrendered, and we are avenged; and that suffices." As a public policy this attitude, which refused to consider the underlying reasons for the revolution, resulted in exile for many, special taxes and fines on all revolutionaries and shooting at Austrian will anyone possessing arms, once even a butcher who had a knife. And instead of bringing peace it led, inevitably, to one incident after another. In Milan on 18 August, the Emperor Franz Josef's birthday, a glovemaker decorated her window with the Austrian eagle, presumably to stimulate sales. Instead it gathered a hostile patriotic crowd that hissed and hooted while Austrian officers in a café opposite applauded. Eventually soldiers dispersed the crowd, but for taking part in such a political demonstration fifteen men were flogged by soldiers and also two women, one of whom was a seventeen-year-old girl from Florence who had "laughed during the transaction." No wounds were healed by such a policy, and the people more than ever solidified in opposition. They expressed their resentment as best they could. At Pavia the Austrians ordered the theatre to open and declared, "If anybody by criminal political obstinancy should persist in not frequenting the theatre, such conduct should be regarded as the silent demonstration of a criminal disposition which merited to be sought out and punished." As the wits observed, government subsidy of the arts could take various forms.

Verdi, in common with the other citizens of Parma, was fortunate that his state was sufficiently small and geographically out of the main scene of Austrian operations so that it was allowed to preserve its nominal independence. In fact Austria, by insisting on its rights in Lombardy and Venetia under the treaties of the Congress of Vienna, was committed to preserving, at least in form, the independence of Parma, guaranteed by the same treaties. Duke Carlo III, who had acceded to the Ducal throne on his father's abdication, was not popular, but the Parmigiani recognized that after the Piedmontese they were the most fortunate of Italians. And at least in the first years following the patriotic disasters of 1849 they remained politically quiet.

Parma's comparative isolation and consequent peace was magnified in its country towns like Busseto where soldiers were seldom seen, and because of it Verdi, for all of his anguish over Italy, could continue his personal life uninterrupted. Manzoni in Milan, for example, had a difficult time meeting the Austrian fines and finally was reduced to giving up his carriage. Verdi paid no such penalty for his political views, and for him the material things of life continued to wax. Even with unsettled conditions in Italy his operas, playing all over the world, assured him a steady income. By now he was probably the richest man in Busseto, and although he lived without ostentation, the kind of arrangements he was able to make for himself and his family left no doubt in the minds of the Bussetani that, whether they liked him or not, Verdi had become their chief citizen.

From Paris in May Verdi had written his father instructions about making payments on the farm at Sant' Agata. Muzio, who was in Busseto, was to read and explain the letter to Carlo Verdi, who would receive the money from Ricordi. Verdi planned to move his parents into a small house that would soon be ready on the farm while he himself would live, at least for the time being, in the Palazzo Cavalli on Busseto's main street. This house, known today as the Palazzo Orlandi, is still the handsomest palazzo in the town. Carlo Verdi was delighted with it all. In dictating to Muzio a receipt for Ricordi he exclaimed: "Heaven made me a father, and a father lucky and happy in a son that honors me and his district (il suo paese), and I thank him for it each day and pray God to make him walk the road that makes men happy." To Verdi himself Carlo wrote, via Muzio, the first news from the farm:

The deliveries of the calves were almost all easy; only one cow remains and she will deliver in a few days, and then I will organize the stalls . . .

Your mother is very happy to be in the country and would not wish to live again in Busseto; she has arranged to bring your bed to Sant' Agata in case you wish, and I hope you will, to come live with us and enjoy your beautiful possessions . . .

Any modern city dweller would consider Busseto, with the fields right to the walls, buried in the country, but evidently Luigia Verdi did not consider a stone street, however short, with the fields however near, the same thing at all as her own chickens roosting in her own yard.

Verdi arrived in Busseto at the end of August with the first two acts of *Luisa Miller* almost completed and the last act sent to him there by Cammarano. Assuming the late October première, he would have a month for the last act, which he already had well in mind, and another month for the orchestration during the rehearsals in Naples.

He had persuaded Strepponi to leave Paris at the same time and join him at Busseto. Both wished to avoid an epidemic of cholera that had broken out in Paris. The disease was unknown in Europe before

1830, or at least unidentified, and was considered to be an exotic Asian trouble. But with the sudden growth of the cities in the Industrial Age, it arrived in the West. An epidemic at Paris in 1831 had killed 18,400, including the Prime Minister. Paris, terribly overcrowded and with antiquated, medieval buildings, streets and sewers was particularly susceptible to it. The Seine was an open sewer from which drinking water was distributed, mostly through the 1700 public fountains. About one house in five had water piped to it, and in the entire city of over a million inhabitants less than 150 houses had running water above the first floor. Many houses had their own wells, but these were largely contaminated and the water used only for washing. Those who could afford it had purer water delivered each morning, like milk today. About three-quarters of the streets had no underground sewers at all, and the human sewage, collected every night in wagons, often flowed in shallow gutters or directly on the street. What covered sewers there were overflowed with every storm. Paris was known as a smelly city, and its perfume business prospered.

The epidemic of 1849 threatened to be even more serious than that of 1831, and everyone who could left the city. Perhaps, too, Verdi and Strepponi, as patriotic Italians, found living among the French difficult after the betrayal at Rome; certainly Strepponi had an additional reason. Her son, Camillino, was in Florence, and she wanted to plan for his education. Delayed by the war, she had not seen him in some time. She went directly there and then wrote Verdi who was at Busseto. The first part of the letter, which uses throughout the intimate second person singular, tells of her arrangements for the boy and then continues:

Addio, mia gioia! Now that I have finished my business, business too serious to neglect, I would like to be able to fly to your side. You speak to me of the harsh countryside, the poor service, even more you tell me "If it doesn't please you I will have you accompanied (N.B. *You will have me accompanied!*) wherever you wish . . ." But what the devil! At Busseto does one learn how not to love and how not to write with a little affection?

I am not there yet so I still know how to write the way I feel, which is that the country, the service and all will go very well for me because you will be there, you ugly, unworthy monster.

Addio, addio. I have hardly time to tell you that I loathe and embrace you.

N.B. Do not send but come yourself to pick me up at Parma, because I would be most embarrassed to be introduced into your house by someone other than yourself.

The presence of Strepponi in Verdi's house increased the general stir over his return to Busseto. The barefoot boy who had held one of the Monte di Pietà's scholarships and been the town's Music Director was now coming back, buying good farms, a handsome town house, and, said some, flaunting a mistress from Paris. The house and farms might stir envy and revive dislike, but it was the air of scandal that would keep the other emotions simmering. Busseto, with two thousand odd inhabitants, closely hemmed in by its walls, was a very small town.

The situation, which Strepponi recognized as difficult, was one Verdi by the very virtues of his nature was ill-equipped to handle. Characterized when a child as alternately shy and fierce, he had grown into a man demanding nothing from others and in turn refusing all the demands of others, even to the extent sometimes of a few simple sentences. When, the previous year, the impresario Flauto had suggested that Verdi's presence might help a Neapolitan production of *Macbeth,* Verdi had replied:

You think that my presence might influence the success? Do not believe it! I repeat what I have said to you at the beginning, that I am a sort of savage, and if the Neapolitans noticed so many defects in me the first time, it would be no different the second. It is true I have been in Paris now for a year and a half (in the city where one is supposed to acquire good manners) but I must confess I am more of a bear than before. I have been working constantly now for six years, and wandering from country to country, and I have never said a word to a journalist, never begged a friend, never courted rich people to achieve success. Never absolutely never! I shall always despise such methods. I do my operas, as well as I can: for the rest, I let things take their course without ever influencing public opinion to the slightest degree. (etc.)

It was all true, characteristic and admirable; but when Verdi, unable to change his nature, applied the same inflexible standard to his personal relations with the folk of Busseto, an equally glorious result was far less certain. His neighbors were curious about him, eager to know him, to renew old contacts, and to have some slight personal share in his glory. But with the third act of *Luisa Miller* to complete Verdi almost never went out. When he did, it was to go to Sant' Agata to see his parents and to plan further additions and alterations to the buildings. Occasionally he visited the Barezzis. With the possible exception of the Barezzis only Muzio visited him and Strepponi. He lived a simple life of hard work. To have given a party, issued invitations, would have been a mistake, forcing nervous, provincial husbands and wives to take a stand on Strepponi; and there would have been the terrible problem, short of inviting everyone, of selecting guests. But there were other, easier actions that Verdi might have taken but apparently did not. In September at Busseto, about seven in the evening, the people begin to stop work, to stand for a moment in the one main street and exchange the news of the day. If Verdi could have just brought himself to take a little walk at that hour, to say hello, to shake hands, to explain how slowly the opera was going, he might have satisfied the town's curiosity, allowed old friends to feel they were not forgotten and disarmed some of his critics. But he could not easily crush with the crowd and, despising such calculated ways of living, remained always indoors and hard at work. When he left in October for Naples, the town's curiosity was left unsatisfied, festering, and some people began to suggest that Verdi probably felt that he was now too good for the likes of them, honestly married folk.

The première of *Luisa Miller* was delayed until 8 December 1849 because the quarantine regulations of Rome, through which Verdi was passing, held him up for almost a month. The delay also meant that Barezzi, who was accompanying Verdi, had to return from Naples to Busseto before the première, although he probably saw a number of rehearsals. But it gave both men a chance to see Rome under French occupation, and Verdi wrote of it to Escudier: "The affairs of our country are desolating! Italy is now only a vast and beautiful prison! If only you could see this sky, so pure, this climate, so mild, this sea, these mountains, this city, so beautiful!! To the eyes—a paradise; to the heart—an inferno!! The rule of your countrymen in Rome is no better than that of the rest of Italy. The French try to win the favor of the Romans, but so far the latter are most dignified and firm." (etc.)

This firmness was to be one of the ways in which the years after 1848 were to be different from those before. In Milan, for example, the family ties with Vienna were sharply broken. Some cousins remained in Milan; others packed bag and baggage and went to Vienna. Thereafter they did not see each other, and Austrians and Austrian sympathizers who remained in Milan were ostracized. In Rome, when

Pio Nono returned in April 1850, he kept a French garrison in the city. Most Italians now agreed that French and Austrian troops were foreign troops. Complicated theories about the Temporal Power or the concept behind the Austrian Empire ceased to have any practical support among Italian laymen, and all foreign observers began to report to their governments and people that the restored governments of northern and central Italy were no better than military occupations.

Beside the difficulties caused by the delay in Rome, the première of *Luisa Miller* was also soured for Verdi by a farcical row with the directors of the San Carlo in Naples. Cammarano had advised him in view of the precarious finances of the San Carlo to demand his fee before handing over the score. The directors countered by demanding the score, without offering payment, and threatening to have him arrested if he attempted to leave Naples without the government's permission. As the San Carlo was a royal theatre, the government and directors supported each other. Verdi in reply threatened to board a French warship in the bay and ask protection from the Second Republic.

The interesting legal and diplomatic problem presented by an irate Parmigian citizen from the stern of a rowboat, score in hand, requesting the French navy to defend him against the Kingdom of the Two Sicilies, never came to an issue. Faced with resistance and the consequent publicity, the directors, whose position was not very noble, quickly backed down. But the sense of unpleasantness remained.

Producing an opera in Naples was always a trial for Verdi. Neapolitans in general adore intrigue and gossip and are almost violent in the intensity of their emotions. If they take a public figure to heart, they can exhaust and desiccate him with the heat of their attention. At the time of *Alzira* there had been a stream of chatty articles about Verdi designed to satisfy the town's curiosity. Journalists, all seeking interviews, discussed the color of his shoes, black or beige, whether he ate in this café or that, and whether it really was he on the soprano's balcony in the dim twilight. When he walked to the theatre, groups gathered and accompanied him, sometimes chattering questions, sometimes just staring. He did not seek such publicity, lacked the light phrase and manner to turn it away and saw it all as an invasion of his privacy that had nothing to do with any opera. He complained once to Flauto that it was "unworthy either of a serious public or a great city." Now the additional harassment by the government infuriated him, and he left Naples, a week after the première, resolved never to do another opera there.

The opera itself had an immediate success, not spectacular but sound, and it is still played with regularity in Italy. Lacking a patriotic theme its success was purely on its merits as an opera, and these are considerable. Many critics like to say that *Luisa Miller* marks the beginning of a new period in Verdi's artistic development, a "middle period" which includes *Rigoletto, Il Trovatore* and *La Traviata* and which ends with *Un Ballo in Maschera* in 1859. The division is convenient if not taken too seriously. Verdi "developed" as much by refining old habits as adding new. *Aida,* in his "last" period, has an "o patria mia" aria, a chorus calling for war, numerous marches and an unhappy love story, all themes constantly reappearing in Verdi's operas. Where *Luisa Miller* seems new is in its tenderness, and it is sometimes called a study for *La Traviata.* With the war and politics subtracted from the libretto the love story stood alone, requiring Verdi to emphasize a different facet of his character. But the facet already existed and had been displayed, although reticently, in the more domestic scenes of his operas, even such an opera as *La Battaglia di Legnano.*

Musically the opera required Verdi to avoid excessive brass and drum sounds, and his happy use of the rather plaintive woodwind tones gives the score a different sound from its predecessors. The first scene in the "pleasant village," with the mountains and castle in the background and introducing a still happy Luisa, has an airy, pastoral lightness reminiscent of Bellini or Donizetti and yet is infused with the vigor that is peculiarly Verdi's. Structurally the scene forms an effective contrast for the darker scenes to come, and for this Cammarano was largely responsible.

In its general structure the opera follows the usual pattern of the time. Each act has a title: The Love, The Intrigue, and The Poison. Verdi introduces the characters with recitative followed by arias, slow and fast, but those of *Luisa Miller,* when compared to those of *Ernani,* are shorter, more frequently interrupted or shared with other voices, and the recitative introducing them is more melodic and less droning. The change from opera to opera might be slight, but Verdi moved continuously toward emphasizing the drama at the expense of the musical pattern.

One place in *Luisa Miller* where the shift is apparent occurs in the finale to the first act, where for several minutes Verdi has the orchestra carry a melody which no character sings but above which several do a considerable amount of talking in short melodic phrases. This was not a new technique: Donizetti had often put lovely melodies underneath patter songs and dialogue. But Verdi, as might be expected, made the melodies more dramatically appropriate. As a technique it has some obvious advantages. It is more interesting than a mere "tum-tum" accompaniment or one that always plays the tune. And it is flexible: characters can sing and fall silent without individual introductions and closings while the orchestral melody underneath binds the whole together. This flexibility allows the composer, if he wishes, to escape from the trap of the aria with its formal beginnings and endings. This in turn gives the librettist greater freedom: more explanatory matter can be put in, more complicated subjects tackled.

Lastly, the overture to *Luisa Miller,* a good one, is interesting because it is the first in which Verdi took a simple phrase with a dynamic turn in it and treated it first one way and then another with different instruments, rhythms and accompaniments. In the past he had generally orchestrated two contrasting arias from the opera to make a fast-slow-fast medley or had written a short prelude. But he had not tried to develop a theme which no one actually sings in the opera but which yet seems to introduce it appropriately. Of the various styles of introducing an opera this last requires the most purely musical ability, and Verdi with the overture to *Luisa Miller* demonstrated that he could successfully compose any sort of introductory music he wished. His choice of style, therefore, for each of the later operas is quite deliberate and may suggest how he himself approached the work, as one predominantly of drama, mood, or spectacle.

After the first three performances of the opera Verdi left Naples for Busseto. He traveled by steamboat to Genoa and then by coach, the trip taking five days; it can be done today, substituting rail for the coach, in one. He arrived at Busseto in time for Christmas, and there at the Palazzo Orlandi Strepponi once again joined him.

He was full of ideas for new operas, and the day after New Year's he wrote Cammarano a short note:

> The subject I should like and which I suggest is *El Trovador,* a Spanish drama by Gutiérrez. It seems to me very fine, rich in ideas and strong situations. I should like to have two feminine roles. First, the gypsy, a woman of unusual character after whom I want to name the opera. The other part for a secondary singer. So bestir yourself, young man, and get busy. It can't be hard to find the Spanish drama. . . . Addio.

And in September, before leaving for Naples and the production of *Luisa Miller,* he had asked Flauto to suggest Victor Hugo's play *Le Roi s'amuse* as a possible subject to Cammarano. "A wonderful play," he had written, "with tremendous dramatic situations." These two plays eventually became the operas *Il Trovatore* and *Rigoletto.*

In addition to these two ideas in February he sent Cammarano a complete outline of Shakespeare's *King Lear.* In the accompanying letter he insisted: "At first glance *Re Lear* seems so big and intricate a drama that it would be impossible to turn it into an opera; but after examining it I think the difficulties, although great, are not insuperable. You know, we need not make *Re Lear* the sort of opera customary up until now; we can treat it in a wholly new manner without regard to conventions of any sort." He wanted to reduce the principal parts to five—Lear, Cordelia, the Fool, Edmund and Edgar—with secondary parts for Kent, Gloucester, Goneril and Regan. He was bothered by Cammarano's suggestion that Lear's reason for disinheriting Cordelia was "a little infantile" but agreed that the scene in which Gloucester is blinded would certainly have to come out.

The outline itself, the reduction of a play into an opera, is a fascinating document, suggesting how Verdi's mind grasped Shakespeare and also how very close sixteenth-century Elizabethan drama was to nineteenth-century Italian opera. Ready at hand is the oratorical blood and thunder, the aria-like soliloquy, the mad scene, the storm scene, and all the spectacle with trumpets of royalty. Even Shakespeare's last line, a stage direction: "Exeunt, with a dead march," is a call for music.

It is indicative of the breadth of Verdi's reading that he culled the plays from the literature of three foreign nations. But his hopes to use one of them for his next opera came to naught. He had contracted with Ricordi to produce a new opera in November "in one of the leading theatres of Italy (except La Scala of Milan)," and time began to run out, especially as he had agreed to direct a production of *Macbeth* at Bologna in August. Before the trip to Naples he had intended to do the new opera with Cammarano at the San Carlo, but after the imbroglio there he asked Cammarano to continue working on long-range plans while he turned to Piave in Venice for the immediate opera. Ricordi started negotiations to have it produced at Trieste.

The outcome of this sudden collaboration, *Stiffelio,* was not a success. The fault lay more in the opera's subject than the music, but Verdi had found the subject interesting, so the blame cannot be put wholly on Piave who first recommended it. The opera is based on a French play, *Stiffelius,* now forgotten.

The subject concerns the marital difficulties of a German evangelical minister at the beginning of the nineteenth century. His wife has committed adultery, and considerable intrigue and talk of honor fills the first two acts which are set in a gloomy castle and a cemetery. Then in the third act the minister proposes a divorce. He has succeeded in not hating his rival and offers to free his wife to marry her lover. The wife, however, still loves her husband and insists she would rather die than be divorced. In the end, most reluctantly, she agrees to it. The final scene takes place in a church. Just as the minister is about to address the congregation, his eye falls on the Bible, open to the passage where Christ forgives the adulteress. Moved by this portent, the minister then forgives his wife. Presumably they remarry and live happily ever after, although it is not quite clear.

The play, *Stiffelius,* had recently been presented in translation in the Italian theatres. But a play can do more to sketch in a strange background and make unusual characters plausible than can an opera which, because of the music, moves more slowly. Further, Verdi had no ability for writing music in a foreign style. There is nothing Scottish in his *Macbeth* or Spanish in his *Ernani;* nor could he compose anything German or Protestant in feeling for *Stiffelio.* The result was an Italian opera in which the audience was asked to believe first that priests could marry, and then that they could divorce, and lastly that it was a Christian virtue for a husband not to hate the man who seduced his wife. But everyone in the audience knew that a virtuous husband hated his rival, by hook or crook killed him, and then went to his priest to be absolved on penance for acting on just cause. This was being virtuous; this was Christianity.

The libretto struck many as a profanation, and throughout the opera censors cut and changed, particularly in the climactic scene, so that it never played anywhere exactly as Verdi and Piave had intended. Verdi himself seems to have felt that the difficulty with the libretto doomed the opera, for he would do nothing on its behalf.

Aside from the libretto the music was pleasant, and Verdi used much of it seven years later when, at his request, Piave rewrote the text, making it into a drama of knights and ladies in thirteenth-century England. This opera, *Aroldo,* was reasonably successful. But it ought to be impossible to use the same music both for a study of a mystical

German preacher and for a medieval costume drama. *Stiffelio*, like *Alzira*, demonstrated that Verdi, even if he could understand the experience and truth that others sometimes found in religion, could not yet translate it effectively into musical terms.

The unfortunate *Stiffelio* was the last opera Verdi wrote that was wholly unsuccessful. It was the last on which he allowed himself so little time, both to compose the music and to become familiar with characters. Six months before the première he still had never read or seen the play. His best operas, like the next which would be *Rigoletto*, he had mulled over for months or even years. The contractual method of commissioning and producing operas in which the theatre or publisher could present the composer with a strange libretto was slowly changing.

CHAPTER 21

RIGOLETTO

1850–1851; AGE, 37

IN the spring of 1850, while Verdi and Piave were still searching for the libretto that became *Stiffelio,* the directors of the Teatro La Fenice in Venice asked Verdi to do a new opera for the Carnival season 1850–51. He was eager to accept. He had no commitment after the production of *Stiffelio* at Trieste, and he liked working at Venice where he had staged the premières of *Ernani* and *Attila.* The contract as signed called for an *opera seria* of unspecified subject to be staged in February 1851. As the première of *Stiffelio* was scheduled for the preceding November, this left only three months thereafter to prepare the new work, and he and Piave began at once to discuss possible librettos.

Verdi first suggested the Spanish play *El Trovador* or *Kean* by Dumas *père,* both of which he knew well. Later he suggested Hugo's play *Le Roi s'amuse,* and his enthusiasm for it eventually overrode Piave's misgivings. "Oh," he wrote, *Le Roi s'amuse* is one of the greatest subjects and perhaps the greatest drama of modern times. *Tribolet* [eventually renamed *Rigoletto*] is a creation worthy of Shakespeare." Verdi could not offer higher praise.

But Piave and the directors were less sure. The play had caused a scandal in Paris at its première in 1832 and been banned after its first performance. It had never been given since and yet continued to be read, largely because of its notoriety. Verdi could hardly have picked a subject more certain to agitate censors of all kinds, political, religious and those self-appointed to defend "good taste."

The play, a rhetorical, poetic drama in five acts, is set at the court of François I of France. The King, an absolute monarch and libertine, uses his position to satisfy his lust, and his jester, a hunchback named Triboulet, excites and aids him. As the play opens at a court party at the Louvre, the King has recently enjoyed Diane de Poitiers by offering, in return for her favors, to countermand her father's execution. Now for the future he plans to debauch a girl he has seen in church while disguised as a student, and for the present, the wife of M. de Cossé. As the court listens, the King and Triboulet discuss in M. de Cossé's presence how to be rid of him. The courtiers, aristocrats of the bluest blood, are goaded beyond bearing by the presumption of the base-born jester and swear to humble him. They plan to abduct a lady they believe to be his mistress and present her to the King. The act ends as the father of Diane de Poitiers, M. de Saint Vallier, bursts in on the festivities to curse the King. Triboulet mocks the outraged man and is included in the curse.

The language and situations are strong, even brutal, but then, as Hugo argued, so was the history of the period. Most historians discount the comforting legend that Diane lost her virginity to save her father's head and point out unkindly that she became the mistress of François' son, Henri II, and did herself proud for many years with the crown jewels and the château at Chenonceaux. As for François, they say, it would be almost impossible to overdraw his character in any evil respect.

In the second act Triboulet on his way home, musing about the curse, meets a professional cutthroat, Saltabadil, who offers to kill anyone for a price. Triboulet refuses, at least for the moment, and then, left alone, philosophizes on the similarity between himself and the man: one cuts with the sword, the other with a word. Then he curses the courtiers for being even more vile than he, a deformed jester. But as he enters his house, his mood changes, for here is his daughter, Blanche, kept secret from the vile world and who, in the two months since she came up from the country, has been out only to church. The two have a scene in which Hugo presents Triboulet as a tender father. This is followed by one between the girl and the King who, disguised as a student, has bribed the housekeeper to let him into the garden. Blanche, at first terrified and confused, is becoming merely shy when the King is forced to leave at the sound of noise in the street. It is the courtiers who have come to abduct the girl they believe is Triboulet's mistress. They fool Triboulet, who is with them, into thinking that they will abduct Mme. de Cossé from the house next door, and only when the jester hears his daughter's cry as she is carried down the street does he realize that the curse has begun to operate.

In the next act the play and opera differ slightly. The play begins with the courtiers back at the Louvre presenting Blanche, near fainting with terror and only half-dressed, to the King. Still thinking she is Triboulet's mistress, they suggest that what the jester finds pleasing the King may also. In the garden François had learned that she was, in fact, Triboulet's daughter; now Blanche discovers that her young student is the King. Even so she repels his advances and runs into an adjoining room and locks the door. But it is the King's bedroom, and bouncing the key in the palm of his hand, he laughs and then goes in and rapes her.

At the play's première the scene caused a furor, and in the discussion in the years following it was always a focal point for those who objected to the play's cynical view of man and for those who considered it propaganda against a monarchal or even aristocratic form of government. It is the only important scene of the play that Verdi and Piave did not ultimately set in the opera. There the courtiers carry the girl directly to the monarch's chamber and then inform him that she is there. He goes off-stage without confronting the disheveled girl or laughing over the key. It is all more gently done.

Triboulet enters and endeavors by indirect questions to discover where the courtiers have taken Blanche. When he realizes the truth, he alternately curses and pleads with them to restore his daughter to him. They are astounded at the relationship but remain unmoved. At this point in the play Triboulet turns on them and, reciting the names of many of the greatest families in France, rails: "Your mothers gave themselves to their lackeys. You are all bastards."

The line stopped the performance. In the boxes were the nobility, white-faced and furious; in the pit the intellectuals and bourgeois, stamping and hooting with approval. In 1882 when the play, fifty years later to the day, received its second performance in the Paris of the Third Republic, the bourgeois, by then sitting complacently in the boxes, paid it the respect owed a dead issue so happily resolved in their favor. But in 1832 under the monarchy of Louis Philippe the issue was not yet decided, and in the preface to the published edition of the play Hugo insisted that the ban, ostensibly to protect public morals, was in fact a form of political censorship.

After Triboulet curses the courtiers, Blanche runs from the inner room and throws herself into her father's arms. The courtiers retire. Brokenly she explains how she first met the King. Across the back of the stage guards lead Diane de Poitiers' father, M. de Saint Vallier, off to prison. Coming forward for an instant, he gazes at the King's door and regrets that heaven has not yet answered his curse and avenged him on the King. Triboulet swears that he himself will be the instrument of heaven.

Hugo's last two acts, both short, show the curse working itself out, but not as either Triboulet or M. de Saint Vallier intend. Triboulet, in order to disabuse Blanche of her love for François which continues in spite of his assault on her, takes her to Saltabadil's shack outside one of the gates of Paris. There she can hear the King inside singing, in the play as well as the opera, a jingle about the fickleness of women. Through a crack in the wall she can see him, again in disguise, pursuing Saltabadil's sister, Maguelonne. A storm threatens, and the King, with his eye on the girl, arranges to spend the night. Outside Triboulet, having sent Blanche home, arranges the King's murder. Saltabadil is to deliver the body sewn up in a sack at midnight. Maguelonne, however, is unhappy over the deal. She is beginning to like the unknown man who flatters her, and she persuades her brother to kill a substitute if one turns up in time. Blanche, who has crept back to the shack to be near the King, overhears the plot and, by knocking on the door, presents herself as the substitute.

In the play there is a break and a new act; in the opera Verdi joins Hugo's last two acts with a storm scene. Triboulet returns, receives the sack, and is about to roll it triumphantly into the Seine when he hears in the distance the King singing the jingle about the fickleness of women. Furiously he tears open the sack and discovers his daughter. She mumbles a few words and dies, while in answer to Triboulet's cries a crowd gathers. A surgeon comes forward and pronounces Blanche dead, giving as his view that blood from her wound had filled her lungs and suffocated her. Triboulet cries "I have killed my child" and swoons.

This last scene Verdi and Piave changed. In the opera there is no crowd or surgeon and the girl's few dying words are extended into a short duet for father and daughter. Also the jester's last line is changed to "La maledizione" (The curse). This is an improvement as it more forcibly recalls the origin of the tragedy. Hugo himself gave a clue to this in his preface when he insisted that "the real subject of the drama is the curse of M. de Saint Vallier," and Verdi and Paive stressed the curse throughout, even planning to call the opera *La Maledizione*.

Throughout the summer of 1850 Verdi believed that the Austrian censors would approve the libretto. Piave had assured him in May that he had talked privately with some of the persons concerned and that there would be no difficulty. After the première of *Stiffelio,* and only three months before the proposed date for the new opera, the libretto was rejected. The president of the Fenice forwarded to Verdi the official communication which read:

His Excellency the Military Governor Chevalier de Gorzkowski in his respected dispatch of the 26th instant directs me to communicate to you his profound regret that the poet Piave and the celebrated Maestro Verdi have not chosen some other field to display their talents than the revolting immorality and obscene triviality forming the story of the libretto *La Maledizione,* submitted to us for eventual performance at La Fenice.

His Excellency has decided that the performance must be absolutely forbidden and wishes me at the same time to request you not to make further inquiries in this matter.

Discussions continued, however, because in the censor's office was an Italian, a music lover and a friend of Piave, who wanted to hear the opera and kept the channels of inquiry open. Again all the arguments of immorality and politics were raised. Even the proposed title, *La Maledizione,* was offensive either because it was impious or because it emphasized the idea that man could move God to action without the intermediary services of the Church, which was Protestantism. Not a single priest or cross appeared on the stage although Paris was a Catholic city, Blanche's "suicide" was not presented as a sin, and above all, Vice, in the form of the debonair King, was triumphant.

Throughout the discussions, which continued for a month, Verdi remained in Busseto. As long as he was not in Venice, he could not be hurried into any compromise either by the censors or the directors of the Fenice. By letter he argued wisely for his libretto, offering to concede unimportant points and arguing firmly for those which were basic to the drama. He was willing to give up the French court with its historical background, the names of the characters, the scene with the key and the title. He insisted, however, that the monarch be an absolute ruler and a libertine and that he must be cursed for ravishing his subject's daughter. "Without this curse," he wrote the directors, "what point, what meaning is left to the drama?" Later in the same letter, in rejecting some of the censor's arguments about the sack in which Blanche's corpse is concealed, he revealed what first attracted him to the play:

I don't see why the sack has been cut out! What does the sack matter to the police? Are they afraid it won't be effective? Then let me ask: why do they think they know more about it than I? Who can be sure? Who can say this will be effective and that not? We had just such a trouble with the horn in *Ernani:* well, then, did anyone laugh at the sound of the horn? With the sack eliminated, then it is improbable that Triboletto would talk for half an hour to a corpse before a lightning flash reveals it is his daughter.

Finally I see that they object to Triboletto being ugly and a hunchback. A hunchback that sings? Why not! . . . Will it be effective? I don't know, but if I don't know then neither, I repeat, does the man who proposed the change. I find this the most wonderful part: to portray this extremely deformed and ridiculous creature who yet is inwardly passionate and full of love. I chose the subject just for this reason, for all these original qualities and traits, and if they are cut out I shall not be able to compose the music. If they tell me I can leave my music as it is for this censored version, I answer that I do not understand such reasoning, and I tell you frankly that my music, beautiful or ugly, I do not write at random, and I try always to give it character.

Finally on 25 January, only four weeks before the opera was supposed to have its première, the censors approved a revised libretto. In it the French King became the Duke of Mantua, Blanche was transformed from Bianca to Gilda, Saltabadil to Sparafucile, Triboletto to Rigoletto, whose name also became the title of the opera, and the scene with the key was dropped. But on all the important points, including the sack and the hunchback, Verdi won out. Because of the delay the première was rescheduled for 11 March, giving rise to the legend that Verdi composed the entire opera in forty days. In fact, of course, he had been considering it as a libretto as early as September 1849 and had begun work on it, although concurrently with *Stiffelio,* in the spring of 1850. His letter to the directors suggests that he had much of the music thought out in his mind, whether he had actually put it on paper or not.

He did the actual composing at his Palazzo Orlandi in Busseto where he continued to live with Strepponi. Over Christmas, apparently at her suggestion, he had invited his parents to join them in the house. The visit had not been a success. The irregular relationship between Verdi and his Peppina, as he called Strepponi, had rattled his parents. Both had spoken out against Strepponi, directly and by innuendo. With his father there was an additional business problem. In January Verdi found it necessary to write to a fellow Bussetano, a notary, what amounted to a public letter:

From a reliable source I have learned that my father goes about saying that matters have been arranged through you in one of the two following ways, to wit: that I have made him the administrator of my properties or that I have leased them to him.

I do not believe that there can be any misunderstanding between me and you, Sir, nor do I believe that you have proposed any of these ideas. Nevertheless, I should like to repeat for my own peace of mind that I will not consent to either of these proposals. I intend to be separate from my father both in my domestic and business affairs. Finally, I repeat what I said to you yesterday: *as regards the world Carlo Verdi must be one thing and Giuseppe Verdi another.*

Undoubtedly Carlo Verdi at times found it very galling that his son should be so much more affluent than he, and his position of caretaker on his son's farm was inherently ambiguous, both in his own eyes and those of the world. Verdi in February attempted to solve his family difficulties by establishing his parents on a farm at Vidalenzo, which was a short distance beyond Sant' Agata. A rather legalistic document, entitled *The Minutes of the Compromise between Giuseppe and Carlo Verdi,* set forth the terms on which Verdi undertook to support his parents, to pay them an annual pension by quarters and provide them with a suitable horse.

Under Italian custom of the time, and even today, it would be unthinkable for a son not to share his wealth with his parents. But such a formal arrangement is unusual and suggests bitter words. The preamble to the *Minutes* reads: "The undersigned in order to arrange for his own peace of mind and also for the needs of his parents, from whom he intends to separate himself both in his home and in business, obligates himself" (etc.). Plainly Verdi's peace of mind required a number of open fields between himself and his father. Vidalenzo, as it turned out, was a successful solution to the problem. For the moment, to manage his affairs in Busseto and to oversee the construction at Sant' Agata, he gave a power of attorney to his brother-in-law, Giovanni Barezzi. But increasingly, after he finished *Rigoletto,* he was his own estate manager.

Toward the middle of February Verdi went to Venice to begin the rehearsals. The only difficulty was in casting the part of Maddalena, as Sparafucile's sister was now called. None of the contraltos in the company wanted to sing the role because it was a small part and lacked a solo aria. A Mme. Casaloni, otherwise forgotten, finally consented. The rehearsals were conducted as privately as possible, Verdi not

PIAVE

unnaturally wishing to husband the shock of his "effects." Probably with this in mind, rather than fearing the "catchiness" of the tune, he held back from the tenor until the day before the dress rehearsal the jingle on the fickleness of women, "La donna è mobile." The repetition of this little tune by the inconstant Duke, almost the moment after Gilda has been faithful through disillusion unto death, is one of the most superbly placed effects in all of opera. And it does not detract from Verdi's greatness in the opera to give full credit for it to Hugo.

At the première the little tune, for it is really more of a motif than an aria, scored a tremendous success, and immediately thereafter all the Venetians were humming it. Piave, gentle, kind, but as inconstant and licentious as François I, is supposed to have seen one of his ex-mistresses crossing the Piazza San Marco. Hurrying to her side, he began the opening lines when she interrupted him and in perfect meter stated that he was a great Ass.

From the first the opera was recognized, at least by the public, as a masterpiece. But its progress during its first decade was contested by many important critics, censors, and in Paris by Hugo himself, who resented the demotion of his drama into a mere libretto. For six years he succeeded in preventing its production altogether, then it was put on at Théâtre Italien and, in the first year, repeated more than a hundred times. In 1863 the Opéra produced it in French and has been giving it continuously ever since. In time Hugo conceded its success.

The censorship problem continued as long as Italy was divided and ruled by nervous monarchs. The opera played in various cities, with cuts and adjustments in the story, as *Viscardello, Clara di Perth* and *Lionello*. Once in despair Verdi suggested the billboard should read *"Rigoletto,* poetry and music by Don——" with the censor's name inserted.

Some critics disliked the opera because they found in it a new style of singing and form of opera construction which they did not like. Verdi's contract with the Fenice had called for an *opera seria;* he delivered something that at least musically was very different. An *opera seria,* even in 1851, was still based firmly on the aria, as Verdi had constructed *Ernani.* In *Rigoletto,* however, the basic unit is no longer the aria but has become the scene. The experiments begun in *Macbeth* are greatly advanced.

Verdi himself was quite aware of what he was attempting although characteristically he let the opera speak for itself rather than broadcast his theories by publishing a "preface" to the score or giving an interview to a journalist. But the husband of a soprano requested him to compose an additional aria for Gilda, and in refusing, Verdi wrote: "I imagined *Rigoletto* almost without arias and without finales, just an unbroken string of duets; because this form satisfied me."

A comparison between the first act of *Ernani* (p. 130) and that of *Rigoletto* (p. 276) will show the difference in form. There are seven arias in the former, only two in the latter. And neither of these two is in a satisfactory form for a singer who wishes to arouse applause. The Duke's "Questa o quella" is a charming song rather than an aria; it begins without fanfare, has no cadenzas, and ends on a low "A." "Caro nome" for the soprano is no better. It has two cadenzas, but both end very quietly on low, easy notes. And the aria's closing measures, if Verdi's stage directions are followed, are to be sung off-stage. This has always proved to be too much for some sopranos, who either remain doggedly on-stage or else break the back of the aria at the second cadenza by raising the low notes up an octave and thereby misleading the audience into thinking it has ended. Then of course what follows is

SCENE 1 (about 16 mins.)
(a splendid apartment in the Duke's palace)

	introduction	ballet as court dances.
THE DUKE	dialogue (fast)	ballet continues; he discusses the unknown girl, Gilda, with a courtier and admires the Countess Ceprano.
	aria (short and less fast)	"Questa or quella," this girl or that, it hardly matters.
	dialogue (slow)	minuet begins; he flirts with the Countess.
RIGOLETTO	recitative (short and fast)	introductory ballet resumes; he mocks Count Ceprano.
	pause (short and less fast)	ballet, a French périgourdine.
COURTIERS	dialogue (fast)	introductory ballet; one tells the others he has discovered Rigoletto's mistress.
DUKE and RIGOLETTO	dialogue (fast)	ballet continues; they discuss how to be rid of Count Ceprano.
little finale	ensemble (faster)	built on an acceleration of the ballet; Duke, Rigoletto and courtiers in asides.
MONTERONE	recitative (short)	demands an audience with the Duke.
RIGOLETTO	recitative (short)	mocks Monterone.
MONTERONE	recitative (slow, long and melodic)	the curse.
FINALE	ensemble (a little faster)	general horror.

SCENE 2 (about 35 mins.)
(a street, with a wall cut away to show Rigoletto's house and garden)

RIGOLETTO and SPARAFUCILE	dialogue (slow)	over a melody never sung; Sparafucile offers his services as an assassin.
RIGOLETTO	recitative (melodic and varied)	compares himself to Sparafucile; recalls the curse; rails at the courtiers, at his own jesting; recalls the curse.
RIGOLETTO and GILDA	dialogue (fast)	over a melody never sung; they greet each other.
	dialogue (slow, ending faster)	he sings of her mother who died; she comforts him.
	dialogue (varied)	he asks her and the housekeeper if she has stayed concealed; his fears.
	duet (slow)	she sooths him; he urges the housekeeper to be careful.

GILDA and DUKE	dialogue (short)	she and the housekeeper discuss the unknown student.
	duet (slow, ending faster)	he appears; surprise, fright, love, his name, good-by.
GILDA	recitative (very short)	his name.
	aria (slow)	"Caro nome," ending inside the house and with courtiers' voices in the street already started.
FINALE with COURTIERS and RIGOLETTO	dialogue (slow)	over a melody never sung; they confuse Rigoletto into helping them.
	chorus (faster)	they abduct Gilda.
	last lines (fastest)	alone on-stage, he discovers what has happened and cries, "La maledizione."

an anticlimax: Verdi's drama has been pawned for the ready applause of a singing exhibition.

As Verdi decreased the importance of the aria, he emphasized the scene as the larger unit in which the characters come and go. In the first scene of *Rigoletto,* for example, the introductory ballet music constantly reappears, so that all the protagonists, the Duke, Rigoletto and the courtiers, are introduced to the same strain; they are brought literally face to face at the same party in a way the form of *Ernani* could not have encompassed. Critics have complained that the music lacks elegance, sounding too much like Busseto rather than Paris or even Mantua, but its rather feverish gaiety does bind the scene into a unit until Monterone's curse introduces, as it should, a new tone.

In the same way Verdi made a theatrically effective unit out of Rigoletto's meeting with Sparafucile in the second scene. Verdi called the conversation between the two men "a duet," but neither has a tune in the conventional sense, only phrases back and forth. The tune is in the orchestra, and it is a musical whole with an introduction, closing and two verses, the second having a more complicated accompaniment. In a sense Verdi simply moved the aria into the orchestra, leaving the drama, now free of its constrictions, to develop above it. The tune, which is lovely in itself, is perfectly suited to its scene in its ominous, muffled quality. This feeling Verdi increased by scoring it for cello and double bass, both muted. As conspirators' music it is infinitely more successful than the chorus for the courtiers which comes later in the scene and sounds like a Gilbert and Sullivan parody of itself.

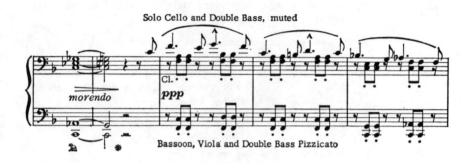

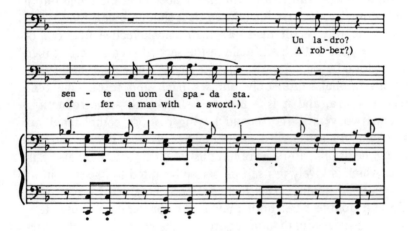

The development of the scene rather than the aria as the unit of construction inevitably cost Verdi his traditional contrast of successive slow and fast arias. But in its place he could contrast the larger scenic units, the quiet of the Sparafucile scene after the court gaiety, and within the scene itself, being free of the purely musical requirements of the aria, he could alternate more rapidly between fast and slow, soft and loud, in the more dramatic conversations and soliloquies. The result may not be equally pleasing, but unquestionably it does give the composer greater freedom to fit the music directly to the words.

Traditionalists of the time complained that Verdi was failing in melodic inspiration: he could write only two arias where once he had written seven; that he was destroying the voice by making it sing mere phrases over an increased orchestra, and that he was thereby driving out of opera singing, in the sense of technique and beauty. Those who liked the new style found it powerful and saw that it was pliable: many more ideas could be encompassed in a recitative or dialogue. The traditional aria was a vignette: the soprano happy or sad; the new style showed her passing from one to the other. This change was reflected even in such a simple thing as the titles for each act: increasingly they were omitted. Such titles as "The Love" and "The Intrigue" simply could not encompass the variety of events and passions encompassed in each act of *Rigoletto*.

The opera is not perfect: the new style is not always maintained; the Duke has one dull aria which is generally cut, and the courtiers' music is often trivial. But beyond this the opera is, for lack of a better word, inspired. And, by universal agreement, Verdi's inspiration reached a unique perfection in the famous quartet in the last act. Here the Duke flatters Maddalena who laughs at him, while outside the shack Gilda laments that he used the same words to her and Rigoletto promises that he will avenge her. Verdi gave each a distinct and appropriate melodic line, and the miracle of the quartet is the clarity with which he is able to keep the four lines distinct and yet harmoniously combined. It is a perfect fusion of music and drama. In most quartets the characters either express the same thought to musically different lines or different thoughts to indistinct and merging lines.

Sometime during the rehearsals or the first performances Verdi remarked of the quartet to Varesi, the Rigoletto, that he probably never could do better. In this particular respect he never did.

CHAPTER 22

LIFE ON THE MAIN STREET
IN BUSSETO

1851–1852; AGE, 37–38

AS always, immediately after the third performance of the opera Verdi left *Rigoletto* and Venice to return to Busseto. Because of the opera's experimental nature he was particularly pleased with its success, but there had been a series of newspaper attacks on Piave for the choice of subject and these distressed him. "Just as if all the blame were not mine," he wrote to Piave, urging the librettist, if he wished, to make a public statement that the composer had "suggested and desired to treat the subject without modification, in the form used, and keeping all of Hugo's dramatic points." But Piave, who was wholly a man of the theatre, rather enjoyed the notoriety and felt secure in the opera's triumphant success.

The attacks, however, represented the fears of a part of Italian society that watched Verdi's actions, public and private, with alarm. These persons, not necessarily priests or even devout, were those who by nature were conventional and supported the accepted forms of living. They saw the most popular artist of the day seeming to condone adultery in *Stiffelio*, rape and suicide in *Rigoletto*, and in both operas by the power of his music making the unconventional, even sinful, life attractive. Those who saw in this an unfortunate trend were even more distressed two years later, when Verdi produced *La Traviata* and made the death of a kept woman a tragedy. None of these good people denied his abilities as a composer, but they questioned whether he applied them to good ends.

So too they questioned his private life with Strepponi. In the bigger cities the question remained abstract, for she had never accompanied him on his trips to produce an opera. But in Busseto where she was present the question blew up, in the spring and summer of 1851, into a real storm and one which, instead of clearing the atmosphere, permanently clouded it.

Most of Busseto, faced with Strepponi in residence for months at a time, had decided to ignore her and Verdi. None, with the exception of Muzio and the men of the Barezzi family and perhaps one or two others, ever called on them; they were excluded from the social life of the town. For Verdi, hard at work first on *Rigoletto* and then on *Il Trovatore,* the isolation had advantages. For Strepponi, running the house and dealing with the town, there were none. On the street people not only would not speak to her, sometimes apparently they were rude. In church no one would sit beside her, and in the house, where she might have expected to rest easy, there were scenes with his parents. In May Strepponi went again to Florence to see her son and from there wrote to Verdi:

I urge you with clasped hands not to connect yourself too intimately with your parents. And I say this, I swear it, not out of willful meanness but because I cannot bear to face any further unpleasantness of the sort I have endured for almost two years! Human nature has shown itself under an aspect so vile in the past troubles that we do better to take every precaution against raising higher the veil that covers our life. Addio, mio Mago (my sorcerer).

It was a private letter about their personal problems, but others stated Strepponi's thought differently and publicly. Strepponi, they said, was driving a wedge between Verdi and his friends and relatives. Because of her he had banished his parents to Vidalenzo. His mother had been ill at the time of the move, and she grew steadily worse thereafter. She died on 28 June. Verdi was stunned. Muzio made the arrangements for the funeral; a few friends called on Verdi, but the great part of the town remained silent in his presence with perhaps a raised eyebrow, as if to say: Well, what did you expect?

The questions the town asked, always without answer, were two: Why had Verdi returned to Busseto with Strepponi? Why didn't he marry her? Sometime in the autumn, when Verdi and Strepponi had gone to Paris, the only man in the town who possibly had a right to demand the answers wrote and did so. The questioning letter is lost or destroyed; the answer exists:

Paris, 21 January 1852

Dearest Father-in-law:

After all these years I did not expect to receive such a cold letter from you and one with, if I am not mistaken, some harsh words. If this letter were not signed *Antonio Barezzi,* that is my benefactor, I would have replied curtly or not at all. But as it bears the name which it will be ever my duty to respect, I will try as best I can to persuade you that I do not deserve such a reproof. To do this I must go back to the past, speak of others, of our town (paese), and the letter will be a little long and boring, but I will be as brief as I can.

I do not believe that, left to yourself, you would have written me a letter that you know could only hurt me. But you live in a town that has the bad habit of meddling in the affairs of others and of disapproving of everything that does not conform to its ideas. I make it a rule not to interfere, uninvited, in the affairs of others, and just for this reason I insist that no one interfere in mine. From this springs the gossip, whispers and disapproval. This freedom of action, observed even in less civilized countries, I have the right to demand in my own. Judge for yourself and judge severely but coldly and dispassionately. What is the harm if I live in an isolated fashion? If I prefer not to pay calls on those with titles? If I do not take part in the festivities and joys of others? If I myself manage my property because it pleases and amuses me? I repeat: what harm is there? In any case no one is injured.

With this said I come to the sentence in your letter: "I know very well that I am not the man to handle your business, because my time has already passed, but for little things would I not still be capable? . . ." If by this you mean that once I used to trust you with serious matters but now use you only on little things, alluding to the letter included with your own, I cannot find a pretext for this; and, though I would do the same for you in a similar case, I simply say it will be a lesson to me for the future. If the sentence is a reproof because I have not burdened you with my affairs during my absence, let me ask you: How could I ever be so indiscreet as to give you such a heavy duty when you never even set foot in your own fields, because your business is already so large? Should I have burdened Giovannino? But isn't it true that last year, during the time I was at Venice, I gave him a full power of attorney in writing, and he never once set foot in Sant' Agata? Nor do I blame him. He was perfectly right. He had his own affairs, important enough, and therefore could not take care of mine.

So much for my opinions, my actions, my wishes, my life—I was about to say my public life. And since we are started making revelations, I have no hesitation to raise the curtain that hides the mysteries closed within four walls and to tell you about my life at home. I have nothing to hide.

In my house there lives a lady, free and independent, who like me prefers a solitary life and who has the means to satisfy her every need. Neither I, nor she must account for our actions; and who knows what our relations are? What are our business affairs? What are the ties? What rights I have over her and she over me? Who knows whether or not she is my wife? And if she is, who knows what reasons or ideas there may be for not announcing it publicly? Who knows if it is good or bad? Could it not be a good thing? And even if it were a bad thing, who has the right to damn us? I will say this, however, in my house she is entitled to equal or greater respect than I, and no one is allowed to fail in it for whatever reason; and finally she has every right to it by her conduct, her mind and the special courtesy she always shows to others.

With this long chitter-chatter I have meant only to say that I claim my freedom of action, because all men have a right to it and because my nature rebels at conforming to others; and you who are so good, so just and have so much heart, must not let yourself be influenced nor adopt the standards of a town that in my opinion—it must be said!—sometime ago would not deign to have me as its organist and now whispers wildly and wrongly about my affairs. This cannot continue; but if it must, then I am the man to defend myself. The world is very large, and the loss of 20 or 30 thousand francs will not stop me from finding another country. In this letter nothing should offend you; but if anything should, consider it not written, because I swear on my honor, I do not intend to pain you in any way. I have always and do now consider you my benefactor, and I make it my honor and my boast. Addio, addio! With all my usual friendship.

The letter does not answer the questions which Barezzi obviously asked, and perhaps the most moving thing about it, aside from Verdi's obvious distress, is just that Barezzi did accept it as an answer. He had asked for the truth and been denied it, a shock to which most men would respond by withdrawing their support and friendship. Barezzi did not. He could not suspend the judgment of the town, but he could his own, and thereafter, as though the questions had never been asked and the answers denied, he accepted Strepponi on Verdi's terms. Perhaps he heard in the letter, so uncharacteristic in its hedging, a cry of despair.

The questions, however, are important and remain for speculation, for neither Verdi nor Strepponi ever suggested the answers. The privacy so imperiously demanded was not relaxed, even after death.

Why did Verdi bring Strepponi and his experiment in free living to Busseto rather than some other town? Everything would seem to have been a reason against it. It was the town in which he had grown up and which had once already split in factions over him. It was the town in which he had married and which was filled with his first wife's relatives. His parents lived there. And it was a small town. The answer probably is that Busseto and the surrounding countryside was his "paese," his "district" or "neck of the woods."

The concept behind the word "paese" is almost impossible to translate. It includes not only a sense of identity by locality, an area which may or may not include small towns; but also an identity by language, the dialect; and by customs, which saints are revered. In Sicily it even includes an identity by which blood feud the family or village is a party to. The strength of the bond is most easily seen among displaced Italians, immigrants in the United States or England, who group them-

selves tightly by "paese," rejoicing whenever another "paesano" arrives to help them dominate the street or section of the town. The chief of police in Los Angeles even has a map of Sicily on his office wall to help solve local murders by reference to village feuds started years before in Sicily.

The emotional pull of a man's "paese" was just as strong in the Po Valley as elsewhere. In a country constantly overrun and ruled by foreigners it was the basic loyalty. Verdi's father rejoiced that his son was an honor, not to Italy or even to Parma, but to his "paese." And in his letter to Barezzi Verdi threatened, if forced to leave, to go to another country, "patria," not merely another town. In nineteenth-century Italy there was almost no movement from one country district to another. So that it is probably fair to say that from the moment Verdi decided to buy a farm it never occurred to him, or to anyone else, that he would buy it anywhere but in or near Busseto. If a man's life was to have problems, where better could he meet them than on his home ground?

But why Verdi did not marry Strepponi is more difficult and the speculations less satisfactory. They had been living together openly for four years; if Verdi would not conform to the world, neither would he attempt to deceive it. In the world of his business, the theatre, she was recognized as his wife in all but name. She acted on occasion as

BUSSETO

his agent, sometimes as his secretary, and often added charming notes on his letters: "I greatly suspect that Verdi *always* leaves my good wishes for you in his pen." And once after asking Piave, please, to return Verdi to Busseto a little less of a bear, she closed: "Verdi is howling that he wants the letter, so I have time only to press your hands and say . . ." (then the letter breaks off).

In Busseto, like the married ladies who were her neighbors, she ran the house, bossed the large staff and arranged for Verdi to be free from the details of living. Once years later she remarked: "After all, everybody can't write *Aida*. Someone must pack and unpack the trunks."

She unquestionably appreciated his music, and some of her comments on it are extremely perceptive. She had, after all, been among the very first to recognize the quality inherent in *Oberto* and she had sung Abigaille in the première of *Nabucco*. But if she admired and understood him as an artist, she loved him as a man.

That which makes the world raise its hat to you is something to which I never, or almost never, give a thought. I swear to you, and you will not find it difficult to believe me, that often I feel a sort of surprise that you know about music.

Though it is a divine art, of which your genius is worthy, the magic qualities in you that fascinate me, that I adore, are your character, your heart, your indulgence toward the errors of others while being, at the same time, so hard on yourself—your charitableness, filled with shyness and mystery—your proud independence—your boyish simplicity—all qualities appropriate in one who has been able to preserve in himself a fierce virginity of ideas and sentiments in the midst of the sewer of humanity.

Oh, mio Verdi, I am not worthy of you! Your love for me is an act of charity, a balm for a heart that is often filled with sadness when it appears to be happy. Keep on loving me, love me even after death, that I may present myself before God's Throne of Judgment rich in your love and in your prayers, oh, my redeemer!

The relationship the letter suggests is surely one based on a profound love of the sort to which the Church would happily give its blessing. Further, the life the two of them led in Busseto was, except for the lack of clerical blessing, entirely respectable, even dull. Verdi worked hard; they never went out, and no one called. Merely as a matter of practicality there must have been many times when not to be married was a nuisance, and a seemingly unnecessary one. Why did they balk at it?

The reason must have been important; all the superficial ones, such as Verdi thought it was only a "temporary" affair, can easily be disposed of. And of the two, Strepponi or Verdi, the most reasonable speculations suggest the reason was important to him. In a letter written in 1872 to a Neapolitan friend Strepponi described their respective religious attitudes as they then were:

Verdi thinks too highly of you not to listen to what you tell him, and in spite of the fact you are a doctor, he counts you a believer in things of the spirit. But between ourselves, he himself is the strangest phenomenon in the world. He is an artist, not a doctor. Everyone agrees that nature endowed him with the divine fire of genius; he is a paragon of honesty, he understands and feels the most delicate and exalted sentiments. Yet this *rascal* claims, with a calm obstinancy that infuriates me, to be, not an outright atheist, but a very doubtful believer. I rave at him about the marvels of sky, earth and sea, etc. . . . It's wasted breath. He laughs in my face, and my oratory, my divine enthusiasms, are ignored. "You are mad," he says. And unfortunately he says it in good faith.

In another letter, also written in 1872, she stated to the Contessa Maffei:

There is no doubt that religious belief (not priestcraft) and the Gospel doctrine of grace and charity lead the spirit to regions of great calm and serenity where one finds the strength to walk with rectitude, where, too, one learns forgiveness for sinners and the charity to bring them back to the fold. (etc.)

Verdi is busy with the grotto and the garden. He is well and in a very good humor. Happy man, may God give him many years of happiness! For some virtuous natures belief in God is a necessity; others, equally perfect, while observing strictly every precept of the highest moral code, are happier believing nothing. Manzoni and Verdi! These two men give me food for thought:—my imperfections and my ignorance, alas, leave me incapable of solving so obscure a problem.

These letters, although written twenty years later, are the best clues to their religious attitudes in 1852. Verdi never changed in his agnosticism; Strepponi seems always to have "believed" and, as she grew older, to have become more at ease with the organized side of the Church, the "priestcraft." Of the two she suffered the more from not marrying and also had the more positive religious views. The great majority of biographers have, therefore, suspected that the one who did not want to marry was Verdi.

His agnosticism might be the reason except that he never made an issue of it beyond refusing to accompany her to church. He would drive her to the door in the carriage, but he would not go in. Yet he never published pamphlets or in any way took a public stand on it. A generation earlier the English poet, Shelley, for example, had sometimes written after his name in hotel ledgers: "Democrat, great lover of mankind, and atheist." Verdi seems generally to have avoided discussing his beliefs even with his friends.

Even more damaging to such a theory is, of course, that he married Margherita in church and that, finally, in 1859 he married Strepponi. Again neither he nor she ever revealed why they suddenly left Busseto for a small village in Piedmont and were married, ten years too late to avoid being pilloried for not doing so. And without any reasonable theories, speculation moves into the supernatural.

One theory suggests that Verdi was superstitious, that, after the death of Margherita and the children, he felt any wife of his was doomed, and he did not wish to put Strepponi into that position. Undoubtedly many Italians at the time, particularly those with simple backgrounds, were superstitious, but agnostics and sceptics generally were not. And there is no evidence that Verdi, who was interested in scientific farming, was bedeviled with irrational beliefs.

Another rather supernatural explanation is that Verdi made a vow to the dying Margherita that he would not remarry. Such vows were common at the time among country folk and were often demanded by a dying mother to protect her children against a stepmother. Custom required the husband to make the vow but then allowed a priest to absolve him from it. According to this theory, which is based on what Strepponi herself supposedly told a friend in Florence, Verdi gave such a vow and held it sacred, not because it was sworn in God's name, but because it was to a person he loved. But being an agnostic, he did not feel that the Church could absolve him from it. Further, his wife's last words were not the sort of thing he could discuss with the world or even Barezzi. He did tell Strepponi because she had a right to know why he would not marry her. As 1859 approached, when he was older, more sophisticated, and the necessity for getting married even more pressing, she persuaded him to allow their common friend, the Bishop of Florence, who acted less as a priest than a layman expert in vows, to release him from it. After which they married in a Catholic ceremony.

The theory is attractive if only because so neat, but like all the others, it is unsupported by any direct evidence. All the protagonists are dead, including Strepponi's friend in Florence, the Contessa Carlotta Collacchioni. The story exists by oral tradition. Curiously enough, in Manzoni's *I Promessi Sposi* the heroine, Lucia, vows not to marry if the Madonna will preserve her from a rape. The Madonna does, and Lucia's fiancé, Renzo, with difficulty persuades her to allow a priest to absolve her from the vow. This was the book Verdi exclaimed was "as true as the *truth.*"

But the town of Busseto could not be expected to divine recondite reasons why Verdi and Strepponi chose to live as they did, and as punishment it immured them in their privacy with hostility and disapproval. Their social life, first in the Palazzo Orlandi and then out at Sant' Agata, revolved almost entirely around visitors from outside, such as Ricordi or Piave. The isolation was harder on her than him. He had a genuine interest in the farm and the land, and when he was composing he had time for nothing else. But even he began to recognize that moving from Milan to Busseto had left him peculiarly alone. He no longer saw the Maffeis, although he continued to correspond with both of them. With other friends, such as Mme. Appiani or the poet Carcano, he exchanged an occasional letter, generally asking for news. In a letter to the Contessa Maffei at this time he regretted that his friend the Contessa della Somaglia no longer wrote him: "Now even this friendship is ended, and the blame is not hers but mine, all mine, or rather of destiny, which in strange ways robs me one by one of everything I love."

Men generally blame destiny when events happen which they do not understand or cannot control, and Verdi's reference to it here suggests that he had not thought out all the consequences of his move to Busseto with Strepponi before he undertook it. Whether the Contessa della Somaglia approved of his life or not was beside the point; the fact was that he had arranged it in such a way that it would be extremely difficult for her to see anything of him. They might meet in Paris; but she could not visit him at Busseto with Strepponi as the unmarried hostess, and he would not go to Milan. Verdi had, in fact, except for a rare friend like the Contessa Maffei who was willing to undertake a magnificent correspondence, effectively abandoned Milan and the stimulation its artistic and social circles could give him. This may have been good, allowing him to develop his talents completely in his own way, or bad, confining him to his established patterns, such as constantly using Piave as a librettist, or both at once. But whatever conclusion the argument reaches, it has as a premise that the move to Busseto under the particular circumstances, seemingly a purely personal decision, was important in Verdi's artistic development.

CHAPTER 23

IL TROVATORE

1852–1853; AGE, 38–39

VERDI and Strepponi spent the winter of 1851–52 in Paris, but even before leaving Busseto in the autumn he had begun work on his next opera, which was *Il Trovatore*. In April the previous spring, only a month after the première of *Rigoletto,* he received from Cammarano an outline of the Spanish play *El Trovador*. He was not happy with it and promptly wrote out one of his own which he sent to Cammarano. "As a man of talent and exceptional character," he wrote, "you will not mind if I, a very low fellow, take the liberty of saying that if we cannot do our opera with all the novelty and bizarre quality of the play, we'd better give it up." The trouble he had taken with the outline, however, showed that he would give it up only reluctantly.

The bizarre quality that appealed to Verdi was inherent in the play itself and not merely exotic color stuck onto a conventional drama. As such it gave the play, and ultimately the opera, a fundamental strength; it also ingrained, at least for the opera, some serious difficulties that neither Verdi nor Cammarano could smooth out.

The story concerns a gypsy woman, Azucena, whose mother had been burned at the stake by the local lord, a Count. To avenge her mother Azucena stole one of the Count's babies, a boy, and, returning to the stake where her mother died, rekindled the fire. There in the confusion and passion of vengeance she burned her own child instead of the Count's.

This mistake strikes a twentieth-century audience as absolutely incredible. The audiences in the 1830s, however, must have accepted it as, at least, possible. The play was a tremendous success, and it and others like it were considered serious drama. The Romantic Age in the theatre was one of passionate excess; gypsies were prevalent and thought to be particularly passionate; if no one in the audience knew exactly what horror might result from seeing a mother burn at the stake, at least from looking at Goya's etchings on the "Disasters of War" they knew that passion was blind and capable of any horror conceivable.

But aside from the theatrical problem of probability the incident presented Verdi and Cammarano with an additional one of time: the incident is only a prologue, taking place twenty-odd years before the story proper begins. Neither Verdi nor Cammarano saw any way to present it except in narration. It was far too climactic a scene to open the opera, yet as the prologue it had to come first. In the end they had a soldier tell the story to his fellows. In spite of Verdi's efforts it is a dull scene, as narratives generally are. The first rule of dramatic writing, whether for opera or play, can be stated simply as: "Show them; don't tell them."

For violating this first rule Verdi and Cammarano had to pay still another penalty. By substituting a soldier narrating in place of Azucena in action, her first appearance, although the opera's most important character, was postponed until the third scene. By then the audience, started falsely, has promoted the subplot, the love story, into a position of equal if not greater importance than the main theme of the opera, the gypsy's revenge.

The love story is a conventional costume drama of duels, vows and death by poison. Azucena has raised the old Count's son as her own, and he now is a famous warrior, Manrico. He loves one of the Queen's ladies-in-waiting, Leonora, but at the moment he is a rebel and visits her disguised as a troubador, a *trovatore*. Leonora is also loved by the old Count's other son and heir, the present Count di Luna. The rivals thus are brothers although no one but Azucena knows it. Her plan is to use one brother to kill the other and so be revenged on the House of Luna.

The plan miscarries. Instead of Manrico killing the Count, it is the other way round. Making the best of a bad situation, Azucena triumphantly tells the Count that he has killed his brother, and he is duly horrified. To some extent Azucena is revenged, but only at the cost of sacrificing the one person she loves.

The bizarre quality that Verdi liked in the story was the tug of conflicting emotions in Azucena. In his outline for Cammarano he wrote and then underlined: *"You must conserve to the very end the two great passions of this woman:* her love for Manrico and her ferocious thirst to avenge her mother. When Manrico is dead, her feeling of vengeance becomes overwhelming and she cries triumphantly: 'Yes . . . he was your brother! . . . Fool! . . . You are avenged, Mother!' " And these became Azucena's last words as she swoons at the end of the opera.

The situation is very like that in *Rigoletto,* and even the quality of the two leading characters is the same. Both are built on contrast: the loving father who is a foul-mouthed jester, the loving mother who is a daughter filled with hate. In *Ernani* the contrast is almost entirely between the characters: Ernani is good and Silva bad. Verdi no longer found such plays interesting; to a friend he complained they were "monotonous," capable, literally, of only a single tone.

In Paris in the winter of 1852 Verdi saw another play which could provide him with the sort of contrast that he liked. It was the dramatization by Dumas *fils* of his novel, *La Dame aux Camélias.* The novel had appeared in 1848, and Verdi evidently had read it, for even before the play appeared he occasionally mentioned it as a possible opera. Here the contrast lay in the character of a lady of the demimonde, a woman supporting herself by the proceeds of love and yet capable of sacrificing her only true love for an innocent girl she had never met. Dumas' dramatization was extremely effective. The novel had been successful, but the play caused a sensation. Undoubtedly seeing it on the stage re-enforced Verdi's tentative beliefs that there was a good opera libretto in the story. When he returned to Busseto in March, still working on *Il Trovatore,* he had the characters of *La Dame aux Camélias* well in mind and probably had begun to think of them in musical terms. Within almost exactly a year they became *La Traviata.*

Busseto was no more friendly to Verdi and Strepponi on their return than before, and she at least must have regretted leaving Paris. Always it was her favorite city and the only one in which, at least at this time, she could be happy. She spoke perfect French, had a circle of friends there who liked her, and it was, simply, Europe's most exciting city. She never considered herself anything but Italian, but she had little interest in politics and felt less of the patriotic tug that constantly pulled Verdi back to Italy. Nor, having grown up in a variety of cities, did she have any feeling about the soil. She endured Busseto only because Verdi lived there and she wished to live with him. When she could persuade him to go to Paris, she tried to do so. She now undoubtedly was delighted that he had agreed with the directors of the

Opéra to do a new opera for November or December 1854. It was in the future, but it was a firm commitment. And there undoubtedly would be more.

In fact their life in Busseto was easier, even if some of the reasons for it were sad. The death of Verdi's mother the previous summer had removed one source of criticism, and now the sickness of his father, temporarily at least, silenced another. Also Barezzi, after receiving and pondering Verdi's letter, began slowly to resume his old relationship. A loss was Muzio who, when in Busseto, had regularly visited them and had now gone to Brussels to be the director of its Théâtre Italien. There were gentlemen visitors, mostly impresarios or agents. There was talk of a new production of *Stiffelio* with a revised last act for Bologna. Ricordi came down from Milan to plead for a new opera for La Scala. But Verdi, who had received reports of a poor production there of *Macbeth,* refused. The only offer he accepted was from the Teatro Fenice in Venice for a new opera in the spring of 1853. The libretto was not specified, and throughout the summer Verdi and Piave corresponded over possibilities. Verdi was reluctant to suggest *La Dame aux Camélias* because he felt the Fenice company lacked a suitable soprano and there did not seem to be one available. But in the end this was the libretto chosen.

Politically the countryside remained quiet. In April there had been a demonstration at Cremona, the nearest large town to Busseto and just across the Po in Lombardy. Someone had displayed an Austrian flag in the main square, and, presumably on signal, all the windows facing the square slammed their shutters closed and symbolically turned their backside to the Imperial emblem. That night the theatre was empty. The Austrians issued bulletins and scolded but stopped short of actual reprisals. The hostilities were over; the Italians had no arms. But their hate was openly professed by dragging, sullen obedience.

Parma continued to be better off than its neighbors. Duke Carlo III, the son of the "dandy," grew increasingly unpopular, particularly as he reintroduced flogging. This was a punishment used by the Austrian army, and the Parmigiani considered it a barbarism. But except for this Carlo III was considered to be a nonentity, a pawn to be used, if possible, as a defense against Austria. He was only thirty and personally attractive, although arrogant. His weakness for women was well-known and considered far less serious than his desire to lead an army. In the absence of a war he constantly reviewed his troops, which probably cooled their loyalty, and designed better-looking parade uniforms, which perhaps increased it. The important middle class in the city of Parma hoped to be able to ignore him, to spread their business enterprises throughout northern Italy and thereby to tighten their ties to Lombardy, Venetia and, especially, independent Piedmont. Rabid followers of Mazzini, mostly among the poorer sections in the city, hated him as a monarch preventing the birth of a republic, and they plotted against him. He retaliated with secret police and public flogging.

On 17 July Cammarano died. His friends in Naples had expected it, for he had been ill for some time. But for Verdi, who only learned of it three weeks later, it was a horrible surprise. To a friend in Naples, Cesare de Sanctis, he wrote: "I was thunderstruck by the sad news of Cammarano. I can't describe the depth of my sorrow. I read of his death not in a letter from a friend but in a stupid, theatrical paper! You loved him as much as I and will understand the feelings I cannot put in words. Poor Cammarano! What a loss!"

Verdi had contracted to pay Cammarano five hundred ducats for the completed libretto. Now, although the outline was complete, it lacked verses for part of the third and all of the fourth act, and of course there were always last-minute changes to be made. But De Sanctis advised Verdi that Cammarano, the gentle, vague poet, had left his wife and children very little on which to live, and so Verdi paid the widow six hundred ducats for the work done. Through De Sanctis he engaged a young Neapolitan poet, Leone Emanuele Bardare, to collect the papers from Cammarano's house and finish the libretto.

Verdi had never contracted formally with any theatre for the première of *Il Trovatore*. Because of Cammarano's connection with the San Carlo, he had considered that first. But even before Cammarano died, he had opened negotiations with the Teatro Apollo in Rome. As far as Verdi was concerned, the choice of theatre turned on the singers available to each. The Apollo was an important theatre in Rome, although not quite as grand as the Teatro Argentina which had staged the premières of *I Due Foscari* and *La Battaglia di Legnano*. But the impresario at the Apollo, Cencio Jacovacci, happened to have the best company of singers, although Verdi was nervous about the mezzo-soprano for Azucena, "that Azucena to whom I attach so much importance!" The première was scheduled for 19 January 1853.

The première of *La Traviata* was to follow less than two months later, on 6 March, requiring Verdi to compose much of it while he worked on *Il Trovatore*. At Rome he even had a piano moved into his hotel room, so that after the rehearsals during the day of one opera, he could work at night on the melodies of the other. During all this period, as always, Verdi suffered with a sore throat and, a new ailment, an attack of rheumatism in his arm.

Verdi went to Rome by boat, Genoa to Civitavecchia, and Strepponi accompanied him, but only as far as Livorno. From there she went to Florence to see her son. She and Verdi exchanged letters almost every day, and hers which have been preserved are long and eloquent. They are filled with gossip, some of it witty and sharp, about singers she had seen, with advice about his arm, and, above all, with love.

Mio caro Verdi, I will confess my weakness to you. This separation has been harder to bear than the others. Without you I am a body without a soul. I am (and you know it) different from those others who need frequent separations to stimulate their love. I could be with you year after year without becoming bored or satiated. On the contrary since we have been together for a long time I feel the parting more, though you make me hope it will be short. (etc.)

Sometimes what must have been a deep fear comes to the surface:

We will not have children (since God perhaps punishes me for my sins by denying me, before I die, any legitimate joys!) But then, if you have no children by me, I hope you will not grieve me by having them by another woman. (etc.)

In Rome Verdi hardly went out at all. He saw something of his friend, the sculptor Luccardi, but after the rehearsals and his work on *La Traviata* there was little time. Besides, Rome in the winter of 1852–53 had a gloomy air of despair, at least for those of Verdi's political persuasion. In 1850 Pio Nono had returned to Rome through the same Lateran Gate by which he had escaped in disguise in 1848. French troops had escorted him to the Vatican which he now made his home instead of the more exposed Quirinal Palace. His experiment with liberalism was over, and the government of the Papal States returned in its essentials to what it had been under Gregory XVI in the 1830s.

A historian of Rome, Luigi Carlo Farini, described the restored government in a letter written in December 1852 to Gladstone in England. Farini was a Moderate, opposed equally to the extreme clerics and the republicans, and his appraisal represents a moderate view.

The Government is, as formerly, purely clerical, for the Cardinal Secretary of State is the only real Minister; Cardinals and Prelates prevail, if not in number, at any rate in authority, in the Council of State and in the Consultà of Finance; Cardinals and Prelates govern the Provinces; the clergy alone have the administration of all that relates to instruction, charity, diplomacy, justice, censorship and the police. The finances are ruined; commerce and traffic at the very lowest ebb; smuggling has sprung to life again; all the immunities, all the jurisdiction of the clergy are restored. Taxes and rates are imposed in abundance, without rule or measure. There is neither public nor private safety; no moral authority, no real army, no railroads, no telegraphs. Studies are neglected; there is not a breath of liberty, not a hope of tranquil life; two foreign armies; a permanent state of siege, atrocious acts of revenge, factions raging, universal discontent; such is the Papal Government at the present day.

But Pio Nono did not spend all his time oppressing his political subjects. He was also the spiritual father to Catholics all over the world, and some of his spiritual acts at this time were important both spiritually and politically. In 1850 he abolished the regime of apostolic vicariates in England and established a regular diocesan hierarchy, putting the first cardinal in England since Wolsey under Henry VIII. Three years later he did the same thing for Holland. In both countries, predominantly Protestant, his acts raised a storm of popular protest. He was burned in effigy; the British Prime Minister was forced to complain of "Papal Aggression," and in Holland the cabinet was forced to resign. From a purely political point of view the acts were unfortunately timed, as they cost Pio Nono important political support in a period when he needed it. From a spiritual point of view they were a suitable outward symbol of what amounted to a Catholic spiritual revival throughout Europe, including the Protestant countries.

Everywhere, for example, devout Catholic laymen eagerly awaited Pio Nono's definition of the Dogma of the Immaculate Conception of the Blessed Virgin Mary.

After six years of study he proclaimed it in December 1854 in St. Peter's: the Virgin Mary at the moment of her conception, which was in the normal, human manner, was miraculously exempted from the taint of original sin. To commemorate the occasion Pio Nono erected a tall column topped by a statue of the Virgin in the Piazza di Spagna.

Both sides of Rome's split personality continued to grow incompatibly side by side: the Catholic and the Italian city. The devout came, heard the proclamation and saw the column; others, like Verdi, came and saw only what Farini reported.

Four years earlier in Rome, almost to the week, Verdi had conducted the première of *La Battaglia di Legnano*. The atmosphere then, with the Pope already fled and the Republic about to be proclaimed, had been one of mass hysteria. The première of *Il Trovatore* on 19 January was, by comparison, sedate. The Tiber had flooded streets near the theatre, and the impresario had raised the prices. Even so, orderly lines had formed by eight in the morning, and by noon the house was sold out. According to a Roman critic who was present: "The public listened to every number in religious silence, applauding at each interval and demanding the repetition of the finale of the third act and the whole of the fourth." As a composer Verdi must have been pleased, for the music was given a fair chance to make its effect; as a perfectionist he was disappointed in the singers, the baritone in particular suffering from an attack of nerves. The singers did well enough, however, for the opera to be recognized as a masterpiece, and it at once began to play all over the world, as fast as Ricordi could mail out copies of the score and singers learn their parts.

The opera is marvelously romantic, opening with a soft roll on the drums, repeated twice, a loud cascade of forceful notes, a silence, and then three times a muffled, distant call on the horn to tragic love and chivalry. In form it is a direct descendant of *Ernani* but in a line which does not include the experiments of *Macbeth* and *Rigoletto*. In *Il Trovatore* the unit of construction is still the aria introduced by a few lines of recitative and expressing a single emotion. No character moves like Rigoletto through a succession of emotions, scornful pride to broken supplication, while staying within a single melodic unit. In *Ernani* the succession of arias had made the drama somewhat static. Verdi and Cammarano avoided this "concert" feeling in *Il Trovatore* by reducing the number of arias, blending them far more skillfully into each other, and finally by making the arias themselves shorter and more vigorous. The pace of *Il Trovatore* is extraordinary. At a good performance the audience arrives at the end breathless with excitement and almost believing it has seen a drama unfold before its eyes.

In fact it has not. In *Il Trovatore* until the last act almost everything of importance happens off-stage, which is a reason the story seems unclear. In *Rigoletto* it is possible to know nothing but what is presented on-stage and have the story make perfect sense. Each scene, even the last, begins almost immediately where the preceding one ended, and all four stay firmly in Mantua. No character need sing a narrative aria to explain what happened during the interval. But in *Il Trovatore* there are eight scenes with their locales scattered widely over Spain, and in the intervals duels and battles are fought, weeks and months pass, and the characters journey to the next improbable place for them to turn up. The first arias sung by the bass, the soprano, the mezzo-soprano and the tenor are all narrative arias describing vital scenes that took place off-stage. This incredible hurdle Verdi cleared partly by the brilliance of his melodies and partly by his and Cammarano's skill in working up the story in such a way that the arias evolve naturally out of the action and seem to advance it.

The libretto of *Il Trovatore* is generally castigated as the most ludicrously confused of Italian opera. But it is so only to persons who either do not understand Italian or will not take the trouble to read the libretto in translation. Verdi and Cammarano can hardly be blamed that English-speaking audiences do not catch all the lines or that the basic premise, Azucena's mistake, now seems so improbable. They can be blamed for skimping on the exposition; the opera is short and a few more minutes scattered through four acts would not hurt it. But the criticism overlooks the fact that Verdi and Cammarano created a viable libretto. When Verdi, working with Piave, attempted to make operas out of two other sprawling Spanish plays, *Simone Boccanegra* and *La Fuerza di Sino,* the result each time was a disaster. For each Verdi had to hire another poet to remake the libretto after the first performances. Piave's success with *Rigoletto* was really Hugo's. *Le Roi s'amuse* is in the tradition of the French "well-made play" in which there are no ends left loose and nothing need be assumed as all is explained as it goes along. In transforming the play into the opera Piave had almost nothing to do but translate the French lines into Italian and occasionally to condense the longer speeches. Cammarano's problem was far more difficult. The Spanish play was filled with minor characters, irrelevancies, scenes of local color and derring-do. He had to cut characters out, transpose scenes and make up speeches. All in all, he did it very successfully. Every operagoer must regret that the Good Lord in his confusion took Cammarano and left Piave.

But the greatest skill in placing arias cannot save one that is intrinsically dull, and what has preserved *Il Trovatore* as one of the world's most popular operas is the aptness and brilliance of its melodies. Verdi's sketches show that he worked hard on them, trying different rhythms, keys and endings. They are brilliant in the castrati tradition. Every voice from soprano to bass and even the chorus is expected to be agile and able to trill. Azucena has a trill lasting four and a third measures; she is also asked to hit a high "C," which is almost fabulous for a mezzo-soprano. The baritone must hold what is for him a high "G" while sounding "sweet," and the soprano is asked to run down the seventeen notes from high "C" to low "A" and at the orchestra's speed, not her own. Beginning with the première, all but the most exceptional singers have been unable to sing the arias as written, yet it has made no difference to the popularity of the melodies. Their secret seems to be partly that they are often waltzes, basically simple and catchy, and partly that Verdi succeeded so perfectly in fusing the words and the music. The melody becomes not the report of an emotion but the emotion itself. When the Count di Luna in his "Il balen" bursts out, "Ah, l'amor, l'amor," the audience does not mentally take note that the baritone is in love; its own chest collectively swells with the frustrated emotion, and for the moment it is in love. Verdi's gift for this sort of melodic writing is variously called his integrity, his passion, or more prosaically, his gift for melody. There is no exact word for it perhaps because the gift so seldom occurs and no one is exactly certain how it operates.

Some aspects of it, however, can be analyzed, such as Verdi's theatrical re-enforcement of his melodies. One of the most famous scenes in opera is the "Miserere" in *Il Trovatore*. In it Manrico, the troubador, is imprisoned in a tower which rises to one side of the stage. Through the grilled window his voice, as he sings to himself, literally floats down to the audience. He is hoping that his love, Leonora, will not forget him and bidding her farewell. At stage level, the foot of the tower, is Leonora, protesting to a man who cannot hear her that she can never forget him and aghast at the sound of monks' voices off-stage chanting the "Miserere" for Manrico's soul, soon to depart. The two voices and chorus are deliberately placed in different corners and levels of the stage to emphasize the contrast and drama between them. The placement is re-enforced by the musical accompaniment. The monks sing to a somber tolling bell, Leonora to a very quiet but ominous rum-te-te-tum in the orchestra, while Manrico's voice soars out over a very clear throb-throb on a harp. Each is presented, first alone, and then together. The audience, as though sitting before so many stereophonic loudspeakers, merges the sound in its ears. When the visual scene is added, the theatrical impact is tremendous. At the première a Roman critic reported that the scene was too much for the sensibilities of several ladies who were forced to leave.

During its first decade the opera was constantly criticized for the grimness of its story. Those who could made witty jokes about it; others wrote moralizing complaints that surprised Verdi. To his friend the Contessa Maffei he wrote: "People say the opera is too sad and there are too many deaths in it. But after all, death is all there is in life. What else is there?"

CHAPTER 24

LA TRAVIATA

1853; AGE, 39

VERDI returned to Busseto again via Genoa and by ship; Strepponi boarded at Livorno, and they arrived back at the Palazzo Orlandi in the last days of January. This time the repairs and alterations on the house at Sant' Agata were completed, or at least far enough along, so that they could move in. Thereafter it was their home, although for almost twenty years Verdi continued to keep it upset with additions and alterations. Once Strepponi wrote rather plaintively to the Contessa Maffei: "I cannot tell you how often during the building operations beds, wardrobes and furniture danced from room to room. It is enough to say that except for the kitchen, the cellar and the stables, we have slept and eaten our meals in every nook in the house." And she regretted with a housewife's pride having once served a meal to some distinguished statesmen in a dining room where the swallows still were nesting.

In that first winter, however, with the première of *La Traviata* only five weeks off, Verdi had no time or attention for anything but the opera. He was more than ever nervous about the cast, particularly the soprano, Fanny Salvini-Donatelli. He wrote the president of the Teatro Fenice that the reports he heard of her from Paris were so discouraging that they ought to make every effort to find another soprano. He particularly recommended Rosina Penco who had just created the role of Leonora in *Il Trovatore*. "She has," he urged, "a beautiful figure, intelligence and stage presence. The very best qualities for *La Traviata*." But the management could not engage her. Soon thereafter Verdi received an anonymous letter from Venice predicting a fiasco unless he could change the soprano and the bass. "I know it, I know it," Verdi wrote to Piave. But the première was scheduled, and Verdi's contract gave him the right to demand another soprano only if he did so before a date that was already past.

On 6 February, while Verdi was at work in Busseto, a disastrous attempt at revolution broke out in Milan. It was organized by Mazzini through his secret societies and required as the premise for its success the capture of a fortress with a garrison of 12,000 Austrian soldiers. As shock troops the societies organized some 500 men, each of whom had a complicated, daring assignment to complete in order for there to be even the slightest hope of temporary success. The revolution was to be announced to the Milanese at the moment of attack by a lengthy proclamation beginning: "The mission of the National Committee is finished; yours begins. The last word which today your brothers send to you is insurrection . . ." (etc.)

As might have been expected, not all the 500 men turned out, and of those that did many failed in their assignments. The Milanese in general were horrified at what was immediately judged to be a futile, foolish action, and they refused to assist the revolutionaries. Only two barricades appeared briefly, and the insurrection was put down in a few hours. Ten Austrians were killed or wounded, but Marshal Radetzky promptly hanged eighteen Italians and the following July condemned many more to various punishments.

Although the city as a whole had not aided the revolutionaries, Radetzky declared it to be in a state of siege, closed all the gates, and expelled all strangers he considered suspicious. On 13 February Emperor Franz Josef confiscated all the goods and real estate of the men involved and imposed on the city the obligation of supporting during the balance of their lives all the wounded and the families of those Austrians killed. He also required the city to raise a contribution to be given to the garrison as extra pay on account of the insurrection.

The attempt's complete failure with its waste of lives and inevitable Austrian reprisals was, in the long run, more important than any temporary success it could possibly have achieved. Because it occurred in Milan, it was widely discussed; and because Mazzini himself was directly involved, albeit from a distance, it discredited him with his republican followers everywhere, not as a prophet of Italy united, free and republican, but as a man of action with a program for obtaining it. Thereafter north Italians of every shade of republicanism began to agree that isolated spasms of revolt could never achieve the first, indispensable step to freedom: the defeat of the Austrian army. In the coming years they began to desert Mazzini and make common cause against Austria with the monarchists who favored uniting northern Italy under Vittorio Emanuele of Piedmont.

There were practical reasons why this was the best course possible. Of all the north Italian states only Piedmont was independent of Austria, and only there could plans be discussed, arms bought and troops trained. Only in Piedmont was there a monarch who could make any claim to being Italian and therefore acceptable to citizens of Parma, Modena, Tuscany and Lombardy-Venetia. And finally, only Piedmont could pursue an independent foreign policy that might succeed in allying foreign arms against Austria. Increasingly and with regret this last was recognized as necessary.

But there were also strong, emotional reasons which led some to look on Piedmont with distrust. Chief among these was the increasingly bitter argument there between the Church and the State. The Church existed in Piedmont in medieval numbers and splendor, and as in medieval times it had its own court, the "Foro Ecclesiastico," for the trial of any priest who violated the state's laws. This duplicated the state system but not exactly, so that laymen complained that the law was not the same for every man. After a series of negotiations with Pio Nono that came to naught the cabinet of Turin submitted a bill to the Parliament there abolishing the ecclesiastical court. The bill passed both houses, aided by a speech in the Chamber of Deputies by an aristocrat who owned a newspaper, Count Camillo Cavour. The bill was extremely popular in Piedmont, and some of its popularity adhered to Cavour, who had hitherto been a somewhat isolated deputy.

But the difficulties over the bill and Cavour's connection with it did not stop when it became law. A few months later Count Pietro di Santa Rosa, a minister in the cabinet which had presented the bill, died. Cavour was the man's friend and present at his deathbed. From the man's widow Cavour heard how the priest had refused the sacrament to Santa Rosa unless the minister repudiated his support for the law abolishing the Foro Ecclesiastico. Santa Rosa refused and, as a pious Catholic, in terrible distress died unshriven. Cavour wrote an indignant article in his paper, denouncing the party spite which concealed itself under a religious cloak. Large angry crowds gathered in the streets of Turin, and the government feared that if the Archbishop, as rumored, denied Santa Rosa a Christian burial, it would be unable to protect the city's priests. So it sent General La Marmora to interview the Archbishop. The General intimated bluntly that the government intended to hold the Archbishop personally responsible for any disturbance, and the Archbishop after some conversation agreed to allow a Christian burial.

For Cavour the incident was a steppingstone to the cabinet, for he replaced Santa Rosa as Minister of Commerce and Agriculture and also added to those posts that of Minister of the Navy. He was a bachelor and had the time; he also had the ability. In ten years he would prove himself to be the ablest parliamentary statesman Italy ever produced.

For others in Piedmont and those watching from neighboring Italian states the incident was an ill omen, revealing that the seemingly insoluble, Italian problem of the Papal States and Temporal Power existed in a somewhat similar form inside Piedmont. Sending a general to browbeat an archbishop is a form of State-Church relations but obviously not a happy one, not a concordat. Anyone could see that there would be other clashes, even more serious, which would divide the people on emotional lines of Church and State allegiance. For men like Santa Rosa, both pious and liberal, it would be a difficult time.

The problem in different guise soon became an international question, the immediate cause being Mazzini's revolt in Milan. One of the Austrian reprisals was an edict sequestrating the property of all Lombard and Venetian patriots who had emigrated after the wars of 1848–49. Many of these had become citizens of Piedmont. The edict violated the terms of Austria's treaty with Piedmont and, in a time when most men's wealth was in land, reduced to penury some of the most famous Italian patriots. What the edict amounted to was the nationalization without compensation of the property of certain individuals who were citizens of Piedmont, not Austria. It was widely thought at the time that the real instigator of the edict was Cardinal Antonelli, Pio Nono's Secretary of State.

Cavour, who was then Prime Minister, protested the edict and, after an exchange of notes, withdrew his ambassador from Vienna, but he could not prevent its enforcement. He did, however, by presenting Piedmont's case calmly and with dignity to the governments of the world, crack the illusion that Austria was upholding treaties and was the only force for peace and orderly government in northern Italy.

Like all other north Italians denied a political life of their own,

Verdi began to follow the news of what was happening in Piedmont almost as though it were already the national government. He had met some of the Lombard emigrants and must have been pleased when the Piedmontese Parliament passed a bill to compensate them in part for their lost property and again when Vittorio Emanuele made two of the most distinguished of them Senators of the Kingdom. About the attempted revolution in Milan he heard directly from Muzio, who had gone there from Brussels to produce his own opera *Claudia* at the Teatro Carcano. The venture was ill-fated, although the critics gave the opera good reviews. But the première was the night after the attempted revolution, and the Austrians almost immediately thereafter closed the theatres. Muzio, knowing Verdi was about to leave for Venice, wrote him a few days later that the countryside was as tranquil as ever and it was possible to travel without danger or difficulty.

Verdi arrived in Venice on 21 February and thirteen days later, on 6 March, *La Traviata* had its première. It was not a success, or as put by one of Verdi's Italian biographers: "The première marked an epoch in the history of colossal fiascos." The second performance did no better.

Verdi sent off terse notes to his friends in which his morale is extraordinarily high. The morning after the première he wrote Muzio: "*La Traviata* last night was a fiasco. Is the fault mine or the singers? Time will tell." Similar notes went off to Tito Ricordi, who was beginning to manage his father's business in Milan, to De Sanctis in Naples, to Luccardi in Rome, and to the conductor Mariani in Genoa: "*La Traviata* has been a great fiasco and worse, they laughed. Now then, what do you want? I am not upset. Either I am wrong or they are. For my part I do not believe the last word on *Traviata* was spoken last night. They will see it again and we shall see! Meanwhile, caro Mariani, record a fiasco."

The audience laughed throughout the last act in which Violetta, the lady of pleasure, wasted with consumption and too weak even to change her clothes, expires. Mme. Fanny Salvini-Donatelli was unfortunately plump and healthy-looking, and apparently every time she attempted a tubercular cough it convulsed the audience. But this is a hurdle many operatic performances have successfully cleared, and more must have been wrong than just the visual illusion.

Verdi clearly felt the singers were partly responsible, and the Venetian critics support him in this. One, after praising the performance of the orchestra, refused to judge the rest of the opera until it was better sung. Apparently not only was the soprano poor, but the tenor had lost his voice, and the baritone felt his role was beneath him. This last was Felice Varesi, who as Verdi's first Rigoletto and first Macbeth should have known better, and his perfunctory performance suggests that for some reason the opera never pulled together for its first production.

One reason may have been time. Verdi arrived in Venice only thirteen days before the première, and he is supposed to have orchestrated the entire opera in that short period. If this can be true, if he arrived without a note of the orchestration done, then he can have spent very little time at the rehearsals explaining and directing what he wanted. Indeed, Verdi's part in the production is something of a mystery. Dumas *fils* had written a contemporary play, and in a letter Verdi wrote before the première he described the opera as "a subject from our own time. Another man perhaps would not have composed it because of the costumes, of the period, or a thousand other foolish objections." Plainly Verdi originally intended it to be done as a contemporary opera, yet at the première the opera's period was set back to the early 1700s. It is curious that Verdi, so positive over the horn in *Ernani* and the sack in *Rigoletto,* never murmured in a letter, either before or after the production, about the decision to change the period. It may be that he was so busy finishing the opera's music that he had no time for its production; and what should have been produced with the greatest care as a new type of opera in a contemporary setting, which was most unusual, was instead hustled onto the stage as just another costume drama by men who did not understand the opera and were too rushed to study it.

For more than a year it lay dormant without a performance anywhere. Verdi told Ricordi not to rent out parts for a production unless he, Verdi, could direct it, and he considered the idea of a production at Rome where he felt the audience was sympathetic. But before he had done more than inquire about singers, his Venetian friends led by a violinist, Antonio Gallo, asked for permission to try the opera again in Venice. Gallo planned to put it on in the Teatro San Benedetto which his family owned. It was a smaller theatre than the Fenice but almost equally famous. Gallo planned to keep the 1700 period, to have Piave direct the production and to have unlimited rehearsals. Verdi at first was hesitant, but he could, after all, hardly reject such a demonstration of friendship and faith in his work. Gallo collected good singers, rehearsed them, and on 6 May 1854, fourteen months after its première, he presented *La Traviata* again to the Venetians. This time the opera had a tremendous success, leading Verdi, who was then in Paris, to observe dryly that the same audience as before was seeing the same opera. But at least its history thereafter was different, for it immediately began to play all over the world.

Part of its success, at least in its early years, was its scandal. Dumas' play had caused a sensation in Paris, and Piave had been able to follow it almost exactly, changing only the names of the characters. In the opera Violetta, a young and attractive courtesan, falls genuinely in love with Alfredo, a young man from Provence. She gives up her gay life and friends to live with him outside of Paris. They are not married, but they are extremely happy together. His father has an interview with Violetta in which he asks her to break off with Alfredo because the liaison is jeopardizing the marriage of Alfredo's sister to a suitable young man in Provence. During the interview the father becomes convinced that Violetta genuinely loves Alfredo but points out that with her reputation she cannot marry him and will spoil not only his life but also his sister's. Violetta agrees to sacrifice herself and returns to a life of empty gaiety, telling Alfredo that she no longer loves him. The final act shows Violetta alone, dying of consumption, and waiting for Alfredo, whose father has only just told him of her sacrifice, to come to her. When he arrives, she begins to feel they can begin their life again, but the excitement has exhausted her and she dies in his arms.

Dumas' play had presented the life and emotions of a courtesan without historical trappings, and part of its effect had been its sense of immediacy. Opera, however, was used to historical trappings, and for many years all the productions of *La Traviata* continued to set it in the early 1700s. But this did not affect the fundamental contrast in the drama; the supposedly debased lady performs the noble act. And in whatever period it was set, the opera suggested that unmarried love could be idyllic and noble. As such, many proper persons considered it an assault on marriage, a plea for free love, and were not consoled by the argument that the wages of Violetta's sin were death. For them cause and effect in the opera were not morally related: the death was not venereal. Nice girls also died of consumption. On the other side, those in revolt against the conventions of society found it very "modern" and made it, much to the joy of the impresarios, something of a *cause célèbre*. Toye recounts how "one aristocratic French lady, well-known in cosmopolitan society, was famed for her attendance at performance after performance in various capitals, though the poignancy of her emotion not infrequently caused her to leave the theatre in the course of the evening. Lovers, especially lovers whose love was illicit, attended it in very much the same spirit as they afterward attended performances of *Tristan und Isolde*. In short *La Traviata* became the symbol of revolt against current sexual conventions."

Such an approach to the opera seems very strange today and probably at the time seemed so to Verdi, if he was aware of it. He might also find strange the extent to which some critics since have gone to make the opera autobiographical, casting Barezzi in the father's role as coming between the lovers and then at the end recognizing his mistake. Undoubtedly Verdi's personal experiences contributed to his understanding of life, but beyond that the theory fits uncomfortably on a man thirty-nine years old, vigorous, confidently trying new forms and prepared to wait out a fiasco. He lived a somewhat isolated, unconventional life, but he was hardly that sort of sensitive soul who after a bout with society retires into isolation and croons over his scars until he has created a masterpiece. It is more likely that he saw first in the novel and then in the play the same sort of qualities that appealed to him in *Le Roi s'amuse* and which he had described as having "the most powerful dramatic situations, variety, vitality, pathos; all the dramatic developments result from the frivolous, licentious char-

acter of the Duke." In the same way in *La Traviata* the drama develops out of Violetta's character: her ability to understand what Alfredo means by love is the same ability that betrays her into understanding what his father means by love. After doing *Rigoletto* Verdi must have seen Dumas' play and had the musical outline for *La Traviata* simply leap into his mind. In fact, his sketches for it show very few hesitations or corrections. This is not to suggest that he was not inspired, only that he saw from the first exactly what his music could do. It is also to suggest a reason why he was able to write it in such a short and distracted time and why, although the première was a disaster, he never lost confidence in it. He knew it was as good as *Rigoletto*.

Of course there is no exact correlation between scenes in the two operas, but often the basic musical outline is identical. In the opening preludes to both operas, for example, the orchestra begins with a somber or tragic tone that as the curtain rises changes to one of frivolous gaiety. In *Rigoletto* it is the music associated with the curse contrasted with that of the Duke's court; in *La Traviata* it is the music associated with Violetta's love for Alfredo contrasted with that of her non-love in her kept world. In both operas the musical contrast is theatrically effective and dramatically true, so that on repeated hearings the contrast gains in significance. In the same way Rigoletto's first jesting scene in which he mocks Monterone is followed by Rigoletto at home exhibiting his best qualities; likewise Violetta is shown first at her party, mocking love, and then at her country retreat, preparing nobly to sacrifice her only chance at it. Thereafter the stories proceed less identically, but the same sort of irony is preserved. Violetta, dying, hears gay carnival revelers singing off-stage; and Rigoletto, sack in hand, hears the Duke's voice in the distance. Just as Rigoletto believes he has triumphed, he discovers he has killed his daughter; just as Violetta thinks she will live, she dies.

But although the operas are alike in their basic musical outline, they are very different in their tone. *Rigoletto* is a costume drama with heroic figures against a romantic background; the music in the prelude is associated with a curse, and the opera's theme is *"vendetta!"* *La Traviata* is a bourgeois story set against a realistic background. Violetta and Alfredo's father even argue over who is paying the rent on the country house. It is the most intimate and domestic story Verdi ever set. Even *Luisa Miller*, while a story about a simple girl next door, takes place in a romanticized Tyrol with, literally, a castle in the background. Appropriately Verdi's music for *La Traviata* has an intimate quality. The melodies do not soar in a heroic fashion; many, particularly in the more intimate duets, have a conversational quality and move easily from one emotion to the next. Violetta in her interview with the father, for example, passes from protest over his demand, to grief, to resolution, to a last frenzied outburst. Each mood has a different and appropriate melody, but none is an aria of the kind a soprano could excise for a concert.

La Traviata has arias, however; fewer than *Il Trovatore* but more than *Rigoletto*. Verdi supposedly was asked about this time which of his operas he liked best, and the reply was that as a professional he preferred *Rigoletto* but as an amateur *La Traviata*. The remark, whether true or not, is extremely understandable. Of the two operas *Rigoletto* is the more tightly constructed and the exposition in it is better. *La Traviata* suffers slightly from the same troubles of *Il Trovatore:* important events occur during the intermissions, such as Violetta changing her mind about accepting Alfredo, or the results of the duel between Alfredo and the Baron who wishes to keep Violetta. In form *La Traviata* falls between the other two operas. In its first act (*See* outline p. 312) the first part, as in *Rigoletto,* is constructed over recurring party music which no one actually sings. The exposition is not so clearly set forth although the melody is more attractive. But the aria, the *brindisi* or drinking song, is an old-fashioned concert aria. The orchestra stops, begins a vamp, and the tenor puts aside his efforts to be Alfredo while preparing to stun the audience with a singing exhibition. When the soprano takes over on the second verse, it becomes a competition. It is a glorious tune and, because carefully placed, does not seem too out of place, but it does prefer musical pattern over the drama. Similarly Verdi allows Violetta to end the act with a full-blown, slow-fast aria, a thing he denied to Gilda or Rigoletto. He adapts the old form brilliantly to a more modern purpose, the slow and fast sections reflecting her changing mood so that the contrast is effective musically and dramatically. But he does even more by interrupting it with Alfredo's voice from off-stage, reminding Violetta of love at the very moment she rejects it. In this he repeats the effect he had used so successfully in the "Miserere" by having Alfredo sing only to a throb-throb on the harp. The sudden, clear sound after all the running noise in the orchestra grips the audience's attention even as it does Violetta's and gives a dramatically valid reason why she must drown

ACT 1 *(about 24 mins.)*
(drawing room in Violetta's house; in the center a table set for dinner.)

GUESTS	introduction *(fast)*	party music as the guests enter.
	chorus and dialogue *(fast)*	party music; guests greet Violetta and Alfredo is introduced.
	pause *(fast)*	party music; they sit to dinner.
	chorus and dialogue *(fast)*	party music; Gaston tells Violetta that Alfredo loves her; the Baron tells Flora he dislikes Alfredo; they all call for a drinking song.
VIOLETTA and **ALFREDO**	aria *(less fast)*	the brindisi: first verse by Alfredo; second by Violetta; chorus joining in close.
	dialogue *(less fast)*	waltz in back room as all go to dance except Violetta and Alfredo. He declares his love.
	aria merging into duet *(slow)*	he urges her to love; she is evasive.
	dialogue *(less fast)*	waltz resumes; she agrees to let him return; he leaves.
GUESTS	chorus *(fast)*	party music; guests say "good-by."
VIOLETTA	recitative	strange! how his words moved her.
	aria *(slow)*	Perhaps he is the one her heart has awaited. Ah, Love.
	recitative	
	aria *(fast, first verse)*	"Sempre libera": she must keep her heart free.
	interruption *(to a harp)*	Alfredo off-stage and under her balcony sings as before of love.
	recitative *(very short)*	it is folly.
	aria *(fast, second verse)*	she must be free. (This last, sung as his voice fades, is very brilliant, filled with runs and trills.)

out his voice with a second verse of her fast aria.

The aria itself is in the *Il Trovatore* style of great singing: very brilliant with many trills and runs. Most sopranos, even in their recordings of it, take it rather slowly, fudge the trills, and drop out five or six measures before the end. Then they end, or try to, on a high note which Verdi did not write.

Taken together the three operas, *Rigoletto, Il Trovatore* and *La Traviata,* form a large part of Verdi's claim to greatness. Curiously, not one is a perfect work of art; all have bad moments in their librettos and all are regularly performed with cuts in their music. It seems not to matter. For more than a hundred years they have survived on every operatic stage, often sung by very bad singers. Why should Verdi suddenly have succeeded so brilliantly and so consistently, three times in a row, where before he had not? Sentimentalists like to argue that his life with Strepponi had added a depth to his passion and given him the stability better to realize it. Artistic types will explain that after 1848–49 Verdi finally understood that he could not prostitute his art to patriotism. Critics will analyze the balance at which he had arrived between arias and melodic recitative, and lastly impresarios will add that the operas were written for small theatres, do not require a large orchestra, and are easy to produce: hence they are often produced. But after all the speculations are considered there still remains an area of the inexplicable, the magic of art.

CHAPTER 25

PARIS AND
I VESPRI SICILIANI

1853–1855; AGE, 39–41

AT Venice in the spring of 1853 the second performance of *La Traviata* was as poorly received as the première, and when the tenor fell sick, the directors of the Fenice canceled the remainder scheduled and substituted *Il Corsaro*. Verdi did not wait to see it but left at once for Sant' Agata. In the time that he had been away Strepponi had been ill with intestinal grippe and on a diet of soup and eggs. She wrote him almost every day, reporting what news there was: Barezzi had been to see her twice, his two sons once each; and when the Duke of Busseto, who was Marie Louise's surviving third husband, had passed through the town, Barezzi had gone to meet him with the Philharmonic Society band. The Duke had spoken kindly to "il Signor Antonio," who was still very excited.

Strepponi's remarks in her letters to Verdi about Barezzi are polite, but the ironic phrasing suggests she as yet felt no affection for him. To the sons she was openly hostile, describing the youngest as "a bad lot," apparently because he had bought a carriage and stayed at a lady's house until 4 A.M. She plainly enjoyed refusing to see him when he called because, as she was careful to be the first to explain to Verdi, he arrived at nine o'clock which was too early to visit "a lady." It does not seem to have occurred to her that because the Bussetani had good reason to believe that she was not a lady it was all the more kind of the young man to call at all.

Once back at Sant' Agata Verdi began again to cast about for new librettos. His contract with the Opéra did not require rehearsals to begin until July 1854 or even the libretto to be delivered until the close of 1853, so that he had almost a full year in which to get another opera under way or possibly even produced. From Naples his friend De Sanctis had forwarded a libretto by a poet, Domenico Bolognese, who hoped to become Cammarano's successor. Verdi's answer, considering his very early Goethe songs (p. 62), is interesting:

I have read Signor Bolognese's lines. The point could not be better stated and I agree with him, only I do not take to such subjects. I adore *Faust,* but I don't wish to put it to music. I have studied it a thousand times, but I don't find Faust's character musical . . . musical (understand me well) in the way I feel music. Frankly I don't like the other subjects. There is nothing that lifts them out of the commonplace.

Make a thousand affable remarks to the said Signor Bolognese. (etc.)

Later in May he rejected more suggestions from Bolognese that had come through De Sanctis. He tried to explain what it was he liked about French drama, particularly Hugo, where he felt that "the great characters produced the great situations, and the dramatic effects naturally followed." As it turned out, he never did find a replacement for Cammarano in Naples and, probably as a consequence, never had another Neapolitan première.

In a poet in Venice, however, Verdi seemed to have found a congenial collaborator. The man was Antonio Somma, a lawyer and friend of Gallo and also a successful playwright of tragedies in verse. Somma began, like Bolognese, by suggesting various subjects all of which Verdi rejected because, as he explained: "I don't find in them all the variety my crazy brain desires." But then, on Verdi's suggestion, they began to work on *King Lear* and by September Verdi had a completed libretto. Thereafter for almost three years the two men constantly rewrote it, and their correspondence discussing the various changes is one of the most detailed discussions by Verdi and a librettist of any of his operas, although parodoxically on an opera he never composed.

Always Verdi insisted that they keep it short: "In the theatre long is synonymous with boring; and of all styles boring is the worst." He was appalled at trying to condense the play into three or "at most" four acts and, partly to save time, planned to begin the opera without any overture or prelude, only trumpet flourishes on "long, antique, straight trumpets." Also to save time at one point both Gloucester and Edgar were cut out although their absence left large holes in the story. But an advantage was that it greatly reduced the number of scenes, which Verdi felt was all to the good. "In this the French are right," he exclaimed. "They plan their dramas so they need only one scene for each act. Then the action flows freely without being held up and without anything to distract the attention of the public."

To assist Somma in reducing the number of scenes Verdi was quite willing to have extended recitatives. As he pointed out, he had done some very long ones in *Macbeth* and *Rigoletto*. The danger lay in having too many, one after another. Then they inevitably turned out "long and consequently boring. To speak frankly," he added, "I am very afraid of the first half of the fourth act. I don't know exactly what, but something doesn't satisfy me. It certainly lacks brevity, perhaps clarity, perhaps truth." For Verdi the three ideals were artistically related: there could be no perceivable truth without clarity, and any truth that was clearly perceived could be stated briefly.

He passed the summer at Sant' Agata with Strepponi, corresponding with Somma and others and working on his farm. An accounting of its profit and loss at this time shows that Verdi already had three peasant subtenants, was growing corn and hay, and owned four oxen, seventeen cows, ten bullocks, eleven calves and six rams. He operated at a profit which came largely from the sale of cattle.

The summer was a vacation from music although he never called it or perhaps even thought of it as such. It was his first since the days after *Un Giorno di Regno,* for in the eleven years following the première of *Nabucco* in March 1842 he had composed fifteen operas. Now he planned to escape the worst of the winter at Sant' Agata with a visit to Naples as "a private person," and he wrote De Sanctis to arrange for rooms for himself and Strepponi. Then he changed his plans and left in October for Paris. Just before leaving he celebrated his fortieth birthday.

The Paris to which Verdi and Strepponi returned had a different atmosphere from that of 1848 or even 1851, for it was once again an Imperial city with an Emperor, Napoleon III, holding court in the Tuileries Palace. Napoleon had traveled from President of the Second Republic to Emperor in two steps, the first involving him in a *coup d'état* for which true republicans never forgave him.

The Second Republic, never very strong, had limped to a halt by 1851. Neither republicans nor monarchists were numerous enough to govern alone, yet neither could imagine a compromise. As the months passed without any solution to the stalemate, the possibility of a civil war increased alarmingly.

The circumstance was ideal for an ambitious man who could lead the country safely out of its dilemma. Louis Napoleon, President of the Second Republic, had a program: he wished to restore Bonapartism to France with himself in the leading role, to be Emperor of the French with the blessing of the people. He laid his plans carefully, removing from command all generals who were ardent republicans and ingratiating himself with those he promoted. He proposed to the Assembly that it grant universal (male) suffrage and, led by the conservative monarchists, it refused. Four weeks later during the night of 1–2 December 1851 Napoleon, with his close councilors around him, opened a bundle of papers which he had marked "Rubicon" and gave last instructions. All drumheads in the National Guard were stove in so that an alarm could not be sounded, and even bell ropes in the churches were cut. Nearly seventy leaders in the Assembly and a number of generals were arrested in their beds. A presidential proclamation was printed and posted about Paris. It urged the army and the people to remain calm and obey their President. It declared the Assembly dissolved and universal suffrage restored. It promised to submit the acts of the President to the people for approval or rejection by plebiscite, and it proposed a new constitution.

What few republicans remained at large, among them Hugo, attempted to arouse Parisians to defend the Republic. But the city was apathetic. A few barricades went up, and a few idealists were killed, but the soldiers easily cleared the streets. On the third day the inevitable tragic incident occurred: nervous soldiers fired into a crowd mostly of women and children. This aroused the city, but by then it was too late. Hugo went into exile in Brussels and many others fled to England. The incident marred the myth that Napoleon wished to create: that the coup was bloodless; and from outside of France republicans, and particularly Hugo, never let the world forget that Napoleon came to power by stepping over the bodies of countrymen he had killed.

Three weeks later Napoleon submitted his actions and a new constitution to the country, and both were approved by a vote of 7,440,000 to 646,000. The constitution provided for a president to hold office for ten years. He was to have all the legislative and executive power of the government and to be advised by a Council of State. There was to be a Senate to bring together "the most illustrious personages in

France"; that is, those who had helped Napoleon. And there was to be a Legislative Assembly, elected by universal suffrage and with no powers at all. Napoleon was technically still only President, but he moved at once from the modest Élysée into the Tuileries Palace. He was Emperor in all but name. Verdi's prediction of a new revolution had come to pass.

The final step was taken less than a year later when the people in another plebiscite amended the constitution to make the President an Emperor with office and title hereditary. On 2 December 1852 Napoleon proclaimed the Empire; it was the anniversary of his own *coup d'état* and of the first Napoleon's battle of Austerlitz in 1805 and coronation in 1804.

He took the title, Napoleon III, because Marie Louise's infant son had been proclaimed Emperor Napoleon II on 22 June 1815, following his father's abdication after Waterloo. Napoleon II's reign, which was never properly started, was immediately cut short by the Allied Powers as they entered Paris. But reference to it in 1852 perhaps made Louis Napoleon's coup seem more legitimate in pretending to resume a broken tradition rather than starting a new one. He had no coronation, but in January 1853 he married an aristocratic Spanish lady, Eugenia de Montijo, who, although not royal, was very well born and stunningly beautiful. He was forty-four, famous for his ladies, and yet it was said with some reason to be a love match. The ceremony took place in Notre Dame, and as the Emperor believed in a show for the people it was a gorgeous spectacle of matching horses and colorful uniforms. The Second Empire, most everyone agreed, was at least more entertaining than the drab frock coats of the Second Republic.

Napoleon, however, intended to do more than merely sit a horse well and wear fancy uniforms. He had considered the problems of the Industrial Age and intended to lead France consciously into it. His chief interest was industry, even including mechanical toys, and he recognized that an industrial France would require a reorganized banking and credit system capable of financing railroads, canal systems, and enlarging the ports. As well as these projects he drained the marshes in the Dombes and stopped the sand dunes in the Landes from shifting by plantations of pines. The actual projects were not so extraordinary as their number and the role he granted the government in carrying them out. But one was so inherently spectacular that it caught the imagination of Europe and was a subject of daily conversation for twenty years. This was the rebuilding of Paris.

Early in June of 1853 Napoleon appointed a French Protestant from Alsace, Georges Haussmann, Prefect of the Seine and gave him a map of Paris. On it Napoleon had drawn in four colors the various streets he proposed to build in order that the city could be more beautiful and better adapted for living and business; the colors showed the priority he gave to each project. In the following months as Haussmann considered the implications of the map, the colored streets slashing through thousands of houses, he realized that many acres at a time in the heart of Paris would be cleared and that he could create an entirely new water system for the city, both for drinking and sewage. The ideas of the two men re-enforced each other, and their project became the first planned assault on the problems of a great, modern city. As such it has had an influence on city planning ever since, and at the time the energy it represented was a sign that France, not Austria, would in the coming years be the leader in Europe.

Haussmann began by making the first accurate map of Paris showing all its street elevations. The importance of a few inches grade in a sewer, one way or the other, can easily be imagined. To map the city in the winter of 1854 he erected on many of the street corners wooden towers that stretched above the rooftops and from which surveyors could triangulate the entire city within the *octroi* walls. These were the walls with sixty gates at which a levy, the *octroi,* was collected on goods entering Paris. The third act of Puccini's *La Bohème* takes place at such a gate. In 1860 the walls were destroyed, but for many months the farmers' horses continued to stop where the gates had been. The present second ring of boulevards follows the line of the *octroi* walls.

It was impossible for anyone not to see the triangulation towers, and they aroused the greatest speculation. Newspapers published cartoons of tightrope walkers carrying messages between them or of artillery shooting the surveyors up to their posts. Everyone talked heatedly of what he understood to be Haussmann's plans.

Verdi took great interest in the work. He went out to the new Bois de Boulogne to inspect the two artificial lakes and the new planting and also down to the Louvre to see the slum between it and the Tuileries demolished. Work progressed very slowly as everything had to be done by hand and the building "season" stopped during the winter. Many of the workers came from other departments, particularly from one in the middle of France, Creuse, which developed a reputation for providing good stone masons. During the building boom about one half of that department's physically fit men, or about 40,000, would trek to Paris for the season and then home again. Such an army arriving and departing posed an economic problem both to Paris and Creuse and an economic delight for the tavern keepers on the road between. After several trips the men often stayed in Paris where the population steadily increased, until by 1856 it was more than a million and a half. Milan in the same year was still well under 200,000 and even fifty years later had only just passed a half-million. The Paris Opéra, officially renamed the Théâtre Impérial de l'Opéra, was the leading theatre in Europe if only because it was in the biggest and most glamorous city.

Verdi, however, found working with the Opéra exasperating. After a few months of it he wrote to the Contessa Maffei that he had "a ferocious desire to go home." The trouble lay partly in the libretto which the Opéra had given him. It was by Eugène Scribe who was thought at the time to be the greatest French librettist and who had done the librettos for Meyerbeer's *Les Huguenots* and Halévy's *La Juive,* both of which had played steadily at the Opéra for almost twenty years. For Verdi Scribe created a story called *Les Vêpres Siciliennes,* or *The Sicilian Vespers;* ultimately the opera became best known under its Italian title *I Vespri Siciliani.*

Verdi's difficulty with the libretto went deeper than uncertainty over French words and their intonation; it reflected the conflict between two opposed views of opera, his and Scribe's. Verdi had arrived at a point where he wanted to keep the action swift, clear and expressing some sort of truth about the characters and his feelings for them. His aim in writing an opera was to induce in the audience the same passion that he felt himself.

Scribe's aim, at least as shown in the works he created for the Opéra, was something quite different. The Opéra was the largest theatre in France and with a character all its own. Every tourist, French or foreign, visited it to see the spectacles put on by the government, for it was a state theatre. The tradition, as largely developed by Scribe, required every opera to have at least one full-length ballet with as many shorter dances as possible; to have five acts so that the tourist would get his money's worth in a long show; to make use of the enormous stage with huge spectacular scenes filled with two or three separate choruses singing back and forth at each other; and lastly, if possible, to have one scene in which the scenery collapsed to the ground or burned up. The purpose was to entertain the audience; to have it admire rather than to feel. The closest thing to the Opéra today, beside its continuing self, is the Radio City Music Hall in New York which at every show offers its patrons an electric organ, a symphony orchestra, a huge choir, a ballet corps, tap dancers, various other acts and a mild movie, all presented in a rather unrelated fashion in a fabulous theatre. Perhaps the greatest difference between the Opéra and the Music Hall is that in New York the President of the United States and his cabinet do not attend the show whereas in Paris the Emperor and his court did. In fact they were part of it. In a time when the theatres were still lit with candles and the house lights could not be dimmed the boxes and their occupants were always interesting.

Scribe's librettos, tailored to these requirements, usually turned on some historical incident. In *Les Huguenots* it was the Massacre of St. Bartholomew which took place in Paris on 24 August 1572 and in which the Catholic party at the French court undertook, on the ringing of the tocsin, to murder all the Huguenot leaders. The story allowed Meyerbeer to compose contrasting choruses for the Huguenot and Catholic groups and to set the scenes in Paris and at two châteaux, one of which was Chenonceaux. In the scene at the latter the hero is brought on-stage blindfolded so that he will not see what the audience clearly can, a ballet of ladies bathing in the river. And then after the court and conspiratorial scenes, and the love scenes, there is the Massacre, starting with a delicious shiver for the audience as the tocsin rings and ending an act later with a deafening rattle on-stage of small-arms fire.

In another of their operas, *Le Prophète,* Scribe and Meyerbeer made use of an Anabaptist uprising in Münster in 1534. In this, in order to take advantage of a current craze, the ballet was put on roller skates and sent whisking around the back of the stage on what was supposed to be a frozen lake. In the fourth act a full-scale coronation was presented in the Münster cathedral in which the historic John of Leyden was crowned king of a new Zion even as the German Emperor marched against him. And in the last act there was a bacchanalian banquet in which John, the Prophet, sets fire to the hall so that the powder magazines underneath can explode with a terrific blast, toppling all the scenery and leaving the audience gasping for fear that one of the singers will be knocked on the head.

It is extraordinary how much interesting music Meyerbeer was able to get into these spectacles. The Coronation March in *Le Prophète* is as good as any of Verdi's marches in *Aida;* the skating ballet is still used by ballet companies, and occasionally, as in Act IV of *Les Huguenots* where the Catholic conspirators bless their daggers, he succeeded in making the music very dramatic. None of his competitors could match him except Halévy who succeeded with one opera, *La Juive,* for which Scribe once again was the librettist. In it the contrasting groups again are religious, Christian versus Jew, and the Cardinal in the finale unwittingly orders his daughter, lost many years earlier, to be boiled in a tub of oil.

The form of Scribe's libretto for Verdi was predictable, and Verdi knew, even before he went to Paris, that he would not be given a tight musical drama like *Rigoletto* or *La Traviata*. Even so, he was dissatisfied with the libretto which he received, partly because he felt it made a travesty out of an actual historical event.

The massacre known to history as the Sicilian Vespers took place in Palermo on the Monday evening after Easter, 30 March 1282. The ruler of Sicily was Charles of Anjou, King of Naples. He was a brother of Saint Louis of France and had with the aid of several Popes successfully made himself King of Naples and Sicily and the most powerful, able ruler in the Mediterranean and all of Europe. Charles was not liked by his subjects because he had displaced a popular dynasty, the Hohenstaufen, and introduced French lords, soldiers and tax agents. Charles was equally unpopular with the Emperor Michael Palaeologus in Byzantium because he had assembled an enormous fleet and army in Naples and Messina to capture Byzantium and the Eastern Empire. Michael had almost no defense except diplomacy and money, and he offered the money where he thought it would do the most good: to the King of Aragon whose prime minister was a Neapolitan doctor exiled by Charles. This man, John of Procida, organized the Sicilian uprising which started with the massacre of all Frenchmen in Palermo. Soon the whole island was freed, Charles's fleet at Messina destroyed, the expedition to capture Byzantium canceled, and a general European war started. Michael smiled and wrote in his diary: "If I should claim I was God's instrument in bringing freedom to the Sicilians, I should only be stating the truth." The event was of European significance, and Dante, who lived throughout the period, happily assigned the actors their places in Heaven or Hell.

In his operas for Meyerbeer Scribe successfully suggested the larger European background to the particular story, but in his libretto for Verdi he somehow failed. The massacre in *I Vespri Siciliani* emerges as a meaningless incident daubed with some exotic Sicilian color. The reason may be, as Verdi discovered only years later, that the libretto was not originally written around the Sicilian massacre. Scribe had done it first for Donizetti in 1840 as *Il Duca d'Alba,* a story of the Spanish occupation of the Netherlands in 1573. Donizetti composed some of the music but never completed the opera before he died in 1848. As no one had seen it, Scribe took the story, which presumably belonged to Donizetti's estate, dubbed it into another period where it did not particularly well fit, and sold it to Verdi as a new libretto.

Verdi had trouble with it from the start. In the spring of 1854 he wrote his old friend Mme. Appiani: "I am composing very slowly, or better to say I'm not composing at all. I don't know why, but I do know the libretto is right there in the same place." Later he exclaimed by mail to De Sanctis: "A work at the Opéra is enough to stun a bull. Five hours of music? . . . Ooof! I will begin the rehearsals when Cruvelli comes, at the beginning of October. It will go on-stage when it can."

The rehearsals began, but then the soprano, Cruvelli, disappeared. She was the current favorite in Paris, and there was the greatest excitement. In London the Strand Theatre produced a farce, "Where's Cruvelli?" but it did not discover the lady.

While the search continued, an incident occurred that must have troubled Verdi because it broke a friendship of long standing. Mme. Appiani wrote Strepponi a letter and evidently addressed the envelope to "Giuseppina Strepponi" which was, after all, the only name to which Strepponi was entitled. It is hard to know just what lay behind Verdi's answer, but his friendship with Mme. Appiani was evidently another casualty of his life with Strepponi.

By chance, by pure chance your letter reached Peppina. As the address you used is unknown at the door of this house, your gracious letter ran the danger of going astray if, I repeat, chance had not led me to the postman who, seeing the name ended in "i," asked me about it. I took the letter and carried it to its destination. Peppina told me that, as she has renounced arts and letters and does not keep up any correspondence except with her family and a few very intimate friends, she would be grateful if I would make her excuses and reply to a letter so *spirituelle.* So here I am, I who cannot write like you or Peppina, in the greatest embarrassment about how to reply to a letter so well written, so fine and, I myself repeat, so *spirituelle*. But I, with my rough style, can make no parade of wit or spirit, so I will briefly state that we are in a great hurry to pack our bags, that La Cruvelli's flight from the Opéra has obliged me to ask to be released from the contract and that I shall go straight to Busseto but shall only stay there a few days. Where shall I go then? I couldn't say! Now that you have all my news, I press your hands.

But before he could leave Paris, if he truly intended to, Cruvelli reappeared without any explanation and began to sing again. The public surmised, without being corrected, that she had taken an antici-patory honeymoon with a Baron Vigier, whom she later married. The escapade delighted the Parisians and had a good effect at the box office. It also indicates the lack of discipline at the Opéra. The schedule of performances and rehearsals was thrown off and the première of the year's most important opera delayed. Verdi suggested that he and the directors cancel his contract, but they would not.

Verdi's relations with the Opéra steadily grew worse, and finally in January 1855, after he had been in Paris fourteen months, he wrote the director, Louis Crosnier, to suggest again that the contract be canceled. The letter, written in French, is a sad testament of an artist entangled in a system that fundamentally cared little about art.

I feel it my duty to let no more time pass without making a few obser-vations concerning *Les Vêpres Siciliennes*.

It is at the same time sad and mortifying for me that M. Scribe will not take the trouble to improve the fifth act which everyone agrees is unin-teresting. I am not unaware that M. Scribe has a thousand other things to do, which perhaps are dearer to him than my opera! . . . but if I had been able to foresee his complete indifference, I would have stayed in my coun-try, where, truth to tell, I was not doing so badly.

I had hoped that M. Scribe would manage to end the drama with one of those moving scenes (since the situation, I think, is ripe for it) which start up tears and are almost assured of success. Notice, Sir, that this would have improved the entire work which has nothing pathetic in it except for the *romanza* in the fourth act.

I had hoped that M. Scribe would have had the goodness to appear from time to time at the rehearsals to watch out for certain troublesome words or lines that are difficult or hard to sing: to see if he couldn't touch up the numbers or the acts etc. etc. For example, the second, third and fourth acts all have the same form: an aria, a duet, a finale . . .

Finally, I expected M. Scribe, as he promised me at the start, would change everything that attacks the honor of the Italians.

The more I consider this point, the more I am persuaded that it is dangerous. M. Scribe offends the French since they are massacred; he offends the Italians by altering the historic character of Procida, according to the Scribe system, into a common conspirator and thrusting the inevitable dagger into his hand.

Mon Dieu! In the history of every people there are good deeds and crimes, and we are no worse than the others. In any case I am an Italian above all and, come what may, I will never become an accomplice in injuring my country.

It remains for me to say a word about the rehearsals in the foyer. Here and there I hear words, observations which if not altogether wounding are at least out of place. I am not used to this and I will not endure it.

It is possible that there are persons who do not find my music worthy of the Opéra; it is possible that others do not think their roles worthy of their talents; it is possible that for my part I find the performance and style of singing other than what I would have wished! . . . Finally it seems to me (or I am strangely mistaken) that we are not one in the manner of feeling and interpreting the music, and without perfect accord there can be no *possible success.*

With that he went on again to urge that the production be canceled without penalty on either side, and he closed with the postscript: "Excuse my bad French. The important thing is that you understand." But neither the director nor Scribe could see that there was anything to understand. Scribe, although he may have changed a word or two, made none of the fundamental changes in the libretto that Verdi suggested, and the rehearsals dragged on with frequent flare-ups for another five months. Finally on 13 June 1855 *Les Vêpres Siciliennes* had its première. The Opéra had functioned just exactly as it always had in the past, and it had produced an opera by a distinguished composer in time for the first Paris Exposition, a project of the industrial-minded Emperor. It was left to Verdi and posterity to regret that the Opéra had not produced a better work, an early *Aida* instead of merely a *Les Vêpres Siciliennes.* The opportunity was there.

The opera had a strong initial success. Hundreds of Italians went to Paris for the Exposition and applauded it as the best national exhibit. French composers who had complained that an Italian had been commissioned to compose what amounted to the Exposition opera conceded that he had done a good job. Verdi's own judgment was cautious. To the Contessa Maffei he wrote: "It seems to me that *Les Vêpres*

Siciliennes is not going too badly." He was more enthusiastic over a statue of Spartacus by Vela in one of the Italian rooms in the Exposition.

The opera was immediately translated into Italian and as *I Vespri Siciliani* began to play around the world. In Italy, where the censors often felt it dangerous to have the Sicilians shown in a successful revolt, the locale was changed to Portugal and the title to *Giovanna de Guzman*. Today, under its original title, it is still given frequently in Italy, but it is not one of Verdi's best works in spite of an excellent overture, good ballet music and some stunning duets and arias.

The trouble lies in the five-act, bloated form of French grand opera. An uncut *Les Huguenots* runs about seven hours and so is generally given without its last act. Even then what remains is often cut. Halévy's *La Juive* originally ran more than five and a half hours and today is always given in a cut version. Verdi's grand opera is shorter than either of these, but it is harder to cut because less repetitious; the excess stuffing is more evenly distributed. It is most noticeable in the recitatives, in the links between verses within the arias and in the grand choruses, all of which sound inflated rather than inspired. When given today the opera is almost always shorn of its ballet and with bits taken out here and there, enough to make the libretto even more preposterous but preserving some excellent music.

Evidence that the basic form is at fault may lie in the fact that no French grand opera has held the stage in anything approaching its original form. The best French operas, *Carmen, Manon, Faust* or *Pelléas et Mélisande* were all written for the Opéra-Comique or the Théâtre-Lyrique where the traditions were very different from the Opéra. If Verdi had been less great he might well have started with the smaller theatre and had a happier result. But competition with Meyerbeer and a première at the Opéra were inevitable, whether Verdi wanted it or not. Rossini and Donizetti had set the course, and Verdi could not refuse to run it. Whether he triumphed in his first effort was a question for others to decide; he himself felt bruised and defeated.

CHAPTER 26

PIEDMONT, COPYRIGHT
AND TWO BAD OPERAS

1855–1857; AGE, 41–43

WHILE Verdi was in Paris composing and directing *I Vespri Siciliani*, the problem of Church-State relations in Piedmont again came to a crisis and, as before, with such extraordinarily inflammatory side incidents that the attention of much of the Catholic world was drawn to Turin. Most Italians, consciously or not, used the events there to decide the sort of state they wanted for Italy in the future, one dominated by the Church or by some form of secular government.

The particular issue was a bill introduced into Parliament by the cabinet and therefore with the King's approval. Its purpose was to abolish all religious orders and communities except those dedicated to education, preaching or care of the sick. This was slightly more than half of the 608 convents in Piedmont. The bill further proposed to forbid the establishment of any new orders except by special legislation, to limit the number of orders existing and to suppress a number of chapters of collegiate churches and simple benefices. With the property formerly held by the orders the bill proposed that the State establish an Ecclesiastical Bank to provide life pensions to the dispossessed monks and nuns and also to supplement the stipends of some of the poorest of the clergy. Further funds for this last purpose were to be realized by reducing the salaries of the archbishops and bishops and by imposing an ad valorem tax on the richer of the church benefices.

The bill was an extreme measure, but it was not hasty. The government at Turin had attempted, always unsuccessfully, to negotiate a concordat with Rome readjusting the position of the Church within the State. Now it proposed to present the problem to the Parliament in the expectation that it would act in favor of the State.

The Church's position in Piedmont was medieval in its numbers, splendor and power. The House of Savoy had always been known for its piety, and on its return to power after Napoleon's downfall in 1814 it had lavished every sort of benefit on the Church. By 1840 Piedmont had become the example of a perfectly governed state as Rome conceived it. The Jesuits controlled the lower education; the bishops, the universities. Church censorship controlled the publication of books and papers as well as their importation. Church courts had jurisdiction of any suit involving its interest, and offenses against religion such as sacrilege or absence from church were part of the State's penal code. Power might technically reside in the King, but the Church exercised it.

Further, simply as a percentage of the population the numbers of priests, monks and nuns in Piedmont were extraordinary. In a country of just under 5 million there were 23,000 ecclesiastics of every kind; about 1 monk to every 670 laymen, 1 nun to every 1695, and 1 priest to every 214. In the United States in 1962 the ratio between priests and Catholic laymen was about 1 to 775. In 1855 Piedmont had 41 bishops and archbishops, and Belgium with a population of 4½ million had 6.

Many Piedmontese felt the numbers were a social evil, allowing too many men to escape the duties of citizenship. They referred to the contemplative orders as "the useless orders" and in deploring the begging orders spoke of "able-bodied idleness" which they felt was out of place in a poor country. In one of his speeches Cavour quoted a study of the Swiss cantons which demonstrated that the prosperity of each was in an inverse ratio to the number of begging friars it contained.

The wealth of the Church was even more extraordinary. Its estimated income from lands and endowments, apart from what it received in fees, collections, or subsidies was about one-thirteenth of the national revenue. And the individual income of the hierarchy was on the same scale. The Archbishop of Turin, for example, received an income twice that of the Archbishop of Paris and almost as large as those of all six Belgian bishops combined. It was almost seven times the salary of a cabinet minister and eight and one-half times that of the chief justice on the highest Piedmont court. Meanwhile many parochial priests in Piedmont were paid almost nothing. The bill proposed to reduce the salaries of the bishops and archbishops and use the balance to pay the poorer priests.

The bishops at once protested to the King. "The law," they said, "is based on principles that the Church can never admit." And in a secret Consistory at Rome Pio Nono pronounced an Allocution against the proposed law. At the Consistory various documents were circulated setting forth the premises of the Church's position and published by the Pope as his justification for opposing the bill. Cavour also circulated them as his reason for supporting it. The most important of the premises were:

A State cannot be given or receive a Constitution that has the effect of subjecting the persons and goods of ecclesiastics to all the laws of the State. Equality of Law cannot be applied to ecclesiastical persons and property.

The liberty of the Press is not reconcilable with the Catholic religion in a Catholic State.

The State has no right to require that the provisions of Rome, outside matters of faith, are subject to royal approval before becoming effective.

The anticlericalism of the times, in which Verdi shared, can only be understood in the light of these premises which were not idle theories but the basis of government in Turin and Naples as well as Rome. With the premises, as the bishops had said, no compromise was possible, and the deputies and senators in Turin realized that one side, Church or State, would have to be victorious. It was no longer possible to evade the issue; the collision of principles was head on.

The debate on the bill began on 9 January 1855. The first speaker against it was Cavour's elder brother who held the family title of Marquis. He angrily castigated the hypocrisy of presenting the bill as a financial measure when in fact it was a confiscation, and he evoked the shade of Padre Cristoforo from Manzoni's *I Promessi Sposi* to plead for the threatened friars. Later a furious old man, Count Solara della Margherita, who for eighteen years had been Carlo Alberto's Foreign Minister, thundered a simple question: were they Catholics or not? To pass a bill not approved by the Church was to cease, *ipso facto*, to be Catholics. The Count's question was simple, clear, and in every house in Piedmont it was debated. As brothers differed the talk often came perilously close to violence.

Then the Queen Mother died, Carlo Alberto's widow, whose life had been a tragedy and whose greatest joy had been an order of contemplative nuns which she had supported. After the royal funeral the Chamber reassembled only to hear that Queen Adelaide, to whom Verdi in 1842 had dedicated *Nabucco,* had also died. Again the Chamber adjourned, reassembled, and the debate resumed, but a fortnight later the King's brother, the Duke of Genoa, died.

Vittorio Emanuele was a simple, elemental man, not unlike his mountain peasants. His manners, by Paris standards, were rough, his speech abrupt, and his heart unsophisticated. He had an eye for the ladies and yet was unaffectedly fond of his family. His favorite sport was hunting mountain goat, and he liked the company of military men. He did not like lawyers, diplomatic or parliamentary maneuvering, and although in time he came to trust Cavour, he never liked him. Now, as the debate began yet again, the country watched its King. It was known that the successive deaths had left him emotionally bankrupt, apathetic and peculiarly open to influence. The House of Savoy was the oldest in Europe, and the King was proud of it. Like his ancestors he was pious, although a friend described him as having "the piety of a brigand." Oppressed by his loss and pressured by his clerical advisers who appealed to his pride and piety, he might refuse to sign the bill or use his influence against it. A cry of despair came from the King. "They tell me," he said, "that God has punished me: that he has taken my mother, my wife and my brother because I have consented to these laws; they threaten me with still worse; but do they not know that a sovereign who would win happiness hereafter must try to make his people on this earth happy?"

Vittorio Emanuele's popular title was "Il Re galantuomo," or "the honest King." He had earned it by his blunt speech and by refusing under pressure from Austria to repudiate the constitution his father had granted. Now once again he stood by his word and, after hesitating, let it be known that he would sign the bill. But his personal tragedy was not yet over. In May, just two weeks before the bill was presented to him, his youngest son, Vittorio Emanuele, died. Soon thereafter the Pope excommunicated him and everyone else concerned in passing the bill.

The "Law of the Convents," as it was called, was as important in the history of the Risorgimento as any of the battles. By it Piedmont with its King's approval undertook to become a secular state. The step was taken slowly, and everyone who wished was given a chance to air his argument either in Parliament, the papers or private conversation. The bill was first presented in November and not finally passed until the following May. Unquestionably within that time the majority of the Piedmontese became convinced of its necessity if Piedmont was to become a modern state. Everywhere Italians compared Piedmont's energy and recovery after 1848 with the continued depression and military occupation of the Papal States, and the discrepancy each year became greater. Piedmont set the pattern for Italy not only in military leadership but in its political and economic development.

The fact that it did so made it very much easier for republicans like the Contessa Maffei and Verdi to desert Mazzini and their republican principles in order to support a constitutional monarchy. It is not possible to set an exact date on which Verdi changed his allegiance, but he generally agreed with the views of the Contessa and she changed hers sometime during 1854, the year after Mazzini's abortive revolution in Milan and the year in which Cavour introduced the bill on the convents. Her friends twitted her on her political inconstancy. But she evidently argued her reasons persuasively for she converted a number of "pure" republicans and among them, probably, Verdi.

In the military world Cavour had succeeded in allying Piedmont with England, France and Austria in the Crimean War against Russia. At first no one but Vittorio Emanuele had supported him in this plan, for it was quite outside the field of the average Piedmontese's vision to see how Piedmont could weaken Austria in Lombardy-Venetia by fighting beside her in the Crimea. Particularly on the Left orators agitated opposition to the dispatch of troops, and Cavour was unable to answer their arguments without revealing to Austria what he hoped to accomplish and thereby spoiling the opportunity. So he limited himself to general remarks on "glory" and "valor" which would show the world that Italians were not all skulking assassins. The speech gained force by reason of an incident just the previous year in Parma that Austria had delighted in presenting to the world as typically "Italian."

Duke Carlo III had announced that he would lead his well-dressed army of 6,000 to Crimea and had imposed a forced loan on his subjects to pay for the expedition. The protest had been immediate and unanimous, both by official petitions and angry squibs on walls. The Duke had chosen to ignore all warnings, and one Sunday afternoon, 26 March 1854, had started on a walk accompanied only by an orderly.

On the way back to the palace he had stopped to watch a ballerina leaning out of a window. As he gazed up, an assassin stabbed, and twenty-four hours later the Duke was dead.

This time Mazzini was not responsible for the murder, but his doctrines and adherents were blamed in particular and the Italian temperament in general. Cavour wished to show Europe that Italians could be orderly and responsible and that Piedmont had achieved sufficient political stability to govern itself properly and could support an army in the field for more than a month. The best stage for such a demonstration happened to be in the Crimea, and in April 1855 an expeditionary force of Piedmontese sailed for there.

For weeks there was no news and then only that the English never tired of admiring the organization and neatness of the Piedmontese camp which was brightened everywhere with little gardens. Finally in August on the Tchernaya there was a battle in which the Piedmontese were engaged. In Paris where Verdi heard the news the French dispatch closed with the words that the Piedmontese had "fought gloriously." It was a warm evening, and everyone poured out of their houses onto the boulevards. Windows were illuminated and French, English and Piedmontese flags hung out to the wind. The sidewalks soon became so crowded it was impossible to move, and the crowds stood, cheering the various flags. There were many Italians in the city, visitors to the Exposition and exiles who had not been in Italy since 1848. They sought each other out and celebrated. The Tchernaya was not one of the war's great battles, but for the Italians it was a turning point in their national morale and, no less important, in their relations with France.

Before the Tchernaya Napoleon III was the hated "man of 2 December" who by a coup had destroyed a French Republic and even before that had sent a French army to destroy the Roman Republic. Now as an ally he seemed less evil. As Emperor he could still help Italy and as an autocrat might be in a better position to do so. The French army in Rome could neither be forgiven nor forgotten, but it could be put second to getting the Austrians out of Lombardy-Venetia. The rapprochement with France was one benefit for Italy of Piedmont's venture in the Crimea.

Another, but more indirect, was the shift in the balance of power among the larger countries. England had not been allied with France for more than two hundred years. Her traditional friends were Austria and Russia. The new alignment gave Austria the problem of deciding which old ally to fight, England or Russia, for both considered Austrian neutrality merely a dodge to help the enemy. After months of hesitation Austria reluctantly joined the English, but she got little credit for it and her position in Europe was more isolated than it had been in a hundred years. And Russia, which had helped Austria put down the Hungarian revolution only six years earlier, was furious. Italians suddenly realized that Cavour had improved Piedmont's position at Austria's expense.

Verdi stayed on in Paris throughout the summer of the Exposition to settle some business problems and recover his health, for after the siege at the Opéra with *I Vespri Siciliani* he suffered from his usual sore throat and stomach trouble. His business problems involved a changing copyright law, pirated productions playing even in Paris and an altercation with his publishers. To Tito Ricordi he wrote: "I wish to lodge a bitter complaint about the printed editions of my most recent operas, done with very little care and full of mistakes; and above all that you did not withdraw the first edition of *La Traviata*. That is inexcusable negligence!" (etc.) More than a hundred years later scholars still complained about the Ricordi editions of the operas and gravely demonstrated that each new one included more interpretative markings than the last and sometimes even altered notes and the directions on how to play them, viz., staccato or legato. The trend with each new edition has, unfortunately, been to vulgarize the music by ironing all the subtleties out of it. The publication of music, however, is a difficult business, and Ricordi in 1855 was as good as any house in Italy. Verdi continued to complain but he never seriously considered changing publishers, although several like Lucca would have been delighted to offer him special inducements.

Verdi's difficulties with his publishers were partly the result of a slow change in the production and composition of opera which was altering the relationships between composer, publisher and impresario. Another aspect of this change was the greatly increased problem of pirated productions and the lack of adequate copyright laws.

What was happening was that the world was growing smaller, and a successful composer was thereby magnified. On the seas the clipper ships made transatlantic crossings swift and certain, and within Europe the railroads had begun to tie the principal cities to within hours of each other. In Mozart's time productions of an opera in Prague and

Vienna with a few cities in between made an opera a success. In Rossini's time the pond had widened, but for Verdi in 1855 it included all of Europe and parts of North and South America.

It was an area no composer or impresario could police. Copyright laws were conflicting or, more often, nonexistent, and royalties were frequently collected only on the threat of court action. At the start of Rossini's career, 1810–20, the composer had no royalty or copyright in his work. The opera belonged for a period of two years to the impresario who commissioned it; after that it became public property. The composer hoped for another commission to start the cycle again, and neither he nor the impresario cared for any financial reason what happened to the previous opera after the first two years. The publisher of it cared, but at the time the printing of music was so difficult that generally only the most popular arias were printed. This meant that of any opera there often existed for the orchestra and singers only the original manuscript parts, so that an opera tended to move slowly from the town in which it was born and then only in the company of the impresario. The system put pressure on a composer to compose and partially explains the enormous output of Rossini and Donizetti.

But as the nineteenth century progressed, inventions made the printing of music more practical and improving communications made it increasingly easy for a publisher to have twenty or thirty printed scores out on rent in as many cities. Then the publisher cared very much about copyrights and royalties, as also did the composer, for then the commission from the impresario for the original production in a single city was often nothing compared to the continuing royalties from all over the world. But to collect the royalties required having agents in the cities and enforceable copyright laws. Otherwise an enterprising impresario produced a version of the original in a "pirated production." An extreme example of this occurred in the United States in 1879 when New York had eight simultaneous productions of *H.M.S. Pinafore,* all unauthorized.

Inevitably over the years power, as divided between composer, publisher and impresario, tended to shift toward the publisher. The impresario cared little or nothing about pirated productions outside his own city, and the composer's pocketbook could not afford to keep agents in every city. The publisher, however, both cared and could afford the agents because he could combine under a single agent in any city protection for all his composers. Some agents like the Escudier Brothers in Paris set themselves up as independent contractors, but sooner or later most became employees of a publishing house.

A result of this shift of power was that a composer began to contract to compose an opera directly with a publisher rather than with an impresario. Verdi's first such contract had been with Lucca for what eventually became *Il Corsaro*. The contract merely stated that the opera was to be performed "in one of the leading theatres of Italy by a first-class company in Carnival of 1848 or within the year 1849." When he had composed it, Verdi mailed it to Lucca. In the coming years hundreds of younger composers would mail in entries in various opera composition contests run by publishers who would then undertake to get the best produced in an opera house somewhere. Even the established composers often completed the work for the publisher before knowing what theatre or singers might be available for it.

An unexpected and, some argue, tragic result of all this was that a composer increasingly composed his opera in the solitude of a retreat rather than the hurly-burly of an opera house. Perhaps polish was gained; certainly experience was lost. Composers who could not only compose but also direct the staging and conduct the orchestra became extremely rare.

Verdi, living through the change, had some of the best and worst of both systems. As a young man he had the experience of composing and producing operas on occasion as a craft; in his old age he had as much time and solitude as he required with the additional advantage of being able to demand any theatre or singers he wanted as well as being able to direct them in rehearsal. On the other hand, in 1855 he had to some extent to defend himself against the pirates because the House of Ricordi was not yet as powerful as it would become. He went twice to London to prevent an unauthorized production of *Il Trovatore*, and in Paris he started a suit against the manager of the Théâtre Italien who had suggested that either he accept a reduced royalty or have the operas produced from pirated Spanish editions and receive no royalties at all.

In his efforts to protect his rights Verdi was hindered by being a citizen of Parma which, as a small country, had no representatives at foreign courts and had no reciprocal treaties with France or England. To his lawyer in Busseto he wrote:

In my two trips to London they suggested I become a citizen of either England, France or even Piedmont (since France and Piedmont have treaties with England) but I wish to be what I am, a peasant from Le

LUISA MARIA DI BORBONE

Roncole, and I prefer to ask my government to make a treaty with England. The Parmigiani government has nothing to lose by such a treaty since it is purely artistic and literary: it will have only to take the trouble to ask for it through its representative in England who is, I believe, the ambassador of Austria or Spain (etc.).

Verdi asked the lawyer on his next trip to Parma (to see if the government would act).

The government of Parma since the assassination of Duke Carlo III was a regency in which the Duke's widow, Luisa Maria di Borbone, ruled in the name of her ten-year-old son, Roberto. Like the lady of reversed name who preceded her, Marie Louise, Luisa Maria's rule, which lasted until the duchy was about to join Piedmont, was mild and sensible. Her Austrian advisers wished to make an object lesson out of the Duke's assassination, and she prevented it. She made better appointments than her husband, dismissed the English jockey, Ward, and when the time came to leave Parma, did so with dignity and grace. The kingdom was better ruled, in the nineteenth century at least, by its Duchesses than by its Dukes. The government, however, did not act at once on Verdi's suggestion, and his problems continued.

Verdi returned to Sant' Agata at the end of December just as *I Vespri Siciliani* began its tour of Italy at the Teatro Ducale in Parma. He had no immediate plans other than to revise the libretto of *Stiffelio* with

336

the possibility of doing it during the summer at Bologna. It and *La Battaglia di Legnano* seem to have been the only two operas about which he had any regrets at this time. His best were fabulously successful; the less good were still vigorously alive, and only *Alzira, Il Corsaro* and the two before *Nabucco* were statistics in history with a rare revival. Both *La Battaglia di Legnano* and *Stiffelio* had good music and yet were effectively hobbled by censorship trouble; and in *Stiffelio* the libretto itself was poor.

After the fall of the Roman Republic *La Battaglia di Legnano* had been turned into a story about a Dutch revolt against the Spanish occupation of the Netherlands in the sixteenth century. The change, in which the music was left untouched, was not successful. The Dutch, who in fact were solid burghers and sang Calvinist and Lutheran hymns, were presented to passionate, searing Italian music with what was obviously a monkish chorus in the background. The transformation did not fit, and from time to time Verdi thought of recasting it. But the original music and libretto were well suited to each other, and in the end he did not disturb them. The opera had been conceived as an Italian propaganda piece, and perhaps he came to feel that it could best survive only as such. Recently it has had a number of revivals, including one in modern dress set in the German-occupied Italy of World War II. More typically, La Scala used it to open its season in December 1962 as part of the national celebrations of the centenary of Italian unity.

But *Stiffelio* with its German evangelical background had an unsuitable libretto to start with and seemed more profitable to reform. Verdi planned to do a new last act and make any other changes that might be necessary. Piave, who had done the original libretto, came for a visit to Sant' Agata, bringing with him a Maltese spaniel for Strepponi and a plan for adapting the music of *Stiffelio* to a story about a medieval crusader. Verdi was dubious but allowed himself to be persuaded, and Piave began recasting the story into the thirteenth century and changing the locale from Germany to England.

In March 1856 Verdi, who had never seen a production of *La Traviata* since its abortive première, went to Venice to stage and conduct its return to the Teatro Fenice. The occasion, as far as any theatrical performance can be, was guaranteed its success, and a result of the general euphoria was a contract with the Fenice for a new opera to be produced the following spring. Verdi seems to have had in mind from the first using another Spanish play by Gutierrez who had written *El Trovador*. This one was called *Simone Boccanegra* and recounted the history of an ex-pirate of that name who became Doge of the Genoese Republic. Piave was to do the libretto, but as usual Verdi's was the dominant hand.

The première of it on 12 March 1857 was not a success, and subsequent performances did no better. The critics scolded the audience and admired Verdi's use of the orchestra and his eloquent recitative, but the audience evidently found the recitative long and boring and the libretto extremely muddled. Neither Verdi nor Piave had been able to compress the sprawling play into a musical drama in which the motives and actions were clear; perhaps even Cammarano could not have done so. The opera with Verdi conducting had a moderate success later in Naples and Reggio, but it failed in Milan, and Parma did not even try it. Twenty-four years later Verdi presented it again but completely revised in music and libretto, and this is the version given today. Until then it was scored, at least by the public, as one of his fiascos.

Besides the libretto part of the first version's difficulty undoubtedly was that Verdi had not given enough time to it. In the ten months between signing the contract and producing the opera he had not only fashioned the libretto for it but gone to Paris to see about his law suit, on to London, then back to Paris where he had watched over a production of *La Traviata* at the Théâtre Italien and assisted a production in French at the Opéra of *Il Trovatore*. For this last he wrote a ballet to be inserted in the third act and slightly lengthened the finale in order to give greater importance to Azucena, the gypsy. At the same time he was putting the final touches on the revised *Stiffelio* for a première at Rimini in the following August. When he arrived in Venice in February before the première of *Simone Boccanegra*, he had the final act and all the orchestration to complete. He was still spending "years in the galley" except that now, instead of shuttling around the cities of Italy to earn new commissions, he was hurrying between the capitals of countries to protect his royalties either by suits in court or by superintending the productions in the theatres.

The première of the revised *Stiffelio*, renamed *Aroldo*, was more successful. Rimini, a small town on the Adriatic, was opening a new opera house, and regardless of the opera the event would have been gala. The townsfolk had hoped to have a new opera based on their most famous citizen, Francesca, but the local impresario, the brothers Marzi, had done almost as well by obtaining not only a Verdi première but Verdi himself to direct it, Piave to stage it, and Angelo Mariani, the best conductor in Italy, to conduct it. The excitement ran very high and music lovers began to pour into the town. The local swells invited the visiting great to put up at their villas, and Piave, of course, accepted and reveled in the luxury. But Verdi and Strepponi, although invited, stayed at the hotel "in two large rooms, poorly furnished." The citizens of Rimini seem to have decided simply to ignore the moral question and to treat Verdi and Strepponi as man and wife. They themselves had evidently come to some sort of decision about it, for she now signed her letters "Giuseppina Verdi" and used his initial on her handkerchiefs. She also began in this year, with *Simone Boccanegra* in Venice, to accompany him to his Italian premières. But even so they did not marry for yet another two years.

The revised opera, *Aroldo,* excited less applause than the new opera house. The libretto was still at fault and in some ways worse than before. Piave's efforts had turned a badly realized plot into a ludicrous one. The German evangelical minister who, after wrestling with his emotions, finally forgives his wife's adultery is a possible character although perhaps one that could not be popular in Italy. Piave's solution to this problem was to divide the character in two: Aroldo, the crusader, and Briano, a hermit. On the crusade Briano saved Aroldo's life, and the two men have sworn never to be separated. Aroldo passionately rejects his erring wife, Mina. Briano, ever at Aroldo's side, urges him to forgive her. Briano is easily the most trying character in any Verdi opera.

Similarly the last scene in *Stiffelio* had shown the minister giving his sermon and moved to forgive his wife when his eye fell on the Bible open to the story of Christ and the adulterous woman. In *Aroldo* Piave has transferred everyone in the last act, for some hidden reason, from Kent to the shores of Loch Lomond. There as Aroldo again rejects Mina, Briano predictably urges: "Let him without sin cast the first stone." And the scene in which the husband forces the wife to agree to divorce him was kept intact although absolutely inconceivable in the rough-and-tumble thirteenth century. The result was a libretto as unreal as any operetta fantasy and a far cry from the drama of *Rigoletto* or *La Traviata.*

The music, however, was considerably better than the libretto and kept the opera alive for a number of years. Parma, for example, while rejecting the wholly new *Simone Boccanegra,* chose *Aroldo* to open its next season. But inevitably there arises the question of why Verdi entangled himself with such a libretto.

Part of the answer undoubtedly lies in the tradition of contracting to produce an opera for a particular season and then turning it out regardless of time or inspiration. But beyond that Verdi seems to have lacked a sure sense of the craft of a libretto. His sense of theatre in isolated effects such as the sudden off-stage voice or contrasting emotions almost never failed him and often extended to whole scenes. But of the framework within which the effects or scenes were set he was much less sure. Bonavia in his short biography observed:

Verdi had the knowledge and instinct—not education. Had he had the advantage of a literary training he could never have accepted the librettos of *Trovatore* or *Boccanegra.* In *Trovatore* we see the effects of romanticism on a mind powerful and responsive but untrained, and therefore apt to err in judging the values of facts and words. His is the romanticism of the masses, ever ready to listen to a tale of adventure, no matter how improbable; awed by the supernatural, by mystery, by the glamor of valor and power. (etc.)

Verdi, like most men, without being able himself to write a well-made play could recognize that *Le Roi s'amuse* was well constructed and thereby gained power. As Bonavia suggests, most university drama students, after taking the right courses, could probably construct better plays than the self-educated Verdi; but almost certainly they could not infuse them with anything like his passion. Posterity can only regret that fate, after guiding Verdi into *Rigoletto* and *La Traviata* at the beginning of the decade, then teased him into dramas which excited his passion without providing a good framework to contain it. For neither he nor Piave, singly or together, seemed to be able to construct one.

CHAPTER 27

UN BALLO IN MASCHERA

1857–1859; AGE, 43–45

FOR more than a year before he had produced his new *Simone Bocca-negra* and the revised *Aroldo* Verdi had been corresponding with a friend in Naples, Vincenzo Torelli, about the possibility of producing a *King Lear* at the Teatro San Carlo. Verdi was anxious to present it in Italy where he felt the audience was most sympathetic to the kind of musical drama he intended, but he also wanted a large stage for it. Except for La Scala in Milan, which he refused to consider, there was only the San Carlo in Naples. Torelli, who was actually a partner of the impresario there and acted as the management's secretary, informed Verdi when new productions might be possible and which singers available.

The casting, as always, worried Verdi and in August 1856, on one of his trips to Paris over the law suit, he asked the soprano Maria Piccolomini if she would care to sing Cordelia. She was eager to do it, and Verdi planned to introduce her to Naples in *La Traviata,* for she was famous for her Violetta, and then to follow her debut with the première of *King Lear.* For the men's voices he was satisfied with the members of the San Carlo company which at the time was one of the strongest in Italy. On the basis of these hopes and intending to do *King Lear,* he signed a contract with the San Carlo in which he undertook to compose an unspecified grand opera of not less than three acts for production in January 1858. The impresario agreed to provide sets, costumes and stage machinery "worthy of so illustrious a maestro and such a spectacle." (The contract is set out in Appendix E, p. 583.)

The San Carlo, however, did not succeed in signing Piccolomini for the season, and Verdi refused to be satisfied with any of the substitutes offered. In the end he put *King Lear* aside and began a frantic search for another libretto as the contract, which had not specified the opera, was still binding. He soon had breached its terms by failing before June 1857 to send the libretto to the management for submission to the censor, and by the time of the *Aroldo* première in August he still had not decided between Hugo's *Ruy Blas,* another Spanish play by Gutiérrez and a libretto by Scribe already used by Auber and Mercadante.

The management at the San Carlo thought Verdi was being unnecessarily finicky about the soprano, and Torelli at the end of September urged: "Give us *King Lear* since even if another time you could have a better Cordelia, you will never have a better baritone, tenor or bass . . . Put your genius to work; I hear that *La Traviata* —a real musical-social revolution—was composed in a short time. I hope you will do a second *Traviata* for us." Though the argument was reasonable and the libretto ready, Verdi still refused. It is hard not to believe that he was deliberately seeking an excuse to put it aside. Possibly he felt he could never realize in the theatre what he heard in his mind. Years later in 1896, after he had composed his last opera, he offered all his material on *King Lear* to Pietro Mascagni, already famous for his *Cavalleria Rusticana.* Mascagni asked him why he had never done the music and then later reported: "Verdi closed his eyes for an instant, perhaps to remember, perhaps to forget. Then softly and slowly he replied, 'The scene in which King Lear finds himself on the heath terrified me.' "

Perhaps because of the shortness of time Verdi ultimately in October chose the Scribe story, which was already a libretto and in the usual Opéra five-act form. Antonio Somma, with whom Verdi had been corresponding about *King Lear,* agreed to redo it, although realizing that his job, aside from compressing the five acts into three, was not much more than that of a translator.

Scribe's libretto as usual was based on a historical event, the assassination in 1792 of Gustavus III of Sweden. The king was shot in the back by a Count Anckarström at a masked ball in the Stockholm opera house. Gustavus was an exceptional man and king. He came to the throne in a period of anarchy, survived by several daring coups and succeeded in making himself and Sweden powerful to the point where in a great naval battle he defeated Russia. While doing all this he managed to write excellent historical essays, revitalize the Swedish theatre with some of its best plays and found the Swedish Academy, which today awards the Nobel Prize for Literature. He was unhappily married to a Danish princess and when shot was only just forty-six.

To explain why such a paragon should be shot Scribe had to find something more satisfying for the Opéra audience than the merely true political reason, and he invented a love story involving Count Anckarström's wife and the King. He also promoted Anckarström from his historical position of dissident noble to that of the King's best friend and prime minister, thus allowing the King and the Countess throughout the opera to struggle with the hoary conflict of love versus honor. The change also allowed Anckarström to have the standard French drama "recognition" scene in which he discovers his wife with the King and thereafter joins the conspirators instead of exposing them. As Verdi observed to Torelli: "It is grandiose and vast; it is beautiful. But also it has the conventional formulas of all operas, which have always displeased me and which I now find insufferable."

But even though Scribe lacked the genius to create characters like Macbeth or even Rigoletto, his Gustave existed inside a libretto fundamentally well-constructed and easily shorn of its excessive ballets and padding. Verdi and Somma, once the decision was made, worked swiftly and, apparently, almost contemporaneously, so that the entire opera, libretto and music, was done in about two and a half months between the end of October and New Year's Day, 1858. Although he must have recognized the dangers of haste, on the whole Verdi approved of such bursts of energy because, he felt, they contributed to an opera's stylistic unity.

The opera, as Verdi and Somma wrote it, first presents King Gustavo at a morning levee of his court. He is a gay, confident ruler, planning a masked ball for the following night and happily daydreaming of the Countess Anckarström. He covers his mental absence by laughing equally at the quips of a fresh page, Oscar, and the warnings of a new conspiracy by his prime minister, Anckarström. The main problem of the levee, however, is whether the King, as recommended by his Chief Justice, should banish a Negro sorceress who by her prophecies is agitating the people. Oscar, the page, defends the lady, and Gustavo decides, much to the concern of Anckarström, to judge for himself by a visit to the sorceress that very afternoon. He will go in disguise and urges the court to follow him.

Gustavo arrives first, watches Ulrica, the sorceress, dazzle the crowd with her call to the devil and palm readings, and then hides in order to overhear a private interview between Ulrica and the Countess Anckarström. The Countess, Amelia, enters in great distress. She wants a cure for a love that has destroyed her peace and which she does not want. Ulrica prescribes a particular herb that grows only at the foot of the gibbet outside the town and which must be picked at midnight. Amelia is terrified but determined to get it that very night, and Gustavo, convinced that she loves him, promises himself (and the audience, for nothing can be promised silently in opera) to meet her there.

The balance of the scene is taken up with Ulrica prophesying to Gustavo before the people and court, which has arrived in disguise, that he will be killed and soon by the next man who shakes his hand. Gustavo laughingly offers to shake hands with anyone there, but all refuse except Anckarström, who arrived too late to hear the prophecy. Scribe built the scene, which is superbly theatrical, around rumors reported by historians that shortly before the assassination of Gustavus a fortuneteller had predicted his death to him.

The Countess, Amelia, arriving at the gibbet, has a moment of despair, an appeal to the Lord, and then is terrified by the arrival of Gustavo. A love duet begins, more interesting than usual because the lovers are neither young nor in agreement. Amelia struggles to be true to her husband and child and denies she loves the King. As Gustavo forces her to confess the truth, Anckarström himself appears only steps ahead of the conspirators. He insists Gustavo leave and agrees to take the trembling, veiled lady back to the city gate without questioning her. Gustavo escapes, but the conspirators trap Anckarström and the lady and threaten to kill him unless he reveals her identity. He refuses, and to save him Amelia unveils. At the sight of the prime minister having a midnight rendezvous at the gibbet with his wife, the conspirators burst out laughing. Stunned by the public humiliation and deception, Anckarström asks the leaders of the conspirators, two counts, to meet with him at his house in the morning. As he leaves in a mounting fury, with Amelia in despair, the mocking laughter follows him. As a finale it is more subtly effective than the sort of vendetta cabaletta Verdi gave to the outraged husbands and lovers of his earlier operas. And undoubtedly one reason he was attracted to Scribe's libretto was because of the light air with which it surrounded its darker doings. The laughing conspirators and smart-aleck page were quite outside the conventional operatic melodrama and furnished the sort of variety and contrast he sought.

The last act opens the next morning in the library of Anckarström's house. He tells Amelia that she must die, but after she goes off, he gazes at a portrait of Gustavo and realizes that the King is more to blame than Amelia. Again Verdi avoided a conventional vendetta aria. Anckarström, a baritone, expresses his dignified accusation of betrayal to the portrait but then goes on to lament the loss forever of his domestic bliss, the source of his strength and happiness. Even revenge and the King's death, he realizes, will not fill the void within him. Anckarström's tragedy, which here is perfectly expressed, is an important theme of the opera. Mostly Verdi and Somma contented themselves with paring Scribe's libretto, but this aria they added to it, giving a depth to the story that Scribe did not plumb.

Anckarström then admits the two leading conspirators, Counts Horn and Ribbing, joins their plot, and puts the three names in an urn to decide by lot who will strike the blow. And this is historically true: Count Anckarström was selected by lot. In the opera Amelia, who has come in to announce Oscar, is forced to do the drawing. Then Oscar enters, pertly invites them all to the masked ball and chatters of how gay it will be, as the conspirators mutter that it will be the King's funeral dance and as the Countess despairs. Again the situation gives Verdi a chance to contrast the various voices and emotions.

In a short scene, also with a historical basis, Gustavo receives a note warning him against the ball. Historically the note came from an ex-officer of the Royal Guards who had had second thoughts; in the opera the audience understands it comes from Amelia. But Gustavo ignores it. Sobered by what he thinks was merely a close escape, he has decided to send Anckarström to Finland as his ambassador, and the ball will be his last chance to see Amelia before she leaves with her husband.

In Auber's opera to Scribe's libretto, the ball, as might be expected of anything done for the Opéra, is an enormous spectacle running on for 114 pages of the score and stopping the action dead while the *corps de ballet* cavorts. Verdi and Somma moved the ball to the back of the stage while keeping the action moving in front of it. The swirl of dancers brings first one group and then another to the fore. Anckarström plagues Oscar to reveal the King's disguise on the plea of urgent state business. The Countess urges the King to leave at once. Then the conspirators see him, and Anckarström strikes. The King lives long enough to proclaim the Countess' innocence, to forgive his enemies, and then dies. In fact he lived thirteen days and Anckarström was first tortured by the administration and then executed.

It is an excellent libretto. The action of the story covers a consecutive thirty-six hours and runs smoothly from scene to scene; nothing happens off-stage requiring a narrative aria; and although no character develops or reveals any great depths in the opera, neither does any by his actions violate his given personality. Once again in the careful construction of the French theatre Verdi found a good frame in which to enclose his musical passion.

From the first Verdi expected to have trouble with the censors, but he seems to have expected to be able to resolve the objections as he had with *Rigoletto,* largely by a change of locale and names. But where *Rigoletto* had merely exhibited a rape by royalty followed by a miscarriage of justice, in his new opera Verdi wanted to show a successful regicide. There was a considerable difference, and the political temper of the times did nothing to minimize it. Not only was the murder of Verdi's sovereign, the Duke of Parma, a case in point, but the general atmosphere of Europe was more explosive than in 1851.

The Crimean War had ended in a Congress of nations held, significantly, in Paris not Vienna. France was again Europe's leading power, and it boded ill for Austria's hold over its dependent kingdoms. At the Congress Cavour, representing Piedmont, had listened while the Great Powers adjusted the results for which the war was fought, such as the rights of navigation on the length of the Danube. Then he managed, over Austria's objection, to have them discuss what should be done for Italy. Even the question was an insult, but its discussion was a threat to Austria, the Pope and the Bourbons in Naples. Piedmont gained no territorial advantages from its Crimean expedition, but it gained enormous European prestige. And whereas in 1848 Austria had successfully posed as the champion of order in Italy, eight years later Cavour had recast it in the role of villain and had led the great powers, England, France and even Russia, to hiss at it. Most Italians recognized that though Cavour's diplomacy was only talk, it was still a triumph. For talk is often the prelude to an enforced change.

Cavour also used the time in Paris to talk with many of the Italian exiles there, always trying to minimize party differences by explaining his policy for Piedmont and Italy. One of the most influential exiles was Daniele Manin, a republican and hero of the defense of Venice in 1848–49. After a series of interviews with Cavour he began to urge republicans to support the House of Savoy. In a famous letter which he knew would be made public, he wrote: "Convinced that it is above all necessary to make Italy, the republican party says to the House of Savoy—*Make Italy and I am with you, if not, no!*" The remark became a slogan, for Manin's prestige was great with all groups. Garibaldians liked his heroic defense of Venice, and constitutionalists admired his strict adherence to the rule of law in times of stress.

A few months later, directly influenced by Manin and after an interview with Cavour, Garibaldi let it be known that he too would fight under Vittorio Emanuele to make Italy. Garibaldi's adherence to Cavour's program for a united front was important, for in the event of a war with Austria Garibaldi would be able to raise a volunteer army faster than anyone else. And Cavour not only wanted the army but some control over it. Garibaldi, for his part, gained the army of Piedmont as an ally and, by semi-official recognition, a better chance of getting arms. Political differences, however, between the men and the views they represented were only submerged, not eradicated. As a radical republican Garibaldi was strongly anti-clerical, and he intended to unite all of Italy, including every inch of Rome which he had defended against the Pope. Cavour, who saw the international problems, was more of a pragmatist, ready to unite Italy bit by bit. He counted on French aid, but Garibaldi still saw in Napoleon III only the "man of 2 December" who had restored the Pope to Rome. But with Italy still unmade the differences seemed less important than the common purpose.

Another ally for Cavour and of great practical value was the National Society, a secret group that had recruited to itself the best of Mazzini's secret societies and was determined not to waste its young men on foolish uprisings. Here too Manin's influence was important, and in the fall of 1856 the Society's secretary, Gìuseppe La Farina, asked Cavour for an interview. Cavour as Prime Minister of Piedmont could not be seen with La Farina, and the interview was arranged for 6 A.M. in Cavour's bedroom. In the best operatic tradition La Farina was admitted from the street by means of a secret staircase. Both men explained what they hoped for Italy, and thereafter La Farina frequently mounted the narrow stair, not to receive orders, but to keep Cavour informed of the Society's activities. Verdi's librettos which today seem so melodramatic were often no more so than the life of the times.

Cavour's success in merging the various groups working for unity and independence into a single force under the House of Savoy greatly simplified the issues before the country. It also isolated his greatest competitor, Mazzini, who ceased after 1857 to be a practical threat either to Cavour or Austria. Republicans and patriots still honored Mazzini for his vision and his loyalty to it, but for its realization they turned elsewhere. Others, too, realized they were being isolated. Franz Josef, Pio Nono and King Ferdinando at Naples saw that European opinion had turned against them and that there was a new alignment of powers. The strength of the patriots lay in their ability to compromise in order to achieve at least part of what they wanted; the ultimate weakness of Austria, the Pope and the Bourbons of Naples lay in their refusal to adjust in any way to a political pressure until it finally grew so powerful it cracked them asunder.

In 1857 Austria, with more political sense than the other two, seemed about to change its policy. Franz Josef made a tour to Milan and Venice. He granted pardons, forgave punitive taxes and started a public works program. But his reception was cold. At Padua the Mayor from the first carriage urged the silent onlookers to cheer the third carriage in which were the Emperor and the Empress. Dutifully the people shouted "Viva la terza carrozza!" Franz Josef even retired Radetzky, replacing him with the Archduke Maximilian, who later briefly became the Emperor of Mexico. But Manzoni refused to admit Maximilian when he called, and the Contessa Maffei and her friends organized social bans and even duels for anyone attending one of the Archduke's functions. And in the end most of the reforms were allowed to die. Maximilian was eager to make them work, but Franz Josef, once he returned to Vienna, was not. The Austrian government no longer had the inclination or ability to rule except by repression. While at Naples King Ferdinando one day insisted on taking an impassible road. "I may break, but I do not bend," he observed, and soon thereafter his carriage sank immovably into a sandy river bed.

Not unnaturally, as the pressure from Piedmont increased, censors in the other Italian states grew more nervous and arbitrary. Every incident increased their industry, and unfortunately for Verdi on the very day that he arrived in Naples, 14 January 1858, in Paris a follower

CAVOUR

of Mazzini named Felice Orsini attempted to blow up Napoleon III and his Empress on their way to the Opéra. Orsini threw his bomb accurately under the carriage, but it did not explode. Another did, but among the crowd. Napoleon, after a short delay, continued on to the Opéra where he arrived in time to hear the famous chorus of oaths in Rossini's *William Tell*. Napoleon was most popular in the country and small towns and least so in republican Paris; not a cheer greeted him as he entered his box although the audience by then knew of the attempt on his life.

The incident caused a sensation throughout Europe. It checked for a time the growing sympathy for Italy and Piedmont and inspired the smaller monarchs to rule, where possible, with an even firmer hand. King Ferdinando had himself, only a year earlier, been the object of an attempted assassination when at a military review, as he was riding by the ranks, a private had lunged at him with a bayonet. The pistol case on his saddle saved Ferdinando from all but a small wound, but the audacity of the attack was shocking. The Neapolitan censor had no intention of permitting the San Carlo to present on its stage a suc-

349

cessful attempt at regicide.

In October, after considering a prose draft sent ahead by Verdi, the censor informed the impresario, Alberti, that the subject of the new opera had been vetoed. It was not a question of adjusting lines and changing names; the subject, the opera itself, was refused a license. Alberti was appalled and decided not to tell Verdi for fear he would stop work on the music; perhaps Alberti hoped that some sort of adjustment with the censor would become possible as time passed and pressure for the production mounted. But when Verdi, Strepponi and her spaniel, Loulou, arrived in Naples, Verdi believed that the censor had only required certain adjustments which he and Somma had already made. They had changed the locale from Sweden to Stettin, the period from the eighteenth to the seventeenth century and the title from *Gustavo III* to *La Vendetta in Domino*. For almost two weeks Verdi continued to believe all was well, and only when he began to choose the cast did he discover the truth: that in spite of all of Alberti's efforts the censor still vetoed the subject, and that he had first vetoed it months earlier.

Verdi eased his fury somewhat by writing friends. To Luccardi in Rome he stated bluntly: "I'm in a real Hell!" To Somma he explained the very least that the censors would demand by way of changes and what the probable result would be:

They have proposed these adjustments (and this is a concession):

1. Change the protagonist into an ordinary gentleman with no suggestion of sovereignty;
2. Change the wife into a sister;
3. Soften the witch's scene, changing it to a period when people believed in them;
4. No ball;
5. The murder off-stage;
6. Cut the scene of drawing the lots.
And then, and then, and then!! . . .

As you will suppose these changes cannot be accepted; therefore no more opera: therefore the subscribers will not pay two installments; therefore the government will withhold the subsidy; therefore the impresario will sue everyone and threatens me with damages of 50,000 ducats!! . . . What a hell! . . . Write me at once at once and give me your opinion.

Then began one of those curious legal monstrosities in which, because the law has no provision for suing the common enemy, friends sue each other. What both Verdi and Alberti really wanted was a joint suit against the censor, requiring him to show why his action was not arbitrary and capricious and asking the court to order him to issue a license for the production of the opera. But under Neapolitan law it was not possible to sue the censor and was forbidden to discuss his work in any court action. As a result the suit that developed between Verdi and Alberti progressed by a series of somewhat artificial claims and counterclaims in which at one point Verdi was threatened with arrest and prison.

The real issue of the suit, beneath the surface sparring, was that Verdi had the music to the opera, actual physical possession of it, and Alberti wanted it. To get it he had prepared a libretto based on Verdi's but meeting all the censor's requirements. With this in hand Alberti went to court, arguing that he had the theatre and singers ready, a libretto approved by the censor, and only the music was lacking because it was being wrongfully withheld. Verdi planned to defend by showing that Alberti had misled him as to the changes required by the censors and that therefore the music he had composed could not be artistically fitted to the libretto which Alberti had later prepared. Given Verdi's temperament, the main defense inevitably would be the artistic one although perhaps the least suitable for a law court.

With his lawyer Verdi prepared a ninety-page folio in which the two librettos were printed in adjacent columns. Alberti's was entitled *Adelia degli Adimari* and was set in fourteenth-century Florence. Verdi's comments, which run all over the margins, begin with the title which he insists "expresses nothing." Then he adds: "In this *Adelia* the name of the librettist is omitted. Praise be to the management! It has not wished to blame anyone for this artistic murder."

But most of the comments are more serious: "The palace has become a simple house: with this the opera is deprived of any sense of luxury." Or, "Judge for yourself if the notes put under the word *muori* can remain under the word *dorme*. Between sleeping and death there should be some difference!" He was particularly scathing of putting the opera back to the fourteenth century, although he had just finished doing the same thing with *Aroldo*. Still in principle "every age obviously has its own characteristics: the men of the fifteenth century had customs and sentiments different from those of the nineteenth; nor do men from the North resemble those from the South. And therefore the musical characteristics of these people are totally different. Take for example a Neapolitan song and a Swedish song and you will see the difference. A composer can, must stress these distinctions."

Oscar, the page, had been turned into a soldier but with his pert lines left largely the same and fitting most incongruously into an older man's speech. Forbidden the ball, Alberti had substituted a banquet, and as no one had ever heard of or tried a masked banquet, there were no masks. As Verdi's lawyer summed up: "Everyone recognizes everyone else; thus all the stage play is lost and nothing which is said has any sense."

The suit caused a scandal. Neither party was above reproach, but because the censor was involved and Alberti was indirectly taking the censor's part, most Neapolitans sided with Verdi. Crowds gathered under his balcony to cheer him, and his friend, Torelli, resigned as secretary of the management. Under pressure from the government the suit was settled out of court. The original contract was dissolved, and Verdi agreed to return in the autumn to stage *Simone Boccanegra,* which Naples had never seen. At the end of April Verdi and Strepponi embarked for home, taking with them the musical score which Alberti had hoped to produce.

The time in Naples was not entirely wasted. Verdi enlarged his group of friends, all of whom accepted Strepponi as his wife. The circle which had started with Cammarano's friend De Sanctis, a businessman, now included a painter, Domenico Morelli; a musically minded aristocrat, Baron Genovesi; and a caricaturist, Melchiorre Delfico, whose weekly pictures * had relieved some of Verdi's exasperation. But besides enjoying these friendships Verdi had, after the law suit began, started secret negotiations with the impresario Jacovacci in Rome to have the première of the Gustavo opera at the Teatro Apollo. And they had come to an agreement, subject to the libretto being approved by the Papal censor.

Verdi spent the summer at Sant' Agata. He worked on his farm, had the conductor Mariani down for several weeks of shooting, and in October returned with Strepponi to Naples where this time everything went well and *Simone Boccanegra* scored a success. Meanwhile Jacovacci had succeeded in securing the Papal censor's approval of the Gustavo libretto's subject and scenes in general, provided the

* A selection of them from this period and Verdi's return for *Simone Boccanegra* are reproduced following page 362.

locale was set outside of Europe. But there could be a ball and draw-ing of lots. Verdi wrote Somma, suggesting the locale be North or South America or perhaps the Caucasus. They finally settled on Co-lonial Boston in the eighteenth century. In all the censor required some sixty lines be changed, and Verdi gave in quickly. He was tired of the opera and felt that another suit would be "ridiculous." Strep-poni, after observing to a friend that the proposed cast was not good, added: "In any case, I want the première of this opera to be over with because it is the second year now it's been talked about." Finally, for the third time the opera's title was changed, to *Un Ballo in Maschera,* and the première set for 17 February 1859.

Verdi and Strepponi arrived in Rome about a month before and in a time of increasing political excitement. There had been rumors the previous summer that Cavour had met Napoleon III secretly at the little French town of Plombières and formed an alliance for war against Austria. No one knew anything for certain as neither of the parties talked, but it was public knowledge that Napoleon at his New Year's Day levee had remarked to the Austrian ambassador: "I regret that my relations with Austria are not as good as I could wish." And the remark, perhaps innocently intended, was widely interpreted as a step toward war. It was re-enforced by the perfectly open prepa-rations for the marriage of Vittorio Emanuele's fifteen-year-old daugh-ter, Clotilde, to Napoleon's first cousin, "Plonplon," the son of Prince Jerome. Everyone understood that the marriage was a dynastic al-liance as "Plonplon" was more than twenty years older than Clotilde and generally considered to be a difficult and embittered man. But the wedding was announced and on 30 January 1859 took place in the Royal Chapel at Turin. Even more important, on 10 January Vittorio Emanuele had opened the Parliament with a speech in which he closed firmly, clearly and with great pride: "If Piedmont, small in territory, yet counts for something in the Councils of Europe, it is because of the greatness of the ideals it represents and the sympathies it inspires. This position doubtless creates for us many dangers, yet, while we respect treaties, we cannot remain insensible to the cry of grief that reaches us from so many parts of Italy." The effect was tremendous. In the parliamentary galleries, packed with exiles, amidst all the frantic applause men who had waited for years began to weep. The "cry of grief," *il grido di dolore,* went round Europe, until in Vienna they wondered if war had not already been declared.

Verdi, already a symbol of patriotic aspiration, now became even more so. Repressed Italians in all the cities suddenly realized that his name was an acrostic for *Vittorio Emanuele Re d'Italia,* and *Viva Verdi!* was scratched on walls and shouted in the streets. Where his operas were being performed the audience called endlessly for the composer, particularly if Austrians were present. And where Verdi himself was present, crowds often gathered spontaneously and broke into cheers.

The première of *Un Ballo in Maschera,* however, was a sound musical success. In spite of Strepponi's fears the women's voices were adequate if not distinguished and the men were exceptionally good, particularly the tenor Gaetano Fraschini. He sang in more Verdi premières, five, than any other singer, although he was hardly lucky in *Alzira, Il Corsaro* and *Stiffelio.* But in *La Battaglia di Legnano* and particularly in *Un Ballo in Maschera* he was fortunate. The role of Gustavo, the gay yet passionate King, has the most variety to it of any tenor role Verdi wrote. It requires more elegance and delicacy than the Duke in *Rigoletto* and at the same time, in its love scene, more agitated passion. In the scene with Ulrica, the sorceress, the tenor has an aria in which he must change his voice and style to sing as the sailor he is disguised to be. And soon after, when Ulrica has prophesied his death, he must laugh at her in the style of an amused but sceptical aristocrat. The title role in *Otello* is undoubtedly more noble, but it is not more varied.

The opera as a whole compounded such variety, particularly in the flip page boy who was an entirely new sort of character for Verdi and for Italian opera in general. Musically it was tightly constructed and in fact is one of the shortest of Verdi's successful operas. Yet all the actions and motives of the characters are presented clearly. To contemporaries the most excitingly different thing about it was Verdi's sudden skill with the orchestra. *Un Ballo in Maschera* is the first opera in which Verdi caught up to the best of his time in orchestration. The sudden leap in skill seems magnified to ears unacquainted with the operas between *La Traviata* and *Un Ballo in Maschera.* The scoring for *I Vespri Siciliani,* for example, is plainly a stage between the two. But the advance is not less astonishing for being gradual, and its cause probably lies in Verdi's experiences in Paris where the best orchestras were considerably better than any in Italy. Whatever the reason, the orchestral sound in *Un Ballo in Maschera* even today is interesting in itself, rich and sometimes subtle.

The opera has always been popular, although not so much so as *Rigoletto, Il Trovatore* or *La Traviata*. One reason is simply that it is more difficult to produce. The orchestra must play better and the singers sing better, or they are more obviously not up to it. Casting the King and the Page is difficult, and the ball without a good stage director can be a disaster. It needs good scenery or, to paraphrase Verdi, all the luxury goes out of it. For all these reasons except in Italy the smaller opera houses are apt not to attempt it.

To a lesser extent the change of locale to Colonial Boston has hurt it, particularly for English-speaking people acquainted with Boston's history. Italian productions from the first have wallowed in a luxury unheard of in Boston with sixty-foot tapestries on the wall, marble staircases and perhaps, as a concession to history, a few wooden beams in the ceiling. But the effect has been that of Stockholm, not Boston. English-speaking operagoers, however, have been faced with some ludicrous changes in name and race that, regardless of the scenery, have kept the inconsistency before them. The aristocratic Counts Horn and Ribbing have become plain Sam and Tom, and Anckarström, a Creole. Businessmen inclined to think opera is ridiculous see *Un Ballo in Maschera* and often are convinced of it. Music lovers have solved the problem by mentally removing the locale to some mythical kingdom. Recently an increasing number of impresarios have aided them by returning the opera's setting to Stockholm and the names to Gustavo, Anckarström, etc.

The opera first played in Boston, its foster home, when Emanuele Muzio, who had been invited to New York by its Academy of Music, took a troupe from there on tour. The bulletins in Boston, after puffing the opera in the orotund style of the period, pointed out that: "In Europe the ELITE of the Opera HABITUÉS have been accustomed to attend the Opera with Dominoes, and have frequently entered upon the stage and united in the CONCLUDING GRAND BAL MASQUE." This consisted of a number of extraneous dances and a galop written by Muzio, all of which was to be squeezed, as in Auber's opera, into the last scene.

The performance took place in Boston's Academy of Music on 15 March 1861. Even though seven Southern states had already seceded

MUZIO

from the Union and Fort Sumter would soon be fired on, Boston's musical best turned out for the opera and apparently enjoyed themselves. The critics praised it highly and with perception. But of the dancing by the ELITE of Boston's opera HABITUÉS one critic remarked, "The Masquerade Ball was a total failure," and another that it "caused amusement, if nothing more." Verdi would have said that Muzio had got what he deserved.

CHAPTER 28

PUBLIC LIFE AND MARRIAGE
AS ITALY IS MADE

1859–1860; AGE, 45–47

FOLLOWING the première of *Un Ballo in Maschera* Verdi and Strepponi stayed on in Rome for several weeks. Since she had begun to accompany him on his trips, or perhaps just because he himself was getting older, his style of living had changed and he traveled less abruptly. For his stay in Rome, through his friend Luccardi, he had rented a house, hired a cook and brought several of his own servants. Strepponi, as at Sant' Agata, managed a household designed to keep him comfortable and free to work. Even if they had had children, the routine of his life would have been no different.

In a social sense Verdi was becoming a great man, one who simply because of the size of his household had an impact on any community he entered. But his style of living was not extraordinary. At the time most families traveled as a household, and many took their own servants with them even to hotels. The arrival of such a caravan was always hard work for its friends, and men made demands on each other that today would seem rather high. Verdi, for example, asked Luccardi not only to rent the house and install an upright piano but also on the actual day of arrival to have a man at the carriage post to conduct him and Strepponi to their new home where the fire was to be lit and the supper laid. Such was an arrival.

A departure was much the same except that custom required the visitors then to do something handsome by their friends. On leaving Naples Verdi gave a husband a watch while Strepponi gave the wife a bracelet. Care was taken to make the gift suitable, and if someone had a collection of something, every effort would be made to add to it. A favorite of the time was autograph letters of the great men of the past. After departure there was always a flurry of letters giving thanks, inquiring about uncertain health and imposing last burdens. Verdi, after leaving Naples, asked De Sanctis, who was coming later to Rome, to find "the thermometer that I forgot in the room where the piano was, and which is hanging beside the door into the bedroom." Then he explained "It's not for its value that I care but only because I have had it a long time."

Friends undertook to rent houses and employ servants for each other perhaps partly because they had the leisure to do it but also because there was an obvious need for it. The kind of communication that is done today directly with the hotel was then almost impossible. The telegraph was only just beginning and was used almost exclusively by the governments. The postal service was certain but in any rural area very slow. Busseto, although a market town, still had no post office at all. Twice a week a man rode into town, picked up and delivered what few letters there might be, visited with friends and then rode on to the next town. From even smaller Sant' Agata Verdi could not dicker with a hotel in Naples, and he naturally turned to his friends there for help.

Besides, with rare exceptions, the hotels in Italy were still simple lodgings for the night and offering food only as good as the signora, lazy or talented, might provide. The dirt could be appalling, particularly in the south where the people were said to comprehend the supernatural more easily than soap. One Sicilian hostess of the time, when asked to clean a knife, "spat upon a brick, rubbed the knife upon it, rinsed the blade in a pail of dirty water, and then dried it on her hair."

But even friends could not make everything perfect for travelers, and in a letter Strepponi privately complained that the house Luccardi had rented for them at Rome was "very ugly." And since he had "rented it for the entire Carnival season, we are obliged to remain."

While they stayed on in Rome, an anti-Austrian demonstration took place in Milan. The occasion was the funeral of Emilio Dandolo, who had fought at the Engineers' Barracks in the Cinque Giornate and the next year, although a monarchist, had defended the Roman Republic under Garibaldi. He had written a history of the siege of Rome, and his book describing the heroism of the defenders had been widely read in the Po Valley. At his funeral, which took place on 22 February

1859, an enormous crowd gathered outside the church in order to follow the bier to the cemetery. The coffin carried a crown of red and white camellias interspersed with green leaves, being the colors of Piedmont, and the crowd, on seeing it, shouted, jostled, wept and sang until the noise became a prolonged roar, frantic and terrible. The police and Austrian troops prudently disappeared.

The funeral was hailed in northern Italy as a decisive moral defeat for the Austrians, and they themselves compounded its effect by attempting to arrest the men connected with it. Most of them, in spite of the increased number of Hussars patrolling the Ticino River, managed to cross into Piedmont where Cavour and the most distinguished generals and statesmen promptly organized a memorial service for Dandolo.

Cavour was now in a position of trying to provoke Austria to attack him. He had a treaty with France which, while secret, was well suspected and under the terms of which Napoleon III had promised to defend Piedmont against every aggressive act of Austria. Napoleon would go no further to help Piedmont and was beginning to feel that he was already too rash. The great mass of Frenchmen were totally uninterested in his Italian plans. The clerical party, of which the Empress was a leader, saw no good in Piedmont and much in the Pope's Temporal Power. The businessmen were happy with the increasing prosperity in France and saw nothing to be gained by a war. The only persons at all favorable to the Emperor were his usual enemies, the republicans, and their support was tempered with demands for reform at home. In addition the other powers, fearing French influence in Italy and Napoleonic designs in Europe, tended to be against him. But the treaty did exist, and the Emperor, although weakly, reiterated that he was a man of his word.

Cavour had a number of grounds on which he hoped to provoke Austria to attack. One was simply that Piedmont was mobilizing, recalling men into the army and passing war appropriation bills. In addition refugees, more than a hundred a day, were arriving in Piedmont and volunteering to fight. The number is small compared to modern figures, but for the period, when men moved around less, it was high. The fact that Piedmont could recruit a volunteer army of more than 12,000 able-bodied refugees was a judgment on conditions in Italy. And although Austria had the right by treaty to demand the return of the men from Lombardy-Venetia, to do so was to draw attention to those conditions. Instead it, too, called men up for service, doubled the garrisons in Lombardy and passed war bills.

The other powers meanwhile, particularly Russia and England, fluttered anxious notes through their embassies and tried to persuade both Piedmont and Austria to settle their differences at a congress. There was nothing Cavour wanted less than more talk. For the moment he had his ally in France, and if time passed, he would almost certainly lose it. While the great powers made proposals and counter-proposals, he locked himself in his room and waited, too nervous to see anyone. In fact, he seems to have had a day of despair, a sort of spasm of nervous revulsion. His nephew, for whom he had cared, had been killed fighting the Austrians in 1848, and Cavour had ever after, to remind himself of the tragic waste of war, kept the bloodstained uniform in a glass case in his bedroom. Now he had prepared another war in which many more young men would be killed. Yet only so could Italy be made and a purpose saved from the deeds of those already dead.

Finally Austria refused the last proposal. Franz Josef apparently was swayed by his military advisers rather than his statesmen, and on 23 April 1859 Austria delivered an ultimatum to Piedmont demanding that it disarm or Austria would declare war. Cavour had three days in which to answer. The ultimatum was an aggressive act, and Napoleon began to send French troops into Piedmont. On 26 April Cavour handed Piedmont's reply to the Austrian envoys, and the war technically began. The Austrians, however, without Radetzky to lead them, moved very slowly, and Napoleon and Vittorio Emanuele were able to fight in Lombardy. Garibaldi with three thousand men operated on the extreme right flank, harassing the Austrians around the lakes and aiming to cut their supply lines in the Adige Valley. On 4 June there was a major battle at Magenta which opened the way to Milan, and four days later the King and Emperor made a triumphal entry into a city frantic with excitement. The older inhabitants could remember when the first Napoleon had swept down out of the Alps and founded a Kingdom of Italy. Now it seemed to be happening again.

Magenta was not a decisive battle, but the Austrians retreated toward the Quadrilateral and from Tuscany, Parma and Modena the Grand Dukes and Duchesses fled to join them. In the Romagna the Papal Legate left Bologna for Rome. At Sant' Agata Verdi, returned from Rome, started a subscription to raise money for the wounded

NAPOLEON III

and after signing himself up first went in order to his wife, who made her own contribution, his father, his head farmer, his lawyer and his father-in-law. The farmer subscribed 5 francs and Verdi, 550. If the Austrians won and returned to Parma, there would be no question of where Verdi had stood.

Like most Italians his excitement after Magenta rose very high. To the Contessa Maffei he wrote:

Who would have believed that our allies could be so generous. For myself I confess and say *mea grandissima culpa,* since I was unable to believe in the French coming into Italy and spilling their blood for us without some idea of conquest. On the first point I was wrong; I hope and wish to be wrong on the second. I hope Napoleon will not go back on his proclamation in Milan. Then I will adore him even more than I have adored George Washington, and, blessing the great nation of the French, I will endure willingly all their "blague," their insolent "politesse" and the contempt they have for everything that is not French.

The next large battle, again indecisive, was fought at Solferino on 24 June. With 310,000 men engaged, it was the greatest battle in Europe since Leipzig in 1813 when the Allied armies defeated Napoleon I. Again the French were fighting the Austrians and both sides were led by Emperors, for after Magenta Franz Josef himself had taken command. On the French side, somewhat to Napoleon's chagrin, Vittorio Emanuele began to emerge as the royal hero. He enjoyed fighting and often succeeded in getting himself into the thick of it. Napoleon, while personally courageous, had a more complicated character. The campaign had forced him to recognize that he was neither a great general nor even a good soldier. The carnage of the battles had appalled him, and he could not ignore it simply by physical action or sleep.

He was also bothered, the further he advanced toward the Quadrilateral, by an increasing number of political difficulties both at home and in Italy. In France the people reveled in the glory of the French arms. The campaign was the first in which the telegraph made continuous contemporaneous bulletins possible, and Napoleon and his staff edited a series of golden prose communiqués that read like verses of the *Marseillaise*. But the success so grandiloquently reported led many in France to declare that everything possible to France's advantage had already been accomplished. The clerical party with the Empress as a conduit protested that the Papal States were being thrown into a turmoil, and realists pointed out that Napoleon was creating a strong, united Italy on France's southeastern border. His own party begged him not to risk losing everything on another battle. Legitimate monarchies could lose a battle and survive, but not those based on a coup. "In France," as the Empress observed on fleeing from Paris in 1870, "it is necessary not to be unfortunate."

In Italy Napoleon's difficulty was that Cavour and not he controlled the political situation. The presence in Italy of Piedmont with a liberal, constitutional government, a capable king and brilliant statesman was a crucial difference between the French liberating invasion of 1859 and those under Napoleon I at the turn of the century. When Napoleon III drove the Austrians out of a Lombard town, its people cheered him ecstatically. But they addressed their petitions for union with Piedmont to Cavour. Even worse, towns in Tuscany and the Romagna, where French arms had not yet been, were doing the same thing.

There were other difficulties. The Quadrilateral was strong and the Austrian armies still intact. The Italian peasants, as always, had refused to rise and considered the French as bad as the Austrians. And across the Alps far to the north the Prussians began troop movements. The result, as Napoleon pondered these facts, was the secret treaty of Villafranca. The terms were in brief:

VERDI, STREPPONI AND LOULOU ARRIVE IN NAPLES

(Top) NEAPOLITANS HOPING TO GET INTO A REHEARSAL; *(bottom)*
STRATAGEMS OF FRIENDS TO GET INTO A REHEARSAL

REHEARSALS

VERDI MEETS A FRIEND, IL BARONE GENOVESI

(Top) VERDI AND GENOVESI COOK RICE AND MACARONI; *(bottom)*
SIGHT-SEEING TRIP WITH FRIENDS TO THE BLUE GROTTO

(Top) VERDI SICK IN BED; *(bottom)* MERCADANTE PRESENTS VERDI
TO THE PUPILS OF THE CONSERVATORY

(Top) DE SANCTIS SHOWS VERDI A SPOT FOR HIS HONEYMOON; *(middle)*
VERDI AND DELFICO ADMIRE THE BAY OF NAPLES; *(bottom)* DELFICO
PAYS HOMAGE TO STREPPONI

VERDI AND LOULOU

(1) Austria and France to favor the creation of an Italian Confederation with the Pope as honorary President.

(2) Austria to cede Lombardy to France which would turn it over to Piedmont. Austria to retain Venetia.

(3) The Dukes of Tuscany and Modena to return to their states, but without using force, and to proclaim a general amnesty.

(4) Austria and France to ask the Pope to make indispensable reforms in the Papal States.

(5) A general amnesty.

The treaty, which was technically only an armistice preparatory to a more formal treaty, was the work of France and Austria, and Napoleon presented it to Vittorio Emanuele as a *fait accompli*. Cavour, when he learned the terms, argued passionately against signing it, but Vittorio Emanuele realistically pointed out that he had no choice: he could not fight France and Austria. And, after all, Lombardy and quite probably Parma, which had not been specifically mentioned, were something: half a loaf. But Cavour would have none of it and offered his resignation, which was accepted. The King then went off to sign the terms. The only concession he could wring from the two Emperors was the right to add after his signature "en ce qui me concerne" or "in that which concerns me." In the coming months Italians would insist this excused him from assisting the birth of a confederation or the return of the Dukes.

The news of Villafranca stunned the Italians and then began to divide them. The Milanese could not help rejoicing for they finally were free of the Austrians, but for the others, the Venetians, Parmigiani, Modenese, Tuscans and those of the Papal States in the Romagna around Bologna, it seemed a terrible betrayal. Republicans accused monarchists and monarchists the French. In a letter to the Contessa Maffei Verdi asked: "Isn't Venice Italy too? After such a victory, what a result! So much blood for nothing! Poor deluded youth! And Garibaldi who even sacrificed his long-standing convictions to fight for a king has not achieved his goal!

"It is enough to drive a man mad! I am writing in the greatest anger." (etc.)

The succeeding weeks were a time of the greatest confusion, and the success of the various smaller states in governing themselves, often under the most difficult conditions, contributed greatly to the final outcome. Cavour, before Villafranca, had appointed temporary administrators to run Parma, Modena and Romagna. In Tuscany the administrator was less important than the local strong man, Baron Ricasoli, who announced firmly to the world that Tuscany would not unite with Piedmont but would merge with it to form part of a new Kingdom of Italy. After Villafranca the administrators, by invitation of the local inhabitants, stayed on as dictators, theoretically not tied to Turin and constantly announcing that they would fight rather than have the Dukes and Duchesses back. Their actions embarrassed everyone, Napoleon, Vittorio Emanuele, and even Franz Josef who had agreed not to use force to return the Dukes. Cavour privately urged on the administrators.

In August Parma, voting for the first time with universal (male) suffrage, joined itself with neighboring Modena. In the first week of September the men again went to the polls to vote for representatives to an Assembly in Parma. In this election Verdi was a candidate for his district. At Busseto the ballot boxes, as was customary, were set up in the church of Santa Maria degli Angeli and presided over by the Mayor and the priest. The band went to meet Verdi and played him into the church. After the count he was declared to be elected and again later at the Assembly in Parma was selected with four others to carry the result of its deliberations to Vittorio Emanuele. These were, not surprisingly: (1) the deposition of the Bourbon dynasty, (2) a dictatorship under the former temporary royal administrator, and (3) union with Piedmont.

The King neither accepted nor rejected the delegation's offer of union. It was a time when official and unofficial remarks were very different, but the public demonstrations in Turin left no doubt that the Piedmontese also desired union. For the moment, however, Parma, Modena and Tuscany continued to exist in a political vacuum.

While Verdi was in Turin, he visited Cavour who was in retirement on his estate at Leri, about twenty-five miles to the northeast of Turin. The visit was arranged, apparently at Verdi's request, by the British Ambassador, Sir James Hudson, who was more used to taking out cabinet ministers than composers. Cavour was a monotone and did not pretend to be interested in music. But he was interested in Verdi as a political power and a great Italian, and both men shared a profound interest in agriculture. The land at Leri is flat and monotonous and except for the Alps in the distance is very like the land at Busseto. Cavour's crops included rice, beets, maize and silk; he also raised cattle. To it all he brought new methods applied on a large scale so that the farms at Leri had become revolutionary models for Italy while at the same time making Cavour very rich. The men undoubtedly talked about politics and probably also about fertilizer. Verdi's bread-and-butter letter read:

Busseto 21 September 1859

Your Excellency:

Please excuse my boldness and the inconvenience I may cause you with these few lines. I had wished for a long time to make the personal acquaintance of the Prometheus of our people, nor did I despair of finding an opportunity to fulfill my great desire. But what I had not dared to hope for was the frank and kindly reception with which Your Excellency deigned to honor me.

I left there deeply moved! I shall never forget your Leri where I had the honor of shaking the hand of the great statesman, the first citizen, the man whom every Italian will call the father of his country. May Your Excellency graciously accept these sincere words from a simple artist, who can boast of only one virtue: that he loves and always has loved his native land.

To which Cavour replied: "It is a great reward for the difficulties suffered to know that I have the affectionate sympathy of a fellow-citizen who has helped to keep Italy's name honored in Europe."

The election which sent Verdi to the Assembly at Parma and from there on to Turin to meet Cavour was held on 4 September. The previous week on 29 August 1859 Verdi and Strepponi were married in the small town of Collonges-sous-Salève near the Swiss border of the province of Savoy. The common language in that part of Piedmont was French and the certificate, like Verdi's baptismal certificate, names him "Joseph" Verdi; Strepponi is "Josephine." She signed in the French fashion, but he made his usual "G. Verdi." He was forty-five and she forty-three.

Unfortunately, because a clerk misread the month in making a copy of the original certificate, the date is often given as 29 *April* instead of August. This would have Verdi and Strepponi marrying on the day fighting started in the spring and at a time when probably, because of troop movements, they could not have traveled from Parma to Savoy.

There are a number of mysteries about the marriage in addition to the great one of why it took place now rather than before. The ceremony, for example, was not performed by the local priest but by an Abbé Mermillod who accompanied the couple in a carriage from Geneva to Collonges. Mermillod eventually became a bishop and finally in 1890 a cardinal, so that he evidently, even as an abbé, was a priest of some importance. As neither Verdi nor Strepponi were in the habit of going to Geneva or had any known business there, it seems probable that they went with the purpose of meeting this priest. From a letter Verdi wrote ten years later, which is the only evidence of the details of the ceremony, it seems probable that the arrangements, if not also the purpose, were primarily Strepponi's. Verdi wrote the letter to a friend when he was trying to establish that the marriage had taken place in order to adopt the daughter of one of his cousins. Even allowing for frustration with legal forms, his tone is harsh, suggesting that neither the priest nor the ceremony was important to him. Verdi wrote:

That priest Mermillot [sic], Rector of Notre Dame in Geneva, who engaged to do everything necessary, wished to celebrate the marriage (sending the local parish-priest out for a walk) perhaps so that He [sic] would not have to share the fee. (etc.)

It is certain that the marriage was celebrated and registered at Collange or Collenge before two witnesses, very distinguished persons, the peasant and the carriage driver who took us from Geneva to Collange. (etc.)

I would prefer to validate this marriage rather than to have another before our authorities, and however . . . I must try to have these documents legalized. Let me first try to find this Mermillot . . . It was he himself, Mermillot, who suggested holding the wedding in Collange so that it would be recognized civilly. He could have done it just as well in his Catholic church with only the religious ceremony in mind.

Beyond these few details, everything is speculation. Perhaps with the war threatening to start again at any minute he wanted to insure that Strepponi would, in the case of his death, at least have the legal rights of a widow to his property. Or perhaps his decision to stand for public office influenced him. He must have realized that he would be elected and that as one of Parma's most distinguished citizens he would, in all probability, be sent to Turin where life would be easier and he could be a more effective representative of Parma if he had conformed to the customs of society. But whatever the reason for the marriage, it made no difference to his way of life. He did not broadcast that he now was married or even refer to it in writing his friends, and the act so long delayed did not change his relations with Busseto.

In the months following the marriage Italy continued in a state of armistice pending a more formal treaty and congress to decide its political future. Verdi and Strepponi stayed at Sant' Agata where, except for his three-week trip to Turin, he worked on his farm. Finally a treaty was signed in Zurich in November, but as it only embodied the preliminary terms agreed to earlier, it did not touch on the larger problems. Lombardy passed to Napoleon who relinquished it to Piedmont. But French troops remained in Lombardy, Austrian in Venetia, and an army of Swiss mercenaries held all but Romagna for the Pope. At Rome there were still more French troops. The smaller states, to keep order and make a show of force, had recruited National Guards, but arms were often lacking, and at Busseto Verdi, through his friend Mariani in Genoa, bought 172 rifles for the town militia.

It was a period of calm which everyone recognized could not last. Most north Italians wanted to unify everything north of the Papal States, including the Romagna, into a Kingdom of Italy under Vittorio Emanuele. Some, and most important Garibaldi and Mazzini, wanted to unify the entire peninsula, even including Rome. Napoleon wanted an independent Kingdom of Northern Italy, restricted to the Po Valley, and a Kingdom of Central Italy, based on Tuscany. For the latter he proposed his cousin "Plonplon" and Clotilde of Savoy as rulers. This would give France a greater voice in Italian affairs and put a buffer between Piedmont and the Papal States. Napoleon, as the Italians were begining to realize, was willing to have them independent but not unified. Before Villafranca Cavour's aim had been to get France into Italy in order to drive the Austrians out. This had been largely accomplished in that all the Austrian troops were now in Venetia and restricted by the armistice and treaty terms from leaving. Now the problem had become how to persuade France to leave Italy and to agree not to intervene while Piedmont unified the little states, including Tuscany.

Vittorio Emanuele recalled Cavour to the ministry in January 1860, and the news of it was celebrated in Florence and all the cities of the Po Valley. Even in Genoa, where Verdi had taken Strepponi to spend the winter months and which was probably the most republican city in Italy, the news of Cavour's recall was popular. He was plainly the best statesman, and his replacement had been able to govern largely by refusing to convene Parliament, which would have promptly unseated him. If the news of Cavour's return to power was not so popular in Rome or Naples it was because there his demonstrated ability was considered to be hostile. His interview with Vittorio Emanuele, who was sick in bed, was stiff but satisfactory. Both King and servant recognized that each needed and perforce had to work with the other.

The only bait that Cavour could offer Napoleon for non-intervention while Piedmont merged North and Central Italy into one state were the two provinces of Savoy and Nice. Savoy had always been a mountain kingdom looking down on the valleys of the Rhone and the Po, and French kings had traditionally worried about their neighbor on the mountains who could almost see over the gates of Lyon and down into Cannes. Savoy was French-speaking and, although loyal to the person of its King, it was fundamentally French in sympathy and disapproving of his Italian ventures. Nice, much smaller, was very different. There the native language was a Ligurian dialect very like that spoken in Genoa, and although many of the inhabitants, like Garibaldi who was born there, also spoke French, their political sympathy was to the old republican tradition of Genoa. They were not personally loyal to Vittorio Emanuele, but they were sympathetic toward his aim of uniting Italy. Savoy, Cavour knew, could be traded without much opposition from Italians, but Nice would raise a storm. Napoleon, however, insisted on controlling the mountains of both.

When Cavour had met secretly with Napoleon at Plombières in 1858, the two men had agreed that the price of the French alliance was to be Savoy and perhaps Nice. The price to France was to assist in freeing Italy from the Alps to the Adriatic, and Napoleon, on first setting foot in Italy, had molded "the mountains to the sea" into a series of grand proclamations. When for political reasons he had been forced to halt before Venetia, he had remarked privately to Vittorio Emanuele that Piedmont should pay for the war but retain its provinces. He was, however, still eager for them as the most tangible benefit of the war he could exhibit to his people.

With Cavour again in office bargaining for the provinces resumed. The negotiations and even the treaty were secret, but everyone suspected the terms, and Garibaldi, who was certain to be against any such bargain, sent an emissary to the King to ask if Nice was to be ceded to France. The King was instructed to "answer me at once by telegraph Yes or No!" Vittorio Emanuele, after recovering from the shock of such a blunt demand, replied: "Very well, yes! But tell the General that not only Nice but Savoy as well! And that if I can reconcile myself to lose the cradle of my family and my race, he can do the same."

Cavour signed the treaty secretly, which by Piedmontese law was unconstitutional, but he insisted that for it to be effective the new Parliament, which would convene in April, must approve it. With the treaty signed Napoleon permitted Tuscany, Modena, Parma and the Romagna to unite with Piedmont in a new Kingdom of Italy. The French troops in Lombardy deterred any action by the Austrians, and when the Pope published a bull of major excommunication against Vittorio Emanuele, Cavour and others for their part in annexing Romagna, Napoleon refused to allow it to be published in France.

Meanwhile Vittorio Emanuele started on a tour of the annexed states, and at Busseto, where he was scheduled to make a short stop, the citizens decided to honor him with the gift of a rifled cannon, horse and gun carriage. Then someone suggested that even better would be a cantata by the town's most distinguished citizen. Verdi, in a letter to the town fathers, promptly disagreed:

28 April 1860

Illustrious Sirs:

The town of Busseto was most praiseworthy in voting to give the King a cannon, which he certainly will prefer to some other gift. I wish that every paese might imitate the example, for not by festivals and illuminations but by arms and soldiers will we become strong, respected and masters in our own house. We must not forget that foreigners, powerful and threatening, are everywhere in Italy. (etc.)

And he went on to explain that he could not accept Busseto's invitation to compose a cantata to honor Vittorio Emanuele without offending Milan and Turin, whose similar requests he had already refused.

Verdi's and Strepponi's relations with Busseto were at their best during these years. Perhaps the fact of their marriage helped, but more likely it was the common bond of patriotism. Verdi had stood for public office and been elected. He had circulated the subscription to help the wounded, and now Strepponi served on a committee to raise money among the women of Busseto for a gift to the King. She was only moderately successful and explained to the parent committee in Bologna that there had been too many subscriptions in recent months, which was undoubtedly true. But successful or not, one result of the war and the unification of the country was that both she and Verdi took a greater part in the life of their community than they ever had before or would thereafter.

The King's tour, in which the small towns were so interested, took place while the Parliament in Turin was adjourned. It had been the first Parliament in which Tuscans, Piedmontese, Lombards and Parmigiani sat side by side as Italians. The questions they considered were momentous, but above all one stood out: the proposed cession of Nice and Savoy to France. Garibaldi early in April started a speech on Nice and was ruled out of order, on Cavour's motion, for raising the question before the Chamber had elected its officers. But Garibaldi could not be silenced forever, and a week later in a short speech he questioned both the legality and morality of Cavour's treaty with Napoleon. His speech was restrained and, in its legalistic approach, plainly not entirely his own; he spoke for many in the opposition, particularly republicans.

The issue he raised was not resolved until after the King's tour and the adjournment, during which a plebiscite had been held in Nice. In it the inhabitants voted 25,743 to 160 for annexation to France. There was no question that French agents had influenced the voting, but even so it may have reflected the majority opinion. Parliament thought so or at least was convinced by Cavour's explanation of why it was necessary to sacrifice the two provinces. The Chamber of Deputies voted to ratify the treaty, 229 to 33 with 23 abstentions. Garibaldi was not present. He had already started fighting in Sicily: if Napoleon was to be paid for uniting Italy, then he, Garibaldi, would see to it that it was truly united, all of it. He would not be satisfied with any of Cavour's cautionary half loaves.

Again, as at Rome, Garibaldi fashioned out of a seemingly foolish expedition a success beyond the world's wildest imaginings. With slightly more than a thousand volunteers, as many old muskets on which even the bayonets did not fit properly and five cannon he steamed secretly out of Genoa early in May. After a false stop in Tuscany he landed in Sicily and by the end of the month had taken its capital, Palermo, from 24,000 Neapolitan troops supported by their

GARIBALDI

Navy. "By God," Verdi wrote to Mariani, "there really is a man to kneel to."

But Garibaldi did not stop in Sicily. It took him through July to clear the island of Neapolitan garrisons and then, as more volunteers with better weapons joined him, he evaded the Neapolitan Navy, crossed the Straits of Messina and marched on Naples. By September he had taken the city, and Francesco II, still with some 50,000 troops, had retreated to Gaeta, where for the moment he tied down Garibaldi and his irrepressible volunteers.

Garibaldi's success was almost entirely of his own making. He was able to take advantage of local grievances, but largely it was the purity of his motives—he wanted only to unite Italy—that inspired his men to be heroes. He also led them brilliantly, so that by the time they reached Naples they believed, as did everyone else, that they were invincible. But his success raised its own problems, and it was with relief that Cavour, Vittorio Emanuele and many other heads wiser than Garibaldi saw him stopped.

Garibaldi constantly proclaimed that he would continue on to Rome and make it the capital of united Italy. Yet there were still French troops in Rome, and no one doubted that Napoleon, under pressure at home and answering pleas from abroad, would send more to defend it. Piedmont could not risk becoming embroiled with France on two fronts while Austria, still in Venetia, looked for an opportunity to retake Lombardy. But there were also domestic reasons for relief. Garibaldi's volunteers were almost entirely republicans, and their feats were eclipsing Vittorio Emanuele. It was beginning to appear as though the republicans were going to unite Italy without Vittorio Emanuele and then crown him merely as an act of favor. Such an event, aside from lacerating the King's pride, would greatly weaken his position as monarch under a constitution. And in another way Garibaldi was threatening the constitutional form of government that Cavour held so precious. Garibaldi ruled Sicily and southern Italy as a dictator and proclaimed that it was the only suitable form of government for such a primitive region. He was agreeable to having the dictator be responsible in some fashion to the King, but he was anxious to save the area from being administered by the Parliament, which he despised as a meeting of small, evil men lacking in love of Italy.

Garibaldi's very success, however, gave Cavour the chance to present himself and Vittorio Emanuele to Europe as the best hope for peace and order in Italy. No one knew where Garibaldi would stop or what he and his red shirts might not attempt. So Cavour sent agents to Napoleon with a proposition to which he agreed, largely because it seemed to offer the only stable solution to the problem of Garibaldi. Vittorio Emanuele was to lead the Piedmontese army down through the eastern part of what remained of the Papal States. These were two provinces known as the Marches and Umbria, and they were to become part of Piedmont. But the western part, known as the Patrimony of St. Peter, including Rome, was to remain with the Pope. Then once down into the Kingdom of the Two Sicilies, Vittorio Emanuele, as Garibaldi's monarch and with an army larger than the volunteers, would "absorb the revolution" and prevent any attack on Rome. To make sure that Austria did not attack while Vittorio Emanuele and the main body of troops were in the south, Cavour kept a few divisions at home and arranged with Kossuth, if necessary, to pay all the expenses of a Magyar uprising in Hungary.

Events went as planned. In September the Piedmontese under General Cialdini started down through the Marches, defeating the

THE UNIFICATION OF ITALY IN THE YEARS 1859–60

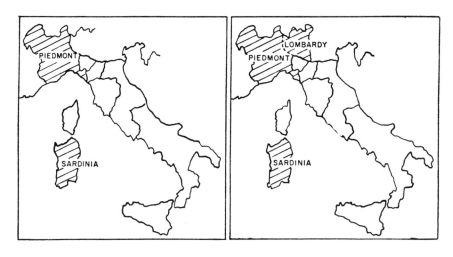

At the beginning of 1859   After July 1859

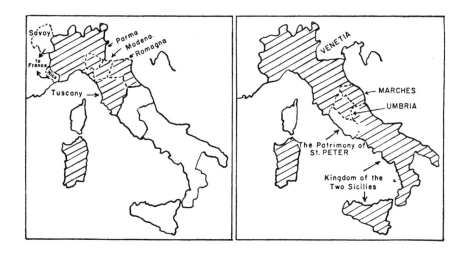

After March 1860   After October 1860

small Papal armies and capturing the fortresses. North and south Italy were at last to be joined. Verdi excitedly wrote to Mariani of Cialdini and Garibaldi: "Those are composers! And what operas! What finales! To the sound of guns!"

Some towns in the Papal States rose in advance of Cialdini and themselves drove out the Papal garrisons. Meanwhile along the Volturno River Garibaldi defeated the Neapolitan army in a complicated, two-day battle which preserved Naples and demonstrated that he was a great deal more of a general than just a guerilla leader. The battle of the Volturno was possibly the most important of the war. If the Neapolitan army had been able to re-establish Francesco II on his throne in Naples the governments of Europe would never have allowed Vittorio Emanuele to continue with the fiction of quelling Garibaldi, and of course the shift in morale following a Garibaldi defeat would have been enormous, both in the volunteers and the Neapolitan army.

But although events went as planned and although north and south Italy were united, Garibaldi and his men felt they had been cheated of Rome. They considered they had been stopped not by the Neapolitans but by Cavour who interposed the army of Piedmont between them and their goal, forcing them to be "absorbed" or fight the Piedmontese. The latter was unthinkable to Garibaldi, but he bitterly resented the choice being forced on him.

Another unexpected repercussion arose out of the personalities and prejudices of the chief actors. Vittorio Emanuele and the officers of his army were jealous of the success of Garibaldi and his irregulars and disliked their radical, republican leanings. When Garibaldi, on order, assembled his men for a farewell review by their King, for whom they had won half of Italy, the King left them standing in the sun and never appeared.

He sent no apology or explanation and never later offered one. He would not even write a proclamation thanking the men. Nor would his commanding general, Fanti, sign such a document; someone lower in rank had to be found. The public incident, which was soon known all over Italy, was the first awful sign that Vittorio Emanuele was too small a man to act with wisdom the enlarged role Cavour and Garibaldi had prepared for him.

All his life Garibaldi blamed Cavour for the insult to his men, and most unfairly. The evidence is perfectly clear that Cavour, who was himself constantly snubbed by the military, had foreseen the possibility of such an incident and tried to guard against it. But Garibaldi, blinded by his fury over the cession of Nice, forgave the King and blamed wrongly the man who had tried to avert the disaster. For it was a disaster for the monarchy. Every volunteer who could walk had assembled for the review, and each in his home town for the rest of his life would be a hero. If in 1946 the Italian people lightly voted to depose the House of Savoy and adopt a republican form of government, it was partly because of their collective memory of the inadequacies of the first King of Italy.

In the following weeks the King offered Garibaldi various rewards for his service, including a dowry for his daughter, a castle, or a steamer to set himself up in business. But all these Garibaldi refused, and when he resigned his command and left Naples for his farm on the island of Caprera, he carried away with him only a bag of seed corn. Strepponi, writing a friend at Naples, asked: "Do you love Giuseppe of Caprera? I hope so. It is impossible that you should not be an enthusiastic admirer of the purest and greatest hero since the world was created."

CHAPTER 29

A DEPUTY TO THE
FIRST PARLIAMENT OF THE
KINGDOM OF ITALY

1861; AGE, 47

THE speed with which Italy was united, after so many years of division, left the country in a state of amazed confusion. At the beginning of 1859 only Piedmont was independent, and two years later only Venetia and the Patrimony of St. Peter (*See* map, p. 373) were outside the new Kingdom of Italy. In the fortress city of Gaeta Francesco II, the last Bourbon of Naples, still held out but plainly not for long. In the two years four kingdoms had joined Piedmont and half each of two more. The problems of absorption and readjustment were enormous. Everywhere there was conflicting coinage, law and tradition. Even weights and measures varied. Many felt that to hold elections and convene a national Parliament in the midst of such confusion would merely add to it. Cavour, however, felt it would unify the country, bring the malcontents into a forum where parties and policies could be formed, glorify the King in his role as constitutional monarch and, above all, give himself a chance to exert his influence where he was strongest. Elections were set for the end of January with the right to vote, as in Piedmont, dependent on property or intellectual qualifications. About 450,000 out of some eleven million men qualified. Parliament was to convene in Turin in February.

Verdi, who was at Sant' Agata as the year began, resisted suggestions that he represent Busseto and its district, known as the Borgo San Donnino, at the first national Parliament. An acquaintance of his, Giovanni Minghelli-Vanni, who was a lawyer and more politically experienced, had announced himself for the post and had Verdi's support. But then Cavour wrote Verdi a personal letter, urging him to stand for election, and there began a comedy of small-town politics.

Verdi promptly went to Turin to explain to Cavour that as an artist he had neither the ability nor the desire to be a Deputy, particularly as he lacked the patience to sit through the speeches. While Verdi was gone, Minghelli-Vanni wrote to him at Sant' Agata to inquire for a last time if he intended to stand for the post, and Strepponi, the dutiful wife, replied that Verdi had authorized her to state that he did not. But in Turin Verdi met with Cavour and was persuaded or flattered into believing that it was his duty to Italy in its first years to endure the speeches in order to lend the Parliament some of the luster of his international reputation. So Verdi returned to Sant' Agata and, making a liar out of his wife, announced himself as a candidate.

A true politician would have accepted the false position as merely one of the trials of political life. But when Minghelli-Vanni, not unnaturally, inquired which of the conflicting announcements he should believe, Verdi, with characteristic honesty, undertook to explain his position. He succeeded only in sounding stuffy. "My trip to Turin had no other purpose than the desire to free myself of it (standing for office), and you know it. I was not successful and am most desolate over it, the more so since you are so much better prepared for the parliamentary battles than the artist, who has only his poor name to recommend him." With such an endorsement Minghelli-Vanni may well have wondered why Verdi did not withdraw.

Verdi continued:

I suggested you, spoke warmly for you at Busseto, knowing I'd procure for my paese a true Italian, an honest man, and a Deputy whose abilities could aid the good cause. I have not campaigned, I will not campaign, nor will I take a step to insure my election. I will serve, although at a heavy sacrifice to myself, if I am elected; and you know the reasons why I must do so.

Nevertheless I am resolved to resign as soon as I can. This letter, that I authorize you to show to whoever dares injure you with innuendos, must suffice to justify yourself and calm your mind. As for the remedy proposed to me, to have myself nominated in another district; forgive me, but it is against my principles. Doing that, I would be *campaigning* to be elected and I repeat for the hundredth time: I am forced to accept the nomination, but I shall not campaign nor put myself up in any district.

If you succeed in putting me in a minority, being elected yourself, and freeing me from this duty, I will not find sufficient words to thank you for such a great service. You would do a favor to the Chamber, a pleasure to yourself, and the very greatest pleasure to

G. VERDI

But Verdi could not leave well enough alone. When Minghelli-Vanni wrote a few days later to say that he did not hold Verdi responsible for any of the political intrigues against him, Verdi, for one of the few times in his life, became pompous: "You have known me too short a time or you would know how my sense of dignity is developed to the point of pride and my scorn for political intrigue to disgust." And again he repeated how ill-equipped he was to be a Deputy, how little he wished to be one, and how he was forced to accept the nomination. In the end Verdi was elected by a margin of 339–206, and he and Strepponi prepared to go to Turin. The desk assigned to him in the Chamber was in the second row on the main aisle to the left, facing the Speaker. Except for an isolated conservative in front of him he was completely surrounded by other members of Cavour's ministerial party.

The Parliament convened on 18 February, only five days after the Neapolitan army capitulated at Gaeta. Francesco II of Naples and his Queen, Maria Sophia, had stayed with their troops to the last day and graced the city's defense with an air of chivalry and romance. They were only twenty-four and twenty, and two years earlier they had been the last royal couple in history to be married by proxy. She was a Bavarian princess, a younger sister of the Empress of Austria and almost as beautiful. At Gaeta she proved herself brave, and each day when she appeared on the ramparts, the men cheered her. At the end when she and Francesco left on a French cutter to take refuge in Rome, the men wept.

In a military sense the defense of Gaeta had always been hopeless, and in Turin many of the politicians talked of it with contempt. But some of the wiser ones saw in it a sign of the troubles coming in the south of Italy. A large part of the Neapolitan army, civil service and society had not welcomed the Piedmontese. And many who had welcomed Garibaldi as a liberator considered Vittorio Emanuele a foreign conqueror. Francesco and his Queen, unlike the Grand Dukes, had a genuine following in their country, and they had fled, not to Vienna or Paris, but only just across the border to Rome.

At Turin, however, the problems of the future were put aside in

VITTORIO EMANUELE II

the excitement of the moment. The King opened Parliament with a brief speech from the throne in which he mentioned the parts played by France, Garibaldi and the Piedmontese forces in unifying Italy, and he invited the Chambers to devise such laws that the military unification would become a lasting political union. On 17 March Parliament unanimously confirmed the decree proclaiming Vittorio Emanuele King of Italy. In the general jubilation there was one sour note, which has confused tourists ever since. The King counted himself as Vittorio Emanuele *Second,* not *First,* in order to keep his sequence in the line of Savoy. It was a small point, but one that a King, who had been willing to sacrifice the province, ought to have been willing to make in the interest of unity. There were many, not only republicans, who felt that Italy was being subordinated to Savoy.

Ten days later Cavour concluded a series of speeches in which he discussed the problem of Church and State in the new kingdom. His program and goal were summarized by the phrase, "a Free Church in a Free State," and to this end he had been in secret negotiation with Pio Nono throughout the winter.

Even today the phrase on its face carries more meaning to persons with the political experience of England or the United States in their background than to Italians who for centuries have been accustomed to a complete overlapping between Church and State. In the United States, for example, it is assumed, merely because of custom, that a bishop will not seek to be elected to Congress. In nineteenth-century Italy, where even the election booths were set up in churches, the assumption was quite different. Any powerful man, cleric or layman, was expected to protect his interest by actively participating in the controlling political body. What Cavour proposed was a separation of Church and State, allowing each to be free within its own sphere, spiritual and political. He saw such a concept at work in England and heard it praised by laymen and priests known as "Liberal Catholics" in France and Bavaria. He planned to introduce it into Italy, but most Italians, whether peasant, man of Parliament, or Pope, had neither the intellectual capacity to imagine how such a foreign concept could work nor the opportunity to see it working elsewhere. In all his life Pio Nono, except for a one-year mission to Chile as a very young man, never set foot out of central Italy.

What Cavour offered Pio Nono in return for surrendering the remainder of his Temporal Power was close to what finally in 1929 Pius XI accepted under the concordat known as the Lateran Treaty. But 1861 was too soon; the negotiations failed, and Cavour's agent was given twenty-four hours to leave Rome. Very little is known of the Church's side of the discussions as the Vatican has denied historians access to the papers, but evidently some cardinals thought the proposal reasonable and wise.

An immediate result of its rejection was that Cavour in his speeches publicly proclaimed the doctrine of a Free Church in a Free State as the only possible solution to the problem of Rome and called on the Pope to accept it. At the same time he proclaimed that Rome must be the capital of the new kingdom, and the Parliament passed a resolution to that effect.

Verdi, who attended the sessions regularly, voted for it if only because he was not very independently minded and always voted exactly as did Cavour. "That way," he remarked, "I can be absolutely certain of not making a mistake." As a composer, however, he offered an expert's opinion to Cavour who, even in the midst of organizing a new kingdom, was considering plans for the government to continue the former Austrian and royal subsidies of the theatres and music schools. Verdi advised that the three leading theatres in Rome, Milan and Naples should have the choruses and orchestras maintained by the government. He was apparently willing to have the soloists and composers fend for themselves. Perhaps he felt that with three theatres in a position to produce opera continually, any good singer or composer would have a chance to be heard. He also wanted the conservatories to offer evening courses in singing free to the public provided the students agreed to put themselves at the disposal of the local theatres. Cavour expected to propose some sort of legislation at a later date.

After the speech on Rome, Verdi spoke with Cavour about resigning from the Chamber.

"It seems to me time I should be going about my business."

"No," replied Cavour, "let us go first to Rome."

"Are we going there?"

"Yes."

And then Verdi's undiplomatic nature rushed ahead: "When?"

"Oh, when, when! . . . Soon."

So Verdi stayed on in Turin, enduring the speeches and on occasion amusing himself by turning the political wrangles into musical notes. In his spare time he considered doing an opera on Victor Hugo's *Ruy Blas* for the Imperial Theatre at St. Petersburg. Eventually this project, using another libretto, resulted in *La Forza del Destino,* and in the memory of the politically inspired musical notes lay the seeds which twenty years later came to flower in the council-chamber scene of his revision of *Simone Boccanegra.*

In the first week of April Garibaldi came to Turin. He had spent the winter on Caprera where he had named his horses after his victories and the donkeys after the enemies of Italy still holding part of her sacred soil: Franz Josef, Napoleon and Pio Nono. Although he had retired to Caprera, he had received many visitors, particularly from the republican Left, and he had followed events on the peninsula closely. He came to Turin with a grievance.

The cause was the treatment of his volunteers by the government. Vittorio Emanuele had promised, too freely, that Garibaldi's army would be kept intact, but Cavour for diplomatic reasons and the regular officers of the Piedmontese army for reasons of administration and jealousy had declared it impossible. Instead, the better men were offered places in the regular army and the others given an honorarium and dismissed. The program was probably the only one possible, but in carrying it out the Piedmontese officers treated the volunteers with contempt and preferred their former enemies of the Neapolitan army over them. Garibaldi was enraged for his men and because he saw that without the volunteers there would be no campaign to free Rome or Venice in the spring.

For a number of days after he arrived in Turin he kept to his hotel with an attack of rheumatism. He had an interview with the King who was unable to influence him. He talked regularly with the republican leaders, and everyone knew that he planned to attack the government. In the Chamber the Deputies waited eagerly for him to appear.

On the afternoon of 18 April, as General Fanti was speaking to justify his treatment of the volunteers, cheering in the streets announced Garibaldi's coming. Fanti continued although the Deputies hardly heard him, they looked so hard at the door. But Garibaldi, who had an operatic sense of drama, did not come in the main entrance; instead, by a side door, he entered suddenly at the topmost row of seats on the Left. Against the black frock coats his red shirt and poncho moved like a tear in the cloth. He limped slightly, and friends helped him to his seat. For five minutes the cheering continued, then order being restored, he took the oath of Deputy and was seated.

The debate on the army continued. After Fanti several Deputies spoke and none very well. Then Garibaldi rose. From his seat he could be seen clearly by all the Deputies. In one hand he held several sheets of paper on which his speech was written. To read it he put on his glasses. He began slowly. His rich and beautiful voice filled the hall. Then he lost his place, struggled to find it on the sheets and finally put them aside. He began to speak his mind. Anger made the words pour out in a torrent of abuse. Vendetta on Cavour, who had tried to compromise the expedition to Sicily, who had opposed the fight for national unity, who had taken the fruits of the Thousand and then treated them with contempt! "Never," he cried, referring to Nice, "can I grasp the hand of the man who has made me a foreigner in Italy." Then sweeping along over the cheers and protest, he returned to his beloved volunteers. "I ought above all," he said, "relate their glorious feats. The prodigies they achieved were only stopped when the cold and treacherous hand of this very ministry sought to foment a fratricidal war . . ."

The words left his lips and returned in a roar of sound. Deputies everywhere leaped up, protesting, cheering, gesticulating. Cavour, who had borne everything till now, at the accusation of sending the Piedmontese army to fight the volunteers, pounded the ministerial table, demanding an apology. His face was fiery red. From his seat Garibaldi bellowed again, "Yes, a fratricidal war!" The Deputies poured down the aisles into the small space before the President's dais. One Garibaldian tried to strike Cavour and was hustled out. The President suspended the meeting.

When it resumed a quarter of an hour later Garibaldi still had the floor. He continued in the same style, and when Fanti attempted to answer him, tempers began again to shorten. Then Nino Bixio, a favorite of Garibaldi, and known as the Second of the Thousand, made a moving plea for peace.

Cavour rose at once. He spoke quietly, although his face betrayed the strain. Regarding Nice, he said, "I believe that I performed a painful duty, the most painful of my life, when I advised the King and proposed to Parliament the cession of Nice and Savoy to France. From what I myself have suffered I can understand what General Garibaldi has felt, and if he cannot pardon me for this act I cannot reproach him for it." Then he passed quietly on to explain the government's bill on the volunteers. When the applause ended, he added: "Deeply as I feel the injustice of certain charges made against me, I accept without hesitation the appeal made to me by General Bixio. For me the first part of this sitting is as though it had not happened."

The Chamber looked to Garibaldi to quit his seat and grasp Cavour's hand. But he would not move. Sometime later at the King's request Cavour agreed to meet Garibaldi in an interview at the Palazzo Reale. After Garibaldi's public announcement that he would never shake Cavour's hand, Cavour kindly did not advance it. And he reported to a friend that Garibaldi had kept his own "under his Prophet's mantle." Verdi throughout was Cavour's man and, although sympathetic to some of Garibaldi's grievances, considered that his actions in the Chamber put him in the wrong.

Not long after a friend warned Cavour that he looked ill, and Cavour wearily admitted that he had not been well since the *maledetta* struggle with Garibaldi. His nights were sleepless; he was troubled by vomiting, and his stamina was exhausted by overwork. At the end of May he took to his bed. The doctors, unable to diagnose the trouble, ordered him bled, and whatever the disease, the excessive bleeding, five times in four days, made recovery impossible. The King came to see him, and so also did a friar who had promised absolution, although Cavour was excommunicated. On the morning of 6 June 1861 he died.

Verdi at the time was at Sant' Agata and about to leave for Turin where he expected to have an interview with Cavour on the question of subsidies for the theatres. He also planned to report on what he had heard from friends in Naples about discontent there with the government's policy. But on hearing of Cavour's death he put off his return. He felt he could not go through the official services without breaking down.

Instead, both as a friend of Cavour and as a Deputy to the Parliament, he organized at his own expense a memorial service in Busseto. To his friend and fellow-Deputy, Opprandino Arrivabene, he wrote:

The service for Cavour was celebrated Thursday with all the pomp you could desire from this small paese. The priest officiated without charge, which is no small thing. I was present at the funeral service in full mourning, but the real mourning was in my heart. Between us, I was not able to keep back the tears and I cried like a boy . . . Poor Cavour! and poor us . . . (etc.)

Verdi in this instance was unfairly harsh in his grudging appreciation of the priest. The members of the Philharmonic Society who had played had insisted on being paid.

Cavour's death was recognized throughout Italy as a national disaster. The people sensed, and correctly, that the country had no other statesman or parliamentarian of his caliber. A corresponding disaster in the American Revolution, in which thirteen states united at a time when they were unusually rich in brilliant men, would have required the deaths of at least Franklin, Hamilton and Madison. And what remained to the new Italy was generally not the equal of its American counterpart. Vittorio Emanuele, for all of some excellent qualities, lacked the breadth of character and intelligence of Washington, and the surviving political leaders were not the equals of Monroe, the two Adamses, or Jefferson.

With Cavour's death Verdi's activity as a politician declined, and he resumed, more and more, his former role of interested spectator, always professing that he understood nothing about politics and yet continually making shrewd and even wise comments on it. He was to finish out the term of his office, dutifully going to Turin when he could, but refusing to stand for re-election. His allegiance to Cavour had been personal rather than based on party, and he did not transfer it to any of Cavour's successors. Verdi's short political career was, like his taste in reading, an instinctive response to greatness. He had followed Cavour into the strange field of parliamentary government; on Cavour's death he retreated gradually to the more familiar fields of his farm and his music.

Part IV

CHAPTER 30

LA FORZA DEL DESTINO AND THE INNO DELLI NAZIONI

1861–1863; AGE, 47–49

SOON after Cavour's death in June 1861 Verdi returned to Turin for a session of Parliament and while there signed a contract with the Imperial Theatre in St. Petersburg to compose an opera for the following winter. He had first planned to set Hugo's poetic drama *Ruy Blas,* but the management of the theatre had disapproved. Its verdict was relayed to Verdi by telegram and without reasons given. But they are not hard to imagine. *Ruy Blas* is one of Hugo's most effective plays, and it presents a valet of seventeenth-century Spain who loves his Queen. When he is used by a grandee to degrade her, he kills himself and the grandee. The political message of the play is clear: the aristocracy is vile and the future belongs to the People who are, in fact, far more noble. The Tsar, Alexander II, was personally rather liberal and probably knew nothing about the decision which some official of the management had made in his name, but as it well reflected the official atmosphere of St. Petersburg, Verdi did not attempt to reverse it. Instead, after casting around, he settled on a Spanish drama, *Don Alvaro, o La Fuerza del Sino,* which was accepted by the management.

The play, by the Duke of Rivas, had first been presented in Madrid in 1835 and with enormous success. Like Hugo's *Hernani* in Paris, *Don Alvaro* had established romanticism in Madrid and had a historic importance aside from its dramatic merits. Verdi seems to have considered it as a possible libretto as early as 1859. Now he began with Piave as librettist to make an opera of it, calling it by its second title, *La Forza del Destino,* or *The Force of Destiny.*

He worked throughout the summer at Sant' Agata while Strepponi

The letter opposite is an example of Verdi's extremely scratchy handwriting, which was never better and frequently much worse. It was written six days after Cavour's death, to which it refers, and on the official stationery of the Chamber of Deputies. The Chamber's crest is just visible in the upper left-hand corner.

In Italian the letter reads:

Caro Tamberlick

Torino 12 giugno 1861

arrivo in questo momento a Torino e trovo qui la vostra lettera e le scritture giacenti qui da qualche giorno.

La sventura che ci coglie è così grande che io non mi posso riavere. Non ho testa nè a leggere nè a parlare d' affari. Vi scriverò da qui a qualche giorno; del resto ritenete la cosa come fatta; metterò il paragrafo che domandate salvo il caso di malattia.

In quanto ai due drammi spagnuoliche m'indicate di leggere, fatemi il piacere di mandarmeli sotto fascia perchè qui non li troverei. Mandatemeli a Torino e prestissimo.

Di gran cuore addio addio

aff.

G. VERDI

In English:

Dear Tamberlick

Turin 12 June 1861

I am just this moment arrived in Turin, and I find here your letter and the contract which have been here several days.

The misfortune that has hit us is so great that I cannot get over it. I haven't the mind to read or speak of business. I will write you from here in a few days; besides, consider it done; I will insert the paragraph you want excepting the possibility of my falling ill.

As for the two Spanish plays you want me to read, please send them to me by registered mail as I won't be able to find them here. Send them to me here at Turin and as fast as possible.

Heartily good-by good-by

affec.

G. VERDI

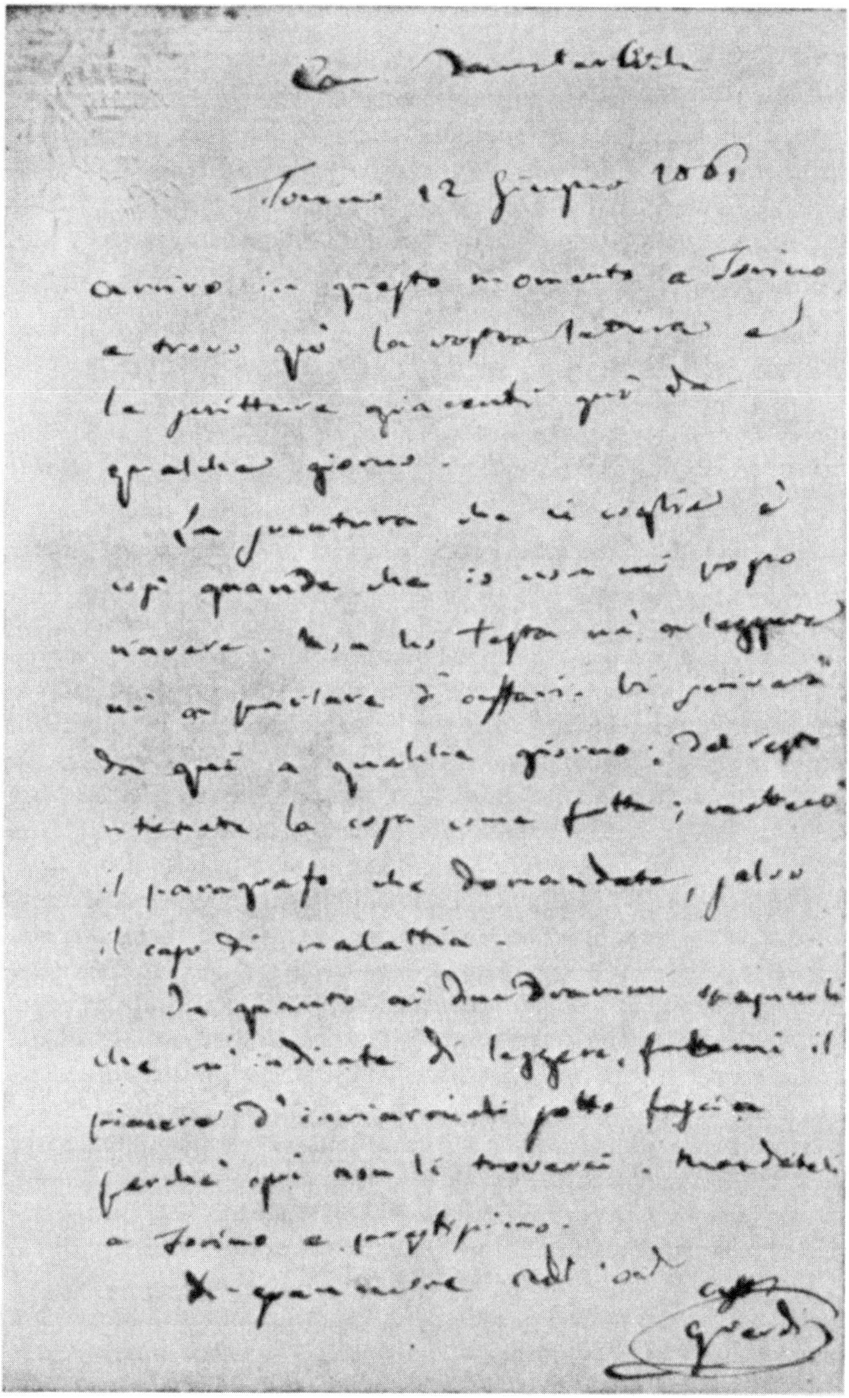

Car Durand…

Torino 12 Giugno 1861

Arrivo in questo momento a Torino
e trovo qui la vostra lettera e
le pitture giacenti qui da
qualche giorno.

La pittura che ci spedite è
così grande che io non mi so po…
… Ma le spese né … né
… per … parlare d'affari vi scriverò
da qui a qualche giorno. Del resto
… la cosa come fatta; vedremo
il paragrafo che domandate, salvo
il caso di malattia.

In quanto ai due… spagnoli
che mi indicate di leggere, fatemi il
piacere d'inviarmeli sotto fascia
perché qui non li troverò. Mandateli
a Torino e prestissimo.

Di gran cuore vostro

Verdi

made arrangements for the-trip, even to ordering the wine in advance: 100 bottles of ordinary Bordeaux for their daily meals, 20 bottles of a good Bordeaux and 20 bottles of champagne for the more special occasions. They expected to be in St. Petersburg from November through January, and as had become their habit, they planned to take two servants with them. Strepponi therefore ordered shipments of rice, macaroni, cheese and salami for four. And as she explained to a friend:

The noodles and macaroni will have to be very well cooked to keep him in a good humor in the midst of all the ice and furs! For my part, to avoid any trouble, I plan to let him be right in everything from the middle of October through January, for I know that while he is composing and rehearsing the opera is not the moment to persuade him that he may be wrong even once!

It was possible, on reaching Paris, to travel to St. Petersburg entirely by rail as the Russians had recently completed their end of the long line stretching between the two capitals. Only three years earlier when Dumas *père* had made the trip, he had been forced to choose between a carriage in Poland or the more comfortable steamers that ran from Stettin to St. Petersburg. Arriving by sea had a certain advantage, for the river Neva, about six times as wide as the Seine at Paris, gives St. Petersburg, built on flat, swampy land, its best claim to grandeur. But the river freezes hard for more than a third of the year, and Verdi in December could not have arrived by boat.

The city has always impressed its visitors with an indefinable tragic air that seems to belittle the beings living in it. In the extreme northern latitude the sun's rays slant in almost horizontally; the flat land stretches away to an infinitely distant horizon, and the canals and rivers with their cold, silent water seem to flow on in a self-contained life excluding man. If nature is not actively hostile, it is certainly uncaring, and man and the city both seem lost in the great, cold wilderness of the Russian north. Many cities have been built out of the sufferings of men, but so many laborers lost their lives in building Peter the Great's city on piles sunk in the cold marshes that it alone has kept the reputation of being built on bones.

Ever since its founding in 1703 Italian architects and musicians had lived and worked in St. Petersburg, and Verdi's visit to it, although a long trip, was not extraordinary. Italians had steadily dominated the opera there and only recently been challenged by German and Russian musicians. The leading tenor at the Imperial Theatre was an Italian, Enrico Tamberlic, who had sung for most of his career outside of Italy. He had acted as an intermediary between the management and Verdi in the negotiations leading up to the contract, and he had done so with considerable skill and patience. Verdi and Strepponi knew several of the other singers there and, of course, had introductions through the management to the city's society, but their particular friend was Tamberlic.

As usual, rehearsals began soon after Verdi arrived, and several weeks later the soprano fell sick. The première was postponed, but she did not improve and no suitable replacement could be found. Finally, at Verdi's suggestion, the première was rescheduled for the following autumn. Meanwhile he and Strepponi made a few sight-seeing trips and then in February started for home.

When he had got as far as Germany, he wrote Tamberlic:

Here I am at Berlin after a trip without sinister events except the appalling cold from Dunaburg to Kovno. We travelled 3 or 4 miles in an uncovered train in 33 degrees of cold to join the train of a Grand Duke who had stopped at the fort.—It is a terrible thing to be at the disposition of others, even a Grand Duke!—Now I understand the meaning of *cold,* and there was a moment when I seemed to feel in my head all the swords of the Russian army. If I could believe in another world, an inferno of ice as Papa Dante says, I would begin tomorrow to recite the *rosary* and *miserere* and ask pardon for all my sins done and not done. The railway carriages that took us from Dunaburg to Kovno were not heated and even the wine—a good wine of 5 rubles the bottle—turned to ice. We spent the night at Kovno. The food and bed were dreadful, but at least there we were warm. On arriving the following morning at the frontier, for us an *oasis,* all our troubles disappeared. There a kind official, most kind, very very kind, to whom you had telegraphed when I arrived at Petersburg—and I thank you for it with all my soul—excused me from all the boredoms of customs and passports and arranged for us to have an entire room in a carriage which brought us easily here. So ends the sad story!—After which I declare, protest, swear and bet that next year I will not leave Petersburg if the cold passes six degrees. I would rather stay there till the month of May. What will I do in all that time? I don't know . . . I will amuse myself, bore myself, curse, perhaps write . . . Yes, I shall write something we must sing in Campidoglio oh Rome Rome! . . . when will that day arrive! The dream of twenty years of life.

Pay my respects to Madame de Bourkoff and tell her that I hope in

London to regain her esteem that I lost by half, as she said to me! . . . But suppose at London I lose the other half? . . . then it would be better to stay home. (etc.)

Verdi expected to see the lady in London because he had accepted an invitation to represent Italy at the London Exhibition. The directors of it had asked Meyerbeer, who came originally from Berlin, to represent Germany; Auber, France; Sterndale-Bennet, England; and Rossini, Italy. But Rossini had refused on the ground of age, and the directors had appealed to Verdi not to let Italy go unrepresented. It was the sort of commission Verdi refused if he could. After the battle of Magenta he had politely evaded invitations from both La Scala and the city of Milan to compose a cantata to honor Napoleon III. And later he had refused similar invitations from Turin, Milan and Busseto to honor Vittorio Emanuele. But among musical entries for an international exhibition he evidently believed the new Kingdom of Italy should be represented. Perhaps he felt it was the sort of thing Cavour would have wanted him to do.

The cantata Verdi composed, the *Inno delle Nazioni,* or *Hymn of the Nations,* is set to a text by Arrigo Boito, a young Milanese recommended by the Contessa Maffei. Verdi, who was in Paris, met with Boito several times and gave the young man at the end of their collaboration a watch with the injunction to make good use of time. The cantata requires a chorus of the people and a solo voice, "the bard," and is closely tied to the events of 1859–60. The chorus rejoices that for the world a new reign of love is beginning, and the bard continues, explaining that out of the fury of battle God has willed a new brotherhood of man. Chorus and bard then join in a prayer that is marvelously secular. After a slight nod to the Lord, blessings are asked on England, "queen of the sea and ancient symbol of liberty," on France "which generously shed its blood for an enslaved land," and on Italy, "oh patria mia." Prussia, although represented musically at the Exhibition, was ignored. It had done nothing for Italy.

The cantata runs about fourteen minutes, and because he had just been rehearsing with Tamberlic in St. Petersburg and knew the tenor would be in London during the Exhibition, Verdi composed the bard's part with Tamberlic specifically in mind. It requires a strong, dramatic voice that will ring out over the chorus. The music is appropriately stirring and, like Tschaikowsky's *1812 Overture,* for the last half presents national songs first separately and then combined. England is represented by *God Save the Queen,* France by *La Marseillaise,* and Italy by Novara's setting of what was known as *Mameli's Hymn.* At the time Verdi's choice of anthems was considered rather startling and a sign of his inveterate republicanism. *Partant pour la Syrie* and not *La Marseillaise* was the national anthem of the French Empire, and *Mameli's Hymn,* written and composed in 1847, was simply a popular republican song particularly associated with the defense of the Roman Republic. Today, when both France and Italy are republics, *La Marseillaise* and *Mameli's Hymn* are their national anthems.

Verdi and Strepponi left for London in April, and on arriving there he was at once plunged into a controversy. The musical director of the Exhibition, Michael Costa, refused to perform Verdi's cantata on the ground that it was not a purely orchestral work as commissioned. This may have been true, but, as Verdi pointed out, some variety was necessary for the good of them all. Meyerbeer submitted a string of marches ending with *Rule Britannia;* Auber, an *Overture;* and Sterndale-Bennet, an *Ode.* Newspapers at the time hinted that the real cause of the trouble was Costa's jealousy of Verdi. Costa was a Neapolitan who had made his career in England, becoming one of its best conductors and composers, and he perhaps felt that he should have represented Italy. When a local impresario arranged to give the cantata in a theatre, Costa in his role as director of the opera at Covent Garden refused to release Tamberlic to sing it. So Verdi rewrote the bard's part for a soprano, and the public, which generally had sided against Costa, made the cantata a success for a number of performances. Thereafter it does not seem to have been performed until Toscanini resurrected it for a concert in the Milan arena during World War I. A newspaper described the occasion as "an explosion of patriotism." Again during World War II Toscanini used it as a concert for the benefit of the Red Cross in New York's Madison Square Garden and in a United States propaganda film he made shortly before. For this he added to the end of it in honor of Russia and the United States the *Internationale* and the *Star-Spangled Banner,* and in this version a recording of it has been issued. The fact that the cantata requires singers has kept it out of the repertory of concert orchestras, so that when it is occasionally revived it can make an impression. It is not great music although better than either Tchaikowsky's *1812 Overture* or Beethoven's *Wellington's Victory,* celebrating a Napoleonic defeat in Spain.

Perhaps what Verdi enjoyed most in his stay in London was buying two guns, a carbine and a small double-barreled shotgun, and he wrote excitedly to Mariani in Genoa, inviting him to Sant' Agata to try them. There were duck in the marshes along the Po, and a specialty around Busseto was quail. These last were not as large as the American quail but about the size of a large robin or squab. They were as often netted as shot and were generally served whole, roasted or broiled, on a bed of rice. Verdi prided himself on preparing a delicate rice, and one of Delfico's caricatures shows him in a kitchen at Naples cooking it.

On the way back to Sant' Agata Strepponi fell sick in Genoa, and then at home one after another of the servants came down with a fever known as the tertian ague. To Verdi's embarrassment he had to put off Mariani's visit and also one from the British Ambassador, Sir James Hudson, who was another hunter. To add to his troubles Strepponi's sister in Cremona fell ill, and the dog, Loulou, died. In his garden Verdi put up a small shaft of marble over Loulou's grave and had inscribed on it: "To the memory of one of my most faithful friends." In her bedroom Strepponi kept an oil portrait of the dog, painted on the trip to Naples in 1858.

The dog was Strepponi's and in her letters she spelled his name "Loulou"; Verdi, in his, "Lulu." It is a small example of the sort of independence they preserved even after they married. Always she bought her clothes out of her own money, made her own contributions to charity and kept quite separate accounts from him. They did not consider their marriage a merger of all their interests, and they did not do everything together.

It was a troubled summer politically for Italy, and for a time there even seemed to be a possibility of civil war in the south. The immediate trouble arose out of the restlessness and prestige of Garibaldi and the ineptness and even duplicity of the government in handling him. The more long-range trouble lay in the Parliament's inability or reluctance to grapple with the problems of the south.

The Kingdom of the Two Sicilies at the time of its annexation to Piedmont and the other northern states had been the biggest geographically, the largest in population and the richest in an absolute sense. At the same time much of its land was useless without draining and irrigation, its population had a high proportion of peasants, all desperately poor, and its per capita wealth was the lowest of the various states. The difference between the two areas is symbolized by the fact that Piedmont in the year of unification had more than half of the railroad mileage in all of Italy. And what there was around Naples, about a hundred miles, did not operate on saints' days or in Holy Week, and although the countryside was mountainous, no tunnels were allowed lest in their darkness public morality should suffer. Inevitably on unification when, overnight, all the customs barriers dropped, the Piedmontese industries operating in the suddenly enlarged market tended to put the more delicate Neapolitan industries out of business. This even was true in Parma and Modena. Further, Naples lost all that went with being a capital, such as the government employment, the court, or being the primary naval base. On top of this Francesco II and Pio Nono in Rome financed guerilla warfare in the mountains where it was almost impossible to track men down. At the time, of 1,848 villages in the old southern kingdom, 1,621 had no roads at all. The result was that the government at Turin, in trying to rule the discontented, suffering area, resorted to press censorship and martial law, in fact the same sort of oppressive government it claimed to have driven out. It was accused with justice of operating without understanding or charity.

Vittorio Emanuele might have done much, but he neither understood nor cared for the people of the south and he made it plain. One of Cavour's first appointments to Sicily had written back to him: "Our Southerners need to know the person *materially* and to see it, in order to love it . . . Four or five promenades . . . would arouse greater sympathy for the King, than four or five acts of civic virtue or military valor . . . *Garibaldi showed himself lavishly.*" And Garibaldi, not the King, was the hero of the south. Legends about him grew naturally and were nurtured by his followers until the simplest peasants readily confused him with Christ come the second time.

From these troubled waters the King and cabinet somehow hoped to fish out Rome and Venice. But without Cavour they had no considered plan. They surreptitiously urged Garibaldi on to raise another army of volunteers in Sicily and allowed him to cross the Straits and begin the march north to Naples and Rome. But they had not thought out how to achieve what they wanted, and when the great powers, particularly France, protested, they lost their nerve. On 29 August the regular army located Garibaldi and his ragged volunteers on Aspromonte in Calabria and fired on them. Garibaldi's men were under orders not to fire on their countrymen and most obeyed, but several, on seeing their neighbors hit, fired back. In all seven soldiers and five volunteers were killed. Deliberate aim seems to have been taken at Garibaldi personally, for he was hit twice, most seriously in the ankle. Sitting on a rock he lit a cigar and calmly ordered his men to amputate at once if necessary. Taken prisoner, he was treated as a traitor. The government issued seventy-six medals for valor to its soldiers and promoted the colonel in charge to general. But most of Italy was disgusted. Royal proclamations were torn down and government officials hissed. In the end the government simply let Garibaldi go free, in spite of the terrible example it set the country in political responsibility, both Garibaldi's and the government's. But it did not dare try him for treason or discipline him, for everyone suspected that it had not only connived and encouraged but actually aided him.

Even so, Verdi held Garibaldi rather than the government responsible. Verdi was, depending on the point of view, either growing in wisdom or merely more conservative with age and acquired wealth. Perhaps also now that Italy had an Italian government he felt Italians should support it. Strepponi, who probably reflected Verdi's thoughts, wrote tartly to a friend after Aspromonte: "As for the simple Garibaldi, he has dropped far in the opinion of right-thinking persons."

Just two weeks before the incident at Aspromonte Verdi refused to consider a performance of his *Inno delle Nazioni* in Italy because of the "imminent danger of civil war." He was also preparing to leave soon for St. Petersburg where the delayed première of *La Forza del Destino* was scheduled for early November. This time when he and Strepponi arrived, the city's odd habit of painting its churches green, its prohibition against smoking in the streets, and the long stretches of wooden paving, all seemed familiar. Most of their acquaintances from the previous visit had returned, and, as the rehearsals went well, Verdi and Strepponi had an enjoyable time.

The première was on 10 November 1862 and presented an opera different in several important respects from the one generally heard today. The opera was successful in St. Petersburg, but even so Verdi evidently was dissatisfied with it. In the next seven years he allowed only a single production of it in Italy, at Rome where entitled *Don Alvaro* it was moderately successful. Meanwhile it played in New York, Vienna, Buenos Aires, London, and with Fraschini as Alvaro had a great success in Madrid. Nevertheless Verdi revised it.

The St. Petersburg version, like the play, tells the story of Don

Alvaro, a Spaniard pursued by an implacable, evil destiny. As the opera opens, Don Alvaro is attempting to elope with his betrothed, Leonora, and wholly without intent kills her father. In fact his gun fires accidentally and fatally at the very moment he is throwing it to the ground as a symbol that he will not bear arms against the old man. In his intent, honor and remorse, Don Alvaro is everything that Don Giovanni, who also kills his lady's father in the first scene, is not.

Thereafter nothing goes right for Don Alvaro. He and Leonora flee, but they are separated by a crowd in Seville and he believes her dead. He goes to Italy under an assumed name and fights with Leonora's brother, who has provoked a duel to avenge the family. Don Alvaro wins and, believing he has killed the brother, calls himself cursed and rushes off into battle to get himself killed.

But both he and the brother survive, and Don Alvaro retires to a monastery in Spain. There the vengeful brother finds him, provokes another duel and again is wounded. Alvaro rushes to a hermit nearby to ask him to absolve the dying brother. The hermit, by *forza della coincidenza,* turns out to be Leonora in disguise, and as she attempts to aid her brother, he recognizes and stabs her. He dies, then she dies, and finally as a procession of monks arrive chanting a "Miserere," the despairing Alvaro jumps off a cliff to his death.

The Duke of Rivas' play has the same qualities as Gutiérrez's *El Trovador* from which Verdi and Cammarano had made *Il Trovatore.* Both plays offer great blobs of passion mixed with scenes of local color, gypsies, monks and townfolk. Both are constructed episodically, more in the style of an epic poem than a play. Much of importance happens off-stage; loose ends are left unraveled, and nothing is too improbable to be taken seriously. In fact the "acts" are more like "cantos," in that they strive less for cumulative effect than for individual impact. In this respect, at least, *La Forza del Destino* is the antithesis of *Rigoletto.*

The changes Verdi made in the opera suggest that he felt it had failed as a drama, which it inherently was not, and would do better as a series of episodes, which it really was. In the St. Petersburg version described above the emphasis is primarily on Don Alvaro. The opera started with a short, gloomy prelude which ended with the suicide music foreshadowing Alvaro's unhappy end. In the revision Verdi replaced this with an eight-minute, potpourri overture that ends in an accelerating galop of excitement. The suicide music is gone because of changes in the final scene. There Alvaro still curses Heaven, but now he is reproved by the dying Leonora and a single monk who has replaced the original version's procession. Leonora, in the most saintly way, dies as Alvaro at her feet agrees to live out the life destiny still may have in store for him. The scene is Leonora's rather than Alvaro's, and a picture of triumphant piety has replaced one of furious despair.

In the preceding act Verdi changed the order of scenes so that it no longer ended with Alvaro believing that he has killed Leonora's brother and rushing into battle to get himself killed. This note of despair Verdi pushed back into the middle of the act and brought to the end an interlude of gay life among the camp followers. The change has the same effect as substituting the brilliant overture for the gloomy prelude.

Taken all together, the changes weaken the dramatic core of the opera, destiny's pursuit of Alvaro, and strengthen its episodic character. An indication of this is that producers, taking their cue from Verdi, constantly cut and shift scenes in an effort to reduce the four sprawling acts with several changes of scene to something more manageable. Generally the scenes of local color are cut, the monks distributing food to the poor, the camp followers whooping it up in Italy, or tavern life in Spain. But the more that is cut, the more unsatisfactory and improbable seems the drama that remains. The libretto is, alas, incurably defective.

The music, however, is extraordinary, particularly in two respects unusual for Verdi. The first is his success with the religious scenes. Leonora separated from Don Alvaro by the crowd in Seville and believing he has gone off to Peru, takes refuge in a monastery. In a series of numbers she prays to the Virgin, explains her plight to the Father Superior, and persuades him that it is God's will that she be a hermit attached to the monastery. The Father Superior gathers the monks together, introduces the "hermit" to them, and in a choral finale all agree never to disturb "him" in his solitude as the Virgin will protect Her child. The scene is one of the opera's most effective because the music, although unabashedly theatrical, sustains throughout a sense of humility, awe and reverence. Verdi as far back as *Nabucco* and particularly in *I Lombardi* had composed prayers and religious choruses. But these succeeded, when they did, more for their theatrical impact or the beauty of their musical lines rather than for any religious quality in them. But with the convent scene from *La*

Forza del Destino Verdi succeeded in sustaining a genuinely religious tone. Evidence of this is that such a discriminating conductor as Bruno Walter sometimes performed it during Holy Week.

The other point of special interest in the opera is the sense of humor with which Verdi treated Fra Melitone, one of the monks. Melitone is a peevish man, lazy and decidedly unelevated by his religion. When the Father Superior dismisses him so that he will not overhear Leonora's troubles, Melitone mutters, "Always secrets! And only these holy ones can know them. We others are so many cabbages." Like Oscar, the page in *Un Ballo in Maschera,* Melitone provides a contrasting air of comedy throughout the opera. Verdi's ability to depict all types of men was increasing.

The opera has been steadily popular in Italy and in recent years increasingly so elsewhere. But not so much for the technical points as for its fantastic wealth of melody. As in *Ernani* and *Il Trovatore,* the Spanish subject seems to have particularly inspired Verdi. In the Romantic Age Spain fascinated many European artists; perhaps because it conserved, in a more primitive state, passions which, in their own countries, had been weakened by community living. The country and its drama seem to have excited Verdi in this fashion. Another side of him could see that the well-constructed French plays had a different and perhaps greater power to which he responded with more sophistication. But to the Spanish plays he responded simply by matching their raw, elemental passion with equally straightforward passionate melody. As operas *Ernani, Il Trovatore,* or *La Forza del Destino* are easy to criticize or even ridicule until discussion reaches the theatrical success of the melodies. Then the critic's squeaky voice is overwhelmed by the roar of public approval.

But for seven years, except for the one production at Rome, Verdi withheld the opera from the Italian public, and they knew nothing of it except that it existed.

CHAPTER 31

MACBETH REVISED
AND THE CHANGING TIMES

1863–1865; AGE, 49–51

AFTER the performances of *La Forza del Destino* in Russia Verdi and Strepponi went directly to Madrid for the opera's première there. Then, as they had done in Russia, they spent several weeks seeing the country. They traveled mostly in Andalusia where they visited Seville, Cordova, Granada and Cadiz, and at Xeres Verdi bought a cask of the famous wine and had it shipped to Sant' Agata. At the end of the trip they returned directly to Paris, for Verdi had agreed with the Opéra to stage and direct rehearsals of a new production of *I Vespri Siciliani*. The Opéra had wanted to do *La Forza del Destino*, but Verdi, uncertain about the opera and unhappy over the singers available for it, had refused.

The rehearsals for *I Vespri Siciliani* went badly. It was July and hot. Verdi asked the orchestra to repeat a section he felt had gone too fast, and the men played it with exaggerated slowness. According to a footnote in one of the earliest biographies, that of Pougin-Folchetto, published in 1881, Verdi rapped the music stand and then said to the management's representative:

"This is a bad joke!"

The gentleman, a M. Dietsch, replied, "Well, these men don't believe there is any need for this rehearsal."

"You don't say!"

"Look, they have their business interests . . ."

"Ah," Verdi exclaimed. "They have their business interests which are other than those of this opera . . . So be it."

And he put on his hat and walked out.

The incident caused a scandal. Verdi had in the past year been elected a foreign member of the French Institute and thereby attained a certain hallowed position in the eyes of the authorities. Peaceful overtures were made toward him and M. Dietsch was eventually removed. But Verdi did not return. For a while he examined the new buildings in Paris, the new boulevards and parks, and then he returned to Sant' Agata.

His difficulties with the Opéra, as he well knew, involved not a single man but an approach to artistic business. The French government, whether republican or Napoleonic, subsidized the Opéra and appointed its officials. In the long list of its directors holding office during Verdi's maturity there is not one of any artistic importance. They all operated by press release, promotional stunt and hired applause, and the best composers, foreign and French, with the exception of Meyerbeer, did their best work elsewhere. The Opéra, as the most important theatre in the city that functioned as the capital of Europe, was the goal of composers everywhere, but it was more famous for its intrigue and bureaucratic slights and snubs than the quality of its productions.

This atmosphere spilled out into the audience whose interests it reflected. The Parisians and French provincials, who made up the bulk of the audience, cared less about the quality of music they heard than its setting: Was the Empress present? Did she approve? What was the position of the Jockey Club? Was it more chic to admire this soprano or that?

The answers to such non-musical questions often determined an opera's fate, at least in Paris. Only two years before Verdi's incident the Opéra had finally capitulated to Wagner and his supporters and produced *Tannhäuser,* sixteen years after its première in Dresden. But the Jockey Club, the popular name for the "Society for the Encouragement of the Improvement of Horse Breeding in France," had taken a stand against the opera because its only ballet occurred in the first act. "Les Jockeys," many of whom supported ballerinas, did not wish to have to hurry their dinners in order to see their favorites pirouette in fetching costumes. They informed the Opéra's director of the problem, and he tried to explain it to Wagner. But Wagner was stupidly artistic: he could see only that in the first-act "Venusberg" scene a ballet was suitable, whereas in the second-act "Tournament of Song" one was not. He refused to make any changes. "Les

Jockeys," among whom were several important government officials, thereupon organized their protest. The première passed unmolested, but at the second and third performances, naturally after the first act, hooting and howling broke out in all parts of the theatre and continued to the final curtain. At the second performance the Empress, who was known to favor the opera, remained resolutely seated in her box. No one had eyes or ears for what was happening on-stage. After the third performance Wagner withdrew the opera, and it was produced again at the great French theatre only thirty-four years later, in 1895.

Verdi had not been in Paris during the *Tannhäuser* performances, but his agent, Escudier, had described them in a letter and he certainly heard about them from his Parisian friends who attended Rossini's Saturday-night music parties. Verdi had not met Wagner, and it seems probable that even in 1863 he had not heard any of his music, at least as played by an orchestra. *Lohengrin* was the first of Wagner's operas to be produced in England (1875) or Italy (1871). Wagner was still best known for his polemical writings although, of course, people did not hesitate to discuss the music which they had not heard. Probably the first of Wagner's music Verdi heard was the overture to *Tannhäuser,* played at a concert in Paris in 1865.

Quite independent of Wagner in Germany there was the beginning of a school of "new" music in Italy. Its adherents were the best of the recent graduates of the Conservatory in Milan, and the most articulate of these was Arrigo Boito who had composed the text for Verdi's *Inno delle Nazioni.* Being a writer as well as a musician, Boito became the spokesman for his fellows. He argued, quite correctly, that in Italy the practice of instrumental music had fallen behind that of Germany and France, and he urged that chamber-music groups be established such as he had heard in France. In opera he urged that melodrama be put aside for true drama, by which he meant librettos in which the characters were psychologically true and rounded and not merely manipulated to create exciting situations. In one article he pointed out how much better *Rigoletto* was than *I Lombardi,* and on this point Verdi would have agreed with him. For Verdi, in fits and starts and without theorizing about it in public, was steadily tending toward the same conclusions as Boito.

But Boito was only twenty-one and wrote in a youthful flamboyant style that often submerged his meaning in a surge of rhetoric. And

BOITO

on one occasion his rhetoric became offensive to the point of horrifying his friends and alienating Verdi, quite unnecessarily. Perhaps more important, he offended the journalists and opera lovers who supported Verdi and thereby helped to create an unnecessary division in the Italian musical world.

The occasion was a dinner in the autumn of 1863 to honor Franco Faccio, another young Conservatory graduate, whose opera *I Profughi Fiamminghi* had just been produced at La Scala. Perhaps the fact that it had been only moderately successful excited Boito, but at the proper moment at the feast he rose, glass in hand, and gave a toast to Italian Art. The words were obviously premeditated, for they flowed out as an ode in the four-line stanzas of sapphic meter.

One stanza proposed: "Here's to the health of Italian Art. May it soon escape, young and healthy, from the encircling limitations of the old and idiotic ways."

Another prophesied: "Perhaps he is already born, modest and pure, who will resurrect art on its altar, that altar now stained like the wall of a whore house." (The image Boito evoked was that of the brothel's outside wall, discolored and noxious, where the men, emerging with their lust satisfied, generally stop to urinate.)

Shortly thereafter the entire ode was published, clearly with Boito's approval, for he must have given the text to the editor. Boito nowhere identified who was responsible for the "old and idiotic" ways, or who had peed on the altar, but everyone understood both references to be to Verdi. Certainly the savior was Faccio, in whose honor the ode was written.

Faccio, who like Boito had met Verdi in Paris, was appalled, and he wrote directly to Verdi, expressing the honor in which he held him. He also asked the Contessa Maffei, whose letter of introduction to Verdi he had used, to write Verdi on his behalf. The Contessa's letter Verdi answered at once.

Referring to Faccio's opera, he said:

I know there has been much talk about this opera, too much I think; and I have read a newspaper article where I found big words about *Art, Esthetics, Revelations* and the *Future,* etc., etc. I confess (great ignoramus that I am!) that I understood none of it . . . On the other hand I am not acquainted with Faccio's talent or his opera; and I don't want to know it in order to avoid discussion or judging it, things I detest because the most useless in the world. *Discussions* never convinced anyone; *judgments* are generally wrong. Finally if Faccio, as his friends say (and even Verdi believes Boito's eulogy is for Faccio) has found new ways, and if Faccio is destined to put Art back on the altar now *fouled with the stink of a whorehouse,* so much the better for him and for the public. If he's *straying,* as others assert, then may he put himself back on the right road, if he so thinks, and the road seems right to him.

To Tito Ricordi, who had also written him, Verdi observed: "If I among others have dirtied the altar, as Boito says, then let him clean it and I will be the first to come and light a candle."

Shortly thereafter Verdi wrote a polite letter to Faccio, wishing him good luck with his career. The incident was closed, except that in a society as small as that of the Po Valley the discussion went on, and whether Verdi liked the role or not, in everyone's mind he was cast as leader of the old guard.

His isolated way of life and the longer period between each new opera, particularly with *La Forza del Destino* withheld, seemed to confirm the opinion that he was half-retired. He served as a Deputy in Parliament, managed his farm which he had enlarged and planned new additions to his house and garden. The house he wished to have comfortable, and when he had made it so he ceased to fuss over it. The garden, however, was a continual interest and his particular pride. It exists today just as he left it and is more of a park than garden, covering about two acres with closely planted trees and shrubs. The fashion in parks at the time, which Haussmann, in redesigning Paris, both followed and helped to set, was that of an informal English park with a serpentine pond and, if possible, a grotto. The best grottoes in the new Paris parks were even furnished with artificial stalactites and stalagmites. Verdi did not attempt such professional touches, but he built a small grotto, about twenty feet in diameter and shaped like a beehive. It has two entrances curving in from opposite sides and screened inside from each other, so that a hermit escaping by one cannot be seen by a visitor entering the other. The pond lies lazily looking up at the sky, and between the willows and poplars the paths come down to its edge and then retreat again. Mostly the paths wander in leisurely curves, but two are straight alleys, each leading down to a gate letting out onto a plowed field. For the Villa Verdi was a profitable, working farm, and if the improvements to the house and park progressed slowly, it was because most of the workmen, including Verdi, spent most of the day out in the fields.

But even the park could not make the winters at Sant' Agata anything but "brutta," cold, wet and windy. And although Verdi would have been happy to stay trudging over his fields, for Strepponi's sake they began to spend their winters regularly in Genoa, renting an apartment with a view of the harbor and close to their friend Mariani. Genoa, protected by the mountains encircling it, has a warm climate. Palm trees line its streets, and flowers bloom all winter. Verdi particularly liked it because the Genoese were interested in their business and left him undisturbed. Also he could go easily by train from Genoa to Turin for the sessions of Parliament.

Verdi's travels to Russia and Spain had caused him to be absent from the sessions for most of two years, but whenever he was in Italy, he attended regularly and served on committees. Yet when elections for a new Parliament were announced for June 1865, Verdi did not stand. He considered, as he wrote to Piave, that he had neither the aptitude nor talent to be a Deputy and was "completely lacking in the necessary patience."

One difficulty with any form of parliamentary government is that it irresistibly attracts a nation's windbags by providing them a forum in which their puffings cannot be brusquely stopped. This difficulty was compounded in the Italian Parliament because, in the first rush of freedom, most Deputies were against restrictions of any sort. They also lacked the experience of their British counterparts in making the parliamentary system work. The Piedmontese Deputies, who had at least had twelve years' experience, were swamped when the entire peninsula began sending Deputies to Turin. Another difficulty, partly arising from the others, was that no party emerged strong enough to rule alone and impose a party discipline. In the four years after Cavour's death there were five different prime ministers. Government was by coalition and personality, and consistent policies were sacrificed to expediency. This difficulty has continued to plague the Italian Parliament to the present day. With the exception of Mussolini, a somewhat special case, only Depretis, 1881–87, and De Gasperi, 1945–53, have managed to repeat Cavour's hold on the office. Of the forty-eight other terms of office, in the period 1860–1960, thirty-seven have been for approximately two years or less, and of these, twenty-five for about a year or less. To Verdi and his contemporaries, as they watched the government change hands five times in four years, it seemed as though their representatives thought more of maneuvering to get into office or to stay there than of governing the country. Garibaldi in 1863 had resigned his seat in disgust. When Verdi took his seat as a Deputy for the last time, in 1865, he still believed firmly in a republican form of government, but he too was somewhat disenchanted with the men operating it. His disappointment and frustration reflected the mood of the country.

In these years his musical career seemed to have come to a standstill or at least passed into the hands of others. Fraschini, the tenor, had gone from Madrid to Paris where he had scored a tremendous success at the Théâtre Italien in *La Traviata*. So much so that two years later the Théâtre Lyrique produced the opera in French as *Violetta* and had an equal success. Verdi was pleased and agreed to revise *Macbeth* for another production in French at the Théâtre Lyrique. The idea had originated with Escudier, who suspected that of all the early operas Verdi would be most eager to revise *Macbeth*. Meanwhile in Italy his better operas continued as popular as ever, with the standard of perfection for performance set by the productions Mariani staged and conducted at the opera houses in Genoa and Bologna. Earlier Mariani had produced an exceptional *Un Ballo in Maschera* at Bologna, and then in the autumn of 1864 he revived *Ernani* there for a new soprano, Teresa Stolz, who came from Bohemia. La Stolz, as she was immediately christened, sent both the crowd and critics into ecstasies. She was tall with large features well balanced, so that she had a statuesque beauty. Her voice was strong, clear and suited to dramatic roles, particularly those by Verdi, of which she made a specialty. Mariani cast her for as many productions as he could, and the gossips began to whisper that his interest was more than artistic.

But performances by others, however pleasing, were not the same thing as composition, and although Verdi toyed with several ideas, the only one he realized was the revision of *Macbeth*. Strepponi hoped he would go to Paris for the rehearsals, for as she wrote to Escudier, in Sant' Agata she was *"royally* bored." But instead Verdi went to Turin for his last session as a Deputy, and then the two of them went on to Genoa.

The revised *Macbeth* was remarkably unsuccessful, both in Paris and elsewhere. In Paris it ran for only fourteen performances, and elsewhere the new version replaced the old in an occasional revival but never came close to touching the popularity of the more successful operas. Verdi was disappointed. He wrote to Escudier: "When all is said and done, *Macbeth* was a fiasco. Amen. I admit, though, that I did not expect it. I was thinking I had not done too badly, but it seems I was wrong."

The troubles were various. Musically the revision was only half successful in that it was not sweeping enough. To ears grown familiar to the sonorities of *Un Ballo in Maschera* or the delicacy of *La Traviata,* some of what Verdi left unrevised sounded painfully like a caricature of himself. The new sections were neatly done but without any particular brilliance, and the old parts presented the same old problems. In spite of Boito insisting that the public was ready for true, psychological drama, of which some of the scenes between Macbeth and his Lady were good examples, the receipts at the box office showed plainly the public was not.

The Parisians had flocked to the Théâtre Lyrique to hear Gounod's *Faust* which in its original form with spoken dialogue connecting the waltz melodies was almost an operetta. Lady Macbeth at the same theatre, shattered by her crime and dying unredeemed, was not such a satisfying picture to them as Marguerite asking the angels to carry her soul to heaven and being redeemed right before their eyes. The revised *Macbeth* also, most unfortunately, had to compete with the première of Meyerbeer's last opera, *L'Africaine,* at the Opéra. The Parisians had waited twenty-seven years for *L'Africaine,* and Meyerbeer had finally finished it only to die as it went into rehearsal. The timing of his death, though not of Meyerbeer's choosing, nevertheless suited the publicity-minded directors of the Opéra, and they whipped the Parisians up to a froth of excitement over the première.

The opera is in the usual five-act form and, uncut, runs for more than six hours. The first two acts are set in Portugal, the third on shipboard, and the last two somewhere in East India. The opportunity for contrasting scenery could hardly be greater, and the shipboard scene alone is one of the most complicated in opera, calling for a lengthwise section of the vessel to reveal the interior decks and cabins. But that was just the beginning. The carpentry had to be flexible enough to toss and roll as a violent storm broke on the vessel and yet remain firm enough, after being dashed on a reef, to support hordes of savages clambering over the rail to massacre all the Portuguese. Against such genocide *Macbeth* with its single murder, discreetly off-stage, and dreary old Glamis castle, scene after scene, could not begin to compete.

As always Verdi took his defeat silently. He protested only to Escudier in a private letter and then only when one of the French critics accused him of not knowing his Shakespeare. Carried away by his indignation, he incriminated himself with his spelling: "Perhaps I did not render *Macbeth* well, but that I don't know, that I don't understand Shaspeare, no, by God, no! He is one of my favorite poets. I have had him in my hands from my earliest childhood and I read and re-read him continually."

That same spring in Genoa, Boito and Faccio presented their attempt to make an opera of Shakespeare with *Amleto,* the music by Faccio and libretto by Boito. It was not a great success although the production, with Mariani conducting, was excellent and all the "intellectuals" from Milan rallied to the première and chattered afterward how good it had been. Verdi did not go, but his friends like Mariani and Piave promptly wrote him their opinions, which generally were unenthusiastic. This might have been expected from his friends, but the proof of the pudding was in the eating. *Amleto* was given one other production at La Scala in 1871 and never thereafter revived.

But Faccio's failure was no consolation to Verdi, for it did nothing to help Verdi devise a form for new operas which would satisfy his own artistic feelings as well as the public's taste. Rossini's biographers, for example, agree that one reason Rossini wrote no operas after *William Tell* in 1829 was that he felt himself to be increasingly out of touch with public taste. When younger he had often followed a success with a fiasco, but he had never doubted he knew what the public wanted and how to provide it with artistic examples. With the beginning of romantic opera he was less sure, and in 1865 he was still alive, living in Paris and occasionally composing lovely music but no longer anything as vast and uncertain as an opera.

Bellini in his ten operas with a single fiasco had, in his melancholy vocal melodies, perfectly expressed a moment in the Romantic Age. Then he had died just as in the improved drama and orchestration of *I Puritani* he began to face the next moment. Donizetti also by death escaped having to make any real change, although his later operas show him consciously moving toward Verdi's more dramatic style. Verdi himself, without having gone to the Conservatory, could see that his own style had changed: through 1848, operas on patriotic themes with set numbers; thereafter, a more fluid form in which a more melodic recitative joined set numbers more dramatically apt to make a more even and continuous flow of music. He had changed and with him the audience. The year 1848 with its abortive revolutions had perceptibly altered the social and artistic atmosphere in Italy and even more so had the year of its political unification. Younger musicians like Boito did not hesitate to predict that Verdi could not keep abreast of the times even as some of Boito's political counterparts insisted that Garibaldi, with his abortive campaign in Aspromonte and constant rumblings about Rome and Venice, no longer could see what was good for Italy.

The problem of keeping abreast, or even better just ahead of the times, is one that every artist presenting himself to the public faces consciously, for the general rule surviving a rare exception is that no work of art can have a timeless success unless it first has a success in its own time. Artists claiming to work for an audience yet to be born are deluding themselves.

How to keep abreast each artist decides according to his nature. If he is a doctrinaire, he will be determinedly in the avant-garde, flogging the public with polemics. Traditional natures keep returning to the great classics, believing that he who reads well will write well, in words or sound. Instinctive artists pretend, sometimes sincerely, that the problem does not exist. Verdi was a mixture of the last two. When he could be persuaded to give his views on musical education, he put the greatest emphasis on Palestrina and Marcello, two of the great choral composers in Italian music. And he advised "Attend but few performances of contemporary opera." To his friend Torelli, in Naples, he wrote about Torelli's son who wanted to be a dramatist:

He should imitate no one, especially not the great; and now, now only (may the schoolteachers forgive me for it) can he stop studying them. Let him lay his hand on his heart and study *that;* and if he has the true stuff of an artist that will tell him all. He mustn't be puffed by praise, nor frightened by blame. When criticism, even the most honest, confronts him . . . let him always go straight on.

Criticism has its function; it judges and must judge according to established rules and forms. The artist must peer into the future, see in its *chaos* new worlds, and if on the new road he sees far, far ahead a *tiny* light, let not the surrounding darkness terrify him. Let him walk on, and if sometimes he stumbles and falls, let him get up and go always straight on. It's a good thing sometimes, a fall, even for a headmaster . . . But good Lord what am I prating about here? (etc.)

Verdi, however, kept abreast of his times in more ways than he perhaps realized. Darwin, for example, published his *On the Origin of Species,* one of the most important books of the century, in 1859. Verdi in 1865, with no Italian translation yet in print, ordered a copy to be sent to him in either the French translation or the original English. Few artists are so quick to keep up with science in a second language.

And when he went to Paris he always examined whatever new thing Haussmann had done: gaslights replacing oil for the streets; spring water, brought for miles on aqueducts, replacing filtered river water; or the Avenue Richard Lenoir with a park down its center built over a working canal which had been lowered twenty feet to avoid a multitude of individual bridges. When some years later a building boom began in Italy he followed the construction in Milan and Genoa with the same interest, particularly in Genoa where his friend, the engineer Giuseppe De Amicis, was in charge of much of it. By inspecting the new housing and discussing sewage systems Verdi saw what was happening in Italy: the enormous increase in population, the growth of the cities and the middle class in them, and the almost complete obliteration of the aristocrats with their way of life, education and faults.

In keeping abreast he was well served by the diversity of his friends. Besides Mariani and Ricordi in the musical world, his particular cronies were De Amicis, an engineer; Opprandino Arrivabene, a journalist; Giuseppe Piroli, a lawyer and politician; and that astute woman of the world, the Contessa Maffei. In Rome and Naples there were groups of friends centered on Luccardi, a sculptor, and De Sanctis, a man of business. And Verdi himself was a farmer. His view of the world, for a composer, had an unusually wide angle.

Keeping up with new music he found more difficult. As he confessed to Arrivabene, reading orchestral scores was not much help as he could not take in music "by eye." But if new music that interested him was scheduled for a concert, he would go if he could. In Italy it was difficult, for his presence was apt to start a demonstration, which he disliked. And he heard most of his new music in Paris. When he and Strepponi were in Paris in the fall of 1865 he went to a concert to hear the overture to *Tannhäuser* and to the Opéra to hear *L'Africaine*. The opera, he felt, was "not one of Meyerbeer's best," and the overture he found confusing. To the Contessa Maffei he privately confessed he thought Wagner "mad."

He had gone to Paris to stage a revised version of *La Forza del Destino* at the Opéra and also to discuss the possibility of a new opera. After his stomping out his return took some persuasion by Escudier, but the Opéra was the leading opera house of the time, paid the best commissions, and planned to perform the new opera during the next Paris Exposition in 1867. The infamous Dietsch had been replaced, and the director and Escudier assured Verdi that this time the atmosphere would be different. The projected revision of *La Forza del Destino* fell through; Verdi and the director could not agree on the changes, and Verdi again was dubious about the singers available for it. For the new opera several subjects were discussed including *King Lear,* which Verdi felt was "magnificent but not spectacular enough for the Opéra." He evidently wanted to make a drama, not a spectacle of it. In the end he agreed to an opera based on Schiller's *Don Carlos,* and when he returned to Sant' Agata in March 1866 he had the completed libretto and had already begun work on the score. Under the terms of the contract he was to complete the opera by the end of June and be in Paris to start rehearsals immediately thereafter. The première was set down for November.

CHAPTER 32

DON CARLO

1865–1867; AGE, 51–53

THROUGHOUT March and April Verdi worked hard on *Don Carlo*, even leaving to others the breaking of his foal "Gisella." But in May the threat of another Italian-Austrian war interrupted him. This time, he felt, it might be fought in the area of Parma as the Italian armies crossed the Po into Venetia or, worse, as the Austrians crossed into Italy. To avoid the possibility of being caught between armies he and Strepponi retired to Genoa. Through Escudier in Paris he asked the Opéra to agree to a delay in turning over the score. He had already finished the third act and was started on the fourth. "With that done," he explained to Escudier, "I shall consider the opera finished, because the fifth act will be and must be written in a flash [un momento]. I know that this flash does not come every day, but in eight or fifteen days one ought to come."

One of the most interesting side benefits for posterity of Verdi's political life was a remark he made to Quintino Sella, the Deputy who sat next to him in the Chamber. Sella, trained as a geologist, became one of Italy's best economists and served in a number of cabinets between 1862 and 1876 as the Minister of Finance. He asked Verdi: "When you are composing one of your stupendous pieces of music, how does the idea present itself to your mind? Do you work out the main theme first and then add an accompaniment to it, and then afterward consider the nature of the accompaniment, whether it shall be for flutes or violins and so forth?" Verdi interrupted, "No, no, no. The idea comes complete, and above all I feel the color of which you speak, whether it should be for flutes, violins and so forth. My difficulty is in writing down the musical thought quickly enough to capture it in its integrity just as it comes into my mind."

But for the idea to come at all, to have its moment of being heard whole, there were evidently days of necessary trial.

The war which Verdi feared is known in history as the Austro-Prussian War or the Seven Weeks War, lasting from 15 June to 23 August 1866. It was deliberately provoked by Bismarck in order to expel Austria from the German Confederation, and at its end, although Prussia took no territory from Austria, it annexed the smaller German states of Hanover, Hesse-Kassel, Nassau and Frankfurt. The unification of Germany under Prussian leadership had begun.

Italy, which had secretly allied itself with Prussia, played a minor and humiliating part in the war. The generals of the Italian armies refused to co-operate with each other, and one foolishly attempting to attack the Quadrilateral was defeated at Custozza. The battle was hardly more than a skirmish, but the morale of the men was so low and the apprehension of the generals so great they did nothing more, except for Garibaldi. He, despite the obstacles raised before him by the regular army, succeeded with volunteers, among whom were both Boito and Faccio, in capturing much of the Trentino, the area through which the Adige flows. His campaign was the only Italian success in the war, for the navy fared even worse than the army. In the battle of Lissa, the first large engagement between ironclad steam fleets, the Austrians with seven ships defeated the Italians with fourteen. The Italian admiral even contrived not to be on his flagship when it was rammed and sunk. Fortunately the Prussians defeated the Austrians at Sadowa, and Bismarck quickly made peace. By its terms Austria gave Venetia to France, and Napoleon III, after the inevitable plebiscite, turned it over to Italy. Garibaldi was forced to withdraw from the Trentino which remained with Austria, as did also the Istrian Peninsula with Trieste and Fiume.

The Italian people, particularly the north Italians, were humiliated and disgusted. The admiral was court-martialed, and the generals, although spared, demeaned themselves with public accusations and retorts. The defeat, for no one pretended there was any victory, shook the people's confidence in the armed forces and even the King. For it was clear that in his appointments he had often ignored merit to advance favorites and had held back Garibaldi in order not to be dwarfed by his general's prestige.

Verdi was so upset at what he took to be the national dishonor that he asked the Opéra to cancel the contract for *Don Carlo*. (The opera's

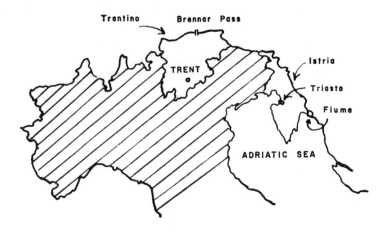

*The shaded area shows the northeastern boundary of Italy from 1866 to
1919. After World War I it acquired the Trentino and the Istrian Peninsula.
It acquired Fiume in 1924. After World War II it lost Fiume and most of
Istria to Yugoslavia.*

title is generally spelled without the final "s"). As Verdi explained to
Arrivabene, "Imagine what it is like to be a patriotic Italian and find
one's self in Paris now." But the Opéra refused, and Verdi and Strepponi set out for Paris as the war ended in the final weeks of August.
They planned to go by Cauterets in the Pyrenees, where they hoped
the hot sulphur waters would ease Verdi's throat which was very sore.

The war had come too soon for Italy, which was still struggling to
make a nation of itself. In some respects it has a superficial resemblance
to the United States War of 1812 in which that young country associated chauvinism with unpreparedness, confused the appropriate roles
of the civilian and military in wartime, and to its immense surprise and
chagrin lost its capital to the more experienced British. Italy had more
excuse, for its problems were greater than those facing the United
States. And although Italian leadership was poor, much of the disaster
was founded in the more basic difficulties of the new country: its
regionalism and conflict with the Church.

Many of the difficulties of amalgamating into one nation areas differing in racial stock, language and tradition could only disappear in
time. Lamarmora, one of the unfortunate generals, was the last prime
minister of the country, 1864–66, who as an adult had to learn Italian

as a new language. Among the uneducated, such as in the ranks of the army, any communication had often to be put in two tongues. Centuries of suspicion did not disappear at once, and within the army Piedmontese and Neapolitan soldiers often regarded each other with hostility.

The position of the Neapolitan soldier was doubly difficult in that the brigandage in the south, which frequently had assumed the proportions of a civil war, had ended only in 1865. The brutality of the hit-and-run fighting had left southern peasants and landowners embittered with each other and hostile to the national government. In the five-year campaign more men perished of fighting and malaria than in all the battles of the Risorgimento. But the fact that the national army had finally defeated the adherents of Francesco II as well as a number of simple outlaws did not mean the government had found any solution to the more difficult problems of poverty and ill-health. And the people remained sullen and hostile.

Even between northern Italians there were bitter differences. In September 1864 Italy had signed a convention with France by which Napoleon III agreed to withdraw his troops from Rome if Italy agreed to transfer its capital to Florence as a pledge that it had given up its designs on Rome. No one, except perhaps Napoleon, believed that Italy had done so more than temporarily, but the decline in property values in Turin and rise in those at Florence were permanent enough to cause severe riots in one and smug rejoicings in the other. The move, a large undertaking, was done most efficiently within six months. It was a move toward developing a greater sense of unity, but as Florence was short of Rome, many felt it was purposeless and merely cost the Parliament its sense of tradition in Turin.

Over all and cutting through all the regions was the problem of the Church. In the south it had helped to finance the civil war and used its priests and bishops to transfer orders and information. This was relatively simple and expected. Church property was often confiscated, its orders suppressed, and its finances regulated, even as they had been in Piedmont. It was considered natural that the Church should defend itself, and most Italians believed that in time it and the State would come to some sort of agreement resulting in a concordat. Meanwhile Vittorio Emanuele, as the head of the State, continued under a bull of major excommunication while corresponding regularly with the Pope and while his people still counted themselves good

Catholics and for the most part went regularly to Mass. When Pio Nono had disciplined the friar who had given absolution to Cavour, most Italians approved, for there was nothing else the Pope could do. But they had also approved when the State granted the friar a pension. It was all perhaps illogical, but it was very much in the tradition of Italian history.

But in December 1864 Pio Nono had issued an encyclical accompanied by a Syllabus of Errors that seemed to preclude any accommodation between Church and State in Italy at any foreseeable time. Further, it condemned the premises on which the most liberal states of the time were founded and as such seemed an incredibly reactionary attack on all that was best in the nineteenth century.

The Syllabus, strictly speaking, was a private letter addressed to bishops everywhere as a guide for instructing Catholics. It begins: "A Syllabus, containing the principal Errors of our times" (etc.), and then lists eighty propositions which Pio Nono considered erroneous. Among those condemning such things as pantheism, Bible societies and communism were others which stigmatized freedom of conscience and religious toleration (No. 77), freedom of discussion and the press (No. 79), and finally (No. 80) the idea that "The Roman Pontiff can and should reconcile and harmonize himself with progress, liberalism and recent civilization." ("Romanus Pontifex potest ac debet cum progressa, cum liberalismo et cum recenti civilitate sese reconciliare et componere.")

The language was harsh and the denunciations sweeping; the Syllabus everywhere, among Catholics as well as others, aroused indignation and confusion. Neither subsided when the Bishop of Orléans tried to explain that the Pope had in mind the principles for "the perfect society" rather than those that might be expedient or even just for an existing society. Many Europeans and Americans had come to believe that toleration and freedom of thought and press were ideal principles and the only ones on which a "perfect society" could exist. The Syllabus strengthened and heartened the authoritarian party within the Church; it also strengthened the anti-clerical party outside it. And in conjunction with other actions by Pio Nono, notably a Brief in which he restricted the freedom of scientific research for Catholics, the Syllabus ended any sort of "Liberal-Catholic" movement within the Church that might have reached an agreement with the moderates of the State. Monarchists and republicans had been able to compromise conflicting ideals to achieve a unified Italy; the Church, believing its ideals were God-given, rejected any compromise. Its position created enormous difficulties for the new Kingdom of Italy; it also generated a constant and lively discussion of which Church policies were God-given and truly religious and which merely self-serving and political. As Vincent Sheehan remarked in *Orpheus at Eighty:* "The true religious miracle of the age took place against Pius IX and the entire machinery of the Church: it was that the Italian people could oppose the Church in politics, systematically and steadily for two or three or four decades, and *still* remain devoutly, overwhelmingly Catholic."

In a Europe arguing the issue of Church and State Schiller's play *Don Carlos* undoubtedly struck Verdi and his librettists as an ideal subject for an opera. It discussed the same issue but at several centuries remove, at the court of Spain under Philip II and the Inquisition; thus it combined topicality with the glamor of great days past. Schiller's play, which he called a "dramatic poem," is an embodiment of his belief in liberalism and hatred of tyranny. Its characters and situations are not historically accurate but transformed, in typical Romantic fashion, to express in a seemingly self-contained, ancient world what were really Schiller's private, modern emotions.

The historical Don Carlos, Philip II's son and heir, was a pathetic young man, physically and mentally twisted, violent, cruel and wholly unable to adjust to the environment into which he was born. All his short life he carried one shoulder higher than the other, as a child had a speech defect, and at eighteen still weighed only seventy-six pounds. His antagonism to his father, the source of all regulation and prohibition, was that of a frustrated child, uncertain and unreasonable. After a fall downstairs which was followed by a primitive brain operation his violence increased, and he is supposed to have made at least six homicidal attacks on men who had denied him something. He planned to escape to Flanders, which was in revolt against Philip, and foolishly revealed his plan to his uncle who could only tell Philip. Shortly thereafter Don Carlos was arrested by his father in person and imprisoned; six months later he died. Protestant princes at once claimed that Philip had ordered his son's death. Protestant historians have echoed the charge, and their Catholic opponents denied it. Without conclusive evidence the wrangle continues.

Schiller idealized this unhappy prince into a young man, sound of limb and mind, hating tyranny and opposed to his father as the em-

DON CARLO

bodiment of it. In the play Don Carlos is all for liberty and wants to go to Flanders to give the people freedom, of conscience as well as person. Even more liberal than Don Carlos is his friend, the Marquis of Posa, who dares to tell Philip directly that his policy of repression and the Inquisition will make a graveyard of Flanders even as it has of Granada in Spain. Historically the Marquis of Posa is an impossibility: any man who felt as he did, much less voiced his opinions, could not have existed at Philip's Court. But in the play his humane ideals are nobly expressed and he is an attractive character. Philip is drawn to him, wants him for a friend, and warns him to beware of the Inquisition. Philip is a man torn between his sense of duty as he has learned it from the Church and his natural desire to be humane as stimulated by the Marquis of Posa. His character is the most interesting in the play, and Schiller wrote of it: "I do not know what sort of monster one expects when Philip II is mentioned. My drama collapses when such a monster is found in it."

Schiller further humanizes Philip by presenting him as a husband eager for his wife's love and fearing that she prefers his son. To present this Schiller creates an elaborate story that has no historical basis. In the play Philip's third and current queen, Elisabetta di Valois, had first been betrothed to Don Carlos, Philip's son by his first wife. Then for reasons of state Elisabetta had been required to marry the King rather than his heir. But while betrothed Elisabetta and Don Carlos had met and fallen in love. Nevertheless, married to Philip, she had been faithful to him. But Philip cannot be sure, and what ultimately makes him hand Don Carlos over to the Inquisition for imprisonment and death is a mixture of political duty as instructed by the Grand Inquisitor and simple jealousy.

The triangular relationship in the play is awkwardly presented and not very convincing. Don Carlos constantly calls Elisabetta "Mother," which was the etiquette of the Court, but when taken in connection with Don Carlos' peculiar antagonism to his father, it suggests that perhaps Schiller was groping toward the presentation of a Freudian Oedipus complex. But with Freud still in the future, Schiller lacked the vocabulary to explore the psychological concepts clearly in his own mind and to reveal them to the audience.

Verdi and his librettists evidently found the triangular relationship confusing, for to clarify it they added to the story a new first act which served as a prologue. In it they present Elisabetta as a young girl at the Court of France meeting with Don Carlo, her betrothed. The two spend an idyllic afternoon together only to be separated forever by the arrival of the Spanish Ambassador who claims her hand for Philip. In the play this is only mentioned. Making it explicit in the opera lessened a confusion but also a subtlety. Philip and his son are closer now to the stock "rivals" of Italian opera.

Another subtlety unfortunately hammered into a stock operatic situation involved an important lady of the Court, the Princess of Eboli. She, too, was a historic person, a lady of great beauty who because of a riding accident wore a black patch over one eye. In the play she has been Philip's mistress but is in love with Don Carlos. She sends him a note setting an assignation, and he, thinking the note from the Queen, appears at the appointed place. There is no confusion of identity, but in the course of the conversational fencing each discovers the other's guilty secret. It is one of the play's best scenes, each line doing double duty as the characters understand it differently. In the opera the subtlety is replaced by a case of mistaken identity. Don Carlo carries on a long conversation with a veiled lady whom he persists in believing is the Queen, although her figure and mezzo-soprano voice proclaim clearly that she is Eboli. At this point the audience can fairly ask if it is supposed to take the opera seriously.

To meet the Opéra's requirements for a spectacular scene the librettists added an auto-da-fé in the great square of Madrid. Philip and his Court come to see the heretics burned. There is contrasted choral singing between the Spaniards and some Flemish burghers who are present and a colorful procession of monks and heretics. The former carry crucifixes and Bibles; the latter, as in history, walk barefoot, hold long green candles and wear "sanbenitos," short smocks with red crosses on the front and back. The play had scenes whose only purpose was grandeur and the opera's spectacle fits easily into the story.

Finally, a change for the worse was made to the play's closing line. It ends with Philip handing his son over to the Grand Inquisitor: "I have done my duty. Now do yours." The librettists followed this exactly except that as the Inquisitorial guards step forward, a mysterious monk appears and whisks Don Carlo away. It is suggested that the monk is Philip's father, the Emperor Charles V, but who he is or why he appears is never made clear, and the opera closes on a sudden, unnecessary confusion. As it occupies less than twelve bars on the final page of the score, some producers omit the monk and end the opera like the play.

The libretto had an obvious appeal for Verdi. It offered a hymn against tyranny and in Philip a great character. In this mind Verdi heard Philip as a bass, as he had heard Attila. But there was more than just Philip, for most of the characters had more than one side to them. There was Elisabetta as the Queen, as the young wife of a middle-aged man and as a lonely French woman in a hostile Spanish Court. If every side to her lot was unhappy, there were at least differences and gradations, each of which contributed to the ultimate tragedy. She was not simply the soprano for whom the tenor alternately raged and pined and about whom the audience knew nothing except that she was the soprano. In this respect *Don Carlo* is a better opera than *Il Trovatore:* it has more depth. In the same way it is better than *La Traviata* which, although it probed deeply into Violetta, did so in a private world. *Don Carlo* attempts to probe just as deeply into its characters' private emotions while at the same time recognizing the public world in which they live and which shapes them.

Verdi was conscious that he was attempting something new, and he was nervous. In June 1866 when the war was just beginning he wrote to Escudier: "Composed in the midst of flame and fire, either this opera will be better than the others or a horrible thing."

The rehearsals went well except that in the middle of them Verdi's father died at Vidalenzo. He had been sick and was eighty-two years old, so that his death was not unexpected. Yet Verdi felt it deeply and for a number of days gave up coaching the singers. He worried about the fate of his aunt, aged eighty-three, who had a granddaughter of seven. Both had been living with his father, and he wrote to Sant' Agata to have them moved in there. Then he worried about them left to the care of his servants. "You can just imagine," he wrote to the Contessa Maffei, "whether I, who have so little faith in anything, can have any in the reliability of two servants now practically masters in my house." (etc.)

Finally on 11 March 1867 *Don Carlo* had its première. Verdi did not wait for the second performance but started at once for Sant' Agata. Within a week he was home attending to his family and bossing the spring planting on his farms.

The opera was neither a success nor a failure. Verdi, on the basis of the première, wrote Arrivabene: "It was not a success! I don't know what the future may hold, but I shouldn't be surprised if things were to change." (etc.) Verdi was both too cautious and too hopeful. The opera was performed throughout the balance of the Exposition year forty-three times, hardly a failure; and yet the Opéra in his lifetime never revived it, hardly a success. In the same period *I Vespri Siciliani* was revived twice.

Everyone had an opinion as to why *Don Carlo* was not more of a success. Partisan Italians complained of a nationalist opposition. Once again French composers and critics, supposedly angered at Verdi being asked to compose for an Exposition, were accused of intriguing against the opera. But this kind of opposition, if it ever existed, was certainly defeated by the number of performances.

More important, and unquestionably a fact, was that the Empress Eugénie disliked the opera. She was a Spaniard, an ardent Catholic, and had the Pope as godfather to her son. She found the opera offensive. There comes a moment when Philip is talking with the Grand Inquisitor and tells him to hold his tongue, "Tais-toi, prêtre." At that moment the Empress ostentatiously turned her back on the stage, and those influenced by such actions considered themselves instructed. Again, measured against forty-three performances, the action was unimportant, yet it attached to the opera, seemingly forever, a suggestion that it is somehow anti-Catholic. When in 1950 the Metropolian presented *Don Carlo* for the first time in twenty-eight years, pickets from various Catholic societies paraded before the doors. Interrogated by a reporter, they confessed they had not seen the opera but understood that it was "against the Church."

Unquestionably from a musical point of view the Opéra production was poor. Soon after the première Mariani at Bologna and Costa in London each produced the opera with fewer rehearsals and greater artistic success. At the Opéra the orchestra played with a languid beat and the chorus was sloppy. Strepponi observed to a friend about the Opéra: "They spend twenty-four hours deciding if Faure or Sax etc. ought to raise a finger or a whole hand." The essentials were ignored.

But when every reason was considered and the defects put right, the fact still remained that *Don Carlo* had, at best, an uneasy success. In trying to please everyone, it combined various forms of opera and completely satisfied no one. Those who liked Meyerbeer enjoyed the spectacle; the traditionalists liked certain favorite arias, and the avant-garde enthused over Verdi's new technique for handling conversation. The discussion on liberty, for example, between the Marquis of Posa and Philip was set not as a burst of lyrical effusion, an aria, but as a dialogue. Verdi was accused of imitating Wagner. This irritated him, and he wrote to Escudier: "If the critics had paid more attention, they would have seen that I was striving for the same effect in the trio from *Ernani*, in the sleepwalking scene in *Macbeth* and in many other numbers . . . But the question is not whether the music of *Don Carlo* belongs to a system but whether it is good or bad. That question is clear and simple and above all the right one to ask." (etc.)

The charge of imitation was unfair. It was to be another four years before Verdi saw his first Wagner opera, and what he had done in *Don Carlo* was anyway rather different from what Wagner was attempting. But Wagner's star was rising, and for a while everything was judged by its light.

The discussion turned, however, on the way Verdi handled his dialogues. In the opera there are three of them extended enough to form short but complete dramas by themselves: Elisabetta's interview with Don Carlo, Posa's with Philip, and Philip's with the Grand Inquisitor. The musical technique underlying them, as Verdi observed, harks back directly to his earlier operas, particularly to *Rigoletto* and the scene in which Rigoletto meets Sparafucile.

As there, in the dialogues of *Don Carlo* Verdi often put the tune in the orchestra while having the singers converse in snatches of the melody or even merely declaim on notes that have a special relation to it. Thus when the Grand Inquisitor enters he is accompanied by a melody in the orchestra which is also used to end the scene as he goes out.

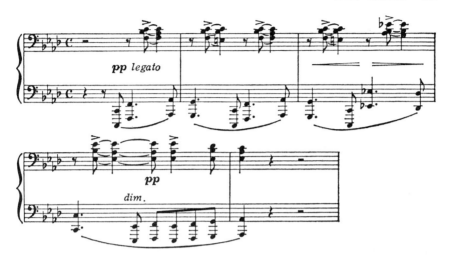

No one ever sings the melody, but the next two examples show how Verdi relates their declamation to the harmony of it. In the first Philip declaims steadily on A flat, "Se il figlio," etc., which is the dominating tone of the melody at that moment. Notice how it regularly occurs as the top note of the accompanying chords and how in the octave melody of the bass the highest note coming just before Philip begins, the "lead-off" note, is an A flat. Then notice how on "la tua mano" Verdi makes the voice follow the drop in the accompaniment from G flat to F. This little turn gives a slight feeling of finality to the words. The audience senses that Philip has finished the sentence.

In the second example Philip actually follows the melody but only for three notes. Then he begins another declamation.

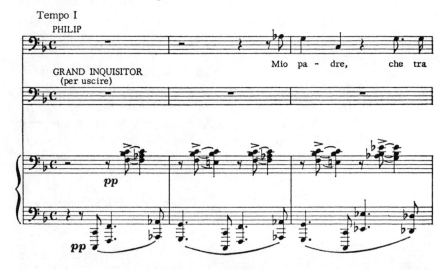

In the theatre the dialogue sounds melodic yet it is neither melody nor recitative in the older style. No one is tempted to whistle Philip's line. The style of writing was best described as "music drama," and at the words everyone cried "Wagner." But Verdi did not use his themes as Wagner did his. When the Grand Inquisitor appears later in the opera, his music is not a transformation or development of his previous music. Nor, for the most part, were Verdi's melodies or "themes" suitable for this sort of treatment. They are too long and too individual. Wagner's themes are generally short or of a kind that can be easily truncated.

But for the time being the charge of imitating Wagner stuck to Verdi. Critics wrote learned articles about it with, of course, the implication that better than the imitation was the real thing. At the same time all Europeans began to take an increased interest in all things German. This was partly because of the rise of Prussia and the fascination and fear of Bismarck, but it included all kinds of cultural activities, particularly German philosophy and music. In Italy Boito and Faccio with their emphasis on chamber music were manifestations of it. In "keeping abreast" everyone turned increasingly to see what was happening in Germany. Italian opera as it had been practiced in the past was said to be on the decline, and as evidence of it, Verdi's last really successful opera, some persons argued, was *La Traviata,* now fifteen years old. Verdi said nothing publicly, but the half-success of *Don Carlo* disappointed him and for several years he turned down all suggestions for operas and worked instead on his farm.

ONE OF VERDI'S FARMS

CHAPTER 33

MANZONI AND ROSSINI

1867–1869; AGE, 53–56

VERDI'S mood after *Don Carlo* was black; he was both grieved and puzzled over the opera's fitful success. In the coming year it was to do well in Bologna and Milan but to fail in Bordeaux, Brussels and Darmstadt. The rule seemed to be that with the best singers and conductors it could succeed but that, unlike *Rigoletto* or *La Traviata,* it could not carry itself in the provinces. On the national scene he raged over the indecisive government. It was impossible to forget the disasters of Custozza and Lissa, for during the spring elections Garibaldi made them a national issue, speaking from balconies to enormous crowds and insisting the defeats could be wiped out only by a national uprising to take Rome. In his family life Verdi felt the loss of his father and was forced to recognize that Barezzi, who was almost eighty, was also dying. To the Contessa Maffei he observed: "This is an ill-fated year for me, like 1840!"

In his black moods Verdi was his most bearish. He would rise early, stomp out into his fields, scold his farm help and exhaust himself with physical labor. In the house Strepponi would hardly hear a word from him. Outside the men would mutter that it was a bad day and those who could would find something to do in the furthest field. His men regarded him as one of themselves and more with envy than admiration. Once from behind a hedge he heard one tell another: "He draws little hooks on paper and then buys possessions." It all seemed improbable, but they could understand and respect his ability as a farmer. Like Cavour, he had made his farms models for his district.

Since Strepponi could not tramp the fields, Sant' Agata was often a lonely place for her, particularly when Verdi was in a silent mood. So they decided to make a permanent second home in Genoa, where

Verdi rented unfurnished the *piano nobile* of the Palazzo Sauli at No. 13 Via San Giacomo. In the same building Mariani, who had found the apartment for Verdi, kept some rooms on the top floor for himself as Verdi's subtenant. In May Strepponi left Verdi farming at Sant' Agata while she went to Milan to buy furniture.

Without telling Verdi of her plan she did more. She called on the Contessa Maffei. The two ladies had never met, although for more than twenty years Strepponi had watched the letters between Verdi and the Contessa leave and enter the house. The Contessa's letters often contained a greeting for Strepponi, and she in turn sometimes added her good wishes in Verdi's letters. But without a meeting mere politeness could develop into nothing more, and Strepponi must often have been sadly aware that she had no place in one of Verdi's most important and satisfying relationships. They had invited the Contessa to Sant' Agata the previous year, but she had been unable to come. So now Strepponi, unannounced, called on her.

The two ladies liked each other at sight, and both later reported that at first meeting they literally fell into each other's arms, laughing, chatting and even weeping a bit. During the visit the Contessa suggested she introduce Strepponi to Manzoni, for she knew Verdi considered him to be one of the two greatest living Italians. The other was Rossini, whom Verdi had met often in Paris. But Manzoni he had never met. And although he would often ask the Contessa for news of Manzoni, he never would ask for an introduction, respecting the other man's privacy as carefully as he guarded his own. If he had known of the Contessa's suggestion to Strepponi, he probably would have tried to dissuade both women from it. But Strepponi, who also knew Verdi's feelings about Manzoni, was delighted with the suggestion and bore away from her visit a photograph of the great man on which he had written: "To Giuseppe Verdi, a glory of Italy, from a decrepit Lombard writer."

Strepponi then described her arrival back at Sant' Agata to the Contessa, whom she was already addressing as "Clarina" and using the familiar "tu":

Verdi was waiting for me at the station at Alseno with little Filomena [the seven-year-old girl he had taken into his house after his father's death]. As soon as we were in the carriage he asked me about my family and what success I'd had in Milan with the furniture. I said that I had shopped around a great deal without finding anything much I wanted, that

I had seen the Ricordis, Piave and his family, and that, although short of time if he'd given me a letter to you, I'd have presented myself, in spite of a certain reluctance because of the *embonpoint* which for the last three years has kept me from sitting in the circle of ladies of sentiment. While he was laughing and calling me *capricciosa* (a flattering term he uses for young girls, which I have not been for some time), I slipt your note gently out of my bag and tossed it on his knees. He glanced at it and looked up with a grin so broad I could see a row of white all the way back to his wisdom teeth! Then with a rush like a cavalry charge I told him how you had received me, how you had gone out with me (something very unusual for you), how foolish I'd been to waste twenty years before knowing you, and he kept repeating, "It doesn't surprise me, it doesn't surprise me; I know Clarina." And wishing to add one last turn I said in an offhand way: "if you go to Milan, you must call on Manzoni. He expects you, and I was there with her the other day." Pouf! The shock was so great and unexpected that I didn't know whether to open the doors of the carriage to give him air or to shut it lest in a burst of surprise and joy he might leap out. He turned first red, then pale, and began to perspire; he took off his hat and kneaded it so hard he almost made a cake of it. But more (and this is just between us) the very stern, proud bear of Busseto had tears in his eyes, and we were both so moved, so upset, that we sat there for ten minutes in complete silence. (etc.)

Verdi's reverence for Manzoni has some of the simple, all-inclusive and ridiculous quality of that of a schoolboy for his hero. He inextricably entwined Manzoni the man and the myth in a way that he did not with Rossini. The reason may lie partly in Manzoni's background and way of life. Verdi and likewise Rossini in the previous generation had both been born to humble parents. Both had scrambled around in life and, in making a success, had learned a little something. But Manzoni by birthright had the sort of education that Verdi undoubtedly felt he could never achieve. Manzoni's grandfather, Cesare Beccaria, was an eminent economist and jurist who had an international reputation for his work on the punishment of criminals. Manzoni's mother had taken him to Paris where between 1805 and 1810 he had immersed himself in French literature and thought and met most of the leading political and religious philosophers of the time. He moved by right of birth and the quality of his mind in a world that was remote from Verdi's and yet was the world which had started Italy on the road to unification and independence and also provided its first martyrs in men like Count Confalonieri.

Manzoni's world had also given him the breadth of culture to write a book like *I Promessi Sposi* in which the peasants, townfolk, clergy and aristocracy all seem equally real in their faults and virtues. Verdi was aware that in *I Lombardi* or even in *Rigoletto* he had not achieved such reality for his characters or their world. In *Don Carlo* he had plumbed deeper than in *Rigoletto* but without popular success. Some of Verdi's admiration was for Manzoni the artist.

He also admired Manzoni the man, modest and retiring. In fact, Manzoni was morbidly shy, but Verdi saw him as an artist working without personal publicity and promotional stunts. Manzoni is known to have made only one speech in public, during the Cinque Giornate, and even privately he deprecated his own works. He made very few public gestures, but those he did were important. The only time he went to Turin to vote as a Senator, for example, was to support changing the capital from Turin to Florence. Many persons in the Po Valley criticized him for this, and because of his political attitude the Church looked on him with suspicion even though he had undertaken to defend it against the Calvinist historian, Sismondi.

Many, including Verdi, thought of him as a holy man, a "sant' uomo," and the Contessa used to visit him every Sunday after Mass and afterward make notes on their conversations. He seemed to be a man who by reason and faith had attained an inner peace or moral repose in the passions of life. His quiet manner and his retired yet public life seemed to confirm this. Actually he was not so fortunate. Even in his eighties he was still searching for such a peace and sometimes lost sight of it altogether. Once in his extreme old age when he saw a carriage spatter an old woman with mud he hissed through its window, "Porci di siori" (filthy gentry). But few men saw such flare-ups. With six years left to live and already eighty-three, he seemed to most a symbol of the past as well as of the future, a kindly old gentleman and artist who had ordered his life so perfectly that he was already living his immortality. The Milanese, who were proud of him, made up a jingle, still current, linking him with their cathedral, the Duomo, as one of the two sights of the city:

> Un tempio e un uomo
> Manzoni ed il Duomo.

Verdi framed Manzoni's photograph and hung it in his bedroom, but he still could not bring himself to write the great man directly.

Instead he wrote to the Contessa, asking her to thank Manzoni for him and enclosing a photograph of himself. On it he wrote: "I esteem and admire you as much as one can esteem and admire anyone on this earth, both as a man and a true honor of our country so continually troubled. You are a saint, Don Alessandro!" But he still envied Strepponi for having actually met and talked with the great man.

That summer, on 21 July, Barezzi died. Like Manzoni, he was an old man, seventy-nine, and Verdi and Strepponi had put off a trip to Paris in order to remain with him. As far back as January Verdi had written the Contessa:

He has been better for three or four days; but I can see that it is only a respite of life for a few days, and no more! Poor old man, who has wanted everything good for me! And poor me who will have him only a little longer and then will see him no more!

You know that I owe him everything, everything, everything. And to him alone, not to others, as they have tried to make out. I can see him still (and this was many years ago) at a time when I had finished school. My father had declared he could not support me at the University of Parma, and I had decided to return to the village where I was born. This good old man, knowing this, said to me: "You were born for something better and not to sell salt and work the earth. Ask the Monte di Pietà for the small sum of 25 francs a month for four years, and I will make up the rest. You shall go to the Conservatory in Milan and, when you are able, you can pay back the money spent for you."

And so it was. You see how generous, how good and loving he was! I've known many men but never one better! He has loved me as much as his sons, and I have loved him as my father.

When the final day came, Verdi and Strepponi hastened into Busseto and arrived in time. Barezzi was in bed, weak but quiet. They sat for a time beside him. Then he raised his eyes and, turning his head, gazed longingly at the piano. Verdi rose and went to it. Softly he began the chorus of the captive Jews in *Nabucco*, "Va, pensiero . . ." his first great success and of all his music Barezzi's favorite. The old man raised his hand as if to bless him and died murmuring "O, mio Verdi! mio Verdi!"

Ordinarily Verdi did not announce family news to his friends except as it might come in the course of a letter. But on Barezzi's death he sent short notes, just a few stricken sentences, to Mariani, Piave, Luccardi, Arrivabene and Piroli. Then to get away from Busseto he and Strepponi, together with Mariani, went to Paris to see the Exposition. Mariani also wanted to see *Don Carlo* at the Opéra, for he was going to do it at Bologna in the autumn, but for Verdi and Strepponi the trip was purely for pleasure and to see the sights.

The particular sight of Paris in the Exposition year was the new system of collector sewers which carried the rain and waste water from the streets and dumped it into the Seine below the city. Hugo's *Les Misérables* had been published in 1862, and its dramatic account of Jean Valjean's underground escape through the old system had stirred everyone's interest. Now Haussmann and his engineers had built a new system, the best in the world, which was large enough to allow small boats and cars to run inside it and keep it clean with mechanical devices. During the Exposition special boats and cars were provided on stated days for visitors, and so successful were the tours that the city has continued them to this day.

Another sight of interest to Verdi was the new building for the Opéra. Work on it had gone on for six years behind the high wooden screens Parisian builders generally erect around their structures. But in the Exposition year the screens on the south side, the front, were removed. The building was still only a shell, but everyone had an opinion on its artistic merits, generally to the effect that it looked like a cluttered sideboard. This building, designed by Garnier and opened in 1874, is the present home of the Opéra.

But even the distractions of Paris during the Exposition could not entirely divert Verdi's attention from the farm at home. To the man in charge he wrote:

Let me tell you now in private that it would be better not to write letters so empty of news: a week is a long time! . . . You tell me, for example, the expenses come to 518.06 lire and you need 276 lire; but, Good Lord! tell me for what and how you spent so much, and how and why you need 276 lire.

And you don't tell me anything of my house and servants! . . . or are they all dead? And how is the coachman? What's he doing? Is it true that my old coachman, Carlo, died at Piacenza? And just incidentally how is the cholera at home? All these things are important and I ought to be told about them. I will be leaving Paris soon. Write me as soon as you receive this letter and answer everything I've asked you.

In others he gave directions for exercising the horses, forbade the men to use the machinery without him, and complained that each man "pulled only his own rope" and so there was no co-operation. Soon thereafter he returned to Sant' Agata and took charge again himself. But like most absentee landlords, he was more impressed with what had not been done than with what had.

That autumn in September the national government arrested Garibaldi, who was raising volunteers in Florence for a march on Rome, and sent him back to Caprera. The situation was distressingly like that before Aspromonte in 1862. No one, neither the general, the King, nor his minister, who had returned to office, seemed to have learned anything from the previous disaster. Once again Garibaldi was privately urged on while publicly rebuked, and the people, noting that Garibaldi was not too closely guarded or the volunteers dispersed, assumed that the rebuke was only a ruse. In October Garibaldi, in the style of a Dumas novel, escaped from Caprera, returned to Florence and started with his troops for the Papal frontier. At the same time Napoleon III announced that, in as much as the Italian government would not protect the Papal States, he would return the French army to Rome. Faced with a direct challenge from France, Vittorio Emanuele lost his nerve and sent his army into the Papal States "to restore order." Many volunteers, realizing that they would have to fight not only the Papal army but also those of France and Italy, decided the cause was hopeless and deserted. In Rome and the rest of the Papal States no one moved to aid Garibaldi even after he took the fortified town of Monterotondo. Daily his situation became more perilous. Because of Vittorio Emanuele's action he had no base from which to organize his supplies or to which he could retreat. There was not even a San Marino where, as in 1849, he could quietly disperse his men. On 3 November 1867 in sight of Rome he fought the Battle of Mentana against French and Papal forces and was decisively defeated. He and what men were not taken prisoner straggled back across the frontier, and again the Italian government arrested him. Garibaldi felt he had been betrayed and used the word "treachery." The people believed him, and again as after Aspromonte the government did not dare to bring him to trial. He was returned to Caprera where for the next three years he remained in retirement, closely watched.

The campaign permanently embittered Garibaldi against the government, and his attitude influenced many. Neither he nor the government was without fault, but Garibaldi, irresponsible as he was and growing old and arthritic, was at least without meanness. Not so much can be said of the government, which had neither the competence nor the courage to put through its policy. The minister took refuge in resigning his post as though he really believed that as long as he was not in office he was not responsible for events he had set in motion. But even he seems better than the King, who confessed to the British and French ministers that he had planned to use Garibaldi's invasion not only as an excuse to take Rome, in the guise of restoring order, but also to "massacre" the volunteers. Vittorio Emanuele, the Re Galantuomo, was visibly shrinking in his middle age into a cowardly, incompetent king whose best feats were accomplished out hunting and in bed. "Too much the father of his country," the wits sniggered.

The real losers in the affair were the Italian people who began to suspect that constitutional government was necessarily ineffective government. Many began to hold the government in contempt and to long for a strong man to enforce strong measures.

For Verdi the ill-fated year held still another disaster. In December Piave, who had moved to Milan to become the resident stage director at La Scala, had an apoplectic stroke on his way to a rehearsal. Verdi's first thought was to go to Milan, but Piave's wife advised against it. Piave was completely paralyzed and unconscious. He was to linger on for eight years, recovering slightly, but never able to move or speak. Verdi never went to see him, but he was generous financially, paying many of the expenses and settling a small estate on Piave's daughter. He also organized an Album of Songs for Piave's benefit and bludgeoned contributions for it out of Auber, Cagnoni, Mercadante, Ricci and Thomas. His own contribution was a gay number entitled *Stornello,* which means simply "a ditty" or "folk song." In it a discarded lover tells his lady he can get along quite well without her. The subject and style reflects the lighter atmosphere of Italian society in 1868 than in the more serious times under the Austrian domination. No one now wrote songs about exile, seduction or death with the intensity Verdi had tried to achieve in his songs published thirty years before.

Verdi and Strepponi spent the winter of 1867–68 at Genoa, which had made him an honorary citizen. The new apartment and furniture were a success, and they enjoyed moving in, although evidently there were some domestic squabbles. In a diary which Strepponi kept briefly the entry for 3 January 1868 reads:

We played billiards, as nearly always these last days. He occupied himself in being a carpenter, locksmith and playing the piano. He found nothing to complain of or grumble about! My God! it would be so easy to be happy when one has health and a little money! Why isn't he always like that, instead of finding fault no matter what I do, *while what I do is done always with one and the same intention*—to make his life comfortable, pleasant and serene?!!

The next day, according to the diary, was a bad one: he told her that it wasn't what she said but how she said it that irritated him, and he complained that she prided herself on being a "perfect wife," so that he couldn't say anything about the housekeeping without offending her. The trouble may have been the cook. Verdi, like most Parmigiani, was a gourmet, and he thought Strepponi's latest choice for cook was a disaster.

A bright spot in the winter was the success of *Don Carlo* at La Scala, and if Verdi had wanted he might have rejoiced over the fiasco of Boito's *Mefistofele* at the same theatre a few weeks earlier. But even in his letters he would not comment. He had not seen the opera; he refused to judge it. The opera had two performances, the second because of its length being spread over two nights. Each performance was completed in a near riot. Partisans of the old and new music went to the theatre to give battle, and any merits the opera may have had were ignored. After the second performance, on police order, the management withdrew the opera. *Don Carlo,* on the other hand, scored a genuine success, although some of it was attributed to the personal magnetism of Teresa Stolz who had been coached by Mariani for the Bologna production early in the autumn. The rule for the opera held true: with an outstanding production it could succeed.

In the spring Verdi went to Milan for the first time in twenty years, since immediately after the Cinque Giornate in 1848. His purpose was primarily to meet Manzoni. The Contessa Maffei had come for a visit to Sant' Agata, the first time she and Verdi had met since 1848, and then gone away with Verdi's promise that he would come.

He found Milan very changed, bigger and more beautiful. In the center of the city the Galleria was being built, and it at once became one of the city's chief sights. Everywhere, as in Paris, streets were being widened into boulevards, canals and streams covered and old gates torn down. Many regretted the passing of the older city with its simple classical style, for the new architecture, following that of

Paris, was heavy and often pretentious. Even the puniest building tried to have at least one stone balcony hang, however clumsily, to its face. But the widened streets and open areas in front of La Scala and the Duomo were an impressive improvement.

Neither Verdi nor Manzoni recorded what they said to each other at their interview. Tradition among the guides in Manzoni's house says that Manzoni entertained Verdi in his study on the ground floor from which the windows look out on the green trees and shrubs of the large interior court shared with the neighboring houses. The study itself is a small, paneled room with bookshelves, a desk, tables and two comfortable chairs before the fire. According to the tradition, the two men sat facing each other and Manzoni began with, "Verdi, you are a great man." To which Verdi replied fervently, "But you are a saintly man." There tradition stops, but the conversation may hardly have gone further. Manzoni was often silent and stuttering among strangers, and Verdi was very likely overcome by the immensity of the moment. If the conversation did go on, they almost certainly did not talk about music, for Manzoni often confessed that he cared nothing for it. Once he had even sent his gardener out to stop the birds twittering. The subjects on which he talked best were religion, language and the French Revolution, and the influence of all or any in the modern world.

Manzoni impressed Verdi in much the way he had expected to be impressed. Immediately on his return to Sant' Agata he wrote to the Contessa:

What can I say of Manzoni? How to describe the extraordinary, indefinable sensation the presence of that saint, as you call him, produced in me. I would have gone down on my knee before him if we were allowed to worship men. They say it is wrong to do it and it may be; although we raise up on altars many that have neither the talent nor virtue of Manzoni and indeed are rascals.

To all his friends he stressed Manzoni's stature as an artist and as a "saintly man." The phrase recurs constantly. By it he seems to have meant not so much self-denial as self-control, a virtue passionate natures are apt to admire greatly. Considering the depths of his passions, Verdi's self-control on the whole was excellent. He exploded on occasion in the theatre, but generally the artistic end he pursued was plain and no one took offense. He had the reputation of being a bear, but in all the productions he staged there is no record of a singer or conductor refusing to work with him or even complaining privately that he was impossible. Most, and generally the best, were devoted to him. But there was one area in his life in which Verdi seemed unable to act with the saintly moderation he so admired in Manzoni. This area involved anything he conceived to be an invasion of his privacy. He had fought with Busseto over his relations with Strepponi; now he fought with it again over its opera house.

This last was a project which had been simmering since 1845, sputtered into an angry crisis in 1865 and finally came to fruition three years later. The town fathers wanted to build a small opera house and name it after Verdi. From the first he had been against it although Barezzi and the music lovers had favored it. The town's motives were mixed: undoubtedly some men primarily wanted to honor Verdi, others to have a proper setting in which to hear the dominant form in Italian music, and still others merely to use Verdi and his connections to make something of Busseto and thereby money for themselves. There was talk of having him compose an opera for the opening night, of having him import the leading singers of the world for a season in which presumably he, Mariani and Piave would all have a hand as they had at Rimini for the opening of its Teatro Nuovo with *Aroldo*. Even more because Verdi was a citizen of Busseto who had enjoyed a scholarship from its Monte di Pietà, there was talk of exactly how much he ought to contribute to the theatre's construction. Nothing could have been calculated to have galled him more.

In 1865 in preparation for a meeting of the town council Verdi had put his objections in a letter of which he kept a copy. The addressee is not stated, but it probably was Barezzi who was a member of the Commission for the Theatre. In the letter Verdi pointed out that he had never agreed to have the theatre named for him and that it was absurd to think he would ask singers such as Patti or Fraschini to give up singing in Paris for Busseto. Then he rushed on to what really infuriated him:

How about it! Are they to dispose of me, my favor and property without talking to me or consulting me? But this is more than an inconvenience: it is an insult. It's an insult because it is as if to say: *Why should we consult him? Oh! He'll do it . . . he'll have to do it!* What right have they to do this?

I know that many, speaking of me, murmur a phrase which I don't know whether it is more ridiculous or unworthy . . . : *We made him!* Words that leaped to my ear just the last time I was in Busseto eight or ten days ago.

I repeat that it is ridiculous and unworthy. Ridiculous because I can reply: "Then why don't you make some more?" Unworthy, because all they did was execute a legacy [the funds of the Monte di Pietà came from wills]. But if they throw this aid in my face I can still reply: "Gentlemen, I have received a four year stipend of 25 francs a month, 1200 francs in all. Thirty-two years have past. Let us make an accounting of principle and interest and I will pay it all off."

The moral indebtedness will remain. Yes. But I raise my head and say with pride: "Gentlemen, I have carried your name with honor into all parts of the world. That is well worth 1200 francs!" Hard words, but fair!

See to what a point things come when men don't weigh their words or follow customary courtesy. I would not have wished for this scandal and I would have given anything to avoid it. Evidence of this is in my conciliatory propositions that I offer the Commission and town council through Dr. Angelo Carrara. Whatever may be the result I never wish to speak of the matter again . . . I ask only one thing from all of you! *Peace;* if you wish, even *oblivion.*

But even the conciliatory propositions contained a thorny problem. Verdi offered his name for the theatre and 10,000 lire toward its construction. The contribution, however, was not cash but the cancellation of a debt the town owed him. A few years earlier the town had lacked the money to repair a bridge on the road to the Villa Verdi, and he advanced the necessary funds. Immediately thereafter the town began to hedge about repaying the debt. Verdi then had put a chain across the bridge which he considered his until paid for. One of his arguments against the theatre was that the town could not afford to build it or to support it thereafter.

But nevertheless the Teatro Verdi had its grand opening on 15 August 1868. The theatre is tiny. The seats are removable, but ordinarily the center aisle sweeps past all of nine rows to the orchestra pit. At the widest on either side are seven seats. At the back this has shrunk to three or four, so that the floor of the house seats just over a hundred. Surrounding this are two tiers of boxes and gallery, all topped by the usual painted ceiling and chandelier. The stage simply cannot contain broad gestures, yet Toscanini once put an *Aida* on it. But for all the theatre's cozy charm it is not very useful. Festival performances in Busseto today are apt to take place in the piazza directly in front of it. There a full orchestra can be used and a larger audience accommodated. Verdi's objections to the theatre made him unpopular, but he was right.

The theatre opened with a performance of *Rigoletto*. Before that the orchestra played an overture, *La Capricciosa,* which according to the program was composed by Verdi at the age of twelve, and then the curtain rose to reveal a large bust of Verdi surrounded with flowers and crowned with a wreath sent from admirers in Rome. Everyone wore something green. Verdi's box which the town had given him was empty. He and Strepponi two weeks before had left for Genoa and then gone to a spa in the Apennines. He would have no part of the festivities. Later, after receiving an anonymous letter reportedly "nasty and impertinent," he sold the box for 2000 lire.

Verdi's actions throughout seem graceless, particularly the sale of the box. They are understandable only in the light of his lifelong loathing of personal publicity. Whether in Naples or Paris, he continually refused to let impresarios turn him into a lure for his operas,

VILLA VERDI

and undoubtedly this was all he saw in the town's project. It also offended his sense of financial appropriateness. A small town that could not even repair its bridges had no business building an opera house. But this was nothing compared to the invasion of his privacy, and he complained to his friends in letters that he was "an exile from his own house." The day after the season ended, on 16 September, he returned home to Sant' Agata, arriving in time for lunch.

Verdi's relations with Busseto were perhaps the only area in which Strepponi was not a good wife for him. She did nothing to smooth ruffled feathers or even to see that Verdi's point of view was presented in the community. A different wife might have used the Barezzis and Dr. Carrera to meet the most congenial people and be at home to some if not all the town. Perhaps something could have been done to lessen the friction. Verdi might perhaps have been persuaded to use the box once. But Strepponi positively worked against any partial reconciliation. She never forgave the Bussetani for their rejection of her in those first years. Once to Escudier she compared them unfavorably to her dog, Loulou. But to use Verdi's phraseology: What right had she to expect any other reception? She arrived in town as a woman who out of wedlock lived first with Merelli and then with Verdi. Was forgiveness to be only for her errors and not for those of the townspeople? Yet in spite of her unquestionably genuine religious beliefs she behaved as if it were so. The emotional scars of the rejection were too much for her. And behind them lay a permanent difficulty: she found the country people boring. For Verdi she would endure the country, but its people she could not. At various times she wrote to Escudier in her favorite city, Paris: "I am no longer young, it is true, but the intellectual life continues in every age, and here there is, alas! absolutely none"; and later, "in the midst of these cretins." (etc.) For her there could be no reconciliation with Busseto, for each meeting was a new exasperation of boredom. She could not talk of the beets, the breaking of horses, or where the shooting was good along the Po. And after the fiasco of Busseto's Teatro Verdi the division between him and the town petrified. He became a sort of local eccentric that everyone accepted yet no one knew.

Hardly had Verdi returned to Sant' Agata after the imbroglio over the opera house when two more blows fell on him, the first of an intensely personal kind. After Barezzi's death Verdi had asked a friend to search in Milan for the graves of his first wife, Margherita, and his son, Icilio. The report came back that the graves had long since been opened and the bones interred in a common mound. In Busseto the grave of his daughter, Virginia, had also been lost, perhaps in the same way. All that he had of the past, kept in a little copper box, were the marriage rings he and Margherita had exchanged together with two other pieces of her jewelry. To these he added a lock of Barezzi's hair. On the box he wrote "Mementoes of my poor family."

Another link with the past was severed when Rossini died in Paris on 13 November 1868. The private loss was not great: the men had never been intimate, but they had been friends. Rossini had once written in a letter: "Rossini, ex-composer and pianist of the fourth class, to the illustrious composer Verdi, pianist of the fifth class." The public loss, however, Verdi felt keenly. He wrote to the Contessa: "Rossini's reputation was the most widespread and popular of our time; it was one of the glories of Italy. When the other like it [Manzoni's] no longer exists, what will remain to us? Our ministers and the exploits of Lissa and Custozza!" Even before the services for Rossini were held in Paris Verdi had suggested publicly in the *Gazzetta Musicale* of Milan that the musicians of Italy unite to honor Rossini. Perhaps he also hoped by a fitting memorial to remind the world that there was more to Italy than just Lissa and Custozza.

His plan was to have the leading Italian composers combine in writing a Requiem to be performed on the first anniversary of Rossini's death. The composers would be chosen by lot from a large list and each would do some part of the Mass, such as the *Requiem,* the *Dies Irae,* or the *Libera Me.* The Mass would be performed only once and at Bologna, which Verdi pointed out was Rossini's "musical home." After the performance the Mass, which Verdi recognized would lack artistic unity, would be sealed up in the archives of Bologna's Liceo Musico and never again taken out except perhaps if some future generation wished to honor Rossini with another performance. The idea was to honor Rossini. No one would be paid for his composition or his services as a singer or instrumentalist.

The idea was enthusiastically received. There were, of course, those who complained that Verdi was pushing himself forward by suggesting it, and other ideas were suggested. But the Civic Committee and Philharmonic Academy of Bologna were enthusiastic, and in Milan a commission, of which Verdi was not a member, was formed to distribute the various parts by lot. Giulio Ricordi, the son of Tito and the third of the family with whom Verdi had dealt, was its secretary. The fact that most of the composers drawn are unknown outside of Italy indicates the immensity of Verdi's pre-eminence among them. They were: Buzzolla, Bazzini, Pedrotti, Cagnoni, F. Ricci, Nini, Coccia, Gaspari, Platania, Petrella, Mabellini; and to Verdi, or so the committee said, fell the closing section, the *Libera Me*. The deadline for the compositions was set for 15 September 1869.

Meanwhile Verdi's trips to Milan and activities over the Rossini Mass began to bear fruit in another direction. For a long time Ricordi had been urging Verdi to finish his revisions of *La Forza del Destino* and present it at La Scala. The theatre had just been through one of its worst seasons with the fiasco of Boito's *Mefistofele,* and its financial troubles were aggravated by the refusal of the Italian government to take on the annual subsidy which the Austrians had always paid. Ricordi even arranged for the Mayor of Milan, who was also chairman of the La Scala board of directors, to plead with Verdi. He undoubtedly was flattered, but it was also something he wanted to do, and the board agreed to have Teresa Stolz and an excellent tenor, Mario Tiberini. Verdi agreed and, even more, consented to direct the rehearsals. It would be the first time in twenty-four years he had worked at La Scala; it also would be the first time he worked with one of his most famous interpreters, La Stolz.

The revised opera had its première on a Saturday night, 27 February 1869, before an enthusiastic audience for most of whom the opera was entirely new. The revisions, as pointed out earlier (p. 400), emphasized song over drama, and compared to *Don Carlo,* which opened the season, it was an old-fashioned opera. Yet the great mass of the public plainly preferred it. "It is a strange thing," Verdi observed, "and at the same time discouraging! While everyone cries *Reform, Progress,* in general the public applauds and the singers prefer arias, romances and songs!" He was writing to Antonio Gallo, whose faith in *La Traviata* had given that opera its first successful performances, and he added: "This way we aren't getting anywhere. Either the composers must go back, or all the rest take a step forward." It was exactly the problem facing Italian composers: they had not yet persuaded the audience to accompany the composers in moving away from musical pattern, arias and romances, toward musical drama.

But *La Forza del Destino* with its arias and duets did not pose the problem and, released at last by Verdi, it soon entered the repertory of even provincial theatres. The audiences in them, as in the past, were ready to sit through a confused libretto in order to hear an aria well sung. Even the bloopers made in the orchestra by second-rate players seemed to lose themselves satisfactorily in the general excitement of the music.

Verdi next turned his attention to the *Libera Me* for the Rossini Mass, and he had it ready in good time. The scheduled performance of the Mass, however, grew more and more doubtful as the summer passed. The difficulty was not with the composers but the performers. Verdi hoped to use the chorus that Mariani was about to conduct at a Festival honoring Rossini in his birthplace, Pesaro. Evidently Verdi and perhaps even the committee in Milan managing the Bologna project expected Mariani to arrange for this chorus to sing also at Bologna. But as Mariani protested in a letter to Verdi: "I didn't assemble it, it doesn't depend on me, and I have no power over it." This was strictly true; the manager of the Festival at Pesaro had assembled the chorus just as he had hired Mariani to conduct it. Yet Mariani, who had agreed to conduct the Mass at Bologna, was the musical director of the Pesaro Festival, and his influence, if he had cared to exert it, might have been decisive. He did nothing, and neither Verdi nor the committee in Milan did anything; after the Pesaro Festival the chorus, specially assembled, disbanded.

The alternative was to use the chorus of the Teatro Communale at Bologna. Mariani, who had conducted it for several seasons, considered it inadequate for a Festival performance of a Mass, and he had written so to Verdi several months earlier. But even the possibility of using that chorus was lost when the impresario of the theatre refused to lend his orchestra or performers without being paid because he was "a poor man with six children and a living to make."

Meanwhile the time until the first anniversary of Rossini's death grew shorter. Desperately the committee suggested a performance in another city or possibly in Bologna but after the anniversary date. Verdi argued strongly against both ideas. The Mass was not an artistic unity and its only purpose was to honor Rossini. Better not to give it at all than to dilute its purpose. The committee reluctantly agreed and returned the parts to the various composers.

Verdi blamed Mariani and unfairly. It was not, after all, the conductor's job to organize the performance. But Verdi was bitterly disappointed. The project had turned into a public fiasco that seemed to slight Rossini, one of the glories of Italy, and to reflect poorly on the nobility of Italian music and musicians. It seemed, in a way, the artistic counterpart of Lissa and Custozza.

CHAPTER 34

THE YEAR 1870–71

AGE, 57

THE success of *La Forza del Destino* at La Scala reinforced several of Verdi's strongest convictions about how to produce opera. He himself had worked over the costumes and staging as well as conducting the musical rehearsals, so that every part of the production reflected his concept of the opera. And he had communicated his passion not only to the soloists, whom he acknowledged were excellent, but also to the chorus and orchestra, which had played with "incredible precision and fire." It was the lack of just such an artistic unity and enthusiasm which he felt had sabotaged *Don Carlo* at the Opéra.

He expressed this in a letter to Camille Du Locle in Paris and at the same time indirectly said he would never compose for the Opéra again. Du Locle had been one of the librettists for *Don Carlo* and now was constantly suggesting new possibilities. In rejecting a play called *Froufrou,* Verdi wrote:

But *hélas!* it's not the work of writing an opera nor the taste of the Parisian public that holds me back, but the certainty that in Paris I can never have my music performed the way I want.

It is a curious thing that a composer must always see his ideas contested and his conceptions disfigured! In your opera houses (without intending an epigram) there are too many connoisseurs! Each one must apply his standard and his taste and, what is worse, according to a *system,* without considering the individuality and character of the composer. Each one must give an opinion, voice a doubt, and the composer who lives for long in such an atmosphere of doubt soon loses his confidence. He ends by correcting and adjusting or, more exactly, by spoiling his work. At any rate he finally has in hand not an opera of inspiration but a *mosaic,* as beautiful as you may wish but still a *mosaic.*

You may reply that the Opéra has produced a string of masterpieces this way. Granted if you wish, but they would be better yet if the joining and adjusting of the pieces were less noticeable. No one denies that Rossini had genius! But, in spite of it all, there hovers in *William Tell* that fatal atmosphere of the Opéra. Sometimes, although less than in other composers, you feel that there is too much here and too little there. The musical flow is not so free and confident as in the *Barbiere*.

I don't mean by this to deny what you have achieved up there. I mean only to say that I cannot again crawl under the Caudine yoke of your theatres when I know I cannot have a real success unless I write as I feel, free from pressure and without worrying about writing for Paris rather than the world of the moon. Besides the singers must sing not as they but as I wish, and the chorus "which in Paris is very good" must do the same. In fact everything must be done my way; one will over all, mine. That seems a little tyrannical! . . . and perhaps it is. But if the opera is an inspiration, there is one idea to it, and everything must conform to that *one*. You will say perhaps that nothing prevents me from achieving all this in Paris. In Italy it can be done, or at least I can always do it; but in France, no.

For instance if I arrive in the foyer of an Italian theatre, no one dares to express an opinion, a judgement, before understanding the work thoroughly. And no one makes silly requests. They respect the opera and the composer and leave the decision to the public. But now in the foyer of the Opéra after four chords whispering starts on all sides: *"Oh, ce n'est pas bon . . . c'est commun . . . ce n'est pas de bon goût . . . ça n'ira pas à Paris . . ."* What significance have such poor words as *commun . . . bon goût . . . Paris . . .* if you have a work of art that ought to be universal!

The conclusion from all this is that I am no composer for Paris. I do not know whether I lack the talent, but I do know that my artistic ideas are very different from yours. I believe in *Inspiration;* you believe in *construction.* For purposes of argument I admit your criterion, but I want the enthusiasm you lack, in feeling and judgment. I want the essence of art in whatever form it may take: not the *compromise,* the artifice, or the *system* that you prefer. Am I wrong? Am I right? Be that as it may, I am right to say that my ideas are different from yours and to add that my backbone, unlike that of many others, is too inflexible for me to give up and deny my convictions which are rooted very deep. (etc.)

In fact Verdi never did compose again for the Opéra although Du Locle, refusing to be discouraged, continued to send ideas and suggested composing for the Opéra-Comique. Perhaps with that theatre in mind Verdi considered a Spanish comedy which he asked Du Locle to send to him. Along with it, early in 1870, came an "Egyptian sketch" of four pages. This was the beginning of *Aida*. Verdi took to it at once. "It is well done," he wrote, "with a magnificent *mise en scène,* and two or three situations which, if not the most original, are very good indeed."

The sketch had a complicated history. Du Locle had made it, reducing into scenario form a story written by an Auguste Edouard Mariette, a French Egyptologist. Mariette had published his story in a limited edition and persuaded the Khedive of Egypt that it should be made into an opera to celebrate the opening of the Suez Canal. But time had passed and the canal had already formally opened with a ceremony at Port Said on 16 November 1869. The next day sixty-eight ships of various nationalities, led by the *Aigle* with the Empress Eugénie aboard, had started through the cut and two days later steamed into Suez. Since then the canal had been in daily operation.

But the idea of an opera to celebrate the opening of the canal clung to Mariette's story, and he allowed Du Locle to make a scenario of it, only with a Cairo première in mind, so that the sketch came to Verdi with a number of conditions attached. Beside the Cairo première, the opera was required to be ready by December for performance in January 1871. This was a short time, less than a year, in which to compose an opera that Verdi wanted to make of "vast proportions (as if for the *Grande Boutique*)" or "Big Box," as Verdi called the Opéra.

The conditions did not disturb Verdi. He would be allowed to choose the singers, if available, and the conductor. Du Locle would prepare the libretto in French, but Verdi could select the Italian translator and would compose directly to an Italian text. In every respect except for the première in Cairo it would be an Italian opera, and Verdi always thought of it as such. The connection with the Suez Canal, tenuous at best, he completely ignored and made no attempt to honor or even mention in the opera. The shortness of time he seems never to have thought a problem. By the end of June Du Locle's French outline was complete, but no Italian verses yet existed, and to meet the terms of his contract Verdi would have less than six months in which to work over the libretto and compose the music. Against this was the fact that he already had in mind the scenes of the story and their general color or, as he called it, "tinta."

For the Italian verses Verdi hired Antonio Ghislanzoni, an eccentric who at various times had worked as a baritone, journalist and a writer of poetry, novels and plays. At the moment he was the editor of the *Gazzetta Musicale*, published in Milan by Ricordi, and he had written the necessary verses for the revision of *La Forza del Destino*. Now Verdi asked him to Sant' Agata to discuss the libretto. He came in July which, beyond the quiet of Sant' Agata, was to be an extraordinary month.

In Rome the Twentieth Ecumenical Council of the Church, known as the "Vatican" Council and the last until 1962, began its eighth month in session. Some persons feared and others hoped that the assembled bishops of the Church, more than 700 in all, would make the Syllabus of Errors affirmative and proclaim it a dogma of the Church. The possibility was widely discussed in Europe, and no one was certain what the result of such an action might be: perhaps no more than another literary blast at the liberal ideas and hopes of the nineteenth century, or perhaps the first step toward a crusade in which it became the duty of Catholics, in Italy as elsewhere, to fight for the recovery of the full Temporal Power.

Another purpose of the Council, it was rumored, was the enunciation of Papal infallibility as a dogma. The possibility of this was equally agitating to many, particularly state governments. For the dogma would be retroactive, and the various states remembered only too well the political theory on which Innocent III acted: that earthly monarchs must be in all things subject to the Pope. Pio Nono was known to favor the enunciation of Papal infallibility.

The Council proceeded slowly with its work, and it soon became evident that nothing would be done with the Syllabus of Errors but that the main issue would be Papal infallibility, which was part of more general reorganization of the Church. Undoubtedly most of the bishops believed the generally accepted tradition of the infallibility of the Pope; the issue was whether it was "opportune" to enunciate the dogma. Roughly speaking, the bishops who thought it "inopportune," perhaps a fifth of the total number, were those in the closest contact with the Protestants and the Greek Orthodox. Those for it were led by Cardinal Manning of England, a convert to Catholicism, and important support was offered by the Jesuits, the traditional defenders of the Papacy against independently minded bishops. Pio Nono had hoped the Council would proclaim the dogma by acclamation, but this was never possible. After considerable tactical maneuvering by Manning and the application of Papal pressure the vote was 451 for,

88 against and 62 conditionally favoring. On the last vote after the bulk of the opposing bishops had withdrawn, the count was 433 to 2.

The most important part of the official statement of the doctrine reads: "The Roman Pontiff when he speaks *ex cathedra,* that is, when he in the exercise of his office of his supreme Apostolic Authority, decides that a doctrine concerning faith or morals is to be held by the entire Church, he possesses, in consequence of the divine aid promised him in St. Peter, that infallibility with which the Divine Savior wished to have His Church furnished for the definition of doctrines concerning faith or morals; and therefore such definitions of the Roman Pontiff are irreformable of themselves, and not in consequence of the Church's consent."

The beginning was not very exciting; the last eight words were revolutionary. The concept embedded in them caused the opposing bishops far more concern than the mere enunciation of Papal infallibility. In future the Pope would be less one bishop among his peers and more their superior. Actually Pio Nono had put through a major reorganization of the Church, centralizing authority in himself and vastly increasing the power of the administration in Rome. Some such reorganization undoubtedly was necessary. Better communications and the shrinking world required either far more frequent Councils with all their complicated machinery, a sort of permanent house of bishops, or a more powerful executive in the Pope. But many priests as well as laymen regretted that the reorganization was put through by an anti-liberal Pope who placed increasing reliance on the Jesuits, generally considered the most reactionary of the Church's orders. In the coming years the Church-State battle in Austria, France and Germany would grow more bitter while continuing so in Italy. An immediate result in Germany was the repudiation of the Church by a group calling themselves "Old Catholics"; it was a new schism.

On 18 July 1870 Pio Nono proclaimed the dogma of Papal infallibility, and on the next day France, egged on by Bismarck, declared war on Prussia. The apparent cause was the possibility of a German prince on the throne of Spain, but Bismarck's real purpose was a war with France, the traditional German enemy, which would bring those German states still outside the Prussian orbit into it. These were chiefly Bavaria, Württemberg and Baden. Bismarck's plan succeeded, and in the first week of August German soldiers crossed into France. Almost immediately thereafter Napoleon withdrew the French army

THE VATICAN COUNCIL

from Rome to defend France. To protect what was left of the Papal States Pio Nono had his own army of 13,000 men.

At Sant' Agata Verdi followed the war anxiously. He grieved over the French defeats and reminded his friends that a victorious Prussia meant a permanently constituted German Empire, as great a threat to Europe and Italy as ever Austria had been. In this he was somewhat out of step with general opinion which equated Bismarck with Cavour and was eager to see the superior French and their Emperor humilated.

On 2 September came the battle of Sedan in which the Prussians captured most of the French army and Napoleon himself. On the news of it a bloodless revolution took place in Paris and the Second Empire, in its twentieth year, gave way to the Third Republic. The Empress Eugénie crept out of the Tuileries into a private cab, spent the night at the home of her American dentist, and the next day sailed to England on a small, private yacht. For French republicans like Hugo, still in self-imposed exile, the passing of one era into the next was a great day, and soon every French town of any size had in it somewhere a "Rue 4 Septembre." But Paris would have to undergo two sieges before the Republic could enjoy its capital. The first was by the Prussians and began on 19 September.

On the same day Pio Nono made his last journey through Rome. After Sedan Vittorio Emanuele had sent an ambassador to the Pope to say that in view of the Franco-Prussian War the King felt it necessary to occupy the Patrimony of St. Peter in order to prevent revolutionary uprisings. Pio Nono told the ambassador that his masters were "whited sepulchres and vipers," and that while he was neither a prophet nor the son of the prophet he could assure Vittorio Emanuele that he would not enter Rome. It was strong language, and as the startled ambassador retreated, Pio Nono added: "But that assurance is not infallible."

The Italian troops were expected to enter on the twentieth, and on the nineteenth Pio Nono reviewed his small army at the Lateran Gate from which twenty-two years earlier he had escaped to Gaeta. He intended to make a token resistance, so that the world would know he submitted under protest. While the troops watched he slowly mounted the *Scala Santa* on his knees. At the top he prayed in a voice all could hear and then turned and blessed the troops. It was the last act of a Pope in Papal Rome. The next day after a short bombardment the Pope withdrew into the Vatican, and Vittorio Emanuele's troops took over the city in the name of the Italian government. The Papal State, the oldest sovereignty in Europe, had passed out of existence.

Only one country, Ecuador, protested the violation of the Pope's territory. The great Catholic powers, France, Austria and Germany, murmured that they would protect the Pope's dignity and spiritual power but pointedly omitted any reference to his land. Their attention was elsewhere, and they were unenthusiastic with the results of the Vatican Council. For Italians it was a great day but spoiled by the rather backhanded way in which it was brought about. Except for those actually in Rome, the change of sovereignty seemed hardly more than a minor episode in a much larger drama being played out at Paris, the capital of Europe.

There one of the leading republicans, Léon Gambetta, escaped in a balloon over the encircling German lines and went to Tours, where he raised new armies, supplied them after a fashion and directed the resistance. Each new French defeat wounded Verdi again, and when he was not working on *Aida* he wrote despairing letters to his friends. To the Contessa he wrote:

This disaster for France desolates my heart as it must yours. It is true that the self-praise, impertinence, presumption of the French was and, in spite of all their miseries, is insufferable. But after all France gave liberty and civilization to the modern world. If she falls, let's not fool ourselves, all our liberty and civilization will fall too. Let our literary men and politicians sing of the knowledge, the science, and (God forgive them) the arts of these conquerors. But if they looked a little closer, they'd see that in the conqueror's veins still flows the ancient blood of the Goths, that these men are monstrously proud, hard, intolerant, contemptuous of everything not German, and rapacious without limit. Men of brains but without heart; a strong race but not civilized.

And that King [William I of Prussia] who is always talking of God and Divine Providence, with whose help he is destroying the best part of Europe! He thinks he's destined to reform the morals and punish the vices of the modern world! What a fine missionary! Old Attila (another of these missionaries) stopped his march before the majesty of the capital of the old world; but this new one is about to bombard the capital of the modern world. And now that Bismarck says that Paris will be spared, I fear more than ever that at least in part it will be destroyed. Why? I cannot imagine. Perhaps so that such a beautiful capital can no longer exist since they themselves will never succeed in building its equal. Poor Paris! that I saw so merry, so lovely and splendid last April.

And us? I would have liked a more generous policy, *which might have paid a debt of gratitude.* A hundred thousand of our soldiers might have been able to save France and us. In any event I would have preferred to sign a peace, conquered alongside of France, rather than to escape by an inertia which in the future will be our dishonor. We will not avoid a European war and we will be *devoured*. It will not come tomorrow, but it will come. A pretext is easily found: perhaps Rome . . . the Mediterranean . . . And why not the Adriatic which they've already proclaimed a German sea?

The business at Rome is a great event but it leaves me cold; perhaps because I feel it will cause trouble, domestic as well as foreign. I cannot imagine side by side Parliament and the College of Cardinals, a free press and the Inquisition, the Civil Code and the Syllabus of Errors; and because it frightens me to see our government ruling by chance and trusting . . . to time. Suppose tomorrow we get a shrewd Pope, astute, a real clever fellow, as Rome has often had, he would ruin us. I cannot see the Pope and King of Italy together except in this letter.

I have no more paper. Forgive the *Speech*. It is a release for me. I see everything very black, but even so I haven't told you half the troubles I fear.

In the midst of these events which Verdi found so depressing he hammered out the libretto with Ghislanzoni and began on the music. His letters to Ghislanzoni show Verdi all but writing the libretto. He requested this or that meter, here and there so many lines, and on occasion he demanded a specific word. Ghislanzoni made some good suggestions, but the spirit and often the letter of the line was, in the end, Verdi's. More than any of his other operas *Aida* is the result of his mind alone, his discipline and his imagination.

By the middle of November he had finished it. It had taken him four months in all, with about a month spent on each act. He was ready, as his contract required, to deliver the score in December for performance in January 1871. But now the siege of Paris made this impossible, for the scenery, which had been built there, could not be gotten out. Verdi had the right under the contract, if for any reason the Cairo première did not take place, to produce the opera outside of Egypt any time after July 1871. With the siege dragging on it began to look as though La Scala, which was planning a production for February 1871, might well be able to delay it six months and then present the world première. The Egyptians appealed to Verdi to consider the siege an "Act of God," stopping time for its duration. Verdi agreed to the extent he was able. The February production at La Scala was canceled, as the Egyptians anyway would have had a right to demand, and Verdi agreed not to authorize any others before the following winter at La Scala, for which certain artists he had suggested had already been hired. For the moment *Aida* was put aside, and Verdi, who had gone with Strepponi to Genoa for the winter, turned his mind to other things.

One of these was the post of director at the Conservatory in Naples. Mercadante, who had held it for many years, had died, and Verdi was immediately invited to replace him. The Conservatories at Milan, Parma and Naples were the best in Italy, and of them Naples had the most distinguished history. The post of director there was the highest academic position in the Italian musical world. Verdi refused. In a letter to his Neapolitan friend De Sanctis he put it bluntly: he would be a stormy petrel trying to make changes, and the academic types would not like it. To the Conservatory itself he presented different reasons but no less true: his life and business were at Sant' Agata and he needed to keep his time free to compose. He added that he should have told the students: "Practice the fugue constantly and persistently until you are tired of it and until your hand becomes strong and supple enough to bend the notes to your will." Perhaps he remembered his own training under Lavigna, but it was characteristic of him to add "to your will." He expected the students to want to say something definite, not merely to run on in a musical vein. He recommended studying Palestrina, a few of his contemporaries and Marcello. Verdi's curriculum would have been basic rather than modern, and his closing sentence which was much publicized, "Let us turn back to the past; it will be a step forward," became something of a battle cry.

Because of it and his position in Italian music he was asked to preside over a government commission to recommend reforms in the curriculums of the various Conservatories. He refused at first, pointing out that in his opinion rules such as the commission might recommend were less important than good men. What the Conservatory at Naples needed was a good director, not advice. But distinguished men put pressure on him, and in the end he gave in. His views on education are not very startling, for like most men who have carried their schooling on into adult life and made a success out of it, he thought the next generation should do just as he had. The danger in this, of course, is that the next generation merely repeats the mistakes of its predecessor.

Lavigna, for example, had taught Verdi much about fugues and little about instrumentation, and in a letter to his friend Piroli Verdi insisted it was not necessary to teach instrumentation: the student could pick it up on his own. This, of course, is ridiculous. It had taken Verdi some twenty operas, including trips to Paris and London, to learn how to make good use of the instruments. The purpose of a Conservatory is to offer the same knowledge at less expense in time and money. In the same way Verdi always stressed the need for the students to have a broad literary background. He had given himself one, and it was important to him. Yet it would seem that literature, far more than instrumentation, is a subject which can safely be left to the music student's own time and pleasure.

Verdi was right to avoid the academic life just as he was right not to answer Boito and other critics in articles theorizing about music. He was not equipped for either job. And it was a source of strength to him that he never confused the form his musical gifts should take: to compose dramatic music and produce it in a theatre.

Throughout the winter Verdi stayed at Genoa and grieved over France. In January the German Empire was proclaimed in the Hall of Mirrors at Versailles, and at the end of the month Paris capitulated. South of it resistance continued, and Garibaldi, now that Napoleon was out and a republic back in, went off to fight for France, much to its embarrassment. But the government gave him five thousand men and he won some small victories. In the elections to the French National Assembly, which was meeting in Bordeaux, Garibaldi was elected in six districts, and he went to the Assembly meetings in February. He wanted to register a public vote for republicanism, which he could not do in Italy, and another against the new German Emperor, who was trampling on liberty. But he was greeted with protests, and when he rose to speak, he was shouted down. In disgust he returned to Caprera. A month later in the Assembly Hugo attempted to defend Garibaldi and suggested that the Deputies disliked him because he was the only general on the French side to capture a German flag. But Hugo himself was shouted down, and he, too, went off in disgust.

The truth was that the Third Republic at this point in its history was "a republic without any republicans." The great majority of the Deputies wanted peace with Germany and were prepared to sacrifice Alsace and half of Lorraine to obtain it. They also wanted peace

HUGO

within France and associated republicanism with war and social disorder. So, Bonapartism for the moment being disgraced, they flirted with restoring the Bourbon monarchy. But immediately the old problem arose: which line of the Bourbon family? The elder branch, the "legitimists," stretching from the guillotined Louis XVI through Charles X to his grandson, the Comte de Chambord; or the Orléanist line, the junior and more liberal branch, stretching through Louis Philippe to his grandson, Philippe, Comte de Paris. While debating the subject the Assembly fixed the seat of government at Versailles and moved there, almost as if eighty years of history were to be wiped out. Paris, fiercely patriotic, wanting to continue the war, and also determinedly republican, would not give up its guns to the men at Versailles. In March the "Commune of Paris" was formed and the city's second siege began while the scenery for *Aida* continued to be trapped within it.

The term "commune" has nothing to do with "communism" but is the medieval term for chartered cities. The insurrection at Paris was partly an explosion of wounded patriotism: the Parisians would never forgive Bismarck for demanding that his troops parade down the Champs Elysées. It also was an attempt to defend the Republic, threatened by its monarchist Deputies, and other "communes" were formed at Marseilles, Toulouse, Saint-Etienne and Le Creusot. And in all these cities the movement was partly a desire for local autonomy. But the provinces refused to follow the lead of Paris, which soon found itself alone, besieged by a French army of 130,000 troops while a German army, encamped close by, watched. The situation was infuriating and hopeless. The moderate elements in the city gradually withdrew their support, so that the Commune became increasingly proletarian and socialist. The bourgeoisie insisted all the "Communards" were "red fiends"; during the last days of the siege in May the leaders of the Commune seemed to run amok and act like the enemies of society they were said to be. They shot sixty-seven hostages, among them the Archbishop of Paris, and they burned the Tuileries, the Hôtel de Ville and the Palais de Justice. But the red fury was nothing compared to the vengeance of the bourgeoisie.

When the government troops entered the city, the seventy-two-year-old Adolphe Thiers was in control at Versailles. He believed that "the vile multitude," as he called them, should be kept down. The troops executed thousands of Communards; the estimates vary from 13,000 to 36,000. Among them were women and children, who could have had no part in directing the city's defense. The greatest number were killed against a wall in the Père Lachaise cemetery. Thousands more were deported without trial to New Caledonia. The proletariat in Paris has never forgiven or forgotten, and a hundred years later the implacable class hatred created by Thiers is still a political force.

The people of Europe responded to the slaughter at Paris largely in terms of their political sympathies. Verdi was stunned. To his sculptor friend, Luccardi, in Rome he wrote:

Events in France are painful and astounding. Principles pushed to extremes lead only to disorder. France, or rather Paris, pushed both good and evil to extremes, and these are the results. The same thing will happen to us, if we don't learn how to control ourselves. You have an example under your eyes. Your priests' refusal to compromise over the dogma of *infallibility* is causing a schism in Germany. Your priests certainly are priests, but they aren't Christians. The Papal Court couldn't find a word of pity for those poor martyrs of Paris, and that is really scandalous. (etc.)

In Brussels Hugo offered his house where he was staying as a refuge for the beaten, terrified Communards who were streaming across the border into Belgium. He received many letters of congratulations; yet one night a mob attacked his house. The incident was not serious, but the Belgian government issued a decree asking "one Victor Hugo, man of letters, sixty-nine years of age, to leave this kingdom, without delay, never to return." Many Belgians protested. Hugo and his family, however, had to pack their bags and go.

By July events everywhere had settled so that Europe could assess the change in itself. There was a new Germany overshadowing Austria, a weakened France and, finally, a unified Italy with its capital at Rome. The Papal State had disappeared and with it a host of problems. Just what the new ones would be was not yet clear. Verdi's attention meanwhile began to focus on the première of *Aida*. It would be at Cairo in December. Six weeks later in February there would be another production with different scenery and almost certainly different singers at La Scala.

CHAPTER 35

AIDA

1871–1872; AGE, 57–58

WITH the premières of *Aida* for Cairo and Milan scheduled barely a month apart, it was likely, if not inevitable, that two entirely different casts would have to be assembled and rehearsed. Verdi showed no preference between the two, although he refused to go to Cairo either to stage the production or to attend its first night. But he agreed, if possible, to coach the singers and conductor before they left Italy, and he made it plain that he refused only in order to avoid the winter voyage and unwanted publicity in a strange city.

The two premières together with the first performance in Italy of *Lohengrin* were, for Italians, the most important musical events of the year, and artists and conductors jockeyed for positions. Verdi recommended Stolz and Mariani as the best soprano and conductor, and the impresario in Cairo tried to sign them for his season. But both had previous commitments which they would not break. Stolz eventually sang in the première at Milan, but a cabal there against Mariani kept him from conducting and he went as usual to Bologna for the *Lohengrin*. In the end Boito's friend, Franco Faccio, conducted *Aida* at La Scala, and it was one of the great occasions of his career.

In the old days Verdi would have conducted the first three performances himself and then turned the post over to some man whose name often would not even be noted in the program. But as the scores had grown more complicated, requiring larger and better orchestras, conducting had become more of a specialty. Composers less frequently conducted their own works, and when Boito had conducted at the première of his *Mefistofele* in 1868, it had been considered rather unusual and one cause of the opera's fiasco. The change in custom had occurred gradually in the twenty years after 1848 and, at least in

Italy, largely because of Mariani who by the example of his achievements had greatly raised the standard of orchestral playing and conducting everywhere.

Verdi's relations with Mariani grew worse, at least on Verdi's side, after the fiasco of the Rossini Mass. For a time they continued to correspond, but Verdi gradually broke with Mariani to the point where he deliberately avoided his former friend, even though in Genoa they lived in the same house. This distressed Mariani who tried through long, defensive letters and the good offices of friends to explain himself and re-establish their old relationship. But the more Mariani tried, the more he irritated Verdi. It was a time to let well enough alone, and yet this was just what Mariani, who was by nature effusive and sometimes a little silly, could never do. The more he discussed his problem with Verdi, the more Verdi resented it, particularly when Mariani discussed it with third persons.

Verdi also was increasingly irritated with Mariani on purely artistic grounds, for the conductor, like several since, thought of himself as a "creator" and sometimes performed the music in a way to express his own rather than the composer's intent. This infuriated Verdi, who once pointed out in detail to Ricordi how Mariani had changed the character of the overture to *La Forza del Destino* by having the brasses boom out. The passage instead of being a quiet song had become a "warlike fanfare, which has nothing to do with the opera's subject in which all warlike matters are mere episodes." Such effects for effect's sake, Verdi felt, led to the "baroque and untrue." The art of opera, he pointed out, had only just freed itself from the tyranny of the singer and his interpretations and now was about to substitute the tyranny of the conductor and his. Verdi, predictably, wanted a single "creator," the composer.

In addition to these reasons, comparatively clear-cut, there were others in the complicated tangle of personal relations between Stolz and Mariani and the two of them and Verdi. There is no question that Stolz had been Mariani's mistress until about 1870 when the affair began to cool. She probably found distressing Mariani's refusal or inability to confine himself to her. He was extremely good-looking with a great shock of black hair, and the ladies found him fascinating. She may also have been disturbed that Mariani's temper was becoming shorter and more violent. He had, although no one at the time knew it, cancer of the bladder, extremely painful and in less than three years

MARIANI

fatal. It seems probable from the existing letters that Verdi and Strepponi had urged Stolz to break off with Mariani, and late in 1871, soon after a three-week visit to Sant' Agata, she wrote him that in future their only tie would be one of "simple friendship as between fellow artists." Sometime, too, as their affection cooled, she asked Mariani to return her savings which she had given him to invest. This he did, but he was slow about it, and it is the sort of thing Verdi, with his careful sense of money, would think was inexcusable.

Cutting into this tangle was the fact that Mariani had agreed to conduct and produce Wagner's *Lohengrin* at Bologna in November 1871. Even announcement of the production caused tremendous excitement as it was the first production in Italy of any of Wagner's operas. Out of the fact gossips were able to spin an incredible web of musical intrigue: Wagner's Italian publisher was Lucca, with whom Verdi had fought over *Il Corsaro;* Verdi and Strepponi had separated La Stolz from Mariani; and Mariani had therefore, out of spite, preferred *Lohengrin* to *Aida*. These suggestions, however ridiculous, were not only whispered but openly discussed. Against them both men maintained a public silence. In his letters Verdi never mentions Mariani except as a conductor; Mariani's letters are more self-pitying. But his position was worse. He had lost a mistress he hoped to marry and a friend. Underneath the self-pity and justification sounds a desperate cry for affection lost. Work was not enough to fill the void.

The Italian première of *Lohengrin* took place first, before *Aida,* on 1 November 1871. The opera scored a real success, not just on its first night when its supporters could be expected to boost it, but throughout the season. The critics praised Mariani's production, extolled Wagner and declared a new era in music had begun. Three weeks after the première Verdi, who had never yet seen a Wagner opera, tried to see a performance without anyone knowing it. But as he got off the train at Bologna, he came face to face with Mariani, who was waiting to meet a friend. Ruffled at being caught so soon, Verdi gruffly refused to let Mariani carry his bag. He also begged Mariani not to reveal to anyone that he had come to Bologna. Then he went off quickly with Ricordi's agent who had a cab waiting.

In a letter written the next day Mariani described the performance of *Lohengrin* that night. It did not go well. Even in the first act the chorus and soloists were nervous and sloppy. When Mariani scolded them in the intermission, all they could think of was that Verdi was in the house. In box twenty-three of the second row, they said. "Go look." Mariani said it was not so, but he would not look. In the front of the box were two undistinguished men, but behind them and visible from the stage, if not the audience, was Verdi. He had brought a score of the opera and was making notes. He did not stir in the intermissions.

After the second act a man, identified as Ricordi's agent, shouted "Viva il Maestro Verdi," and the house applauded for almost a quarter of an hour. Verdi refused to show himself or acknowledge the applause in any way even though urged by the Mayor. Mariani thought Verdi was right in this, and it is interesting that he also assumes Ricordi's agent started the demonstration without Verdi's knowledge. After the performance Verdi left quickly and returned the next day to Sant' Agata. He never saw Mariani again.

The score with Verdi's notes on the performance exists and shows 114 remarks which he himself summarized as "Mediocre impression. The music is beautiful when it is clear and expresses an idea. The action moves as slowly as the words and therefore is boring. Beautiful effects with the instruments. Abuse of held notes with consequent heaviness. Mediocre performance. Much *verve* but without poetry or delicacy. In the difficult points always bad."

On the Prelude to Act I he wrote at the beginning: "too loud," and then, "doesn't explain itself"; later: "beautiful clarinet and flute" and "all too loud"; and at the end of it: "beautiful but heavy with the continuously held high notes on the violins." On the bridal chorus he wrote: "perhaps a little too fast as it lacks the desired poetry and calm." Mariani in his letter states unequivocally that the performance was poor, and plainly Verdi agreed. The fact kept the comments less interesting than they might have been.

Seven weeks later, on Christmas Eve, *Aida* had its Cairo première. Although there were no political figures such as the Empress Eugénie, who had been at the formal opening of the canal two years earlier, it was still a gala occasion. The Khedive had invited the leading musical critics from Paris and Milan, and the newspapers treated it as a great event. At the performance the harem put in an appearance en bloc and occupied three boxes on the first tier. The opera had a great success which it repeated on 8 February 1872 at La Scala. For this second production Verdi wrote an overture to replace the prelude but then decided not to use it. He did, however, add Aida's aria at the beginning of Act III, "O cieli azzurri," or as it is often called from the recitative introducing it, "O patria mia." It has remained in the score ever since.

The success of *Aida* has been so prodigious that it gives off an air of inevitability, concealing the work that achieved it. But after the failure of the revised *Macbeth* and the fitful success of *Don Carlo* Verdi insisted to his librettist: "I repeat now for the twentieth time that *the only thing I'm looking for is success.*" Then he went on to rewrite a scene, discussing meters, lines and words while urging: "Have patience."

What finally emerged was a grand opera in the Paris style but clipped and pruned with such care that it seemed all flower and no stalk. This was achieved partly by keeping the story extremely simple, and the decision to do so was a deliberate retreat from the complications of *Don Carlo*. Aida, for example, is an Ethiopian slave serving Amneris, the Egyptian princess. Both love Radames, an Egyptian soldier, who because of his military feats is officially engaged to Amneris. Yet he loves the slave, Aida. One facet of this triangle Verdi ignores altogether. In no slave society that has ever existed has a member of the ruling class been able to entertain honorable intentions toward a slave. Such a thought, when made public, invariably declasses the man and raises a host of social problems. In *Don Carlo* this was the sort of reality Verdi had included: the etiquette of the Spanish Court which caused, in part, Don Carlo, Elisabetta and Philip to behave as they did. In *Aida* all such realities are ignored. As a result the characters, even Aida, are rather flat, and although the action is set in Egypt, it really takes place in a never-never land in which Verdi can manipulate the characters as he wants. For some this is a weakness in the libretto.

Its strength is the clarity and speed with which Verdi brings his flat characters together to make dramatic situations. The opera starts with a priest telling Radames that the King will soon announce the general chosen to lead the Egyptians against the Ethiopians. Radames hopes it will be he and looks forward to telling Aida how he fought for her. In his aria, "Celeste Aida," he proclaims his love for her, and he does *not* consider that defeating her people may be a poor way to show it. For that is not the situation Verdi has in mind: it would delay the action. Instead, he rushes it ahead by producing Amneris, who suggests hopefully that Radames is thinking of love. His confusion convinces her that he was but also leads her to suspect that she is not the loved one. Who could it be? Aida then enters, and in a trio Radames expresses his fear that Amneris will discover he loves Aida, Amneris declares her jealousy, and Aida sings of her unhappy lot at being a slave and hopelessly in love. Before the first scene is more than eleven minutes old Verdi has given his tenor a gorgeous aria and brought his three leading characters together in a trio that perfectly expresses the problem of the opera. In *Il Trovatore,* another opera of dramatic situation rather than character, Verdi took much longer to reach the same point, in the trio ending Act I, and the issues and background were much less clear.

As a result of this speed Verdi has considerable time free to devote to the pomp and pageantry of grand opera. But even this he makes do a double duty. The King enters with his court assembled to hear a messenger report that the Ethiopians have attacked, led by Amonasro. At the name the courtiers exclaim "Il Re" (the King himself), but Aida gasps to the audience "Mio padre." Necessary information has been given the audience, not by a narrative aria but by two words, easily understood, which come naturally out of a tense situation. Meanwhile everyone sings a fine march, banners are waved, and the scene ends with a rattling chorus calling for war, "Guerra," just as had similar scenes in every Italian opera since Bellini's *Norma*. Some of the audience hearing *Aida* for the first time in Cairo and Milan relaxed happily with the familiar, old form. There was going to be no nonsense about "new music" in *Aida*.

Actually, of course, there was considerable "new music" in *Aida*, but it was presented in what seemed to be the old forms and made palatable by a succession of good melodies. The first act of *La Traviata* had ended with a scene for Violetta, establishing her as the most important character and the one whose mood and point of view would dominate the opera. Verdi used the same technique in *Aida*. As the King and his court leave the hall after the declaration of war, Aida is left on-stage alone to declare her problem directly to the audience. In *La Traviata* Violetta had done this in the traditional musical style of the time (*See* p. 312): recitative, slow aria, recitative, fast aria. But for *Aida* Verdi used a different style, one he had developed largely through operas like *Rigoletto* and *Macbeth*. It is more declamatory, preferring the drama of the words over the musical pattern of the aria with its more formal beginning, middle and end.

At the end of the chorus calling for war Amneris had given Radames an Egyptian standard and urged him: "Ritorna Vincitor" (Return victorious). Everyone had repeated it, even Aida who had been carried away by the emotion of the moment. But left alone on the stage she begins her soliloquy, the climax of the opera's first scene, by repeating the words and then wondering in horror how she could wish Radames to defeat her father and brothers. The question is posed in vigorous declamation. Then to a swift tune she wishes the words unspoken and the Egyptians destroyed. It is a "tune" rather than an "aria" because it lasts only seventeen measures. Yet it is not merely melodic recitative; it has a definite beginning, middle and end, so that the thought is presented in a melodic unit. Her next thought, however, is of Radames. How can she wish him defeated and dead? A contrasting tune, soft with love, presents the thought. Again it is merely seventeen measures long. She sees no way out of her dilemma: whichever gods she calls upon, Egyptian or Ethiopian, it is a crime. It is best to die. A broken tune expresses her confusion. Finally, in a tune whose double length and breadth of phrasing establishes it as the climax, Aida calls on the gods to let her die.

Obviously such a method of composing a scene puts an enormous demand on melodic invention. Violetta had required only two arias, each using a second verse, and some connecting recitative. Aida needed four distinct tunes, clear-cut and compact. A large part of the opera's success lies in Verdi's incredible ability to supply them. When he arrived at his final scene, a point where musical-comedy composers are desperately offering reprises, Verdi filled the tiny, eight-minute scene with three new tunes, all contrasting and apt to the changing mood.

Not everything was cast in the form of tunes. Verdi was ready to use a formal aria where it seemed to fit. Radames' "Celeste Aida" is one, starting with recitative and then moving into the aria itself which continues for fifty-one measures, or just three times as long as one of Aida's typical tunes. It has a beginning, contrasting middle and an end which repeats the words and melody of the beginning to a more complicated accompaniment in the orchestra. The effect is static: it is the tenor in love to a beautiful musical pattern while the drama stands still. Verdi was also prepared to use the slow-fast formula ending with the jumpy cabaletta. He assured the librettist: "I have no aversion to cabalettas, but I must always have a situation and justification for them." So in Act III, when Aida tries to persuade Radames to desert Egypt and flee with her to Ethiopia, she describes the cool forests there to a soft, languid melody. But when he finally resolves to go with her, they express the decision in an impassioned cabaletta which in performance generally ends with them running downstage to receive applause before remembering to head for the wings and Ethiopia. Verdi deliberately included something for everyone, and part of the opera's success lies in its happy balance of musical pattern and drama. No matter what the fashion of the moment might be in musical appreciation, *Aida* offered several stunning examples.

The style of even the formal arias, however, was changing. Teresa Stolz as Aida was a different sort of soprano from Strepponi as Abigaille in *Nabucco*. The change can be seen in a comparison of Aida's final tune in which she calls on the gods to let her die and similar climactic arias for the sopranos in *La Traviata* (disc., p. 312) and *Macbeth* (illus., p. 186). In Aida's opening and closing phrases there are no fancy turns, runs or enormous jumps.

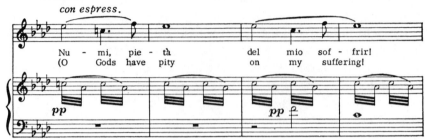

The phrases are as simple as a child's song. Greater reliance is put on the words and coloring the voice to suit them than on its agility or the graceful or forceful effect of the notes' pattern. The drama is expressed differently and, the fashion of the time declared, more dramatically.

Of course, not all the arias are as simple as Aida's appeal to the gods. The one Verdi inserted for the Milan production, "O cieli azzuri," is more in the old style, allowing the soprano to show off her voice with grace notes that must be sung clearly and a soft high C with thereafter a sudden drop down the scale of almost two octaves.

Even so it is technically easier than Lady Macbeth's runs, and often today the dramatic soprano who can make something of Aida cannot also whirl her way through Lady Macbeth's coloratura. As the composers gradually changed their style, the singers gradually changed their techniques. But their job did not become any easier. Eight years earlier Verdi had lamented in a letter to Luccardi: "You don't have to be able to do coloratura to sing *La Forza del Destino,* but you must have a soul, and understand the *words* and express them." Many sopranos have found acquiring a soul more difficult even than a technique.

ACT 1 SCENE 1 (about 24 mins.)

(A hall in the King's palace at Memphis, on either side a colonade with statues and shrubs, and to the back a gate through which can be seen temples, palaces and the Pyramids.)

PRIEST and RADAMES	dialogue	Rumor declares Ethiopia has invaded Egypt. Isis has selected and the King will announce who is to be Egypt's general.
RADAMES	recitative (fast, and to trumpets)	Suppose it were he. He would fight for Aida.
	aria (slow, and to strings)	"Celeste Aida, forma divina," etc.
RADAMES and AMNERIS	dialogue	She wonders what he is thinking of. He replies "war." And when she insinuates "love," his confusion reveals she was right and that he does not love her.
	duet (fast and very short)	Each expresses his agitation.
AIDA, AMNERIS and RADAMES	dialogue (very melodic)	Amneris suspects Aida is her rival for Radames. She asks sweetly why Aida cries, and Aida answers, "The war."
	trio (fast and longer)	Aida bewails that war dooms her love. Amneris determines to discover the truth about Radames and Aida, and he fears Amneris will spoil his plans.
KING, and ALL	fanfare	The King arrives.
	recitative	The messenger reports the Ethiopians are led by Amonasro. Aida in an aside reveals he is her father.
	chorus (very short)	Interrupts with cries for war.
	recitative (very short)	The King announces Radames will be the general.
	chorus (slow)	Led by the King, all sing a march, "Su del Nilo . . ." in which others, in asides, express their thoughts.
	chorus (fast)	They call for war, "Guerra."
AIDA	recitative (very strong declamation)	"Ritorna Vincitor!" How can she wish him to return victorious over her father and brothers!
	tune (very short and fast)	Let the Ethiopians win.
	tune (short and slow)	But then Radames would die.
	tune (short and slow)	She can hope for neither side to win and perhaps had best die herself.
	tune (longer and slow)	Gods, have pity on her. "Numi, pietà." (ending on a low "C").

The seeds of the new style existed in Verdi's earliest work or, put differently, what remained constant in his work was greater than what changed. In *Aida,* as in the first songs from Goethe's *Faust* (p. 62), Verdi expected to project the soprano's state of soul by her voice. Aida's plea, like Marguerite's lament, has only the very lightest accompaniment. And wherever in *Aida* the voice sounds, it is supreme, always dominating the orchestra. Wagner in *Tristan und Isolde,* which had its première in 1865, had created something quite different. The voice in Isolde's "Liebestod," for example, loses itself at times in the orchestral sound and, particularly toward the end, much of the melody's excitement is carried by the orchestra which continues after Isolde dies. The musical climax is in the orchestra pit rather than on-stage. In Verdi the climax is always in a voice.

Even the way in which Verdi constructed his scenes remained basically the same, although so much more subtly done that it often seemed different. In *Ernani* (p. 130) each character had come on-stage and declaimed some fact in recitative. The fact then led the character into an emotion based on it which was then expressed in an aria. The same thing happens in *Aida* (p. 470), but it is done with greater depth and variety. The recitative leading into "Celeste Aida," for example, goes very quickly and to trumpets, presenting the military, active side of Radames. The aria is slower, softer and to strings, showing Radames in love. The contrast is effective and crystal-clear. Even those who do not understand the words grasp the idea. Like the pageantry, Verdi has made the recitative do double duty: it still serves as a trigger to the aria but now also adds something by way of contrast. Verdi worked particularly hard on the recitatives, wanting them to merge imperceptibly, if possible, into the arias. He succeeded by making them either very short or very melodic, so that an audience feels much of the time that the melodic flow is never broken. This was one reason the critics of the day were misled into announcing that in *Aida* as well as *Don Carlo* Verdi was imitating Wagner. For one of Wagner's principles, which he announced but did not always follow, was that the melodic line should be "continuous," without breaks for the beginnings and ends of arias. Verdi, less theoretical by nature, made no announcements but recognized that long, unmelodic recitative tended to be boring.

Finally, in its atmosphere or soul *Aida* expresses the same Verdi who found in Goethe's *Faust* the suffering Marguerite, in *Nabucco* the cry of the captive Jews, or could write after *Il Trovatore:* "But after all, death is all there is in life. What else is there?" In *Aida,* he wrote his librettist, he wanted to avoid a conventional death scene as Aida and Radames are sealed into the tomb. There was to be no more struggle with life or protest as in *Il Trovatore.* The librettist was to avoid words like: "My senses fail me. I go on before you. Wait for me! She is dead! And I still live! etc. etc." "I want something," Verdi wrote, "sweet, ethereal, a quiet, short duet, a *farewell to life.* Aida should then sink quietly into Radames' arms. Meanwhile Amneris, kneeling above on the stone sealing the tomb, should sing a *Requiescat in pace,* etc." Verdi's view of life continued pessimistic and melancholy. The only change, if it really was one, came in the note of resignation after the struggle. If he had composed *Aida* earlier, he would have closed the curtain on Amneris cursing heaven.

Almost certainly none of this concerns the general public, at least not consciously. It goes to *Aida* primarily for the color and noise of the spectacles. The triumphal scene is the best of its kind yet written, largely because of its clarity and sense of direction. The clarity is equally the result of the libretto and the distinctive quality of the melodies Verdi gave to the various groups. With the simplest stage gestures anyone in the audience can understand that the Ethiopian prisoners are begging for mercy, that the Egyptian people support their plea, and that the Egyptian priests do not. In the great mass of sound the words are indistinguishable, but the melodies stand out and contrast clearly.

The scene also has a sense of direction, of "getting somewhere," because Verdi managed in the libretto to keep the drama moving ahead. An extraordinary amount happens at the parade. Radames is officially betrothed to Amneris with consequent anguish to Aida. Amonasro appears for the first time with the Ethiopian prisoners, and although he is in disguise, Aida's recognition identifies him for the audience. Her anguish over Radames is replaced by relief over her father's safety, only to turn into fear for his life as the priests recommend execution. Everyone, of course, expresses an opinion, and when because of Radames the King announces that Amonasro will be kept as a hostage and so will live, Aida has another series of emotions. So that beside all the elephants, zebras and dancers an impresario can cram onto the stage, there is considerable drama, much more than Meyerbeer had in his skaters' ballet or fiery banquet in *Le Prophète.* And it is this close connection with the drama, together with the vigorous music, which makes it possible for operagoers to see the triumphal scene as often as they do. Each repetition is or can be different depending on the artists doing it, and it never becomes merely spectacle, which seen once or twice is seen often enough.

Verdi had immense pleasure in the success of *Aida,* particularly in the Milan production over which he had taken great care. In the spring, because he felt a tie to Parma, he took the soloists and Faccio there and directed another production on the smaller stage. Then he retired to Sant' Agata and followed the opera's fortunes from a distance.

Some of Verdi's pleasure in *Aida* seemed to lie in the charms of his leading lady, Teresa Stolz. There is no doubt that Verdi found the lady attractive. He had worked with her now on both *La Forza del Destino* and *Aida,* and he had invited her on several occasions to Sant' Agata. To the gossip which had first started a year earlier about Verdi, Mariani and the Bologna *Lohengrin* there was now added a suggestion of sexual intrigue. Everyone, including Strepponi and Mariani, could see that Verdi blossomed in the lady's company. Nevertheless, neither Strepponi nor Mariani thought there was an affair.

Mariani wrote a friend in a letter about Verdi: "All I'll say is that if the gossip about him and another person, who also treated me badly, were true, they would both deserve contempt." The balance of the letter indicates clearly, although indirectly, that Mariani thought they deserved better.

Strepponi expressed her feelings more obliquely. During the season at Parma and thereafter from Padua and Brescia, Stolz wrote Verdi almost twice a week about the performances and the arrangements for her next visit to Sant' Agata. The letters are quite proper, even businesslike, and do not use the intimate form of address. But in the corner of one of them Strepponi wrote: "Sixteen letters!! in a short time!! what *activity!*" Although Verdi was almost sixty and Stolz forty, Strepponi was evidently watching, nervously and with care. So was Mariani who, of course, did not know he would soon be dead. And so was the general public. Verdi at the time was either unaware of the gossip or determined to ignore it. He successfully gave the appearance of being more interested in the productions of his opera, and what he saw and heard often disturbed him.

Conductors made cuts; singers transposed arias down and even changed the melodic lines. In a fury he wrote Ricordi suggesting that the opera be withdrawn and absolutely forbidding any changes to be made in it. But he did not lose his sense of humor altogether. When a man from Reggio wrote enclosing a bill for the cost of going to Parma to see *Aida,* which he had found a bore, Verdi paid it. But he demanded in return a written declaration from the gentleman promising never to hear another new opera by Verdi.

But more disturbing even than the poor productions or the fact that in all Italy there seemed to be one man who did not like the opera was the critical chatter that continued endlessly in musical columns and journals. Its constant theme was that in an effort to keep up with new music Verdi was imitating Wagner. Verdi exploded to Ricordi: "A fine result after thirty-five years to wind up as an imitator!!!"

It is hard today to see why critics and to some extent the public cared so passionately about the issue, which was very artificial. But Wagner had suddenly loomed on the musical scene even as had the German Empire on the European. Everyone talked about Wagner, and his numerous theories positively bred disciples to explain and spread them. Mariani followed his production of *Lohengrin* with one a year later of *Tannhäuser,* and the discussion, comparisons and gossip went right on. Verdi's friend in Naples, De Sanctis, wrote him about an article Torelli was preparing, and Verdi replied:

I read in the *Omnibus* two words which anger me. I don't want to *excuse* myself for being anyone's *disciple.* I am what I am. Every man can think of me what he wishes.

And you are, I repeat, a pretentious bigwig with your Italian music. No, no, there is no Italian music, nor German, nor Turkish . . . but there is MUSIC!! Don't harrass me with these definitions. It is useless! I write as I please and as I feel. I don't believe in the past or the present. I detest all schools, because they all lead to conventionalism. I don't idolize any individual, but I love beautiful music when it is really beautiful, whoever wrote it.

"Progress of Art!!" More meaningless words! It is a thing that moves by itself. If the author is a man of genius, he will make art progress without seeking or wishing to do it.

So tell Torelli to say on his own whatever he wants, and that I shall not defend myself, nor do I want the jokes I make in private to be exposed to the public.

But there lay just the trouble. After *Aida* he was so famous, so successful, so much the leading Italian composer that his privacy, which he considered his by birthright, no longer existed. The invasion of it,

WAGNER

first started by Busseto and defeated, was now taken up by all of Italy.
He was determined to preserve it. He would not lend his name to a
Philharmonic-Dramatic Society in Busseto, would not exhibit himself in Trieste to help a production of *Aida,* and would not defend
himself or his operas in literary jousts. He was a farmer. He would grow
beets and raise horses and be seen regularly at the market in Cremona.

CHAPTER 36

THE MANZONI *REQUIEM*

1872–1875; AGE, 58–61

THROUGHOUT the summer of 1872 Verdi's attention, when not on his farm, was on the production of his operas, particularly the last three. He had gone himself to Parma, but the first *Aida* in Padua he supervised by mail. He persuaded the impresario, probably without much difficulty, to use the scene painter, stage manager, chorus, properties and costumes from Parma, and he also persuaded Faccio to conduct and La Stolz to sing. The result was a great success with enormous receipts at the box office, and the impresario took the trouble to call on Verdi at Sant' Agata in order to thank him. Next, again by mail, Verdi produced *La Forza del Destino* at Brescia, and again the theatre made money. The money was important to everyone, for the opera houses in Italy were increasingly in the red.

Various reasons were offered for this: subsidies from all sources were less or nonexistent; the operas, with their emphasis on drama rather than stand-still singing, were more complicated to produce; and composers wrote for larger orchestras, requiring better players and more rehearsals. Verdi could see the truth in these reasons, and he still advocated subsidies by the State for at least the three most important theatres in Milan, Rome and Naples. But a more basic reason for the poor performances, he felt and stated, was that the persons involved in them were either too stupid or too lazy to improve them. This view did not make him popular in the opera houses. Once when a double-bass player at La Scala declared at a rehearsal that a certain passage was unplayable, Verdi wired to Parma, and the next day a fat, countrified musician arrived. The La Scala orchestra laughed until the man played the passage through without fault. But it learned nothing from the lesson.

The problem of the lazy, incompetent musician has always plagued opera houses. When Toscanini first came to La Scala in 1898 he fired more than forty *comprimari,* singers of secondary roles. The action caused a scandal, but it also began a rise in the theatre's fortunes, artistic and financial, which were at rock bottom: a closed house. Today such a wholesale house cleaning would be impossible, although every important house could use it; but the unions which would prevent it have only complicated, not created, the problem. For Verdi the public was right to refuse to pay money for a second-rate show. His solution to the problem lay in energy and talent, his own or men he had worked with and felt he could trust. For *Aida* he had a two-man team, a designer and director, whom he used to stage the opera at Milan, Parma, Padua, Rome, Paris and London. It is indicative of the problems of La Scala that both men were Parmigiani from the Teatro Regio. Verdi himself went to Naples to produce the opera. Strepponi went with him.

Verdi's plan for Naples was to produce *Don Carlo* first, in December, and while that was running to rehearse *Aida* for a première early the next year, 1873. Stolz was to sing in both, but shortly after *Don Carlo* opened she fell ill, and the rehearsals and première of *Aida* were postponed for several weeks. Left suddenly in a hotel with nothing to do, Verdi composed a short *String Quartet in E Minor.* Sometime in the week after the first performance of *Aida,* which had its usual success, he invited his friends to a surprise concert at his hotel, and the *Quartet* was presented. Not unexpectedly everyone insisted it was charming, and the players repeated it.

In fact, it is charming, light and amusingly operatic in its melodies and dramatic accompaniments. It does not pretend or achieve any great depth as music, and Verdi himself considered it of "little importance." For a number of years he would not allow it to be published or performed anywhere, but as requests for it continued to come in and Ricordi was eager to publish it, he finally agreed. And in 1877 there were public performances of it in Paris, Cologne, Vienna, Milan, and of course many in private by amateurs who simply enjoyed playing it.

Verdi never, however, attempted to make anything of it and quite correctly recognized that it was no better than hundreds of other quartets by less famous composers. The interest in it arose from the fact that he had written it, and it neither enhanced nor damaged his reputation as a musician. Rather it was and is an interesting irrelevancy to his career and as such is still occasionally played.

On 9 April 1873, after almost five months in Naples, Verdi and Strepponi left for Sant' Agata. It had been five months in which they both had seen a great deal of Teresa Stolz, and again there had been gossip about Verdi and his leading lady. Strepponi in her first letter from Sant' Agata to De Sanctis in Naples made the usual remarks about how much she regretted leaving and then enclosed a small card on which she wrote:

I would be curious to know if the gossip on that matter of which you told me all Naples was talking has come to the ears of La S . . .

If by chance you mention this infamous and foolish gossip and learn something, it will be enough in writing me to say on a separate piece of paper: "She knows that."

Strepponi wrote the final three words in English. If, as seems probable, the "La S . . ." was Teresa Stolz, Strepponi was keeping a close, feminine watch on her while at the same time discounting the gossip as gossip.

Verdi also wrote De Sanctis, but his letter merely describes the trip north. His mind, apparently, was mostly filled with thoughts about the theatre, particularly about the problem of poor productions. In a farewell note to the Mayor of Naples he advised:

The greatest thing you can do for the San Carlo would be to put through the reforms demanded by the needs of art today. The careless and ignorant way of putting on operas in recent years is no longer possible.

Later he wrote to a friend in Rome:

I know that at Rome they are thinking of reorganizing the theatre, and I wish the reformers really understood that modern opera has very different requirements from that of the past, and that to achieve success, a good ensemble is absolutely necessary. Consequently, the direction should be entrusted only to two men who must be capable and energetic. One should direct all musical matters: singers, chorus, orchestra, etc.; the other, scenic matters: costumes, property, scenery, production, etc. These two men must decide everything and assume all the responsibility. Only then is there any hope of a good performance and a success.

Verdi also had suggestions for the design of opera houses, many of which were being altered as gas replaced candles in the chandeliers and footlights. At La Scala he was particularly anxious to be rid of the stage boxes in which spectators sat between the orchestra and the singers: "It is impossible today to tolerate horrible tailcoats and white ties among Egyptian, Assyrian and Druid costumes." In conjunction with this the curtain could be moved out to the footlights. He also wanted to sink the orchestra in a pit: "The idea is not mine, but Wagner's, and it is excellent." At the time the orchestra generally sat on the same level as the audience, forming a hedge between it and the stage "with the harps, double basses and the windmill arms of the conductor jutting into the air." As a place to sit the orchestra floor only began to become fashionable after these changes were made.

The introduction of gas to replace candles, which occurred in most of the larger theatres during the 1870s, was a major revolution in theatre construction and affected even the kind of operas composed. For the first time the house lights could easily be dimmed and the auditorium made much darker than the stage. In another twenty years electricity would make it possible to put the auditorium in total darkness and relight it easily and safely.

Dimming the house lights greatly emphasized the musical side of a performance over the social parade connected with it. Under candles, which once lit had to remain so, the audience visited in boxes, waved and whispered during the performance as well as in the intermission. Kings and Emperors who hated music sat in boxes for an act or two because they could be seen the whole time. The opera house was as much a social as musical center of a city. Gas and later electricity changed this. With the audience sitting in darkness unmusical Kings and Emperors decided the intermission was simply not worth the agony of the music, and society began to go elsewhere, to show itself off where it could be seen. Music lovers rejoiced, for the gabbling noise of society had always been infuriating. But the cost was great, and part of the financial difficulty of the opera houses in Italy arose from the fact that they were losing part of their audience. Verdi's operas reflect the change and span it. His early operas were lit by candle, *Aida* by gas, and *Falstaff,* his last, by electricity. His later works are far more purely musical than, say, *I Lombardi* or *La Battaglia di Legnano.* From a musical point of view this was undoubtedly a good thing, but his extraordinary national prominence, which even such successful composers as Puccini or Wagner could not begin to equal, had its roots in a time when an opera house was more than just a house for music. And that time was passing.

Verdi's thinking, however, was conditioned by it, and when Manzoni, at the age of eighty-nine, died on 22 May 1873, it was characteristic of Verdi to begin to think at once of how to use music to honor one of Italy's great public figures, even though Manzoni himself was not a musician.

Manzoni's death was not a surprise. Two weeks before on his way to early-morning Mass he had slipped on the steps of the church of San Fedele and been carried home unconscious. Then, as all of educated Italy watched and waited, he fell into a state of alternating mania and delirium with occasional flashes of his old wit. When a visitor asked him why it was he got things all mixed up, he replied: "If I knew why it was, I wouldn't get them mixed up." The last thing he read was a few pages of Propertius.

His body was laid in state in the Town Hall of Milan and a funeral procession held on the sixth day after his death. All the shops were closed, memorial odes put in their windows and pasted on the walls, and the people packed the streets from the Town Hall to the cemetery. A squadron of cavalry and groups of scholastic and workers' organizations preceded the bier. Vittorio Emanuele sent two princes of the blood to carry the flanking cords, and they were aided by the Presidents of the Senate and the Chamber and the Ministers for Education and Foreign Affairs. The bier itself was drawn by six horses.

Verdi did not attend the funeral. To Ricordi he confessed he was too moved. To the Contessa he wrote: "Now all is over! and with him ends, the most pure, the most holy, the greatest of our glories. I have read many papers. Not one speaks fittingly of him. Many words, but none deeply felt. There is no lack of gibes. Even at him! Oh, what a wretched race we are!"

The gibes came mostly from clerical papers. One published an attack on Manzoni as a bad Catholic, arguing that he had insulted the Pope by accepting an honorary citizenship of Rome. Another found a "fine poison" in his books: "Manzoni was never straight in his thoughts." The head of the Jesuits in Milan said bluntly: "He was a born revolutionary." Pio Nono said nothing.

A week after the funeral Verdi went to Milan and visited Manzoni's grave alone. Then through Ricordi he proposed to the Mayor of Milan that he write a Requiem Mass to honor Manzoni on the first anniversary of his death; Verdi to pay the expenses of preparing and printing the music, the city to pay the cost of its performance on the anniversary date. Thereafter the Requiem would belong to Verdi. The city accepted, and the following week Verdi returned to Sant' Agata.

Obviously his approach to this Requiem Mass was influenced by his experience with the one he had dropped to honor Rossini. This time he began not with a public letter but privately. No committee was appointed or other composers or conductors involved. Verdi kept everything in his own hand. He would compose the entire Mass, select the singers and chorus, rehearse them and conduct them in performance. He could even select the hall in which the performance would be given. The only restrictions were that it must be in Milan and on the anniversary date. And there was never any question of locking the Mass away after the single commemorative performance. This one, composed by a single man, would have artistic unity and if successful would be available for public performance like any other of Verdi's works.

While these details were being agreed upon, Mariani, still in Verdi's eyes the villain in the history of the *Requiem* for Rossini, died in Genoa. Verdi did not attend the funeral but exclaimed when told of Mariani's death: "What a misfortune for art." Mariani died in horrible pain, without a friend by him and almost without a doctor, while the great love of his life, Teresa Stolz, was in Ancona, singing in *Aida*. It was a sad, bitter end to a great career.

For his Manzoni *Requiem* Verdi supposedly started with a final and important section already composed, the *Libera Me* he had done for the Rossini *Requiem*. But, to snatch a conclusion from the scholars without recapitulating their evidence, it seems he largely rewrote it although retaining many of his ideas. So it is fair to say that the Manzoni *Requiem* is a single work and not two pieces fitted together.

Verdi began work on it in Paris where he and Strepponi spent the summer. It was their first visit since the days of the Commune, and the ruins of the Tuileries and other buildings burned saddened him. But at the same time he took long walks in the working-class sections of La Villette and Belleville, parts of Paris where many of the Communards had lived but which few tourists bothered to examine.

Baron Haussmann, whose vision and energy had created a new and beautiful city out of the soiled and smelly Paris of the 1840s, had been forced from office in January 1870, only eight months before Napoleon and the Empire fell. Thereafter neither the city nor the state undertook any new projects and, what with the disasters of the war, barely finished those already begun. The new house for the Opéra was completed in 1874 and opened the next year with an evening of operatic selections from dead composers, thus offending no one. There were the overtures to Rossini's *William Tell* and Auber's *La Muette de Portici,* two acts of Halévy's *La Juive* and a scene from Meyerbeer's *Les Huguenots.* The only concession to the living was the ballet *La Source* by the *Chef de Chant* of the Opéra, Léo Delibes.

The merits and defects of Haussmann's city have been argued since it first began to appear in the 1850s. Many persons complain of the heavy, pretentious style of architecture which was enforced on builders by law. Others point out that some of the conceptions are mechanical or so vast they can make no impression. The Place de l'Étoile, for example, is most impressive from the air where it can be taken in with a single view. Against these objections most men will insist on the city's beauty, its parks and boulevards, and professional city planners will point out that for the first time men concerned themselves with city planning: parks, sewers and water supply. Napoleon and Haussmann believed a big, modern, industrial city could be beautiful, and that it was important for it to be so. Perhaps these premises on which they planned were ultimately of greater moment than anything they achieved.

France itself in the summer of 1873 was still a "republic without any republicans." The majority of Deputies were royalist sympathizers and might well take the opportunity offered by the drafting of a new constitution to declare France a constitutional monarchy. What held them back was the terms which the leading pretender demanded. He was the Comte de Chambord, representing the legitimist line. The Comte de Paris, representing the Orléanists, had agreed to support his fifty-three-year-old cousin who was a bachelor and without an heir provided the throne passed to the Orléans line on Chambord's death. This compromise seemed to insure a monarchy for France. Napoleon III had died in England in January, and his son, the Prince Imperial, was too young to be a political force. The republicans were still regarded as sources of war and social disorder. But the Comte de Chambord turned out to lack any political sense. He viewed his return as a "Restoration" to things as they were sometime before 1789. He insisted, for example, that the tricolor flag be replaced by the royal fleur-de-lis on a white field, and he kept issuing manifestos which horrified all but the most hardened monarchists. He succeeded in pro-

THE OPÉRA

ducing a stalemate: monarchists controlled the Chamber but had no candidate. Eventually in 1875 the Chamber produced its new constitution, drawn up on the British model. There was a position for a "president" which could easily be retitled "king." But it never was. The royalists missed the tide in 1873, and gradually the republicans captured their republic by winning in local elections until they controlled both Chambers and the presidency. This Third Republic was the first in France to last more than ten years and survived until 1940 when it fell in World War II. But for the remaining years of Verdi's life France, which he considered the source of liberty, was a republic and the only one of any size in Europe.

Verdi had finished his *Requiem* by April when he sent the score to Ricordi, and soon thereafter he went to Milan to determine where it should be given. He selected the Church of San Marco as having the best proportions and acoustics for the size choir and orchestra he would use, and the première was given there on 22 May 1874, the first anniversary of Manzoni's death.

The occasion was one of the rare public events to be a success in every way. Manzoni, the most distinguished literary figure in the history of Milan, was honored by having international attention focused on him; the city through its officials was everywhere credited with having done the right thing; and for the occasion Verdi produced a masterpiece. The performance, all critics agreed, was excellent. Stolz was the soprano soloist and Verdi conducted. There was an orchestra of a hundred and a chorus of one hundred and twenty. The church is not very large and could not begin to contain the number of persons who tried to get in. Three days later Verdi conducted another performance, but this time at La Scala, and this was followed by still two more conducted by Faccio. The atmosphere of the first performance at La Scala was very different from that in San Marco. For La Scala, for example, Stolz changed from subdued clothing to a dress of blue silk trimmed with white velvet. The mezzo-soprano, Maria Waldmann, wore solid pink. Everything was applauded, and three sections were encored. At its end amid wild applause a silver crown "on an elegant cushion" was presented to Verdi.

Some persons objected that Manzoni was slighted by the honors and attention given to Verdi who merely used Manzoni to push himself forward. The argument soon reaches the curious and delightful conclusion that Manzoni would have been better honored if Verdi had produced something less good; perhaps something really bad, so that the whole thing could be dismissed in a paragraph.

More to the point was the argument that Verdi had not written ecclesiastical music although using an ecclesiastical text. Critics, musical and otherwise, at the time and ever since have raised this point and divided on its importance. The Roman Church took an official stand in 1903 when Pope Pius X issued an encyclical, "Motu proprio," setting out the requirements for ecclesiastical music and by definition excluding many nineteenth-century Masses, among them the *Requiem*. The Church wanted what most persons think of as religious music: liturgical texts set to counterpoint, fugues or imitations using melodies that, however vigorous, do not distract the listener from the religious message of the service. Verdi violated these canons and departed from what many expected of religious music, both in the character and form of his melody, which was extremely dramatic, and also in the "message" of his *Requiem*. For what Verdi emphasized in the text was quite different from what other composers had done before him or from what, perhaps, the Church would ideally like to have emphasized.

There is no one text for a Requiem to which all composers stick. Brahms, for example, extracted seven texts in German from the Lutheran Bible and composed *A German Requiem* of which the purpose or message was to give comfort, after the death of some loved person, to those left living. But Requiems in the Italian or French tradition use Latin texts from the Roman Catholic liturgy and have as their purpose the winning of peace, by the prayers of the living, for those already dead. Verdi's *Requiem* starts out, at least, within this Latin tradition.

In the Roman Catholic Church the Requiem Mass is said on "All Souls' Day," 2 November, and also can be said on public occasions or at the funeral of an individual or the anniversary of his death. Cherubini's *Requiem in C Minor,* for example, was first performed in the Abbey of St. Denis on 21 January 1817, the twenty-fourth anniversary of Louis XVI's execution. Berlioz's *Requiem* or *Grande Messe des Morts* had its first performance in La Chapelle of the Hôtel des Invalides on 5 December 1837. Originally its purpose had been to commemorate the men killed in the revolution of July 1830, but by the time of its performance it was commemorating French soldiers killed in the capture of Constantine in Algeria. But not all Requiems were composed for such public occasions. Mozart's *Requiem,* his last composition, was a private commission by a man who wanted the work performed for his deceased wife. He is supposed also to have planned to palm it off as his own work, which was why he sent around a mysterious "man in gray" who refused to reveal his principal. Mozart, falling ill, believed the "man in gray" was a portent and that he was really composing the *Requiem* for himself, or so the romantic nineteenth century loved to believe. Mozart's grieving widow, however, was simply practical. She saw the *Requiem* was not quite complete, persuaded a friend to finish it, and then, insisting that Mozart himself had done all the work, collected the full commission.

Berlioz, Cherubini and Mozart all used the same text which consists of that part of the Requiem Mass traditionally set to music. The central part of it is the *Dies Irae,* the *Day of Wrath,* which is a medieval poem by Thomas of Celano, a friend of St. Francis of Assisi. Thomas in his poem recites a vision of Judgment Day calculated to terrify a listener into virtue. To this usual text Verdi added a last section, the *Libera Me,* which, although not an integral part of the Mass, sometimes followed it on solemn occasions and sometimes was set to music. He also expanded the *Dies Irae* by repeating certain of its crucial lines out of order and, by emphasizing them, bound his *Requiem* tightly together. Berlioz, Cherubini and Mozart had each composed his *Requiem* to be used as part of a service although today all three are generally performed independently in a concert hall. But Verdi from the first imagined his as a purely musical work.

Verdi's text is set out on pp. 488–491. Those lines which he either repeated, inserted or added to the more "usual" text which Mozart used are underlined; those words he emphasized by a musical climax or repetition are set in capitals.

It would be best if the text were read with imagination and over and over as Verdi did all his texts before he set them. But in the interest of speed, notice the primitive imagery that runs throughout. The living want the dead to have peace and light. The texts are very old and come from a time when the night with its darkness was terrifying. Men lay down at night not sure the sun would rise again. Eclipses panicked whole nations, and the worst thing to be imagined was eternal night. Artificial light, fire, was a blessing and a curse; it kept men warm, but every child knew the pain of being burned; once extinguished, it was hard to start; its source was not understood; it was a miracle; it was from God, who could use it to bless, by banishing night, or to punish, by burning. The wise and the frightened prayed and tried to buy God's favor by sacrificing their animals. To make their prayers louder, to reach further into the night, they often gathered in groups, chanting and dancing around a fire.

This was all years ago, and Verdi, faced with a nineteenth-century, musically sophisticated audience, did not intend to entertain them with a tone poem depicting pastoral life among the savages. But he did intend to involve them emotionally in a drama which they all felt they knew backward and forward and need pay no attention to. He succeeded not only by the excellence of his music but by stirring in the audience the ancient feelings and fears of primitive man peering nervously into the night, trying to find his God and establish some sort of relationship with him. By the end of his *Requiem* Verdi has his singers and audience praying for peace and light, not for the dead, but for themselves, the living.

He begins in the *Requiem and Kyrie* in a quiet ecclesiastical style, the sort of music and approach to the text that everyone expected. The music is lovely; the soloists are introduced, and the whole builds up into a mass of sound through which the lines of the various voices remain admirably clear.

But then comes Thomas of Celano with his vision of the Last Judgment, and Verdi knocks the world apart with the violence of his music. Four cracks of doom from the orchestra, and the voices begin the dizzy slide into blackness. No one can possibly not pay attention. Mozart had set the first six lines of the poem in order and then repeated them. Verdi greatly emphasized the first line, the idea of wrath, and he kept bringing it back throughout the section, giving the whole a constant undertone of terror. In both Berlioz and Mozart the musical climax of the poem comes on "Rex Tremendae Majestatis," making the poem primarily one in praise of God. Verdi, on the other hand, emphasized the *Salva Me* which with the constantly recurring *Dies Irae* makes the poem one of an individual's terror on the Day of Judgment. It is as though an angry God had come down in the holocaust and, standing on the altar, was pointing a fiery finger at "you, you and you: damned"; while of the people some pressed forward, others knelt where they were, and all called out to Jesus: "Save me."

REQUIEM AND KYRIE

Requiem aeternam dona eis, Domine, et lux perpetua luceat eis. Te decet hymnus Deus in Sion, et tibi reddetur vótum in Jerusalem. Exaudi orationem meam, ad te omnis caro veniet. Requiem aeternam dona eis, Domine, et lux perpetua luceat eis.

Kyrie eleison. Christe eleison. Kyrie eleison.

Give them eternal peace, Lord, and let perpetual light shine on them. A hymn becomes you God in Sion, and to you a vow will be made in Jerusalem. Hear my plea, to thee all flesh will come. Give them eternal peace, Lord, and let perpetual light shine on them.

Lord, have mercy upon us. Christ, have mercy upon us. Lord, have mercy upon us.

DIES IRAE

DIES IRAE, DIES ILLA
    solvet saeclum in favilla,
    teste David cum Sibylla.

Quantus tremor est futurus,
    quando judex est venturus,
    cuncta stricte discussurus.

TUBA MIRUM SPARGENS SONUM

    per sepulchra regionum,
    coget omnes ante thronum.

MORS stupebit et natura
    cum resurget creatura
    judicanti responsura.

Liber scriptus proferetur,
    in quo totum continetur
    unde mundus judicetur.

Dies Irae

Judex ergo cum sedebit,
    quiquid latet,
    apparebit;

Dies Irae
    NIL inultum remanebit.

Dies Irae

DIES IRAE, DIES ILLA
    solvet saeclum in favilla,
    teste David cum Sibylla,

DAY OF WRATH, THAT DAY
    shall dissolve the world in ash
    as David and the Sibyl promise.

How great the terror will be
    when the judge is about to come
    on whose word everything hangs.

THE TRUMPET, SCATTERING ITS
    AWFUL SOUND
    through the graves of earth
    drives all before the throne.

DEATH and nature will be astounded
    when everything created will rise up
    to answer to the judge.

The book of record will be brought out,
    in which everything is entered
    from which the world will be judged.

Day of Wrath

Then when the judge takes his seat,
    whatever is hidden, will appear;

Day of Wrath
    NOTHING will go unpunished.

Day of Wrath

DAY OF WRATH, THAT DAY
    shall dissolve the world in ash,
    as David and the Sibyl promise.

Quid sum, miser, tunc dicturus?
  quem patronum rogaturus,
  cum vix justus sit securus?

REX TREMENDAE MAJESTATIS,
  qui salvandos salvas gratis,
  SALVA ME, fons pietatis.

Recordare, Jesu pie,
  quod sum causa tuae viae,
  ne me perdas illa die.

Quaereus me sedisti lassus,
  redemisti crucem passus;

  tantus labor non sit cassus.

Juste judex ultionis,
  donum fac remissionis
  ante diem rationis.

Ingemisco tamquam reus,
  culpa rebet vultus meus;
  supplicanti parce Deus.

Qui Mariam absolvisti,
  et latronem exaudisti,
  mihi quoque spem dedisti.

Preces meae non sunt dignae,
  sed tu bonus fac benigne,
  ne perenni cremer igne.

Inter oves locum praesta,
  et ab haedis me sequestra
  statuens in parte dextra.

Confutatis maledictis,
  flammis acrivus addictis,
  voca me cum benedictis.

Oro supplex et acclinis,
  cor contritum quasi cinis,

  gere curam mei finis.

DIES IRAE, DIES ILLA
  solvet saeclum in favilla,
  teste David cum Sibylla,

What am I, miserable man, then to say?
  to what protector will I turn,
  when even the just man is scarcely safe?

KING OF DREADFUL MAJESTY,
  who saves those needing it for nothing,
  SAVE ME, you fount of pity.

Remember, Jesus holy one,
  that I am the reason for your life,
  so that you won't destroy me on that
    day.

Seeking me you have sat down weary;
  suffering on the cross you have bought
    me free.
  let not so much labor be for nothing.

You impartial judge of punishment,
  make a gift of remission
  before the day of accounting.

I groan as when I'm guilty; . .
  my sins make my face red; . .
  God, spare the supplicant.

You who absolved Mary
  and listened to the thief,
  have also given me hope.

My prayers are not worthy,
  but you good Lord kindly make them so,
  lest I be burned in the everlasting fire.

Save me a place with the sheep,
  and take me away from the goats,
  putting me on your right-hand side.

When the wicked are overthrown
  and given to the crackling flames,
  call me with the blessed.

I beg as a suppliant and relying on you,
  my heart almost burned out with re-
    morse;
  take pity on my end.

DAY OF WRATH, THAT DAY
  shall dissolve the world in ash
  as David and the Sibyl promise.

Lacrymosa dies illa,
   qua resurget ex favilla
   judicandus homo reus.

Huic ergo parce Deus.
   pie Jesu Domine,
   dona eis REQUIEM.

Amen.

That tearful day
   in which shall rise out of the dust
   the guilty man to be judged

Spare him then, God.
   holy Jesus Lord
   give them PEACE.

Amen.

DOMINE JESU

Domine Jesu Christe, Rex Gloriae, libera animas omnium fidelium defunctorum de poenis inferni, et de profundo lacu. Libera eas de ore leonis, ne absorbeat eas Tartarus, ne cadant in obscurum. Sed signifer sanctus Michael repraesentet eas in lucem sanctam; quam olim Abrahae promisisti et semini ejus.

Hostias et preces tibi, Domine, laudis offerimus: tu suscipe pro animabus illis quarum hodie memoriam facimus. Fac eas, Domine, de morte transire ad vitam; quam olim Abrahae promisisti et semini ejus.

Lord Jesus Christ, King of Glory, free the souls of all the faithful dead from the punishments of Hell and the bottomless pit. Free them from the mouth of the lion so that Hell will not gulp them down nor will they fall into darkness. But let holy Michael, the standard-bearer, lead them into the holy light; as you once promised to Abraham and his children.

Animals and prayers to you, Lord, we offer in praise; take them for the benefit of those souls whom we are remembering today. Make them, Lord, go from death to life; as you once promised to Abraham and his children.

SANCTUS

Sanctus, sanctus, sanctus Dominus Deus Sabaoth. Pleni sunt coeli et terra gloria tua. Hosanna in excelsis. Benedictus, qui venit in nomine Domini. Hosana in excelsis.

Holy, holy, holy Lord God of hosts. The heavens and earth are filled with your glory. Hosanna in the highest. Blessed is he who comes in the name of the Lord. Hosanna in the highest.

AGNUS DEI

Agnus Dei, qui tollis peccata mundi, dona eis requiem. Agnus Dei, qui tollis peccata mundi, dona eis requiem sempiternam.

Lamb of God, who takes away the sins of the world, give them peace. Lamb of God, who takes away the sins of the world, give them peace everlasting.

LUX AETERNA

Lux aeterna luceat eis, Domine, cum Sanctis tuis in aeternum, quia pius es. Requiem aeternam dona eis, Domine, et lux perpetua luceat eis.

Let eternal light shine on them, Lord, with your saints in eternity, because you are kind. Give them eternal peace, Lord, and let perpetual light shine on them.

LIBERA ME

Libera me, Domine, de morte aeterna, in die illa tremenda, quando coeli movendi sunt et terra; dum veneris judicare saeculum per ignem.

Tremens factus sum ego et timeo, dum discussio venerit atque ventura ira, quando coeli movendi sunt et terra.

DIES IRAE, DIES ILLA, calamitatis et miseriae, dies magna et amara valde; dum veneris judicare saeculum per ignem.

Requiem aeternam dona eis, Domine, et lux perpetua luceat eis.

LIBERA ME, Domine, de morte aeterna, in die illa tremenda, quando coeli movendi sunt et terra; dum veneris judicare saeculum per ignem.

LIBERA ME.

Free me, Lord, from eternal death on that terrifying day when the heavens and earth are shattered; when you will have come to judge the age with fire.

I tremble and am afraid at the judgment that will have come and the wrath to follow, when the heavens and earth are shattered.

DAY OF WRATH, THAT DAY of calamity and misery, the day so great and very bitter; when you will have come to judge the age with fire.

Give them eternal peace, Lord, and let perpetual light shine on them.

FREE ME, Lord, from eternal death on that terrifying day when the heavens and earth are shattered; when you will have come to judge the age with fire.

FREE ME

The succeeding verses Verdi gave to his soloists, intensifying the idea of an individual appeal. Berlioz throughout used his chorus, and Mozart, even when he used his soloists, made them sing as a quartet. The effect is to keep the poem more liturgical; the appeal is channeled through the church service and is for everyone. As such it has less immediate intensity for its audience.

Verdi closes the poem, after a last glimpse at the *Dies Irae,* on long decrescendo covering the last six lines. The effect is of a vision fading; gradually, as the thought and possibility of personal damnation recedes, the soloists and audience begin to remember where they are and why they gathered. And they end by praying for the dead.

The next sections are more liturgical in their feeling and also in the settings Verdi provided for them. His fugue for double chorus in the *Sanctus* is a perfect example of the ecclesiastical style in music, and if it is a touch more vigorous than most, it may be the better for it. In the *Sanctus* occurs the phrase "Hosanna in excelsis," and in his *Requiem* Berlioz greatly emphasized it, making of it a musical climax to correspond with the previous "Rex Tremendae Majestatis." Verdi keeps all these middle sections short and subdued in comparison to his *Dies Irae.* To balance that earlier climax he has the *Libera Me,* which does not appear in Berlioz at all.

Verdi's final section plunges the singers and audience back into the personal drama as though someone had said the wrong thing and God suddenly reappeared. The soprano is the soloist, asking to be freed from eternal death, and at the mention of judgment by fire, the *Dies Irae* begins to build up in the orchestra. Suddenly it bursts out in all its fury, terrifying and awful, and the broken suppliants almost sob their request of peace and light for the dead. But then, as in the *Dies Irae* section, their thoughts turn to themselves: "Libera me, libera me." Verdi expresses this as a finale, using a fugue sung by the chorus. Each voice enters with the words "libera me" set to a heavily accented "skip-stamp-stamp" rhythm or "Dum-dee-Dum-Dum."

This is a very simple rhythmic pattern, the kind in which when repeated, anyone, savage or sophisticated, instinctively joins. Verdi pounds on it as the voices enter, as the phrase reoccurs, and in the orchestra. He directs that it be sung "allegro risoluto"; that is, at the speed of one who is "merry" and "with resolution." In the orchestra he uses it as he did the "screw-turn" figures in the finales of his early operas, to give the fugue a strong sense of forward motion by sounding whenever the voices stop for breath or hold long notes. The simple rhythm, constantly repeated while the melody above it varies, soon has the audience and singers joined in a common bond, like a lot of savages around a fire stamping away their fears. "Libera me," they sing, calling on the magic of music and words to save them from the terror of the unknown. But magic even in a group does not answer an individual's fears. One by one they fall silent, drop their neighbor's hand and peer out into the night, alone. "Free me, Lord," the soprano pleads alone, "from eternal death on that awful day." "Free me," each one breathes. "Free me."

Of course Verdi, when he composed the *Requiem,* did not think of savage tribes stomping out their fears or even of medieval men who believed in the exact truth of Thomas of Celano's vision. Nor does an audience hear it in such pictorial detail. The methods of music are different and more general. But musicologists have shown that its basic qualities, particularly rhythm, are deeply embedded in man's emotional and religious feelings, and these Verdi quite deliberately stirred. The audience, whether it intellectually wants to or not, becomes emotionally involved in the sheer rush of sound in the final fugue and, like the chorus and soloists, asks for some sort of emotional release. This Verdi, also quite deliberately, refuses to give it. There is no sudden burst into a sunny amen, no vision of a kind God or promise of intercession; there is only dwindling power and continued uncertainty. Such, said Verdi, is man's lot in life.

No church gives such an answer; they all offer some happy solution to the quest for assurance that life and life after death have certainty and meaning. In this respect Verdi's *Requiem* is not a religious work, and the Roman Church is quite right to ban it (*See* Appendix F). In not offering a clear solution Verdi reflected the increasing uncertainty of the end of the nineteenth century when Darwin and the new science were shaking traditional beliefs. And Verdi, who anyway had never held them, was far too honest an artist to fake an ending to his *Requiem* that he did not himself feel. On this point his wife, already quoted on Verdi's religious beliefs (p. 287), wrote wisely to a friend:

They have all talked so much of the more, or less, religious spirit of this sacred music, of not having followed the style of Mozart, of Cherubini, etc. etc. I say that a man like Verdi must write like Verdi, that is according to how he feels and interprets the texts. And if the religions themselves have a beginning, a development, some modifications or transformations etc. according to the times and peoples, evidently the religious spirit and works that express it must carry the stamp of their time and (if you agree) of an individual personality. I'd have simply rejected a *Mass* by Verdi that had been modeled on A, B, or C!! Perhaps I'm talking nonsense. (etc.)

But even if the *Requiem* is agnostic in that it does not offer a Catholic, Lutheran or Hindu resolution to the fears it raises, it is religious in the sense that it recognizes the fears and needs of man and suggests that there is some sort of Creator or Being with whom man ought to develop a relationship.

Many persons, however, did not bother their heads with whether Verdi's music was more or less religious; they simply enjoyed it. And it was as good if not better than *Aida,* just as melodic, as dramatically apt, and possibly even better orchestrated. Every Italian had known the texts since earliest childhood, and to have them suddenly set to glorious melodies almost made popular songs of them. So much so that Verdi insisted Ricordi use the law to prevent unauthorized and mutilated performances of it. At Bologna four pianos had been substituted for the orchestra, and at Ferrara, a military band. But any amateur could buy the vocal score and bawl the tenor solo, "Ingemisco," to his heart's content.

The popularity of the *Requiem* led some to doubt its worth. Hans von Bülow, an outstanding German pianist and conductor who was also an important disciple of Wagner, disliked it even before he had heard a note of it. He happened to be in Milan at the time of the première and published in the papers a letter in which he stated for those who cared: "Hans von Bülow was not present at the show [sic] presented yesterday in San Marco. Hans von Bülow must not be counted among the foreigners gathered in Milan to hear Verdi's sacred music." And on the eve of the première he had written to Germany, as soon was general knowledge in Italy, "Verdi, the omnipotent corruptor of artistic taste in Italy, hopes to sweep away the last remains of Rossini's immortality which inconveniences him. His latest opera, in ecclesiastical dress, will be exposed, after the first fictitious compliment to the memory of the poet, for three evenings to the world's admiration. After that it will go accompanied by the trained soloists to Paris, the aesthetic Rome of the Italians." (For "trained" Bülow used the German word applicable to circus animals.) Lastly he added: "A hasty, stolen glance at this emanation from *Trovatore* and *Traviata* took away any desire to attend this Festival."

It was offensive and on its face uninformed. Brahms, after hearing of Bülow's opinions, examined the score and observed: "Bülow has blundered, since this could be done only by a genius." As most of Europe agreed with Brahms, Bülow soon found himself without an audience, an appalling situation for an egotist, and years later with newspaper fanfare he reversed himself.

After the La Scala performances Verdi took the *Requiem* to Paris where there were seven more at the Opéra Comique. These were so successful that Ricordi and Escudier arranged a tour for the spring of 1875, and Verdi agreed to conduct and Stolz and Waldmann to sing. Before leaving for Paris, first city on the tour, Verdi, the careful farmer, wrote out exact instructions for his bailiff:

The youngest colt should be continually in harness and never allowed to break its trot, which must always be slow and gentle. You will see that next year he will go splendidly, perhaps as well as the other. And as for the other, take great care he does not develop some vice. He is a horse who is very much above himself and, being at the same time very quick, he might easily come to some harm.

In Paris there were again seven performances, and the French government made Verdi a Commander of the Legion of Honor. In London there were three in Albert Hall with a chorus of twelve hundred, and in Vienna four combined with two of *Aida* for a Verdi festival. Vienna was a considerably smaller city than London or Paris, and for the *Requiem* to be able to fill the Hofoper at high prices on hot June nights was considered extraordinary. While there Verdi received the medal of the Franz-Josef Order and also went to see *Tannhäuser*. It was his first visit to Vienna since April of 1843 when Merelli had produced *Nabucco*.

At the time of the *Requiem* tour Verdi was in his sixty-second year, and in many ways both he and others considered it the climax of his career. He had proved himself as a composer in more fields than one, as a conductor and choral director, and by taking his music to foreign capitals a worthy successor to Rossini. Verdi himself probably never thought it and certainly never said it, but others did. With Rossini and Manzoni both dead, Verdi was now the chief glory of Italy. In fact he was the only one, for it was a sterile period in the other arts and the political figures like Garibaldi were either tarnished or not very great.

CHAPTER 37

STOLZ, BOITO AND
SIMONE BOCCANEGRA REVISED

1875–1881; AGE, 61–67

IN the months following the tour with the *Requiem* the persistent gossip about Verdi and Teresa Stolz came to a head with the publication of a serial article in a Florentine journal, *Rivista Independente*. The installments began with an editorial promising "to tell the truth" about the Verdi-Stolz-Mariani relations "without passion or prejudice." The article then described Stolz's career as entirely the creation of Mariani, called her "an accomplished courtesan," and accused her of deserting Mariani for Verdi because the latter had more money. Verdi was portrayed throughout as something of a fool: "Poor fame, poor name, how low you have been brought!"

The article's climax was an account of Verdi visiting Stolz in a hotel room in Milan. There "a little later the amorous couple stretched themselves out, or rather did not stretch themselves out but accommodated themselves, made themselves comfortable, sat themselves, on a soft sofa." The writer then confessed that he had not been in the room because the door was locked, but "the fact is" that Verdi "in the heat of the struggle" lost his wallet. He eventually recovered it when, at the suggestion of a waiter, a search was made of the sofa. And there was more, equally unpleasant in tone although not so sensational.

After the publication of the first installment Strepponi wrote Stolz who was then singing in the *Requiem* at Florence. The letter sounds as though either Strepponi had seen the article herself or had heard of it from Stolz. In the midst of a longer letter Strepponi wrote:

By now you will have arrived at Florence where I think it best to address this letter. That you love us I know, or rather we know, we believe it, we rejoice in believing it, and we have faith that in you we will never be disappointed. That we love you you know, you believe it, you rejoice in believing it, and you may be certain that towards you we shall continue the same as long as we live. So, my dear Teresa, the fear of *being in the way,* because you saw in me a touch of sadness, is a fear to put by that which made you, for fear of disturbing us, go to your room almost at sunset with the famous phrase: *If you'll excuse me, I'll retire.* You are never too much with us as long as you and we remain the honest, loyal hearts we are. With this and a kiss I close the paragraph.

If Stolz was upset, she can hardly have imagined a more wonderful letter to receive. If Strepponi was upset, she concealed it magnificently. Even after three years of gossip in September 1875 Strepponi was able, apparently, to dismiss the articles, confidently and magnanimously, as malicious libel. But in the following spring, when she, Verdi and Teresa Stolz were in Paris for the first performances there of *Aida,* she confided some doubts to her notebook in which she often wrote out first drafts of her letters. This particular letter has no date although it follows, after a blank page, one dated 21 April 1876. There is no way of knowing when she wrote it or whether, having put her thoughts once on paper, she delivered them recopied to Verdi or, on second thought, closed the book and kept her peace.

The letter with the canceled words indicated reads:

It did not seem to me to be a suitable day for you to visit a lady who is neither your wife, daughter, nor sister . . . and the observation escaped me. I realized at once it had irritated you. This irritation hurt me, for as the lady is neither sick nor about to give a performance it seemed to me you could go twenty-four hours without seeing her, especially since I had taken the trouble myself to go up to her room to ask after her; which I told you as soon as I returned.

I don't know if there is or is not anything in it . . . I do know that since 1872 there have been on your part [erased: "febrile"] periods of assiduity and attentions that could not be taken by any woman in a sense more flattering. [erased: "I know that I have not failed with this lady in courtesy and cordiality."] I know how I have always been disposed to love her openly and sincerely. You know how you have paid me back: with hard, violent, wounding words. You cannot control yourself, when I open my spirit to the hope that you will see this lady and things as they are.

If there is anything in it . . . [erased: "If you find this lady so seductive."] Be frank and say so without humiliating me with these excessive deferences.

If there is nothing in it . . . be more calm in your attentions [erased: "Don't be so agitated"], be natural and less exclusive. Think sometimes that I, your wife, scorning past gossip, am at this very moment living *à trois* and have the right if not to your caresses at least to your regard. Is it too much? How was my disposition the first twenty days? Calm and merry, and that was because you were cordial.

Behind all the smoke was there a fire? Strepponi's notes would seem to indicate there was not. Verdi responded perhaps foolishly and evidently extravagantly to the attention bestowed on him by a genuinely admiring lady twenty years his junior. But Strepponi, in reviewing the four years in which Verdi and Stolz had seen something of each other, accused her husband only of "febrile periods of assiduity and attentions." His behavior may have wounded his wife and raised a storm of gossip, but it hardly seems that of a man involved in a passionate love affair. (*See* Appendix G, p. 588.)

With the close of the season in Paris, Stolz went off to sing in Russia, and Verdi and Strepponi returned to Sant' Agata. The tension between them over Stolz gradually eased, and she continued to be a friend of both although for a while she saw less of them. After she retired and lived permanently in Milan, she became one of their five or six intimate friends who accompanied them on trips and visited them regularly. And for this successful, happy conclusion to a difficult situation Strepponi deserves the credit.

After the season in Paris Verdi's attention continued to be on the productions of his work. He had gone to Paris to do *Aida* at the Théâtre Italien because Paris was the musical capital of Europe. But he refused, in spite of a good fee, to go to the outposts of St. Petersburg and Moscow even though Stolz was going. He went, however, the next year to Cologne to conduct the *Requiem* because Cologne was in Germany where he was particularly anxious to have his music well presented and because Ricordi, to Verdi's fury, had canceled the Berlin performances on the original *Requiem* tour. At Cologne, where he was the guest of honor, the ladies of the chorus presented him with a baton of ivory inlaid with silver, and other ladies, on behalf of the city, gave him a crown of silver and gold leaves. He was remarkably docile under all the attention, probably because both the *Requiem* and the *String Quartet* had gone well.

In Italy operatic performances continued to be sloppy, and Verdi's relations with his publishing house grew strained. He wrote often and

VERDI IN 1888

VERDI IN 1886
(*from a portrait by G. Boldini in the*
Galleria Nazionale d'Arte Moderna in Rome)

VERDI IN 1886
(*from a portrait by G. Boldini
in the Casa di Riposo in Milan*)

STREPPONI IN 1890

STREPPONI IN 1896

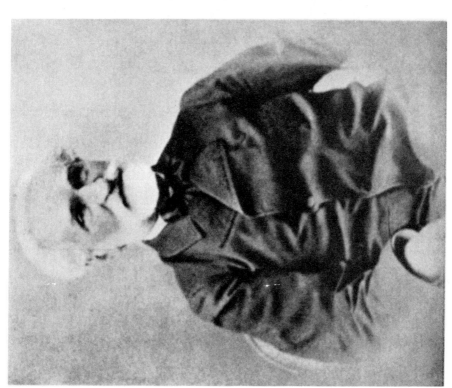

VERDI IN 1893

VERDI AND BOITO AT SANT' AGATA

VERDI IN 1899

VERDI IN 1900
(*one of the last photographs*)

angrily to Ricordi whom he felt was making money both at the cost of art and of Verdi. On the latter point the word "stealing" was never used, just "irregularities" in the accounts. "I don't know what they would be called in legal terms," Strepponi observed, writing in the role of buffer between Verdi and the publishers. But the deeper Verdi dug into the records the more furious he became, and he finally sent a man to Milan to collect all his contracts with the firm and between Ricordi and the various theatres from *Rigoletto* on. It was a quarter of a century of business, 1851–75. Verdi went through every contract and account himself during the summer at Sant' Agata. At the end of it he agreed to settle for 50,000 lire in back commissions. It was less than Ricordi owed him, but it was still an enormous sum. The fact that Verdi continued to do business with the firm must indicate that, whatever he thought of Tito Ricordi as a businessman, he did not think him personally dishonest. But beginning at this time Tito's son, Giulio, began to represent the firm in its dealings with Verdi.

But Verdi's anger with Ricordi was only partly over the money due to him. He also considered the publishers spineless in defending art and unimaginative in spreading it by example. As Strepponi patiently explained to Giulio, the House of Ricordi often saved a penny and lost a pound. When Verdi had wanted to take *Aida* on a tour of Germany, Ricordi had first agreed to risk money on it and then had withdrawn. As a result the tour had been canceled. The firm did not or could not see that one good production would stimulate others and that it would more than get its money back in the greater sale and rental of scores.

Nor, apparently, could it see any advantage to itself in defending art. Verdi, who had in the past disciplined La Scala, was quite prepared again to withhold the right to perform an opera until a particular theatre could show that it had assembled an adequate cast, chorus and orchestra. Ricordi, however, did not investigate each theatre's roster and substitutions but rented out the scores to any that asked. Then, when cuts and transpositions had been made, some friend of Verdi's would write him that at Naples or Bergamo such and such had been done, and Verdi would fly into a fury: "I am still stunned to think the House of Ricordi's agent could have allowed such an outrage."

In the tussle between art and business within the House of Ricordi art unquestionably took a severe drubbing. No one prefers bad performances to good and the Ricordis, father and son, undoubtedly attempted to use what influence they had to see that Verdi's operas were well produced. But they never, for example, made a *cause célèbre* out of an impresario's mutilations such as Verdi had done with the censor's cuts in *Un Ballo in Maschera*. And they could well have done so. There were other publishing houses in Italy, notably Lucca, but by 1875 the House of Ricordi was the most powerful, and any steps taken to defend art would have rallied composers to it, not driven them away. But it did nothing, and Verdi at Sant' Agata raged and fumed while trying "to distinguish between Tito Ricordi and Ricordi the publisher."

Lacking some action by the Ricordis, there was no altogether happy solution to the problem. It simply got more or less aggravating as theatrical circumstances and Verdi's personal relations with the Ricordis changed. Of the three generations with whom he had done business he got along best with the last, Giulio, Tito's son. Giulio, an accomplished writer and composer of light music, began to take an active part in the business about 1870 when he was thirty years old. He was more flexible than his father in dealing with Verdi, or perhaps being in a younger generation gave him an advantage. Verdi was often cantankerous, and his demands were sometimes unreasonable. But like

THE RICORDIS

ERK

GIOVANNI

all men he was susceptible to the flattery of attention, and this the younger Giulio could more naturally provide. Between contemporaries there is apt to be some reluctance to make allowance for each other. With Giovanni, the grandfather, a man of Rossini's generation, Verdi had been all business; with Tito, whom he knew more personally, he tended to quarrel; but with Giulio he developed a real, personal relationship, largely because the younger man, who visited often at Sant' Agata, worked hard on it.

The house at Sant' Agata, known locally as the Villa Verdi, had now assumed the shape which it has today. Across the front to the east (*See* map, pp. 502–503) run the dining room, billiard room, library, a smaller and then a larger living room. Above these in Verdi's time in each corner with double exposure were the guest bedrooms. The one to the north was normally reserved for men, Giulio Ricordi and later Boito; the one to the south for ladies, most often Stolz. Along the south on the ground floor, and facing directly into the park, were a dressing room for Strepponi, her bedroom, his bedroom, his dressing room and study and then the greenhouse, as the living quarters merged directly into the stables. It was comfortable without being grand. The one chandelier was a skimpy affair, and there was no fancy marble work anywhere. The furniture, which his heirs have kept as he left it, is all

TITO   GIULIO

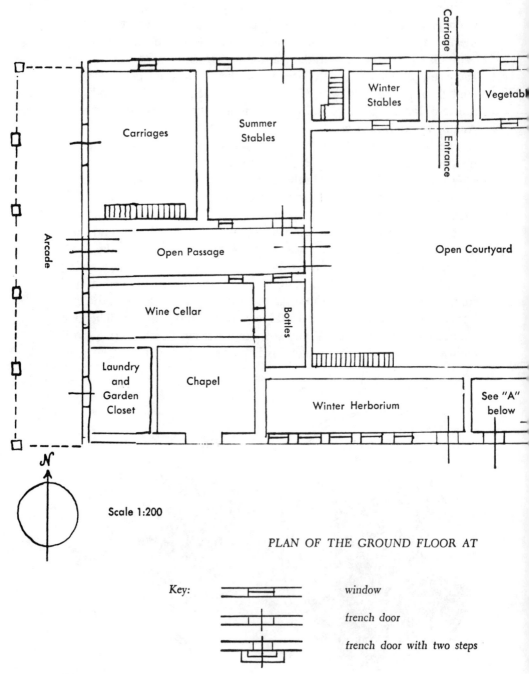

Carriage

Winter Stables

Vegetab[l]

Carriage Entrance

Carriages

Summer Stables

Arcade

Open Passage

Open Courtyard

Wine Cellar

Bottles

Laundry and Garden Closet

Chapel

Winter Herborium

See "A" below

N

Scale 1:200

PLAN OF THE GROUND FLOOR AT

Key:

window

french door

french door with two steps

502

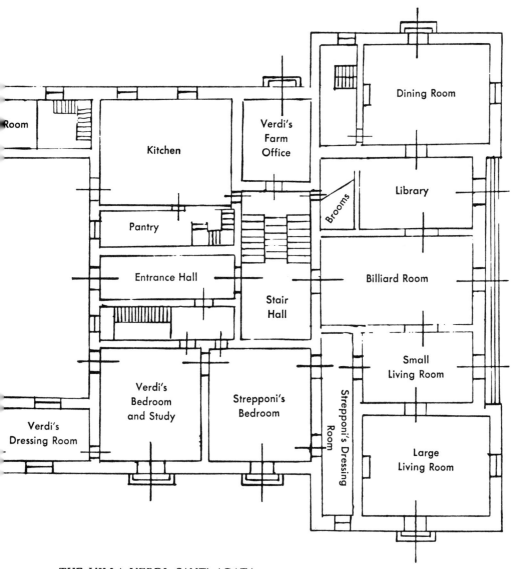

THE VILLA VERDI, SANT' AGATA

"A": During Verdi's life this room was part of the herborium. After his death it was separated from that and made into a replica of the room in the Grand Hotel in Milan in which he died. The bed, washstand and other furniture were brought from Milan, and even wallpaper of the same pattern was put on the walls. This room together with Verdi's and Strepponi's dressing and bed rooms, kept just as they were during their lives, are open to the public. The descendants of their adopted daughter, Maria Carrara, live in the rest of the house.

curlicue Victorian with heavy drapes and gilt picture frames on the walls. And in the living room there is only a small upright piano known as "Strepponi's piano." In Verdi's bedroom was a grand piano at which he worked and at which he did not entertain his guests. There were no musical evenings at Verdi's house with himself the center of attention.

The villa at Sant' Agata was Verdi's home in a way that no other place could possibly be. He and Strepponi had adopted the little girl, Filomena, whom he had taken into his house after his father's death. They had educated her, called her Maria and in every way treated her as a daughter. She was actually his first cousin once removed, a grandchild of Carlo Verdi's younger brother. In 1878, when she was nineteen, she married Alberto Carrara, the son of Verdi's lawyer in Busseto. The wedding was held in the chapel Verdi had just built in his house, and he gave the bride away. Strepponi, rather pathetically in view of her own early life, saw the bride as "a true symbol of virginity" and wept and smiled with the other relatives at the bride's "first kiss."

Verdi was delighted with the groom. Not only was the young man of the "paese," but he was "serious and honest, and comes from a family more honored than one can imagine. Maria," Verdi explained to a friend, "was born like me into poverty and could not ask for a better marriage. I believe that in her new lot, perhaps not the richest but comfortable, she will be very happy." The next year like any other grandfather he was writing his friends: "You know our Maria has a beautiful baby. I can't describe the joy of everyone, especially of Peppina [Strepponi] and the Carrara family. I pray only that this little baby girl will not one day or another be suffocated . . . by kisses."

This family life was a source of great satisfaction to Verdi who saw life, although a musician, in terms of being a man of property and family. At the same time neither he nor Strepponi considered the baby a reason for changing their habits. Every winter they continued to leave Busseto for Genoa where they had moved from the Palazzo Sauli to the Palazzo Doria-Pamphily which had an even better view of the harbor and a magnificent garden.

When they first moved into it in 1874, they had an apartment on the third floor. Then three years later they moved to the second, which had larger rooms and an enormous terrace stretching down one wing toward the harbor which was at the foot of the garden. Their apartment consisted of some twenty rooms, all of which Strepponi furnished and provided with the necessary linen, silver and glass. Thereafter Verdi spent some part of almost every winter there, generally arriving in December or January and returning to Sant' Agata in April. His life, now that both he and Strepponi were in their sixties, began to assume a pattern broken only by an occasional trip to Paris.

In 1875 he went briefly to Rome to take his oath as a Senator of the Kingdom. In the first parliaments at Turin he had been a Deputy and Manzoni a Senator. But as time took a toll among the elderly great, Verdi stepped up to join them. The decree confirming his appointment spoke second of his great artistic merits and first of the size of the tax he paid. The order shocked music lovers, who felt it reflected poorly on the glory of art, but in a way it was a true reflection of the atmosphere of the times.

It was a prosperous decade for northern Italy, Florence and Rome. Business was accelerating, towns burgeoning, and the politics, with the Austrians gone, were more pork-barrel than idealistic. At least it was a prosperous time for the upper and middle classes which controlled the property and the government. Under the constitution only men over twenty-five who were literate and also paid a fairly large amount in direct taxes could vote, and they amounted in 1871 to about 530,000 out of twenty-seven million Italians, or about 1.98 per cent. Almost 73 per cent of the population, including almost all southern Italians outside of Naples and Palermo, were disqualified for illiteracy. At the time Verdi was appointed a Senator, democracy in Italy was restricted largely to the more prosperous townspeople. They had led the fight for independence and unity and were, naturally, the first to benefit by it.

The benefits, however, gradually seeped down. In 1882 there was a Reform Act which extended the franchise to all men over twenty-one who were literate and greatly reduced the taxation requirement. Under this act two million voters registered, raising the percentage to 6.97 per cent, still a small figure, but at the same time the number of illiterates had dropped to 63 per cent, a greater accomplishment than many men realized. But even after 1882 there was a strong emphasis in the country on property and position. Manzoni had been a member of the minor nobility, and the peasants saw nothing extraordinary or exciting in his being a Senator. But Verdi, because of his peasant origin, was quite different. To the men on the bottom trying to improve their lot he shone with a special luster having nothing to do with his musical accomplishments. The decree, however inadvertently, reflected this.

It was signed by Vittorio Emanuele, who died three years later, in January 1878. He was only fifty-eight, still vigorous, and his death of a fever was a surprise. Pio Nono, when he heard the King was dying, sent a priest authorized to lift the ban of excommunication, thus enabling the King to have the last sacraments. Further, Pio Nono allowed him to be given a Christian burial in the Pantheon, but only on the understanding that he would not be called "King of Italy" in the liturgical prayers.

The King's death moved the country, but rather less than the monarchists and royal family would have liked. In spite of all their efforts at propaganda, Vittorio Emanuele never quite succeeded in establishing himself in his countrymen's hearts. Among the illiterate many, Garibaldi was the "father of his country," and among the educated few, Cavour or perhaps even Mazzini. These men had all initiated ideas or action and been true leaders; Vittorio Emanuele had followed and reaped where they had sown. At his death the country mourned, as the government instructed it to do, but probably most men who thought of it all felt, more than grief, a smug relief that the government now was so organized that the King's death would not, even could not, initiate a drastic change in policy. Umberto I succeeded, and the country went on about its business.

But the feeling was very different the next month when Pio Nono died at the age of eighty-five. He had been the Pope for almost thirty-two years, the longest reign in Papal history. He had been the object of passionate defense and furious attack throughout the entire period, and he actually controlled Papal policy. His successor might make changes, but in fact there were none. The new Pope, Leo XIII, continued to consider himself a prisoner in the Vatican and refused to come to any agreement with the State over their respective roles in Italian life. Even in death Pio Nono was embroiled in the struggle which had dominated his life.

Pio Nono's death came for Verdi at a time when all his friends seemed to be dying: Piave, finally released from his suffering; at Rome, his friend Luccardi; even Solera, whom Verdi had not seen for years. In a letter to the Contessa Verdi wailed:

PIO NONO

Everyone is dying! Everyone! And now the Pope! Certainly I am not for the Pope of the *Syllabus,* but I am for the Pope of the amnesty, and of the *Benedite, Gran Dio, l'Italia* . . . Without him who knows where we'd be now.

They have accused him of retreating, of lacking courage, and of not knowing how to wield the sword of Julius II. But what luck! Supposing in 1848 he had been able to chase the Austrians from Italy, what would we have now? A government of priests! Anarchy probably and dismemberment! Better as it is! Everything that he has done good or bad has helped the country. And at heart he was a good man, and a good *Italiano;* better than many of those others who cry *Patria, Patria,* and . . . So may this poor Pope have peace! (etc.)

The many deaths made Verdi feel old and perhaps gave him a charity he would not otherwise have had. He was kind but not sensible in arguing that Pio Nono's "bad" policy had helped Italy. Many more argued that it had not even helped the Church; that by being rigid when it should have been flexible it had strengthened the reactionaries within the Church while driving the moderates out. In reaction, both France and Italy in the last quarter of the century at times elected bitterly anti-clerical governments whose treatment of the Church in matters relating to education, public support and freedom proved to be far more severe than what the Church would probably have experienced at the hands of the moderates with whom it had flatly refused to deal in the middle of the century. And by constantly opposing the social and economic trends of the century the Church sacrificed its contact and influence with the great new class of industrial workers that was coming to the fore in the rapidly expanding towns. Pio Nono's successor, Leo XIII, saw that Marx and Engels knew more of the problems and desires of these people than did the priests, and in his encyclicals Leo attempted to give the Church a voice in industrial relations. But the Church had a late start, and most workers considered it to be hopelessly on the side of reaction. It was strong in poor, agricultural areas: Spain, Ireland and French Canada; it was weak in the industrial areas: the Po Valley, northern Germany and metropolitan France. Yet these areas, for better or worse, dominated the future.

This was one side of the picture; on the other was the undeniable fact that under Pio Nono the Church had become more religious. Perhaps because it was so under attack, those who clung to it did so even harder. It ceased to be a refuge for unwanted daughters or younger sons; bishops who could not recite the Mass became extinct. Cardinal Antonelli, Pio Nono's Secretary of State, left a fortune to his family, and everyone was genuinely shocked. The proclamations of the Dogma of the Immaculate Conception, of the Papal Infallibility and the Ecumenical Council were all important events, for better or worse, in the spiritual history of the Church. The question men and historians debated then and since is whether the spiritual acts need necessarily have been coupled with the political acts.

The deaths of Solera and Piave, although Verdi had seen neither in many years, emphasized a problem which Verdi was slow to recognize: he no longer had any professional librettists working for him. Piave had been one of the last with *La Forza del Destino* in 1862. Du Locle had done *Don Carlo* and provided the basic scenario for *Aida,* but Verdi had steadily rejected every other idea Du Locle had offered while announcing that he would never again compose for the French theatres. Not unnaturally Du Locle had turned his attention elsewhere. After *Aida* Verdi had done the *Requiem* which had not required a librettist. Ghislanzoni, who had revised *La Forza del Destino* and done the verses for *Aida,* was the logical candidate for the position, but he was either uninterested in it or perhaps too busy doing librettos for other composers. The result was that no one was stimulating Verdi with suggestions, not idle ideas but suggestions thought out and fitted to his talents.

His friends worried over it. He was behaving as though he had retired. When the Contessa prodded him about his music, he replied: "Are you serious about *my moral obligation to compose?* No, no, you're joking, since you know as well as I that *the account is settled.* Which is to say that I have always scrupulously fulfilled every obligation undertaken. The public has equally done its duty, greeting every work with loud whistles or applause etc. No one has a right to complain, and I repeat again: *the account is settled.*" And the five years following the *Requiem* were the least productive in Verdi's career.

But he could not scare off the Contessa with his huffing about rights and duties, and she prodded him again. This time he evasively reminded her of the criticism raised by *Aida* and the accusations that he was imitating Wagner. Then he passed on to other subjects, and his friends, including Strepponi, suspected that he had nothing particular in mind. Gradually they fell into a conspiracy to start him working again. Once when Giulio Ricordi wrote to Verdi, suggesting that he write an opera for Adelina Patti, Ricordi at the same time wrote to Strepponi, tactfully asking her to use her influence. Verdi rejected the idea, but she replied to Ricordi in a way to suggest that, although the time was not then ripe, she would help when it was. A link was forged between Milan and Sant' Agata. In Milan there were Ricordi, Faccio, Boito and the Contessa in whose salon the others often met. It is not known who had the idea first, but the plan was to have a reconciliation between Boito and Verdi and have them do a Shakespearean opera. Boito, who had long since revised his opinion of Verdi, was eager and probably suggested the subject. He knew that both he and Verdi honored Shakespeare above all other poets, and he had already done one libretto from the plays, the *Amleto* for Faccio. There are no recorded minutes of the conspiracy, but the way events in July of 1879 worked out suggests that some of them, at least, were premeditated.

Verdi went to Milan to conduct a performance of the *Requiem* at La Scala. It was a benefit for victims of the spring floods in the Po Valley, and it was also Teresa Stolz's last appearance. For fifteen years, since her debut under Mariani in 1865, she had been the leading soprano in Italy and particularly associated with Verdi's music. Now she wished to retire and enjoy a social life in Milan. She and Verdi would continue to see each other, but for both the last artistic endeavor together was a trying experience.

In Milan Verdi and Strepponi stayed at the Grand Hotel on the old Corsia del Giardino which had recently been renamed the Via Alessandro Manzoni. Down the street was La Scala, and almost directly opposite the hotel was the Via Bigli on which both the Contessa and Teresa Stolz lived. Verdi stayed regularly at the Grand Hotel, one of the city's best and the first to have an elevator.

One night Verdi and Strepponi had Faccio and Ricordi to dinner in their suite. The talk turned, or was cleverly led, to Shakespeare, the play *Othello* and Boito. Urged on by Ricordi and Faccio, and almost certainly after coffee and a cigar, Verdi agreed to meet Boito whom he had not seen since Paris in 1862, seventeen years earlier. The next day Faccio brought Boito around, and three days later Boito gave Verdi a scenario of *Othello* as an opera.

Three days is fast work, and it is unlikely that Boito started from scratch. Also the conversation at the dinner table does not seem to have revolved around *which* play; that seems to have been decided. Of course Verdi had already tried *Macbeth* twice, Boito had done *Hamlet*, and Verdi had a known block about doing *King Lear*. Of the great ones that were left, *Julius Caesar* had no soprano roles, and Gounod had recently done *Romeo and Juliet*. There were, perhaps, *Troilus and Cressida*, *Othello*, or *Antony and Cleopatra*. The first is a bitter, cynical play, in a vein totally foreign to Verdi's passionate commitment to life, and he himself apparently never considered it. *Antony and Cleopatra* he had considered, but perhaps Boito reasoned another Egyptian subject would come too soon after *Aida*. There remained *Othello, the Moor of Venice*, a good Italian subject which Rossini had made into an excellent opera, but in 1816 and in a very different style. It is hard not to believe that Faccio, Ricordi and Boito had discussed these ideas beforehand and agreed to concentrate on *Othello*, or that Boito had agreed to stand by in Milan with his ideas in order, ready to present them if the occasion arose.

Verdi read the scenario and liked it. "Put it into verse," he said; "it will always be good for you, for me, or someone else."

Ricordi urged Boito to do it at once and tried to wangle an invitation for the two of them to Sant' Agata to discuss the "chocolate scheme," as they called it. But Verdi was much more cautious and wrote to Ricordi:

A visit from you with a friend, who just now would be Boito, will always be a pleasure. But on this point let me speak clearly and plainly. A visit from him would commit me too far, and I absolutely do not wish to commit myself. (etc.)

If you come now with Boito, I will be obliged to read the libretto he has brought. If I find it completely satisfactory, then I am somewhat committed to go on with it. If I find it good and suggest some modifications that Boito makes, I'm even more committed. If, in spite of its virtues, I don't like it, it would be too harsh to tell him so directly.

No no . . . You have already gone too far, and we must stop before there is gossip and prejudice. In my opinion the best course (if you agree and its suits Boito) is for him to send me the finished poem, so I can read it and give my opinion of it on reflection and without any obligation on either side. Once these thorny difficulties are smoothed I will be most happy to see you here with Boito. (etc.)

So Boito started to work, and Ricordi visited Sant' Agata alone. He followed the new director of the Opéra who had persuaded Verdi to stage and conduct a French version of *Aida* in the coming winter. There was much talk about that and also of a *Pater Noster* and *Ave Maria* that Verdi had just completed for a concert in Milan the following spring. But Ricordi was most interested in the "chocolate scheme" and Boito, still kept at a distance, was extremely eager to discuss it. After Ricordi left, Strepponi wrote him a letter of warning and advice:

In the hope of bringing some peace, I will whisper a little secret into the ear of Giulio, provided he doesn't make it common knowledge. About the twentieth of November, we will be in Milan for a few days, and this seems to be a good moment for Boito to talk at length and in quiet with Verdi without arousing the attention and interest of the curious.

Between us, as far as Boito has written the *Africano* [her term for libretto] it seems well done and to Verdi's liking. I am sure the rest will be done as well. So let him finish the poem in peace, abandoning himself (without self-torture) to his fantasy. As soon as he is finished, let him send the poem without hesitation or delay to Verdi, before he goes to Milan. That way Verdi will be able to read it in peace and organize his thoughts in advance. I repeat, the first impression is good; the modifications and polishing will come after.

I hope and have faith in the saying, "Anything is good that works well," and in this way we will succeed here. Therefore don't write or speak to Verdi of your fears, hopes or problems. I add: don't even tell him that I wrote you on this point. I think it best not to give him the slightest, even distant feeling of pressure. Let us let the water find its own way to the sea. (etc.)

But it was to take a long time. Verdi went to Milan, on to Genoa and finally to Paris for the *Aida,* all the while protesting that he liked the poem but refusing to commit himself to anything. His letters show him almost morbidly shy of discussing it and terrified that the newspapers and the public would hear of it. Secretly he began looking at suitable costumes and pictures, trying to visualize the characters and setting in his mind; publicly he seemed wholly occupied with other things.

The *Aida* in French for the Opéra had an enormous success, as great as in Italian in 1876 at the Théâtre Italien. For both productions Verdi had directed the rehearsals. But without his guiding hand the Théâtre Italien had no success. Escudier, who had gained control of it, had put on an unsuccessful *La Forza del Destino* and then tried to revive *Aida* with inadequate singers. As a result the theatre, after being the showcase in Paris for Italian music for years, closed. Muzio, its conductor, was left without a post and was reduced to teaching singing. The following year the theatre burned and was never rebuilt. Verdi, who had prophesied poor productions and disaster, blamed Escudier. The fact that no one ever revived the Théâtre Italien perhaps was a symptom that Italian opera was losing its dominant position.

Back in Milan on 18 April 1880 Verdi heard his *Pater Noster* and *Ave Maria* sung at a concert of the Orchestral Society, a new musical group in Milan which had organized itself with Faccio as conductor to give concerts, mostly of instrumental music. It had taken the La Scala orchestra under Faccio to the Paris Exposition in 1878 and scored a success. Then in April of 1879 it had asked Verdi to be its honorary president, and he had declined. In his letter he had suggested that perhaps vocal as well as instrumental music should be cultivated, particularly as vocal music was more in the Italian tradition. This was an opinion Verdi held consistently, strongly and at least partially in response to the influence of Wagner and the general admiration for German orchestral music. On receiving Verdi's letter Faccio probably immediately planned to devote one concert the following year to vocal music, certain he could persuade Verdi to compose something for it.

In both works, as Verdi wrote a friend, "the verses are (hats off!) by Dante." So that the *Pater Noster* is actually a *Padre Nostro*, and the common, Italian words give both prayers an intimate quality. The *Ave Maria* is for solo soprano and a string quartet. It is lovely, but not so lovely as the *Ave Maria* he was to give Desdemona in *Otello*, and the later prayer has obscured the earlier one. The *Pater Noster* is less obviously operatic but still plainly by Verdi. It calls either for a five-part chorus or five voices, two sopranos, contralto, tenor and bass. Like the *Ave Maria*, it is well done but lacks some ultimate touch to distinguish it from the many, many other equally good musical settings of the prayer.

After the concert in Milan the business of life again caught up Verdi, much to Ricordi's distress. There was still no commitment on Boito's libretto and, so far as Ricordi could see, no work being done. Once again he suggested a visit to Sant' Agata, accompanied by Boito, but Strepponi warned him away: "Verdi does not yet, in spite of the very good verses, have his ideas clear and without clear ideas he will decide now, or at any rate later, never to compose. Considering everything, I believe frankly it is better to leave things, at least for the moment, just as they are, wrapping the Moor in as great a silence as possible."

Ricordi followed her advice, and instead of talking of *Otello*, he suggested to Verdi the possibility of revising *Simone Boccanegra*, which had failed at its première in 1857 and was almost never performed. Verdi was interested. He had some "clear" ideas for revising the libretto and was prepared to begin work at once if a librettist could be found. Ricordi promptly suggested Boito and proposed further that the revised opera be presented at La Scala the following March, which allowed about six months for the work of the revision.

The shortness of time seemed to stimulate Verdi. He was so full of ideas which he began to pour on Boito that he hardly noticed the other man's reluctance to take on the job. The libretto as Piave had left it was a jumble of mistaken identities, off-stage poisonings and unexplained motives; in sum, everything Boito thought old-fashioned and preposterous. But Verdi's ideas were good and his enthusiasm infectious. By February Boito was urging Verdi to polish and improve where Verdi would have left well enough alone, and they were still making changes when rehearsals began. The revised work had its première as the last opera of the season on 24 March 1881 and in its ten performances scored a real success. The production was excellent and the cast outstanding, particularly the baritone, Victor Maurel, in the title role.

It is a general rule that great operas never emerge from the revision of bad ones, and Verdi was well aware of it. As he had explained to Boito in the beginning: "The table is shaky, but, by putting a leg or two in order, I think it can be made to stand upright." This limited objective Verdi achieved. The second version is better than the first in every respect and is the most successful revision of an opera Verdi ever made. Before it the opera was dead; after it, the opera has had a continuous life.

Its defects are similar to those of *Il Trovatore,* also based on a play by Gutiérrez. Both require a prologue or explanation to set forth what happened in the years before the main drama begins. In *Il Trovatore* Verdi used a narrative aria to describe the past; in *Simone Boccanegra* he actually presents the happenings in a prologue set "twenty-five years before" Act I. The technique is more dramatic but still not altogether successful. No baritone can make his voice suddenly sound twenty-five years older, and it should. A twentieth-century composer, used to movie techniques, and with far greater gradation possible in lighting, might have tried a "flash back" and used a different singer with a lighter voice and more youthful figure. But the problem, which the theatre of Verdis' time was not equipped to solve, was inherent in Gutiérrez' sprawling plays, and no amount of tinkering by Boito and Verdi could altogether eradicate its effects. As in *Il Trovatore,* too much in *Simone Boccanegra* takes place off-stage and has to be reported in awkward asides or quick remarks that pass before the audience can grasp their significance.

The opera's virtues center on the title role. Boccanegra is a historical figure and important in the medieval history of Genoa. He was a member of the minor nobility but from the first led the plebeian party. As a sort of compromise and reform candidate he twice served as Doge of the city. His second term, from 1356 to 1363, ended with his death, after a banquet to honor the King of Cyprus. It was generally believed that he was poisoned. Under him Genoa had a successful foreign policy and some of its few years of peace. Gutiérrez used this

historical background largely to give titles to his characters and to determine the cut of their costumes. Verdi and Boito put it directly onto
the stage with a magnificent scene set in the city's Council Chamber.
The plebeian and patrician parties wrangle in the Chamber while the
people riot in the streets, and over all Boccanegra tries to exert his
statesmanship. This portrayal of medieval politics and statesmanship
gives the opera a depth greater than Gutiérrez's simpler romance contained. Boccanegra, like Philip in *Don Carlo,* is shown as a man existing in a particular time and place and attempting to deal with the
forces which make him as much as he makes them. And the scenes
with his daughter, simple, loving and human, gain a poignancy by
contrast. Few operas attempt to put politics on the stage, and part of
the distinction of both *Don Carlo* and *Simone Boccanegra* lies in the
larger reality with which each surrounds its characters.

Musically *Simone Boccanegra* is uneven. Verdi wrote considerable
new music, such as for the new Council Chamber scene, and some he
reorchestrated. But what he did not touch sometimes sounds suddenly ludicrous and out of place, such as the chorus which ends the
prologue. Much of what he left, however, is adequate or better, and
the new music is excellent, melodic, dramatic and orchestrated with
the skill Verdi had been steadily developing.

In all his operas Verdi used his orchestra primarily to establish the
atmosphere of a scene and within the scene to give emphasis to the
text. Ideally for both purposes, which anyway tend to reinforce each
other, each change in the dramatic situation should have some change
in the orchestral color, figure and harmony. In his early operas which
were dominated by arias Verdi's orchestration tended to fall into a
repetitious, supporting pattern: an introduction by woodwinds setting
an atmosphere, which changed to strings as the voice entered. Then
as the singer breathed, Verdi might fill the gap with a figure or a
phrase by the woodwind. Elvira's aria in *Ernani* is in this form. The
orchestral pattern, not very interesting to begin with, was made less
so by Verdi's tendency to have the instruments play by groups. Thus
all the strings play together and become the proverbial "guitar accompaniment." He used the instruments singly sometimes to carry the tune
underneath the voice and lend it the instrument's quality: to make a
singer sound loving Verdi accompanied him with a clarinet; martial,
a trumpet.

But as he grew more experienced he began to do more with the individual instruments. At the same time, as the musical pattern of the aria grew more flexible, he was able to make the underlying orchestral pattern less rigid. It is almost possible, opera by opera, to see Verdi freeing yet another instrument from the domination of its group and discovering its unique qualities. Among the first was the clarinet as Violetta writes her letter in *La Traviata,* the brasses throughout *Don Carlo,* and the bass drum at "Mors Stupebit" in the *Requiem.* In *Aida* he created a marvelously atmospheric night by the Nile out of a single flute and the strings, largely violins, made to make unique sounds. In *Simone Boccanegra* he continued his orchestral development so that quite apart from the vocal writing some of the orchestral sounds haunt the memory—the shimmering atmosphere of daybreak on the Mediterranean or the menace of a curse launched over a solo bass clarinet, an unusual and difficult instrument to use but one whose sound is therefore all the more arresting.

The success of *Simone Boccanegra* merely confirmed what Ricordi, Boito and the others all knew: that Verdi, although he thought of himself as old, was actually adding to his powers. His only weakness was in the construction of his librettos, and this Boito hoped to strengthen. Otherwise there seemed to be no limit to his imagination and his ability to support it by continuous self-improvement. As Bernard Shaw once said of him: "It is not often that a man's strength is so immense that he can remain an athlete after bartering half of it to old age for experience."

CHAPTER 38

OTELLO

1881–1887; AGE, 67–73

AFTER the success of *Simone Boccanegra,* everyone hoped that Verdi would start in at once on Boito's libretto which the newspapers generally referred to as "Boito's *Iago.*" Boito himself never discussed it publicly, nor did Verdi. But others did, particularly those in the theatre, and out of bits of truth and surmise journalists made up stories for the public. Probably Ricordi occasionally leaked a word about it to keep the subject alive and pressure on Verdi. And Verdi himself occasionally made a slip. Once during the rehearsals of *Simone Boccanegra* he had been particularly pleased with Victor Maurel, the baritone, and he had exclaimed something like: "If God gives me health, I'll write *Iago* for you." After which there were knowing looks, and Maurel, treasuring the words as a promise, tried to make them binding by making them public on every conceivable occasion.

But in spite of the hopes Verdi seemed little inclined to satisfy them. In 1883 he was seventy, and that year his great rival, Wagner, who was the same age, died in Venice. Verdi, who had never met him and was in Genoa, wrote a note to Ricordi. His thought, without beginning or end, seems breathed whole onto the paper:

Sad Sad Sad!
Vagner is dead!
When I read of it yesterday in the paper I was, I tell you, stunned. Let's not talk of it.—A great personality has disappeared! A name that leaves a most powerful mark on the History of Art!

He was genuinely moved. The script is shaky, the punctuation lacking, and he spelled Wagner's name as he pronounced it, with a "V," as if the thought wrote itself. Only in the last line did Verdi's conscious mind intrude. He had written merely "powerful" (potente) and he scratched it out to write "most powerful" (potentissima).

But while Verdi was quite ready to acknowledge Wagner's greatness, he was still prepared to battle the man's influence on Italian music. The same month that Wagner died Verdi wrote his friend Piroli to explain why he had refused to serve on a government commission for music and drama:

Today you can't find either teachers or students who are not infected with *Germanism* and it would not even be possible to form a Commission free of this disease which, like all others, must run its course. (etc.) Our music is different from German music, whose symphonies can survive in large halls, and quartets in small rooms. Our music, I say, has its seat principally in the theatre. Now the theatres without government aid cannot exist. It is a fact no one can deny. They must all soon close and if one can hang on to life, it is an exception. La Scala, even La Scala, perhaps will close next year.

The only hope Verdi could see lay either in subsidy, so that impresarios would not be forced into poorer and poorer productions, or in some "new man, an artist of genius, young and uninfluenced by schools." But when his friends insisted that he was the man and pointedly regretted that he had not written an opera in more than ten years, he treated it as a joke and went on about his farm, muttering to himself about the world and art and probably not very happy.

When the Contessa's husband in all but name, Carlo Tenca, died in the autumn, Verdi wrote her a letter that, while perhaps honestly reflecting his feelings, can hardly have lightened hers:

I have heard all, admired your courage and can well understand, now the first nervous agitation is passed, the heaviness in your heart. There are no words that can give comfort in such misfortune. And I will not say to you that one stupid word "courage": a word that has always angered me when said in my direction. We need more than that! Comfort you will find only in the strength of your soul and firmness of spirit. (etc.)

Now the years are beginning to pile up and I think . . . I think that life is the most stupid of all things and, even worse, useless. What are we doing? What have we done? What will we do? After considering all, the answer is humiliating and very sad:

NOTHING!

Addio, mia cara Clarina. Let us avoid and hold off as long as possible the sad things in life and love each other well as long as we can . . .

It is tempting to search for some medical reason, even change of life, to explain his melancholia in these years. It runs steadily through his letters, darkening every subject discussed, art, politics, or life. Yet when commiserating with friends on their aches and pains, he generally stated that his own health had never been better. And in fact it was extraordinarily good.

A more likely reason for his depression was that the world as he knew it was rapidly changing. Figures who had seemed indestructible and had furnished a lifetime with passions for and against were suddenly no more, and no person or cause in the coming generation could quite take their place. On Caprera Garibaldi, in his last years almost immobilized by arthritis, died requesting that he be cremated on a pyre under the open sky. In a note to his will he advised his wife that she would need plenty of wood. But the authorities intervened, on the ground that a cremation would offend other persons' religious sensibilities, and he was given an incongruous state burial with which, now that he was safely dead, royalty and politicians hastened to associate themselves.

In Paris, writing, talking and making love to the very end, Hugo died in his eighty-fourth year of a congestion of the lungs. His final death rattle was said to be "like the sound of pebbles dragged backward by the sea." His funeral was extraordinary: an entire city stopped to mourn and honor him, not so much because he had been a republican, gone into exile, and then returned, but because with his great rolling words he had expressed more completely than anyone else the universal feelings of love and grief, of duty and defeat, of triumph and the greatness of mercy. His body lay in state under the Arc de Triomphe and then was buried in the Panthéon. On the day it was moved twelve young French poets formed a guard of honor, and as two million people watched and followed the hearse, there arose from their lips a multitudinous murmur of verse, of words, Hugo's words, which he had driven into their hearts and which in grief they now gave back to him.

Verdi read of it in the paper and must have thought of the many plays of Hugo he had almost set and of the two that he had: *Ernani* and *Rigoletto*. He had instinctively understood the passionate rhetoric of Hugo's plays and been able to draw the best from them. He was less sure now that he understood what men wanted or thought important. He was aware that his taste in painting and sculpture, which was for a sentimental realism, was already old-fashioned. Rodin's statues, for example, seem to have made no impression on him, and he no longer seems to have considered contemporary plays as possibilities for an opera. It was a symptom that he was becoming a spectator rather than an actor in Italian life. And when the impresario at Vienna suggested that he revise *Don Carlo* to make it shorter, he agreed. Once again he put off *Otello,* a new work, to tidy up an old one.

He continued, however, to look around him, to read and to go to expositions where the new way of life was collected and put on exhibition. He had refused an invitation to be a member of the organizing committee of the Paris Exposition of 1878 and in the end had not even gone to it. But he went to the great industrial fair in Milan in 1881 which marked the emergence of the Po Valley as a European industrial area. The Galleria Vittorio Emanuele, still at the center of the city's life, was then a symbol of the new age. Built of iron and glass and lit by more than two thousand gas jets, it spanned an area in a wholly new style, and to see the dome being lit at night was one of the sights of the city. There, more than a hundred feet in the air, a small engine carrying a flame ran round a circular track igniting the jets above it. The engine was set in motion by clockwork and took a minute and a half to complete its run.

Three years later Turin had an Exposition and again Verdi went, going on from there with Strepponi to the mineral baths at Montecatini. Thereafter they returned to them almost every year, generally in July. The pattern of their life was now fixed, and in some ways these years were their happiest. They both enjoyed Maria Carrara's family at Busseto and saw almost no one else in the town; at Genoa they were more social, and in Milan were some of their best friends. His health was better than hers, but her spirit was more serene. She had always believed in Catholicism although at times, like Verdi, had been very out of sorts with its priesthood. But in these years she found a confessor she particularly liked, and her religion became a source of strength and satisfaction to her. Her serenity counterbalanced his spasms of gloom and irritation.

He found his fame a burden to him. At Turin he had gone to a concert which Faccio was conducting, and he had been recognized and given a long ovation. In Milan he had to persuade the hotel manager not to put a plaque with his name on the door to his suite. More difficult were the musical honors. La Scala unveiled statues in its lobby of Bellini and himself, and he managed to avoid being present without giving offense. And most difficult of all were the matters involving money. From Florence came a proposal that he give 10,000 lire toward the new façade of the cathedral. The proposal also, as if it were quite incidental, suggested that Verdi's likeness be enshrined in a medallion on the façade. He excused himself because people might say, "not unreasonably," that he had bought the honor. Also, he insisted, he could not afford it.

But there was no limit to what people thought he could afford. He read one day in the Milan paper, the *Corriere della Sera,* that he had proposed "to restore the Church of Sant' Agata, which is in bad repair," and he hastily wrote the architect in charge that he had made no such proposal and had no such intention. He considered the article a form of blackmail to force him to make a contribution.

The difficulty was that there really did seem to be no limit to what he could do. In the past he had given scholarships for students in the Busseto school. He had advanced 10,000 lire to construct one of the town's bridges, and the advance had turned into a gift toward the town's opera house. More recently he had built three new dairy farms merely to give employment in bad years to some two hundred men and to prevent "emigration from my village." And now he was building a hospital with twelve beds at Vidalenzo because the nearest hospital in the area was at Piacenza and many of the sick could not afford to go there. In short, Verdi had all the troubles of a man known to be rich and sometimes generous. Every petitioner thought he had a right to ask and, when refused, grumbled.

Verdi undoubtedly was rude to some. He had a bearish temperament, and there are stories of occasional gruff remarks and brusque letters. But he never lost a sense of justice about money. When he considered a person or cause had a demand on him, he paid. Floods, for example, were a common disaster, and he always contributed to their relief; rent—and he had suffered for it as a young man—was to be paid on the first of the month, not the tenth or the thirtieth; and even in small matters his sense of justice prevailed. Once when he was leaving Turin for Montecatini, a carriage driver almost caused him to miss his train. In a fury Verdi refused to give the man a tip. But then a few days later, his anger past, he sent the money by letter.

But his sense of justice could not relieve him of the irritation of constant appeals and journalistic blackmail. When the Vienna première of the revised *Don Carlo* fell through and one at La Scala was substituted, a story in the *Corriere della Sera* implied that Verdi would direct the rehearsals and attend the opening performances. Such a rumor pleased the La Scala box office, but to avoid contributing to the false impression Verdi appealed to Ricordi to publish a denial. The truth was that he would attend only some of the rehearsals: "Nothing else, nothing else! Absolutely *nothing else!!!*"

The revision had the same fitful success as the original version. Verdi had added some new music, most successfully a new prelude to the old Act III. To make the opera shorter he had cut out, principally, the ballet and the entire first act in which Don Carlo and Elisabetta meet at Fontainebleau. He could argue that both had been additions to the play and he was merely hewing more closely to his source. But musically the first act contained many seeds which flowered later, and the revision cost the bloomings much of their identity. In the same way the structural curve of the opera was broken. The original version began with Don Carlo first meeting Elisabetta and ended with their final separation. The revision, beginning with Don Carlo and the Marquis of Posa, starts well along the curve and with a number of unexplained questions. These Verdi tried to answer by taking Don Carlo's love music from the old first act, turning it into a memory-narrative aria, and inserting it into the middle of the new first act. But it is no substitute for seeing Don Carlo and Elisabetta meet and begin to love. Ultimately, without Verdi's participation, a third version of the opera appeared, restoring the first act, but retaining the other revisions. This made it once again a long opera and one offering no obvious and satisfactory cuts to impresarios. In spite of even Verdi's efforts it remains a difficult opera to produce but with some of his most fascinating music.

In the months after it Verdi began for the first time to work with concentration on Boito's libretto, which he now was calling by its final name, *Otello.* He took almost two full years over it, from the autumn of 1884 to 1886, during which time he lived in his regular pattern of about eight months at Sant' Agata and four in Genoa, with occasional trips to Paris and Montecatini.

Deaths among his friends continued to upset him. He felt each loss deeply, particularly that of Giulio Carcano, whose translations of Shakespeare he read. He described to the Contessa the last time he had seen Carcano:

It was Sunday. About one o'clock I went to his house and found him bustling around as if to go out. "Don't go to any trouble," I said. And he answered with adorable simplicity: "My dear Verdi, I am still one of those who go to Mass on Sunday." All right, all right; and I went with him to the church door. "Till we meet again . . ." and I will meet him no more!! Alas, alas.

A few days after Carcano died, his daughter delivered to Verdi her father's copy of the first edition of *I Promessi Sposi,* which Manzoni had inscribed. It had been one of Carcano's last requests, made literally on his deathbed. Verdi was overcome. And even before he could get used to that loss, Andrea Maffei died.

Beside these recurring shocks of personal loss, the politics of the time kept him agitated and depressed. Both domestically and in foreign policy the country was moving in directions of which Verdi disapproved, so that each morning the newspaper headline was apt to start him off in a bad temper.

Cavour's generation, to which Verdi belonged, had always considered France to be Italy's natural ally, and while France had often scolded Italy and at times even deserted it, the alliance over the years had been fruitful; not only politically in the unification of Italy, but economically in that France was the best market for Italian goods, particularly such agricultural products as olive oil. It had also been fruitful aesthetically in such exchanges as the Théâtre Italien in Paris and the enormous sale of French books in Italy. For Verdi Paris, even after 1870 and the Battle of Sedan, continued to be the capital of Europe and a French alliance seemed axiomatic.

But to the younger generation, which now dominated the Parliament, Berlin and not Paris was the capital of Europe. As in art so in politics, and the royal house and monarchists who admired the German Empire more than the French Republic strongly supported the trend. The Italian army was reorganized, not unnaturally after Sedan, on the Prussian model, and Italian statesmen, frustrated by years of being unable to come to any agreement with the Church, imitated Bismarck's anti-clerical legislation and, where they could, his authoritarian methods. Finally in 1882 Italy had joined German and Austria in a Triple Alliance.

Many Italians thought it strange for Italy to ally itself with Austria which still held the Trentino and Trieste, and others insisted that the Germans would never develop an appetite for olive oil. In fact, there were hardly any benefits for Italy except the prestige of being the partner of Germany, the strongest and most advanced state in Europe. But the King, who had a special prerogative in the field of foreign policy, was for it, and so was Parliament, composed largely of lawyers who came from towns and often understood little about Italy's needs and problems. Verdi was not necessarily wiser than the lawyers, but in his farming he partook of the great national industry which employed by far the most people. At the Milan Exposition he could see the results of the subsidies and tariffs industries enjoyed, and he knew nothing similar was being done for the peasants, the great majority of whom owned no land, were lucky if employed for half the year, and were luckier still if they could emigrate. Instinctively he distrusted the empty prestige of the Triple Alliance as an answer to the country's problems.

Some progress was made, more in the field of education than of agriculture. The potential effects of the Industrial Revolution in the north were barely imagined, but over the years it became plain that it was making the rich richer and the peasants even poorer. As money became more plentiful, land values rose, and those who had no money had even less chance of ever buying their pitiful plot of land. In the same way, as transportation improved, distant but more efficient farms in France and the Po Valley began to compete successfully with local but inefficient farms in southern Italy. And in the last two decades of the century began the great exodus of southern Italians to the United States as their peasant, agricultural society was brutally overturned by the beginnings of industry.

The Parliament was handicapped in its efforts and even desires to deal with the problem by the absence from it of some of the country's most responsible social thinkers. These were some of the followers of Mazzini who refused to swear allegiance to the monarchy and therefore could not sit in Parliament and the devout Catholics who obeyed their Church's edict not to do so. From 1868 to 1919 Pio Nono's direction that Catholics were not to be "electors or elected" remained in force. Those who obeyed it met in Catholic congresses held in various cities throughout the last three decades of the century. But whatever wisdom and experience the congresses may have contained was largely lost to the country as a whole.

In every field with which Verdi was concerned, agriculture, foreign policy, music and the theatre, he saw vital problems being ignored while prestige was pursued in Berlin and a *Germanism,* perhaps suitable for its own country, was mistakenly applied to Italian life and art. Yet one of the most extraordinary facts of *Otello* is that in it there is no trace of Verdi's gloom and despair. Nor is there any autumnal glow of an old man looking back on love and passionate jealousy, either trying to remember how it was or philosophizing that it was not so important as it seemed. With the opera Verdi reached an extreme opposite from *Nabucco* or *I Lombardi*. Whereas then his music had been tied emotionally to the times and even Aida's aria "O patria mia" is tinged with them, *Otello* is pure, timeless art. The music, of course, may go out of fashion, but not because of choruses calling for the capture of Trieste or arias extolling nationalism. In the opera Verdi and Boito examined love, jealousy and a man's disintegration in their essence.

The composition of it went remarkably smoothly. Verdi had one flare-up at Boito when a newspaper misquoted Boito as regretting that he could not set the libretto himself. Boito was in Naples at the time, supervising a production of his revised *Mefistofele,* and Verdi wrote to Faccio in Milan to get at the truth of it. And through Faccio Verdi stiffly offered Boito the libretto if he wanted it. But Boito was able to explain and the incident closed, leaving Verdi looking unduly touchy.

As he got into the opera, his spirits rose. Even the Contessa's death in July 1886 could not shake him. She died of meningitis, and although Verdi hurried to Milan, she had lost consciousness and did not recognize him. So ended a forty-four-year friendship between a remarkable man and an equally remarkable woman. A half-truth about Italian life that foreigners tend to swallow whole is that women have no place in it outside their family and home. But some part of the other half of the truth is exhibited in such women as the Contessa, who with her salon and friendships played a direct part in Italian politics and art.

Three months later, as he finished the opera, Verdi was writing positively gaily to Arrivabene: "So away with melancholy, and get well soon, for I hope to embrace you next spring when, my work finished, I shall come to Rome. I'm a bit tired, but I am well. I've completely finished *Otello!* Now . . . *à la grace de Dieu!*" (etc.) But he did not say what he had in mind, and a month before the opera's première Arrivabene died.

Verdi directed the rehearsals himself and reportedly like the young man he was no longer. When the tenor playing Otello killed himself with insufficient passion, Verdi is supposed to have taken the knife,

TAMAGNO, THE FIRST OTELLO

stabbed himself at the top of the dais steps, and rolled to the stage floor. He had insisted that no one, absolutely no one, be admitted during the rehearsals, and he had by contract reserved the right to cancel the performances even after the dress rehearsal. Fortunately no such thing happened. At the première on 5 February 1887 Faccio conducted, Maurel sang Iago, and in the orchestra pit a nineteen-year-old Toscanini, who had come specially from Parma to see and work under Verdi, played the second cello.

All successful premières are much the same: the glitter and the lights, the excited cries and the sense of an event. Perhaps this last was heightened at the première of *Otello* because it was the first new opera by Verdi in sixteen years, generally assumed to be his last, and characterized by everyone but himself as the Italian answer to German opera. It had a triumphant success, and even many days later when Toscanini was returning to Parma, the sounds of it again suddenly flooded his mind. So that when he reached home and found his mother asleep in bed, he woke her up, insisting: *"Otello* is a masterpiece. Get down on your knees, Mother, and say Viva Verdi." And he forced the poor, bewildered woman to kneel beside him and repeat "Viva Verdi!"

But for Verdi the work now finished left a void. Sitting with his friends in the hotel after the première was over, he grew melancholic. "I feel," he said, "as if I'd fired my last cartridge. Oh, the solitude of Sant' Agata, so alive in the past with the creatures of my imagination which, well or ill, I put into music. Tonight the public has torn the veil that hid my last mysteries. I have nothing left."

They protested, Faccio, Boito, Stolz, Ricordi; they spoke of his glory. Probably Strepponi only smiled. But he would have none of it. Finally he relented somewhat: "If I were thirty years younger I'd begin a new opera tomorrow, if Boito provided the libretto."

As Verdi implied, Boito's libretto for *Otello* was exceptional, by far the best Verdi had ever set. As always he had made suggestions, some of which Boito followed, but the conception was Boito's as were also the construction and beauty of the lines. The lines were a bonus, but the construction was basic.

Boito's problem was to take Shakespeare's play, five acts filled with words, and compress it so that it would move sufficiently faster to allow time for the music to expand in the lyrical passages. He did it largely by omitting Shakespeare's first act set in Venice and in which Othello defends his elopement with Desdemona before the Doge and Senators assembled in the Doge's palace. It took a strong artistic conscience for an Italian to give up all the theatrical splendor of Venice at its height, and Verdi without Boito probably could not have done it. But the cut allowed Boito to set the entire action in Cyprus and to have each act follow its predecessor almost directly in time. This unity of place and almost of time gives the opera the same dramatic punch Hugo achieved for Verdi in *Rigoletto*. The characters carry their emotions over from one act to the next, so that the opera presents a continuous emotional curve from the first scene to the last. Otello's disintegration is relentlessly pursued.

Boito also changed the personalities of the characters. Iago is simplified. His motives in Shakespeare are somewhat unclear, and clues to them are scattered throughout the play. Boito compressed and generalized them into an aria, Iago's "Credo," in which Iago scorns honesty and virtue as fantasy. The only truth is death and after it: nothing. He is evil because he enjoys it, having been created in the image of a cruel God. Boito, with an opera on the subject, was steeped in Goethe's *Faust,* and his Iago is a brother to Mephistopheles who cries: "I am the Spirit that Denies!" Boito wanted to have Iago watch the love scene between Otello and Desdemona, all the while muttering that he would destroy their love. But Verdi made Boito take Iago out. Apparently Verdi thought the "Credo" was enough to explain Iago and wanted an undistracted love scene to establish what a great love was destroyed.

Desdemona's character Boito expanded greatly. In Shakespeare she is a bewildered innocent who understands almost nothing of what goes on around her or in Othello. In the opera she is a full-grown Italian woman, understanding jealousy, capable of adultery and of answering the charge against her. In Shakespeare when Othello calls her false to her face, she bleats: "to whom, my lord, with whom? How am I false?" In the opera she replies, with stage direction: "(looking firmly at him) I am honest." Desdemona's gain was in part Otello's loss. In Shakespeare Othello, dealing with a sort of child-bride, is, as an adult, prosecutor, judge and jury of her supposed crime. In his soliloquy, "It is the cause," he identifies himself directly with abstract justice, and his arrogance in so doing makes the ultimate truth even more devastating. In the opera he is more simply the aggrieved husband. Abstract justice is not involved, perhaps because as a general rule Italians tend to see actions and emotions in human rather than abstract terms.

Finally, although in both play and opera Otello strikes Desdemona and almost strangles Iago, in the opera he has a much greater air about him of ill-suppressed violence. This is partly the result of Boito's compression of the play. Scenes which Shakespeare could insert to slow the rise of jealousy in Othello, Boito had to cut. And in the opera Otello passes quickly, almost too quickly, from love to furious jealousy. As a result he seems to be a volatile, violent man. It is hard to see how Boito could have avoided this cast to the character. But another reason for it lies in the very nature of music, particularly Verdi's music. Whenever a melodic phrase wells up and dies down, there is a suggestion of strain and suppression; and Verdi particularly liked such contrast and passion. Inevitably his Otello would be a man of passion and violence.

But whether the opera is greater than the play is one of those inconclusive, interminable arguments best left to those who like them.

In its musical construction, for which Boito with the libretto is as much responsible as Verdi, the opera moves far toward preferring the drama over musical pattern. The first act opens (*see* p. 529) with a furious storm in the midst of which Otello appears, delivers two lines of recitative and goes off. Forty years earlier no tenor would have countenanced such an entrance, just recitative without any aria or cabaletta. What was the point of learning to sing? Yet it is probably the most impressive entrance in opera. The sudden silence in the storm filled with Otello's clarion announcement of victory suggests that he

ACT I (about 31 mins.)

(outside the Castle on Cyprus and facing the harbor. A tavern to one side)

THE STORM	chorus, fast and tense	Will Otello's ship make the harbor? God help it.
OTELLO	recitative	"Rejoice. The Turks are defeated" (two sentences in all). He enters the castle.
CYPRIOTS	chorus, fast and relaxing	"Vittoria."
IAGO and RODERIGO	recitative, into tune, into recitative, into tune	He promises to help Roderigo win Desdemona and complains of Cassio being promoted before him. He leads Roderigo aside to talk.
CYPRIOTS	chorus	They settle for the evening around a fire.
IAGO CASSIO RODERIGO CYPRIOTS	dialogue; aria, for several voices and chorus	Iago urges Cassio to drink. The drinking song; at the end of it Cassio is drunk and is angered by Roderigo's laughter.
OTELLO and OTHERS	dialogue with chorus; recitative	Cassio and Roderigo fight while Cypriots call for help. Otello appears, stops the fight, demotes Cassio and dismisses the crowd.
OTELLO and DESDEMONA	dialogue in tunes ending with broken phrases over an orchestral melody	They talk of their love, growing more ardent until they kiss twice and go into the castle together.

is the storm's equal, that he can quell even the heavens. The effect, carefully prepared, is so dramatic that the memory of it, Otello in his glory, lasts throughout the opera to Otello at the end.

Boito achieves the effect without stopping the action for an aria. In fact, although he introduces all three main characters in the act, he gives none an aria. In the corresponding scene of *Aida* (p. 470) Verdi had given one each to Radames and Aida, and of course in *Ernani* (p. 130) all four main characters came on to their own recitative and aria. But in *Otello* the drama is more tightly meshed, and even Iago's drinking song, the closest thing to an aria, the baritone has to share with two tenors and the chorus. No one is on-stage who is not actively involved in the drama, and the leading singers are pre-eminent because of their roles in the drama rather than by virtuoso performances on the voice. As a result the drama evolves quickly and intensely. Boito slows it twice: once as the chorus settles around the fire, and then at the end of the act as Otello and Desdemona talk of their love. The first is sometimes criticized for slowing the action unnecessarily, but it may be needed to rest the audience after the exhausting pace at which the opera has opened. The second, the love scene, like Otello's entrance, is made so effective that it haunts the rest of the opera. Its climax comes as Otello asks for a kiss, "un bacio," and the orchestra swells with a phrase, ardent and tender, that Verdi brings back when Otello dies upon a kiss at the end of the opera.

Boito's construction of the act abandoned completely the older style of slow-fast arias building to a fast, brilliant climax, and to contemporaries the opera seemed quite revolutionary. In place of the old style Boito substituted the natural pace of the drama, which he altered only occasionally to permit some moments of lyrical effusion. This method required Verdi to follow the words with his music far more closely than he ever had before, and in setting *Otello* he wrote out the libretto several times and memorized the words until their individual rhythms and those of the phrases were absolutely sure in his mind.

In setting the words Verdi used all the skill he had been developing in making recitative melodic and using instruments to underline the emphasis. He achieved an extraordinarily subtle and evocative musical line underpinning the many, many words, for *Otello*, while not one of Verdi's longest operas, is one of the most dense. But the number of words may have cost him something. There are moments in Acts II and III when the non-professional operagoer's attention begins to flag. There is a quartet in Act II which, unless it has the very best singers, is apt not to come off and similarly a septet in the finale to Act III. Neither grips the non-professional listener with anything like the force of the quartet in *Rigoletto* or the sextet in the triumphal scene of *Aida.* The reason is not clear. Verdi may have simply been less inspired melodically. Or the number of words and thoughts, the complications of the drama, may have begun to interfere. In the *Rigoletto* quartet each character had one idea which he repeated by repeating the words over and over. This made it easy for Verdi to build an individual musical pattern for each character, and the four patterns remain clear when sounded together. In the *Otello* quartet each character has several ideas to express and hence very much less time for word repetition. The musical patterns are far less distinct and tend to get lost when sounded together. With bad singers the *Otello* quartet completely breaks down, yet the *Rigoletto* quartet never fails to sing itself. It may be that Verdi and Boito had tipped the balance so far away from musical pattern and toward drama that such forms as a quartet or septet not only seemed out of place in the drama but also failed to communicate anything.

The opera, however, can carry its few weak spots with a fraction of its strength. Verdi by now had every conceivable sort of technique at his command, so that he could take a soliloquy and move it along almost as fast as the spoken word and yet have it musically fascinating. In the third act, for example, after Otello has raged at Desdemona, he is left alone and desolated by what he thinks is the truth. Brokenly he exclaims he could have withstood captivity, dishonor, anything but loss of faith in Desdemona. He ends screaming that she must confess her crime and then he will kill her. Verdi begins very quietly, and probably few in the audience realize that for eighteen measures he has the voice declaim on only two notes, moving occasionally from one to the other. The impression is one of anguished melody, which in fact is wholly in the orchestra while Verdi husbands the voice until later. The melody is no more than a descending figure on the violins, supported largely by the cellos and a bassoon. But so perfectly is it worked in with the declamation that the two seem less a voice over a tune than a vocal melody.

Further into the soliloquy Verdi shifts the voice into a simple tune and reduces the orchestra to a mere tremor as an accompaniment. This method, as well as declaiming on two relatively low notes, permits the words to be heard distinctly. Then as Otello's anger mounts, his voice rises slowly from note to note while underneath Verdi works an insistent figure. Finally Otello flies apart: "Dannazione!" and "Confessione! Confessione!" He explodes the words out, and the orchestra replies with percussive blows.

The virtue, of course, is not in the number of techniques but in the skill with which Verdi applied them to reinforce the text. In the earlier operas the audience often sat back and wallowed in the glorious melodies and rhythms. In *Otello* the audience often sits forward, hanging on the words and quite unaware of how powerfully the music is working on it.

Critics generally cite *Otello* as the greatest of Italian romantic operas. In it Verdi seemed to achieve the sort of musical drama at which he had aimed since *Macbeth*. The trend toward drama was not original with Verdi; its roots stretch back to Mozart and Rossini, particularly in its romantic roots to *William Tell*. But if Rossini started important ideas about operatic style and form, he did not push them far before he retired. And neither Bellini nor Donizetti, both of whom died young, achieved the authority to conduct an operatic revolution. Verdi did, and in *Otello* he finally achieved a musical drama which avoids the stop and go of recitative and aria, a drama in which the music is continuous and the lyrical moments seem to swell naturally out of it.

Verdi achieved this within the tradition of Italian Opera, although everyone said it could not be done and that Italian opera would have to reconstruct itself within Wagner's German frame. But *Otello* is wholly Italian in its origins, and critics at the première recognized it as such; there was no more talk about Verdi imitating Wagner. In *Otello* the voice is still supreme, although now supported by instruments used with a subtlety Bellini, Donizetti, or even Verdi as a young man could never have imagined. Further, in *Otello* Verdi made use of all the stock in trade of Italian opera, such as the storm scene, the victory chorus and the drinking song, and gave them dramatic purpose as well as beauty for beauty's sake. His musical line continued to be melodic and in the typically Italian style of a longer rather than shorter phrase. The drama is sung, even in dialogues back and forth, rather than being musically spoken, a style which German composers increasingly approached.

Finally, in *Otello* Verdi expressed the essence of the Romantic Age of which he along with Hugo, Schiller, Wagner and a man like Garibaldi were all a part. The opera is typically Romantic in its exploitation of nature as the background for man, as in the scenes of storm, fire and calm night in the first act; in its emphasis on the emotions rather than reason, and in its passionate approach to love. Above all, it reflects the artistic as well as political thinking of the Romantic Age in its premise that man can be immensely noble and because of it suffer terrible tragedy. The potential nobility of man is a constant theme in Verdi's operas. No matter how he might despair of man in private, when he came to composing an opera he made man noble, capable of greatness in love, sacrifice and death. Life for all men would certainly end in death, but each, Verdi seemed to say, could make of his passage toward it something glorious.

CHAPTER 39

FALSTAFF

1887–1893; AGE, 73–79

VERDI'S next and last opera, *Falstaff*, was conceived and composed with less difficulty than *Otello* which had first been suggested in 1879, then postponed for the revisions of *Simone Boccanegra* and *Don Carlo*, and finally finished in 1887, eight years after its inception. With *Falstaff* there were to be no musical interruptions, and from the time Boito first produced the libretto in 1889 until the opera's première in 1893 Verdi worked on nothing else.

Naturally, immediately after the *Otello* première, everyone urged Verdi to start at once on another opera, and the impresario at La Scala suggested a comedy based on *Don Quixote*. Boito, however, remained silent; perhaps because he had just embarked on an affair with the actress, Eleonora Duse, or perhaps out of a feeling that it would be better to let Verdi rest for a bit and work in his fields before presenting him with another idea. After *Otello* Verdi never considered any librettist other than Boito, and so when he returned to Sant' Agata soon after the première he resumed for almost two and a half years his life as a country squire with the winters in Genoa. He tended his farm, refused to go to Rome for the première there of *Otello,* supervised the construction of his little hospital and complained in private letters of the state of the Italian nation.

But if the postman carried complaints out, he also brought some in, and to a Signor Rocchi of Perugia, otherwise unknown, Verdi replied:

Sir!

You allow yourself to give me a lecture which I do not accept.
I ask you in turn:
Why do you who don't know me, send me one of your works?
And why should I spend time on it?

Do you know how many letters, pamphlets, and compositions I receive every day from all over the world? Am I supposed to answer them all?

It is my duty, you say; but I say on the contrary it would be sheer *tyranny* to demand that I waste my time answering all the letters and examining all the pamphlets and compositions, almost always foolish and futile.

P.S. I do not recall your book exactly. But if it was sent in August it must be at my estate, and I will send it to you as soon as I return there.

And back at Sant' Agata in the autumn the little hospital opened, and the beds were immediately filled. Verdi had followed the construction as carefully as he did any of his farm buildings, insisting that nothing unnecessary be added, refusing to have his name appear over the door, and persuading Streponi to see to the furniture, linen and utensils. The hospital stands today, still serving the local people, and identified only by the single word "Ospedale."

But it is difficult to do good, and within less than two months Verdi, who had gone to Genoa, was writing the hospital's director:

I think it right to warn you that I have had bad reports from the hospital at Villanova, and I hope and wish they are not true. Here is what they are saying:

1. That the food is skimpy.

2. The wine even more so (although the cellar is well stocked!)

3. That the milk costs more than it's worth and that it is not whole milk.

4. That the oil is of the commonest kind, with a bad effect on both food and lighting.

5. That they wanted to buy half-spoiled rice and coarse, dark native spaghetti.

6. That funeral expenses are charged, even to persons of absolutely no means.

7. Many more things which for the sake of brevity I won't mention.

I am far away and can say nothing to this; I can neither believe nor disbelieve it; but in any case these reports distress me extremely and make me wonder if I cannot achieve the purpose for which I devoted part of my fortune to endowing this charitable foundation.

I think that the hospital is sufficiently well provided and that no small economies should be necessary. But to tell you the truth, rather than hear more of these complaints I would prefer that the hospital be closed and nothing more said about it.

But I hope that none of this is true, and that you will be so kind as to reassure me at once with a couple of words.

The hospital continued to be full as country people particularly suffered an economic depression. The government had begun a five-year tariff war with France which hurt the poorer and more backward Italy far more than its richer neighbor. The Prime Minister was one of Garibaldi's lieutenants, Francesco Crispi, a Sicilian with a strong personality and sense of destiny about himself. His mistress, disguised as a boy, had been the only woman to accompany "The Thousand," and in 1877 he had been forced to retire briefly from politics when an opponent revealed that he had married a lady in a mock ceremony under a forged signature and then had left her after twenty years to legitimize his daughter by another woman. But no one seriously held this against him. Many Italians found it amusing and romantic, the action of a strong man who dared to do what others only dreamed of. As a follower of Garibaldi he pulled many radicals into supporting the government, and as a strong man he was popular with the monarchists and army. Many of his ideas for internal reforms were liberal, but he had a tendency to introduce them by violent means. His answer to the increasing social unrest was apt to be a police squad rather than a policy to remove the cause. As the poor and dispossessed, particularly in the south, began to riot, Verdi in Genoa wrote to his friend Piroli, now a Senator:

Tell me something you who find yourself in the bustle of a riot! Sad events that will unhappily have a sequel! If they repress them, make arrests and exile the leaders, it will serve no purpose. In the crowd certainly there are always agitators, bad ones, thieves, but also there is almost always *Hunger.*

I do not like politics, but I admit its necessity, the theory, the form of Government, Patriotism, Dignity, etc., etc., but first of all *a man must live.* From my window every day I see a ship and sometimes two, each carrying at least a thousand emigrants! *Poverty and Hunger!* I see in the country landlords of a few years ago now become peasants, day-laborers, and emigrants (poverty and hunger). The rich, whose fortune decreases every year, can no longer spend as before, and so *poverty and hunger!*

And how can we go forward? It is not our industry that will save us from ruin! . . . Perhaps, you, you politician, will say that "there is no other road." Well then, if it's to be so, then let's get ready for riot and disorder, first in one city, then in another, then in the villages and countryside, and then *Le déluge!*

Italian music lovers who are also Communists say with a laugh that, come the revolution, they will have no trouble proving Verdi was a

Communist all along. Certainly it is attractive that, as he approached eighty and was comparatively rich, he did not retreat into yachting or polo or hire gamekeepers to beat the poachers off his land. Instead when hard times hit his *paese,* he reduced rents on his farms while at the same time improving them, started a new system of irrigation, reclaimed swamps along the Po, built dairy farms and a hospital. In short, he ran his own public works program. His social conscience was unusual among Italians of the time. Garibaldi had it and constantly preached that the greatest danger facing the newly unified country was the enormous gap between the rich and the poor. Some politicians managed to see this and recognize that the peasants must have some stake in the new State or they would eventually destroy it. But they grasped the idea only as a matter of intellect and, lacking Garibaldi's or Verdi's emotional intensity, they did little.

Others argued that the emigration was a good thing, not only a safety valve but a form of colonization and spreading of Italian culture. In a sense it was, but of course the strong and able left while the weak and poor remained, and the money sent back in the mail was no recompense for the brains and ability lost. Without some action by Parliament the pressure could only build up, and in time, although Piroli did not live to see it, Verdi had to watch his gloomy prophecy of a *déluge* almost come true.

But meanwhile one day in July 1889 when Verdi was at the baths at Montecatini there came by mail from Boito the outline for the libretto of *Falstaff.* Verdi took to it instantly. Falstaff was one of his favorite Shakespearean characters, and he had wanted to do a comedy for years, if only to prove that he could and thereby avenge the ancient defeat of *Un Giorno di Regno.* He began at once to reread all the plays in which Falstaff appears: *The Merry Wives of Windsor, Henry IV, Parts I and II,* and the report of his death in *Henry V.* Two days later he wrote to Boito in Milan protesting, rather weakly, that he was very old, that he might not finish it, that it might interfere with Boito finishing his own opera, *Nerone.* But he could not keep from giving himself away in capital letters. "What a joy!" he wrote, "to be able to say to the public:

"HERE WE ARE AGAIN!!
COME SEE US!"

And Boito was ready by return mail with an answer for everything. His opera *Nerone* was, after all, his own problem. As for Verdi's age:

Writing a comic opera I don't believe will tire you. A tragedy makes its composer *truly suffer,* the thought gives rise to grief that morbidly agitates the nerves. But the joke and laughter of a comedy exhilarate the mind and body. "A smile adds a thread to the web of life." I don't know if I've quoted Foscolo correctly, but the idea is true.

Back to Milan by return mail went Verdi's answer:

Dear Boito:

Amen; and so be it! Let us then do *Falstaff!* Let's not think at the moment of the obstacles, my age, and illnesses! I want only to keep it the most profound secret: a word I underline three times to tell you that no one must know anything of it . . .

But wait . . . Peppina, I do believe, knew it even before we did! . . . But don't worry: she will keep the secret: when women have the talent for secrets, they have it even stronger than us.

Strepponi would have had to be far less astute than she was not to have guessed what was afoot, what with all the pulling of Shakespeare off the shelf and letters to and from Boito in every post. She in turn might have made an observation about the talent of men for secrets, but instead she dutifully fended off all inquiries for two years. Even Ricordi knew nothing of the opera. He, like most men, assumed that Verdi at seventy-four had completed his career with *Otello.*

In those years Verdi worked at *Falstaff,* sometimes more and sometimes less, but never more than two hours a day, for he had read that this was enough of concentrated work for a man of his age. By March of 1890 he had completed the first act, and the only problem, on which he appealed to Boito, had been the placing of accents on the strange English words "Falstaff," "Norfolk" and "Windsor." Otherwise he had been able to set the text exactly as Boito had written it, without any problems of meter or dramatic effects. Considering how he had harassed Piave and the others, he could pay no greater compliment to Boito's libretto.

Meanwhile as the leader of Italian music he received an invitation to become an honorary member of the Musical Society of the Beethoven House in Bonn and accepted, although deploring the publicity, because "it concerns Beethoven! At whose great name we must all prostrate ourselves in reverence!" And several years later in 1892 he appeared at La Scala to conduct the Prayer from Rossini's *Mosè* at a concert celebrating the Rossini centennial. When invited, he had groaned over displaying his person, and the ovation as he walked out on the stage had held up the program, he felt, far too long. But for Rossini he had done it, and it was the last time he conducted in public.

When La Scala, however, planned a jubilee to honor the fiftieth anniversary of Verdi's first opera, *Oberto,* he refused to have anything to do with the idea. Various suggestions were put forward as to what might be done, and he found them all bad. "A concert of assorted operatic pieces?" he wrote to Boito. "Good God, how horrible!" As for a revival of *Oberto* itself, he felt that in fifty years the audience had changed and wanted something different, and in any event, *Oberto* was not a very good opera. To revive it was foolish artistically and financially. There was even talk of creating a national foundation in his name which might award stipends to young composers or underwrite the productions of first operas. Verdi foresaw endless difficulties: who would guarantee the quality of the opera or the quality of the production? Privately he urged Boito to quash the idea.

In the end on 17 November 1889, fifty years to the day after its première, La Scala revived *Oberto.* Verdi did not attend, but at Sant' Agata he received messages of congratulation from the King, Crispi, the poet Carducci and thousands of less well-known persons who sincerely believed he was their country's greatest glory. He was moved by the demonstration and attempted to acknowledge many of the messages.

Just a year later Muzio died in Paris, alone and in circumstances that agitated Verdi strongly; for Muzio's life in his last years had been neither happy nor successful. When in America he had married a lady considerably younger than himself, and they had had a child. Verdi and Strepponi were the godparents. But the child had died, the wife drifted away, and Muzio had lived in Paris alone. After the Théâtre Italien had failed, he had been unable to place himself elsewhere as a conductor and gave singing lessons. Finally he had died in a hospital without a friend beside him.

He named Verdi the executor of his will and in a note written a few days before his death apologized for the imposition. The will, which he wrote himself, is in the style of the times and reflects the simplicity which Muzio never lost:

This is my Credo and my Will.

I believe with heart and soul in all that my Mother believed and taught me and whom I have always venerated and adored. I lived in the Catholic religion and I still proclaim in this hour the name of God, because it is God whom I adore. Feeling myself to be very sick and believing that I will die in Paris . . . (etc.)

And he went on to ask that he be buried near his mother in Busseto. He mentioned Verdi several times, once in explaining that he wished to follow Verdi's good example in setting up a small scholarship for students to be administered by the Monte di Pietà, and again with regard to Verdi's letters, all of which he had saved: "It is my *absolute wish* that all of them be burned, because I do not wish them to become objects of gift or, in time, of commerce, traded for profit for their autographs." And they were all burned, causing the greatest single gap in Verdi's correspondence.

Undoubtedly this is what Verdi wanted done with his letters, and it is touching that Muzio, who shared Verdi's peasant background, should have been the only one of his friends with the sensitivity and regard for him to do it. But posterity can only regret the loss. Muzio was a conductor, not particularly outstanding, who specialized in Verdi's operas. Probably some of the letters contained explanations of what Verdi intended in his music and advice on how to achieve it.

With Muzio the last of Verdi's old friends in his own generation died. With the exception of Strepponi, none who had seen the first *Oberto* or *Nabucco* survived to see *Falstaff*. Of the men in the younger generation or singers such as Teresa Stolz, now grown fat and jolly, none could remember a time when Verdi had not been the most popular composer in Italy. And it seems fitting that Strepponi, who had been the first to support *Oberto,* may also have been the first to announce the imminence of *Falstaff*.

The story goes that one night in November 1890, after Verdi had finished the first act and outlined the second and third, he gave a dinner in his hotel in Milan for his friends. Among the guests were, of course, Ricordi and Boito and also Ricordi's married daughter, Ginetta, who was plainly pregnant. After dinner Verdi called for some spumante, and Strepponi rose to propose a toast. "I drink," she said, "to the large belly," and hesitated on the word. As Ginetta began to blush, Strepponi smiled and added, "who is 'Falstaff' and whom Verdi finished yesterday evening."

In fact Verdi was a long way from being finished. But he presumably had reached a point at which he had confidence that he would finish and thought it was time to think of signing artists and La Scala

MAUREL

for the première, still two years off.

In reaching it the opera had the usual number of difficulties. Boito's attention was diverted by Faccio's decline into insanity, which required Boito for more than a year to take on Faccio's post as director of the Conservatory at Parma in order to retain the salary for Faccio's expenses. Verdi at times lost interest and wrote to Ricordi that he had no intention of keeping to any dates or binding himself in any way, and of course to the general public he repeated this endlessly. He also insisted that he had not composed the opera with any singers in mind, but he never considered anyone but Maurel for the title role. After Teresa Stolz retired, Maurel became the outstanding interpreter of Verdi. He first came to Verdi's attention as Amonasro in the Opéra's production of *Aida* in 1880. After that he had sung the title role in the première of the revised *Simone Boccanegra* and Iago in the première of *Otello*. There is no reason to think, in spite of Verdi's denial, that he did not create the role of Falstaff with Maurel in mind. Maurel had a good baritone voice, but Verdi liked him for his ability to act, which suited Verdi's increasing emphasis on the drama and would be especially important in a comedy.

Maurel, however, along with others connected with the La Scala production began to demand enormous fees. Maurel even wanted a monopoly on the role, which was tantamount to demanding the right to determine when and where the opera would be produced. In the face of such arrogance Verdi remained remarkably calm and contented himself with some sensible remarks and the observation that he could, after all, burn the opera. No one thought he would go that far, but it was quite possible that he would withhold the production altogether or give it to some other city or theatre. And the demands dwindled. Verdi, however, again retained the right to cancel the production even after the dress rehearsal.

The première on 9 February 1893, like *Otello* before it, was one of the great musical events of its decade. The occasion was perhaps a shade less exciting than that of *Otello,* and the reason may have been that everyone was certain it would be a masterwork. With *Otello,* which had been his first new opera in sixteen years, there had been a doubt. With *Falstaff* there was none. Also comedy is by its nature less stirring than tragedy, and the audience was interested and excited rather than wildly enthusiastic.

The performance was not perfect. Evidently the final scene in Windsor Park failed for some reason, and several critics complained that La Scala was too large, which it is, for such intimate and witty comedy. Even the orchestra was not without fault. The double-bass section, for example, could not play a passage in the final act, and during the rehearsals Verdi had agreed that only the first-desk man should attempt it. This threw the balance off and, worse, the man got the rhythm wrong. But Verdi had accepted it as the best La Scala could do. These imperfections in detail, however, did not obscure the fact that a masterwork had been added to Italian opera, and foreign critics writing home said so unequivocally.

Although in his eightieth year, Verdi had spent hours each day at the rehearsals and then more hours back at his hotel dealing with all the admirers, friends, critics, bores and telegrams. Strepponi marveled at his resilience, as did all the journalists who wrote articles on everything from his clothes to his digestion. He survived the journalistic invasion of his privacy with remarkable good humor. The rehearsals, while they continued, exhilarated him, and he evidently had determined to go through the ordeal of the traditional first three performances with the best grace he could. He took endless curtain calls, appeared on the balcony of his hotel and answered hundreds of congratulatory notes and telegrams. Only a rumor agitated him into action. A newspaper declared that the government intended to give him the title of "Marquis of Busseto." Verdi telegraphed at once and in horror to the Minister of Education who replied that the rumor had no basis.

The excitement did not end with La Scala. Verdi agreed to accompany the production to Rome and direct the rehearsals there even though he knew perfectly well the sort of reception he was letting himself in for. But again he seems to have made no objection. He was genuinely happy with his comedy's success, realistically aware of his position in the country and at the moment had nothing else to do. Any man likes to be a success, and his wife generally likes it even more. Undoubtedly Strepponi urged him to go. She was always proud of him. Once when he had played part of *Otello* for Ricordi, she had remarked in her dialect: "My Verdi is still good!" Of *Falstaff* she had written to her sister: "We are witnessing the advent of a new combination of poetry and music. We shall see what is the verdict of the Respectable Public." Rome was the country's capital, and the governmental part of the public, including the King, was there.

Verdi went from Genoa to Rome by train, accompanied by Strepponi, Stolz and Ricordi. To avoid demonstrations at either end or along the line the times of departure and arrival were kept secret. It made no difference. The Mayor of Rome in the robes of his office, together with several thousand persons more, met every train that came from Genoa. Finally at 11:38 P.M. Verdi arrived. The crowd surged forward; the Mayor was jostled aside, and Verdi was, with difficulty, smuggled into a toolshed and after a time out to a carriage. From the station to the Hotel Quirinale crowds lined the street and refused to go home until he had appeared at his window. The hotel later put up a plaque to commemorate the night, and so did some railway official in the toolshed: "In this room Giuseppe Verdi took shelter from the impetuous enthusiasm of the crowd on his arrival in Rome, 13 April 1893." The toolshed and station have long since disappeared, but the plaque has been preserved in the Rome Museum.

The demonstrations continued. The city council made him an honorary citizen; he had an interview with King Umberto, and the theatre orchestra played a serenade outside his window, including the overtures to *Nabucco* and *Giovanna d'Arco,* excerpts from *I Lombardi* and *La Forza del Destino,* and the prelude to the last act of *La Traviata.* As in Milan, he attended the three traditional performances. At the première he sat in an armchair in the wings, and at the end of the second act he was invited to the royal box where King Umberto, in full view of the audience, introduced him to Queen Margherita. Then Their

Majesties led him to the front of the box while they themselves retired. In a box in the tier below with Stolz and Ricordi sat Strepponi. The mores of the time and place did not permit her as a fallen woman to have any part in the social pageant.

Finally it was all over, and Verdi and Strepponi went home. From Sant' Agata he watched the La Scala troupe, with an occasional change of cast and using local orchestras, tour most of Italy and go on to Vienna and Berlin. He himself went to Paris the following spring for a production in French with Maurel at the Opéra Comique, and there was more adulation and applause. By then he had made two revisions in the score, in the second and third acts, and considered the opera to be on its own, to succeed or not but either way without special attention. Characteristically, after making the revisions, he destroyed the original versions in the score, so it is impossible to know how his second thoughts differed from the first. But probably he wanted to clarify the characters' motives and the musical lines underlying them. As a general rule operatic comedies are at their best when music and motives are at their clearest.

With *Falstaff,* unlike *Otello,* there is no question that Boito improved on his Shakespearean source, *The Merry Wives of Windsor.* There is a tradition that Queen Elizabeth asked to see Falstaff in love and that Shakespeare wrote his play hurriedly to satisfy what amounted to a royal command. The result was and is a prosaic farce built of stock characters and on a series of repetitious episodes involving a fat man, any fat man, for the Falstaff of the comedy has none of the unique characteristics he exhibits in the chronicle plays of *King Henry IV, Parts I and II.* Boito's problem was to cut down the number of episodes while intensifying those he kept and at the same time to build up the characters, particularly that of Falstaff.

He succeeded by reducing the episodes to two and working the action in such a way that he could bring in many of Falstaff's best and most famous speeches in the chronicle plays. For the episodes he cut out nine irrelevant characters and the entire sequence in which Falstaff masquerades as the fat woman of Brentford. He retained the laundry-basket episode in which the merry wives, mocking Falstaff's advances, succeed in dumping him into the Thames and also, as the opera's finale, the nocturnal meeting under the oak in Windsor Park. Boito directed the action so that Falstaff's speech on honor became the finale of the first scene; he also combined parts of several others into a new speech on the vile world and benefits of drink, which he used to open the last act. Besides these two monologues he incorporated many touches here and there to make his Falstaff Shakespearean. The result is probably what Queen Elizabeth had in mind when she put her request: an exhibit of the great Shakespearean character in love. Given Falstaff's limitless self-esteem and cynical realism, his power with words and awful puns, the result should have been a comedy ranging from witty observations on the way of the world to romping farce. And Boito succeeded where Shakespeare, perhaps hurried, failed.

Presented with a libretto in which wit and words were to be of great importance Verdi carried his musical style even further toward drama and away from musical pattern. In *Falstaff* there are not only no arias, there are almost no tunes. There is also no recitative. The unit now has become the melodic phrase, which lasts only as long as the verbal phrase requires, and no scheme or outline can reveal the construction of an act short of printing almost the entire text. The musical result is an almost continuous melodic line broken only rarely for ensembles, such as when the merry wives chatter together. This new musical line without aria or recitative is what Strepponi meant when she wrote to her sister of "a new combination of poetry and music."

Verdi supported his musical line in *Falstaff* as he had in *Otello* but with even greater orchestral skill and conciseness. The opera is shorter and more dense than *Otello,* and in fact the whole of it takes less time in performance than the last act of Wagner's *Die Meistersinger.* Where Wagner unfolds his opera slowly and luxuriantly, with every detail examined and revealed, Verdi shimmers or dances his past the audience's ear and eye, startling its imagination with almost every note and yet never stopping to reveal all that has been suggested. The speed of *Falstaff* has always been held by some as a count against it. There are no moments of repose in which the audience and music can catch their breath. Others, of course, rejoice that at last someone showed that operatic music does not, by its very nature, have to dawdle.

What rank *Falstaff* holds among Verdi's operas depends greatly on who is assigning the positions. A majority of musicians, critics and professional operagoers declare that, along with *Otello,* it is his best. And between the two it is merely a question of preferring tragedy or comedy, with *Falstaff* holding an edge on orchestral skill. Yet the casual

operagoer has seldom seen the opera, and outside of Italy many persons, who know perfectly well that Verdi composed *Aida,* have never heard of *Falstaff*.

The explanation lies partly in the problem of translation. The opera is a witty comedy; the fat knight loves words and plays and puns with them outrageously. For anyone who does not understand Italian, and understand it well, the wit is totally lost. What few laughs remain are in the farce, which in non-Italian-speaking countries is often grossly overplayed and thereby obliterates the subtleties in the music. A few statistics will show the problem.

At La Scala, for the period 1900–1960, *Falstaff* ranked fourth among Verdi's operas in number of performances, which, considering most persons prefer operatic tragedy to comedy, is very high. It followed *Aida, Rigoletto* and *La Traviata*. But for the same period at the Metropolitan, where it is given in Italian to an English-speaking audience, it ranked ninth, following the three mentioned above and also, in order, *Il Trovatore, Otello, La Forza del Destino, Un Ballo in Maschera* and *Don Carlo*. Even more startling, for the same period at La Scala it tied with *Carmen* for tenth place among the operas most frequently performed, but at the Metropolitan it was sixtieth.

The discrepancy, however, cannot be entirely explained in terms of language. For even in Italy in opera houses other than La Scala, which has a special interest in *Falstaff*, the opera ranks only seventh or eighth in popularity among Verdi's works and is generally well down on any over-all list of performances. Some critics and many casual operagoers explain this by insisting that a melodic phrase is no substitute for a tune or an aria. These persons argue that in *Falstaff* Verdi tipped the balance too far away from musical pattern and toward drama. They rejoice that Puccini refused to follow Verdi's lead in this and complain of the many composers lacking Verdi's skill who have written operas in which the music thumps and squeaks along under a lot of words without adding anything of value to them. Some years ago this minority was strengthened by the support of Igor Stravinsky who, turning his coat, stated in a lecture at Harvard: "I am beginning to think, in full agreement with the general public, that melody must keep its place at the summit of the hierarchy of elements that make up music." He went on to speak of *Falstaff* as a "deterioration of the genius that gave us *Rigoletto, Il Trovatore, Aida* and *La Traviata.*" And he did not include *Otello* as a flowering of that genius.

The word "deterioration" may be misapplied. There is no evidence that Verdi did not achieve exactly what he intended with *Falstaff*. It happens not to be universally popular. But then neither is Michelangelo's "Last Judgment" if compared to the sentimental Madonnas that sell by the millions in reproductions. To what extent popularity is a gauge of artistic value is a question men are apt to decide in terms that support their prejudices. Verdi placed a high value on box-office receipts, and even in the first year after the première he recognized that *Falstaff*, while it made money, was not as popular as he had hoped. This grieved him and in a way that all the praise from professional musicians could not quite assuage, although he must have laughed that he who in his youth had been dismissed as vulgar had ended in being praised by the fastidious.

If he had written another opera, what direction would it have taken? A swing back toward musical pattern? The only certainty is that he would have done something different, for even with *Falstaff* at seventy-nine he did not repeat his *Otello* of six years before.

CHAPTER 40

THE LAST YEARS: STREPPONI'S DEATH

1893–1897; AGE, 79–84

THE excitement of *Falstaff* in Milan and Rome exhausted Verdi and at the same time, as Boito had predicted, exhilarated him. He followed the tour with letters to Edoardo Mascheroni, the conductor, that sparkle with gaiety. The opera ends as the merry wives outsmart Falstaff under Herne's Oak in Windsor Park, and then all the characters, led by Falstaff, step forward to the footlights and finish with a philosophic fugue: "Tutto nel mondo è burla." "All the world's a joke. Man was born laughing, swung this way and that by his heart and his head. All men are ridiculous; each laughs at the other, but he laughs best who laughs the last."

"Tutto nel mondo è burla" became a refrain, chanted by operagoers to each other and by Verdi in his letters. In Rome he had worn his years so lightly he had seemed capable of anything, even another opera. And once when he had half in jest mentioned it, Boito had promptly suggested *Antony and Cleopatra*. He had just finished a translation into Italian for Eleonora Duse and began to reduce it into a libretto. But as the months went by and Verdi passed eighty, nothing came of it; and there gradually emerged, at least among his intimate friends, a sense that this time he really had composed his last opera. When Emma Zilli, who had sung one of the merry wives, wrote him a Christmas letter, he replied:

Do you remember the third performance of *Falstaff?* I took leave of you all; and you were all a little moved, especially you and Pasqua . . . Imagine what that farewell was for me. It meant: "We will never meet again as artists!!!"

We did meet again, it's true, in Milan, and at Genoa and Rome; but memory always went back to that third night, which meant:

Tutto è finito!

And he had earlier used the same phrase, "All is ended," in a note which Toscanini found only twenty-five years later in the manuscript of the opera and which Verdi must have written before sending the score on to Ricordi. In it with the intimacy of creation he addresses Falstaff by his first name:

Le ultime note del Falstaff	*The last notes of Falstaff*
Tutto è finito!	All is ended!
Va, va, vecchio John . . .	Go, go, old John . . .
Cammina per la tua via,	Be off on your way,
Fin che tu puoi . . .	As far as you can . . .
Divertente tipo di briccone;	Laughable type of a rogue;
Eternamente vero, sotto	Eternally true, under
Maschera diversa, in ogni	Varying guise in every
Tempo, in ogni lugo!!	Time and place!!
Va . . . Va . . .	Go . . . Go . . .
Cammina cammina	Be off Be off
Addio!!!	Farewell!!!

Age takes its toll, and opera, with voice, orchestra and scenery, is the most complicated form of music to compose. If for a moment at Rome Verdi considered another opera, he later did nothing to realize it. He seems to have felt in his heart that *Falstaff* was the last.

He did not intend, however, to cease composing, and he began soon after on some ballet music for *Otello*. The directors of the Opéra wished to be the first to produce that opera in Paris and had proposed a production in Italian for the same winter that *Falstaff* had opened at the Opéra Comique. But Verdi had refused. The two operas would compete with each other, and what with Maurel singing *Falstaff* in French at the Opéra Comique, the *Otello* in a foreign language at the Opéra would suffer. Besides, as he had written the directors, it was traditional at the Opéra for all operas to be in the national language and include a ballet. And with new music as bait he succeeded in postponing the production to the following autumn. Meanwhile, at the same time he composed the ballet music, he undertook to shorten the finale to Act III which would follow it. He was always conscious of time and the span of an audience's attention. When he had played over the first act of *Falstaff* for Ricordi and discovered it ran for forty-two minutes, he had gloomily observed that it was "two minutes too long." Now for the ballet music he blocked out the choreography and set the whole to run five minutes and fifty-nine seconds, not a second longer.

The French chose the occasion of the Parisian première of *Otello* to honor their forty-seven-year association with Verdi. It had started in 1847 when he had revised *I Lombardi* and added a ballet so that the Opéra could present it as *Jérusalem*. Now in 1894 in a new building, but still the Opéra, there was *Otello* with Maurel as Iago. Verdi had not wanted to go, but Boito had insisted and perhaps also Strepponi, who had always loved Paris. The night of the première the President of the Third Republic came to the Opéra, invited Verdi to his box, told him he had been awarded the Grand Cross of the Legion of Honor and then, taking him by the hand, led him forward to present him to the audience. He was eighty-one. His hair, moustache and beard were now uniformly white and a little whispy. He still stood straight, and his trim figure made him seem slighter than he really was. He had never been handsome, but with age had come a look of distinction. Now as he acknowledged the applause, quietly turning his head this way and that, he seemed curiously vital. Everyone there could sing not one or two but many of his melodies, and his clear eye and slowly turning head seemed to promise an inexhaustible supply, endlessly churning within him.

The festivities continued all week. Several days later, representing Italian music, he attended a memorial service for Gounod. The following day both he and Strepponi were guests of honor at a State banquet given by Republic's President in the Elysée Palace.

The honors back and forth were only just. French music and Verdi had done much for each other. Like all operatic composers in the nineteenth century he had struggled to reach Paris, and once there, he had learned much. The Opéra was always exasperating, but there were other orchestras in Paris that were the best in Europe, and with them Verdi heard possibilities of disciplined sound unimagined in Italy. He heard Meyerbeer's dramatic orchestration and, even more important, that of Berlioz, who perhaps more than any other composer created the modern orchestra and its enormous range of sound. Much of the ink and passion spilled to prove that Verdi imitated Wagner would have been better used examining their mutual debt to French music and performances of the 1840s. For Verdi there was also the

debt to French drama which had given him the librettos for *Ernani,
Rigoletto, La Traviata* and indirectly for *Un Ballo in Maschera* and
even *Aida.* And lastly there was the city itself. He did not love it; he
was not a cosmopolite, and he truly loved only his own paese. Yet he
considered Paris the fount of freedom and civilization in modern
Europe and held it in a special regard. It was there that he had first
lived with Strepponi, and in Paris the State invited her to share his
honors; in provincial Rome it did not.

After the third performance of *Otello* in Paris Verdi and Strepponi
returned to Genoa where they spent the winter. In January they went
to Milan for several weeks for Verdi to consult Camillo Boito, the
librettist's elder brother and an architect. An idea had been gestating
for several years in Verdi's mind. He had done much for his paese
with the hospital, scholarships and farm work, and his thoughts had
turned to the other great area commanding his love, the theatre. He saw
that many musicians, singers, conductors and instrumentalists, ended
their days in poverty. Most German houses offered assured wages and,
after ten years of service in them, a pension. The Italian houses had
nothing comparable. They still operated under a system of impresarios
who, without support from the cities or State, were gradually going
bankrupt and in the process ruining the average musician who could
not demand a large fee.

There have always been persons who argue that any really good musician will end his life famous and rich. Verdi himself is often offered
as an example, but even among the great the argument fails with Mozart, who was buried in a pauper's grave. And among the less great it
totally ignores the economic realities of life in an opera house. Verdi
knew that along with the musicians too lazy to practice their parts or
merely unendowed with the virtue of thrift there were many others,
competent and responsible, who still faced old age with little more
than their memories.

In 1889 he had bought a plot of land outside the Porta Magenta of
Milan with the idea of building a hospital and convalescent home. At
the time he had consulted only Camillo Boito, and for several years
no one knew anything about it, not even that Verdi had bought the
land. Meanwhile Arrigo Boito had produced the libretto for *Falstaff,*
and Verdi had put any thought of building aside while he composed
the opera. But that done, he returned to the project, substituting for the
idea of a hospital and convalescent home one of a rest home large

enough to house and feed a hundred musicians. Camillo Boito's first drawings put the sleeping quarters in dormitories, but this struck Verdi as too institutional. He wanted double bedrooms so that the old people could assist each other, if necessary, during the night and yet with a partition between the beds for privacy. But the estimated cost of such an arrangement staggered him, and he asked Boito to eliminate the partition so that each room would need only a single window and door.

Boito redrew the plans, and in 1896 construction began on a two-story building designed to hold a hundred musicians. Verdi later stipulated that the ratio was to be sixty men to forty women and that they were to be "Italian citizens who have reached the age of sixty-five, have practiced the art of music professionally, and find themselves in a state of poverty." He also set up an order of priority for admission which, not unnaturally, put composers first; and then in order, singers, conductors, choir leaders and orchestra players. Boito had suggested the building be called an "Asylum," but Verdi thought it too harsh and decided on "Casa di Riposo per Musicisti" or "House of Rest for Musicians." This has generally been shortened to "Casa di Riposo" or, as it is often called by the Milanese, merely "Casa Verdi."

With the actual ground-breaking the newspapers published a rash of stories, and there was no more secrecy about the project. But at least the stories on it had some basis in fact. The previous summer, merely because Verdi had written to a musical librarian asking for a copy of a vocal solo on Dante's character "Ugolino," there had been a round of stories that he and Boito planned an opera on the subject. *Falstaff*, one paper intoned, "is the triumph of yesterday and *Ugolino* that of tomorrow. We have it from a reliable source" (etc.), but it was all quite wrong.

Verdi was, however, composing. It was the habit of a lifetime, and he would never altogether lose it. He once had written Mascheroni, the conductor: "Every man has his destiny: one to be a donkey all his life, another to be a cuckold, one to be rich and another poor. As for myself, with my tongue in my mouth like a mad dog, I'm fated to work to the last gasp!"

It was his practice to do some work on music every day, even if very little, and when he was not working on an opera, he did exercises just as he had done for Lavigna and Provesi. But beyond these he had started to set two ecclesiastical texts, the *Te Deum Laudamus* and *Stabat Mater Dolorosa*. The latter, like the *Dies Irae*, is a medieval

The letter opposite is Verdi's reply, in the year of the Otello première in Paris, to someone who had asked his opinion of Gounod. Throughout the last half of the nineteenth century Gounod ranked very high with the public and critics and was widely considered to be the French equivalent of Verdi and Wagner. The Khedive of Egypt, for example, had restricted the commission for what later became Aida to one of the three. Verdi wrote:

Genoa 20 Nov. 1894

Monsieur

What can I say about Gounoud?

When a composer has written operas which have been able to achieve a thousandth performance in a single country, there is nothing left for an individual to add to his glory.

Accept, Monsieur, my respectful compliments.

G. VERDI

Verdi, trying hard to be pleasant, marred his effort by misspelling "Gounod.' But he did try and succeeded, with a fine Italian hand, in seeming to say something when he really said very little, a social art he practised with difficulty.

His true opinion of Gounod he had written earlier, in 1878, to his crony, Arrivabene, and it probably was the opinion he still held:

Gounod is a great musician, a great talent, who composes chamber and instrumental music in a superior and individual style. But he is not an artist of dramatic fiber. In his hands Goethe's Faust, although turned into a successful opera, has become small. The same is true of Roméo et Juliette and will be true of Polyeucte. In short, he always does the intimate scene well but always weakens the dramatic situations and draws the characters poorly.

Gênes 20 Nov. 1894

Monsieur

Que pourrai-je dire sur Gounod?

Quand un compositeur a écrit des opéras qui ont pu atteindre la millième représentation dans un seul pays, il n'y a pas d'individu qui puisse rien ajouter à sa gloire —

Agréez, Monsieur, mes compliments respectueux

G. Verdi

poem and describes Mary as she watches her son, Jesus, on the cross. The *Te Deum* is a canticle of praise, the work of a number of poets and probably going back to the fourth or fifth century A.D. Both poems have a periodic place in the Roman Catholic service, and Christian churches of all sects use the *Te Deum* to rejoice over victories in war, most often victories over other Christians.

Granted the decision not to do another opera, it is not surprising that Verdi turned to these poems, set by many other composers before him. Each had a dramatic text of a length that he presumably felt he could encompass, and each also allowed him to do the sort of choral writing in which, with his study of Palestrina, he had become increasingly interested. He also had composed, probably several years earlier, a *Laudi alla Vergine Maria, Praise to the Virgin Mary,* with the text taken from Canto XXXIII of Dante's *Paradiso.* With all three works he insisted, just as he always had with *Otello* and *Falstaff,* that he might never finish them and that he was doing them for his own pleasure. When Arrigo Boito inquired about them early in 1897, Verdi replied in his old discouraged vein: "Just now I cannot say what I want to do. Everything I might do seems to me useless! Now, I haven't the mind to decide anything! . . . In case I finish the instrumentation, I will write to you!"

His mood, as often in the past, was partly the result of the country's predicament which had gone from bad to worse and finally in the Battle of Aduwa in Ethiopia had culminated in disaster. The flamboyant Crispi, whom Verdi had admired as a man who could cut through the parliamentary tangle to get things done, had returned to office as Prime Minister in 1893. His predecessor had proposed economies in the army to release revenue for more urgent civilian programs, and this had lined up against him not only the army and arms manufacturers but also the Court and all the enthusiasts for the Triple Alliance. It may well not have been a majority of the country, but it was a majority in Parliament and Crispi, by refusing to cut back the army, was able to stay in office.

He used the army to back an aggressive colonial policy based on several Red Sea ports which the Italians held and called collectively Eritrea. It was a time when the British were moving into Egypt, the French into Tunis and Morocco, and much of Crispi's interest was in prestige, to demonstrate that Italy was also a great power. His plan was to take over the vast interior of Ethiopia as well as its Red Sea coast, and he began sending military expeditions inland. In the past there had been skirmishing, but Crispi now embarked on large-scale colonial war. Many Italians, including a cabinet minister who resigned, insisted that Italy could not afford it, that the country's first duty was to its "quadrilateral of seventeen million illiterates." The powerful *Corriere della Sera* was against it, and in some areas the peasants ripped up the tracks over which the troops would have to travel to ports of embarkation. But powerful interests backed Crispi, and he pushed the campaign ahead although without proper support or preparation.

It was a desultory war. The terrain was difficult, the climate unhealthy, and the Ethiopians effectively hostile. Finally in March 1896 the Ethiopian King, Menelik, caught an Italian army off guard with inadequate maps, equipment and leadership and slaughtered it. Probably more Italians lost their lives on that one day than in the year of their country's unification.

The news of the disaster at Aduwa drove Crispi from office forever, and the subsequent investigations, like those after Custozza and Lissa in 1866, revealed frightening incompetence in the military commanders and their civilian support. Politicans opposing Crispi pointed out that Eritrea was unsuitable for a colony in any event and had now cost some eight thousand lives and nearly five hundred million lire, all for nothing. The only return was disillusion and bitterness which aggravated the social unrest and fanned the dissatisfaction with parliamentary government. Worse, Crispi and his supporters had so attached the idea of prestige to the campaign that the humiliating defeat left a festering wound in those segments of Italian society that had supported the war. For many Italians "Aduwa" assumed the same emotional charge that "Alsace and Lorraine" contained for many Frenchmen. Just forty years later in 1936 these same elements in Italian society, the army, the monarchists, and those putting a high value on prestige, provided the chief emotional support for Mussolini's Ethiopian war of *revanche*.

But in 1896 these elements were defeated. The Mayor of Milan publicly asked the government to abandon a policy which had so damaged Italy's good name and commerce. Others called Aduwa a salutory defeat for a second-class power puffed up with grandiose ambitions, and among these, although privately, was Verdi. He observed to a friend: "Unfortunately we, too, are in Africa playing the tyrant; we are wrong, and we will pay for it. A fine civilization we have, with all its miseries! Those people don't know what to do with it, and in many ways they are more civilized than we!" But like most Italians, he found the public washing of dirty linen humiliating and tended to deprecate Parliament without fully realizing the extent to which it was successfully working. The country changed its policy on a major issue without a revolution involving executions and riots and ending in a military dictatorship. Considering the incipient violence constantly percolating among the desperately poor, who were the great majority of the population, it was an important accomplishment.

The following year in January 1897 Verdi, whose good health was still a subject for newspaper articles, had his first sign of trouble. One morning in the Palazzo Doria in Genoa Strepponi found him lying motionless in bed and unable to speak. Maria Carrara, the adopted daughter, was staying with them, and she and Strepponi had an excited discussion on whether to call a doctor at once. Strepponi, probably fearing the publicity of an emergency call, was against it, but before they could decide, Verdi signaled that he wanted to write. In a shaky hand he managed "Caffè," and after being served some he began to recover. In a few days he seemed as well as he had been before, and the incident was kept a secret from all except Boito, Ricordi and Mascheroni, who was conducting at the Carlo Felice in Genoa. The newspapers continued to comment on Verdi's exceptional health at eighty-three, and when he and Strepponi went to Montecatini in July, he seemed perfectly well, but she, two years younger, suffered with arthritis. A friend who saw them there wrote in his diary: "She walks with difficulty, all bent over and supporting herself on his arm. Still there is some suggestion of her old beauty. He, on the other hand, what vigor he still has for his eighty-four years! [sic] He has a cloud of white hair which, joined with his beard, forms a sort of halo. He holds himself straight, walks briskly, and turns easily; he talks quickly and can remember facts, dates and names, and set forth his ideas on art clearly." With his friends he was genial and liked to talk on almost any subject. With strangers he tried to be tolerant, although he resented being stared at like "a wild beast" and sometimes with bores he was curt. To a lady who insisted on describing how much she adored *Aida*, he tartly suggested that she buy a ticket to a performance and meanwhile leave the composer alone.

Another hazard for him were autograph hunters who plotted to maneuver him into a signature or better yet into a few bars of music signed. Best of all (like the example below) was a card with the opening notes of the final fugue to *Falstaff*, "Tutto nel mondo è burla."

These were considered, quite incorrectly, to be the last notes he wrote and therefore to have a peculiar significance. A legend was emerging that the gloomy Verdi of burning passion had, at the end of his life, somehow decided that life itself was not suffering but a joke. This confused art with life, a traditional ending of a comic opera with Verdi's personal philosophy. In the years that remained to him he demonstrated that his view of reality had not changed. But the legend was comforting to those who, faced with the enormity of human suffering, stupidity and cruelty, find it easier to giggle than to weep; just as if Voltaire had never written *Candide*.

Soon after they returned to Sant' Agata from Montecatini, Strepponi developed bronchitis and was in bed for several weeks. She recovered but continued to cough and had no appetite. Verdi worried that she ate almost nothing. Then, just before they were to leave for the winter in Genoa, she fell ill again. This time the doctor diagnosed the trouble as pneumonia. For three days she lingered, without fever or pain, and when Verdi brought her a flower she is said to have apologized for not being able to smell it because of her cold. Throughout the morning of 14 November 1897 she visibly failed, and at four that afternoon she died. Verdi kissed her and then left the room. Sometime later a friend came upon him standing motionless near a table, his cheeks flushed and his head down.

In her will Strepponi requested a simple funeral very early in the morning and without any flowers, crowds, or speeches. "I came poor and without pomp into this world, and I would leave it the same way." Then at the end, after all the recital about the funeral, the bequests to friends and the poor of Sant' Agata, and the appointment of her executors, she addressed him directly in a note: "Now, addio, mio Verdi. As we were united in life, may God rejoin our spirits in Heaven."

Everything was done as she asked. The service was held in the cathedral in Busseto at eight in the morning. There were no flowers or music. Teresa Stolz and Ricordi came from Milan; Boito was in Paris and could not come. The church was crowded with Bussetani. After the service others accompanied the coffin to the cemetery in Milan; Verdi returned to the house at Sant' Agata.

A month later from there he observed in a letter to a friend: "Great grief does not demand great expression; it asks for silence, isolation, I would even say the torture of reflection. There is something superficial about all exteriorization; it is a profanation."

Few artists have been as blessed as Verdi in his wife, for she loved him both as an artist and a man, a rare occurrence in the human heart. To have loved him as a man, difficult as he was, perhaps was no more of an accomplishment than many women achieve for other husbands. But her understanding of him as an artist was something quite extraordinary. As an important prima donna she had examined the score of his first opera, *Oberto,* and found in it something to recommend. When fifty-four years later she presided over the composition and première of *Falstaff,* she did so as a full partner in sympathy and understanding. Always she grasped his intent, and her statement of it was often more to the point than that of professional critics.

She was too intelligent to try to influence him which, in any case, was probably impossible. But she seems never to have asked why he did not compose "another *Aida*" or questioned why he risked a failure by changing his style or suggested that he retire on his laurels. Nor, when the reconciliation with Boito was proposed, did she puff up with misplaced loyalty and urge Verdi not to see the man who had insulted him so offensively. What influence she had she used only to keep him composing. She could not follow him all the way into the dark cave of creation, but she always assured him that it was important to go and even, on occasion, conspired to get him started.

It cannot have been easy for her. Once to a friend she let the wish escape: "Oh God! grant that Verdi shall compose no more operas!" His absorption in composing excluded her from his life, sometimes for months. And days of artistic disappointment in the theatre undoubtedly produced snappish evenings at home. Finally, after all the frenzy of trying to finish on time, came the exhilaration of the première which in turn was always followed, whether the opera was successful or not, by an emotional reaction leaving him depressed and with a sense of loss. Yet she never doubted that his composing was the point on which all their life should focus, and for this the world should be grateful.

Undoubtedly her own experience in the theatre helped her as Verdi's wife. She knew how to dress, to mingle in society and talk to men of state. In fact, she was far more cosmopolitan than he. She also could discount theatrical gossip and intrigue. Through all the slander and libel swirling around Verdi and Teresa Stolz she managed to steer a remarkably smooth and sensible course. She never, for example, seems to have suggested that Verdi not take Stolz on tour in the *Requiem* or not cast her so frequently in his operas. She knew the value of an exceptional interpreter. But it must have been a relief when a baritone rather than another soprano emerged as La Stolz's successor.

Whether the far less sophisticated Margherita Barezzi could have done as well by Verdi the artist is doubtful. She might have demonstrated the truth of Wagner's cruel remark that "except in the case of wholly insignificant persons" youthful marriages are always a "terrible mistake." Certainly Verdi's life, if Margherita and the children had lived, would have been different. Probably artistically it would have been less rich, for in this area Strepponi's unusual experience and intelligence was constantly required and effectively used.

CHAPTER 41

THE LAST YEARS: THE *PEZZI SACRI* AND HIS DEATH

1897–1901; AGE, 84–87

THE shock of Strepponi's death shook Verdi physically, and for the first time he began to complain that his hand trembled, his legs would not support him and his eyes were giving out. In the past he had responded to depression or any sort of emotional disaster with increased or even feverish activity, either on his farm or in composing, but now he was eighty-four and old age robbed him of action. He wrote to Mascheroni: "I am not sick, but I am too old! Think of spending your life without being able to do anything! It is very hard."

He continued in his pattern of life, going to his apartment in Genoa for the winter months and to Montecatini for July. Younger friends like Stolz and Boito visited him regularly, and many others wrote. But every place seemed empty without Strepponi, and a younger generation could not share in his memories. Any man fifty years old was only just born in 1848 and knew of that year's events only by hearsay. The old order was not changing; it was quite passed, and he was lonely.

He had two activities. One was the construction of the Casa di Riposo which he followed, as he had all his building projects, with meticulous care. He went often to Milan to consult with Camillo Boito and to watch the building going up. He knew the cost of the materials, why they were used, and how much to the penny the construction would cost. A large part of this he had deposited in a bank as ground had been broken. He had also to figure closely the probable costs of operating the foundation and how to fund it, so that in addition to the architect and construction of the building he was also involved with lawyers setting up the foundation and qualifying it with the city and state government as a charitable organization. In all of this, which continued to the day of his death, Verdi took an active interest, so that around the Casa di Riposo there was never an air of abstract, impersonal charity. The Milanese, who saw Verdi out at the site or near his hotel, knew it was his building and fell easily into calling it the Casa Verdi.

His other activity, for yet another year, continued to be his music. When Strepponi had died, Boito had been in Paris where, without Verdi's knowledge, he was arranging for the première of Verdi's short sacred works which he knew had been completed or very nearly so. Besides the *Te Deum* and *Stabat Mater,* each for chorus and orchestra, these included the slighter *Laudi alla Vergine Maria* on a text from Dante's *Paradiso,* and an *Ave Maria,* both for unaccompanied voices. When Boito had returned to Italy, he presented Verdi with arrangements, lacking only Verdi's approval, for a première by the choral "Société des Concerts" to be given at the Opéra during Easter week in April 1898. Verdi agreed, although maintaining weakly that he had never intended to publish the pieces. Left to himself, he might never have done so, but the action or lack of it would have been an expression of enervating old age rather than a determined purpose. Verdi had always composed for the public; for him composing was not primarily an interior release but an exterior communication. The audience was always in mind and the end at which every work aimed. Boito knew this and generously undertook to make Verdi's arrangements for him. Verdi insisted only that the *Ave Maria* be dropped from the première, although he agreed to publishing it with the others. It is an exercise employing an unusual scale, C, D♭, E, F♯, G♯, A♯, B, C, as it ascends,

CASA DI RIPOSO IN 1900

and the same descending, except that the F♯ becomes natural. Verdi did not consider it "real music"; he once referred to it as a "virtuosity" or "a sort of charade." Nevertheless, because of the odd scale it has a unique, haunting quality.

In January he went to Milan to see Boito and oversee the printing of the music. He found the city far less lonely than Sant' Agata and stayed almost until March, when he left for Genoa. He lived, as always in Milan, in the Grand Hotel where he had an apartment on the second floor. It included a salon with a piano and two bedrooms, one for himself and the other for his cousin whom he had adopted, Maria Carrara-Verdi. Her family was grown and she often stayed with him. When she was not there, Teresa Stolz was just a block away. Every night he had at least one friend in for dinner and after it often more. He was not sleeping well and he liked to talk late in order to keep the nights short. During the day he took long carriage rides, generally out to see the Casa di Riposo. He had planned to go to Paris himself for the première of his *Pezzi Sacri,* or *Sacred Pieces,* but after a series of slight heart attacks he decided against it. Boito went and was followed almost daily by letters from Verdi explaining what he wanted and how he thought Boito might be able to attain it.

The première was a success, and Boito immediately arranged for the first performance in Italy. This was in May at Turin during the Exposition celebrating the fiftieth anniversary, 1848–98, of the Piedmontese constitution, which had in 1860 become that of the Kingdom of Italy. Toscanini conducted and again the *Ave Maria* was omitted. But in most subsequent performances of Verdi's *Pezzi Sacri* it was included and is generally counted today as one of them, although it did not share the same première as the others.

Taken together, the four of them do not make a balanced program. The *Stabat Mater* and *Te Deum,* being for full chorus and orchestra, tend either completely to overshadow the other two unaccompanied works or by comparison with them to seem heavy and turgid. The only reason for gathering them together, which at the time was never stated, though everywhere understood, was that they were Verdi's last compositions. Of the four the most simply beautiful is the *Laudi alla Vergine Maria* for four women's voices, and this was always the most popular on first hearing. But the *Te Deum,* the largest of the four in concept, is also the most impressive musically.

Verdi, as always, approached the text in his own way. Most composers make of it a continuous chant of joy, ranging perhaps from majestic jubilation to introspective worship, but always with a sense of confidence. Verdi heard something else in the words. In 1896, in searching for an ancient example of what he had in mind, he had written to the director of the Cappella Antoniana in Padua:

> I know several old settings of the *Te Deum* and I have heard a few modern ones. But I am not convinced by the interpretation (aside from the music) given the Canticle. It is usually sung at great, solemn festivals, celebrating a victory or a coronation, etc. At the beginning Heaven and Earth rejoice . . . *Sanctus Sanctus Deus Sabaoth.* But half way through the color and tone change . . . *Tu ad liberandum* . . . and Christ is born of the Virgin and appears to mankind . . . *Regnum coelorum* . . . Mankind believes in the *Judex venturus* . . . invokes him *Salvum fac* . . . and ends with a prayer . . . *Dignare Domine die isto* . . . pitiful gloom, distress approaching even terror!

All of which, Verdi felt, had nothing to do with victories and coronations, and neither does his *Te Deum*. It follows closely the scheme outlined in his letter which suggests an ending very like what he had imagined for the close of his *Requiem*. He set the words of the *Te Deum* for double chorus and with almost no repetition or change in their position for emphasis. The greatest changes, which are very slight, all occur at the end where he repeats the *Miserere* and in the last line the "in te speravi." For this last, which he uses to end the work after the two choirs have sung its line in full, he introduces the work's only solo voice, a soprano, which quietly insists: "in you, Lord, have I put my trust." The *Te Deum,* after establishing a confident tone of praise in its first half, moves thereafter toward a final note of uncertainty, as if to say that mankind, which in the end is individuals, can only hope and trust without being sure.

The musical style of the *Te Deum* is more ecclesiastical and less operatic than that of the *Requiem* and in its choral writing reflects Verdi's interest in Palestrina who, he insisted more than ever, was the source of Italian music. But within the more muted and austere bounds he set for his *Te Deum* he developed the music with great subtlety. Like his last operas, it reveals its beauties only on several hearings, and although it started its life with less popular favor than the more obviously dramatic *Stabat Mater* and more lovely *Laudi alla Vergine Maria,* it probably has since passed them in the number of performances.

LATIN

Te Deum laudamus, te Dominum confitemur,
te aeternum Patrem omnis terra veneratur.
Tibi omnes Angeli, tibi coeli et universae potestates,
tibi Cherubim et Seraphim incessabili voce proclamant:
Sanctus, sanctus, sanctus Dominus Deus Sabaoth,
Pleni sunt coeli et terra majestatis gloriae tuae.
Te gloriosus Apostolorum chorus,
te Prophetarum laudabilis numerus,
te Martyrum candidatus laudat exercitus.
Te per orbem terrarum sancta confitetur Ecclesia,
Patrem immensae majestatis,
venerandum tuum verum et unicum Filium,
sanctum quoque Paraclitum Spiritum.

Tu Rex gloriae, Christe,
tu Patris sempiternus es Filius.
Tu ad liberandum suscepturus hominem non horruisti Verginis uterum.
Tu devicto mortis aculeo, aperuisti credentibus regna coelorum.

Tu ad dexteram Dei sedes, in gloria Patris.
Judex crederis esse venturus.
Te ergo quaesumus, tuis famulis subveni, quos pretioso sanguine
    redemisti.
Aeterna fac cum sanctis tuis in gloria munerari.

Salvum fac populum tuum, Domine, et benedic haereditati tuae.
Et rege eos et extolle illos usque in aeternum.
Per singulos dies benedicimus te,
et laudamus nomen tuum, in saeculum et in saeculum saeculi.

Dignare, Domine, die isto sine peccato nos custodire.
Miserere nostri, Domine, miserere nostri.
Fiat misericordia tua, Domine, super nos, quemadmodum speravimus
    in te.
In te [Domine], speravi; non confundar in aeternum.

We praise Thee, O God; we acknowledge Thee to be the Lord.
All the earth doth worship Thee, the Father everlasting.
To Thee all Angels cry aloud; the Heavens, and all the Powers therein;
To Thee Cherubim and Seraphim continually do cry,
Holy, Holy, Holy, Lord God of Sabaoth;
Heaven and earth are full of the Majesty of Thy glory.
The glorious company of the Apostles praise Thee.
The goodly fellowship of the Prophets praise Thee.
The noble army of Martyrs praise Thee.
The holy Church throughout all the world doth acknowledge Thee;
The Father, of an infinite Majesty;
Thine adorable, true, and only Son;
Also the Holy Ghost, the Comforter.

Thou art the King of Glory, O Christ.
Thou art the everlasting Son of the Father.
When Thou tookest upon Thee to deliver man, Thou didst humble
    Thyself to be born of a Virgin.
When Thou hadst overcome the sharpness of death, Thou didst open
    the Kingdom of Heaven to all believers.
Thou sittest at the right hand of God, in the glory of the Father.
We believe that Thou shalt come to be our Judge.
We therefore pray Thee, help Thy servants, whom Thou hast redeemed
    with Thy precious blood.
Make them to be numbered with Thy Saints, in glory everlasting.

O Lord, save Thy people, and bless Thine heritage.
Govern them, and lift them up for ever.
Day by day we magnify Thee;
And we worship Thy name ever, world without end.

Vouchsafe, O Lord, to keep us this day without sin.
O Lord, have mercy upon us, have mercy upon us.
O Lord, let Thy mercy be upon us, as our Trust is in Thee.
O Lord, in Thee have I trusted; let me never be confounded.

Verdi still continued to regard popularity as an important test of any composition's worth. When La Scala performed the *Pezzi Sacri* a year later with empty seats in the house, Verdi insisted to Boito: "When the public does not run to a new production, it is already unsuccessful. Some charitable applause and indulgent reviews as a kindness to the 'Grand Old Man' cannot soften me. No, no. No indulgence or pity. Better to have whistles!" Age might make his hand tremble, but it could not shake the standards by which he judged his own work. But in this case he was too hard on himself. If the *Pezzi Sacri* partially failed in Milan, they succeeded excellently elsewhere, particularly in Germany and England, both of which had a strong tradition of secular choral societies singing in concert halls.

Boito, in writing to Verdi about the lukewarm reception at La Scala, suggested that the difficulty lay in the opera house itself and its audience. "The greatest success was in Turin, and I attribute it to the fact that a concert hall, where *the soloists are not trying to shine,* is a better setting for religious music than an opera house in the course of its season." This continues to be true, and in countries or cities where Verdi is thought of simply in terms of his operas, the *Pezzi Sacri* are almost never performed.

Another trouble at La Scala may have been that Verdi's gloomy prophecy had finally come to pass: the house had closed and remained shut for an entire year. And before that, for a two-year period, it had been rented and run by a musical publisher, Sonzogno, who had produced only those operas he controlled. Among these had been the fabulously successful *Cavalleria Rusticana* but, of course, not one Verdi opera. Finally in 1897–98 no impresario would rent the house and it stayed shut. It was possible to argue with some truth that the fault was the government's, oppressive taxes on the theatre and no subsidy, which even the "barbarian" Austrians had always provided. But it was also true that the tradition of great performances had been lost, even squandered, and the public was exercising its good sense by staying away. Such a tradition, once lost, is only slowly recaptured, and Verdi's *Pezzi Sacri,* coming in the first season after the house was reorganized, may have suffered from being an odd program to put before a suspicious and even hostile public. One newspaper, for example, in praising the music said that the concert itself had been "abominably organized."

In La Scala's reorganization the traditional Italian system of the

TOSCANINI

impresario was abandoned. Instead a group of leading Milanese, including Boito, took over the house as directors, hoping thus to provide it with continuity, and hired a business and artistic director to run it for them. These men were Giulio Gatti-Casazza and Toscanini, and both conducted revolutions in the organization and personnel of their departments. There was considerable opposition, not only from those whose heads had fallen, but even from the general public which grew angry at Toscanini for denying encores of favorite arias. But the improvement was plain. After a performance of *Falstaff* with Antonio Scotti in the title role, Verdi sent Toscanini a telegram: "Thanks, thanks, thanks," which was fulsome praise from Verdi. And there was even improvement in what was not done. After *Norma* had reached its dress rehearsal and the soprano was still inadequate, Toscanini, who had proclaimed her so from the start, refused to conduct the opera, and the production was canceled. The public was not going to be robbed of its money by a lot of cant about the problems of running an opera house.

It was strong medicine, and opposition built up, even on the board of directors. It came to a head one night in 1902 when the audience at the last performance of the season insisted on an encore. Toscanini stood firm, and the tumult grew. Those in the orchestra who resented him smirked; on-stage the tenor watched him nervously, and in the audience men began to abuse him personally. In a fury he turned, threw his baton in their collective face, and stomped out. He had conducted four seasons and immeasurably raised the artistic standards of the performances.

With the performance of the *Pezzi Sacri* at La Scala in 1899 Verdi's active connection with music came to an end. Only one text thereafter seems to have moved him toward a musical expression. These were the words, widely printed, of Queen Margherita's prayer following the assassination of Umberto in July 1900:

O Lord! He sought to do good in this world. He held rancor against none. He always forgave those who did him evil. He sacrificed life to duty and to the good of his country. To his last breath he strived to fulfill his mission.

For his red blood which spurted from three wounds, for the good and just works he accomplished, merciful Lord and just, receive him in your arms and grant him his eternal reward!

Cynics professed it impossible to recognize Umberto except by the three wounds, but Verdi felt the words had the simplicity of the early Fathers of the Church. He heard in them a nobility that he thought worthy of Palestrina, and secretly he began some musical sketches. But he never finished them.

The assassination itself marked the culmination of a tragic decade in Italian history. As Verdi had foreseen, poverty and hunger, both in the cities and countryside, had finally erupted in violence, even in the relatively stable and prosperous north. In 1898 there had been a riot in Parma in which a mob had cut the telegraph wire and smashed all the new electric lights. Rome for several days had been almost in a state of siege with troops posted at every corner, and in Milan eighty people had been killed and minor street fighting lasted for four days.

The government's first response was to blame the socialists whose party had begun to emerge as a force in politics. But the socialists, whose doctrines were extremely confusing, had almost no contact with the illiterate poor who anyway had no interest in such complicated talk. The peasants were simply incoherently angry at a society which seemed to offer them nothing. In their animosity toward a State dominated by the middle class, they were urged on by the Church; and the clericals, far more than the city-bound socialists, agitated the class war that seemed about to begin. The government soon realized this and began to dissolve and ban Catholic as well as socialist organizations.

Umberto's Prime Minister at the time was a General Luigi Pelloux whose actions in attempting to cope with the continual unrest increasingly violated the constitution. Gradually the liberals, the socialists on the Left and the clericals on the Right began to make common cause against him, and in Parliament the young poet D'Annunzio, who had been elected as a Deputy for the extreme Right, ostentatiously crossed the floor of the house and exclaimed: "On one side of Parliament there are men who are half dead, and on the other a few who are alive, so as a man of intellect I shall move toward life." Verdi, following it all from Sant' Agata, wrote Boito: "The goings-on in the Chamber of Deputies are quite incredible! . . . What about D'Annunzio?"

Finally in June 1900 Pelloux was forced from office, a victory for constitutional government, and the assassination of Umberto the following month shocked the country into a realization of how close to disaster it was veering. Gradually, aided by a measure of prosperity, it righted itself without abandoning its constitution and, in fact, re-enforcing it with a court decision that certain acts of the executive were unconstitutional. Many Italians, constantly comparing Italy to France and England, saw only the troubles in which Italy seemed forever to flounder. They often underestimated what was in fact being accomplished, even without strong leadership.

The country, in spite of the strains tending to split it apart, was gradually drawing together, and the spread of a common language was a symptom of it. Even after forty years of unity most peasants still spoke only dialects and many of the better educated spoke "Italian" with difficulty. But there was no question, as there is in Belgium today, of what was the national language to be taught in the schools, used in the courts and in Parliament. General Pelloux, for example, had been born in 1839 in the old province of Savoy where French was the native language. He spoke it perfectly and Italian with a bad accent, but he governed in Italian. Mazzini, Garibaldi, Manzoni and Cavour had succeeded in making one nation out of many states, diverse in language, culture and wealth, and by doing so they had benefited all in the end. Italy for all its troubles avoided those worse evils that plagued the Balkan states, too small to support their fierce independence and too proud to merge it with their neighbor.

On Umberto's death his son Vittorio Emanuele III succeeded to the throne. Verdi years before had dedicated *Nabucco* to the new King's grandmother. It all seemed very far in the past, and he wondered to a friend, "Why am I still in this world?" He was eighty-seven in October 1900, and although the doctors insisted he was not sick, everything tired him. He did not complain of it for, as he observed, "it is only natural!" But as a consequence his letters grew very short, and he had to be wheeled around his park at Sant' Agata.

In December he left for the Grand Hotel in Milan where he spent Christmas with his adopted daughter Maria Carrara-Verdi, Stolz, Boito and members of the Ricordi family. And there four weeks later, on 21 January 1901, as he was sitting on the edge of the bed and buttoning his waistcoat he had a stroke. He fell backward on the bed, senseless and his right side paralyzed.

He survived until ten minutes before three in the morning of 27 January. In the five intervening days the full pageant of an Italian death watch was played out. Inside the hotel friends gathered in the bedroom and watched and waited and carried word out to those in the salon or the corridors. Strangers tried to force their way in to have a look. A priest was summoned, administered Extreme Unction, was sent away and summoned again. The hotel drenched itself in black. Telegrams poured in. An artist drew deathbed sketches; the man in charge of death masks was alerted. Outside the hotel a silent crowd waited, and straw was put on the street to quiet the carriage wheels.

Through it all Verdi lay motionless except for the rise and fall of his chest. He never recovered consciousness, or spoke, or made a sign. To the crowd around his bed, watching, he seemed to be asleep. This was the peaceful, outward show; Boito, more imaginatively, described the inner drama. He wrote:

He carried away with him a great quantity of light and vital warmth. We had all basked in the sun of his Olympian old age. He died magnificently like a fighter redoubtable and mute. The silence of death fell on him a week before he died. With his head bent, his eyebrows set, he seemed to measure with half-shut eyes an unknown and formidable adversary, calculating in his mind the force that he could summon up in opposition. Thus he put up a heroic resistance. The breathing of his great chest sustained him for four days and three nights; on the fourth night the sound of his breathing still filled the room; but what a struggle, poor maestro! How magnificently he fought up to the last moment! In the course of my life I have lost persons whom I idolized, when grief was stronger than resignation. But I have never experienced such a feeling of hate against death, such loathing for its mysterious, blind, stupid, triumphant, infamous power. For such a feeling to be aroused in me I had to await the end of this old man.

Preparations had been launched for a great public funeral, but in his will, which, unlike Muzio, he began without any statement of faith or preamble, he asked that his funeral be "very modest, either at dawn or the time of the Ave Maria in the evening, and without music and singing." And so it was done. At six-thirty on a damp, foggy morning his coffin, borne on a simple hearse and preceded by a single crucifix, was transported to the city's cemetery. A small crowd quietly followed and joined another at the cemetery, standing a distance from the grave. The simple service was swift, and he was buried as he requested beside Strepponi and "without music and singing." The terms of his will were known, but many in the crowd, seeing the coffin in the gray dawn go slowly into the ground, began to weep and in their emotion they forgot, or thought he would not mind, or could no longer resist what welled up inside them. So that those by the grave as they turned to go heard a sort of chorale softly begin, the lament from *Nabucco,* sung now for Verdi himself: "Va, pensiero sull' ali dorate":

Go, thought, on golden wings;
Go, rest yourself on the slopes and hills
Where, soft and warm, murmur
the sweet breezes of our native soil.

Greet the banks of the Jordan,
The fallen towers of Zion . . .
Oh my country so beautiful and lost
O memory so dear and fatal!

Golden harp of the prophetic bards
Why do you hang mute on the willow?
Rekindle memories in our breast,
Speak to us of the time that was!

O as with the fates of Solomon
You make a sigh of cruel lament.
O may the Lord inspire you to a song
That infuses suffering with strength.

Later there was another funeral. Verdi had also asked in his will that he and Strepponi be buried in the Casa di Riposo, but this, as he must have known, required authorization by the State. In his case there was no question about it, and the permission was granted immediately. Arrangements were made to move the two coffins from the cemetery on 28 February. But if the city and state had felt constrained to follow Verdi's wishes on the first internment, they did not for the second. Enormous preparations were made. Toscanini and a choir of eight hundred stood outside the cemetery chapel prepared to burst into "Va, pensiero" as the two coffins left it for the Casa di Riposo. Troops of cavalry kept the crowd back. The coffins were carried on a specially constructed catafalque. All the balconies along the way were draped in black. Princes of the Blood, Ministers of State and representatives of Italian cities marched in the procession. Many cities sent huge floral tributes arranged in appropriate symbols and pulled by horses. Two hundred thousand people, in fact all those in Milan not actually marching, are said to have lined the streets and at various times hummed or sung his music as his coffin passed or as they waited for it and remembered.

The old thought back to their youth, to days that seemed truly great and beautiful. To have been born in a country divided and enslaved, to have carried in one's heart an ideal of unity and freedom and to have shared in the achievement of them was to have been born at a good time. In Verdi the last great figure of the Risorgimento died, and the movement itself with all its idealism and heroism faded into the past, to be marveled at, read of in books, and its actors envied for the passion and commitment with which they had lived their lives. For many in the crowd, recalling the thrill on first hearing those great, swinging choruses, the coffin carried with it to the grave part of their country's history.

For others he was above all the composer of the human heart, of love and grief, despair and joy, the simplest human emotions. With the magic of his music he had touched depths of feeling often unsuspected in those who listened and by it had declared to them the universality of their human condition. For many who had been surprised to tears for Violetta or lured to sympathy for Rigoletto he had literally stretched the bounds of their humanity. To be alive, to love, he seemed to say, was to suffer; and in the largeness of his understanding and compassion, as D'Annunzio wrote in a famous memorial ode, "He wept and loved for all."

Even men who knew him only through his music felt with Boito the loss of his "vital warmth." Yet it remained in his music, for his art and life were one, exhibiting the same integrity, the same concern for people and the same sense of adventure. His growth in both was extraordinary. Peasants like himself marveled that he could rise so far in the world, and musicians today still wonder at the distance between *Oberto* and *Falstaff*.

The vitality of this growth permeates his music. Among his works each man has a favorite opera, scene or even aria, fast or slow, loud or soft, but in them all and in Verdi's career taken as a whole there is a sense of energy called variously: passion, sweep or even masculinity. Others have composed music more graceful, less obvious, or more beautiful; but few have equaled the sheer vitality of Verdi's music. It is not surprising that Garibaldi on his way to Sicily sang it. It is active music for active men.

This same vitality runs through his career. After *Il Trovatore* and *La Traviata* he could have composed endless variations on them, made an easy fortune and been easily famous. Instead he always chose, after *Aida,* after the *Requiem,* and at seventy-four after *Otello,* to go on to something new, to risk a failure and the whistles of the crowd. Such daring is thrilling, the source of it as mysterious as life itself, and the energy underlying it the most exciting quality in his life and art. For the ability to grow, to change, to adapt one's self without loss of integrity is the essence of being alive, and men instinctively respect and admire it.

Among the great figures of nineteenth-century Italy only Verdi had this quality. Manzoni's creative urge exhausted itself early, and Vittorio Emanuele's good start soon dwindled into pretense. Political events passed Mazzini by; death cut off Cavour's career and came too late to save Garibaldi from marring his. Verdi alone continued into the new age after 1860 still adding to his glory. And when death finally came to him, his last work, the Casa di Riposo, although it had already begun to accept applications, had still to open officially. Like his music, it is alive today, housing a hundred musicians and largely supported by the royalties of his operas which he bequeathed to it.

At every anniversary of his birth, death or intervening dates of importance Italians have celebrated him both as a man and a musician. His music has already once gone out of fashion and then returned, and it certainly will do so again. But his life is a constant example of purpose and integrity.

Appendices

THE OPERA *ROCESTER*

IT IS possible that the opera Verdi intended for the Teatro dei Filo-drammatici in 1836 and later offered to the Teatro Regio in Parma was not *Oberto* but a work of which nothing exists today but its title, *Rocester*. Whether this was actually a different opera from *Oberto* or was transformed by revisions into *Oberto* is a scholar's quarrel. Gatti, Abbiati and Toye have argued that *Rocester* was the original of the much revised *Oberto,* while Walker argues that the two are quite separate. My own opinion is that there is not enough evidence to support either conclusion.

Not a note or a word of *Rocester* can be identified; it exists solely as a title. Verdi, just before going to Parma in October 1837, wrote to Massini: "Oh, I should have liked to produce *Rocester* at Milan!" In several preceding letters to Massini he talks merely of "the opera," and in one he says that "the opera" is completed except for "short passages." In all he uses the title twice, both times in the letter quoted. In 1879 when he described his first years in Milan to Giulio Ricordi he declared his first opera was *Oberto* and composed during this period.

Beside Verdi only one other contemporary mentions *Rocester* and that is Giuseppe Demaldè, a friend of Verdi's in Busseto and at one time treasurer of the Monte di Pietà. In his unpublished notes on Verdi's early years, "Cenni biografici," Demaldè states that Verdi completed *Rocester* in the spring of 1838. Then he goes on to say: "What happened to it in the end I cannot say. It seems, however, that the librettist objected to the verses and opposed a production on the ground that in the autumn of 1839 *Oberto* was being produced at La Scala" (etc.).

These few references are all the direct evidence about *Rocester,* and the identity of the fastidious librettist is yet another problem. On such uncertain sand no argument has yet stood for long, and the identity and fate of *Rocester* is still an open question.

Purely for convenience I have identified "the opera" on which Verdi was working in these years, 1835 to 1837, as *Oberto.*

VERDI'S READING

VERDI had a library at Sant' Agata of several thousand volumes, most of which he evidently had read. By his bed he kept a small standing bookcase about four feet high. The top of the case and the second shelf were devoted to the works he read most frequently. The books on these shelves were never changed except where noted below.

THE TOP

1. The complete string quartets of Mozart, Haydn and Beethoven. (These were pocket size and simply bound. He used to slip one into his pocket whenever he went out.)
2. Schiller's complete plays, translated into Italian by Andrea Maffei. (Vols. 1 & 2 were bound together; 3 & 4 were in the library, and he occasionally would replace one with the other.)
3. Shakespeare's complete works, translated into Italian by Giulio Carcano.
4. Dante's complete works.

SHELF #2

1. Milton's *Paradise Lost,* translated into Italian by Andrea Maffei.
2. Shakespeare's complete works, translated into Italian by Carlo Rusconi.
3. Byron's complete works, translated into Italian by Carlo Rusconi.
4. Holy Bible in the King James Version.
5. Dictionary of Dates and Events (in 6 vols.).
6. Three French and Italian dictionaries.
7. *Estetica della Musica* by Amintore Galli.
   (But as this was not published until 1900 it seems likely it was a movable prop.)

This shelf he constantly changed, and most of the books on it when he died were only recently published. There were forty-one titles in all, many of them presentation copies of poems or studies of him and his operas. The pages on these are almost invariably uncut. Some of the more interesting titles which he seems to have read were:

1. *Histoire de La Notation Musicale* by Ernest David and Mathis Lussey.
2. *Dell' Udito Schediasmi Musicali* by G. Branzoli.
3. *Riccardo Wagner, studio critico-biografico* by E. Schure.
4. *Impressions Musicales et Littéraires* by Camille Bellaigue.
5. *Etudes Musicales et Nouvelles Silhouettes des Musiciens* by Camille Bellaigue.

This was the bottom shelf and used as a catchall for magazines and odd-sized publications.

STREPPONI'S ILLEGITIMATE CHILDREN

THERE has never been any doubt that before Strepponi met Verdi in 1839, she had already borne an illegitimate child. The fact first appeared in print in a biography of Verdi published in 1904, three years after his death and about as soon as biographers could be expected to start discussing such a fact. But in the intervening years it was known, although not widely. In 1839 Strepponi had sung before a succession of audiences that could see she was pregnant, and the fact was well recorded in memory and private letters. Its resurrection was inevitable.

There has, however, always been doubt as to the father, and even today there is no positive identification. There are two hypotheses. The older, set forth as a conclusion by Gatti and most subsequent biographers, casts as the father Bartolomeo Merelli, the impresario. The argument starts with a tradition handed down in the Barezzi family that Verdi one night at La Scala, in pointing out Strepponi to Marianna Barezzi, his sister-in-law, mentioned that Strepponi was said to have had a son by Merelli. To this biographers added, supposedly as history, an account of how Merelli managed Strepponi's career, introduced her to Vienna and Milan and thereby made her the leading Italian soprano of the years 1836 to 1842. During this time the two, supposedly, were constantly together.

The newer hypothesis, put forward by Frank Walker in *The Man Verdi,* casts as the father Napoleone Moriani, the tenor. In attacking the older hypothesis Walker, of course, can do nothing to prove or disprove the tradition handed down in the Barezzi family, but he has demonstrated, most successfully in my opinion, that the supporting history is fantasy. During these years Merelli did not establish Strepponi's career, and they were not frequently together. Walker, by a most admirable and laborious reconstruction of her career, has been able to isolate the times in which she bore the children, for it now appears there were two born and a third lost in miscarriage. The dates show that Moriani and not Merelli had the opportunity to be the father.

The argument is further supported by Strepponi's and Merelli's correspondence with her manager, Alessandro Lanari, who was based in Florence. The support is not strong because Strepponi was extremely guarded in her letters, and they do more to clear Merelli than to charge Moriani. Neither she nor anyone else ever identifies the father by name, even though Lanari arranged for him to settle a fairly large sum on her. But what clues the letters contain seem to point to Moriani. On this tangled question I have followed Walker.

But it is important to point out that in this case history may know more than those who lived it. It is perfectly possible that everyone, including Verdi, *thought* Merelli was the father of the child.

According to Walker's research the children were:

1) a son, Camillino, born about February 1838.
2) one lost in miscarriage in February 1839.
3) a child born about December 1841.

Nothing whatever, not even the sex, is known of the child born in 1841. Presumably it died young, or at least it is only charitable to Strepponi to suppose so. The first, Camillino, is mentioned in a few of her letters, and in 1849 she left Verdi at Busseto to go to Florence and arrange for the boy's education. Soon thereafter all references to Camillino cease, and perhaps he too died. If so, Strepponi kept her grief, if she had any, absolutely private. The children were born, lived and died in mystery. Unquestionably this was her desire. Even in her letters Camillino does not exist as a person.

One last point should be made about the children and their relevance to Verdi's life. The number of them is relatively unimportant. He loved and lived with a lady who had an illegitimate child living. This says much about him. The fact that another illegitimate child had already died and a third been lost in miscarriage does not say much more.

On the other hand, Walker's research has altered the traditional view of Strepponi. In the past, with only a single illegitimate child, and that fathered by the impresario who supposedly controlled her career, she could be regarded as merely another innocent victim of theatrical life. Now, with three pregnancies, the last child conceived when she was twenty-six and an established prima donna, and the father probably only another singer, she seems less innocent, although no less courageous.

APPENDIX D

THE SCREW-TURN FINALES

VERDI used a choral finale with the screw-turn in some form in almost all his operas after *Ernani* and preceding *Rigoletto*. Most persons today are not likely to hear a performance of *I Due Foscari, Attila* or *I Masnadieri,* but in *Macbeth* there is an example of it toward the end of the finale to Act II. Macbeth, the baritone, has the figure. Then in *La Traviata,* where it is beginning to sound old-fashioned and static amidst the better realized drama, a form of it occurs toward the end of the finale that concludes Flora's party in Act II. The two Germonts, baritone and tenor, have the figure. Lastly it appears in *Un Ballo in Maschera* where Verdi has moved it into the orchestra and uses it as a recurring, ominous figure leading up to the King's death in the last act. Verdi, characteristically, had developed a new use for an old trick rather than discarding it.

THE CONTRACT UNDER WHICH VERDI WROTE *UN BALLO IN MASCHERA*

The contract is an example of the impossibility of reducing an artistic undertaking to legal rights and duties. Article 8 is no more than a pre-fabricated quarrel. Yet short of attaching the actual costume designs with specifications for velvet, satin, etc., it says about all that can be said. Similarly, Article 2 did not cover the row that broke out with the censor over Verdi's choice of subject. But it could hardly do so as most of the changes demanded by the censor were without reason and therefore un-foreseeable.

The "Impresa" to which the contract refers is the organization adminis-tering the opera house as opposed to the individual at its head, the im-presario.

CONTRACT BETWEEN THE CAVALIER GIUSEPPE VERDI
AND THE IMPRESARIO OF THE ROYAL THEATRES OF NAPLES

Naples 2 May 1856

With the present document in duplicate original in accordance with the civil law of the Kingdom of the Two Sicilies, we the undersigned Cav. Giuseppe Verdi, Maestro of Music, and Luigi Alberti, Impresario of the Royal Theatres of Naples, have contracted as follows:

Art. 1—The Cav. Giuseppe Verdi engages to compose a grand opera of not less than three acts for the Royal San Carlo Theatre of Naples, the opera to be produced between October 1857 and the end of January 1858 and the Cav. Maestro undertaking to be in Naples in time to deliver the music and direct the rehearsals and staging.

Art. 2—The subject of the libretto and its poet will be the free choice of the Cav. Maestro who will be so kind as to send the subject or the libretto itself in January 1857 * for submission to the Censor of Naples without whose approval the opera cannot be produced.

Art. 3 *

Art. 4—The Cav. Maestro will have the choice of singers for his opera from those under contract to the Impresario.

Art. 5—The Cav. Verdi grants the Impresa of Naples the property rights in the music and libretto for the entire Kingdom of the Two Sicilies throughout which he will have no rights whatsoever, and retaining for himself the property rights in the book and music for Upper Italy and foreign countries, being entitled there to make whatever use of them he may think best; to this end, renouncing the benefits granted to Authors in the Kingdom of the Two Sicilies by the Royal Decree of 7 November 1811, in articles 7 and 8, as well as every author's privilege that may be granted in other, later decrees; by which he grants and gives all said property rights to the Impresario Alberti for the Kingdom of the Two Sicilies who thereby is entitled to make whatever use of them he sees fit without any exception.

Art. 6—The Impresario Alberti will pay the Cav. Maestro Verdi six thousand ducats in hard silver coins from the Bank for the said property rights in the music and book for the Kingdom of the Two Sicilies as well as for his direction of the said opera and the voyage of the Cav. Maestro to Naples. This payment of six thousand ducats will be made as follows: *

Art. 7—The cost of the libretto will be paid half by the Cav. Maestro and half by the Impresa, as generously proposed by the Cav. Maestro.

Art. 8—The opera will be produced by the Impresario as regards the scenery, costumes, stage machinery etc. in a style worthy of so illustrious a Maestro and such a spectacle.

Drawn up in Naples in duplicate originals, 2 May 1856.

LUIGI ALBERTI

* I sign the present contract with the following modifications:

On Art. 2—The subject of the libretto will be sent in the coming month of June 1857.

On Art. 3—I cannot undertake to produce the opera before January 1858: but I will try to do so if possible.

On Art. 6—The 6000 (six thousand) ducats will be paid to me in three equal installments: the first at the first piano rehearsal, the second at the first orchestral rehearsal, the third at the dress rehearsal.

Busseto, 5 February 1857.

L. ALBERTI   G. VERDI

VERDI'S SACRED WORKS AND EXCERPTS FROM THE *MOTU PROPRIO*

Pius X issued the *Motu Proprio* on 22 November 1903 and in it stated in general terms what should be the function and form of ecclesiastical music composed for and performed in Roman Catholic Churches. The statement's title, which can be translated as "on the proper form," comes from its opening Latin words. The statement continues today to be the basis of the Church's policy on ecclesiastical music.

All of Verdi's published sacred works fall foul of the requirements in some way, but this probably would have neither surprised nor disturbed him as there is no evidence that he wrote them for use in churches.

EXCERPTS

§ 3   On these grounds Gregorian Chant has always been regarded as the supreme model for sacred music, so that it is fully legitimate to lay down the following rule: *the more closely a composition for Church approaches in its movement, inspiration and savor the Gregorian form, the more sacred and liturgical it becomes; and the more out of harmony it is with that supreme model, the less worthy it is of the temple.*

§ 6   Among the different kinds of modern music, that which appears less suitable for accompanying the functions of public worship is the theatrical style, which was in the greatest vogue, especially in Italy, during the last century. This of its very nature is diametrically opposed to Gregorian Chant and classic polyphony, and therefore to the most important law of all good sacred music. Besides the intrinsic structure, the rhythm and what is known as the *conventionalism* of this style adapt themselves but badly to the requirements of true liturgical music.

§ 13   On the same principle it follows that singers in church have a real liturgical office, and that therefore women, being incapable of exercising such office, cannot be admitted to form part of the choir. Whenever, then, it is desired to employ the acute voices of sopranos and contraltos, these parts must be taken by boys, according to the most ancient usage of the Church.

§ 19   The employment of the piano is forbidden in church, as is also that of noisy or frivolous instruments such as drums, cymbals, bells and the like.

§ 23   In general it must be considered a very grave abuse when the liturgy in ecclesiastical functions is made to appear secondary to and in a manner at the service of the music, for music is merely a part of the liturgy and its humble handmaid.

APPENDIX G

VERDI AND TERESA STOLZ

POSSIBLY more has been written on whether Verdi did or did not have an affair with Teresa Stolz than on any other single question in his life. In the course of it scholars and biographers have sometimes forgotten that even assuming an affair could be proved, it still would have no demonstrable effect on Verdi's life or music. The fact is, affair or not, he continued to live at Sant' Agata with Strepponi and continued to develop his music along the same lines on which he had started before he met Stolz.

Still, was there an affair? Biographers in the nineteenth century, close to the memory of the libelous articles, generally thought so. More recently, as more and more letters and notebooks have come to light, they have become less certain, particularly as it has become clear that Verdi's break with Mariani antedated any possible affair with Stolz.

Beyond gossip, all the evidence suggesting an affair exists in Strepponi's letters and notebooks. Stolz's letters to Verdi are generally about the theatre and always use the most formal "Lei" style of address. Verdi's letters to Stolz have largely disappeared and those that survive reveal nothing. He uses the "voi" form of address except for one late letter after Strepponi's death when he uses the familiar "tu." In Verdi's letters to others there is never any suggestion of an affair or trouble possibly caused by one in his home. So at the present time what evidence there is comes entirely from Strepponi, who was not a principal. This evidence is best presented by Walker in Chapter 8 of *The Man Verdi,* pp. 393–446.

Walker concludes that Verdi was in love with Stolz but refuses to conclude that she became his mistress. He rather inclines to think she did not. To have done so would have required her to be "about the biggest hypocrite that ever lived," and he finds it "extraordinarily difficult to believe." I agree.

But with his conclusion that Verdi "beyond all doubt" was "in love" with Teresa Stolz I am less happy. Perhaps my disagreement here is over the meaning of "in love." I cannot answer Walker's fifty pages with another fifty here, but I will sketch briefly some of the arguments that can be raised to suggest that while Verdi may have been charmed, fascinated and foolishly overattentive to Stolz, he was hardly "in love" with her.

For example, aside from inviting her frequently to Sant' Agata, he does not seem to have gone out of his way to be with her. He refused a number of offers to stage his operas with her in them, and on two occasions, tours of *Aida* and the *Requiem*, he left the tours and her early in order to return to Sant' Agata with Strepponi. The fact is that he conducted his career without any special reference to Stolz as a person. They came together at predictable times such as the première of the *Requiem* and the first performances of it and *Aida* in Paris, but I see no move in Verdi's life in these years that can be said to have been caused solely by his desire to be with Teresa Stolz. Is this being "in love"?

Approaching the problem from Stolz's side: As suggested above, I find it hard to believe that she was hypocrite enough to have concealed the truth from everyone for so many years. She liked people, liked to gossip about them and was not a very clever woman. Yet none of her friends seem to have heard anything from her suggesting an affair. The Contessa Maffei, for example, who knew both principals well, who received the most intimate letters from Strepponi, and who was hostess many times over to all three during the rehearsals and performances in Milan, seems never to have suspected one existed.

Further, in May of 1872 or about the time gossip began, Strepponi's notebook contains a summary of a letter to Stolz which reveals that Stolz was considering marrying or living with some Milanese gentleman who was not Verdi. Nothing came of it, but the date is important when considering the evidence presented in Strepponi's letters and notebooks.

Going through these in consecutive order starting in 1868, it is clear that much of the time Strepponi's health was poor. She comments on it, and so does Verdi in his letters. She also seems much of the time to have been unusually depressed. This reached some sort of climax in March of 1874 when she wrote the Contessa Maffei: "Even my religious enthusiasm has vanished and I hardly believe in God when I look at the wonders of creation!" She wrote this at a time when Stolz was singing in Egypt and when Strepponi's spirits, if Stolz was the cause of their depression, might have been expected to rise. In the same way her gloomy desires not to go to Milan for the rehearsals of *La Forza del Destino*, 1869, and *Aida*, 1871, have generally been put down to the presence there of Stolz. Yet before the rehearsals in 1869 Verdi had spent no time in Stolz's company and perhaps had not even met her. And Strepponi herself dates the period of "febrile assiduity" on Verdi's part from 1872 or after the rehearsals of *Aida*. Evidently Strepponi was in a period where life seemed unsatisfactory even before La Stolz appeared as a threat to domestic bliss. May she not then, made nervous by the continual gossip and the libelous articles, have exaggerated the threat?

On reading her notebooks, her life seems a misery because, like most persons, she confided her woes to paper and enjoyed the good days almost without comment. Thus in the notebook for 1868 her entry for 2 January, a good day, is a line; her entry for 4 January, a bad day, is close to forty. And even in her "febrile assiduity" draft letter she confesses to twenty days when she was "calm and merry," which hardly suggests she was then living unhappily *à trois* with Verdi and his mistress.

No doubt she was nervous about La Stolz, and her behavior toward the younger lady, considering the circumstances, was truly magnificent. But in trying to decide whether Verdi was "in love" with Stolz, it is important to remember that the entries in Strepponi's notebooks are those of a prima donna, one skilled in words, subject to periods of depression, and quite humanly presenting herself in her diary as the aggrieved party.

APPENDIX H   RULING HOUSES IN ITALY

THE HAPSBURG-LORRAINE LINE—THE AUSTRIAN SUCCESSION

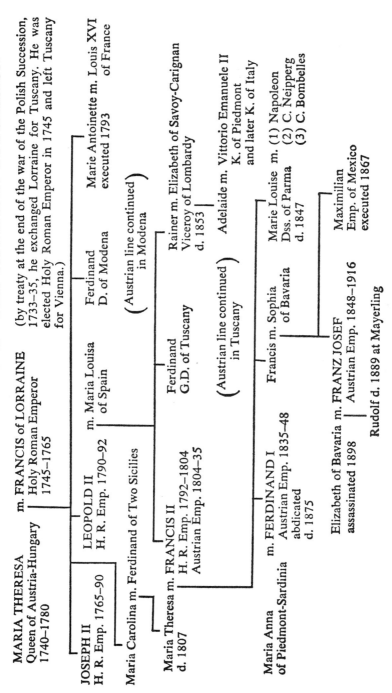

591

DUKES OF PARMA

Pope Paul III (Alessandro Farnese) formed the Duchy of Parma in 1545 by carving it out of the Papal States and giving it to his natural son Pierluigi Farnese. The family was originally Roman and almost all its members were great patrons of the arts. Paul III (1468–1549) employed Michelangelo to decorate the Sistine Chapel. Reigning Dukes are shown in capitals.

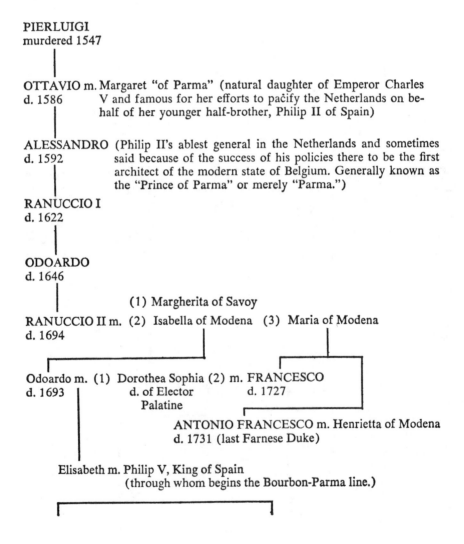

PIERLUIGI
murdered 1547

OTTAVIO m. Margaret "of Parma" (natural daughter of Emperor Charles
d. 1586   V and famous for her efforts to pacify the Netherlands on behalf of her younger half-brother, Philip II of Spain)

ALESSANDRO (Philip II's ablest general in the Netherlands and sometimes
d. 1592   said because of the success of his policies there to be the first
architect of the modern state of Belgium. Generally known as
the "Prince of Parma" or merely "Parma.")

RANUCCIO I
d. 1622

ODOARDO
d. 1646

           (1) Margherita of Savoy

RANUCCIO II m. (2) Isabella of Modena   (3) Maria of Modena
d. 1694

Odoardo m. (1) Dorothea Sophia (2) m. FRANCESCO
d. 1693   d. of Elector   d. 1727
                Palatine

ANTONIO FRANCESCO m. Henrietta of Modena
d. 1731 (last Farnese Duke)

Elisabeth m. Philip V, King of Spain
(through whom begins the Bourbon-Parma line.)

|
CHARLES
(Duke from 1731 to 1736. In 1734
he departed to conquer the kingdom
of Naples for himself and to which
he removed all the Farnese art
treasures. He later became King of
Spain.)

* * *

The Austrians occupied Parma from
1736–1748, during and after the
War of the Polish Succession.

|
PHILIP m. Louise Elizabeth
d. 1765 | eldest d. of Louis XV,
King of France

FERDINAND m. Maria Amalia
d. 1802 | d. of Empress
Maria Theresa of
Austria

Parma governed by France
as "The Department of the Taro"
from 1800–1815

By Congress of Vienna, 1815, Parma given to
MARIE LOUISE
d. 1847
Ex-Empress of France but succession denied to her
son by Napoleon, the Duke of Reichstadt (d. 1832),
and given to the Bourbon-Parma line.

Louis
d. 1803

CARLO II
restored 1847

Parma joined Piedmont in
July 1848 in a Kingdom
of Upper Italy which
survived about two weeks

abdicated 1849

CARLO III
murdered 1854

ROBERTO
(born 1848)
his mother, LUISA MARIA,
acted as Regent,
deposed 1860

HOUSE OF SAVOY

VITTORIO AMADEO III
d. 1796

From a common ancestor seven
generations back

CARLO EMANUELE IV
abdicated 1802
d. 1819
(in a monastery in Rome)

VITTORIO EMANUELE I
abdicated 1821
d. 1824

CARLO FELICE
d. 1831

CARLO ALBERTO m. Theresa of Tuscany
abdicated 1849
d. 1849
(in a monastery
  in Portugal)

(after defeat by Austrians at Novara, 3/23/49)

VITTORIO EMANUELE II m. Adelaide, d. of Archduke Rainer
K. of Piedmont 1849
K. of Italy 1861–78

Viceroy of Lombardy-Venetia

UMBERTO I m. Margherita of Savoy-Genoa (a first cousin)
assassinated 1900

VITTORIO EMANUELE III m. Helena of Montenegro
abd. 1946
d. 1947
(in Egypt)

Emperor of Ethiopia 1936–1943
King of Albania 1939–1943

UMBERTO II m. Marie José of Belgium
abd. 1946
(when the Kingdom of Italy became a Republic)
(as of 1961 living in exile in Portugal)

THE POPES

Pius VII, 1800–1823 (taken prisoner by Napoleon I to Fontainebleau)
Leo XII, 1823–1829
Pius VIII, 1829–1830
Gregory XVI, 1831–1846
Pius IX, "Pio Nono," 1846–1878
Leo XIII, 1878–1903

VERDI'S PUBLISHED WORKS WITH DATES OF THEIR PREMIÈRES AND CASTS OF THEIR OPERAS

Opera	FIRST PERFORMANCE Date, City, Theatre	Librettist
OBERTO, CONTE DI SAN BONI- FACIO	17 Nov. 1839, Milan, Scala	Piazza, Merelli, Solera
UN GIORNO DI REGNO (some- times called "Il finto Stan- islao")	5 Sept. 1840, Milan, Scala	Romani
NABUCODONOSOR (generally called "Nabucco")	9 Mar. 1842, Milan, Scala	Solera
I LOMBARDI ALLA PRIMA CROCIATA (see "Jérusalem" below)	11 Feb. 1843, Milan, Scala	Solera
ERNANI	9 Mar. 1844, Venice, Fenice	Piave
I DUE FOSCARI	3 Nov. 1844, Rome, Argentina	Piave
GIOVANNA d'ARCO	15 Feb. 1845, Milan, Scala	Solera
ALZIRA	12 Aug. 1845, Naples, S. Carlo	Cammarano
ATTILA	17 Mar. 1846, Venice, Fenice	Solera
MACBETH (see below)	14 Mar. 1847, Florence, Pergola	Piave, Maffei
I MASNADIERI	22 July 1847, London, Her Majesty's	Maffei
JÉRUSALEM (being "I Lom- bardi" revised with new num- bers and ballet added)	26 Nov. 1847, Paris, Opéra	Royer, Vaez
IL CORSARO	25 Oct. 1848, Trieste, Grande	Piave
LA BATTAGLIA DI LEGNANO	27 Jan. 1849, Rome, Argentina	Cammarano
LUISA MILLER	8 Dec. 1849, Naples, S. Carlo	Cammarano
STIFFELIO (see "Aroldo" below)	16 Nov. 1850, Trieste, Grande	Piave
RIGOLETTO	11 Mar. 1851, Venice, Fenice	Piave
IL TROVATORE	19 Jan. 1853, Rome, Apollo	Cammarano, Bardare

Source	ARTISTS IN FIRST PERFORMANCE
	Ladies; Men
	Raineri, Shaw; Salvi, Marini
	Raineri, Abbadia; Salvi, Ferlotti, Scalese
	Strepponi, Bellinzaghi; Miraglia, Ronconi, Dérivis
Grossi's poem of the same name	Frezzolini; Guasco, Severi, Dérivis
Hugo's play *Hernani*	Loewe; Guasco, Superchi, Selva
Byron's play *The Two Foscari*	Barbieri-Nini; Roppa, De Bassini
Schiller's play *Die Jungfrau von Orléans*	Frezzolini; Poggi, Collini
Voltaire's play *Alzire*	Tadolini; Fraschini, Coletti
	Loewe; Guasco, Costantini, Marini
Shakespeare's play *Macbeth*	Barbieri-Nini; Brunacci, Varesi, Benedetti
Schiller's play *Die Rauber*	Lind; Gardoni, Coletti, Lablache, Bouché
	Julian-Vangelder; Duprez, Alizard, Prévôt, Brémont
Byron's poem *The Corsair*	Barbieri-Nini, Rampazzini; Fraschini, De Bassini
Méry's play *Battaille de Toulouse*	De Giuli; Fraschini, Collini
Schiller's play *Kabale und Liebe*	Gazzaniga, Salandri; Malvezzi, De Bassini, Arati, Selva
Souvestre's and Bourgeois' play *Stiffelius*	Gazzaniga; Fraschini, Collini
Hugo's play *Le Roi s'amuse*	Brambilla (Teresa), Casaloni; Mirate, Varesi, Pons
Gutiérrez's play *El Trovador*	Penco, Goggi; Boucardé, Guicciardi, Balderi

Opera	FIRST PERFORMANCE Date; City; Theatre	Librettist
LA TRAVIATA	6 Mar. 1853, Venice, Fenice	Piave
(2nd production)	6 May 1854, Venice, S. Benedetto	
LES VÊPRES SICILIENNES (generally called "I Vespri Siciliani")	13 June 1855, Paris, Opéra	Scribe, Duveyrier
SIMONE BOCCANEGRA (see below)	12 Mar. 1857, Venice, Fenice	Piave
AROLDO (being "Stiffelio" revised with new last act)	16 Aug. 1857, Rimini, Nuovo	Piave
UN BALLO IN MASCHERA	17 Feb. 1859, Rome, Apollo	Somma
LA FORZA DEL DESTINO (see below)	10 Nov. 1862, St. Petersburg, Imperial	Piave
MACBETH (orchestration revised, new numbers and ballet added)	21 Apr. 1865, Paris, Lyrique	(Nuitter, Beaumont)
DON CARLO (see below)	11 Mar. 1867, Paris, Opéra	Méry, Du Locle
LA FORZA DEL DESTINO (numbers added; sequence of scenes and last act changed; prelude replaced by overture)	27 Feb. 1869, Milan, Scala	(Ghislanzoni)
AIDA	24 Dec. 1871, Cairo, Opera	Ghislanzoni
(2nd production)	8 Feb. 1872, Milan, Scala	
SIMONE BOCCANEGRA (reorchestrated, text revised and scenes added)	24 Mar. 1881, Milan, Scala	Boito
DON CARLO (reduced from five to four acts)	10 Jan. 1884, Milan, Scala	
OTELLO	5 Feb. 1887, Milan, Scala	Boito
FALSTAFF	9 Feb. 1893, Milan, Scala	Boito

	ARTISTS IN FIRST PERFORMANCE
Source	*Ladies; Men*
Dumas *fils'* play *La Dame aux Camélias*	Salvini-Donatelli; Graziani, Varesi
	Spezia; Landi, Coletti
	Cruvelli, Sannier; Gueymard, Bonnehée, Obin
Gutiérrez' play of the same name	Bendazzi; Negrini, Giraldoni, Vercellini, Echeverria
	Lotti; Pancani, Poggiali, Ferri, Cornago
Scribe's libretto *Gustave III*	Julienne-Dejean, Scotti, Sbriscia; Fraschini, Giraldoni, Bossi, Bernardoni
Duke of Rivas' play *Don Alvaro, o La fuerza de sino*	Barbot, Nantier-Didiée; Tamberlick, Graziani, De Bassini, Angelini
	Rey-Balla; Monjauze, Ismael, Petit
Schiller's play *Don Carlos*	Sax, Gueymard; Morère, Faure, Obin, David, Castelmary
	Stolz, Benza; Tiberini, Colonnese, Rota, Junca
	Pozzoni, Grossi; Mongini, Steller, Medini, Costa
	Stolz, Waldmann; Capponi, Pandolfini, Maini
	D'Angeri; Tamagno, Maurel, Salvati, De Reszke
	Bianchi-Chiatti, Pasqua; Tamagno, Lhérie, Silvestri
Shakespeare's play *Othello*	Pantaleoni; Tamagno, Maurel, Navarrini
Shakespeare's *Henry* plays and *Merry Wives of Windsor*	Sthele, Zilli, Guerrini, Pasqua; Garbin, Pini-Corsi, Maurel

SONGS

FOR SOLO VOICE AND PIANO

Where the song was not published until recently, the first date in the parenthesis is the year of composition; the second, that of publication.

Sei Romanze (1838)
1. Non t'accostar all'urna (Jacopo Vittorelli)
2. More, Elisa, lo stanco poeta (Tommaso Bianchi)
3. In solitaria stanza (Vittorelli)
4. Nell' orror di notte oscura (Carlo Angiolini)
5. Perduta ho la pace (from Goethe's *Faust,* trans. by Luigi Balestra)
6. Deh, pietoso, o addolorata (from Goethe's *Faust,* trans. by Balestra)

L'esule (1839) (Temistocle Solera)
La seduzione (1839) (Balestra)

Chi i bei di m'adduce ancora (1842, 1948) (Goethe, trans. by Balestra)

Album di Sei Romanze (1845)
1. Il tramonto (Andrea Maffei)
2. La zingara (S. Manfredo Maggioni)
3. Ad una stella (Maffei)
4. Lo Spazzocamino (Maggioni)
5. Il Mistero (Felice Romani)
6. Brindisi (Maffei)
Il poveretto (1847) (Maggioni)
L'Abandonée (1849) (Marie or Léon Escudier?)
Fiorellin che sorge appena (1850, 1951) (Piave)
La preghiera del poeta (1858, 1941) (N. Sole)
Il Brigidin (1863, 1941) (Dell' Ongaro)
Stornello (1869) (anon.; Verdi's contribution to the album for Piave's benefit)
Pietà Signor (1894) (Verdi and Boito; Verdi's contribution to an album for the benefit of victims of an earthquake in Sicily and Calabria, 16 Nov. 1894)

FOR THREE VOICES AND FLUTE

Guarda che bianca luna: notturno (1839) (Vittorelli; for soprano, tenor and bass with flute *obbligato*)

SACRED WORKS

Messa da Requiem (1874) for 4 solo voices, chorus and orchestra (to commemorate the first anniversary of the death of Alessandro Manzoni)
Pater Noster (comp. 1878–79?; perf. 1880) for 5 solo voices unaccompanied (Italian text by Dante). It is sometimes sung by a 5-part chorus instead of soloists.
Ave Maria (comp. 1878–79?; perf. 1880) for soprano with string accompaniment (Italian text by Dante).

Ave Maria, on a "scala enigmatica" (comp. 1889; pub. 1895), for 4 soloists. It is sometimes sung by a 4-part chorus instead of soloists.

Stabat Mater (comp. 1896–97; perf. 1898) for chorus and orchestra.

Laudi alla Vergine Maria (comp. 1888; perf. 1898) for 4 women's voices unaccompanied (text from Dante's *Paradiso*, Canto XXXIII). It is sometimes sung by a 4-part women's chorus instead of soloists.

Te Deum (comp. 1895–96; perf. 1898) for double chorus and orchestra.

The last four works are generally known as the *Pezzi Sacri*. But of them only the last three shared a common première.

MISCELLANEOUS WORKS

Suona la tromba (1848), a patriotic hymn (Giuseppe Mameli).

Inno delle Nazioni (1862), a cantata (Arrigo Boito).

String Quartet, E minor (1873).

A SHORT BIBLIOGRAPHY

What follows is a compromise, somewhat uneasy, between a revelation of "sources" and "suggested reading" for anyone whose curiosity has been stirred. With the books on Verdi, I have emphasized "source"; with the others, "suggested reading." Happily the two sometimes combine.

In spite of its length it is a "short" bibliography because with the exception of the most important characters and events I have mentioned only one book on each. Obviously there are other excellent books on the first Napoleon besides that of Mr. Fisher, but his is short, well-written and recently reprinted. I have also omitted such general works as the plays of Hugo or Schiller and also all fiction.

BOOKS ON VERDI

ABBIATI, Franco: *Giuseppe Verdi*. 4 vols. Ricordi, Milano, 1959.
(A "life" with little discussion of his music. Chiefly valuable for the number of letters and documents printed in full or nearly so.)

BONAVIA, Ferruccio: *Verdi*. 120 pp. Dobson, London, 1947.
(A brief "life" with little discussion of his music but much understanding of the man.)

BOTTI, Ferruccio: *Verdi e la religione*. 2nd edition. 91 pp. Anonima Zafferri, Parma, 1940.
(An interesting effort to show Verdi was a "good" Catholic. The argument proceeds largely by ignoring the evidence and relying, in part, on letters ascribed to Strepponi and later shown to have been fabricated by a Lorenzo Alpino, presumably for the same purpose.)

CESARI, Gaetano and LUZIO, Allesandro: *I Copialettere di Giuseppe Verdi*. 729 pp. Milano, 1913.
(Verdi's "copybooks" in which either he or Strepponi entered copies of many of his letters.)

DEMALDÉ, Giuseppe: *Cenni Biografici del Maestro di Musica Giuseppe Verdi*.
(Unpublished and belonging to the Monte di Pietà in Busseto.)
(About ten pages of "memories" by an ex-treasurer of the Monte di Pietà who knew Verdi in his earliest years in Busseto. Demaldé, who knew all the men involved in Verdi's youth, seems to have written these "remembrances" soon after the success of *Nabucco*, and they, together with other unpublished papers at the Monte di Pietà, are the best source for material on Verdi's youth.)

GARIBALDI, Luigi Agostino: *Giuseppe Verdi nelle lettere di Emanuele Muzio ad Antonio Barezzi*. 382 pp. Fratelli Treves, Milano, 1931.
(Verdi during his "years in the galley" as reported by Muzio to Barezzi.)

GATTI, Carlo: *Verdi*. 2 vols. Alpes, Milano, 1931 (new edition in single volume, Mondadori, Milano, 1951).
(The second edition is not a clear improvement over the first and lacks the first's excellent index.)

GATTI, Carlo: *Verdi, The Man and His Music*. 358 pp. Putnam's, New York, 1955. Translated by Elisabeth Abbott.
(A translation of about one-third of Gatti's biography. Generally speaking, the politics and discussions of other Italian music were cut.)

GATTI, Carlo: *Verdi nelle immagini*. 236 pp. Garzanti, Milano, 1941.
(Excellent pictures of Le Roncole, Busseto, Verdi, La Scala and every other place or person associated with Verdi. It was published under the Fascists, and although there is a section on famous interpreters of Verdi, there is no picture or mention anywhere of his greatest, Toscanini.)

HUSSEY, Dyneley: *Verdi*. 312 pp. Dent, London, 1940.
(Emphasis is strongly on the music, not the life, and particularly on the operas from *Rigoletto* on.)

LUZIO, Alessandro: *Carteggi Verdiani*. 4 vols. Accademia Nazionale, Roma, 1947.
(Vol. I: Letters of Verdi and Strepponi to their Neapolitan friends. Vol. II: Extracts from Strepponi's "copialettere" and miscellaneous letters. Vol. III: Verdi's letters to Piroli and some of Piroli's replies. Vol. IV: Miscellaneous letters.)

MILA, Massimo: *Giuseppe Verdi*. 383 pp. Laterza, Bari, 1958.
(A discussion of the music, including that of the early operas, and also of certain aspects of Verdi's character.)

MONALDI, Gino: *Verdi, 1839–1898*. 2nd edition, 279 pp. Bocca, Torino, 1926.
(An early biography quoting a number of contemporary reviews of the premières of the operas and also "memories" such as those of Mme. Barbieri-Nini.)

POUGIN, Arthur: *Giuseppe Verdi, vita aneddotica con rote e aggiunte di Folchetto*. 160 pp. Ricordi, Milano, 1881.
(An early biography with numerous anecdotes quoted or corrected by most later biographers.)

SHEEAN, Vincent: *Orpheus at Eighty*. 351 pp. Random House, New York, 1958.
(A "life" with the emphasis on the person and politics rather than the music. The book starts with Verdi's last night in the opera house and proceeds by flash-backs and -forwards probably confusing to anyone not already familiar with the story and characters.)

TOYE, Francis: *Giuseppe Verdi, His Life and Works*. 414 pp. Knopf, New York, 1946. Paperback, Vintage Books K-82.
(A short "life" followed by a section on the music in which each opera is discussed and its libretto outlined.)

TRAVIS, Francis Irving: *Verdi's Orchestration*, 105 pp. Juris-Verlag, Zürich, 1956.
(Technical and with many musical examples.)

VERDI, *Studie e memorie*. A commemorative volume of articles and eulogies published by the Sindacata Nazionale Fascista Musicisti on the fortieth anniversary of his death. Rome, 1941.
(Valuable for an excellent and detailed chronology of Verdi's life.)

WALKER, Frank: *The Man Verdi*. 510 pp. Knopf, New York, 1962.
(Probably the most important book on Verdi published since Gatti's two-volume biography in 1931. It is not a biography in the usual sense but a scholarly series of essays examining important persons and incidents in Verdi's life. Some of these first appeared as magazine articles and are listed below. No discussion of music.)

WERFEL, Franz and Paul Stefan: *Verdi, the Man in His Letters*. 469 pp. Fischer, New York, 1942. Translated from the German and Italian by Edward Downes and Barrows Mussey.
(A good selection of the letters excellently translated but with some of their dates obviously scrambled.)

YBARRA, T. R.: *Verdi, Miracle Man of Opera*. 306 pp. Harcourt, Brace, New York, 1955.
(A "life" without much depth but exerting a certain fascination as it proceeds from one climactic moment to the next.)

MAGAZINE ARTICLES ON VERDI

"DONIZETTI, VERDI AND MME. APPIANI" by Frank Walker in *Music and Letters*, Jan. 1951, pp. 1–18, London.
(Exposes a confusion in the identity of Mme. Appiani and greatly decreases the likelihood, strongly espoused by Gatti and Sheehan, that Verdi was ever her lover. Donizetti also seems to have been only her friend.)

"Gesù Morì, AN UNKNOWN EARLY VERDI MANUSCRIPT" by Hans F. Redlich and Frank Walker in *The Music Review*, Aug./Nov. 1959, pp. 233–43, Cambridge.
(A discussion of Verdi's earliest works composed while he was in Busseto and almost all of which he succeeded in destroying.)

"MERCADANTE AND VERDI" by Frank Walker in *Music and Letters*, Vol. 33, no. 4, pp. 311–21; and Vol. 34, no. 1, pp. 33–38 (Oct. 1952 & Jan. 1953), London.

Verdi. The magazine of the Institute of Verdi Studies, Parma. All articles are published simultaneously in Italian, English and German.
(In its first year of publication, 1960, all three issues were devoted to *Un Ballo in Maschera;* in its second, all were to be devoted to *La Forza del Destino*.)

"VERDI AND VIENNA" by Frank Walker in *Musical Times*, Sept. 1951, pp. 403–05; continued in subsequent number. London.

"VERDI AS MUSICIAN" by Eric Blom in *Music & Letters*, Vol. 12, no. 4, pp. 329–44 (Oct.), London, 1931.
(Valuable for showing the attitude of English musicians toward Verdi at a time it was beginning to change.)

"VERDIAN FORGERIES" (No. 1) by Frank Walker in *The Music Review*, Vol. 19, no. 4, pp. 273–82 (Nov. 1958), Cambridge.
(Presents evidence that Lorenzo Alpino fabricated eight letters which in two articles he claimed Strepponi had written to her confessor and the Archbishop of Genoa on the subject of Verdi's religion and his relations with Teresa Stolz. The letters purported to show that Verdi was a "good" Catholic and had no intimate relations with Stolz. Contemporary gossip reported the reverse of each. The weight of the evidence now strongly inclines to the conclusion that he was not a "good" Catholic and had no intimate relations with Stolz.)

"VERDIAN FORGERIES" (No. 2) by Frank Walker in *The Music Review*, Vol. 20, no. 1, pp. 28–38 (Feb. 1959), Cambridge.
(Presents evidence that certain letters of Verdi in which he shows hostility to the composer Catalani were fabricated by Lorenzo Alpino.)

"VERDIAN FORGERIES; A SUMMING UP" by John W. Klein in *The Music Review,* Vol. 20, nos. 3/4 (Aug./Nov. 1959), Cambridge.

(Agrees that the letters purporting to be from Strepponi to her confessor and the Archbishop of Milan are fraudulent. Does not agree that the letters supposedly by Verdi about Catalani are fraudulent.)

"VERDI'S ATTITUDE TO HIS CONTEMPORARIES" by John W. Klein in *The Music Review,* Nov. 1949, pp. 264–76, Cambridge.

(Presents evidence of Verdi's hostility toward Catalani. But *see* articles on "Verdian Forgeries" above.)

"VINCENZO GEMITO AND HIS BUST OF VERDI," by Frank Walker in *Music and Letters,* Jan. 1949, pp. 44–55, London.

BOOKS ON MUSIC AND ITS HISTORY

CHORLEY, Henry F.: *Thirty Years' Musical Recollections.* 400 pp. Knopf, New York, 1926.

(Chorley lived from 1808 to 1872 and for the last thirty-five years was one of the best and most powerful critics of music in London. Rossini was his idol, and he had no use for Verdi. His "recollections" are an excellent summary of opera in England from 1830 to 1859.)

COOKE, Deryck: *The Language of Music.* 274 pp. Oxford, London, 1959.

(Technical, with many musical examples taken from Verdi, Wagner and other operatic composers. He discusses how musically to express grief, joy, etc.)

HERIOT, Angus: *The Castrati in Opera.* 227 pp. Secker and Warburg, London, 1956.

HOLST, Imogen: *Tune.* 169 pp. Faber, London, 1962.

(On what makes a tune, i.e., something a man can whistle.)

HUGHES, Spike: *The Toscanini Legacy, a Critical study of Arturo Toscanini's Performances of Beethoven, Verdi and Other Composers.* 340 pp. Putnam, London, 1959.

(A discussion in detail of Toscanini's recordings. Of Verdi's works these include: *Rigoletto* (Act IV), *La Traviata, Un Ballo in Maschera, Aida, Otello, Falstaff,* the *Requiem, Te Deum* and an album of miscellaneous overtures and arias as well as the complete *Inno delle Nazioni.*)

HUGHES, Spike: *Great Opera Houses, a traveler's guide to their history and traditions.* 344 pp. Weidenfeld and Nicolson, London, 1956.

SLONIMSKY, Nicolas: *Music Since 1900,* 3rd ed., 712 pp. Coleman-Ross Company, Inc., New York, 1949.

(Contains the full text of the Vatican's statement, "Motu Proprio," of what constitutes permissible music in the Church. Also has several of the famous Soviet directives on what the U.S.S.R. wants in music.)

TOYE, Francis: *Rossini, a study in Tragi-Comedy.* 217 pp. Knopf, New York, 1947.

(Containing an excellent account of operatic life in Italy at the beginning of the nineteenth century and then later at Paris.)

WALTER, Bruno: *Theme and Variations, an autobiography.* 380 pp. Hamilton, London, 1947.

(Valuable for its descriptions of provincial operatic théatres at the end of the nineteenth century.)

BIOGRAPHY, POLITICS, HISTORY AND LITERATURE

ACTON, Harold: 1) *The Bourbons of Naples (1734–1825)*, 2) *The Last Bourbons of Naples (1825–61)*. 2 vols. Methuen, London, 1961.
(Detailed history of southern Italy and favoring the Bourbons.)

ADAMS, John Clarke and BARILE, Paolo: *The Government of Republican Italy*. 237 pp. Houghton Mifflin Co., Boston, 1961.
(A study of the form of government from 1946 to 1960.)

BEALES, Derek: *England and Italy, 1859–60*. 173 pp. Nelson, London, 1961.
(An examination of British policy in the crucial year of Italian unification and showing it to be less pro-Italian and more anti-French than traditionally thought.)

BERNINI, Ferdinando: *Storia di Parma*. 207 pp. Battei, Parma, 1954.
(A history of Parma.)

CASTELOT, André: *King of Rome, a Biography of Napoleon's Tragic Son*. 378 pp. Harper, New York, 1960. Translated from the French by Robert Baldick.
(Valuable for its account of Marie Louise, the King's mother, in her role as Duchess of Parma.)

CESARESCO, Evelyn Martinengo: *The Liberation of Italy, 1815–1870*. 415 pp. Seeley, London, 1902.

CESARESCO, Evelyn Martinengo: *Cavour*. 220 pp. Macmillan, London, 1898.

COLQUHOUN, Archibald: *Manzoni and His Times*. 260 pp. Dent, London, 1954.

DUMAS, Alexandre *père*: *Adventures in Czarist Russia*. 194 pp. Owen, London, 1960. Translated from the French by A. E. Murch.
(Dumas traveled in Russia only a year before Verdi and wrote a good account of what life there was like.)

FISHER, H. A. L.: *Napoleon*. 211 pp. Oxford, London, 1912.
(An excellent, short introduction to Napoleon I who spread many of the ideas of the French Revolution throughout Europe.)

GUEDALLA, Philip: *The Second Empire, Bonapartism, the Prince, the President, the Emperor*. 440 pp. Putnam's, New York, 1922.
(Witty and swiftly paced, but spurned by many historians as superficial.)

GUÉRARD, Albert: *Napoleon III, a Great Life in Brief*. 207 pp. Knopf, New York, 1955.
(A rehabilitation of Napoleon who had been unduly reviled by republican historians during France's Third Republic.)

HALES, E. E. Y.: *The Catholic Church in the Modern World*. 313 pp. Eyre & Spottiswoode, London, 1958.
(Wholly pro-Church and within the Church wholly pro-Rome, but quiet in tone and valuable for gathering into one place the various threats the Church has faced from 1789 to 1956.)

HALES, E. E. Y.: *Mazzini and the Secret Societies, the Making of a Myth*. 220 pp. Eyre & Spottiswoode, London, 1956.

HALES, E. E. Y.: *Pio Nono, a Study in European Politics and Religion in the Nineteenth Century*. 331 pp. Eyre & Spottiswoode, London, 1956.
(A pro-clerical account of the Risorgimento.)

KING, Bolton: *A History of Italian Unity, Being a Political History of Italy from 1814 to 1871*. 2 vols. Nisbet, London, 1899.
(The pro-liberal account of the Risorgimento.)

MACK SMITH, Denis: *Garibaldi*. 206 pp. Hutchinson, London, 1957.
(Excellent summary of Garibaldi's entire career, good and bad; lacks only, perhaps, a sense of the poetry in the man.)

MACK SMITH, Denis: *Cavour and Garibaldi, a Study in Political Conflict*. 444 pp. University Press, Cambridge, 1954.
(A technical study leaving Cavour looking slightly the worse for it.)

MACK SMITH, Denis: *Italy, a Modern History*. 508 pp. University of Michigan Press, Ann Arbor, 1959.
(From 1860 to 1945.)

MANZONI, Alessandro: *I Promessi Sposi*. 574 pp. Dent, London, 1951. Translated with a biographical study added by Archibald Colquhoun as *The Betrothed, a Tale of XVII Century Milan*.
(The only complete and best translation.)

MAUROIS, André: *Olympio, the Life of Victor Hugo*. 446 pp. Harper, New York, 1956. Translated from the French by Gerard Hopkins.

PARRIS, John: *The Lion of Caprera, a Biography of Giuseppe Garibaldi*. 347 pp. Barker, London, 1962.
(Strongly anti-clerical and somewhat unfair to Napoleon III.)

PINKNEY, David H.: *Napoleon III and the Rebuilding of Paris*. 221 pp. Princeton, Princeton, 1958.

REYNOLDS, Barbara: *The Linguistic Writings of Alessandro Manzoni; a textual and chronological reconstruction*. 225 pp. Heffer, Cambridge, 1950.

RUNCIMAN, Steven: *The Sicilian Vespers, a History of the Mediterranean World in the Later Thirteenth Century*. 293 pp. Cambridge, Cambridge, 1958.

STILLMAN, W. J.: *The Union of Italy, 1815–1895*. 398 pp. Cambridge, Cambridge, 1909.

THAYER, William Roscoe: *The Dawn of Italian Independence; Italy from the Congress of Vienna, 1814, to the Fall of Venice, 1849*. 2 vols. Houghton Mifflin, Boston, 1894.

THAYER, William Roscoe: *The Life and Times of Cavour*. 2 vols. Houghton Mifflin, Boston, 1911.

TREVELYAN, George Macaulay: 1) *Garibaldi's Defence of the Roman Republic (1848–9)*, 2) *Garibaldi and the Thousand (May 1860)*, 3) *Garibaldi and the Making of Italy (June –November 1860)*. 3 vols. Longmans, Green, London, 1911.

TREVES, Giuliana Artom: *The Golden Ring, the Anglo-Florentines, 1847–1862*. 214 pp. Longmans, Green, London, 1956. Translated from the Italian by Sylvia Sprigge.
(The Risorgimento in Florence seen through the eyes of such persons as Elizabeth Barrett Browning, Walter Savage Landor, and Margaret Fuller.)

VENOSTA, Giovanni Visconti: *Memoirs of Youth, Things Seen and Known, 1847–1860*. 444 pp. Houghton Mifflin, Boston, 1914. Translated by William Prall.
(An account of Milan during the Cinque Giornate and thereafter. Venosta was a friend of the Contessa Maffei and knew most of the city's important political figures.)

WALL, Bernard: *Alessandro Manzoni*. 62 pp. Yale, New Haven, 1954.

WHYTE, A. J.: *The Political Life and Letters of Cavour, 1848–1861*. 469 pp. Oxford, London, 1930.

WRIGHT, Gordon: *France in Modern Times, 1760 to the Present.* 598 pp. Murray, London, 1962.
(The end of each section has a chapter devoted to identifying the position of various historians, monarchist, republican, Marxist, etc., and to discussing their views of what happened during the period.)

INDEX

Primary sources, including quotations from letters, are in **boldface type**. Books and musical compositions are indexed under names of authors and composers. Theatres and opera houses are under names of places.

Entries concerning Verdi are listed in several sub-indexes under his name: first, under "Career," a chronological index of his life; second, under "Alphabetical Summary by Subject," an index by subject such as "Religious beliefs and opinions"; third, "Operas"; and fourth, "Other Works." Some entries appear in more than one of the four sub-indexes.

OPERAS